EXCITING WRITING

EXCITING WRITING

Activities for 5 to 11 year olds

Jacqueline Harrett

Paul Chapman Publishing

© Jacqueline Harrett 2006

First published 2006

Apart from any fair dealing for the purposes of research or private study, or criticism or review, as permitted under the Copyright, Designs and Patents Act, 1988, this publication may be reproduced, stored or transmitted in any form, or by any means, only with the prior permission in writing of the publishers, or in the case of reprographic reproduction, in accordance with the terms of licences issued by the Copyright Licensing Agency. Enquiries concerning reproduction outside those terms should be sent to the publishers.

Paul Chapman Publishing
A SAGE Publications Company
1 Oliver's Yard
55 City Road
London EC1Y 1SP

SAGE Publications Inc.
2455 Teller Road
Thousand Oaks, California 91320

SAGE Publications India Pvt Ltd
B-42, Panchsheel Enclave
Post Box 4109
New Delhi 110 017

Library of Congress Control Number: 2006920507

A catalogue record for this book is available from the British Library

ISBN 10 1-4129-1856-1   ISBN 13 978-1-4129-1856-5
ISBN 10 1-4129-1857-X   ISBN 13 978-1-4129-1857-2 (pbk)

Typeset by Pantek Arts Ltd, Maidstone, Kent
Printed in Great Britain by The Cromwell Press, Trowbridge
Printed on paper from sustainable resources

Contents

	About the author	vi
	Dedication	vii
	Acknowledgements	viii
	How to use this book	ix
1	Introduction	1
2	Pictures in the head	3
3	Art as a start	19
4	Picture Books	39
5	Photographs	49
6	Media	63
	References and other information	87
	Glossary	91
	Index	93

About the Author

Jacqueline Harrett is a freelance writer, inspector and educational consultant, with extensive classroom experience in primary, secondary and higher education. A former teacher and lecturer, she has spoken at national exhibitions and conferences as well as working extensively in schools. Jacqueline is currently undertaking research for a PhD on the responses of children to storytelling and story-reading. A passionate advocate for literacy, she is the Welsh representative for the United Kingdom Literacy Association and has written a number of articles and books on literacy and storytelling including *Welsh Tales for the Telling, More Welsh Tales* and *Tell me Another ... Speaking Listening and Learning Through Storytelling*. Jacqueline was born in Northern Ireland but now lives in Wales with her family.

Dedication

To my parents, Norah and Andy, and my family, Doug, Douglas and Felicity, whose love and encouragement are the foundations of my life.

Acknowledgements

My grateful thanks go to the staff and pupils in all the schools I have taught in over the years, especially schools involved in the project.

Pupils whose work is featured in the book are from the following schools:

Howell's Junior School, Llandaff

St Peter and St Paul's Catholic Primary School, Preston

Pontlottyn Primary School, Fochriw

A special mention for Sandra Farmer, Bernadette Woods and Helen Leaman who were really able to pull the rabbit out of the hat!

Last, but not least, a thank you to my husband, Doug, whose artistic eye provided the photographs of the door and castle interior.

How to Use This Book

This is a book written for student teachers, the people who teach them and practising teachers. This book hopes to provide some ideas for them to use as a springboard. The introduction, chapter one, is a brief overview of my reasons for writing the book and my personal viewpoint of literacy teaching, both as an observer and practitioner.

The second chapter, called 'Pictures in the Head' is about storytelling and the use of visualisation to lead children to plan and write more imaginative narratives. I am a firm advocate of oral storytelling and have always found telling and retelling stories in the classroom useful for speaking and listening activities but also as a precursor for writing. It allows children to plan orally before having to write and they find it fun!

The third chapter concentrates on the work of Lowry, Van Gogh and Renoir as the basis for writing and other linked cross-curricular activities. The ideas may be adapted for any artist but as these artists are familiar to most schools it gives a starting point. An introductory biography of the artists is followed by writing ideas linked to various famous paintings – familiar to most teachers.

The next chapter looks at picture books now regarded as another art form. There are so many beautiful picture books available these days that it would be possible to write an epic on this topic. I have chosen two books to concentrate on. The text selected for Key Stage One is Martin Waddell's *Once there were Giants*. The patterned text is ideal for young children and it appeals to both children and adults.

At Key Stage Two the focus is Chris Van Allsburg's, *The Mysteries of Harris Burdick*. This is a picture book with a difference and never fails to arouse discussions and imaginative ideas. Anyone who is unfamiliar with this one will be hooked by the beautiful black and white illustrations.

Photographs are central to the fifth chapter and examples of photographs and some linked ideas are included in this. Digital photography is often used by teachers these days and this chapter encourages use of photography by the children as well. Photography is an art form and the 'Talking Pictures' pack, designed for art-work, is a wonderful resource for narrative writing.

Following on from this the final chapter examines the media and the use of television, video, DVDs, newspapers and even comics. Teaching ideas and some photocopiable material is provided. Nowadays there is a wealth of information available and it is difficult to know what is fact and what is opinion. Examination of the way the media works should give children a more measured approach to thinking about, and writing about, events.

References and resources are listed to help the busy teacher find what is needed. This is a 'dipping in' book, not a definitive guide.

Chapter 1

Introduction

Teaching is at times like being set adrift on white water. Just as you think it is all going to be plain sailing another waterfall appears and you have to take a deep breath and be ready to change course. When the National Literacy Strategy first came into place some teachers felt constricted by the tight format, others welcomed the structure and a whole group of teachers have never thought about how to teach in any other way. Recently the agenda has changed again with the emphasis now on creativity in the classroom and children making links with different areas of learning. Literacy is a key skill needed across the curriculum and teachers are now being prompted to think outside the literacy hour.

This book is a series of writing ideas based on mainly visual stimuli. We are bombarded by the visual wherever we go and children these days are much more visually literate. As Kress (1994:234) says 'non-verbal, visual modes of representation are becoming more dominant in many forms of public communication.' We take the visual for granted but we, as teachers, could make much more of the world of arts and media. Projects involving museums and art galleries across the country have proven that it is possible to link these different disciplines to enhance learning across the curriculum. I have tried to give as broad a view as possible in the following pages and given a 'taster' of activities. Teachers are generally creative so, I am hoping that these few ideas will give a small spark to set imaginations alight in the minds of those who read it.

My own observations and experiences are central to this book. Some people believe that good literacy teaching means following the same pattern year after year. The agenda for creativity is pushing people out of that comfort zone and forcing them to think again. I have worked with numerous teachers and student teachers over the years and the best teaching I have seen is when people let go and are prepared to take risks. Those who can think outside the box are the teachers who inspire and excite children. They are the ones who can keep a class enthralled on a wet Friday afternoon when the rest of the school is crawling up the walls. They are not afraid to throw away the textbook, try something different and give the learning over to the children.

Many of our most renowned writers, such as Phillip Pullman, have been vociferous in condemnation of a curriculum that is more skills based than creative. As teachers we are aware that a balance has to be made and that children need to be able to make sense of their writing. However, this book does not attempt to address issues of spelling and punctuation but concentrates on reasons for writing. Motivation is central to all learning and giving children exciting things to write about is more motivational than turning to a page in a textbook to complete an exercise.

Giving children time to write and reflect and exchange ideas about their writing is central to many of the ideas presented here. Guy Claxton (2002) says that we all need time for reverie. In the Literacy Hour time is restricted and little reflection may be given. However, being aware of the restrictions imposed by the curriculum many of the activities presented will fit into an hour and may be built on during the course of a week, or longer. Using a cross-curricular approach enables children to make connections with their learning in other areas of the curriculum so layering knowledge upon knowledge and consolidating understanding.

Throughout the book I have used examples from children to illustrate points. I anticipate that the children's work will help make this book a 'reader friendly' text, of use to busy professionals and student teachers alike. I am extremely grateful to colleagues, in both England and Wales, who have tried out ideas and given valuable feedback. That is what creativity is all about. It is about moulding ideas to suit the particular class and year group you are teaching. It is about giving children memorable experiences. We all use worksheets and textbooks now and again, and this book provides some examples, but all good practitioners know that this should not be the sole method of teaching. Giving children different texts they can engage with and become excited by is central to literacy teaching.

Einstein said that imagination is more important than knowledge. I hope teachers who read this book will see it as a starting point only, take the ideas further and give their classes more opportunities for exciting writing.

Chapter 2

Pictures in the head

How do you motivate children to want to write and where do you find ideas for writing? These questions are frequently asked by teachers who are struggling to encourage their young charges to produce exciting and legible 'creative writing' in a short period of time. Anyone who writes knows that it is hard work. Writing takes time, energy and a degree of skill. Even writing a letter of complaint or sympathy – forms most adults will be familiar with – takes thought, consideration and a careful drafting and redrafting to ensure the correct tone. How many adults feel competent enough to sit down and write creatively in a spare few minutes, or even hours? Why then do we expect children to be able to write imaginative and exciting stories with minimal experience? For very young children the physical act of putting pencil to paper is tiring and this demanding activity cannot keep pace with their thoughts and ideas. For many youngsters the use of a teacher or another adult as scribe frees them from the necessity of the actual writing and allows the imagination to have full rein.

The words 'imagination' and 'creativity' are used virtually synonymously and we have almost an instinctive feeling for what we mean by these terms. However, if we stop for a moment to consider and define what we mean by 'imagination' and whether 'imagination' and 'creativity' are the same or entirely different concepts it becomes more difficult. Imagination is frequently linked with the idea of 'pictures in the head', although Pinker (1998) warns us not to become too carried away with this. Not everyone has a visual imagination. All teachers of literacy value what is termed as a 'good imagination' and the ability to imagine places and people we have never seen is almost a prerequisite for creative writing. Whether this is a pictorial representation or something more nebulous depends on the individual. It is said that Einstein had a visual imagination and helping children to visualise places and people can enable them to become more creative in terms of their written work. Sometimes simply allowing children to draw their ideas before plunging into writing may help.

Developing the imagination can be seen as a difficult task, especially in those young children who have deprived backgrounds or poor linguistic development. In school, children learn how to read and are read to by the teachers and this literary experience helps them to develop a love of books. Encouraging a love of books and reading in children is essential to their development as literate adults and in enabling them to see beyond their world into the world of the imagination. Creativity is almost a by-product of this development and the creation of something original, in terms of story-writing, may be traced back to the roots of the conscious and

same quiet voice, place them in an imaginary situation. Try to ensure that the situation is one that most of the children will have had some experience of, or if you wish to extend imaginations you may present them with a different scenario.

Perhaps you want each child to be a pebble on a beach and to think about what they are able to see, hear, smell, taste, touch and feel. For children who have never had the opportunity to visit the sea bring the sea to them by the use of shells, seaweed, sand, pebbles and driftwood. Allow them to touch and smell these objects and press a large shell to their ear. Show them pictures and videos of the sea and listen to the sounds. Place a number of small pebbles in a basket and rotate it slowly to give the 'swish-swish' sound of the sea rolling across the stones. Dissolve salt in water and let them taste it, if they wish, to ensure they have some idea of how the sea would taste. Let salt water dry on a piece of cloth or seaweed so that they can feel and see the crunchy, crusty patterns it makes.

Maybe you want them to be a bird in the sky floating high above the world, or an animal in a beautiful garden. If the school does not have a garden then bring in grass, leaves, flowers, vegetables and fresh herbs to handle and experience before trying to visualise. Take the children outside to taste the wind and to hear more keenly the sounds around the school. The secret is not to paint too vivid a picture with your words but to allow them to develop their own visions. Discussion afterwards is essential, as every child will realise that each visualisation, like a dream, is unique. The discussion may be in the whole class or smaller groups. It may or may not be followed by writing, depending on the focus of the lesson. Giving children time to talk and share ideas helps them to develop the imaginative process needed for writing, so try not to be tempted to ask them to write after every session.

Objects

Using different and unusual objects can provoke discussion and inspire ideas for writing. Even quite ordinary items, such as an old walking stick, will enable children to build a picture of a character that may then be used in a narrative. Ask open-ended questions such as:

Who do you think this belonged to?

How old was the person?

What did he/she look like? (Further questions demanding more detail may also be used.)

How did he/she dress?

Where do you think this person lived?

Once children realise that there is no right or wrong answer they will be more willing to express their thoughts and ideas. The sharing of these inventions will provide a base for children who are perhaps not as imaginative and help everyone to develop their own mental picture of the person. This type of activity could also link with a history topic. For example, a medal from World War Two or a copy of a ration book would not only give some sort of evidence base, but also provide a starting point for investigation as well as a talking point for children to develop, and share, creative ideas. A few simple notes, or ideas, could later become the basis for a story.

Storytelling

Building on these visualisation techniques the next step for the teacher to take is to tell stories rather than read them. Years ago the advertisement for Vauxhall cars stated, 'Once bitten, forever smitten'. Storytelling is like that. The easiest stories to tell are the stories you know well. You may decide to tell the class personal anecdotes about you and your family. This always fascinates young children, as they seem to believe that the teacher spends all night in the school and does not really exist outside the school grounds. Sometimes it feels like that! Maguire (2002) believes that personal storytelling helps to improve relationships as well as enhancing communication.

The stories that stem from the oral tradition, such as folk and fairy tales, are usually the easiest to tell as they have a strong plot and there are many different versions from around the world. You can chop and change the story as you please. In fact, changing a traditional story so that it is still recognisable but also unique in some way provokes a tremendous amount of discussion.

Stories may be changed to include familiar names, situations or places. Characters may be added or removed and the 'what if … ' factor introduced. The following story is a retelling of Hansel and Gretel and demonstrates some of these points.

Handsome and Grumpy

Long, long ago lived a woodcutter, his wife and his two children, Handsome and Grumpy. As you may imagine these were not the real names of the children but their nicknames. Handsome was tall like his father and was always smiling. Grumpy, his young sister, although a pretty child, was always complaining about something. The children's mother had died when they were babies and the woodcutter had married again. The children's stepmother did not care for the children and took no joy in them. She was frequently nasty to them and showed them no affection. In fact, she was jealous of the love their father had for them.

The winter was long, dark and miserable. The woodcutter was unable to work because of the weather so they had little money to keep them. They were always hungry and there was little food in the house. Their stepmother was always moaning about how much the children ate and how little they did to help her in the house. One night as Handsome lay awake he overheard his stepmother talking to his father. 'You must take the children deep into the forest tomorrow and leave them there. If you don't we will all starve to death. We are all so hungry and all they do is eat and eat.'

The woodcutter could scarcely believe what his wife was saying. He was horrified and protested at the thought of abandoning his children. The wife was strong and determined and nagged the poor man long into the night until he agreed to her plan. Handsome waited until they were both asleep and crept outside. He gathered a pocketful of little white stones that twinkled in the moonlight and then crept back inside the house and slept.

When the sun rose the next morning the woodcutter took the children with him into the forest. He was sad and his steps were slow and heavy as he led the children deeper and deeper into the forest. He did not notice Handsome drop the little stones on the path as they made their way through the tall trees. Grumpy soon became tired. 'How much further? My feet hurt and I'm hungry.' 'Not much further,' said their father, unable to meet Handsome's bright smile. When they reached the very centre of the forest, the woodcutter stopped and gave each child a piece of dry bread. 'Rest here and eat this,' he told them. 'I have other things to do.'

He hugged his children and walked quickly away. Grumpy sat down on the grass and ate her bread. When she had finished Handsome told her what he had overheard. Grumpy started to cry until Handsome told her about the stones. The children picked some berries and ate them before huddling together under a huge tree. They soon fell fast asleep. When they awoke it was dark and Grumpy

was afraid. 'Oh no, we'll never get home and some horrible wolf will eat us.' 'Don't worry,' said Handsome. 'Look the moon is rising. We will soon be able to see our way home.' Sure enough, they could see the little stones twinkling in the moonlight. They followed the trail of stones and arrived home in the early hours of the morning. Their father was delighted but their stepmother frowned at them.

For a time all was well but one night Handsome overheard his stepmother arguing with his father. 'You must take the children to the forest. We have only enough food for the two of us. They eat so much and if we don't get rid of them soon we will *all* die of starvation.' The woodcutter protested but his wife was strong and argued with him long into the night until he agreed to her plan. When they were asleep Handsome crept downstairs but the door was locked and he could not go out.

The next morning when their stepmother gave them some dry bread to eat Handsome put it in his pockets. When they left for the forest their stepmother came with them to make sure her plan would succeed this time. Handsome walked slowly behind the others and dropped little crumbs of bread along the path so that they could find their way home again. Grumpy was complaining so much that no one noticed.

When they reached the very centre of the forest the woodcutter and his wife lit a fire and told the children to stay there until they came back to fetch them. Grumpy cried and cried until Handsome told her he had left a trail of breadcrumbs. The children put wood on the fire but the branches they picked were damp with all the rain and the fire smouldered and then went out. Grumpy cried some more and the children huddled together and finally slept. It was night when they awoke and the moon was full but they could see no trail of crumbs. The birds of the forest had eaten the bread. Grumpy cried and cried but Handsome comforted her. 'Hush now, don't cry. We will find some way out of the forest. We'll just follow the path.'

They wandered round and round all night but every path looked the same. As the sun arose they found themselves right back at the spot where they had been sleeping. A little frog had been following them for some time and when the children stopped to rest he hopped onto the ground in front of them. 'Look, look at the little frog. What is he doing?' The frog hopped right up to Grumpy's feet. 'Maybe if you kiss him he'll change into a prince.' Grumpy smiled and her whole face changed. She bent down to pick up the frog but he hopped a little way down one of the paths and then stopped. Grumpy frowned. 'I think he wants us to follow him.'

Pulling themselves to their feet the children followed the frog and before long they came to a clearing where they saw a pool surrounded by beautiful flowers. The frog jumped into the water and disappeared. As the children peered into

the water they could see their own reflections. They had never seen themselves before so they thought some other children were in the pool. 'Come out and play with us!' shouted Grumpy. But there was no reply. Handsome heard a noise and looked behind him to see a strange woman dressed all in white. She frowned at them. 'Why are you here? Where have you come from?' Handsome smiled at her and bowed. 'Kind lady, we are lost. Our stepmother does not love us and has left us in the forest to starve to death.' The woman's face softened as she looked at the boy. 'Then come with me and eat your fill.'

She walked away from them and the children ran to keep pace. As they turned a path in the forest they saw a wonderful sight. There, right in front of them, stood a house made of gingerbread. It had sweets all over it and a fence made of lollipops. From inside the house came delicious smells and the children rushed to the door. Inside was a table covered in food and the children soon sat down and ate their fill. The strange woman had vanished but there appeared a very old lady, with long, spidery fingers and a hunched back. 'Who has eaten my food?' 'I'm very sorry,' said Handsome, 'but we were so hungry. We haven't had anything to eat for a long time and the smell was so delicious we couldn't resist it.'

The witch, for witch she was, squinted at them and smiled a horrible, toothless grin. 'That's all right my dears. You can work for your keep.' She grabbed Handsome and put him in a cage in the corner of the room. She pressed her ugly face so close to him that he could smell her stale breath. 'You are a fine looking boy. I will feed you until you are nice and plump.' Grumpy started to cry. 'Stop that noise. You will work hard or I will beat you!' The children were terrified. Their stepmother seemed like an angel compared to this fiend. 'W..W..What are you going to do with my brother?' The witch cackled. 'I'm going to fatten him up and eat him and you can do all the work for me.'

For weeks Grumpy worked and worked all day and halfway through the night. She never complained, as she was so frightened. Handsome was given plates and plates of food while the witch give Grumpy nothing but bones and scraps. Handsome would often pass food to his sister through the bars of the cage when the witch wasn't looking. Every few days the witch would ask Handsome to poke a finger out of the cage to see if he was fat enough to eat. The old hag had very poor eyesight so Handsome gave her a bone to feel. She couldn't understand how he was eating so much and not getting any fatter.

Eventually she grew fed up waiting and decided it was time to eat the boy. She lit the oven and asked Grumpy to see if it was warm enough to roast her brother. 'How do I do that?' asked Grumpy. 'Creep inside, girl.' The witch intended to shut

Grumpy in the oven, roast her and eat her too. 'Inside?' Grumpy pretended not to understand. The witch was impatient and hungry. 'Yes, stupid. Inside. Here, let me show you.' The witch opened the huge oven door and climbed into the edge. Quick as a flash, Grumpy pushed her right into the oven and locked the door. She could hear the witch screaming as the heat inside baked her alive.

Grumpy ran to the cage and opened it to let her brother free. They hugged each other as the screams of the witch stopped and they knew she was dead. The gingerbread house was full of chests of gold and jewels so the children collected some food and as much money and jewels as they could before leaving the house. Outside was the lady that had led them to the house. 'How can I thank you enough?' she asked. 'The witch put a spell on me and forced me to bring lost children to her. She said if I did not do so then she would kill my husband. Come, I shall take you out of this wicked place.' Handsome frowned. He did not trust her. 'I think she is trying to help,' said Grumpy. 'Maybe she will take us to another witch,' said Handsome, but they agreed that they would follow her for a little way. They soon came to the pool and the lady went to the edge of the pool and whistled. The frog appeared. The lady lifted him out of the water and as soon as his feet touched dry land he changed into a tall man. The couple embraced. Apparently the witch had cast a spell over them both and her death had broken the spell.

The four travelled together for many hours and gradually the forest became lighter and there were fewer trees and more flowers growing. At last they came to the edge of the forest and the children could see their home. The strange couple bid them farewell and left them there.

The children were concerned about what their stepmother would say when she saw them but she had left and their father was overjoyed to see his beloved children again. They told him of their adventures and showed him the gold and jewels. Grumpy stopped being grumpy as she realised what a lucky escape they had had. She became the sweetest natured child in the land and smiled all the time, just like her brother. They never had to worry about being hungry again and they were always kind to the creatures of the forest – just in case they turned out to be under a witch's spell!

The End

Following the storytelling the children may be questioned about what they 'saw' in their minds as they listened. However, for the novice storyteller the main problem is not what questions to ask but how to remember the story.

Remembering the story

The easiest way to remember a story is *not* to try and learn it by rote. If you start with a simple story that you know very well, perhaps a favourite from your own childhood, all that will be needed are a few 'hooks' to hang it on. One way to do this is to produce a story skeleton of the main points, or events, in the tale to be told.

Creating a story skeleton may be done in various ways. You need to start by visualising the story and sequencing the pictures in your mind. This is also a useful activity for children to do as a class, in groups, pairs or individually. A few key words linking the pictures and story will help. Take a blank page and think of the key points in the story. Try to keep this to a maximum of six. A story skeleton is just that – the bones of the story. As storyteller you add the flesh to make the story come to life in the minds of the listeners. The wonderful thing about storytelling is that each telling is different from the others as you change emphasis according to the needs of the audience. Writing a story skeleton is a useful class, shared, writing activity and may then be used by the children to further develop their own ideas. It avoids the 'blank page syndrome' and is also a way of planning without going into great detail. It allows flexibility and individuality while giving a clear structure.

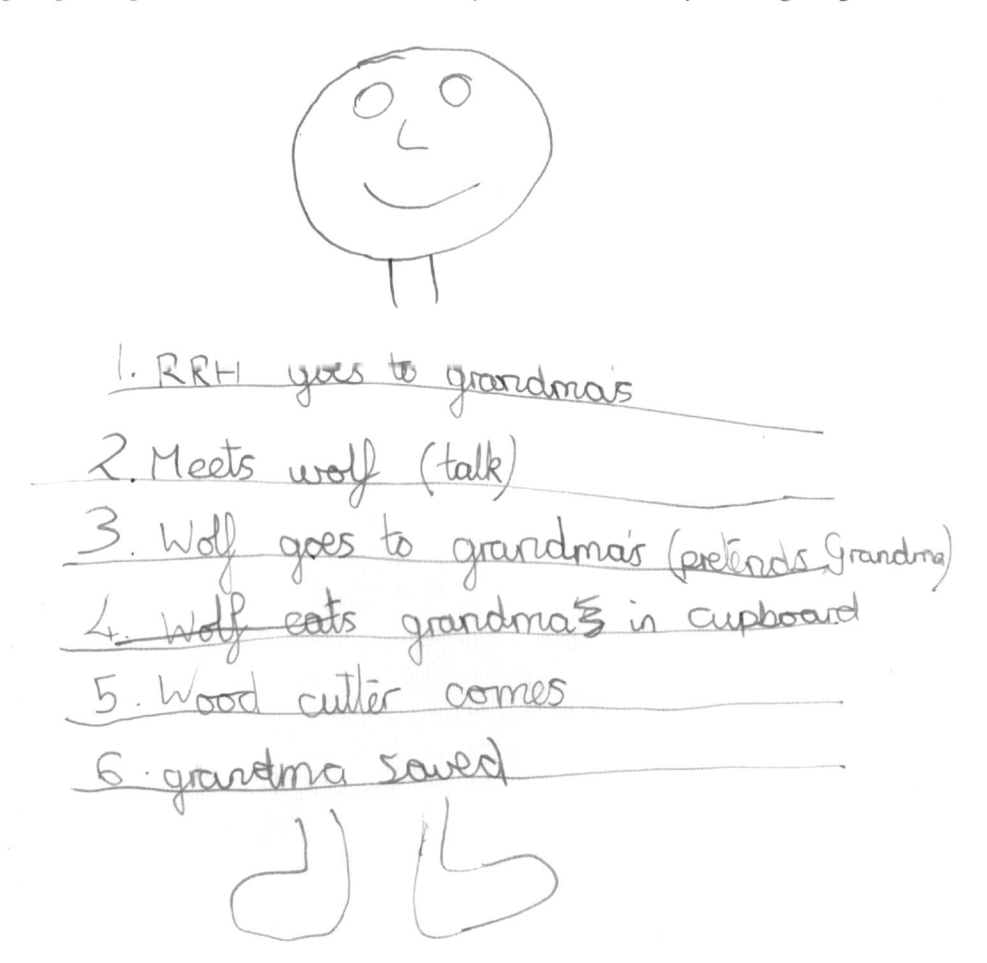

Figure 2.1 Example of a story skeleton

For some children it is fun to make a story skeleton that looks like a skeleton. This skeleton in Figure 2.1 was made in response to the story of Red Riding Hood.

Handsome and Grumpy or *Hansel and Gretel*, if you prefer to stick to the original, may be summarised in the following way:

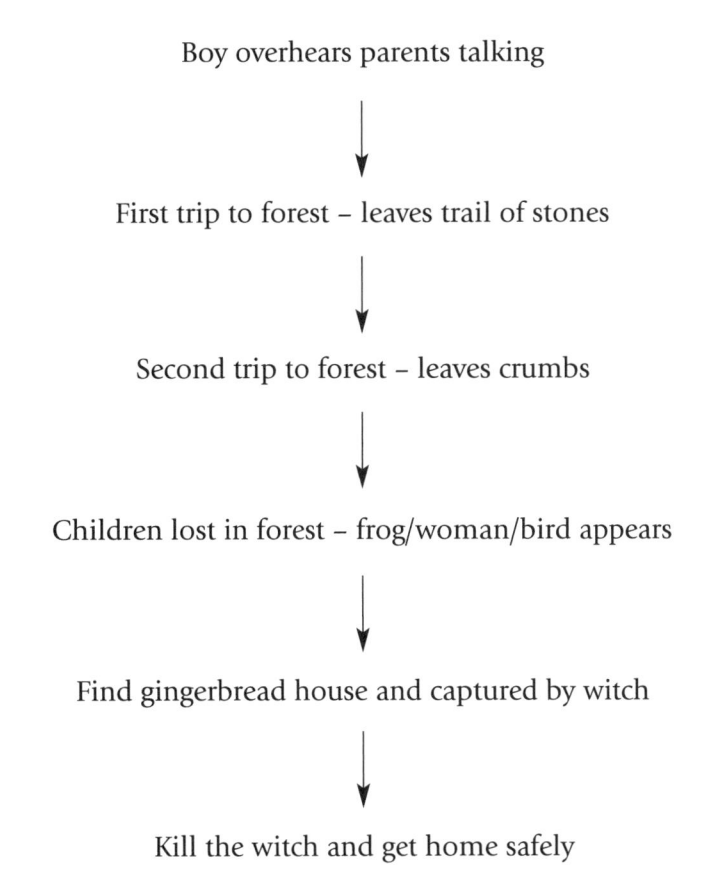

Boy overhears parents talking

↓

First trip to forest – leaves trail of stones

↓

Second trip to forest – leaves crumbs

↓

Children lost in forest – frog/woman/bird appears

↓

Find gingerbread house and captured by witch

↓

Kill the witch and get home safely

The main points are sequenced in note form so there is little to remember. The more complicated parts of the story, such as the description of the walk in the forest or the relationship between the various characters, are left to the storyteller to elaborate during the telling. Asking children to retell stories helps them to develop these techniques and is a useful planning tool for creative writing. It is brief, concise and relieves them of the mammoth task of writing a long and detailed plan.

Some people prefer to make a grid with pictures to help. The following grid in Figure 2.2 (see page 14) was the work of a Year Five child.

Another memory aid, and useful in helping the children to remember events, is to make story maps (see page 15).

Talking, as stated before, is an essential foundation for writing. Without the time to exchange ideas and discuss their thoughts and images children will find it difficult to form artistic views about the stories they are expected to write. The storytelling should be followed by a speaking and listening session, giving children time to reflect and share. The teacher can lead this by posing questions to arouse animated exchanges and giving children the chance to retell the story in pairs or small groups.

EXCITING WRITING

Handsome and Grumpy

Story grid

What do you need to remember?

Stepmum, Grumpy, Handsome, Dad. "Take children into forest to starve." Boy overhears.	Stones in forest. Children get home. Birds eat breadcrumbs. Children get lost.
Meet frog, leads to Kind lady, House of sweets.	Witch — "I love to eat children". Lives in sweet house.
Witch burns in oven. Children escape with gold and jewels.	Frog turns into prince + Kind lady. Show children way home.

Figure 2.2 Example of a grid with pictures

14

2 ■ PICTURES IN THE HEAD

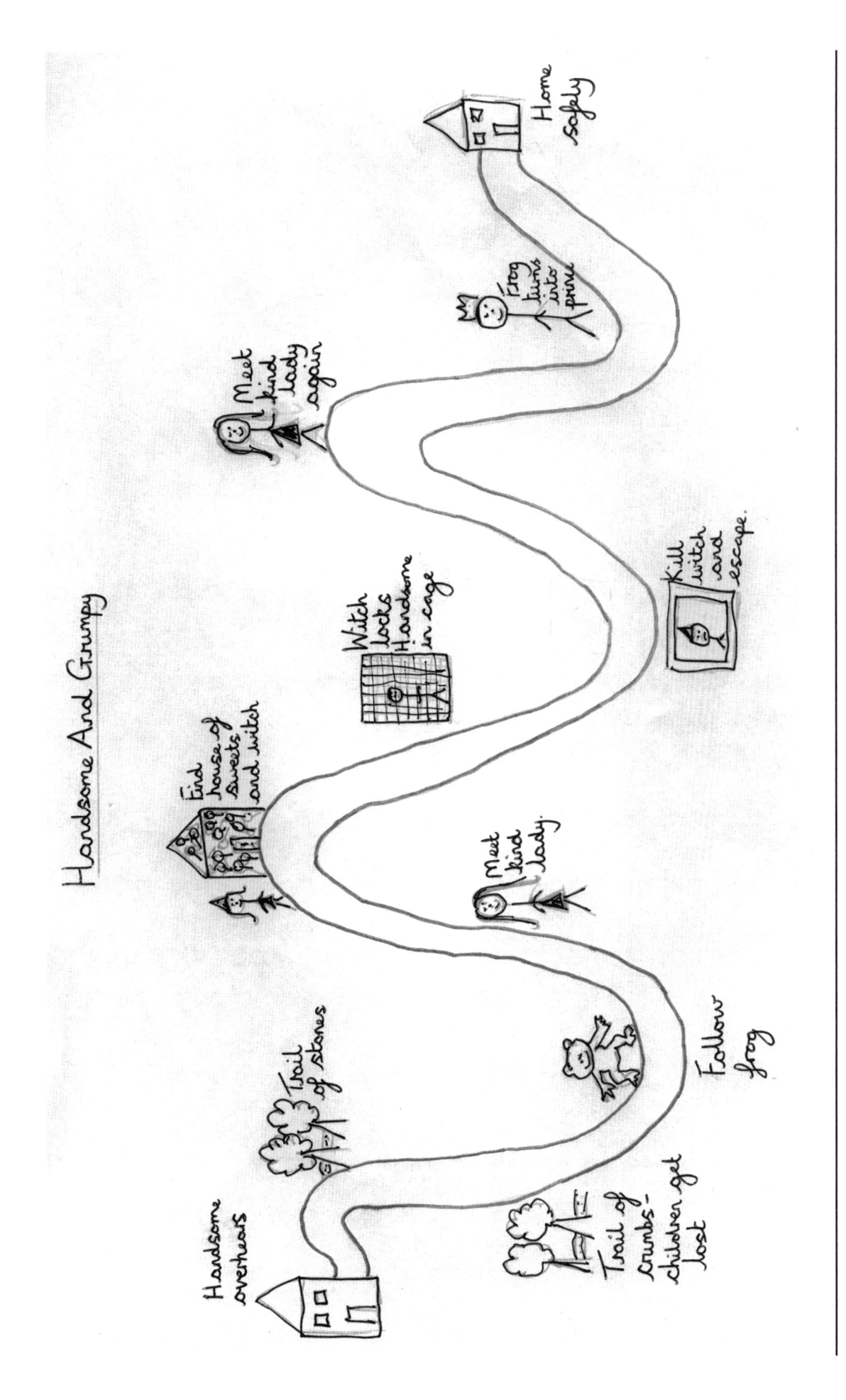

Figure 2.3 Example of a story map

15

Some examples of questions to ask about the story

Key Stage One and Two

- Do you think the title is suitable?
- What do you think the children should have been called?
- Do you think that nicknames are a good idea? Give reasons for your answers.
- This is a version of what story? Have you heard or read any other versions? What are the similarities and what are the differences?
- Are there any other characters or stories that you recognise in this story?
- Who is your favourite character in the story? Why?
- Can you describe what Handsome/Grumpy/the witch/the woodcutter/the stepmother looked like? (This question always produces diverse answers allowing each child to realise that their visual image of the character is different from everyone else's.)

The following are perhaps more suitable for Key Stage Two

- How do you think the woodcutter felt when he abandoned the children?
- Why do you think he gave in to his wife?
- Was the stepmother really wicked or just uncaring? Give reasons for your answer.
- Who could the lady in white have been or what did she represent?
- Who might the frog have been?
- In some versions of this story a bird leads the children to the witch. What other creatures could have been involved? If you were going to write the story would you use a different creature?
- If the witch had all that food why did she want to eat the children?
- Do you think it was right of Grumpy to kill the witch? Did she deserve to have such a horrible death?
- Were the children justified in taking the witch's money after killing her?
- Did you trust the lady in white when she offered to take the children to their home? What did you feel at that point and why?
- Where do you think the stepmother went to and why?
- How do you think their experience changed the children? How would you feel after such a traumatic experience?

The story also lends itself to a range of oral activities to encourage children to become more involved in the story and to extend not only their imaginations, but also their perceptions of the characters and events. Asking open questions about emotions raises issues related to personal, social and moral issues that may be discussed in a 'safe' mode. Reading various examples of the original story of Hansel and Gretel and comparing and contrasting these stories are also good literacy practice. Anthony Browne's picture book version tells the tale whilst supported by wonderfully intense art work.

Oral/Drama Activities

The following ideas may be adjusted for the age range taught. Some topics are more suitable for Key Stage Two so teachers may pick and choose as they see fit depending on the age and ability of the children in the class, bearing in mind that the less academic children often shine during oral based sessions. Links to writing are given in brackets after the oral activities.

- 'Hot-seat' the witch and question her about all the children she has taken and possibly mistreated and eaten. (Write down a list of suitable questions.)

- Someone (possibly a relative) comes to visit the children and their father after they return to the woodcutter's cottage. In a group devise a list of questions for him or her to ask both the children and their father.

- The children are to be interviewed by the local press about their experience in the forest. Role-play the situation. You will need several characters for this: the children; their father; possibly a mediator, such as a social worker or lawyer, and several news reporters. (In a group children decide on the characters and, after the role-play, write a screenplay of the situation.)

- Word of the escapade has travelled further afield and the national, and international, television crews are to interview the children on television. They have a surprise visitor – their stepmother. What happens? Will the children and their father forgive her so the all live happily ever after, or will she create a scene on the show? (As above.)

- The witch's sister appears and threatens to turn the children into frogs, or worse, if they do not give her the money they took. What are they to do? Will they be able to outwit her or appeal to her better nature? Perhaps this witch is not as wicked as her sister. How will they find out and what will happen? Discuss ideas in groups and then act out the situation. (In smaller groups write different versions of this scenario, depending on the perception of the character. Compare and contrast these notes and as a larger group come to some agreement as to the final version.)

- Put the father on trial for neglect of his children. What will the children say in his defence? Will the stepmother be involved in his prosecution? Will the witch? What about the mysterious lady in white and her husband? Whose side are they going to be on? (Each 'character' will write their point of view to be discussed in the court. The language will need to be formal to suit the style of a courtroom drama.)

- The stepmother returns and begs to become part of the family again. Has she really changed or is this just a pretence? The children need to judge for themselves? Act out the scenes following her return. (Write out the arguments the stepmother has for being included in the family again.)

SUMMARY

In this chapter the basis of talking for writing was explored and the use of storytelling in particular. Using traditional stories to provoke discussion on emotional and social issues was an area raised in the teaching ideas. The use of visualisation was explained and the main focus was on narrative. Drama, and writing in role, was another aspect mentioned in this chapter.

Poetry/creative writing – based on the senses after visualisation

Narrative – using a told story as the basis for writing

Story planning/Story grids/Story maps/Story skeletons – using different ways to plan and draft narratives.

Questions – how to write relevant questions

Drama scripts – following drama activities

Formal language/monologue – courtroom drama or monologue written in character's role

Chapter 3

Art as a start

Recent projects involving children and art galleries all over the country have demonstrated only too clearly what may be achieved when different disciplines are joined. Many art galleries and museums have education programmes and the Tate especially has an online course for anyone wishing to develop their subject knowledge on modern art. Great works of art may be examined from different points of view. This enables children to react and respond to the emotions aroused by the study of paintings and sculptures and has proven to be successful in stimulating imagination and creativity.

This chapter will look at the work of three artists whose work is freely available through reproduction on calendars, postcards and prints advertised for sale on websites. This is not a definitive guide, nor intended to be. It is simply an insight into how art may be used as a springboard for writing. Just as each individual's reaction to a story or film is different so one may expect a different response from each child to different pieces of art. Doonan (1993) talks about a 'composite picture' which is made from both illustrations and how one perceives that illustration according to one's personal experiences. Using this theory as a basis one may see how different children could form their own ideas about the characters portrayed in works of art.

Laurence Stephen Lowry

Known as the Pendlebury artist, Laurence Stephen Lowry was born in Manchester in 1887. He was an only child. He moved with his parents to Pendlebury when he was twenty-two and worked as a rent collector and clerk for the Pall Mall Property Company, Manchester. His job enabled him to observe and sketch the different people he saw during his daily work. These sketches would then be mixed together to form composite paintings with buildings from different sketches mixed with various figures.

Lowry was a rather lonely and private person. He attended art classes in the evenings for a number of years and his strongest influence was the work of his teacher, Adolphe Valette, who painted the canals and streets of Manchester in the Impressionist style. Lowry was to use the same inspiration for his own work. The earlier paintings were dark and forbidding but gave way to lighter tones of cream and white with soft shades of rust, blue, brown and grey. He left canvasses unfinished for many years until the white background had yellowed. The figures are often bent and childlike in their simplicity.

As well as his industrial landscapes Lowry also painted a number of seascapes, some devoid of people, reputed to represent his inner desolation following the death of his parents. Prints of Lowry paintings are widely available, as are postcards and calendars, and The Lowry Gallery in Salford stands as testament to his great influence as an artist.

The paintings

Although many of Lowry's paintings could be used as a basis for creative work I have concentrated on three to look at in more detail. The following ideas are not meant to fit neatly into one, or even five, literacy hours but should be selected for use where and when appropriate to the curriculum.

Figure 3.1 Painting by child entitled *Father going home*

This particular painting is interesting as it shows a solitary figure walking along the street, but if one looks carefully it is possible to see a face at the window watching his progress. No age limit is set for the following ideas, as the various abilities of the children involved will dictate what you do or how far you take the project. Similar activities and questions may be used for other Lowry paintings in the same vein such as, *Man lying on a Wall*, or *Gentleman looking at Something*.

Talking

With all written work it is, of course, important to start with talking. Just asking the children what they can see in the picture can start the discussion. With young children beginning with a few closed questions will help them to go forward.

- What is the man wearing?
- What colour is his hat?
- What colour is his coat?
- What is he carrying?
- What has he got around his neck?

Some children will also comment about the fact that he is a funny shape and that he is smoking and may even start to ask questions themselves. This can lead on to more open questions, to which the teacher does not have the answer, thus giving a sense of achievement to the children.

- Where is he going?
- What do you think is in the bag?
- What could he be thinking?
- Who is at the window?
- Is it someone the man knows or just someone watching?
- I wonder what his name is?
- What is his job?

This usually leads to a number of possible answers about the man and what his job could be, whether he has important papers, clothes or just his lunch in his bag. Already children are beginning to build up a character profile of this person and his life.

Narrative

To develop this into a narrative takes a little longer. With the children, the teacher can decide on a suitable name for this person. I did this with my class of seven year olds. We had been reading Ahlberg's *Jeremiah in the Dark Woods* and one little girl decided that he looked like a Jeremiah as he was rather old-fashioned. In this way the children were making links with their previous learning.

Asking children to just write a story about this person may work with some of them, or even some classes, but most will need a starting point. Everyone will have some idea of what they think he is doing or where he is going, so the teacher could work with the whole class or one group at a time on a story starter.

One day Jeremiah Obadiah left home to go to work as usual. He took his bag with him but Stephen, his son, noticed that it was bulging at the seams. Could father have something else in there, instead of his lunch as usual? When Jeremiah did not come home at the usual time that evening they all began to worry. What had happened to him?

Alternatively, the story ending could be given. This works best with older children.

As he returned home that evening Jeremiah smoked his cigarette and thought about what an extraordinary day it had been.

Just why it had been an extraordinary day and what exactly had happened that day are left to speculation. Brainstorming ideas helps to build up the picture.

- When did the story start?
- Had something happened that morning to make the day so eventful? What could it have been?
- Had he witnessed something strange such as a bank robbery; perhaps a film star had spoken to him; he had had a promotion in work; he had met someone important; he had won a lot of money; perhaps he had received bad news?

The possibilities are endless and because no one knows the answers to the questions it becomes even more interesting – a sort of 'Who-dunnit?'

Children Playing

Moving on from solitary figures to groups is a natural progression. Although Lowry often drew individuals he is perhaps better known for his group scenes. *Children Playing* provides such a group and is also a familiar occupation for children. It is something they can relate to easily. This group of four children provides ample opportunity for talking leading to writing. Each individual has a different expression so examining the physical characteristics of each girl, their expressions and dress may begin discussion. Open-ended questions help to stimulate thoughts.

- What game could they be playing?
- Are they on the way to somewhere or back from somewhere?
- Is there a park nearby or do they always play in the street?
- Who do you think is the oldest? Why do you think that?
- Who could be the youngest?
- Do you think they are sisters or just friends?

Role-play

As well as the obvious links to building stories around the children in the picture and their families this painting also lends itself to role-play with younger children. Ask the children to think about what could be happening in the picture. Perhaps the girls are playing a game and have a quarrel. Older children could take this a step further by acting out the argument and then scripting it. The teacher may even play the part of one of the girls in the first instance to start the scene. Grainger and Pickard (2004: 41) describe the teacher in a role as 'the most powerful convention' through which the teacher 'can support, extend and challenge the children's thinking from inside the drama'.

Rhymes

Children often chant rhymes as they play. Children could invent a number chant for these girls to say as they swing their arms and skip along the pavement. It helps if they have a basis from which to start, so some time talking about playground chants and games and even playing a few of these can allow children to understand what is required of them.

Description

The children could choose one figure and write a description of her; 'She has black hair and clothes and red lips. She is wearing grey socks and black ankle boots'.

The descriptions may then be expanded: 'The girl was taller then the others but she did not smile. She pouted, as if sulking, and pursed her bright red lips together, frowning a little. Her hair was flat and straight, cut roughly into a bob. Her clothes were dark and drab although a bit of lace at the neckline added something to an otherwise unremarkable person'. This is best in a shared or guided writing exercise where the teacher can help to extend vocabulary and ideas.

Thought bubbles

Although the conversation between the four girls could be written as part of a story the children could write captions for each girl's spoken words or even thoughts. If the children initially copy the picture themselves it gives them valuable thinking time before they start writing.

Going to the Match, 1953

This painting should appeal to boys because of the subject content. Although they may never have been to a football match they probably will have watched one on television or may have even just witnessed a school match. The excitement building up and the crowd atmosphere could be discussed so that a shared understanding is reached about what actually happens before, during and after the match.

Reports

This particular painting lends itself to different styles of writing as the event could be written from the viewpoint of a player or a spectator. The spectator could be old or young, male or female. After working on the reporting style (see Chapter 6) children could write an imaginary account of the match from a local news reporter's viewpoint.

Commentary

With football matches televised now an examination of the oral style of commentators could be followed by an enactment of a football match or an interview with one of the star players. Internet searching for names and information about players during that era would add an authentic twist to this.

Lists

Even the scores on the back of the newspaper report can provide a reason for writing. Ask a group to compile a list of teams and scores in alphabetical order. The names of the teams could be made up and a touch of alliteration added for extra interest – Avonborough Avengers, Bettlestern Budgers or the Cornweb Cruisers, for example. This provides a lot of fun and gives the less able a chance to contribute.

Cross-curricular links

Art

The most obvious link to make with these painting is through art. *Father coming Home* is a distinct shape with which quite a few techniques may be used. Using A4 black sugar paper ask the children to colour with chalk. The top two thirds of the paper need to be rust coloured and the bottom third chalked in white. They then add the lines for the bricks and the paving slabs, using crayon. This only requires a light touch. Once that is complete they may use paint to add in the figure. A written evaluation of the work can give an extra reason for writing. Using a writing frame for this makes it less of a chore.

Evaluation for painting

My painting:
I found the easiest bit was *choosing the colders*
It was difficult to *Make the shape of to boddy*
What I learnt about using the chalk was *it cept on braking*
What I found out about painting the figure was *it was tricky and intresting*

Figure 3.2 Example of an evaluation sheet

Evaluations may then be mounted along with the gallery of figures. In this way not only are the children writing for a reason they are fulfilling part of the art curriculum by evaluating the mediums they have been using to create the finished product. Using clay, or plasticine, to make 3D models of *Father coming Home* also encourages the children to talk and think about the character.

As mentioned, Lowry would often leave paintings untouched for years until the white canvas had yellowed. He would then add to it and eventually decide it was finished. In school there is not the time to do this but children may paint in thick poster paint on cardboard and leave it to dry thoroughly for a week or so before attempting to add the little matchstick figures so familiar in Lowry's paintings.

Take one of the prints with numerous figures and ask each child to identify a figure to copy – *On the Sands, A Village Square,* or *The Fairground* each provide plenty of individuals to copy and may help the children to relate to their own personal experiences. Discussion about the figures and their actions could well lead to further narratives.

Another way to approach this is to ask children to use fine brushes, and a limited palette of colours, to paint a few different figures. The figures may then be cut out and stuck onto a background to make a collage.

History

Discussion about Lowry inevitably includes the time factor. Lowry lived through two World Wars and recorded some of that destruction in his drawings and paintings. During the Second World War he was a war artist although it is thought that some of his bleaker paintings are a reflection of his feelings of grief following the death of his mother. Paintings such as *St Augustine's Church, Manchester* depict the aftermath of bombing and although photographic and film evidence for the war years is available, this adds an extra dimension to any project on World War Two. One child in response to *The Funeral Party* placed his story at the railway station during evacuation: 'They all knew it was going to be a long jurney. Away from the city, away from their homes and family and away from the war.'

Children Playing could lead to further research on the games children played in the fifties. Grandparents could be consulted and skipping games and playground games from the era introduced as part of a history week, or a playground games week. The clothes people are wearing in the paintings also stimulate discussion. Many of the figures are wearing hats and the predominant colour is black. Compare the styles to modern day clothing and invite the children to talk about how different things would have been in Lowry's day. His landscapes often depict the heavy industry of the north and the factories and mills where crowds flocked to work. Discuss how life might have been for these people. The film and photography of Mitchell and Kenyon, recently shown on television, could give this extra depth and lends itself to discussion about life in those times. This could eventually lead to writing a diary page for one of the factory workers.

Paintings are almost like a moment frozen in time, so thinking about what happened before and after this picture was created is another way to help children to sequence events in time.

- What were the children like five years before or five years after this picture was painted?
- What do you think happened to them?

All these types of questions inspire inquiry and help chronology. Taking some of Lowry's more well known paintings and sequencing them according to date order is also a simple but effective way of encouraging children to see how his work changed and developed during his lifetime.

Geography

Lowry's landscapes are generally composite pictures made up of a number of different places, although some places are mentioned, for example Lincoln, Bargoed and Piccadilly Circus. Looking for these named places on a map encourages the use of an index and co-ordinates for map-reading. Many of his industrial landscapes are almost a bird's eye view. Using something like *Town Centre*, children could draw a map of what they imagine the rest of the town would look like. With younger children this could be done in a more concrete way using blocks or Lego to build up an impression of the town from the painting.

Vincent Van Gogh

Vincent Van Gogh was born in 1853 in the Netherlands but spent much of his life living and painting in France. Although he sold some of his paintings during his lifetime he did not really become famous until after his death in 1890, when he was only thirty-seven. Van Gogh, the son of a minister, depended on the charity of his younger brother Theo for much of his life.

Van Gogh's *Sunflowers* is perhaps his most famous painting but in fact Van Gogh painted a series of these paintings. The influence for his later work came after he was affected by the work of the Impressionists he met in Paris such as Degas and Pissarro. Van Gogh spent a number of months living in Arles with another Impressionist, the artist Gauguin. This was often a stormy relationship and, after one particularly volatile argument, Van Gogh is reputed to have cut off his own ear.

Vincent was unstable. He was ill for many months before his death and spent a great deal of time in an institution in St Remy where he was allowed to paint the scenes from his window. His particular style is easily recognisable and is frequently emulated in schools.

Vincent's bedroom

In the same way that Lowry's paintings have been explored for characterisation so Van Gogh's paintings are a good basis for looking at settings. Although he painted portraits of himself and others, Van Gogh was also a prolific artist of landscapes and interior scenes.

In Vincent's bedroom we can see evidence of how he lived and the simplicity of his life in Arles. Ask the children to be detectives and scrutinise the picture for evidence of how Vincent spent his life there. Pose some questions to stimulate enquiry.

- Who lives here and what do we know about him?
- Is he old/young; tidy/untidy; rich/poor?
- What things are important to this person and how do we know?

The children will question what they can see and may need to be reminded that it is what is missing that tells us as much as what is visible.

- What do the mirror and the things on the table tell us?
- Look at the walls. What do we know about him from the walls?
- What about his clothes?
- Why are there two chairs?
- Does he eat in this room as well as sleep?

> I think that he is old because there is no toys hears qite tidy I think that he is poor because he has small bedroom It makes me feal cold and lonely in side. It may have his own paintings on the wall. It looks like he's an artist. I don't think he has many clothes and it is a very small bedroom with a cold wooden floor he must like to sit in his bedroom looking at how many chairs he's got. I think he likes the colour blue.

Figure 3.3 Example of child's replies

Questioning

After debating these points ask the children to think about questions they would like to ask the person who lives in this room. The questions may be related to his job, his lifestyle, likes and dislikes and so on. Remind the children that this person is from the past so that questions such as 'What is your favourite video?' will not be applicable. The teacher, in the role of Van Gogh, may then respond to the questions.

Letters

The relationship between Vincent and his younger brother Theo was often difficult. The teacher could give the children some information about Vincent's life and concentrate on his relationship with his brother. In role-play the children could then write a letter from Vincent to Theo begging for money.

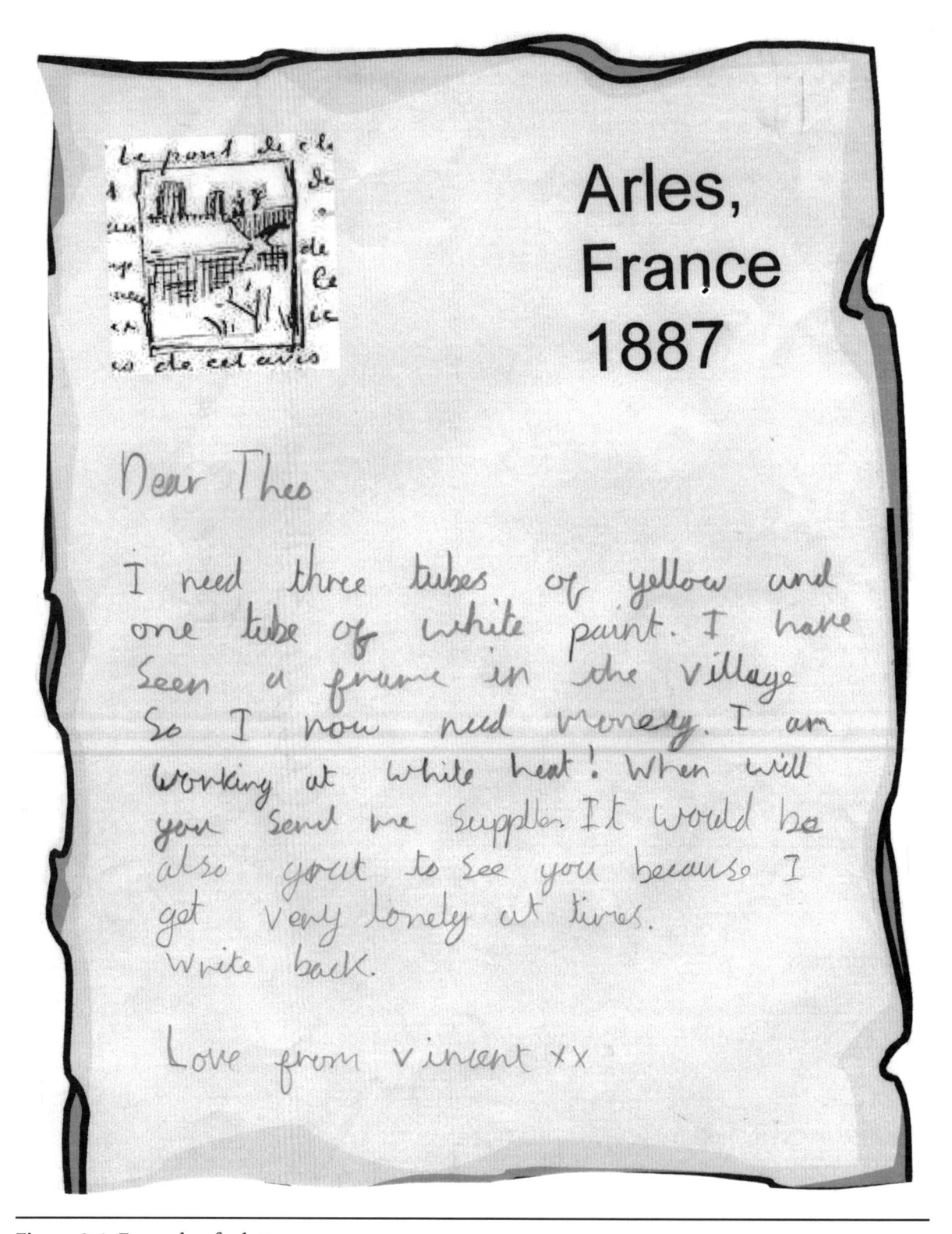

> Arles, France 1887
>
> Dear Theo
>
> I need three tubes of yellow and one tube of white paint. I have seen a frame in the village so I now need money. I am working at white heat! When will you send me supplies. It would be also great to see you because I get very lonely at times. Write back.
>
> Love from Vincent xx

Figure 3.4 Example of a letter

Vincent's house in Arles – *Yellow House*

Description

This vibrant painting contains a number of ingredients to stimulate writing. In the first instance just defining the colours requires the use of descriptive words. The blue of the sky is not just deep blue and begs to be compared to something. Encouraging use of simile and metaphor to classify the colour also introduces the value of using a thesaurus.

The sky was as blue as a kingfisher's wing and had the same luminescent quality.

The sky was peacock blue, so intense you felt you could swim in it.

Describing the yellow house and its position may also be enhanced by personification.

The little house stood strong and upright, its yellow face smiling in the warmth of the sun and its red roof a jaunty hat perched on its proud head.

A house is, of course, where someone lives and this house looks lived in as the shutters are opened. Speculation about who lives there and what do they do raises discussion about this setting. The people in the foreground are dressed in old-fashioned clothes and there are no cars around so we are aware that this is a painting from a different era. What does the shop with the pink shutters sell? Is it bread, groceries or clothes perhaps?

Lists

Decide what sort of a shop it is likely to be. If some of the children have visited France and are aware of small sleepy hamlets then they could perhaps contribute their knowledge about what sorts of shops they have seen. With little transport available the shops then would have to cater for the everyday needs of the people – such as food.

Make a shopping list for the people about to shop there. This may be written vertically, perhaps arranged alphabetically, or from left to right using commas to separate the items. In this way grammar is combined with more creative work.

Poetry

For poetry stimulus the children may imagine that they live in the yellow house. They should describe the sounds and smells experienced every day. This may be written in the form of a poem. Use a writing frame, such as that given in Chapter 2, or just permit the children to write a series of images based on the senses. The following is an example from a Year Five class. The children worked in pairs to share ideas and to discuss their plans before writing.

> *The Yellow House*
>
> This bright yellow house sits
>
> under the deep blue sky
>
> with the relaxing scents of coffee and pie
>
> floating through the spring air.
>
> People walking past this deserted house
>
> as if it wasn't there.
>
> More interested in the food shop next door
>
> Where people are eating.
>
> Poor little house.

Interior of a Restaurant in Arles

Van Gogh painted many pictures of restaurants, both inside and outside, and any of those paintings could be used as the basis for a discussion about food. In the foreground of this particular painting we see the tables set for dinner and some patrons in the background.

Menus

This painting lends itself to writing menus. Ask the children to look at some menus from local restaurants and then to compose one suitable for the restaurant in the painting. If menus are available from French restaurants then it should be noted that the various sections are given titles different to other restaurants. Children may even like to try and write a menu in French, with English explanations. This makes them aware of different languages as well as different writing forms.

Recipes

Restaurants lead on naturally to talking about food and favourite foods. Look at recipes and how they are set out and ask the children to bring in a copy of their favourite recipe to compile into a class book. Take a normal recipe, a cake for example, and use the framework as the basis for inventing an unusual recipe – one for a robot, a dog, an elephant or any other bizarre idea. This gives them practice at writing in a certain format but makes it fun to do.

Starry Night

Van Gogh's use of vibrant colour is obvious in quite a few of his paintings. This vibrancy can only truly be appreciated by seeing the paintings themselves, although the beauty of the night sky is pleasing even in the prints. Fear of the dark is something many children share but this painting shows the dark as belonging to the village that is dwarfed by the beauty of the heavens.

Adventure stories

The sky in this painting is so unusual with the tiny town miniaturised by the swirls of blue and gold sky that one could almost imagine an alien invasion. Again, this is the type of thing that appeals to boys in particular. A visit from outer space may seem incongruous with art from over a hundred years ago, but as a stimulus for narrative it is something that many children could relate to. As always brainstorming ideas and even a shared writing activity to begin the story could be the catalysts for adventure stories. Some children who wrote stories related to this picture projected themselves into the painting. As well as the possibility of meeting aliens the idea that this was pure fantasy came across '… and jumped into space past the bright gold moon and the silver stars and out of the picture'.

What if …

With all good stories the 'what if …' factor is important. Pose a few questions to set minds ticking.

- What if the sky exploded?
- What if this was a different universe?
- What if someone who lived in this village was able to travel to the stars?

Adjective webs

Put a small (thumbnail) copy of the picture in the centre of an A4 page. Draw lines radiating out from this. On each line ask the children to identify something in the picture and write the name (noun) on the line in red ink. Once the nouns have been identified in this way they then have to think of two adjectives to write down describing that noun. This may be done in blue ink. Using the different colours helps to distinguish between nouns and adjectives and the phrases may then be used in narratives.

This is what the start of an adjective web may look like:

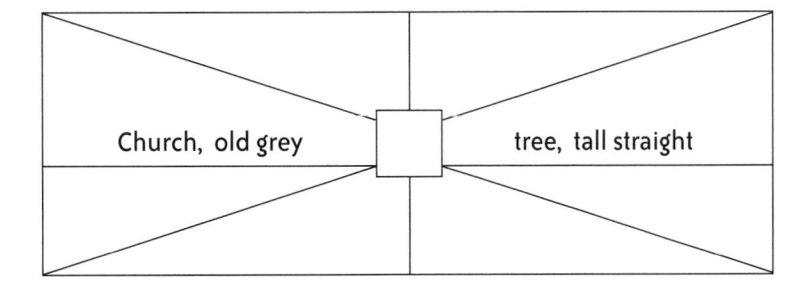

Church, old grey | tree, tall straight

Cross-curricular links

Geography

Many of Van Gogh's paintings are set in France, although he was born in the Netherlands. Ask the children to identify both places on a map of Europe and then to look very closely at the political map of Europe. Questions to ask could be:

- What is the capital of France?
- Why do they have sea walls in the Netherlands?
- Name one town in Holland that you can see on the map.
- Which countries border on France?

Art

Van Gogh's style of painting consisted of many short, sharp strokes and dots of strong colour. Allow the children to experiment with different strokes, brushes and thicknesses of paint. Develop painting techniques allowing each layer of paint to dry first. Give instructions verbally and observe who is able to follow these and how they interpret what you say. This is useful for assessment.

History

Use the internet to find information about life in Van Gogh's time – between 1850 and 1890. Pose specific questions about clothes, transport, who was on the thrones of Europe, what music people enjoyed and anything else of interest. Compile the information into a non-fiction book and alternate between giving a fact and presenting information in question format.

Community links

If there are any restaurants in the area that are willing to forge links with the school take advantage of this by arranging a visit. Often they will have someone who is willing to show groups behind the scenes and maybe even allow children to try their hand at cooking something simple. Designing advertising posters or a children's menu for the restaurant is good experience for the children and often results in favourable publicity for the restaurant.

Pierre-Auguste Renoir

Pierre-Auguste Renoir was born in 1841 and became one of the group of painters known as the Impressionists. His paintings are full of light and colour and are peopled with young friends and lovers. They depict the French middle class at play and his style is full of hope and joy.

The figures in Renoir's paintings have much more personality than those of Lowry so they are perhaps simpler to use as characters in stories. Many of the paintings also involve scenes of

activity, such as *The Umbrellas* or *Luncheon of the Boating Party*, and although the settings are not contemporary the activities still are.

The Umbrellas

In this painting a number of people, including a small girl with a hoop, are grouped together. It has obviously just started to rain as several umbrellas are in evidence and one lady is in the process of putting up her umbrella. The woman in the foreground to the left is carrying a large basket but it is not possible to see its contents.

Figure 3.5 Child's version of *The Umbrellas*

Narratives

One can imagine the hustle and bustle of life in these paintings and it would be easy to build a narrative around the people or the situation. Giving the children a story starter helps to avoid 'blank page' syndrome. In the following example the story starts before the scene in the painting, allowing the children to build up to the scene depicted and then take the story further.

Madame Dupont pulled on her soft leather gloves and fastened the button at the wrist. She looked out of the window and sniffed. 'Well, Marie, it looks as though we will have to take the umbrella. I smell rain in the air.' Marie wrinkled up her little nose and sniffed. She could not understand what Maman was talking about. How could you smell rain? She skipped to the corner and picked up her hoop. Hopefully they could go to the park on their walk today.

What happened after the rain and why the umbrellas were so significant to the story are left to the children. What they need to remember about narratives is that, in general, a story starts with a character who has a problem and the main part of the story revolves around how the problem is to be solved before the resolution and ending. Corden (2002) gives a very comprehensive list of questions one could use to help with narrative writing.

Out of the picture

In her book, *Once upon a Picture*, Sally Swain illustrates what might happen if one of the characters stepped out of the picture and did something different. In this case the little girl with the hoop runs off and finds another child to play with. Using this as an example one could discuss what might happen if one of the characters did something different. For example, the lady with the basket might sit down in the rain and have a picnic or the gentleman with the beard could start singing! Looking at all sorts of strange possibilities like this engages imaginations and gives children ideas about the people in the painting.

Notes

When children plan stories they often write the whole story instead of making notes. Giving them a limited space to make the plan means that they have to use notes. Before writing a narrative on *The Umbrellas* they could use a short planner to make notes for the beginning, middle and end of the story. This could be in the form of an umbrella to make it more appealing and to give them less space to write (see Figure 3.6). Notes have to be crisp and concise.

Figure 3.6 Example of the note-writing

Luncheon of the Boating Party, 1881

This painting is apparently of Renoir's friends enjoying a day out and it depicts a group of young people who have enjoyed a good meal and are engaged in conversation afterwards. Various groups may be observed and homing in on one of these, or a specific person, can lead to different ideas for writing.

Speech/conversation

Imagining the type of conversation between the various members of the luncheon party can lead to work on conversation and punctuation of conversation. Role-play of the situation first helps the children to establish the possible conversations. The young couple on the right are earnestly talking to each other – perhaps they are speaking about something important or maybe they are simply engaged in social chit-chat. The children have to decide for themselves. Dialogue is often used to move narrative forward so examination of extracts from popular

children's novels to establish how this occurs will help before attempting this type of work. Working in pairs to start, the children need a little time to conduct their conversations initially and then they can write down individually the imagined conversation, using a new paragraph for each different person speaking and inverted commas around the spoken words.

Cross-curricular Links

Art

After discussing the techniques the Impressionists used, and perhaps comparing the work of Renoir to that of some of his contemporaries, the children could write a critique of one of the paintings. This could be relatively simple, perhaps six or seven sentences expressing personal preferences and giving a brief description of their favourite painting. Museums and art galleries offering educational tours may have this type of exercise built into their programme of events, so it is worth enquiring locally to find out what is on. Seeing original masterpieces is always more impressive than viewing a print or another kind of reproduction.

Geography

Much of Renoir's work is set in Paris so identifying this city on the map of Europe and then making a fact file about it is one way to combine literacy and geography. Each child in the class could be given a separate question to which they have to find the answer, either through use of reference books or the internet, and the answers would be word-processed to produce an information leaflet.

Community Links

Brochures from the travel agent are a good reference source for information on France. This contact could be expanded by asking the local travel agent to come and speak to the children. Travel agents will be more willing to do this if you do not approach them at a very busy time and if you are obliging enough to send home advertising leaflets for the company. Children may then write their own travel brochures for the city, or indeed any destination.

Conclusion

As stated at the beginning these ideas are simply a start. The works of many more modern artists are also just as suitable for discussion and subsequent writing activities. Edward Hopper's paintings depict scenes from American life that show characters who seem detached from each other, and possibly even reality. They could be regarded as freeze-frames and as such pose questions about the lives and problems of the characters in the paintings.

Jack Vettriano, with his Scottish heritage, is another popular modern day artist. His work decorates posters and cards nationwide. Examining these prints and the scenes and characters in the different settings opens up a whole new world of possible narratives – with a bit of imagination.

Sculptures both classical and modern, or the ethnic carvings found in many high street shops, may also form the basis of a story. Not only do you have the story the sculpture tells but also the story behind it.

- What was the inspiration behind it?
- Who could have made it and why?
- What is that person's story?

The possibilities are endless.

SUMMARY

This chapter looked at some of the paintings of Lowry, Van Gogh and Renoir and how they could be used as stimulus for different types of writing. Ideas were linked to certain named paintings but could be adapted for different ages and abilities. Cross-curricular links were also given so that the key skill of literacy could be joined to different subjects to enhance learning. These links are generally to the humanities. Writing ideas given are as follows:

Questioning – questions posed to elicit imaginative response and encourage children to ask questions

Narratives – stories based on characters and settings, adventure stories, what if ... , out of the picture

Rhyme – related to games

Role-play – used as a stimulus for discussion prior to writing speech in play form and with proper punctuation

Description – use of adjectives and adjective webs, similes and metaphors

Reports/commentary – writing/speaking in reporting style

List and notes – the use of concise types of writing

Letters – writing in role

Poetry – using senses

Menus and recipes – particular forms of writing

CHAPTER 4

Picture Books

'Most of us learn to read through picture books and initially the visual and verbal share prominence. But somewhere along the line the appreciation of pictures gets left behind'. So said founding director H. Nicholas B. Clark at the opening of the Eric Carle Museum of Picture Book Art. In America the importance of picture book art has been brought to the fore by the creation of this museum. This quotation verbalises exactly what happens in schools. Beginner readers are actively encouraged to use pictures as cues. The popularity of the *Oxford Reading Tree* series lies in the graphic illustrations that readers use to help them make sense of the story. However, as children become more fluent readers they regard picture books as 'babyish' and move away from these often carefully crafted and well constructed texts to something more 'wordy'.

Picture books are therefore usually seen as the province of Key Stage One but in this chapter both key stages will be included. Picture books usually tell a good story and as Hughes and Ellis (1998: 28) point out, 'Stories are a good starting point for learning'.

Judith Graham (1995) reminds us that pictures are important for children who are learning to read and that they have been used throughout time as the basis for a story. This is generally accepted in the early years but as children become more competent and independent readers, as mentioned before, pictures no longer have the same focus.

This chapter examines in detail how picture books can enhance learning and imagination for children in primary school. Children are often able to see much more in a picture than an adult and this helps them to ascertain what is going on in a story. Sometimes the pictures tell a different story, as in John Burningham's *Come Away from the Water, Shirley*, where the words and pictures tell contrasting tales. Allowing older children to have access to picture books helps them to realise how important it is to build up the scenes in a narrative. Older pupils may examine picture books and then attempt to write and illustrate their own versions for younger siblings or children. This gives both an audience and a purpose for their writing and they also learn that producing a picture book is not an easy task.

I propose to take two books and look at them in depth to see how they may be used to stimulate writing. Martin Waddell is a significant children's author who writes both for younger children and teenagers. Some of his books for older children are based on the troubles in Northern Ireland, his home country, but he is perhaps better known for his picture books. The following ideas are based on *Once There Were Giants*.

Once There Were Giants by Martin Waddell (Illustrated by Penny Dale)

Synopsis

The story is based on one little girl growing up. In the beginning she is a baby and everyone else is a giant in her eyes. Through a series of pictures and words we see her growing up and marrying. The final scene is almost a flashback to the beginning where the adults are crowded around a baby. This time, however, the baby is hers and she is one of the giants. It is a wonderful description of the circle of life and each page ends with a refrain: 'The one … is me'.

Using the book as a framework

Reading for enjoyment is something that is important for children. It is not just enough that they are able to access texts and decode these. Children who read for pleasure are much more likely to extend their learning in so many ways. It is essential therefore that dissecting them and destroying the emotive response evoked must not diminish the sheer pleasure of listening to stories. The ideas that follow are not based on the usual word, sentence and text level work recommended by the Literacy Strategy. They start with the story and use that as the basis for cross-curricular work, which in turn helps the children to understand the basis of the story.

Children who interact with a story are much more likely to learn something from it than those who listen passively. Unsworth (2001: 168) states that 'while all images construct representational meanings they also simultaneously construct interactive meanings'. This indicates the complex process that occurs when children view illustrations. They are not just looking at what the picture represents but are also relating that image to their own experiences and compositions.

In *Once There Were Giants*, Martin Waddell uses a repetitive refrain, reminiscent of the oral, traditional stories. Although this is important in itself, allowing the children to involve themselves in the reading of the story by joining in, it also serves to stress the importance of the central character in the story. Children enjoy putting themselves into stories so can relate to this easily.

Art/RE

One way to stimulate children to write is to start by asking them to draw a picture of themselves on a special day in their lives. In *More Than Words* (2004), a joint UKLA and QCA publication, the emphasis is on how multimodal texts develop children's understanding and give them a 'repertoire of approaches making appropriate choices to communicate effectively '(p. 10). Through assessment of drawing and writing teachers are also able to develop their understanding of the ideas children are attempting to convey through the 'combined uses of images and words' (p. 10).

Special days are, of course, few and far between for many children in deprived areas. In some schools children can recall lots of special occasions while others cannot remember anything special. For those who need help, talking about the first day at school or in their new class or a birthday may help them to remember a special event in their lives. Even something like receiving a certificate in assembly or a gift from Santa could be the focus.

Once the occasion has been selected then each child has to draw the special event with him or herself, clearly identified in the picture. It is essential to give them plenty of time to do this and to talk to children as they are drawing so that they can explain what they are doing and the finer details of the drawing. At the end of the lesson children can either show their drawing to the class – a good speaking and listening activity – or work in groups to talk about their special day. A teacher talking about special days in relation to different religious festivals can extend this. Some children may identify a religious event such as the baptism of a sibling as the special day, so raising this point naturally.

In the follow up to the drawing session they may be asked to write a sentence, or more depending on the age and ability, to explain what is happening in the picture. With young children, or those with special needs, the teacher can act as scribe. The last line should copy the example from the book by saying 'The one … is me'. If written out on paper, instead of in books, the sheets may then be stuck into a sugar paper book to make a class book of 'Special Days'.

Figure 4.1 Example of writing about 'Special Days'

History

Once There Were Giants also lends itself very easily to history. Children may be encouraged to bring in photos of themselves as babies and to talk about what they can remember. With some children it may be possible to ask them if they really remember the events they are describing or whether they are recounting memories related to them by parents. Thoughts about growing up and any aspirations may be discussed at this point. This in itself can lead to further investigations. If children have aspirations for a certain job then they can be asked what they know about it and what they can find out. This may be recorded on a KWL grid, as described by Wray and Lewis (1997).

What do I **K**now?	**W**hat do I want to know?	What have I **L**earnt?
I want to be a lorry driver because they go around the country	How do they learn to drive lorries?	They have to do special driving tests
	How much do they get paid?	They get about £8 per hour

The concept of chronology may be difficult for some children. Teachers can help with this process by bringing in photographs of themselves as babies, toddlers, youngsters and teenagers to make a timeline. A washing line of clothes worn at certain ages also helps children to develop their sense of chronology in a very visual form.

An obvious development on from this is to make and label a family tree. However, with so many single parents and mixed families this may not be possible. Completing a friendship tree is an alternative. The child draws a picture of himself at the bottom and the various branches of the tree can be a series of pictures and labels of family and friends. In this way all the children are able to produce something that shows their relationship to others. For more advanced writers each label could give extra information about a person. For example: 'This is my Gran. She lives in a flat with her three cats. We visit her every Tuesday after school.'

The history theme may be taken further by making a list of questions for grandparents to answer about their childhoods. The teacher can scribe all the questions and then the class has to vote on which questions they think are the most useful. If the teacher compiles this into a questionnaire format they can take it home to complete and then relate the responses to the class. Typical questions tend to be:

- What sort of toys did you play with?
- Were you ever naughty?
- Who was your favourite friend?
- What sort of presents did you have for your birthday?
- Where did you go on holiday?
- What was your favourite television programme?
- What did you do at school?

- Who was your favourite teacher?
- Did you like school dinners?

The teacher obviously needs to be careful about which questions to include in a worksheet to take home, as grandparents do not want to be totally overwhelmed!

Although this is a book designed for young children, Key Stage Two children may also be involved in writing activities linked to this story. They could be asked to write a special book for siblings illustrated by drawings or even photographs. Each page could identify either a birthday or a special time, such as the first tooth, first step, first time in the paddling pool or other family events. The bottom of each page has the refrain 'The one … is you'. Completing something like this is unique to the individual. Often special needs children, or boys who find writing 'boring', will complete a project like this as it has a particular meaning for them and because of the repetitive refrain the focus on writing is not so stressful.

Geography

Special days do not necessarily happen at home. Ask the children where they were on their special day.

- On the beach?
- Visiting a friend?
- At the swimming pool?
- At school?
- This country somewhere?
- Abroad?

This can lead to looking at maps to identify the different places. If most of the special events took place in the local area a 'bird's eye' view map could be made with children's names marking the places they thought were important. For children who have travelled further afield a country or even a world map may be required.

The Mysteries of Harris Burdick by Chris Van Allsburg

Synopsis

This book is essentially a series of black and white pictures with a facing page containing a title and the beginnings of a first line. All the pictures contain enough detail to encourage discussion and the titles and lines add an extra clue to the mystery. The preface of the book explains the story of Harris Burdick who left these mysterious drawings with a publisher and then was never seen again. This preface is written with such conviction that one is unsure whether the story is true or not. Although I have placed this book as a text to use at Key Stage Two, it may also be of interest at upper Key Stage One.

Using the book as a framework

This is truly a picture book worth owning. For the following activity you will need two copies, one to read and show in its entirety and the other one, unfortunately due to copyright, will have to be cut up so that you will have the individual pictures. This is a dreadful sacrilege for any book but entirely necessary here. The captions you can type up and put on the back or the bottom of the pictures. If you laminate the cut up pages then it will last for years and may be used time and time again with different age groups. As there are 14 pictures in the book you should have enough copies to cater for a class of 28. This book has been used with classes from Year Two to Year Seven and is guaranteed to evoke a response.

In the first instance the teacher will need to explain that this is a picture book but one with a difference. The children have to 'read' the pictures to unravel the mystery. With upper juniors you will almost see the children look at you in disbelief as they generally regard picture books as beneath them. However, once they listen to the preface and see the pictures they will be captivated.

Children are asked to work in pairs in the first instance to discuss what they can see in the pictures and what they think the pictures could be about. This enables children to engage in collaborative discussion and thinking, as Mercer et al. (1999) demonstrated in their research. Each pair has a different picture from the book. If the class exceeds 28 then groups of three may be necessary. Although Mercer and Dawes advocate groups of three for discussion purposes, for this particular exercise I have found paired work to be most effective. Allow 20 minutes for discussion time and give them some pointers to get them started.

- What can you see in the pictures?
- What do you think is happening?
- Does the title or caption help or confuse?
- What is the story behind the picture?

You may need to emphasise that there is no right or wrong answer. For some children, especially those in upper juniors who have been 'trained' to be pupils (Dowling, 1995); this open-ended approach is difficult. Working in pairs, or groups, gives the children confidence to express themselves.

They now have about 25 minutes to produce individual pieces based on their responses to the story. These may be in any format – a poem, a story, a plan for a story, question and answer, or play scripts. The choice is entirely up to them. Children may also need to be reminded that the objective is to produce individual responses and to be creative – not to worry about spelling and punctuation. As Pullman (2005) says 'features of language such as grammar, are things you can correct at proof stage'. Children may adjust these basics on the second draft, or perhaps complete this on the computer.

In the plenary session individuals may explain their pictures and the format they have used in response to their particular pictures. Even special needs pupils have responded in imaginative ways to these pictures. Giving children the chance to share ideas before writing has a positive effect. The following passage is an example from a special needs boy who normally has difficulty writing more than the date and title. It has been typed for legibility but the spelling is original.

The final line is the caption from the picture. It was interesting to see that the boy used this as his final line instead of the beginning.

CAPTAIN TORY

A captain cacherd a little boy for a slave and the, CAPTAIN'S bote apeard forgetting on the main (b x) ship. And captain will tace the litel boy neve to be herd from (Agen x) egen

He swung his lantern three times and slowly the schooner appeared.

Other examples show how some children question what they can see while others are immediately drawn into a narrative.

A Strange Day In July

In this picture it looks like it is night time. Why were they at the beach at night time? Were they hiding there? Who knows, it is all a great mystery. The boy keeps throwing the stones in the water. But the thrid one keeps skipping back. Maybe someone is under there. But why would someone be under there. Maybe it is a animal. Who is the girl. Who knows.

Figure 4.2 Example of child's work

One day a lady was walking to a libory called Mr Lindens Libory she went to the spell ile and picked up a plont book she went to the reception and said "i would like to borrow this book please" Mr. Linden said " that book is donger's we have meny other books please pick a nother". No i will stick to this one thank you she went home and to start to read it was geting late i will turn my lamp on she got in bed and storted to read she fell asleep with the book open when she read it she storted a spell well she was asleep wines grew out of the book and she was never heard of AGAIN!

Figure 4.3 Example of child's work

Of course, the teacher may prefer to use these wonderful pictures in different ways to encourage writing. Any one of the pictures may be used as the focus for a whole-class lesson and a mind map could be made of different ideas linked to the picture which individuals may use as the basis for stories. Alternatively, a play could be built up around the characters seen in the picture and then acted out in groups.

Art

Copy-cat pictures using the illustrations from the book may be completed by children as this requires careful observation and use of sketching and shading. Use of charcoal for some of the drawings may be effective, as long as the child does not smudge this too much. Any work of this type encourages even closer examination of the pictures and so aids understanding. It also encourages thinking about settings and a description of the illustration using various phrases could be attempted as a follow-up to the drawing.

History

Many of the pictures in the book look as if they are from the mid-twentieth century. They may be used as a basis for research about what people wore in those days, how they travelled, what happened in a certain decade. This may coincide with a project on World War Two with the songs from that era used to enhance story-readings based on the pictures. Children could perhaps write their own song lyrics to accompany the pictures, or read their stories to incorporate the music of those times. They could imagine themselves transported back to that era and could write a diary of events for a week in wartime Britain.

Murris and Haynes (2000) regard picture books as a firm basis for children's thinking and philosophising and believe this type of activity is central to enhancing children's capacities for listening and enquiring. Sarah Matthews (2001), who has worked with children on all sorts of activities based on picture books, thinks that they not only enable children to access different levels of meaning in a text but also 'the use of illustration also facilitated the writing of some of those pupils whose learning mode is essentially kinetic'. Alan Hill (2001) says 'pictures have something of the quality of verbs; they convey or are part of the action. But pictures can also have something of the more static quality of nouns, providing a background against or within which the action takes place, providing the added interest of life going on around the central characters and their situations'.

The value of picture books throughout the primary phase and beyond is obvious, not only for the possibilities they bring for creative writing but also for what Unsworth (2001) describes as the 'intersection of language and image in picture books'.

SUMMARY

In this chapter the importance of picture books in the development of the imagination and as a basis for creative writing was deliberated. Two books, **Once There Were Giants** by Martin Waddell and **The Mysteries of Harris Burdick** by Chris Van Allsburg, were used as the basis for exploring ways to engage children in writing of different kinds. Cross-curricular links to other subjects were also covered.

Writing activities were as follows:

Special days: writing personal events – cross-curricular links with art, RE, geography and history

KWL grids: information searching on jobs

Family/friendship tree: writing about people who matter to the child

Questionnaires: questions for grandparents about their childhoods

Free writing: creative responses to pictures in any format

Descriptive writing: copy-cat illustrations to be accompanied by descriptions of settings

Song lyrics: writing song lyrics of the era

Diary writing: diary of a week in a different time

CHAPTER 5

Photographs

Photographs may be an art form as well as illustration. How to use photographs to stimulate discussion and lead into narrative is the basis for this chapter. Digital cameras have made it possible and even desirable to incorporate photography into lessons. Photographs are instant and can be manipulated by use of software so that they become an art form. Even photographs of quite ordinary things may be made to look strange or sinister and can form the basis for discussion and writing. Hobbs (1996) discusses the 'paradoxical nature of images' and asks the questions:

- Do images tell the truth?
- What meanings do different people see in images?
- How do words shape the meanings of images?
- How do the authors of images shape their messages?
- Why do images arouse us emotionally?

Although Hobbs was asking these questions in relation to news based images the questions she raises are of relevance in discussion of any photographic images.

Talking Pictures from the Questions Publishing Company provides a number of striking images that children can use as a basis for discussion. Although this is meant to act as a starting point for art work based on digital photography, some of the images presented just beg to be used as stimulus for creative writing. One photograph, *From the Edge of the Garden* by Karen Ingham, shows a toddler peering through a rain-splattered window – a simple enough picture until one realises he is holding a very sharp knife in his hand. Another particularly strange photograph, '*Untitled* by Patrica Townsend, shows a hand with what appears to be an egg cradled in the palm. The egg has a face so this leads naturally to all sorts of discussion. An image such as an egg in a hand instantly transports one to that far distant land of 'Once upon a time ...'.

Photographs from magazines

Photographs are generally linked with non-fiction writing but they may also be used as the basis for narratives. A glance through a Sunday magazine provides a wealth of resources. An

advertisement for a credit card features a photograph of a house and garden covered in snow while the remaining gardens are lush and green. Think of the questions this poses. Just identifying the difference is the first step for children and prompts them to ask all sorts of questions. The teacher may start them thinking by asking, 'Is there anything strange about this picture?' Once the children can identify the odd nature of the one house covered in snow, just saying, 'I wonder why?' provokes a string of explanations.

Here are some examples from a Year Two class:

> *Somebody just put the snow on that one house.*

> *I think it's all covered in popcorn!*

> *I think they wanted to make it look like Christmas so they put snow all around.*

> *Maybe it just snowed very hard in that one place.*

The picture could be linked to Oscar Wilde's story of *The Selfish Giant* whose garden is always in winter or the children could think of titles for the story themselves. Unusual pictures like this stir the imagination and raise the 'what if' question that is at the base of much narrative. Research by Kendrick and McKay (2001) discovered that children have 'very rich images of literacy' and their interpretations of children's drawings indicate the impressions made by visual forms of different types.

In the same magazine there is a fashion feature and beautiful young women in evening clothes are photographed against icy backdrops. One photograph is particularly striking. It features a woman standing on the lake with a backdrop of a waterfall and snow-dusted cliffs. One immediately thinks of the Snow Queen. The model in question looks wistfully to her right as if she is waiting for someone or something to appear. Who or what will come along is left to the imagination and exchanging ideas about the woman and her fate could form the basis of many different stories, as each child will put their own interpretation on the picture. Working in pairs, or small groups, ask each child to write down one question, or comment, about the photograph and then to share their ideas as a class. If the teacher uses a system, such as the Aidan Chambers *Tell Me* model, then this should provide a rich framework of ideas from which the children may choose to build a story.

The advertisements for pensions showing two halves of the same face with one half aged are wonderful for both art work and characterisation. Give each child half a face and ask him, or her, to draw and shade, with pencil only, the other half of the face.

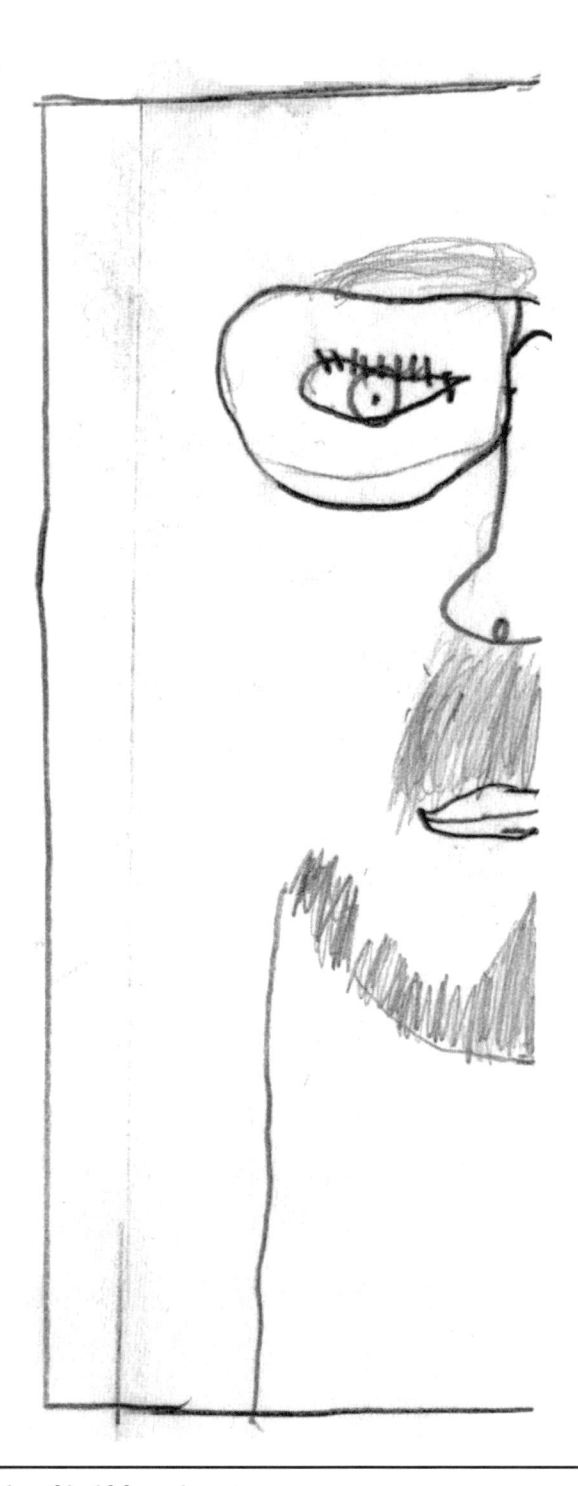

Figure 5.1 Example of half face drawing

The same procedure may be used for any full-page photograph of a face. The face may be cut in half down the centre and each half given to a different child. Putting the two halves together again raises much hilarity and discussion about the finer details of the drawing. By studying the lines and qualities of the face the children start to develop thoughts about the type of person they are drawing and may be encouraged to write a story or just some thoughts about that person.

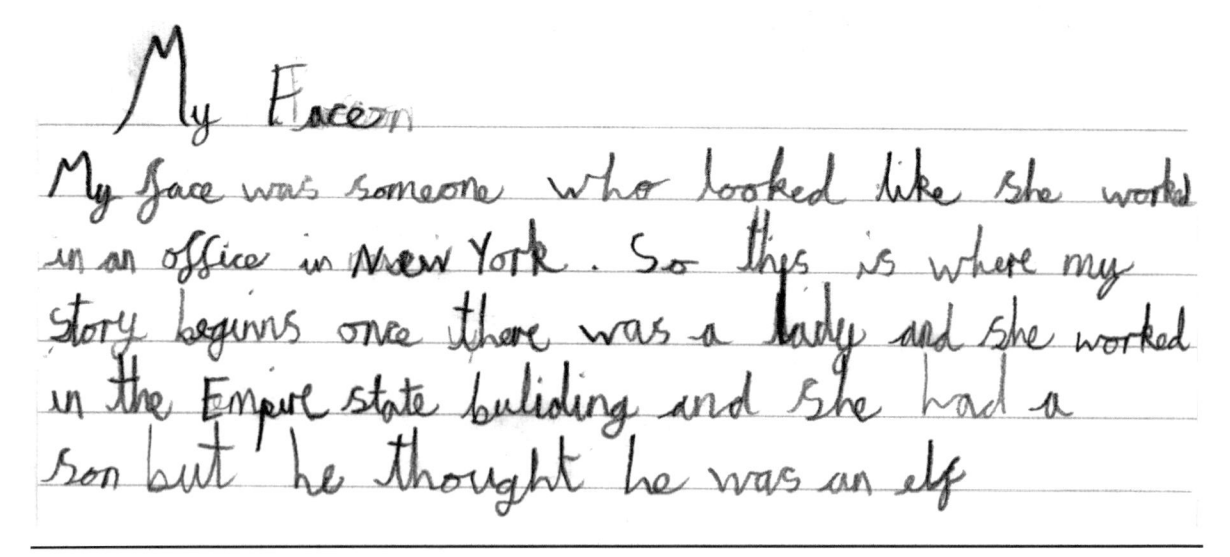

> My Face
>
> My face was someone who looked like she worked in an office in New York. So this is where my story begins once there was a lady and she worked in the Empire state buliding and she had a son but he thought he was an elf

Figure 5.2 Example of child's work

In this example the children were just asked to write a couple of sentences about the person they had drawn and then to start a story with that person as the main character. Giving each child a character profile to complete may be used if preferred. By filling in this type of writing frame children can begin to develop an idea of the personality. The following frame is for use mainly at Key Stage Two. For younger children a simplified version would be required.

Character Profile

Name: _____

Age: _____

Description: _____

Colour of hair: _____   Eyes: _____

Any distinguishing features: _____

Family: _____

Address: _____

Job: _____

Likes: _____
_____

Dislikes: _____
_____

Favourite food: _____

Favourite holiday place: _____

Any special skills: _____

Photocopiable: Exciting Writing: Activities for 5 to 11 year olds
Paul Chapman Publishing © Jacqueline Harrett 2006

Characters and settings

Characters do not have to be people. Many children's books have animals as their main characters and these are very popular. Magazines often contain articles about different animals and beautiful photographs can be incorporated as the basis for non-fiction writing and research on a particular animal or by using the plight of these animals as the basis for a story. When one considers the popularity of *Wind in the Willows*, *Watership Down* and *The Animals of Farthing Wood* for example, there is much to be said for writing from an animal's viewpoint. The characters all display human emotions and other qualities. This genre is, however, difficult for young children and probably best left to older juniors to tackle – after reading several examples.

Magazine and internet photographs (see further information for this chapter) also provide settings for stories. A photograph of a vegetable market in a foreign street, for example Bombay, is alight with vibrant colours. Using this as a basis for discussion one may talk about the senses aroused by this picture. Engaging the senses and trying to imagine the smells, tastes, sounds and textures of the different vegetables, as well as having the visual presentation, are all steps towards poetry writing. For children who have difficulty imagining themselves in such a place, playing some Indian music and bringing examples of suitable herbs and vegetables into school would add an extra dimension to this particular type of photograph. If you teach in a multicultural school then ask the children to bring in any unusual vegetables or herbs they use in their day-to-day cooking. If they have visited different places abroad then discuss their experiences of street markets. Giving children a starter line or a structure often helps them to overcome 'writer's block'.

Shared writing as a class is, of course, an invaluable tool to help children to understand the different requirements of each writing genre and to pool ideas together. Concept or mind maps help children to organise their thoughts more effectively.

Advertisements for foreign holidays often portray unusual sights like the monastery on top of a mountain. Travel brochures often contain evocative photographs of landscapes and buildings rather than standard hotel blocks. If the photograph has a building as part of the landscape then it can pose various questions. Who built this building and why is it in that position? As well as a focal point for setting the scene for a story, this type of photograph may be used for geography and history projects. Finding out more about the country in question involves the use of different reference sources. One could research the country on the internet, for example, or write to the tourist board of the country in question for further information.

Once all the information is assembled it may be presented to the rest of the class in various forms. It could be a powerpoint presentation, thus involving ICT skills, a newspaper item, a brochure, a leaflet or a poster. Facts may be turned into questions – 'Did you know that … ?' If children work in groups on this type of project it enables them to make the most of their particular talents whilst gaining valuable experience from each other on how to improve different skills.

Other sources and ideas

Even photographs of quite ordinary things can tell a story. Many wedding photographers use what is termed 'reportage' in the wedding albums they create. Photographs of hands buttoning up dresses or shoes and half-consumed glasses of wine all have a tale to tell.

This type of thing appeals more to girls than boys but a pair of dirty football boots or a car with a spare wheel sitting beside it may have more man appeal, especially if teamed with a caption linked to a famous footballer or racing driver. Each member of the class can have a different photograph to use or children may work in pairs to discuss ideas before beginning to draft out a storyline. Writing requires thinking and drafting time, as well as writing and editing time, and most children find that a short while spent talking about ideas with a sympathetic partner helps. Making concept maps of ideas, or story maps, and labelling the order of events help children to plan their stories.

Another method to use is to ask the children to take their own photographs of things that interest them. This could be done in the form of a collage of different items of significance to a particular child or just a photograph taken when out for a walk. Even something as ordinary as a footprint can lead to a discussion of ideas for narratives. This photograph of an old door was used as the basis for a story.

Figure 5.3 Photograph of an old door

In many narratives a door leads to a different world. A few simple questions can lead to the sharing of ideas.

- Who lives here?
- What happens when you go through the door?
- Where does it lead?

With a Year Five class this seemed to be the focus for horror stories with strange worlds and whispering voices, as well as signs on the walls in blood saying 'Fear thee who enter for this is death!'

The same photograph, in class discussion with a Year Two class, became the door of dreams and led to some very interesting responses.

Once upon a time there was a DOOR. The door was a very spooky door as it looked. It was a very magical door that took you wherever you dreemed (sic). One day they notest (noticed) that the door was a door of dreams. Now this door was sracht (scratched) and batterd (battered) and rusty. Know (no) one had ever sept thruw (stepped through) this door for 100 years, that's my estermate (estimate). So they opened the door and it was a land of dancers but thay (they) weren't nomal (normal) dancers they were fairy dancers sparkerling (sparkling) and gliserning (glistening). They were gorgeous. We started to dance as well. It put us in a dancey mood.

Another child was obviously influenced by computer games as this extract demonstrates:

Once upon a time there was an old creaky door and long ago a man went through and only person yet. A cople (couple) years later a boy called Kevin opened the door and fell in to a game cube. On the first level it was on the moon and on the moon Kevin met a boy called Charlie and Charlie showed Kevin were a veris selpt (slept). There foot steps were so nosy (noisy) the veris woke up and chased them he zapped them a few times and then they came across another door so they went throoh (through) it. Charlie said 'we must be on the next level' and Kevin said 'woopee'.

This story continued with the Roman level and then the prehistoric level before the fourth level where everything was upside down and 'Well it was a bit weird'. Eventually they found the last door and escaped from the game.

The photograph of the door may also be used as the basis for poetry writing. A 'lift the flap' door with the writing hidden underneath could form an attractive display and adds more excitement to the writing process. Children simply write a list of possibilities and illustrate it appropriately. Younger children may just make a list of characters while older children can incorporate more description.

Behind the door

```
Behind the door hides ...

            A wizard weaving
            spells,
            A mad professor
            mixing potions,
            A dragon awakening
            after a hundred
            years,
            A monster waiting to
            eat you up!
            Look out!
```

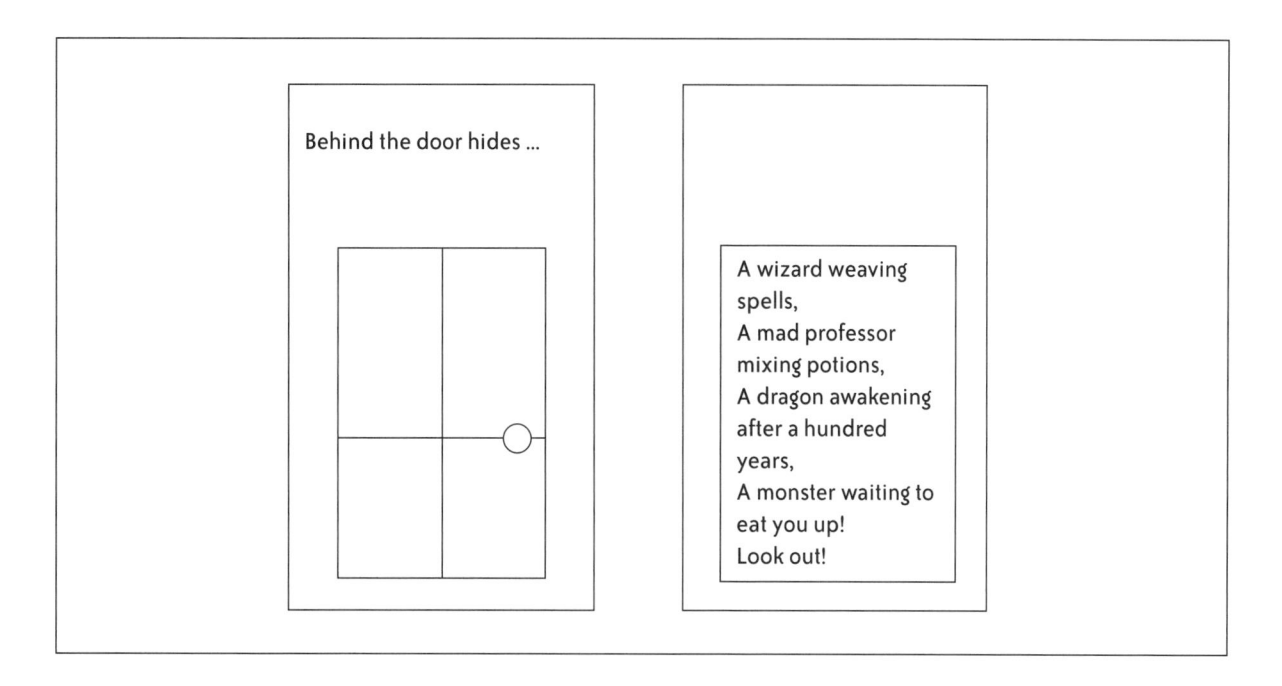

A structure like this is also useful for teaching grammar such as nouns, adjectives and verbs, in a more inspiring way than ploughing through textbook pages and completing exercises at word level. In this way children are actually using grammar to make sense of their writing. They start with a list of nouns and then add adjectives and verbs to produce a fuller picture. Moira Andrew (1996), explains how to approach poetry writing in this way.

Photographs of castles or old historical sites also form a useful link between history and literacy. The following photograph can be used with a simple story starter to lead to narratives. Children learn best if they can make connections with their learning so linking the photograph with a classic story such as *The Gauntlet* by Ronald Welch may also help. In this book Peter finds a gauntlet and is transported back to the fourteenth century. As well as being a gripping story, sure to appeal to boys, this fiction text is full of details related to castles and dress in the past, providing an excellent cross-curricular link.

Figure 5.4 Example of an historical site

Here is one example of a story starter:

James blinked as he entered the hall of the castle. The sun was streaming through the open doorway but he shivered as the damp air inside made him feel uneasy. His foot knocked against something on the muddy floor. Bending down James could see something that looked like a necklace. He lifted it and wiped off some of the mud. It was a cross, shaped out of pewter or something like that, he thought. He felt dizzy and his eyes blurred. James rubbed his eyes and looked around. The hall had changed somehow and a long wooden table stood in the middle. People, in strange costumes, were bustling about all around him where before there had been no one. 'Come on lad. Stop dreaming. There's work to be done. No time for idling.'

It is left to the writer to decide in which century the story is to be set. It could be based on Roman or Tudor times to link with relevant history projects. If this is the case then any information the children have learnt as part of their history may be interwoven with the fictional account of James and his adventures. What happens to his character and how he gets back to his own time are left to the writer. Discussion of ideas and making a story plan before writing are essential. The opportunity to act out stories before writing often enhances the experience and helps children to 'fix' the order of events into their minds before writing. In this way they are able to orally redraft stories before anything is written down (Jones, 1988).

Postcards

Postcards are a tremendous source for cross-curricular links. If you have a selection of postcards from different countries then you have the beginnings for geographical enquiry by grouping them into countries and continents. Writing postcards is different from writing letters. Reading some of the messages on the backs of the cards and discussing why they are different from letters or emails is a way to start.

Alternatively, the teacher could compose two messages; one in typical postcard style and another in over-descriptive prose. If these are used in a shared reading session and then discussed it should highlight for children the genre of writing used. This may be followed in a shared, or guided, writing session by composing a postcard-style message. The children may then design and make postcards of their village, town or city pretending they are visitors. This sort of activity helps children to look positively at their surroundings and to develop an awareness of their own environment.

Gathering postcards from different eras gives an historical theme. For this type of work it may be worth looking at *A Postcard Century* by Tom Phillips. This book contains a variety of postcards illustrating the changes in social attitudes throughout the twentieth century.

Frames

Photographs can often be misleading. Show children how they may be misled by using frames. Make two L-shaped frames out of cardboard and use a photograph from a newspaper or magazine. Frame a small part of the photograph and ask the children to describe what they see and what their perceptions are. This works best with photographs of people in different settings. Frame the person's face first and then gradually move the frames outwards to include more of the background. The more information they are shown, the more depth of understanding they have of that character and setting.

Storyboards

Storyboards can easily be created by using photographs. In some magazines they have a photo story with captions under each picture. Teachers can provide children with this sort of storyboard and ask them to write the narrative. An example of this is shown here.

Figure 5.5 Example of a storyboard

In this simple framework the two characters, the dragon and the owl, meet, have some sort of conversation and then the owl departs. What happened, what was said, why the owl left and everything else to do with this are left to the imagination. This proved very popular with Year Two children who decided that the dragon was after treasure and that owl knew that the key led to a secret cave!

Photograph frames like this may also be used for caption writing. This short, sharp style of writing is often popular with boys as it requires little writing but a great deal of thought if one wishes to make an impact. The 'shoots' may be planned first.

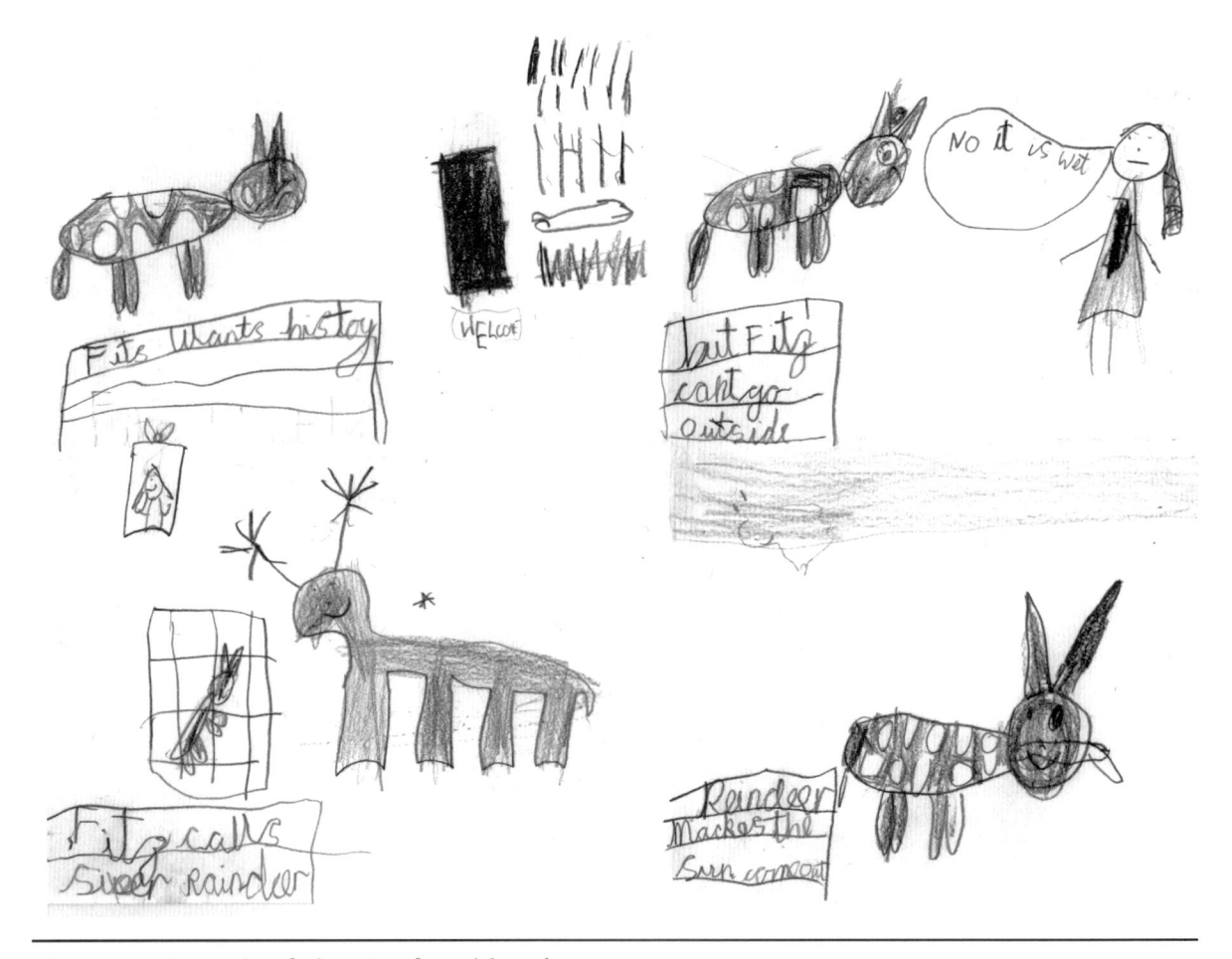

Figure 5.6 Example of planning for a 'shoot'

As shown above, children may design and make their own storyboard backgrounds, take the photographs and write the captions to tell the story. Although the example shown was individual work this may also be a collaborative effort. In fact, working in a group is good for children's speaking and listening activities and also promotes social skills. To do this it is best if children work in groups of between four and six. They need to decide on the characters to feature in the shoot. A maximum of two characters is recommended to begin with. Once they have decided on the storyline they can each draw a part of the background scene and pose the characters in position to take the photographs. If interactive whiteboard technology is available then the storyboard may be presented to the whole class with the group members taking it in turn to act as narrators. Otherwise, photographs may be printed and the story made into a book for the class, and other children in the school, to read and enjoy.

Older children may prefer to take photographs of each other and write the sort of photo story seen in many popular teen magazines. These usually incorporate not only captions but also speech and thought bubbles to indicate what the story is all about and how the characters are feeling about the situation.

Photography is often viewed as simply a form of illustration used in non-fiction books, but in an increasingly digital age it is a technique teachers will need to become more familiar with in order to enhance learning and to excite all children to want to write.

> **SUMMARY**
>
> In this chapter the use of photographs was discussed with an emphasis on characters and settings for narrative. Use of digital cameras in classrooms was mentioned and various photographs with related ideas and some examples of work were included.
>
> Writing ideas given are as follows:
>
> **Questioning** – discussion points raised by images
>
> **Photographs from magazines** – using faces for art and characters as well as settings for narrative and geography links
>
> **Character profiles** – photocopiable worksheet to hold information
>
> **Non-fiction writing** – researching and presenting facts about a country
>
> **Postcards** – writing short notes
>
> **Letter writing** – requesting information about a country from the consulate
>
> **Reportage** – pictures telling stories
>
> **Poetry writing** – using a framework
>
> **Photo storyboards** – children composing their own storyboards using digital photographs
>
> **Captions** – simple captions for picture stories

Chapter 6

Media

This chapter examines some of the devices and designs available to today's teachers to use in the classroom. This is simply touching on a developing form of literacy - a collection of thoughts and ideas to help make the most of a growing body of research.

Television, videos and DVDs

The subject of whether television is beneficial to children's learning is almost as emotive as the teaching of reading. It is one of those topics that really set pulses racing and most people have an opinion on the subject. Whether you are of the belief that television and video are affecting children's ability to listen actively, or that these media sources are a brilliant teaching tool to stimulate imagination and discussion, the fact remains that the media are a part of all our lives (Marsh, 2004). The first part of this chapter examines the use of television, video or DVD in the classroom and how these may be channelled into the teaching of writing.

In many schools television programmes are selected for their educational value and form part of the timetabled curriculum. Teachers who plan lessons around them are conversant with the learning objectives and have a range of follow-up resources to put to good use once the children have watched the programme. Children who have a viewing task will know that they will be expected to recount various points from their viewing and will listen quietly, totally engaged with the programme.

In other schools television provides respite for teachers with sometimes two classes huddled together to watch a programme in the afternoon. There is little discussion other than a few minutes of asking the children what they have watched and which bits they enjoyed. The value of the programme is negligible. Videos exist for 'wet' playtimes and end of term when teachers are sorting out their cupboards and trying to catch up with paperwork.

These two examples are extremes perhaps, but if one asks 'Which experience is better?' there is no doubt that the first school has got it right. Every teacher has resorted to the second example at times, but in general we all know that to achieve the best from this source of media careful planning is needed. A report from the National Literacy Trust in March 2004 (available at www.literacytrust.co.uk) attempted to investigate how television can contribute to the language development of children. Director Neil McClelland commented that in the two to five

year old age range, 'high-quality "educational" programmes designed for their age group can enhance language development'. The overall view from this conference indicated that the quality of the interactions with children and their parents when watching programmes was the important element. A personal study, conducted with a colleague, found that most children watched television with someone but that little interaction followed. It would appear that it is this interaction that is important.

In America growing interest in the subject has led to articles on critical viewing for parents and children. Considine (2004) suggests that teaching children to become critical viewers helps them with their ability to 'read words and worlds'.

As thinking teachers we can see the need to embrace media literacy as an aid to helping children to make sense of the words and pictures that bombard them in our highly visual society. Having put forward the argument that we need to make the most of these types of resources, how can we do this?

Television

Most educational television programmes have some sort of guide to help teachers, so this really requires no further deliberation except to perhaps comment that the creative teacher may wish to adjust ideas according to the needs of their class. 'Soap operas' also provide material of an educational nature. Many of the 'soaps' deal with issues such as teenage pregnancy, drug abuse and homosexuality and could be used as the basis for discussion around these topics in lessons. It is not necessary to watch a whole programme, although at times this may be preferable. A five-minute snippet should suffice as a source for debate. BBC drama series for children may also be seen as a starting point. The scripts for some of these dramas may be obtained and used in class for sessions, leading to groups devising their own scripts. One has to be fairly careful about this type of work though as some children will look on it as an opportunity to swear and shock. However, it does illustrate the point that all television drama begins with the written word.

Popular programmes like these 'soaps' and dramas and US import, *The Simpsons* also give the ideal base from which to explore the use of Standard English, accent and dialect. Pupils, in small discussion groups, identify the accents and make a note of any dialect words used in the clip. This then leads to a compilation of slang or dialect words used by the pupils themselves and highlights their own use of English. An enjoyable activity to follow this is group work where a panel of three interviewers interviews a number of candidates for a job. Pupils take on different persona and use slang or Standard English to conduct the interviews. If videoed and viewed afterwards this really highlights for pupils how their use of spoken language is important. It is more effective than any paper exercise, but can lead on to scriptwriting similar scenes. Alternatively these 'ad lib' sessions could be 'evidenced' by pupils writing a short evaluation of the exercise.

Viewing video and DVD

If teachers wish to use video and DVD as a teaching tool the same types of rules apply. The children need to have a viewing task and to be aware of what that task is prior to watching a short extract. This may seem an obvious point but children often become excited by the idea of a video, so just reminding them what they are looking for before watching can make a difference to their attention to detail.

Film shorts (available at www.bfi.org.uk) provide a wealth of material to use in the classroom. In fact the British Film Institute has a section of its website devoted to education. Most children are familiar with the Disney films, and those like *Shrek* offer endless topics for discussion and writing. Character profiles, letters, invitations, reviews of the film, intertextuality, drama and script writing are only a start. Confining viewing to a small section of a film may not be very popular with a class, but is more useful as a basis to start writing.

In some instances, however, it may be more beneficial to watch the whole film. Many films are based on books and watching a film version that has been read and enjoyed in class adds an extra dimension to how pupils think about the text. Watching the film gives one interpretation of the book and allows for a great deal of discussion on characterisation, atmosphere, settings, and the impact of the visual. Short reviews may be written on the different formats and contrasts and comparisons made between the two different forms.

Infants

Winnie the Pooh

Winnie the Pooh has fans of all ages but the following ideas are slanted towards infants. The viewing task here is to listen for, and make a note of, any unusual words. At the beginning of the story Pooh and his friends decide to go the Wild Woods. On the way they hear a strange noise and speculate on what type of an animal it could be – a woozle, a jagular or a jugosaurus? What these animals look like is up to the imagination. Ask the children to describe the animal and draw only what they say; for example, two pointy ears, sharp fangs, a long tail. They will soon realise that there are huge gaps in the picture. This gives them a visual representation of a description and highlights for them the need to give details in their explanation.

The story begins with a map of the Wild Woods and this may be the basis for geography as well as literacy. The teacher draws the map and provides the children in pairs, with copies of these, so as to follow the path the animals take. Pooh is not very good at writing so needs help with his spelling – another good word activity. This type of simple map may also be used as a story map. Each feature can be linked to an imaginary event – 'Pooh climbed up the tree in search of honey.' The children then have a basis for a sequel to the story. Working in pairs in the first instance gives them the opportunity for discussion and exchange of ideas before settling down to individual writing.

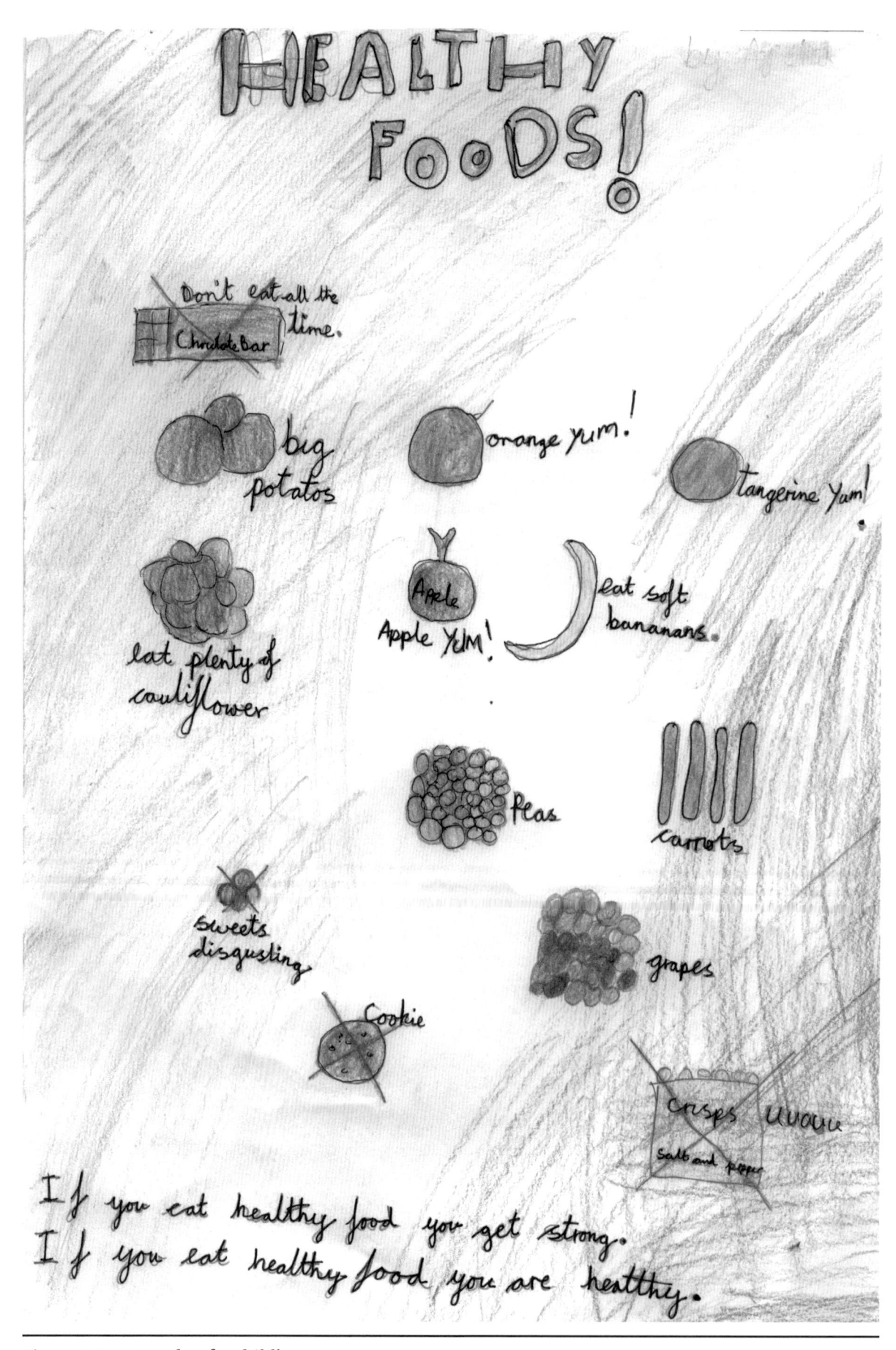

Figure 6.1 Example of a child's poster

Lady and the Tramp

Part of this film shows Tramp having a wash and then deciding where he is going to eat. He looks at various restaurants before making his choice. The children, as their viewing task, need to make a note of which restaurants he considers and why he makes his final choice. The restaurants are from different countries so finding out about these countries and the types of food typical in a French restaurant, for example, can lead to all sorts of other experiences. If there are restaurants near the school the children could perhaps visit in small groups to talk to the owners or to see a typical menu. Some will welcome this sort of link as it brings in extra business for them. Offering them something in exchange, involving the local press for example, is one way to ensure that your partnerships are appreciated on both sides.

If this is not an option open to you then menus from the local Chinese takeaway are just as valuable, if not more so, as the children will be introduced to a different style of writing. This can lead on to the children designing their own menus. The menus may be individual, or if you wish to change the role-play area into a restaurant or café then the children can work in groups to design a suitable menu. The choices are then displayed for all to see and a vote is taken. This is a good introduction to citizenship for young children. The final design may, with the teacher's help, be typed up on the computer with clip art added.

Tramp decides against the fattening pastries for breakfast, so another angle on this theme could be a healthy eating poster. After discussion on the types of food needed for a healthy diet, linked to science, the children need to use pictures and words to promote the message that a balanced diet is essential for good health.

Voices

The different characters in the film are not just denoted by their physical characteristics but by their accents, so the children can talk about the voices used and the way these make them feel. Encourage the use of adjectives and use outlines of the different characters to write the adjectives inside. With lower ability, or younger children, a teacher may need to provide words and meanings to help. Words like 'gruff', for example, may be outside a child's experience. In this case the teacher needs to demonstrate by speaking in a gruff voice and asking the children to imitate. This causes great hilarity but is more certain to remain in the child's consciousness than simply telling them what a word means.

Juniors

The Secret Garden

For older children try watching a short sequence without any sound. The children have to make judgements about the characters and what is happening. A part of *The Secret Garden* was used for this particular activity with Year Six, although something similar could be conducted with any suitable short clip. The scenes used from the film in this instance were the journey in the train, followed by the part where Mary finds that everyone else has disappeared and she is alone. She is discovered by the soldiers and is obviously not very happy about the situation.

The children were told to just watch and make comments on anything they knew about what was happening from viewing the silent pictures. Their observations demonstrated how much children learn from just the visual.

The girl is unhappy.

It is set in olden times. I can tell by the clothes.

The woman does not really like the girl.

The girl is in a temper.

The man looks surprised.

I think that bit is in a different country.

They are quite rich by the look of the furniture.

I think the men are soldiers because they are wearing uniforms.

No one had taught these young viewers how to 'read' video in the way they had been taught how to read. Think how much more discerning these young viewers would become if they were introduced to media studies in their primary years.

Following the viewing the class was split into pairs to write the dialogue for either the scene in the train or the confrontation with the soldier. They were each given 20 minutes for this followed by the chance to act out their particular scene. What was remarkable was the similarity in tone to the original. At the end of the lesson the sequences were shown again, with the sound on this time, and the children were able to evaluate and comment on their work. Further lessons on this discussed the use of camera shots and how music was used to enhance viewing experience.

Film Education also has a very good website and excellent resources to use in the classroom (www.filmeducation.org/resources.html) with a free of charge range linked to literacy and other teaching ideas. A CD of *Madagascar*, for example, was very useful in helping to find out about African animals for a class non-fiction book. Work based on Paul Geraghty's *The Hunter* was supplemented by this lively, interactive CD-rom.

Newspapers

Newspapers are a wonderful resource and may be used from Reception right through to Year Six as the basis for discussion and writing. Many cities operate a 'Newspapers in Education' programme and for a small fee you can have specially designed newspapers delivered to your school complete with ideas on how to use these for class work. With young children just looking at things like the map of the British Isles and identifying where they live provides a start for geography and, as illustrated in the chapter on photographs, the people and places photographed in the newspapers may be used in other ways.

As children become more competent they can develop their ideas further. The National Literacy Strategy identifies news reports as a non-fiction text in Year Five, but children younger than this may be able to write or plan short news reports for a class newspaper. To study newspaper reports as a class, it is probably best if everyone can have a copy of the front page or the whole paper that you are using. If this is not possible then use different copies of the same newspaper whilst working in pairs. Tabloid is better than broadsheet for this as, on a purely practical note, it takes up less space.

One may begin by identifying the physical features of a newspaper:

- How is it different from a book?
- What features can you identify on the front page?
- What is the title?
- What things do you notice about this cover that make it different?

As the class identifies the different features the teacher could scribe these on the board. Although newspapers have a jargon of their own it is not necessary for children to know what is meant by a byline, strapline or other journalistic talk, although some boys may enjoy learning a different 'lingo'. (Local press offices will be able to supply you with a list, or if you have any contacts in the press ask them to visit and talk to the class.)

The next step is to identify the language used in news reports. Ask the class to listen while you read out two accounts of the same event. One should be in narrative form and the other in a report format. The three examples following are in a photocopiable format for teachers to use on an overhead projector.

Example A

It was a dark and miserable evening and Mr Jones had just settled down by the television with a cup of warm cocoa when he thought he heard a noise. Getting unsteadily to his feet, Mr Jones shuffled over to the window to look outside. Imagine his distress when he saw two young lads throwing stones at his greenhouse. Mr Jones shouted at them and banged the window and the youths ran off. He rang the police but it was too late. The youths had escaped and left poor Mr Jones with a dreadful mess to clear up the next morning. The neighbours, who had heard the noise, were horrified as it was not the first time this had happened in their usually quiet neighbourhood.

Photocopiable: Exciting Writing: Activities for 5 to 11 year olds
Paul Chapman Publishing © Jacqueline Harrett 2006

Example B

Yesterday evening a pensioner, Mr John Jones, 83, of West View Drive was distressed when two unknown youths vandalised his greenhouse. The commotion was heard by neighbours, but the police arrived too late to apprehend the youths. This is the third attack on property in the area in the past two weeks.

Example C

It had been one of those days again. John was wandering home without a care in the world when, suddenly, from out of nowhere a huge red lorry swung around the corner and knocked him straight off his bike. He hit his head on the kerb and collapsed in unconsciousness.

The police are interested in any information regarding the accident involving Mr John Jones of Old Road, Newtown, who was found late last night unconscious at the side of the road. People in the vicinity prior to the accident saw a red lorry driving in an erratic fashion. If you have any information regarding this incident please ring 22 44 666.

Ask the children to classify any differences in style and language used. They should identify that the report is not in the same style of writing – much crisper and to the point rather than descriptive. The language also tends to be rather formal. Using copies of the reports they should identify any words they think are more formal and that they possibly do not understand, such as *vicinity*.

The next stage is to look for the five questions that need to be answered in a newspaper report.

- Who?
- What?
- Where?
- When?
- How?

In many newspaper reports the answers are in the first paragraph. Using the three examples given identify the answers to the five questions. The photocopiable sheet below may help them to remember what it is they are looking for and enable them to make brief notes on the reports. After a few minutes – no more than five – the class may feed back and discuss the answers.

Newspaper Reports

WHO was involved?

WHAT happened?

WHERE did it happen?

WHEN did it happen?

HOW did it happen?

Newspaper Reports

This may raise some issues as not everyone may have the same answers to the questions. After looking at the examples given the next step is for groups to take the same five questions and examine the reports in the actual newspapers to locate these answers. Highlighter pens in different colours may be used for this to help with coding. Red for *who*, yellow for *what* and so on.

Fillers

To continue this group work 'fillers' from newspapers may be used. Give the class copies of four or five different fillers and in groups of about six they have to find and record the answers to the five questions. Each group should have all the examples on their sheet, but they have to study only one in depth and then provide the answers for this in the feedback session. It is useful for everyone to have all the examples as it helps during feedback (see the example given below). Again, this should only take a few minutes to maintain the pace of the lesson.

Even though this is virtually the same activity repeated, it is approached in different ways and this helps with consolidation before attempting any writing. Pupils may also look at the titles of the fillers and discuss their suitability, as well as the concise language used in these tiny snippets of journalism. Keeping a fast pace is essential as it also helps children to realise what the life of a busy journalist, with deadlines to keep, must feel like.

Fillers

UFO spotted

Residents lliving in Cumbria last night reported seeing a strange object that looked like a flying saucer.

The Ministry of Defence denied that it was any of their aircraft so speculation on alien visitors is rife in the area.

Strawberry Shortage

The large supermarket stores were in chaos last night as an unprecedented rush for English strawberries left them with empty shelves. The recent floods have caused havoc in the strawberry fields and crops in some areas of the country have been completely destroyed. The traditional Wimbledon treat will have to be supplemented by imported crops from Spain.

More crop circles

A farmer in Wiltshire reported another crop circle, which he claims just appeared overnight at his farm near Devizes. These mysterious circles have been appearing all over the West Country since the beginning of June and baffling all the experts.

Baboon Escapes

There was grave concern last night over the disappearance of a baboon from London Zoo. Hulk, as he is known, was last seen just before the zoo closed to the public at 6pm.

Zoo officials say that he is unlikely to go far but if spotted he should not be approached as he could be dangerous.

Writing

By this stage everyone should have grasped enough basics to help them to write their own report in journalistic style, or at least attempt to do so. Real journalists write to a deadline and with a word or column limit, so using *The Daily News* planning sheet will help children to focus on the task in hand which is to write their own news report. As this is quite a difficult task give each child a photograph, from a magazine or newspaper, of a real person. This gives them a starting point as they have the 'who', once they have given the person a name. It is best not to use a famous person unless you want a regurgitation of something they have already seen or heard in the media. The tiny squares at the side of the sheet are to write brief notes and the column is to write the opening paragraph of the report. Once the task is explained the children can have two minutes' talking time, in pairs, to exchange ideas about how they are going to fill the boxes.

This leads on to individual work. The task is to write the first paragraph of a newspaper report, including the title. Children may use the ideas they have talked about to write notes in the boxes. Then, using that information they must write their paragraph. A time limit for this appeals to boys especially and I would suggest around ten minutes here, as this seems to keep the momentum necessary.

One of the less obvious features of report writing is that it has to be within a certain word limit. As an extension activity they have the challenge of re-drafting to produce an opening of thirty words exactly.

The Daily News

Who?

What?

Where?

When?

How?

Photocopiable: Exciting Writing: Activities for 5 to 11 year olds
Paul Chapman Publishing © Jacqueline Harrett 2006

In the plenary session each group of children should appoint a 'journalist' to read aloud their report. Reflection on the main features and how this was achieved ensures that all the children are clear about the style and format of writing reports.

Extension

Once they have mastered this style of writing they may be encouraged to write their own class newspaper for the rest of the school to read. Although this requires a great deal of organisation it is possible and works best if you hand this responsibility over to the children. Not everyone has to write a news report. Examining the newspaper in detail it can be seen that it contains all sorts of writing – advertisements, sport, recipes, reviews, weather, television pages, lost and found, lonely hearts and so on. Allow the children to compile a list of topics they wish to include and to make choices about what they want to write about. Graham (2003) found that children were more motivated to write when they were given some autonomy.

What they should have identified by this stage is that a report on last week's football match has to be in the third person and not through the eyes of the player. Appoint an editor who will be able to oversee the project, sit back and keep your fingers crossed! I managed to do this with a mixed Year One and Reception class and also with a mixed Year Five and Year Six class, so it does work. The newspaper may be hand-written or word processed and physically stuck on to a sugar paper base or put together entirely on screen. It really depends on the children and their level of computer expertise.

Television

Another way to present news is as a television news report. Taking a printed news story as a beginning children have to work in small groups. Each group must decide who will be the newsreader, cameraman, roving reporter, eye-witness, the person in the story or perhaps a relative. They can suggest characters other than those they have read about as the report will only present them with the bare bones on which to base their story. They will need to make a list of questions to ask. Perhaps one child could be the reporter on the street talking to people and reporting on the news while another is in the studio.

The children are given twenty minutes to work on their presentation to perform to the rest of the class. Collaborative working like this encourages thinking skills and teamwork and the teacher is able to assess these areas by close observation. Sometimes a teacher can learn more about children in a class by this type of observational assessment.

Music

Music may be included in the presentation if this is to be a more polished effort. This could be recorded music or something that the class have composed themselves. Chanting could be one addition. For example, if the report is about something emotive such as a protest against poverty or war the class may be divided into sections to work together to compose rhythms for the chant. They could use body percussion or instruments to indicate the syllables in the words.

Comics

When do children read comics in school? In some schools this is allowed and even encouraged during whole class reading sessions such as ERIC (Everyone Reading In Class) but often comics only ever see the light of day during 'wet' playtimes. However, they may prove to be a valuable aid to literacy. Often boys or children who 'don't like reading' will pick up a comic. Hooking onto children's interests and using these to develop both reading and writing is entirely possible.

In the USA they are beginning to see the value of using comics as teaching aids and to discuss the merits of this. Melissa Ezarik reports on a movement in New York to bring comics into the classroom to motivate children. Dan Tandarich, education chair on the board of trustees for the New York City Comic Book Museum, started a programme in his school that proved to be so successful, especially for poor readers, that it has now spread and materials are available online.

A Comics Books Blog (see http://comicbooks.about.com/b/a/153699.htm) suggested that 'comics require an active participation on the part of the reader to synthesize the dynamic of sequential art as paired with words, creating its own unique visual language'.

For sceptics, the International Reading Association has also links to lesson plans about the genre and putting theory together with practice.

Parts of speech

Comics provide an interesting and different stimulus for writing activities at word, sentence and text level. Identifying the different parts of speech is a simple activity to start. Many comics have a variety of stories. Some of these are comic strip while others may have a longer type of story. Use the longer stories to help children to identify the nouns, verbs and adjectives, as a follow-up activity to more formal lessons on these parts of speech. This could also act as an introduction to the topic if conducted as a class lesson or a guided group session. Concentrate on one type of word to begin with and ask the children to be a 'noun noticer' by finding all the nouns in the story and underlining them with red felt, or gel, pens. This may be completed in pairs or individually. After a few minutes each pair has to feedback to the whole class one specific word they have discovered.

The next step is to search for the adjective. Ask the children to be 'adjective detectives' and with their blue pens to underline all the adjectives they can find. These activities are short and sharp with a competitive element to make it more exciting. Finally, the 'verb vole' seeks all the verbs and underlines them in green. By this stage the children have a very visual picture of how the text is structured and the basics of sentence structure – a painless grammar lesson.

Pupils will enjoy playing with the different coloured pens and may even find some words that have a dual purpose, depending on their role in the sentence. This idea may be extended to include adverbs or pronouns if their teacher thinks it is appropriate at the time. The main benefit is that pupils have a graphic representation of the types of words used in writing.

Another way to approach the same activity is to enlarge the text and cut out the words instead of underlining them. They may then be arranged in columns headed, 'noun', 'verb', or 'adjective'.

EXCITING WRITING

One feature that may be noted during this activity is that there are different types of nouns. If the children make a list of the characters in the comic they will have a register of proper nouns. This may be a paired or individual activity. When the list is complete it could be put into alphabetical order with a short description of each character at the side.

An extension for this activity is to add an adjective describing each character. Asking for an alliterative adjective, or adjectives, can add an extra dimension and result in some very strange descriptions.

Dreadful, dangerous, deadly, dribbling Dennis.

This may be extended into alliterative sentences. I term these 'silly sentences'.

Dreadful, dangerous, deadly, dribbling Dennis drools deafeningly daily.

Speech Marks

Comics are useful for demonstrating the use of speech marks. Many comic strips depend almost entirely on dialogue to move the action forward. If possible, enlarge a suitable version of a comic strip story and read it aloud encouraging the children to join in and use different voices for the characters. The speech bubbles clearly denote how the bubbles contain the actual spoken words. In a shared writing activity the teacher may show the children how to complete a comic strip of four frames. (Look for an interactive version of this online at http://www.read-writethink.org/.) This does not have to be based on a real comic book character, although some children may prefer to use those familiar to them to help design their strip.

The next step is to show how the picture text may be written out as a full story. The words in bubbles will need to be translated into proper speech denoted by speech marks. The teacher should demonstrate this technique in the first instance, as part of a shared or guided writing session. Writing out the text and then drawing around the spoken words helps children to 'see' the purpose of speech marks. A few examples on the board for children to try out, either in the whole-class session or on their own mini-whiteboards in guided group work, demonstrate visually what happens.

Beryl said   (EEK! Is that a rat?)

In this way the children have a graphic view of how speech marks work. It may take a few attempts for some to grasp this idea, but cutting up comic strips to use in this way engages the less able as well as making learning fun. As comics come in all sorts of formats it is also easy to find something to interest all tastes; from superheroes to 'girly' magazines.

Character study

As a very simple look at characters children may identify their favourite and talk about how they look and act. This information could then be made into riddles. Children write a short

description ending with the question 'Who am I?', for the other children to guess. The descriptions may then be made into cards with the questions on one side and the character name or picture on the other, or as mini 'lift the flap' books.

I wear a red jumper.

I like eating honey.

I live in a wood.

I have a friend called Piglet.

Who am I?

Answer: Winnie the Pooh

Sequencing

Comic strips are a good resource to use for sequencing stories. Give individuals, pairs or groups a cut up comic strip story to read, sequence and stick onto paper. It this way they learn about the structure of narrative. As an extension activity children may then have half of a comic strip which they have to finish using a storyboard. If children work in small groups they can pool ideas and share the drawing and writing of the story. The story for each group could be the same, which encourages reading and sharing of ideas in the whole class before they start.

Alternatively, differentiated groups could have various stories in guided writing sessions. The children's finished versions could then be compared to the original published version and similarities and differences noted. A variation of this is to cover a few frames in the middle of the story which the children have to complete. This really makes them think about the narrative.

Using language for persuasion

The art of persuasion is important not only in social contexts where emotional intelligence is crucial to managing oneself and others (Goleman, 1996), but also for looking at topics such as global citizenship. If we wish children to understand our election system, for example, then comics may help children to understand how that system works. Ask the children to choose their favourite comic, or feature from a comic, and to explain to others in their group the reasons for their choice. They must then try to persuade others to agree with their decision by use of persuasive language. Once a winner is declared in each group they proceed to the next stage and write out and present their arguments to the whole class.

This is a collaborative act with everyone in the group supporting their winning competitor, regardless of their own personal preferences. After the presentations a secret ballot may be held during which all may vote for any team member. They should not be constrained by the 'party' they have worked for, but by the use of language and persuasion used in the process. The results of a poll could be displayed as a graph, giving the key skill of numeracy a focus in the lesson.

Letter Writing

Writing for an audience and purpose is important so the children could write letters to the Editor of their favourite comic, explaining individual likes and dislikes. Some comics feature a letters page so this is a viable activity. With some children, the use of a letter frame is the best way to ensure that they complete this task. It is important that the letters are posted, perhaps with a covering letter, in the hope of a reply. To save on postage it is best to confine the activity to two or three favourite comics in the class. The children could use the previous activity on persuasive language to make their decisions. Writing for a purpose really motivates children and if you have a reply it provides a real boost to writing.

Jokes

The joke page is another feature of some comics. The children can make individual books using jokes they have heard or read. Copying directly from the comic is not permitted but they may create a different version of a joke they have seen by changing the characters, for example. The funniest jokes may be selected for the class notice board on 'a joke a day' basis. The other way to use this type of writing is to have all the jokes on separate pieces of paper in a box. This is used as a reward system for good work or behaviour. When someone deserves praise they are permitted to take a joke out of the box and read it to the whole class.

Puzzles

Often comics have a puzzle page. If these activities are cut out and laminated they may be used as handy, extra reading matter. Children may also use them as models for making their own puzzles as they involve reading, discussing, designing and writing. This could be a shared task or an individual extension activity.

Comics may have traditionally poor status as reading matter but they are, nevertheless, part of the reading culture of many children and may have a place in raising literary awareness. They have become more of an acceptable genre and one of the *Oxford Reading Tree Fireflies* actually has a really interesting non-fiction book on 'Comic Illustrators'. As teachers we can access this material and use it to our advantage to increase knowledge and motivation, especially in those children who 'don't like reading'.

SUMMARY

This chapter examined the use of the media in teaching about writing, both fiction and non-fiction. Topics covered included television, film, video and DVD, newspapers and comics. While acknowledging that this is only a taster for what is available for use in the classroom, various styles of writing were encouraged.

Questions – for debates

Scripts – news reports and television dramas

Standard English – making lists of slang and dialect words

Film and book reviews – contrasting and comparing different versions of the same text

Story maps – making a map as a planning tool

News reports – introduction to the five questions used in journalistic style and writing a report

Menus – based on discussion and knowledge (KS1)

Posters – designing and making posters to promote healthy eating

Letter writing – letters to the editor giving opinions

Jokes/puzzles – writing a joke/puzzle page for the class newspaper

Parts of speech – using comics to define the different parts of speech, making lists, alliterative sentences

Riddles – writing simple riddles as an introduction to character study

Sequencing stories/comic strip – mixing up stories and filling the blanks in comic strips

References and Other Information

Chapter One: Introduction

(Web addresses correct at time of publication.)

Claxton, G. (2002) http://observer.guardian.co.uk/magazine/story/0,11913,796509,00.html

Kress, G. (1994) *Learning to write*. London: Routledge

Chapter Two: Pictures in the head

DfEE (1998) National Literacy Strategy. London: DfEE.

Duffy, B. (1998) *Supporting Creativity and Imagination in the Early Years*. Buckingham: OUP.

Maddern, E. (1992) *A Teacher's Guide to Storytelling at Historic Sites*. London: English Heritage Publications.

Maguire, J. (2002) *The Power of Personal Storytelling*. New York: Tarcher/Putman.

Pinker, S. (1998) *How the Mind Works*. London: The Softback Preview

Further information

http://www.storyarts.org
This is a website run by Heather Forest with various information for storytellers, including lesson plans and links to other sites.

www.sfs.org.uk
In Britain the Society for Storytelling has a variety of information about storytelling circles across the country. They also have resources for sale.

Chapter Three: Art as a start

Ahlberg, A. (1999) *Jeremiah in the Dark Woods*. London: Puffin Books.

Corden, R. (2000) *Literacy and Learning Through Talk*. Buckingham : OUP.

Doonan, J. (1993) *Looking at Pictures in Picture Books*. Stroud: Thimble Press.

Graham, J. (1995) *Pictures on the Page*. Sheffield: National Association for Teaching of English (NATE).

Grainger, T. and Pickard, A. (2004) *Drama: Reading, Writing and Speaking Our Way Forward*. United Kingdom Literacy Association (UKLA) Royston, Herts: UKLA.

Swain, S. (2004) *Once upon a Picture*. London: Frances Lincoln Publishers.

🖱 Further information

Edward Hopper: A short biography and examples of his paintings are available from http://www.artchive.com/artchive/H/hopper/mansard.jpg.html

Tate Gallery: Visit the Tate online at www.tate.org.uk for a variety of resources and online courses.

Jack Vettriano: Try www.jackvettriano-prints.com or www.vettriano-art.com for examples of the artist's work.

Mitchell and Kenyon: Stills from their archive collection of photographs are available from http://www.bfi.org.uk/features/mk/gallery/r02_01.html

Pierre Auguste Renoir: A gallery of his work and biographical details may be found at http://www.renoir.org.yu/

Vincent Van Gogh: Prints and calendars are widely available. Biographical details and further pictures may be viewed at http://www.vangoghgallery.com/

Chapter Four: Picture Books

Burningham, J. (1992) *Come Away from the Water, Shirley*. London: Red Fox.

Clarke, H.N.B. (2002) Welcoming address at opening of the Eric Carle Museum of Children's Art (available online at www.picturebookart.org).

Dowling, M. (1995) *Starting School at Four*. London: Paul Chapman Publishers.

Graham, J. (1995) *Pictures on the Page*. Sheffield: National Association for Teaching of English (NATE).

Hill, A. (2001) 'The same only different', *Primary English Magazine*, 7(1), October.

Hughes, A. and Ellis, S. (1998) *Writing it Right: Children Writing 3–8*. Edinburgh: Scottish Consultative Council on the Curriculum.

Matthews, S. (2001) 'Quentin Blake in the classroom', *Primary English Magazine*, 6(5), June.

Meek, M. (1991) *On Being Literate*. London: The Bodley Head.

Mercer, N., Wegerif, R. and Dawes, L. (1999) 'Children's talk and the development of reasoning in the classroom', *British Educational Research Journal*, 25(1), pp. 95–111.

More than Words (2004) A joint UKLA and QCA publication based on collaborative classroom research. Available from UKLA (www.ukla.org) or QCA Publications.

Murris, K. and Haynes, J. (2000) *Storywise: Thinking through Stories*. Puriton: Dialogue Works.

Pullman, P. (2005) 'Common sense has much to learn from moonshine', *Guardian*, 22 January.

Unsworth, L. (2001) *Teaching Multiliteracies Across the Curriculum: Changing Contexts of Text and Image in Classroom Practice*. Buckingham: OUP.

Van Allsburg, C. (1984) *The Mysteries of Harris Burdick*. Boston: Houghton Mifflin Company.

Waddell, M. (2001) *Once There Were Giants*. London: Walker Books.

Wray, D. and Lewis, M. (1997) *Extending Literacy: Children Reading and Writing Non-fiction*. London: Routledge.

Further information

Since writing this chapter I have found a web source for the *Harris Burdick Mysteries*, complete with pictures at http://www.sd35.bc.ca/lm/divmysteries.htm. Not only are there pictures to project from the internet on to the interactive whiteboard, it also gives examples of stories children have written in response to the pictures – all American based.

Chapter Five: Photographs

Andrew, M. (1996) *Paint a Poem*. London: Belair.

Chambers, A. (1993) *Tell Me : Children, Reading and Talk*. Stroud: Thimble Press.

Hobbs, R. (1996) 'Expanding the concept of literacy', in *Media Literacy Review* at http://interact.uoregon.edu/Medialit/mlr/readings/articles/hobbs/expanding.html

Jones, P. (1988) *Lipservice: The Story of Talk in Schools*. Milton Keynes: OUP.

Kendrick, M. and McKay, R. (2001) 'Revisiting children's images of literacy', at http://educ.queensu.ca/~landl/archives/vol51papers/0304_ken_mck/

Phillips, T. (2000) *A Postcard Century: Cards and their Messages*. London: Thames and Hudson.

Unsworth, L. (2001) *Teaching Multiliteracies across the Curriculum: Changing Contexts of Text and Image in Classroom Practice*. Buckingham: Open University Press.

Welch, R. (1999) *The Gauntlet*. Oxford: Oxford University Press.

Wilde, O. (2004) *The Selfish Giant*. London: Puffin Books.

Further information

The National Geographic site at www.nationalgeographic.com has a range of photographs of people and places and even video clips of animals.

Other free photographs are available at www.freefoto.com or free-photographs.net. You need to have some idea of what you are looking for, for example castles, or you could spend hours happily surfing through a wealth of photographs.

'Talking Pictures' is available at www.teachthinking.com. For further details click on online catalogue for information about the photograph pack available.

Chapter Six: Media

Considine, D. (2004) 'Critical viewing and critical thinking skills', at http://www.medialit.org/reading_room/article202.html

Goleman, D. (1996) *Emotional Intelligence*. London: Bloomsbury.

Graham, L. and Johnson, A. (2003) *Children's Writing Journals*. Royston, Herts: UKLA.

Marsh, J. (2004) 'The techno-literacy practices of young children', *Journal of Early Childhood Research*, Vol 2(1) pp 51–66.

Tainui, B. (2003) *Comic Illustrators*. Oxford: OUP Oxford Reading Tree Fireflies.

🖱 Further information

Web based sources

http://www.emints.org/ethemes/resources/S00001222.shtml
Wonderful resources with online cartoons and great links to other material to use in the classroom.

http://www.readwritethink.org/lessons/lesson_view.asp?id=188
Linked to the International Reading Association and gives step by step guidance on how to use these lessons.

Check out reports at www.literacytrust.co.uk

www.bfi.org.uk
Visit the British Film Institute site for a range of ideas and resources, including 'Show us a Story' and 'Story Shorts'.

www.filmeducation.org/resources.html
Film Education has a number of resources, some of them free, to use with all ages. Sign up with it to keep up to date with what is happening in the world of film education.

www.nyccomicbookmuseum.org/
Materials are available online for use in the classroom. This programme was so successful in Dan Tandarich's school that it has now spread to other areas.

See Comic Books Blog at http://comicbooks.about.com/b/a/153699.htm for information and resources.

http://content.educationworld.com/a_curr/profdev/profdev105.shtml
This site is about using comics to aid visual learners.

Glossary

For colleagues who are unfamiliar with the British educational system the following explanations may be of some use.

Key skills: Children throughout their schooling are now assessed on the key skills of communication, mathematical skills, Information Technology, Personal Health and Social Education and problem solving skills.

Key Stage One: This refers to children between the ages of five and seven years old. The key stage is divided into two separate year groups. Year One consists of children between the ages of five and six. Year Two children are between six and seven years old. In England the children in Year Two are given tests of attainment in literacy, mathematics and science at the end of this key stage.

Key Stage Two: Following on from Key Stage One the children between seven and eleven are classed as being in Key Stage Two. There are four year groups in Key Stage Two: years three, four, five, and six. At the end of this key stage children are once again assessed before progressing to secondary school at age eleven.

National Literacy Strategy: In 1998 the National Literacy strategy was introduced in England to ensure that literacy had a dedicated time in the curriculum. The Enhanced Literacy Hour became a requirement in every school. Practice spread to other parts of the U.K. but was not enforced in quite the same manner. Recent reports point to less stringent monitoring of 'The Hour' although many schools still have a strong focus on the 'core' subjects of English, mathematics and science as well as ICT. The frameworks for literacy and numeracy are currently under review. Futherninformation by be obtained by visited the Standards site:

http://www.standards.dfes.gov.uk

Index

Adjectives, 31
Art, 24, 32, 36, 40, 46

CD rom, 68
Characters, 51–54, 82
Comics, 81–84
Commentary, 24
Community links, 32, 36

Description, 23, 29
Drama, 17–18
DVD, 65–68

Geography, 26, 32, 36, 43, 58

History, 25–6, 32, 42, 46

Jokes, 84

KWL grid, 42

Letters, 28, 84
Lists, 24, 29
Lowry, 19–26

Menus, 30
Music, 80

Narrative, 21–22, 31, 45, 54–58
Newspapers, 68–80
Notes, 34

Parts of speech, 57, 81
Poetry writing, 29, 57
Puzzles, 84

Questions, 5, 6, 16–17, 21–22, 26–27, 31–32, 37, 42, 44, 55

RE, 40
Recipes, 30
Renoir, 32–37
Reports, 23
Rhymes, 23
Riddles, 83
Role-play, 23, 67

Science, 67
Storyboards, 59–60
Storytelling, 7–15,
Speech, 35, 82

Talk, 21
Television, 63–64, 80
Thought bubbles, 23, 60

Van Allsburg, 43–46
Van Gogh, 26–32
Video, 63, 65–68
Visualisation, 4–6

Waddell, 40–43

ALSO AVAILABLE FROM PAUL CHAPMAN PUBLISHING

Creative Learning and Teaching in Language and Literacy

Jeni Riley Institute of Education, University of London

This practical guide considers the research evidence that is needed to inform enlightened practice, and offers concrete suggestions and teaching approaches for early years settings and classrooms. This comprehensive book shows the 'what' the 'how' and the 'why' of innovative, creative practice for teaching language and literacy. The author clearly examines how young children learn to use both spoken and written language, and shows how to assess, plan and teach for the effective learning of speaking, listening, reading and writing.

Each chapter includes activities and review questions for further study, and topics covered include:

- Learning to communicate
- Developing spoken language in early years settings and classrooms
- The links between oracy and literacy
- The inter-relatedness of the literacy process
- Teaching literacy holistically
- The assessment of language and literacy
- Supporting literacy in Key Stage 1
- Teaching reading and teaching writing for different purposes
- Children and books
- Teaching children for whom English is an additional language
- Language, literacy, learning and ICT.

Contents

Learning to communicate / Developing spoken language in early years settings and classrooms / The links between oracy and literacy / The inter-relatedness of the literacy process / Teaching literacy holistically / The assessment of language and literacy / Supporting literacy in Key Stage 1 and the teaching of reading for different purposes / Supporting literacy in Key Stage 1 and the teaching of writing for different purposes / Children and books / Teaching children for whom English is an additional language / Language, literacy, learning and ICT

June 2006 · 224 pages
Hardback (1-4129-1985-1) Price £60.00 · Paper (1-4129-1986-X) Price £17.99

Paul Chapman Publishing
A SAGE Publications Company

Visit our website at
www.paulchapmanpublishing.co.uk
to order online and receive free postage and packaging!

ALSO AVAILABLE FROM PAUL CHAPMAN PUBLISHING

Using Drama to Support Literacy

Activities for Children Aged 7 to 14

John Goodwin *Freelance Consultant*

Using ideas and activities already tried and tested in the classroom, this book shows practitioners how imaginative drama lessons and activities can be used to help encourage and improve children's writing, speaking and listening skills.

Perfect for the person who might not be used to leading drama-based activities, this book takes a step-by step approach that will help even the most daunted teacher tackle drama with confidence.

Also included are:

- ideas for suitable writing and drama activities
- advice on lesson planning
- list of useful resources
- examples of children's work and teachers' comments.

Class teachers, teaching assistants, literacy consultants and drama and English co-ordinators looking for practical, fun drama activities to support literacy will find all the help they need in this book.

Contents

HOW TO USE THE BOOK / PLANNING / STRATEGIES / Caption Making / Ceremony / Conscience Alley / Costume or Prop / Dream Pictures / Forum Theatre / Hot Seating / Journeys / Meetings / Mime / Modelling / Movement Sequences / Narrate / Role on the Wall / Sequencing / Sound Collage / Space Building / Speaking Thoughts / Still Image / Teacher in Role / Thought Tracking / Trials / LESSONS IN ACTION / LITERACY / Big Bad Wolf / The Spooky House / …and the Clock Struck 13 / The Key / Mr Wolf and Mr Pig / Poetry of World War 1: Dulce et Decorum Est Christmas 1924 Good Night Mr Tom / PSHE / Stealing // Bullying / HISTORY / The 2nd World War (a) / The 2nd World War (b) / RE / The Christmas Story.

April 2006 · 112 pages
Hardback (1-4129-2050-7) Price £60.00 · Paper (1-4129-2051-5) Price £18.99

Paul Chapman Publishing
A SAGE Publications Company

Visit our website at
www.paulchapmanpublishing.co.uk
to order online and receive free postage and packaging!

ALSO AVAILABLE FROM PAUL CHAPMAN PUBLISHING

Language and Literacy in the Early Years
Third Edition
Marian R Whitehead *Independent Consultant*

'I found this book to be clearly written and exceptionally well organized. Each chapter is prefaced with a glossary of key terms. The book will be invaluable for students, early years professionals and support staff, working to develop spoken language, reading and writing with young children and their families' - ***Child Language Teaching and Therapy***

'This empowering book should be a "must" for anyone working with nought to eight-year-olds' - ***Nursery World***

'This **Third Edition** is a welcome update of an already key text for early years educators. It reflects continuing research over the last 20 years in the field of language and literacy development whilst also embracing recent developments and initiatives which have influenced early years education. **Marian Whitehead** has broadened the context of early years education beyond the classroom, acknowledging the variety of settings and professionals who are now involved in educating and developing young children from birth onwards. The text relates theory and practice in an easily readable form with particularly helpful sections on key terminology and summaries within each chapter. A most useful, practical text which no early years practitioner should be without'
- *JacquelineBarbera, Director of Undergraduate ITT, Liverpool Hope University College*

This **Third Edition** of **Language and Literacy in the Early Years** has been updated to reflect current professional interests and the latest developments in the field. The book provides comprehensive coverage of issues in language, literacy and learning, focusing on the age range from birth to eight years.

The author emphasizes the joy and creativity involved in supporting young children's development as speakers, writers and readers. While taking account of current initiatives and programmes, the author supports flexible teaching methods in what is a complex teaching and learning process.

This book is essential reading for primary and early years students and practitioners in the field of language and literacy including nursery nurses, classroom assistants and Foundation Stage teachers.

Contents
PART ONE: LANGUAGE AND LEARNING / Linguistics: The Study of Language Key Terms Linguistics Grammars Systems and Signs Teaching and Learning Suggestions / Sociolinguistics: Language and Cultures Language Variety Power and Influence Language Change Multilingualism Teaching and Learning Suggestions / Psycholinguistics: Early Language Acquisition Key Terms Early Language Acquisition How Do We Do It? Stages in Speech and Language Development Teaching and Learning Suggestions Language and Thinking Key Terms Views and Perspectives Brainy Babies Teaching and Learning Suggestions / The Early-Years Educator and Knowledge about Language: From Theory to Practice? Language Knowledge and the Educators Language Study in Early Years Settings Language in Social Contexts Multilingualism in Early Years Settings Language Variety and Standard English Language, Thinking and Learning / PART TWO: LITERACY / Narrative and Storying: Key Terms Narrative Storying Teaching and Learning Suggestions / Books and the World of Literature: Key Terms Early Experiences with Books Literature and Becoming Literate Teaching Reading and Supporting Readers Teaching and Learning Suggestions / Early Representation and Emerging Writing: Key Terms Process and Product Literacy, Culture and Schooling Early Representation and Symbolizing Symbols and the Creation of Meanings Emerging Writing Appropriate Practices Teaching and Learning Suggestions / The Early Years Educator and Literacy: The Literacy Approach Getting Started Emerging Literacy Early Literacy and Nursery Curriculum Parents, Families, Communities and Cultures Records and Assessment

2004 · 272 pages
Hardback (0-7619-4469-9) Price £65.00 · Paper (0-7619-4470-2) Price £19.99

Paul Chapman Publishing
A SAGE Publications Company

Visit our website at
www.paulchapmanpublishing.co.uk
to order online and receive free postage and packaging!

FROM LUCKY DUCK BOOKS...

Write Dance

A Progressive Music and Movement Programme for the Development of Pre-Writing and Writing Skills in Children

Ragnhild Oussoren

Pack Includes A4 Book, Video & CD-ROM!

'The author of this book is a very experienced graphologist who has worked on the subject with children for many years. What she has produced is a highly practical resource for early years teachers' - **Special**

'The whole scheme is wonderfully inventive and gives a wealth of ideas to be developed and adapted to suit a particular group of children. It uses a wide range of movements with a greater variety of direction than many pre-writing schemes and encourages the children in their movements quickly as well as rhythmically, with confidence and enjoyment' - **Handwriting Today**

This innovative and exciting programme is widely used across Europe as a way of introducing handwriting using music, movement and exercise. It has been found especially helpful for children with special educational needs, from learning difficulties to dyspraxia.

Psychologists working with youngsters with learning difficulties developed the idea. It was thought that encouraging children to express themselves would empower them and raise their self-esteem. The experts soon noticed that it benefited children of all abilities, and once they started writing, letters were better formed and more legible.

The Write Dance programme is sold as a fully comprehensive package including: Instruction Book, CD music recording and training video. Items can also be bought separately.

Contents

What is Write Dance? / What is Writing Psychology? / Teaching Writing in Sweden in the 1990s / How is the Write Dance Programme Organised? / At What Age Should Write Dance Be Introduced? / Is the Write Dance Method Tied to any Prescribed Style? / The Teaching Principles of Write Dance / The Rhythm of Handwriting / Practical Explanation - Ideas and Tips / Blindfolds / The Writing Movement Test / Learning to Write / Write Dance Daily Practise / The Write Dance Programme / The Volcano / A Walk in the Country, Krongelidong / Circles and Eights / Robot / The Train / The Growing Tree / Silver Wings over the Sea / Cats / Mandala / Carry On...with Write Dance / Clowns and Shy Children / Combining Music with Imaginative Drawings / The Story that Connects all Themes / Write Dance Folding Books / Lectures and Inset Days

A4 Book, Video & CD-ROM
81 Pages

Paul Chapman Publishing
A SAGE Publications Company

WWW.LUCKYDUCK.CO.UK
Order online and receive free postage and packaging!

Your All-in-One Resource

On the CD that accompanies this book, you'll find a fully searchable version of this *Step by Step* book as well as additional resources to extend your learning. The reference library includes the following eBooks and reference materials:

- *Microsoft Computer Dictionary, Fifth Edition*
- Sample chapters and poster from *Look Both Ways: Help Protect Your Family on the Internet* by Linda Criddle
- *Windows Vista Product Guide*

The CD interface has a new look. You can use the tabs for an assortment of tasks:

- Check for book updates (if you have Internet access)
- Install the book's practice file
- Go online for product support or CD support
- Send us feedback

The following screen shot gives you a glimpse of the new interface.

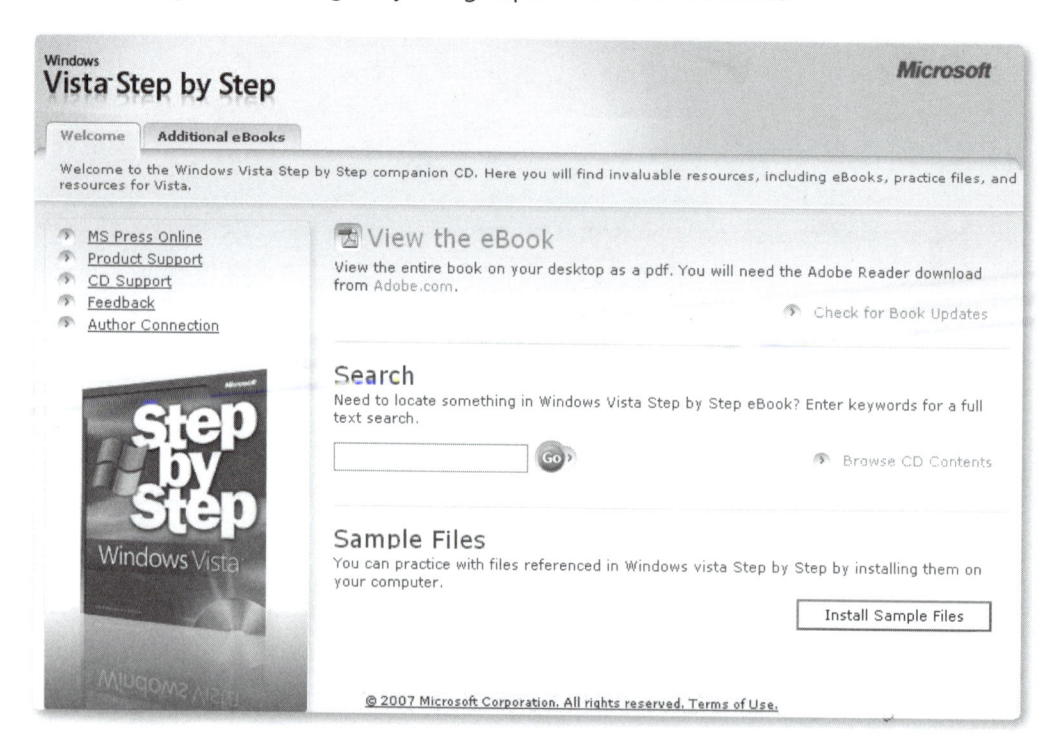

Microsoft® Office Word 2007 Step by Step

Joyce Cox
Joan Preppernau
Online Training Solutions, Inc.

Published by
Microsoft Press
A Division of Microsoft Corporation
One Microsoft Way
Redmond, Washington 98052-6399

Copyright © 2007 by Joyce Cox, Joan Preppernau, and Online Training Solutions, Inc.

All rights reserved. No part of the contents of this book may be reproduced or transmitted in any form or by any means without the written permission of the publisher.

Library of Congress Control Number: 2006937018

Printed and bound in the United States of America.

6 7 8 9 WCT 2 1 0 9

Distributed in Canada by H.B. Fenn and Company Ltd.

A CIP catalogue record for this book is available from the British Library.

Microsoft Press books are available through booksellers and distributors worldwide. For further information about international editions, contact your local Microsoft Corporation office or contact Microsoft Press International directly at fax (425) 936-7329. Visit our Web site at www.microsoft.com/mspress. Send comments to mspinput@microsoft.com.

Microsoft, Microsoft Press, Access, ActiveX, Aero, Calibri, Constantia, Encarta, Excel, Groove, Hotmail, InfoPath, Internet Explorer, MSN, OneNote, Outlook, PowerPoint, SharePoint, SQL Server, Verdana, Visio, Webdings, Windows, Windows Live, Windows Server, and Windows Vista are either registered trademarks or trademarks of Microsoft Corporation in the United States and/or other countries. Other product and company names mentioned herein may be the trademarks of their respective owners.

The example companies, organizations, products, domain names, e-mail addresses, logos, people, places, and events depicted herein are fictitious. No association with any real company, organization, product, domain name, e-mail address, logo, person, place, or event is intended or should be inferred.

This book expresses the author's views and opinions. The information contained in this book is provided without any express, statutory, or implied warranties. Neither the authors, Microsoft Corporation, nor its resellers, or distributors will be held liable for any damages caused or alleged to be caused either directly or indirectly by this book.

Acquisitions Editor: Juliana Aldous Atkinson
Project Editor: Sandra Haynes

Body Part No. X12-48764

Contents

About the Authors ix
Introducing Word 2007 xi
    New Features xii
    Let's Get Started xiv
Information for Readers Running Windows XP xv
    Managing the Practice Files xv
    Using the Start Menu xvi
    Navigating Dialog Boxes xvii
The Microsoft Business Certification Program xix
    Selecting a Certification Path xx
    Becoming a Microsoft Certified Application Specialist xx
    Taking a Microsoft Business Certification Exam xxi
    For More Information xxii
Features and Conventions of This Book xxiii
Using the Companion CD xxv
    What's on the CD? xxv
    Minimum System Requirements xxviii
    Installing the Practice Files xxix
    Using the Practice Files xxx
    Removing and Uninstalling the Practice Files xxxi
Getting Help xxxiii
    Getting Help with This Book and Its Companion CD xxxiii
    Getting Help with Word 2007 xxxiii
    More Information xxxvii
Quick Reference xxxix

What do you think of this book? We want to hear from you!

Microsoft is interested in hearing your feedback so we can continually improve our books and learning resources for you. To participate in a brief online survey, please visit:

www.microsoft.com/learning/booksurvey/

Contents

1 Exploring Word 2007 … 1
Working in the Word Environment … 2
Opening, Moving Around in, and Closing a Document … 10
    Sidebar: Compatibility with Earlier Versions … 15
Displaying Different Views of a Document … 15
Creating and Saving a Document … 23
Previewing and Printing a Document … 27
Key Points … 31

2 Editing and Proofreading Documents … 33
Making Changes to a Document … 34
    Sidebar: What Happened to Overtype? … 35
    Sidebar: About the Clipboard … 40
Inserting Saved Text … 40
    Sidebar: Inserting the Date and Time … 43
Finding the Most Appropriate Word … 43
    Sidebar: Researching Information … 45
    Sidebar: Translating Text … 46
Reorganizing a Document Outline … 46
Finding and Replacing Text … 49
Correcting Spelling and Grammatical Errors … 54
    Sidebar: Viewing Document Statistics … 59
Finalizing a Document … 59
    Sidebar: Adding a Digital Signature … 63
Key Points … 63

3 Changing the Look of Text … 65
Quickly Formatting Text and Paragraphs … 66
Manually Changing the Look of Characters … 68
    Sidebar: More About Case and Character Formatting … 74
Manually Changing the Look of Paragraphs … 75
    Sidebar: Finding and Replacing Formatting … 86
Creating and Modifying Lists … 86
    Sidebar: Formatting Text as You Type … 93
Key Points … 93

4 Changing the Look of a Document — 95

- Changing a Document's Background....................................96
  - Sidebar: Using a Picture as a Watermark........................100
- Changing a Document's Theme 100
- Working with Templates...104
  - Sidebar: Applying a Different Template to an Existing Document 112
- Adding Headers and Footers...113
- Controlling What Appears on Each Page 116
  - Sidebar: Inserting and Formatting Page Numbers 117
- Key Points 121

5 Presenting Information in Columns and Tables — 123

- Presenting Information in Columns 124
- Creating a Tabular List 128
- Presenting Information in a Table..................................130
  - Sidebar: Other Layout Options 138
- Formatting Table Information......................................138
- Performing Calculations in a Table.................................142
  - Sidebar: Creating Table Styles 143
- Using a Table to Control Page Layout 150
  - Sidebar: Deciding How to Insert Excel Data 151
- Key Points 155

6 Working with Graphics, Symbols, and Equations — 157

- Inserting and Modifying Pictures...................................158
  - Sidebar: Organizing Clips.......................................164
- Creating Fancy Text..165
  - Sidebar: Formatting the First Letter of a Paragraph 170
- Drawing and Modifying Shapes.......................................170
- Changing the Relationship of Elements on the Page 176
- Inserting Symbols and Equations 179
- Key Points 185

7 Working with Diagrams and Charts — 187

- Creating a Diagram 188
- Modifying a Diagram 193
- Inserting a Chart 199
- Modifying a Chart 205
- Using Existing Data in a Chart 212
- Key Points 215

8 Working with Longer Documents — 217

- Inserting Ready-Made Document Parts 218
- Creating and Modifying a Table of Contents 226
  - Sidebar: Creating Other Types of Tables 230
- Creating and Modifying an Index 231
- Adding Bookmarks and Cross-References 238
- Adding Hyperlinks 242
- Adding Sources and Compiling a Bibliography 246
  - Sidebar: Adding Footnotes and Endnotes 247
- Key Points 253

9 Creating Form Letters, E-Mail Messages, and Labels — 255

- Understanding Mail Merge 256
- Preparing Data for Mail Merge 257
  - Sidebar: Using an Outlook Contacts List as a Data Source 262
- Preparing a Form Letter 263
- Merging a Form Letter with Its Data Source 267
  - Sidebar: Printing Envelopes 270
- Sending a Personalized E-Mail Message to Multiple Recipients 270
- Creating and Printing Labels 274
- Key Points 277

10 Collaborating with Others — 279

- Sending a Document Directly from Word 280
  - Sidebar: Faxing a Document 283
- Tracking and Managing Document Changes 283
- Adding and Reviewing Comments 287
  - Sidebar: Entering Handwritten Changes 291
- Comparing and Merging Documents 291
- Password-Protecting a Document 294

  Preventing Changes 296
  Using Document Workspaces 299
  Key Points 303

11 Creating Documents for Use Outside of Word   305

  Saving a File in a Different Format 306
    Sidebar: Saving a PDF File 308
    Sidebar: Using Add-Ins 309
  Creating and Modifying a Web Document 310
  Creating a Blog Post 314
    Sidebar: Setting Up a Blog Account 315
  Creating an XML Document 319
    Sidebar: The DOCX Format 327
  Key Points 327

12 Customizing Word   329

  Changing Default Program Options 330
  Making Favorite Word Commands Easily Accessible .336
  Making Commands Available with a Specific Document 342
  Creating a Custom Keyboard Shortcut 344
    Sidebar: Tracking Down Built-In Keyboard Shortcuts 347
  Key Points 347

 Glossary 349

 Index 355

What do you think of this book? We want to hear from you!

Microsoft is interested in hearing your feedback so we can continually improve our books and learning resources for you. To participate in a brief online survey, please visit:

www.microsoft.com/learning/booksurvey/

About the Authors

Joyce Cox

Joyce has 25 years' experience in the development of training materials about technical subjects for non-technical audiences, and is the author of dozens of books about Office and Windows technologies. She is the Vice President of Online Training Solutions, Inc. (OTSI). She was President of and principal author for Online Press, where she developed the *Quick Course* series of computer training books for beginning and intermediate adult learners. She was also the first managing editor of Microsoft Press, an editor for Sybex, and an editor for the University of California. Joyce and her husband Ted live in downtown Bellevue, Washington, and escape as often as they can to their tiny, offline cabin in the Cascade foothills.

Joan Preppernau

Joan has worked in the training and certification industry for 12 years. As President of OTSI, Joan is responsible for guiding the translation of technical information and requirements into useful, relevant, and measurable training, learning, and certification deliverables. Joan is a Microsoft Certified Technical Specialist (MCTS) and Microsoft Certified Application Specialist (MCAS), and the author or co-author of more than a dozen books about Windows and the Microsoft Office system.

Joan has lived and worked in New Zealand, Sweden, Denmark, and various locations in the U.S. during the past 16 years. Having finally discovered the delights of a daily dose of sunshine, Joan is now happily ensconced in America's Finest City—San Diego, California—with her husband Barry and their daughter Trinity.

The Team

This book would not exist without the support of these hard-working members of the OTSI publishing team:

- Susie Bayers
- Jan Bednarczuk
- Jeanne Craver
- Marlene Lambert
- Jaime Odell
- Barry Preppernau
- Jean Trenary
- Lisa Van Every

We are especially thankful to the support staff at home who make it possible for our team members to devote their time and attention to these projects.

As always, Juliana Aldous (Acquisitions Editor) and Sandra Haynes (Series Editor) provided invaluable support on behalf of Microsoft Press.

Online Training Solutions, Inc. (OTSI)

OTSI specializes in the design, creation, and production of Office and Windows training products for information workers and home computer users. For more information about OTSI, visit

www.otsi.com

Introducing Word 2007

Microsoft Office Word 2007 is a sophisticated word processing program that helps you quickly and efficiently author and format all the business and personal documents you are ever likely to need. You can use Word to:

- Create professional-looking documents that incorporate impressive graphics such as charts and diagrams.
- Give documents a consistent look by applying styles and themes that control the font, size, color, and effects of text and the page background.
- Store and reuse ready-made content and formatted elements such as cover pages and sidebars.
- Create personalized e-mail messages and mailings to multiple recipients without repetitive typing.
- Make information in long documents accessible by compiling tables of contents, indexes, and bibliographies.
- Safeguard your documents by controlling who can make changes and the types of changes that may be made, removing personal information, and applying a digital signature.

The 2007 release of Word represents an extensive overhaul and update from previous versions. You'll notice some obvious changes as soon as you start the program, because the top of the program window has a completely new look, described in Chapter 1, "Exploring Word 2007." But the improvements go way beyond changes in appearance. Throughout this book, we include discussions of each new feature that is likely to be useful to you and how and when to use it.

New Features

Because there are so many new features in this version of Word, we don't identify them with a special margin icon as we did in previous versions of this book. We do, however, list them here. If you're upgrading to Word 2007 from a previous version, you're probably most interested in the differences between the old and new versions and how they will affect you, as well as how to find out about them in the quickest possible way. The sections below list new features you will want to be aware of, depending on the version of Word you are upgrading from. To quickly locate information about these features, see the Index at the back of this book.

If You Are Upgrading from Word 2003

If you have been using Word 2003, you will soon realize that Word 2007 is not just an incremental upgrade to what seemed like a pretty comprehensive set of features and tools. In addition to introducing a more efficient approach to working with documents, Word 2007 includes a long list of new and improved features, including the following:

- **The Microsoft Office Fluent Ribbon.** No more hunting through menus, submenus, and dialog boxes. This new interface organizes all the commands most people use most often, making them quickly accessible from tabs at the top of the program window.
- **Live Preview.** See the effect of a formatting option before you apply it.
- **Building blocks.** Think AutoText on steroids! Predefined building blocks include sets of matching cover pages, quote boxes, sidebars, and headers and footers.
- **Style sets and document themes.** Quickly change the look of a document by applying a different style set or theme, previewing its effect before making a selection.
- **SmartArt graphics.** Use this awesome new diagramming tool to create sophisticated diagrams with 3-D shapes, transparency, drop shadows, and other effects.
- **Improved charting.** Enter data in a linked Microsoft Office Excel worksheet and watch as your data is instantly plotted in the chart type of your choosing.
- **Document cleanup.** Have Word check for and remove comments, hidden text, and personal information stored as properties before you declare a document final.
- **New file format.** The new Microsoft Office Open XML Formats reduce file size and help avoid loss of data.

If You Are Upgrading from Word 2002

In addition to the features listed in the previous section, if you're upgrading from Word 2002 (part of the Microsoft Office XP system), you'll want to take note of the following new features that were introduced in Word 2003:

- **Reading Layout view.** View and easily read a document on the screen without needing to print it, and use buttons on the Reading Mode Markup toolbar to make comments, highlights, and revisions.
- **Thumbnails.** Get an overview of a document by displaying small images of its pages.
- **Smart Tags.** Flag items such as names and addresses, and then display a menu of options for performing common tasks with that type of information.
- **Research service.** Locate supporting information in references stored on your computer or on the Internet.
- **Handwriting support.** On a Tablet PC, write your comments in Word documents by hand.
- **Insertion and deletion colors.** When tracking changes and comments in a document, easily distinguish between insertions and deletions and between the changes made by different reviewers.
- **Balloon control.** Independently display or hide revision balloons and comment balloons.
- **Editing and formatting control.** Specify whether and how a document can be modified.
- **Shared workspaces.** Send a file as an attachment and automatically create a workspace on a collaboration site built with Microsoft SharePoint products and technologies.
- **XML capabilities.** Save a Word document as an XML file.
- **Document summaries.** Extract the key points of the document.
- **Readability statistics.** Display statistics that help you gauge the reading level of the document.

If You Are Upgrading from Word 2000

If you are upgrading from Word 2000, you've got a lot of catching up to do, but this upgrade will definitely be worth the effort. In addition to the features listed in the previous sections, the following features and tools, which were added in Word 2002, will be new to you:

- **Styles And Formatting task pane.** Work with paragraph styles and character formatting in an entire document from a single task pane. Create, view, select, apply, and clear formatting from text.
- **Reveal Formatting task pane.** Display the formatting attributes of a text selection.
- **Improved collaboration.** Use the improved Reviewing toolbar when collaborating on documents with colleagues.
- **Improved table and list formatting.** Easily copy, format, and sort tables, and create lists with complex paragraph structures.
- **Improved security interface.** Access security options on a single tab in the Options dialog box.
- **Information protection.** Remove personal information stored as file properties and names associated with comments or tracked changes.

Let's Get Started!

We've been working with Word since its debut, and each version has offered something that made daily document creation a little easier. But this is the first version in a while that has actually had us smiling and even elicited the occasional "Wow!" We look forward to showing you around Microsoft Office Word 2007.

Information for Readers Running Windows XP

The graphics and the operating system–related instructions in this book reflect the Windows Vista user interface. However, Windows Vista is not required; you can also use a computer running Windows XP.

Most of the differences you will encounter when working through the exercises in this book on a computer running Windows XP center around appearance rather than functionality. For example, the Windows Vista Start button is round rather than rectangular and is not labeled with the word *Start*; window frames and window-management buttons look different; and if your system supports Windows Aero, the window frames might be transparent.

In this section, we provide steps for navigating to or through menus and dialog boxes in Windows XP that differ from those provided in the exercises in this book. For the most part, these differences are small enough that you will have no difficulty in completing the exercises.

Managing the Practice Files

The instructions given in the "Using the Companion CD" section are specific to Windows Vista. The only differences when installing, using, uninstalling, and removing the practice files supplied on the companion CD are the default installation location and the uninstall process.

On a computer running Windows Vista, the default installation location of the practice files is *Documents\Microsoft Press\Word2007SBS*. On a computer running Windows XP, the default installation location is *My Documents\Microsoft Press\Word2007SBS*. If your computer is running Windows XP, whenever an exercise tells you to navigate to your *Documents* folder, you should instead go to your *My Documents* folder.

To uninstall the practice files from a computer running Windows XP:

1. On the Windows taskbar, click the **Start** button, and then click **Control Panel**.
2. In **Control Panel**, click (or in Classic view, double-click) **Add or Remove Programs**.

xv

3. In the **Add or Remove Programs** window, click **Microsoft Office Word 2007 Step by Step**, and then click **Remove**.

4. In the **Add or Remove Programs** message box asking you to confirm the deletion, click **Yes**.

> **Important** If you need help installing or uninstalling the practice files, please see the "Getting Help" section later in this book. Microsoft Product Support Services does not provide support for this book or its companion CD.

Using the Start Menu

To start Word 2007 on a computer running Windows XP:

→ Click the **Start** button, point to **All Programs**, click **Microsoft Office**, and then click **Microsoft Office Word 2007**.

Folders on the Windows Vista Start menu expand vertically. Folders on the Windows XP Start menu expand horizontally. You will notice this variation between the images shown in this book and your Start menu.

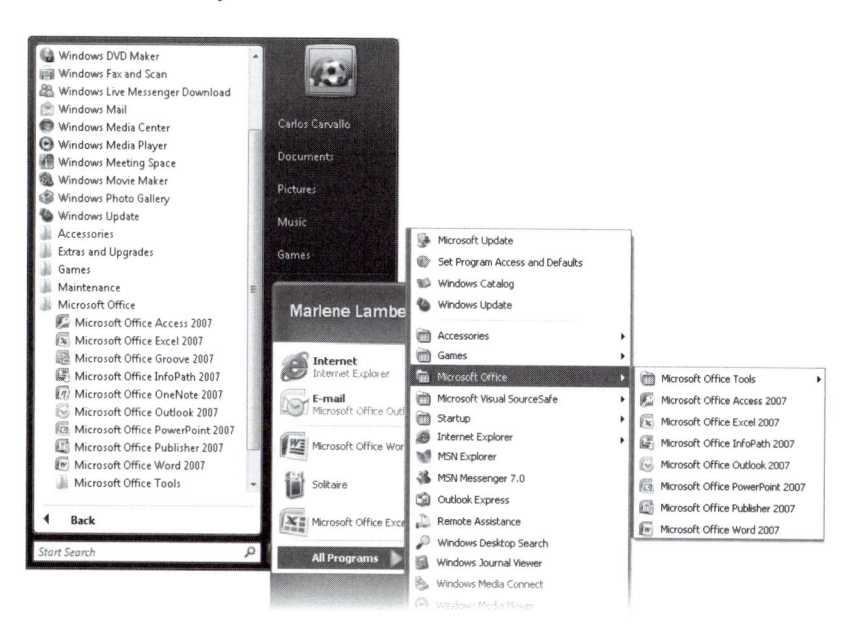

Navigating Dialog Boxes

On a computer running Windows XP, some of the dialog boxes you will work with in the exercises not only look different from the graphics shown in this book but also work differently. These dialog boxes are primarily those that act as an interface between Word and the operating system, including any dialog box in which you navigate to a specific location. For example, here are the Open dialog boxes from Word 2007 running on Windows Vista and Windows XP and some examples of ways to navigate in them.

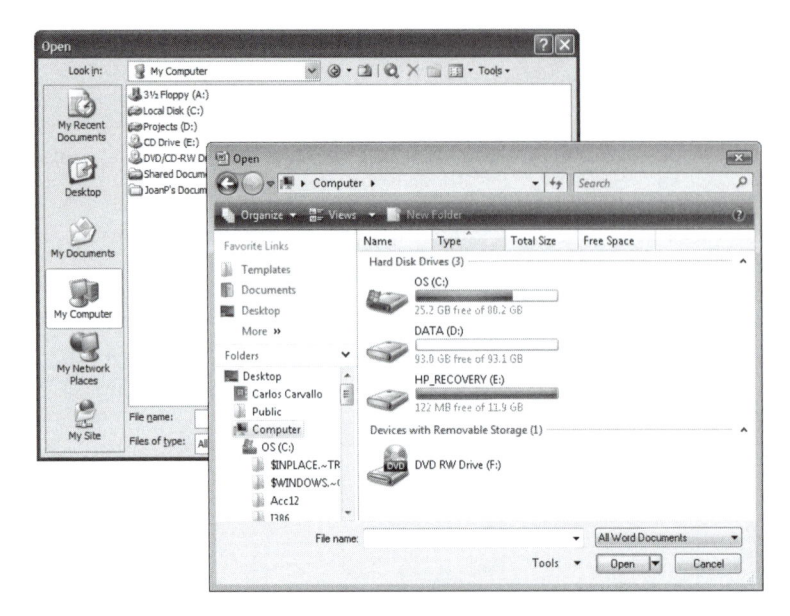

To navigate to the *ExploringWord* folder in Windows Vista:

→ In the **Favorite Links** pane, click **Documents**. Then in the folder content pane, double-click *Microsoft Press*, *Word2007SBS*, and double-click *ExploringWord*.

To move back to the *Word2007SBS* folder in Windows Vista.

→ In the upper-left corner of the dialog box, click the **Back** button.

Back

To navigate to the *ExploringWord* folder in Windows XP:

→ On the **Places** bar, click **My Documents**. Then in the folder content pane, double-click *Microsoft Press*, *Word2007SBS*, and double-click *ExploringWord*.

To move back to the *Word2007SBS* folder in Windows XP:

→ On the toolbar, click the **Up One Level** button.

Up One Level

The Microsoft Business Certification Program

Desktop computing proficiency is becoming increasingly important in today's business world. As a result, when screening, hiring, and training employees, more employers are relying on the objectivity and consistency of technology certification to ensure the competence of their workforce. As an employee or job seeker, you can use technology certification to prove that you already have the skills you need to succeed, saving current and future employers the trouble and expense of training you.

The Microsoft Business Certification (MSBC) program is designed to assist employees in validating their Windows Vista skills and 2007 Microsoft Office program skills. There are two paths to certification:

- A Microsoft Certified Application Specialist (MCAS) is an individual who has demonstrated worldwide skill standards for Windows Vista or for the 2007 Microsoft Office suite through a certification exam in Windows Vista or in one or more of the 2007 Microsoft Office programs, including Microsoft Office Word 2007, Microsoft Office Excel 2007, Microsoft Office PowerPoint 2007, Microsoft Office Outlook 2007, and Microsoft Office Access 2007.

- A Microsoft Certified Application Professional (MCAP) is an individual who has taken his or her knowledge of the 2007 Microsoft Office suite and of Microsoft SharePoint products and technologies to the next level and has demonstrated through a certification exam that he or she can use the collaborative power of the Office suite to accomplish job functions such as *Budget Analysis and Forecasting*, or *Content Management and Collaboration*.

After attaining certification, you can include the MCAS or MCAP logo with the appropriate certification designator on your business cards and other personal promotional materials. This logo attests to the fact that you are proficient in the applications or cross-application skills necessary to achieve the certification.

Selecting a Certification Path

When selecting the Microsoft Business Certification path that you would like to pursue, you should assess the following:

- The program and program version(s) with which you are familiar
- The length of time you have used the program
- Whether you have had formal or informal training in the use of that program

Candidates for MCAS-level certification are expected to successfully complete a wide range of standard business tasks, such as formatting a document or worksheet. Successful candidates generally have six or more months of experience with Windows Vista or the specific Office program, including either formal, instructor-led training or self-study using MCAS-approved books, guides, or interactive computer-based materials.

Candidates for MCAP-level certification are expected to successfully complete more complex, business-oriented tasks utilizing advanced functionality with the combined 2007 Microsoft Office suite of products. Successful candidates generally have between six months and one or more years of experience with the programs, including formal, instructor-led training or self-study using MCAP-approved materials.

Becoming a Microsoft Certified Application Specialist

Every MCAS and MCAP certification exam is developed from a set of exam skill standards that are derived from studies of how Windows Vista and the 2007 Office system programs are used in the workplace. Because these skill standards dictate the scope of each exam, they provide you with critical information about how to prepare for certification.

To become certified as a Microsoft Certified Application Specialist in Word 2007, you must demonstrate proficiency in these six areas:

- **Creating and customizing documents.** You must demonstrate the ability to quickly create and format documents; lay out documents by formatting pages; make documents and content easier to find; and personalize Word 2007 by customizing options.
- **Formatting content.** You must demonstrate the ability to format text and paragraphs, including creating and modifying styles and setting tabs; manipulate text by cutting, copying, and pasting it, and by finding and replacing it; and control pagination with page breaks and sections.

- **Working with visual content.** You must demonstrate the ability to insert and format pictures, clip art, SmartArt graphics, and shapes; insert graphic text by using WordArt, pull quotes, and drop caps; and insert, format, and link text boxes.

- **Organizing content.** You must demonstrate the ability create and use Quick Parts (building blocks); create, modify, and sort lists; create and format tables, including merging and splitting cells and performing calculations; insert and format captions, bibliographies, and tables of figures and authorities; and use mail merge to create form letters, envelopes, and labels.

- **Reviewing documents.** You must demonstrate the ability to move around in a document and switch to a different view; compare and merge documents; and manage tracked changes and work with comments.

- **Sharing and securing content.** You must demonstrate the ability to prepare a document for sharing by saving it in the appropriate format, removing inappropriate or private information, and marking it as final; restrict permissions to a document, set a password, and protect it; and attach a digital signature.

Taking a Microsoft Business Certification Exam

The MCAS and MCAP certification exams for Windows Vista and the 2007 Office system programs are performance-based and require you to complete business-related tasks by using an interactive simulation (a digital model) of the Windows Vista operating system or one or more programs in the Office suite.

Test-Taking Tips

- Follow all instructions provided in each question completely and accurately.
- Enter requested information as it appears in the instructions, but without duplicating the formatting unless you are specifically instructed to do otherwise. For example, the text and values you are asked to enter might appear in the instructions in bold and underlined (for example, **<u>text</u>**), but you should enter the information without applying these formats.
- Close all dialog boxes before proceeding to the next exam question unless you are specifically instructed otherwise.
- Don't close task panes before proceeding to the next exam question unless you are specifically instructed to do otherwise.
- If you are asked to print a document, worksheet, chart, report, or slide, perform the task, but be aware that nothing will actually be printed.

- Don't worry about extra keystrokes or mouse clicks. Your work is scored based on its result, not on the method you use to achieve that result (unless a specific method is indicated in the instructions), and not on the time you take to complete the question.
- If your computer becomes unstable during the exam (for example, if the exam does not respond or the mouse no longer functions) or if a power outage occurs, contact a testing center administrator immediately. The administrator will restart the computer and return the exam to the point where the interruption occurred with your score intact.

Certification

At the conclusion of the exam, you will receive a score report, which you can print with the assistance of the testing center administrator. If your score meets or exceeds the passing standard (the minimum required score), you will be mailed a printed certificate within approximately 14 days.

For More Information

To learn more about the Microsoft Business Certification exams and courseware, visit

www.microsoft.com/learning/mcp/msbc/

Features and Conventions of This Book

This book has been designed to lead you step by step through all the tasks you are most likely to want to perform in Microsoft Office Word 2007. If you start at the beginning and work your way through all the exercises, you will gain enough proficiency to be able to create and work with all the common types of Word documents. However, each topic is self contained. If you have worked with a previous version of Word, or if you completed all the exercises and later need help remembering how to perform a procedure, the following features of this book will help you locate specific information:

- **Detailed table of contents.** A listing of the topics and sidebars within each chapter.
- **Thumb tabs.** Easily locate the beginning of the section or chapter you want.
- **Topic-specific running heads.** Within a chapter, quickly locate the topic you want by looking at the running head of odd-numbered pages.
- **Quick Reference.** General instructions for each procedure covered in specific detail elsewhere in the book. Refresh your memory about a task while working with your own documents.
- **Detailed index.** Look up specific tasks and features and general concepts in the index, which has been carefully crafted with the reader in mind.
- **Companion CD.** Contains the practice files used in the step-by-step exercises, as well as a fully searchable electronic version of this book and other useful resources.

In addition, we provide a glossary of terms for those times when you need to look up the meaning of a word or the definition of a concept.

You can save time when you use this book by understanding how the *Step by Step* series shows special instructions, keys to press, buttons to click, and so on.

Convention	Meaning
CD icon	This icon at the end of a chapter introduction indicates information about the practice files provided on the companion CD for use in the chapter.
USE	This paragraph preceding a step-by-step exercise indicates the practice files that you will use when working through the exercise.
BE SURE TO	This paragraph preceding or following an exercise indicates any requirements you should attend to before beginning the exercise or actions you should take to restore your system after completing the exercise.
OPEN	This paragraph preceding a step-by-step exercise indicates files that you should open before beginning the exercise.
CLOSE	This paragraph following a step-by-step exercise provides instructions for closing open files or programs before moving on to another topic.
1 **2**	Blue numbered steps guide you through step-by-step exercises and Quick Reference versions of procedures.
1 2	Black numbered steps guide you through procedures in sidebars and expository text.
→	An arrow indicates a procedure that has only one step.
See Also	These paragraphs direct you to more information about a given topic in this book or elsewhere.
Troubleshooting	These paragraphs explain how to fix a common problem that might prevent you from continuing with an exercise.
Tip	These paragraphs provide a helpful hint or shortcut that makes working through a task easier, or information about other available options.
Important	These paragraphs point out information that you need to know to complete a procedure.
Save button	The first time you are told to click a button in an exercise, a picture of the button appears in the left margin. If the name of the button does not appear on the button itself, the name appears under the picture.
Enter	In step-by-step exercises, keys you must press appear as they would on a keyboard.
Ctrl + Home	A plus sign (+) between two key names means that you must hold down the first key while you press the second key. For example, "press Ctrl + Home " means "hold down the Ctrl key while you press the Home key."
Program interface elements	In steps, the names of program elements, such as buttons, commands, and dialog boxes, are shown in black bold characters.
User input	Anything you are supposed to type appears in blue bold characters.
Glossary terms	Terms that are explained in the glossary at the end of the book are shown in blue italic characters.

Using the Companion CD

The companion CD included with this book contains the practice files you'll use as you work through the book's exercises, as well as other electronic resources that will help you learn how to use Microsoft Office Word 2007.

What's on the CD?

The following table lists the practice files supplied on the book's CD.

Chapter	Folder\File
Chapter 1: Exploring Word 2007	ExploringWord\Opening.docx ExploringWord\Printing.docs ExploringWord\Viewing1.docx ExploringWord\Viewing2.docx
Chapter 2: Editing and Proofreading Documents	EditingText\Changes.docx EditingText\Finalizing.docx EditingText\FindingText.docx EditingText\FindingWord.docx EditingText\Outline.docx EditingText\SavedText.docx EditingText\Spelling.docx
Chapter 3: Changing the Look of Text	FormattingText\Characters.docx FormattingText\Lists.docx FormattingText\Paragraphs.docx FormattingText\QuickFormatting.docx
Chapter 4: Changing the Look of a Document	FormattingDocs\Background.docx FormattingDocs\ControllingPage.docx FormattingDocs\Header.docx FormattingDocs\Template.docx FormattingDocs\Theme.docx

Chapter	Folder\File
Chapter 5: Presenting Information in Columns and Tables	*CreatingTables\Calculations.docx* *CreatingTables\Columns.docx* *CreatingTables\Loan.xlsx* *CreatingTables\LoanData.xlsx* *CreatingTables\Memo.docx* *CreatingTables\Table.docx* *CreatingTables\TableAsLayout.docx* *CreatingTables\TabularList.docx*
Chapter 6: Working with Graphics, Symbols, and Equations	*CreatingGraphics\Logo.png* *CreatingGraphics\Picture.docx* *CreatingGraphics\Relationships.docx* *CreatingGraphics\Shapes.docx* *CreatingGraphics\Symbols.docx* *CreatingGraphics\WordArt.docx*
Chapter 7: Working with Diagrams and Charts	*CreatingCharts\Chart.docx* *CreatingCharts\Diagram.docx* *CreatingCharts\ExistingData.docx* *CreatingCharts\ModifyingChart.docx* *CreatingCharts\ModifyingDiagram.docx* *CreatingCharts\Sales.xlsx*
Chapter 8: Working with Longer Documents	*Organizing\Bibliography1.docx* *Organizing\Bibliography2.docx* *Organizing\Bookmarks.docx* *Organizing\Contents.docx* *Organizing\Hyperlinks.docx* *Organizing\Index.docx* *Organizing\OtherLogos.docx* *Organizing\Parts.docx*
Chapter 9: Creating Form Letters, E-Mail Messages, and Labels	*Merging\DataSource.xlsx* *Merging\E-mail.docx* *Merging\FormLetter.docx* *Merging\MergingData.docx* *Merging\PreparingData.docx*

Chapter	Folder\File
Chapter 10: Collaborating with Others	*Collaborating\Comments.docx*
	Collaborating\Comparing1.docx
	Collaborating\Comparing2.docx
	Collaborating\Comparing3.docx
	Collaborating\Password.docx
	Collaborating\PreventingChanges.docx
	Collaborating\Sending1.docx
	Collaborating\Sending2.docx
	Collaborating\Sending3.docx
	Collaborating\TrackChanges.docx
	Collaborating\Workspace.docx
Chapter 11: Creating Documents for Use Outside of Word	*WebDocs\Blog.docx*
	WebDocs\Web.docx
	WebDocs\XML.docx
	WebDocs\XMLSchema.xsd
Chapter 12: Customizing Word	*CustomizingWord\Commands.docx*
	CustomizingWord\Toolbar1.docx
	CustomizingWord\Toolbar2.docx

In addition to the practice files, the CD contains some exciting resources that will really enhance your ability to get the most out of using this book and Word 2007, including the following:

- *Microsoft Office Word 2007 Step by Step* eBook
- *Microsoft Computer Dictionary, Fifth Edition* eBook
- Sample chapter and poster from *Look Both Ways: Help Protect Your Family on the Internet* by Linda Criddle
- Windows Vista Product Guide

Important The companion CD for this book does not contain the Word 2007 software. You should purchase and install that program before using this book.

Minimum System Requirements

2007 Microsoft Office System

The 2007 Microsoft Office system includes the following programs:

- Microsoft Office Access 2007
- Microsoft Office Communicator 2007
- Microsoft Office Excel 2007
- Microsoft Office Groove 2007
- Microsoft Office InfoPath 2007
- Microsoft Office OneNote 2007
- Microsoft Office Outlook 2007
- Microsoft Office Outlook 2007 with Business Contact Manager
- Microsoft Office PowerPoint 2007
- Microsoft Office Publisher 2007
- Microsoft Office Word 2007

No single edition of the 2007 Office system installs all of the above programs. Specialty programs available separately include Microsoft Office Project 2007, Microsoft Office SharePoint Designer 2007, and Microsoft Office Visio 2007.

To install and run these programs, your computer needs to meet the following minimum requirements:

- 500 megahertz (MHz) processor
- 256 megabytes (MB) RAM
- CD or DVD drive
- 2 gigabytes (GB) available hard disk space; a portion of this disk space will be freed if you select the option to delete the installation files

> **Tip** Hard disk requirements will vary depending on configuration; custom installation choices may require more or less hard disk space.

- Monitor with 800 × 600 screen resolution; 1024 × 768 or higher recommended
- Keyboard and mouse or compatible pointing device

- Internet connection, 128 kilobits per second (Kbps) or greater, for download and activation of products, accessing Microsoft Office Online and online Help topics, and any other Internet-dependent processes
- Windows Vista or later, Windows XP with Service Pack 2 (SP2), or Windows Server 2003 or later
- Windows Internet Explorer 7 or Microsoft Internet Explorer 6 with service packs

The 2007 Microsoft Office suites, including Office Basic 2007, Office Home & Student 2007, Office Standard 2007, Office Small Business 2007, Office Professional 2007, Office Ultimate 2007, Office Professional Plus 2007, and Office Enterprise 2007, all have similar requirements.

Step-by-Step Exercises

In addition to the hardware, software, and connections required to run the 2007 Microsoft Office system, you will need the following to successfully complete the exercises in this book:

- Word 2007, Excel 2007, and Outlook 2007
- Access to a printer
- 10 MB of available hard disk space for the practice files

Installing the Practice Files

You need to install the practice files in the correct location on your hard disk before you can use them in the exercises. Follow these steps:

1. Remove the companion CD from the envelope at the back of the book, and insert it into the CD drive of your computer.

   The Step By Step Companion CD License Terms appear. Follow the on-screen directions. To use the practice files, you must accept the terms of the license agreement. After you accept the license agreement, a menu screen appears.

   > **Important** If the menu screen does not appear, click the Start button and then click Computer. Display the Folders list in the Navigation Pane, click the icon for your CD drive, and then in the right pane, double-click the StartCD executable file.

2. Click **Install Practice Files**.

3. Click **Next** on the first screen, and then click **Next** to accept the terms of the license agreement on the next screen.

4. If you want to install the practice files to a location other than the default folder (*Documents\Microsoft Press\Word2007SBS*), click the **Change** button, select the new drive and path, and then click **OK**.

> **Important** If you install the practice files to a location other than the default, you will need to substitute that path within the exercises.

5. Click **Next** on the **Choose Destination Location** screen, and then click **Install** on the **Ready to Install the Program** screen to install the selected practice files.

6. After the practice files have been installed, click **Finish**.

7. Close the **Step by Step Companion CD** window, remove the companion CD from the CD drive, and return it to the envelope at the back of the book.

Using the Practice Files

When you install the practice files from the companion CD that accompanies this book, the files are stored on your hard disk in chapter-specific folders within the *Documents\ Microsoft Press\Word2007SBS* folder. Each exercise is preceded by a paragraph that lists the files needed for that exercise and explains any preparations needed before you start working through the exercise. Here are examples:

> **USE** the *FormLetter* document and the *DataSource* workbook. These practice files are located in the *Documents\Microsoft Press\Word2007SBS\Merging* folder.
>
> **BE SURE TO** start Word and display non-printing characters before beginning this exercise.
>
> **OPEN** the *FormLetter* document.

You can browse to the practice files in Windows Explorer by following these steps:

1. On the Windows taskbar, click the **Start** button, and then click **Documents**.

2. In your *Documents* folder, double-click *Microsoft Press*, double-click *Word2007SBS*, and then double-click a specific chapter folder.

You can browse to the practice files from a Word 2007 dialog box by following these steps:

1. On the **Favorite Links** pane in the dialog box, click **Documents**.
2. In your *Documents* folder, double-click *Microsoft Press*, double-click *Word2007SBS*, and then double-click a specific chapter folder.

Removing and Uninstalling the Practice Files

You can free up hard disk space by uninstalling the practice files that were installed from the companion CD. The uninstall process deletes any files that you created in the *Documents\Microsoft Press\Word2007SBS* chapter-specific folders while working through the exercises. Follow these steps:

1. On the Windows taskbar, click the **Start** button, and then click **Control Panel**.
2. In **Control Panel**, under **Programs**, click the **Uninstall a program** task.
3. In the **Programs and Features** window, click **Microsoft Office Word 2007 Step by Step**, and then on the toolbar at the top of the window, click the **Uninstall** button.
4. If the **Programs and Features** message box asking you to confirm the deletion appears, click **Yes**.

See Also If you need additional help installing or uninstalling the practice files, see the "Getting Help" section later in this book.

> **Important** Microsoft Product Support Services does not provide support for this book or its companion CD.

Getting Help

Every effort has been made to ensure the accuracy of this book and the contents of its companion CD. If you do run into problems, please contact the sources listed below.

Getting Help with This Book and Its Companion CD

If your question or issue concerns the content of this book or its companion CD, please first search the online Microsoft Press Knowledge Base, which provides support information for known errors in or corrections to this book, at the following Web site:

www.microsoft.com/mspress/support/search.asp

If you do not find your answer at the online Knowledge Base, send your comments or questions to Microsoft Press Technical Support at:

mspinput@microsoft.com

Getting Help with Word 2007

If your question is about Microsoft Office Word 2007, and not about the content of this Microsoft Press book, your first recourse is the Word Help system. This system is a combination of tools and files stored on your computer when you installed the 2007 Microsoft Office system and, if your computer is connected to the Internet, information available from Microsoft Office Online. There are several ways to find information:

- To find out about an item on the screen, you can display a *ScreenTip*. For example, point to a button to display a ScreenTip giving the button's name, the associated keyboard shortcut, and a description of the button's purpose.

- In the Word program window, you can click the Help button (a question mark in a blue circle) at the right end of the Ribbon to display the Word Help window.

- After opening a dialog box, you can click the Help button (also a question mark) at the right end of the dialog box title bar to display the Word Help window with topics related to the functions of that dialog box already identified.

To practice getting help, you can work through the following exercise.

> **BE SURE TO** start Word before beginning this exercise.

Microsoft Office Word Help

1. At the right end of the Ribbon, click the **Microsoft Office Word Help** button.

   The Word Help window opens.

2. In the list of topics in the **Word Help** window, click **Activating Word**.

   Word Help displays a list of topics related to activating Microsoft Office system programs.

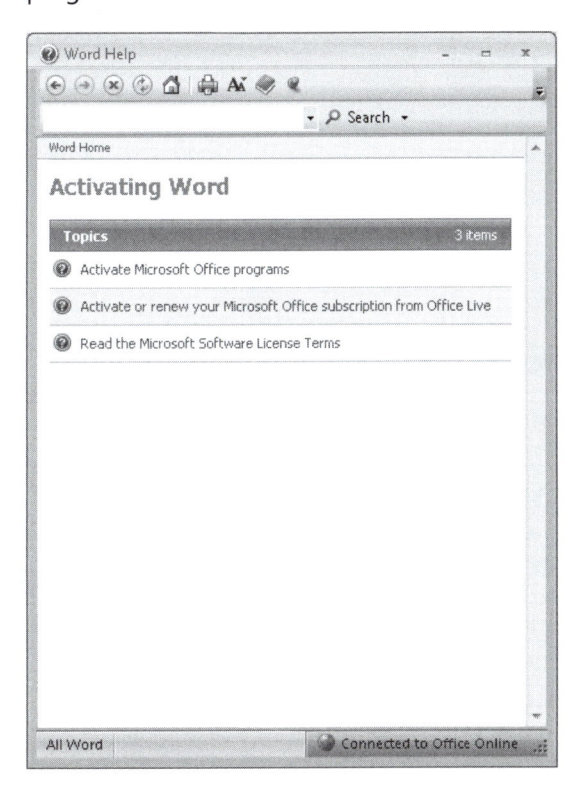

   You can click any topic to display the corresponding information.

Show Table of Contents

3. On the toolbar, click the **Show Table of Contents** button.

   The Table Of Contents appears in the left pane, organized by category, like the table of contents in a book.

Clicking any category (represented by a book icon) displays that category's topics (represented by help icons) as well as any available online training (represented by training icons).

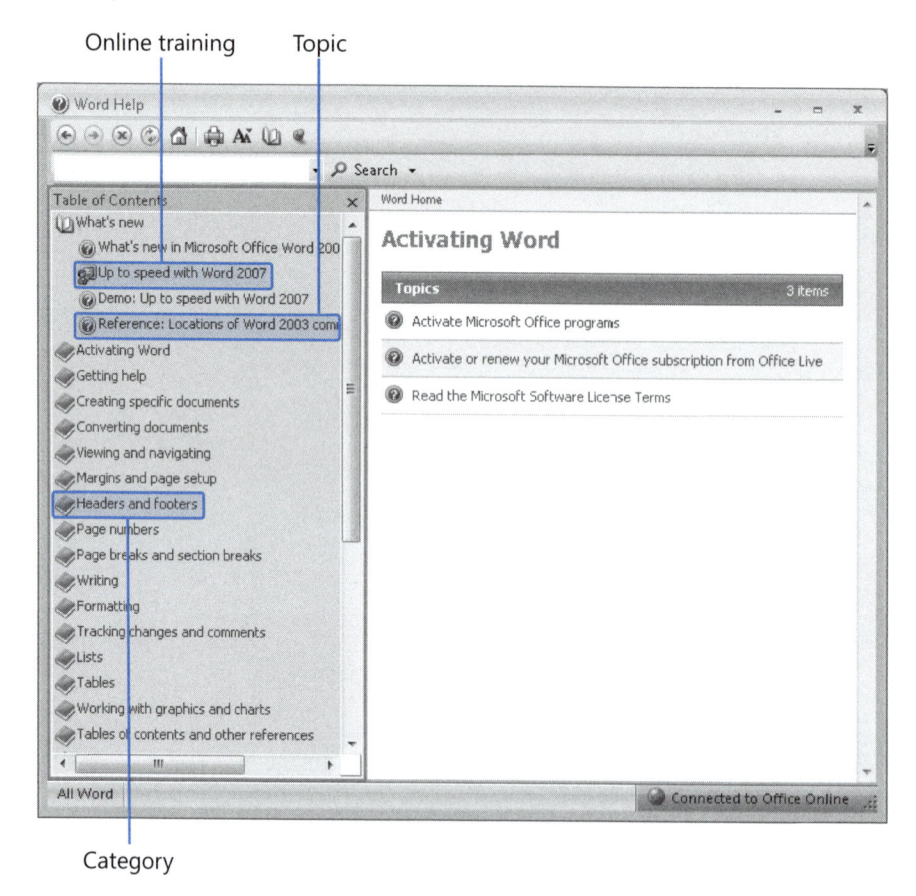

Online training   *Topic*

[Screenshot of Word Help window showing Table of Contents with categories including "Up to speed with Word 2007", "Reference: Locations of Word 2003 com...", "Activating Word", "Getting help", "Creating specific documents", "Converting documents", "Viewing and navigating", "Margins and page setup", "Headers and footers", "Page numbers", "Page breaks and section breaks", "Writing", "Formatting", "Tracking changes and comments", "Lists", "Tables", "Working with graphics and charts", "Tables of contents and other references". Right pane shows Word Home > Activating Word with topics: Activate Microsoft Office programs; Activate or renew your Microsoft Office subscription from Office Live; Read the Microsoft Software License Terms.]

Category

If you're connected to the Internet, Word displays categories, topics, and training available from the Office Online Web site as well as those stored on your computer.

4. In the **Table of Contents**, click a few categories and topics, then click the **Back** and **Forward** buttons to move among the topics you have already viewed.

Back   Forward

5. At the right end of the **Table of Contents** title bar, click the **Close** button.

Close

6. At the top of the **Word Help** window, click the **Type word to search for** box, type Help window, and then press the Enter key.

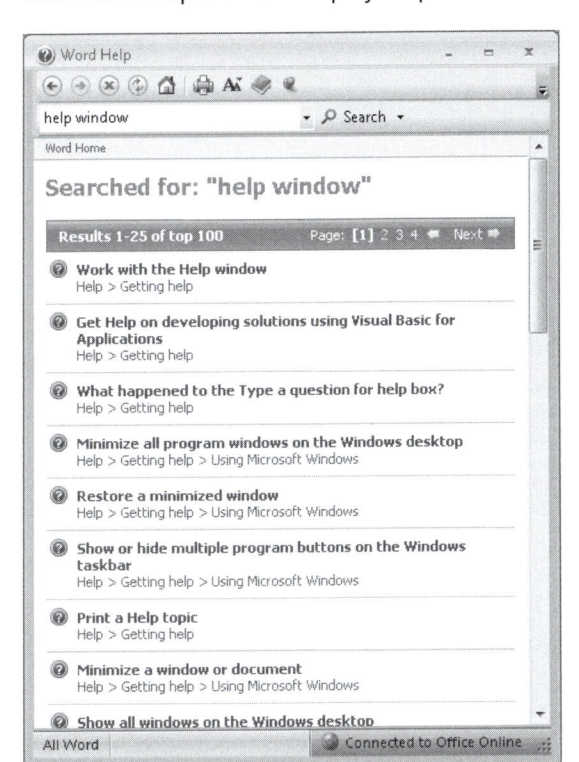

The Word Help window displays topics related to the words you typed.

7. In the results list, click **Print a Help topic**.

   The selected topic appears in the Word Help window, explaining that you can click the Print button on the toolbar to print any topic.

8. Below the title at the top of the topic, click **Show All**.

   Word displays any hidden auxiliary information available in the topic and changes the Show All button to Hide All. You can display or hide an individual item by clicking it. When you click the Print button, Word will print all displayed information.

CLOSE the Word Help window.

More Information

If your question is about Microsoft Office Word 2007 or another Microsoft software product and you cannot find the answer in the product's Help system, please search the appropriate product solution center or the Microsoft Knowledge Base at:

support.microsoft.com

In the United States, Microsoft software product support issues not covered by the Microsoft Knowledge Base are addressed by Microsoft Product Support Services. Location-specific software support options are available from:

support.microsoft.com/gp/selfoverview/

Quick Reference

1 Exploring Word 2007

To start Word

→ Click the **Start** button, click **All Programs**, click **Microsoft Office**, and then click **Microsoft Office Word 2007**.

To open an existing file

1. Click the **Microsoft Office Button**, and then click **Open**.
2. In the **Open** dialog box, navigate to the folder that contains the file you want to open, and then double-click the file.

To move the insertion point to the beginning or end of the document

→ Press [Ctrl]+[Home] or [Ctrl]+[End].

To convert a document created in an earlier version of Word

→ Click the **Microsoft Office Button**, and then click **Convert**.

To view multiple pages

1. On the **View** toolbar, click the **Zoom** button.
2. In the **Zoom** dialog box, click the **Many pages** arrow, select the number of pages, and then click **OK**.

To adjust the magnification of a document

1. On the **View** toolbar, click the **Zoom** button.
2. In the **Zoom** dialog box, click a **Zoom to** percentage or type an amount in the **Percent** box, and then click **OK**.

To display the Document Map

→ On the **View** tab, in the **Show/Hide** group, select the **Document Map** check box.

To display thumbnails of pages

→ On the **View** tab, in the **Show/Hide** group, select the **Thumbnails** check box.

To display or hide non-printing characters

→ On the **Home** tab, in the **Paragraph** group, click the **Show/Hide ¶** button.

To display a document in a different view

→ On the **View** tab, in the **Document Views** group, click the button for the desired view; or

→ Click a view button on the **View** toolbar at the right end of the status bar.

To switch among open documents

→ On the **View** tab, in the **Window** group, click the **Switch Windows** button, and then click the name of the document you want to switch to.

To view multiple open documents

→ On the **View** tab, in the **Window** group, click the **Arrange All** button.

To open a new document

→ Click the **Microsoft Office Button**, click **New**, and then in the **New Document** window, double-click **Blank document**.

To save a document for the first time

1. On the **Quick Access Toolbar**, click the **Save** button; or click the **Microsoft Office Button**, and then click **Save As**.
2. If **Browse Folders** is shown in the lower-left corner of the **Save As** dialog box, click it, and then navigate to the location where you want to save the file.
3. In the **File name** box, type a name for the document, and then click **Save**.

To create a new folder while saving a document

1. Click the **Microsoft Office Button**, and then click **Save As**.
2. In the **Save As** dialog box, navigate to the folder where you want to create the new folder.
3. On the dialog box's toolbar, click the **New Folder** button.
4. Type the name of the new folder, press [Enter], and then click **Open**.
5. In the **File name** box, type a name for the document, and then click **Save**.

To preview how a document will look when printed

→ Click the **Microsoft Office Button**, point to **Print**, and then click **Print Preview**.

To print a document with the default settings

→ Click the **Microsoft Office Button**, point to **Print**, and then click **Quick Print**.

To print a document with custom settings

1. Click the **Microsoft Office Button**, and then click **Print**.
2. In the **Print** dialog box, modify the settings as needed, and then click **OK**.

2 Editing and Proofreading Documents

To select text

- Word: Double-click the word.
- Sentence: Click in the sentence while holding down the [Ctrl] key.
- Paragraph: Triple-click in the paragraph, or double-click in the selection area to the left of the paragraph.
- Block: Click to the left of the first word, hold down the [Shift] key, and then click immediately to the right of the last word or punctuation mark.
- Line: Click in the selection area to the left of the line.
- Document: Triple-click in the selection area.

To delete text

- Select the text, and then press [Del] or [Backspace].

To copy or cut and paste text

1. Select the text, and then on the **Home** tab, in the **Clipboard** group, click the **Copy** or **Cut** button.
2. Click where you want to paste the text, and then in the **Clipboard** group, click the **Paste** button.

To undo an action

- On the **Quick Access Toolbar**, click the **Undo** button.

To move text by dragging

1. Select the text, and then point to the selection.
2. Hold down the mouse button, drag the text to its new location, and then release the mouse button.

To save text as a building block

1. Select the text. Then on the **Insert** tab, in the **Text** group, click the **Quick Parts** button, and then click **Save Selection to Quick Part Gallery**.
2. In the **Create New Building Block** dialog box, type a name for the building block, make any necessary changes to the settings, and then click **OK**.

To insert a building block in a document

- Click where you want to insert the building block. Then either type the name of the building block, and press [F3]; or on the **Insert** tab, in the **Text** group, click the **Quick Parts** button, and select the building block from the **Quick Part** gallery.

To insert the date and time

1. Click where you want the date or time to appear, and then on the **Insert** tab, in the **Text** group, click the **Date & Time** button.
2. In the **Date and Time** dialog box, under **Available formats**, click the format you want, and then click **OK**.

To use the Thesaurus

1. Double-click the word you want to replace, and then on the **Review** tab, in the **Proofing** group, click the **Thesaurus** button.
2. In the **Research** task pane, point to the word you want to insert in place of the selected word, click the arrow that appears, and then click **Insert**.

To research information

1. On the **Review** tab, in the **Proofing** group, click **Research**.
2. In the **Research** task pane, in the **Search for** box, type the research topic.
3. Click the arrow of the box below the **Search for** box, click the resource you want to use, and then in the results list, click a source to view its information.

To translate a word or phrase into another language

1. Select the word or phrase, and then on the **Review** tab, in the **Proofing** group, click the **Translate** button.
2. In the **Translation** area of the **Research** task pane, select the desired languages in the **From** and **To** boxes to display the translation.

To display a document in Outline view

→ On the **View** toolbar, click the **Outline** button.

To display specific heading levels in Outline view

→ On the **Outlining** tab, in the **Outline Tools** group, click the **Show Level** arrow, and in the list, click a heading level.

To collapse or expand heading levels in Outline view

→ Click anywhere in the heading to be collapsed or expanded. Then on the **Outlining** tab, in the **Outline Tools** group, click the **Collapse** or **Expand** button.

To demote or promote headings in Outline view

→ Click the heading to be demoted or promoted. Then on the **Outlining** tab, in the **Outline Tools** group, click the **Demote** or **Promote** button.

To move content in Outline view

→ Collapse the heading whose text you want to move. Then on the **Outlining** tab, in the **Outline Tools** group, click the **Move Up** or **Move Down** button.

To find text

1. On the **Home** tab, in the **Editing** group, click the **Find** button.
2. On the **Find** tab of the **Find and Replace** dialog box, specify the text you want to find, and then click **Find Next**.

To replace text

1. On the **Home** tab, in the **Editing** group, click the **Replace** button.
2. On the **Replace** tab of the **Find and Replace** dialog box, specify the text you want to find and the text you want to replace it with, and then click **Find Next**.
3. Click **Replace** to replace the first instance of the text, **Replace All** to replace all instances, or **Find Next** to leave that instance unchanged and move to the next one.

To check spelling and grammar

1. On the **Review** tab, in the **Proofing** group, click the **Spelling & Grammar** button.
2. In the **Spelling and Grammar dialog** box, click the appropriate buttons to correct the errors Word finds or to add words to the custom dictionary or AutoCorrect list.
3. Click **OK** when Word reaches the end of the Spelling and Grammar check, and then click **Close**.

To remove personal information from a document

1. Click the **Microsoft Office Button**, point to **Prepare**, and then click **Inspect Document**.
2. In the **Document Inspector** dialog box, select the items you want checked, and then click **Inspect**.
3. In the **Document Inspector** summary, click the **Remove All** button to the right of any items you want removed, and then close the **Document Inspector** dialog box.

To mark a document as final

1. Click the **Microsoft Office Button**, point to **Prepare**, and then click **Mark as Final**.
2. Click **OK** in the message box, click **Save**, then click **OK** in the finalization message.

3 Changing the Look of Text

To preview and apply styles

→ Click the paragraph or select the text to which you want to apply a style. Then on the **Home** tab, in the **Styles** group, click the thumbnail of the style you want to apply in the Quick **Styles** gallery.

To change the style set

→ On the **Home** tab, in the **Styles** group, click the **Change Styles** button, click **Style Set**, and then click the set you want to use.

To apply character formatting

→ Select the text. Then on the **Home** tab, in the **Font** group (or on the **Mini toolbar** that appears), click the button of the formatting you want to apply.

To copy formatting

→ Select the text that has the formatting you want to copy. Then on the **Home** tab, in the **Clipboard** group (or on the **Mini toolbar** that appears), click the **Format Painter** button, and select the text to which you want to apply the copied formatting.

To change the font

→ Select the text. Then on the **Home** tab, in the **Font** group, click the **Font** arrow, and click the font you want.

To change the font size

→ Select the text. Then on the **Home** tab, in the **Font** group, click the **Font Size** arrow, and click the font size you want.

To apply text effects

1. Select the text, and then on the **Home** tab, click the **Font** dialog box launcher.
2. In the **Font** dialog box, under **Effects**, select the check box for the effect you want, and then click **OK**.

To clear formatting from text

→ On the **Home** tab, in the **Font** group, click the **Clear Formatting** button.

To change the color of text

→ Select the text. Then on the **Home** tab, in the **Font** group, click the **Font Color** arrow, and in the color palette, click the color you want.

To highlight text with a color

→ Select the text. Then on the **Home** tab, in the **Font** group, click the **Highlight** arrow, and click the color you want.

To select all text with the same formatting

→ Click the formatted text. Then on the **Home** tab, in the **Editing** group, click the **Select** button, and click **Select Text With Similar Formatting**.

To insert a line break

→ Click at the right end of the text where you want the line break to appear. Then on the **Page Layout** tab, in the **Page Setup** group, click the **Breaks** button, and click **Text Wrapping**.

To align paragraphs

→ Click the paragraph, or select multiple paragraphs. Then on the **Home** tab, in the **Paragraph** group, click the **Align Left**, **Center**, **Align Right**, or **Justify** button.

To indent the first line of a paragraph

→ Click the paragraph. Then on the horizontal ruler, drag the **First Line Indent** marker to the location of the indent.

To indent an entire paragraph

→ Click the paragraph, or select multiple paragraphs. Then on the horizontal ruler, drag the **Left Indent** or **Right Indent** marker to the location of the indent.

To increase or decrease indenting

→ Click the paragraph, or select multiple paragraphs. Then in the **Paragraph** group, click the **Increase Indent** or **Decrease Indent** button.

To set a tab stop

→ Click the paragraph, or select multiple paragraphs. Then click the **Tab** button until it displays the type of tab you want, and click the horizontal ruler where you want to set the tab stop for the selected paragraph(s).

To change the position of a tab stop

→ Click the paragraph, or select multiple paragraphs. Then on the horizontal ruler, drag the tab stop to the new mark.

To add a border or shading to a paragraph

1. Click the paragraph. Then on the **Home** tab, in the **Paragraph** group, click the **Borders** arrow, and click **Borders and Shading**.
2. In the **Borders and Shading** dialog box, on the **Borders** tab, click the icon of the border style you want to apply, and then click **OK**.
3. In the **Borders and Shading** dialog box, on the **Shading** tab, click the **Fill** arrow, click the shading color you want, and then click **OK**.

To format paragraphs as a list

→ Select the paragraphs. Then on the **Home** tab, in the **Paragraph** group, click the **Bullets** or **Numbering** button.

To change the style of a list

1. Select the list paragraphs. Then on the **Home** tab, in the **Paragraph** group, click the **Bullets** or **Numbering** arrow.

2. In the **Bullets Library** or **Numbering Library**, click the bullet or number style you want to use.

To change the indent level of a list

→ Select the list paragraphs. Then on the **Home** tab, in the **Paragraph** group, click the **Decrease Indent** or **Increase Indent** button.

To sort items in a list

1. Select the list paragraphs. Then on the **Home** tab, in the **Paragraph** group, click the **Sort** button.
2. In the **Sort Text** dialog box, click the **Type** arrow, and then in the list, click the type of text by which to sort.
3. Select **Ascending** or **Descending**, and then click **OK**.

To create a multilevel list

1. Click where you want to create the list. Then on the **Home** tab, in the **Paragraph** group, click the **Multilevel List** button.
2. In the **Multilevel List** gallery, click the thumbnail of the multilevel list style you want to use.
3. Type the text of the list, pressing [Enter] to create another item at the same level, pressing [Enter] and then [Tab] to create a subordinate item, or pressing [Enter] and then [Shift]+[Tab] to create a higher-level item.

4 Changing the Look of a Document

To add a background color to a document

→ On the **Page Layout** tab, in the **Page Background** group, click the **Page Color** button, and then in the palette, click the background color you want.

To change a document's background fill effects

1. On the **Page Layout** tab, in the **Page Background** group, click the **Page Color** button, and then click **Fill Effects**.
2. In the **Fill Effects** dialog box, click the tab for the type of fill effect you want.
3. Click the options or thumbnails you want, and then click **OK**.

To add a text watermark

→ On the **Page Layout** tab, in the **Page Background** group, click the **Watermark** button, and then click the thumbnail for one of the predefined text watermarks.

or

1. On the **Page Layout** tab, in the **Page Background** group, click the **Watermark** button, and then click **Custom Watermark**.

2. In the **Printed Watermark** dialog box, click **Text watermark**, and then either click the **Text** arrow and click the text you want, or type the text in the **Text** box.
3. Format the text by changing the settings in the **Font**, **Size**, and **Color** boxes.
4. Select a layout option, select or clear the **Semitransparent** check box, and then click **OK**.

To use a picture as a watermark

1. On the **Page Layout** tab, in the **Page Background** group, click the **Watermark** button, and then click **Custom Watermark**.
2. In the **Printed Watermark** dialog box, click **Picture watermark**, and then click **Select Picture**.
3. In the **Insert Picture** dialog box, navigate to the folder where the picture is stored, double-click the name of the picture, and then click **OK**.

To apply a theme

→ On the **Page Layout** tab, in the **Themes** group, click the **Themes** button, and then in the **Themes** gallery, click the theme you want.

To save a custom theme

1. On the **Page Layout** tab, in the **Themes** group, click the **Themes** button, and then click **Save Current Theme**.
2. In the **Save Current Theme** dialog box, in the **File name** box, type a name for the theme, and then click **Save**.

To create a document based on a template

1. Click the **Microsoft Office Button**, click **New**, and then in the left pane of the **New Document** window, click **Installed Templates**.
2. In the center pane, double-click the thumbnail for the template you want.
3. Replace the placeholder text with your own text, and then save the document.

To save a document as a template

1. Click the **Microsoft Office Button**, and then click **Save As**.
2. In the **Save As** dialog box, in the **File name** box, type a name for the template.
3. Click the **Save as type** arrow, and then click **Word Template**.
4. Under **Favorite Links**, click **Templates**, and then click **Save**.

To create a new style

1. Click the text that you want to save as a new style.
2. In the **Styles** group, click the **More** button, and then click **Save Selection as a New Quick Style**.

3. In the **Create New Style from Formatting** dialog box, in the **Name** box, type the new style's name.

4. To make the style available in the template, rather than in only the current document, click **Modify**.

5. At the bottom of the dialog box, click **New documents based on this template**, and then click **OK**.

To apply a different template to a document

1. Display the **Add-Ins** page of the **Word Options** window.

2. In the **Manage** list, click **Templates**. Then click **Go**.

3. In the **Templates and Add-ins** dialog box, under **Document template**, click **Attach**.

4. In the **Attach Template** dialog box, locate and double-click the template you want to attach.

5. In the **Templates and Add-ins** dialog box, select the **Automatically update document styles** check box, and then click **OK**.

To insert a header or footer in a document

1. On the **Insert** tab, in the **Header & Footer** group, click the **Header** or **Footer** button.

2. In the **Header** or **Footer** gallery, click the style you want to use.

3. In the placeholders, type the text you want.

4. On the **Design** contextual tab, in the **Close** group, click the **Close Header and Footer** button.

To insert only a page number

1. On the **Insert** tab, in the **Header & Footer** group, click the **Page Number** button.

2. Point to a position option in the list, and in the gallery, select a page number style.

To change the format of page numbers

1. On the **Insert** tab, in the **Header & Footer** group, click the **Page Number** button, and then click **Format Page Numbers**.

2. In the **Page Number Format** dialog box, click the **Number format** arrow, and then in the list, click the number format you want.

3. Select any other options you want, and then click **OK**.

To prevent widows and orphans

1. Select the paragraphs you want to format. Then on the **Home** tab, click the **Paragraph** dialog box launcher.

2. In the **Paragraph** dialog box, click the **Line and Page Breaks** tab.

3. Select the **Widow/Orphan control** and **Keep lines together** check boxes. Then clear all the other check boxes by clicking them twice, and click **OK**.

Quick Reference **xlix**

To insert a page break
→ Click to the left of where you want to insert the page break. Then on the **Insert** tab, in the **Pages** group, click **Page Break**.

To insert a section break
→ Click to the left of where you want to insert the section break. Then on the **Page Layout** tab, in the **Page Setup** group, click the **Breaks** button, and under **Section Breaks**, click the type of section break you want.

To adjust page margins
→ On the **Page Layout** tab, in the **Page Setup** group, click the **Margins** button, and then click the margin style you want.

5 Presenting Information in Columns and Tables

To format text in multiple columns
→ Select the text. Then on the **Page Layout** tab, in the **Page Setup** group, click the **Columns** button, and click the number of columns you want.

To change the width of columns
1. Click anywhere in the first column. Then on the **Page Layout** tab, in the **Page Setup** group, click the **Columns** button, and then click **More Columns**.
2. Under **Width and spacing**, change the setting in the **Width** column or the **Spacing** column, and then click **OK**.

To hyphenate text automatically
→ On the **Page Layout** tab, in the **Page Setup** group, click the **Hyphenation** button, and then click **Automatic**.

To insert a column break
→ Click where you want the column break to appear. Then on the **Page Layout** tab, in the **Page Setup** group, click the **Breaks** button, and then click **Column**.

To create a tabular list
1. Type the text of the list, pressing [Tab] between each item on a line and pressing [Enter] at the end of each line.
2. Select the lines of the list, change the **Tab** button to the type of tab stop you want, and then click the horizontal ruler where you want to set tab stops that will line up the items in columns.

To insert a table

1. Click where you want to insert the table. Then on the **Insert** tab, in the **Tables** group, click the **Table** button.
2. In the grid, point to the upper-left cell, move the pointer across and down to select the number of columns and rows you want, and click the lower-right cell in the selection.

To merge table cells

→ Select the cells you want to merge. Then on the **Layout** contextual tab, in the **Merge** group, click the **Merge Cells** button.

To add rows to a table

→ Click in the row above or below which you want to add a single row, and then on the **Layout** tab, in the **Rows & Columns** group, click the **Insert Above** or **Insert Below** button; or select the number of rows you want to insert, and then in the **Rows & Columns** group, click the **Insert Above** or **Insert Below** button.

To convert text to a table

1. Select the text you want to convert. Then on the **Insert** tab, in the **Tables** group, click the **Table** button, and click **Convert Text to Table**.
2. In the **Convert Text to Table** dialog box, enter the dimensions of the table in the **Number of columns** and **Number of Rows** boxes, select the type of text separator, and then click **OK**.

To insert a Quick Table

1. Click where you want to insert the table. Then on the **Insert** tab, in the **Tables** group, click the **Table** button, and then point to **Quick Tables**.
2. In the **Quick Tables** gallery, click the table style you want.

To apply a table style

→ Click the table whose style you want to change. Then on the **Design** contextual tab, in the **Table Styles** group, click the style you want in the **Table Styles** gallery.

To total a column of values in a table

1. Click the cell in the table where you want the total to appear.
2. On the **Layout** contextual tab, in the **Data** group, click the **Formula** button.
3. With the SUM formula in the **Formula** box, click **OK** to total the values.

To insert an Excel worksheet

→ Copy the worksheet data in Excel, and then in Word, click where you want to insert the copied data, and on the **Home** tab, in the **Clipboard** group, click the **Paste** button.

or

1. In Excel, copy the worksheet data. Then in Word, click where you want to insert the copied data, and on the **Home** tab, in the **Clipboard** group, click the **Paste** arrow, and click **Paste Special**.
2. In the **Paste Special** dialog box, in the **As** list, click **Microsoft Office Excel Worksheet Object**, click **Paste link**, and then click **OK**.

or

→ Click where you want to insert the worksheet, and then on the **Insert** tab, in the **Tables** group, click the **Table** button, and click **Excel Spreadsheet**.

To draw a table

1. Click where you want to draw the table. Then on the **Insert** tab, in the **Tables** group, click the **Table** button, and then click **Draw Table**.
2. Drag the pointer (which has become a pencil) across and down to create a cell.
3. Point to the upper-right corner of the cell, and drag to create another cell, or draw column and row boundaries inside the first cell.

6 Working with Graphics, Symbols, and Equations

To insert a picture

1. Click where you want to insert the picture. Then on the **Insert** tab, in the **Illustrations** group, click the **Picture** button.
2. Navigate to the folder where the picture is stored, and then double-click the picture to insert it.

To adjust the size of an object

→ Click the object. Then point to one of the handles surrounding the object, and when the pointer becomes a two-headed arrow, drag until the picture is the size you want.

To insert clip art

1. Click where you want to insert the clip art. Then on the **Insert** tab, in the **Illustrations** group, click the **Clip Art** button.
2. In the **Clip Art** task pane, in the **Search for** box, type a word describing what you are looking for, and then click **Go**.
3. In the task pane, click a clip art image to insert it in the document, and then close the task pane.

To move an object

→ Click the object to select it. Then point to the object, and when the pointer changes to a four-headed arrow, drag the object to the new position.

To quickly copy an object

→ Click the object, hold down the `Ctrl` key, and then drag a copy of the object to its new location, releasing first the mouse button and then the `Enter` key.

To insert a WordArt object

1. Click where you want to insert the WordArt. Then on the **Insert** tab, in the **Text** group, click the **WordArt** button.
2. In the **WordArt** gallery, click the style you want.
3. In the **Edit WordArt Text** dialog box, type your text.
4. Set the size and other attributes of the text, and then click **OK**.

To apply a drop cap

→ Click in the paragraph. Then on the **Insert** tab, in the **Text** group, click the **Drop Cap** button, and click the style you want.

To draw a shape

1. On the **Insert** tab, in the **Illustrations** group, click the **Shapes** button, and then click the shape you want.
2. Point where you want the shape to appear, and then drag to draw the shape.

To group drawing objects

1. Hold down the `Ctrl` key, and click each object you want to group.
2. On the **Format** contextual tab, in the **Arrange** group, click the **Group** button, and then click **Group**.

To change the text wrapping of a picture

→ Select the picture. Then on the **Format** contextual tab, in the **Arrange** group, click the **Text Wrapping** button, and click the wrapping style and attributes you want.

To change the position of a picture

→ Select the picture. Then point to the picture, and when the pointer changes to a four-headed arrow, drag the picture to its new location.

or

1. Select the picture. Then on the **Format** contextual tab, in the **Arrange** group, click the **Picture** button, and click **More Layout Options**.
2. In the **Advanced Layout** dialog box, on the **Picture Position** tab, set the position options you want, and then click **OK**.

To insert a symbol

1. Click where you want to insert the symbol. Then on the **Insert** tab, in the **Symbols** group, click the **Symbol** button, and click **More Symbols**.

2. In the **Symbols** dialog box, on the **Symbols** tab, select the font you want.
3. Scroll through the list of symbols until you find the symbol you want, double-click it, and then click **Close**.

To insert an equation
1. Click where you want to insert the equation. Then on the **Insert** tab, in the **Symbols** group, click the **Equation** button.
2. Type your equation in the equation box that appears in the document.

7 Working with Diagrams and Charts

To insert a diagram
1. Click where you want to insert the diagram. Then on the **Insert** tab, in the **Illustrations** group, click the **SmartArt** button.
2. In the **Choose a SmartArt Graphic** dialog box, click the diagram layout you want, and then click **OK**.

To add text to a diagram
→ Click the placeholder text in the **Type your text here** pane or in the diagram shape, and then type your text.

To resize a diagram
→ Drag a sizing handle around the diagram frame, and then drag the handle to increase or decrease the size of the diagram.

To add a shape to a diagram
→ Click the diagram shape above or below which you want the new shape to appear. Then on the **Design** contextual tab, in the **Create Graphic** group, click the **Add Shape** arrow, and in the list, click **Add Shape After**, **Add Shape Before**, **Add Shape Above**, or **Add Shape Below**.

To change the diagram layout
→ Click a blank area in the diagram's frame. Then on the **Design** contextual tab, in the **Layouts** group, click the **More** button, and in the gallery, click the layout you want.

To move a diagram
→ Point to the diagram's frame (not one of the handles), and when the pointer changes to a four-headed arrow, drag the diagram to its new location.

To change the style of a diagram
→ Click a blank area inside the diagram's frame. Then on the **Design** tab, in the **SmartArt Styles** group, click the **More** button, and in the gallery, click the style you want.

To insert a chart

1. On the **Insert** tab, in the **Illustrations** group, click **Chart**.
2. In the **Insert Chart** dialog box, click the category of chart you want, click the style you want, and then click **OK**.

To enter data in a new chart

→ In the Excel worksheet, replace the sample data by clicking a cell, and then typing your own data.

To fit a column to its longest entry

→ Point to the border between two column headings, and when the pointer changes to a double-headed arrow, double-click.

To edit the data in a selected chart

1. On the **Design** tab, in the **Data** group, click the **Edit Data** button.
2. In the Excel worksheet, click the cell you want to edit, type the new data, and then press Enter.

To change the type of a selected chart

1. On the **Design** tab, in the **Type** group, click the **Change Chart Type** button.
2. In the **Change Chart Type** dialog box, click the chart type you want, and then click **OK**.

To change the style of a selected chart

→ On the **Design** tab, in the **Chart Styles** group, click the **More** button, and in the **Chart Styles** gallery, click the style you want.

To turn a chart's gridlines on and off

→ On the **Layout** contextual tab, in the **Axes** group, click the **Gridlines** button, point to **Primary Horizontal Gridlines** or **Primary Vertical Gridlines**, and click the option you want.

8 Working with Longer Documents

To delete a building block

1. In the **Text** group, click **Quick Parts**, and then click **Building Blocks Organizer**.
2. In the **Building blocks** list, select the building block you want to delete, and then click **Delete**.

To create a table of contents based on headings

1. Position the insertion point where you want to insert the table of contents. Then on the **References** tab, in the **Table of Contents** group, click the **Table of Contents** button.
2. In the **Table of Contents** gallery, click the table of contents style you want.

To update a table of contents

1. Click in the table of contents. Then on the **References** tab, in the **Table of Contents** group, click the **Update Table** button.
2. In the **Update Table Of Contents** dialog box, click **Update page numbers only** or **Update entire table**, and then click **OK**.

To insert an index entry

1. Select the word you want to mark. Then on the **References** tab, in the **Index** group, click the **Mark Entry** button.
2. In the **Mark Index Entry** dialog box, click **Mark**.

To create an index

1. Click where you want to insert the index. Then on the **Home** tab, in the **Paragraph** group, click the **Show/Hide** button to turn off the display of non-printing characters.
2. On the **References** tab, in the **Index** group, click **Insert Index**.
3. In the **Index** dialog box, click the **Formats** arrow, click an index format, select any other options you want, and then click **OK**.

To insert a bookmark

1. Select the text or item that you want to bookmark. Then on the **Insert** tab, in the **Links** group, click **Bookmark**.
2. In the **Bookmark** dialog box, in the **Bookmark name** box, type the bookmark name (with no spaces) or select one from the list of bookmarks, and then click **Add**.

To insert a cross-reference

1. Click where you want to insert the cross-reference. Then type the introductory text for the cross reference; for example, *For more information, see*.
2. On the **Insert** tab, in the **Links** group, click the **Cross-reference** button.
3. In the **Cross-reference** dialog box, click the **Reference type** arrow, and then click the type of reference you want.
4. Click the **Insert reference to** arrow, and then click the type of item you are referencing, if necessary.
5. In the **For which** list, click the item you are referencing to, click **Insert**, and then click **Close**.

To insert a hyperlink to another location

1. Select the text or item you want to convert to a hyperlink. Then on the **Insert** tab, in the **Links** group, click **Hyperlink**.
2. In the **Insert Hyperlink** dialog box, select the type of link on the **Link to** bar, and then designate the hyperlink target.
3. Click **Target Frame**, and then in the **Set Target Frame** dialog box, specify where the hyperlink target will be displayed.
4. Click **OK** twice.

To jump to a hyperlink target from a Word document

→ Hold down the Ctrl key, and then click the link.

To edit a hyperlink

1. Right-click the hyperlink, and then click **Edit Hyperlink**.
2. In the **Edit Hyperlink** dialog box, make the necessary changes, and then click **OK**.

To create a footnote or endnote

1. Click where you want to insert the reference mark. Then on the **References** tab, in the **Footnotes** group, click **Insert Footnote** or **Insert Endnote**.
2. In the linked area at the bottom of the page or end of the document or section, type the note text.

To add a new bibliography source to the Source Manager

1. On the **References** tab, in the **Citations & Bibliography** group, click the **Manage Sources** button.
2. In the **Source Manager** dialog box, click **New**.
3. In the **Create Source** dialog box, click the **Type of Source** arrow, and in the list, click the source type. Then enter the bibliography information for the source, and click **OK**.

To insert a bibliography citation in a document

→ Click where you want to insert the citation. Then on the **References** tab, in the **Citations and Bibliography** group, click **Insert Citation**, and in the **Insert Citation** gallery, click the citation you want to insert.

To create a bibliography

→ Click where you want to insert the bibliography. Then on the **References** tab, in the **Citations & Bibliography** group, click the **Bibliography** button, and in the gallery, click the type of bibliography you want.

9 Creating Form Letters, E-Mail Messages, and Labels

To merge a document with an existing data source

1. On the **Mailings** tab, in the **Start Mail Merge** group, click the **Start Mail Merge** button, and then click **Step by Step Mail Merge wizard**.
2. In the **Mail Merge** task pane, select an option in the **Select document type** area, and then click **Next: Starting document**.
3. Click **Use the current document**, and then click **Next: Select recipients**.
4. Click **Use an existing list**, and then click **Browse**.
5. In the **Select Data Source** dialog box, navigate to the location of the data source, and then double-click the file.

To add a record to a data source

1. On the **Mailings** tab, in the **Start Mail Merge** group, click the **Edit Recipient List** button.
2. In the **Mail Merge Recipients** dialog box, in the **Data Source** box, click the data source, and then click **Edit**.
3. In the **Edit Data Source** dialog box, click **New Entry**, enter the new record information into the fields, click **OK**, and then click **Yes** to update the list.

To sort data in a data source

1. On the **Mailings** tab, in the **Start Mail Merge** group, click the **Edit Recipient List** button.
2. In the **Mail Merge Recipients** dialog box, under **Refine Recipient List**, click **Sort**.
3. In the **Filter and Sort** dialog box, click the **Sort by** arrow, and select the field you want to sort by. Then click **Ascending** or **Descending**, and click **OK**.

To filter records in a data source

1. On the **Mailings** tab, in the **Start Mail Merge** group, click the **Edit Recipient List** button.
2. In the **Mail Merge Recipients** dialog box, under **Refine Recipient List**, click **Filter**.
3. In the **Filter and Sort** dialog box, click the **Field** arrow, and select the criteria you want to use for the filter. Then click **OK**.

To insert a merge field into a form letter

1. Click where you want to insert the merge field. Then on the **Mailings** tab, in the **Write and Insert Fields** group, click the button for the field you want to insert.
2. In the dialog box that opens, click **OK** to accept the default settings, or make any changes you want and then click **OK**.

To print an envelope based on an address in a document

1. Select the lines of the address in the document. Then on the **Mailings** tab, in the **Create** group, click the **Envelopes** button.
2. In the **Envelopes and Labels** dialog box, type a return address, if necessary, and make any other necessary selections.
3. Insert an envelope in the printer according to your printer manufacturer's directions, and then click **Print**.

To send personalized e-mail messages

1. Open a new blank document. Then on the **Mailings** tab, in the **Start Mail Merge** group, click the **Start Mail Merge** button, and click **E-mail Messages**.
2. Type the text of the message in the Word document.
3. In the **Start Mail Merge** group, click the **Select Recipients** button, and then designate the data source you want to use.
4. Add any necessary merge fields to the message by using the buttons in the **Write & Insert Fields** group.
5. In the **Finish** group, click the **Finish & Merge** button, and then click **Send E-mail Messages**.
6. In the **Merge to E-mail** dialog box, select **Email_Address** in the **To** box, type a subject in the **Subject line** box, select the mail format, select which records to use, and then click **OK**.

To create mailing labels

1. Open a new blank document. Then on the **Mailings** tab, in the **Start Mail Merge** group, click **Labels**.
2. In the **Label Options** dialog box, select the label vendor and product number you want, and then click **OK**.
3. In the **Start Mail Merge** group, click the **Select Recipients** button, and then designate the data source you want to use.
4. With the insertion point in the first cell on the left, in the **Write & Insert Fields** group, click the **Address block** button.
5. In the **Insert Address Block** dialog box, click **OK** to accept the default settings.
6. In the **Write & Insert Fields** group, click the **Update Labels** button.
7. In the **Preview Results** group, click the **Preview Results** button.
8. In the **Finish & Merge** group, click the **Finish & Merge** button, and select whether you want to merge to a document or the printer.

10 Collaborating with Others

To send a copy of a document as an e-mail attachment

1. On the **Microsoft Office Button** menu, point to **Send**, and then click **E-mail**.
2. In the **To** box, type the e-mail address of the recipient(s), and then click the **Send** button.

To turn change tracking on or off

→ On the **Review** tab, in the **Tracking** group, click the **Track Changes** button.

To display revisions in balloons

→ In the **Tracking** group, click the **Balloons** button, and then in the list, click **Show Revisions in Balloons**.

To show or hide revisions marks

→ In the **Tracking** group, click the **Display for Review** arrow, and then in the list, click **Final Showing Markup** or **Final**.

To accept or reject a change in a document

→ Select the changed text. Then in the **Changes** group, click the **Accept** or **Reject** button.

To move among comments in a document

→ On the **Review** tab, in the **Comments** group, click the **Next** or **Previous** button.

To insert a comment

→ Select the word(s) you want to comment on. Then on the **Review** tab, in the **Comments** group, click the **New Comment** button, and type the comment in the comment balloon.

To delete a comment

→ Click the comment balloon. Then on the **Review** tab, in the **Comments** group, click the **Delete** button.

To open and close the reviewing pane

→ On the **Review** tab, in the **Tracking** group, click the **Reviewing Pane** button.

To edit a comment

→ Click the comment you want to edit, and then type your changes.

To respond to a comment

→ Click the comment balloon. Then on the **Review** tab, in the **Comments** group, click the **New Comment** button, and type your response.

To hide comments

→ On the **Review** tab, in the **Tracking** group, click the **Show Markup** arrow, and then click **Comments**.

To combine versions of a document

1. On the **Review** tab, in the **Compare** group, click the **Compare** button, and then click **Combine**.
2. In the **Combine Documents** dialog box, click the **Original document** arrow, and then in the list, click the name of the original document.
3. Click the **Revised document** arrow, and then in the list, click the name of a different version of the document.
4. In the lower-left corner of the dialog box, click **More**, and then under **Comparison settings**, select the check boxes for the items you want Word to check.
5. Under **Show changes in**, click the option you want, and then click **OK**.

To hide a reviewer's changes

→ On the **Review** tab, in the **Tracking** group, click the **Show Markup** button, point to **Reviewers**, and then click the name of a reviewer whose changes you want to hide.

→ To display hidden changes, in the **Tracking** group, click the **Show Markup** button, point to **Reviewers**, and then click **All Reviewers**.

To accept all changes in a document

→ On the **Review** tab, in the **Changes** group, click the **Accept** arrow, and then click **Accept All Changes in Document**.

To protect a document with a password

1. Click the **Microsoft Office Button**, and then click **Save As**.
2. In the **Save As** dialog box, navigate to the folder where you want to save the file, and then in the **File name** box, type a name for the document.
3. At the bottom of the dialog box, click **Tools**, and then click **General Options**.
4. In the **General Options** dialog box, in the **Password to open** or **Password to modify** box, type a password.
5. Click **OK** to close the **General Options** dialog box.
6. In the **Confirm Password** dialog box, in the **Reenter password to modify** box, type the password again, and then click **OK**.
7. Back in the **Save As** dialog box, click **Save**.

To remove a password

1. Click the **Microsoft Office Button**, click **Save As**, click **Tools**, and then click **General Options**.
2. In the **General Options** dialog box, select the contents of the **Password to open** or **Password to modify** box, press [Del], click **OK**, and then click **Save**.

To restrict formatting and editing

1. On the **Review** tab, in the **Protect** group, click the **Protect Document** button, and then click **Restrict Formatting and Editing**.
2. In the **Restrict Formatting and Editing** task pane, under **Formatting restrictions**, select the **Limit formatting to a selection of styles** check box, and then click **Settings**.
3. Click the **Recommended Minimum** button. Then under **Checked styles are currently allowed**, select the check boxes for other styles you want to include.
4. Under **Formatting**, select the check boxes for any other restrictions you want to set on the document, and then click **OK**.
5. If a message box asks if you want to remove any styles in the document that aren't allowed, click **Yes**.
6. Under **Editing restrictions** in the task pane, select the **Allow only this type of editing in the document** check box.
7. Click the arrow to the right of the box below the check box, and then in the list, click the type of changes you want to allow.
8. Under **Start enforcement** in the task pane, click **Yes, Start Enforcing Protection**.
9. Enter a password if you want, and then click **OK**.

To create a document workspace

1. Open the document for which you want to create a document workspace. Then click the **Microsoft Office Button**, point to **Publish**, and click **Create Document Workspace**.
2. In the **Document Management** task pane, in the **Location for new workspace** box, type the URL of the SharePoint site where you want to create the document workspace, and then click **Create**.
3. If you are asked to supply your user name and password to connect to the site, fill in the **User name** and **Password** boxes, and then click **OK**.

11 Creating Documents for Use Outside of Word

To save a document as a PDF file

1. Install the Save As PDF Or XPS add-in from the Microsoft Downloads site.
2. Click the **Microsoft Office Button**, point to **Save As**, and then click **PDF or XPS**.
3. In the **Publish as PDF or XPS** dialog box, select the file type, change the file name if you want to, and then select the optimal file publishing size.
4. To make additional changes to the format of the published file, click **Options**, make the changes you want, and then click **OK**.
5. In the **Publish as PDF or XPS** dialog box, click **Publish**.

To install an add-in for use in Word

1. Display the **Add-Ins** page of the **Word Options** window.
2. In the **Manage** list, click the type of add-in you want to install. Then click **Go**.
3. In the **Add-Ins** dialog box, click **Add**.
4. In the **Add** dialog box, navigate to the folder containing the add-in you want to install, and double-click the add-in.
5. In the **Add-Ins** dialog box, in the **Checked items are currently loaded** list, select the check box of the new add-in. Then click **OK**.

To save a document as a Web page

1. Open the document you want to save as a Web page. Then click the **Microsoft Office Button**, and click **Save As**.
2. In the **Save As** dialog box, navigate to the folder where you want to save the Web page, and then in the **File name** box, type a name.
3. Click the **Save as type** arrow, and then in the list, click **Web Page**.
4. If you want the Web page title to be something other than what is shown in the dialog box, click **Change Title**, and then in the **Page title** box in the **Set Page Title** dialog box, type a new title, and click **OK**.
5. In the **Save As** dialog box, click **Save**.

To create a blog post

1. Click the **Microsoft Office Button**, and then click **New**.
2. In the **New Document** dialog box, click **New blog post**, and then click **Create**.

To register a blog space

1. In the **Register a Blog Account** dialog box, click **Register Now**.
2. In the **New Blog Account** dialog box, click the **Blog** arrow, select the name of your blog service provider, and then click **Next**.
3. In the **New Account** dialog box, type in the requested information, and click **OK**.

To publish a blog post

1. Open the blog post that you want to publish. Then on the **Blog Post** tab, in the **Blog** group, click the **Publish Entry** button.
2. In the **Connect to Your Space** dialog box, enter your user information, and then click **OK**.

To save a document in XML format

1. Click the **Microsoft Office Button**, and then click **Save As**.
2. In the **Save As** dialog box, navigate to the folder where you want to save the XML file, and then in the **File name** box, type a name.
3. Click the **Save as type** arrow, and then in the list, click **Word XML Document**.
4. In the **Save As** dialog box, click **Save**.

To show the Developer tab on the Ribbon

1. Display the **Popular** page of the **Word Options** window.
2. Under **Top options for working with Word**, select the **Show Developer tab in the Ribbon** check box, and then click **OK**.

12 Customizing Word

To display the Word Options window

→ Click the **Microsoft Office Button**, and then click **Word Options**.

To add a button for a command to the Quick Access Toolbar

1. Click the **Customize Quick Access Toolbar** button.
2. If the command you want to add appears in the list, click it; otherwise, click **More Commands**.
3. Set **Choose command from** to the tab or menu containing the command you want to add. Then click the command in the list below, and click **Add** to move it to the box on the right.
4. Click **OK**.

To create a keyboard shortcut

1. On the **Customize Page** of the **Word Options** window, to the right of **Keyboard shortcuts**, click **Customize**.
2. In the **Customize Keyboard** dialog box, in the **Categories** list, click the name of the tab or menu that contains the command you want, and then in the **Commands** list, click the command.
3. If there is not already a shortcut for the command, click the **Press new shortcut key** box, and then press the keys you want to use for the shortcut.
4. If the shortcut is not already assigned to another command, click **Assign**.

Chapter at a Glance

Work in the Word environment, **page 2**

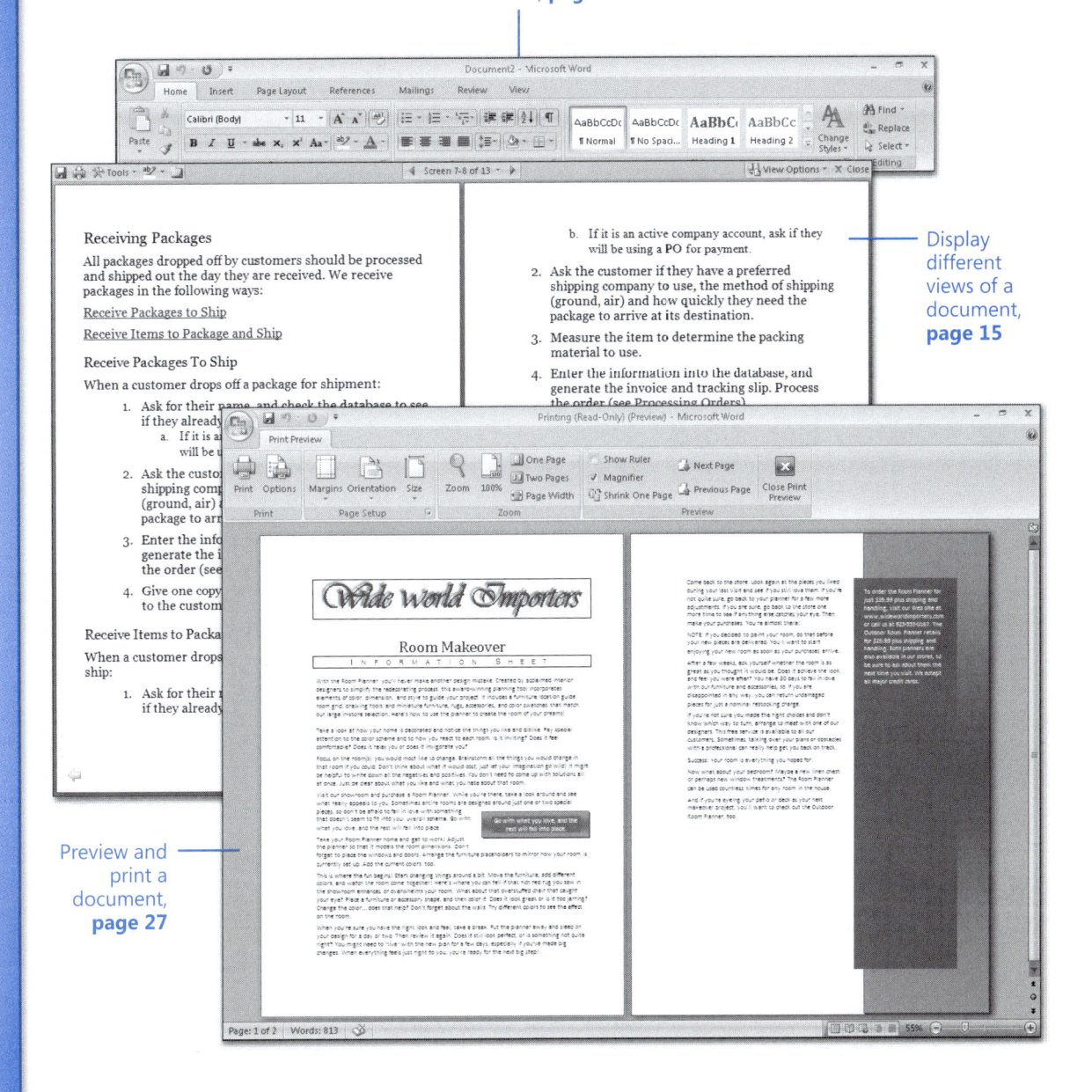

Display different views of a document, **page 15**

Preview and print a document, **page 27**

1 Exploring Word 2007

In this chapter, you will learn to:
- ✔ Work in the Word environment.
- ✔ Open, move around in, and close a document.
- ✔ Display different views of a document.
- ✔ Create and save a document.
- ✔ Preview and print a document.

When you use a computer program to create, edit, and produce text documents, you are *word processing*. Microsoft Office Word 2007 is one of the most sophisticated word-processing programs available today. With Word 2007, it is easier than ever to efficiently create a wide range of business and personal documents, from the simplest letter to the most complex report. Word includes many *desktop publishing* features that you can use to enhance the appearance of documents so that they are appealing and easy to read. The program has been completely redesigned to make these and other powerful features more accessible. As a result, even novice users will be able to work productively in Word after only a brief introduction.

In this chapter, you will first familiarize yourself with the Word working environment. Then you will open an existing Word document, learn ways of moving around in it, and close it. You will explore various ways of viewing documents so that you know which view to use for different tasks and how to tailor the program window to meet your needs. You will create and save a new document and then save an existing document in a different location. Finally, you will preview and print a document.

See Also Do you need only a quick refresher on the topics in this chapter? See the Quick Reference section at the beginning of this book.

Important Before you can use the practice files in this chapter, you need to install them from the book's companion CD to their default location. See "Using the Companion CD" at the beginning of this book for more information.

1

Troubleshooting Graphics and operating system–related instructions in this book reflect the Windows Vista user interface. If your computer is running Windows XP and you experience trouble following the instructions as written, please refer to the "Information for Readers Running Windows XP" section at the beginning of this book.

Working in the Word Environment

As with all programs in the 2007 Microsoft Office release, the most common way to start Word is from the Start menu displayed when you click the Start button at the left end of the Windows taskbar. If Word is the first program in the 2007 Office system that you have used, you are in for a surprise! The look of the program window has changed radically from previous versions.

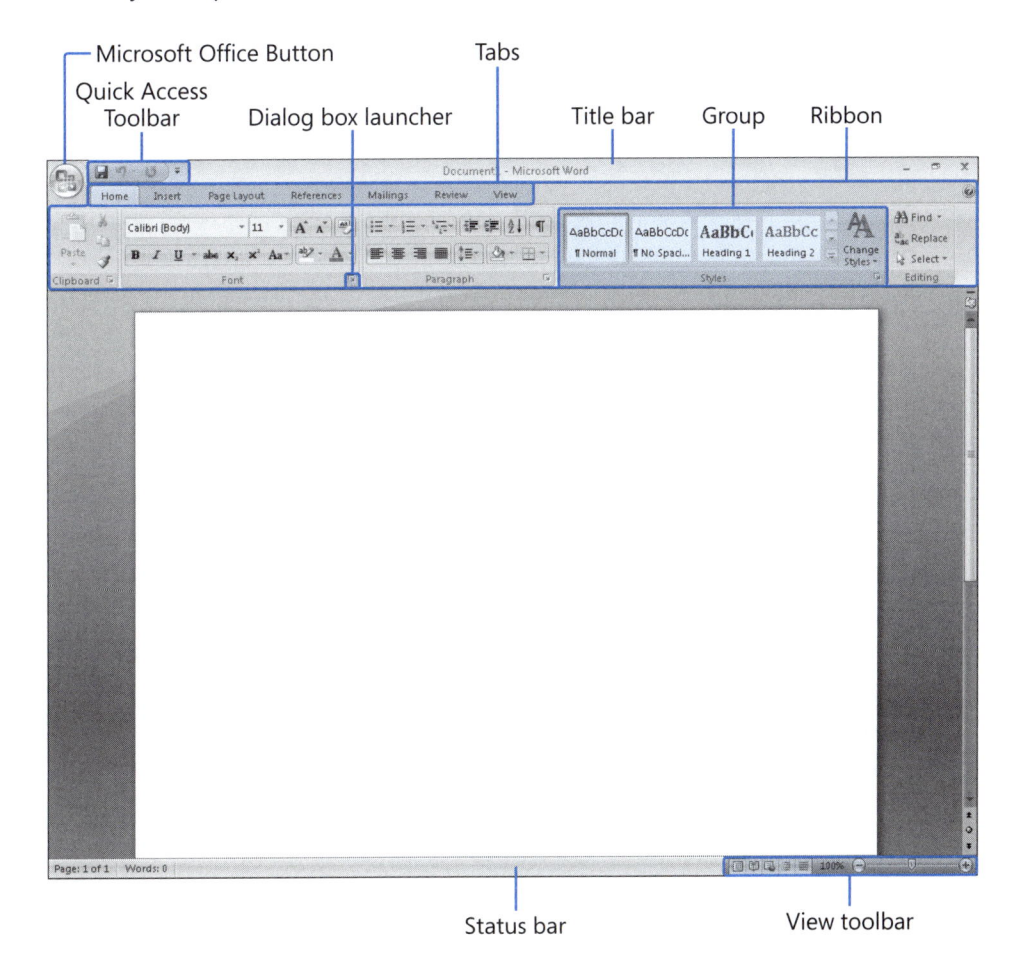

Microsoft Office Button
Quick Access Toolbar
Dialog box launcher
Tabs
Title bar
Group
Ribbon
Status bar
View toolbar

Tip What you see on your screen might not match the graphics in this book exactly. The screens in this book were captured on a monitor set to a resolution of 1024 x 768 pixels with the Windows taskbar is hidden to increase the display space.

The new Word environment is designed to more closely reflect the way people generally work with the program. When you first start Word, this environment consists of the following elements:

Microsoft Office Button

- Commands related to managing Word and Word documents as a whole (rather than document content) are gathered together on a menu that is displayed when you click the *Microsoft Office Button*.
- Commands can be represented as buttons on the *Quick Access Toolbar* to the right of the Microsoft Office Button. By default, this toolbar displays the Save, Undo, and Repeat buttons, but you can customize the toolbar to include any command that you use frequently.

    See Also For information about customizing the Quick Access Toolbar, see "Making Favorite Word Commands Easily Accessible" in Chapter 12, "Customizing Word."

- The *title bar* displays the name of the active document. At the right end of the title bar are the three familiar buttons that have the same function in all Windows programs. You can temporarily hide the Word window by clicking the Minimize button, adjust the size of the window with the Restore Down/Maximize button, and close the active document or exit Word with the Close button.
- Below the title bar is the *Ribbon*, which makes all the capabilities of Word available in one area so that you can work efficiently with the program.
- Commands related to working with document content are represented as buttons on the *tabs* that make up the Ribbon. The Home tab is active by default. Clicking one of the other tabs, such as Insert, displays that tab's buttons.

Tip If Microsoft Office Outlook with Business Contact Manager is installed on your computer, you will have a Business Tools tab in addition to those shown in our graphics.

- On each tab, buttons are organized into *groups*. Depending on the size of the program window, in some groups the button you are likely to use most often is bigger than the rest.

> **Tip** Depending on your screen resolution and the size of the program window, a tab might not have enough room to display all of its groups. In that case, the name of the group resembles a button, and clicking the button displays the group's commands.

[Dialog Box Launcher]

- Related but less common commands are not represented as buttons in the group. Instead they are available in a dialog box, which you can display by clicking the *dialog box launcher* at the right end of the group's title bar.
- Some button names are displayed and some aren't. Pausing the mouse pointer over any button for a few seconds (called *hovering*) displays a *ScreenTip* with not only the button's name but also its function.
- Some buttons have arrows, but not all arrows are alike. If you point to a button and both the button and its arrow are in the same box and are the same color, clicking the button will display options for refining the action of the button. If you point to a button and the button is in one box and its arrow is in a different box with a different shade, clicking the button will carry out that action with the button's current settings. If you want to change those settings, you need to click the arrow to see the available options.

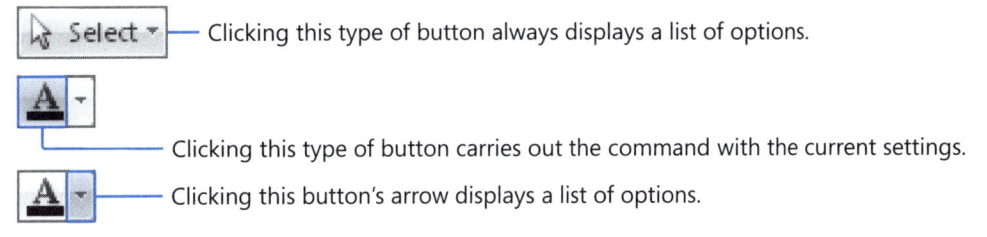

[Select ▼] — Clicking this type of button always displays a list of options.

[A ▼] — Clicking this type of button carries out the command with the current settings.

[A ▼] — Clicking this button's arrow displays a list of options.

- The *Microsoft Office Word Help button* appears at the right end of the Ribbon.
- You create a document in the *document window*. When more than one document is open, each document has its own window.
- Across the bottom of the program window, the *status bar* gives you information about the current document. You can turn on or off the display of an item of information by right-clicking the status bar to display the Customize Status Bar menu, and then clicking that item.

Working in the Word Environment   5

[Customize Status Bar menu screenshot]

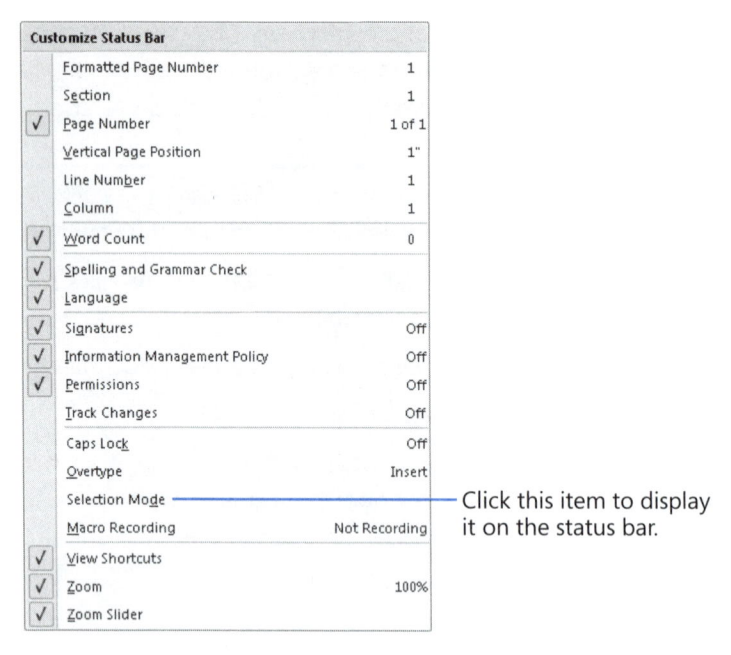

— Click this item to display it on the status bar.

- At the right end of the status bar is the *View toolbar*, which provides tools for adjusting the view of document content.

    See Also For information about adjusting the view of a document, see "Displaying Different Views of a Document" later in this chapter.

The goal of the redesigned environment is to make working on a document more intuitive. Commands for tasks you perform often are no longer hidden on menus or in dialog boxes, and features that you might not have discovered before are now more visible.

For example, when a formatting option has several choices available, they are often displayed in a *gallery* of *thumbnails*. These galleries give you an at-a-glance picture of each choice. If you point to a thumbnail in a gallery, an awesome new feature called *Live Preview* shows you what that choice will look like if you apply it to your document.

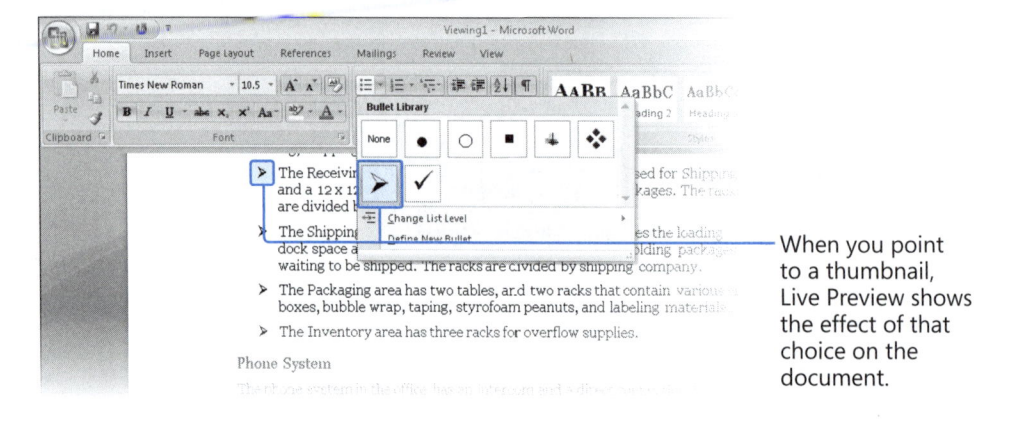

[Screenshot of Word with Bullet Library gallery open]

When you point to a thumbnail, Live Preview shows the effect of that choice on the document.

In this exercise, you will start Word and explore the Microsoft Office Button and the tabs and groups on the Ribbon. Along the way, you will see how to take advantage of galleries and Live Preview. There are no practice files for this exercise.

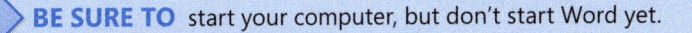

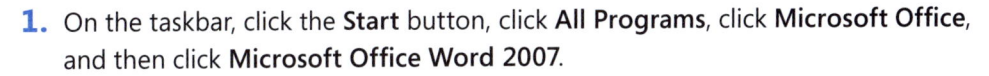

> **BE SURE TO** start your computer, but don't start Word yet.

1. On the taskbar, click the **Start** button, click **All Programs**, click **Microsoft Office**, and then click **Microsoft Office Word 2007**.

   The Word program window opens, displaying a blank document.

2. Click the **Microsoft Office Button**.

   Commands related to managing documents (such as creating, saving, and printing) are available from the menu that opens. This menu, which we refer to throughout this book as the *Office menu*, takes the place of the File menu that appeared in previous versions of Word.

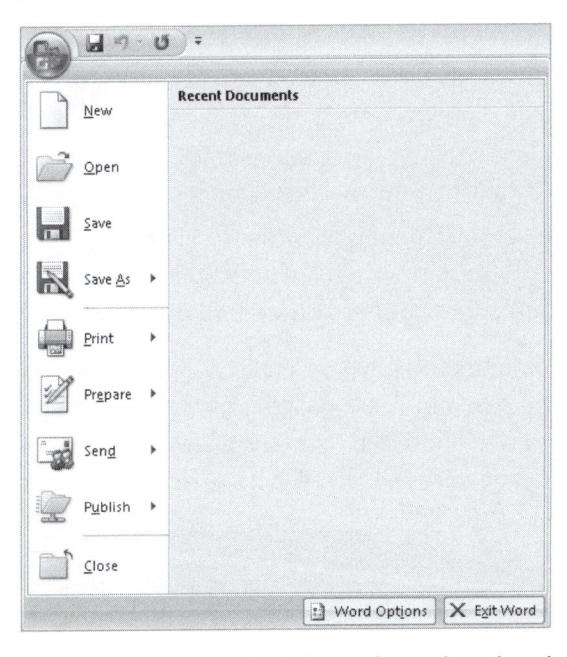

   The commands on the left are for tasks related to the document as a whole. After you have worked with a document, its name appears in the Recent Documents list so that you can quickly open it again. At the bottom of the menu are buttons for changing program options and for quitting Word.

Working in the Word Environment   **7**

See Also For information about changing program options, see "Changing Default Program Options" in Chapter 12, "Customizing Word."

3. Press the Esc key to close the menu.

   On the Ribbon, the Home tab is active. Buttons related to working with document content are organized on this tab in five groups: Clipboard, Font, Paragraph, Styles, and Editing. Only the buttons representing commands that can be performed on the currently selected document element are active.

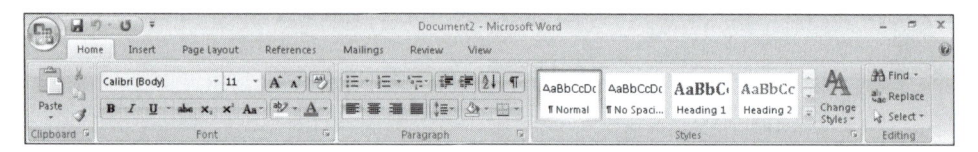

4. Hover the mouse pointer over the active buttons on this tab to display the ScreenTips that name them and describe their functions.

   > **Important** Depending on your screen resolution and the size of the program window, you might see more or fewer buttons in each of the groups, or the buttons you see might be represented by larger or smaller icons than those shown in this book. Experiment with the size of the program window to understand the effect on the appearance of the tabs.

5. Click the **Insert** tab, and then explore its buttons.

   Buttons related to all the items you can insert are organized on this tab in seven groups: Pages, Tables, Illustrations, Links, Header & Footer, Text, and Symbols.

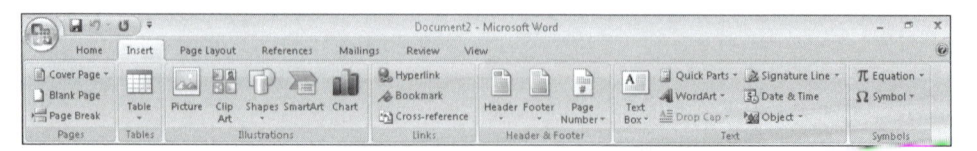

6. Click the **Page Layout** tab, and then explore its buttons.

   Buttons related to the appearance of your document are organized on this tab in five groups: Themes, Page Setup, Page Background, Paragraph, and Arrange.

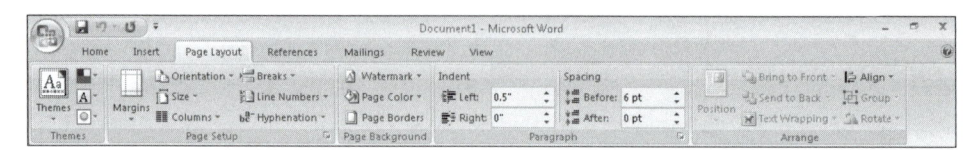

7. In the **Page Setup** group, display the ScreenTip for the **Margins** button.

   The ScreenTip tells you how you can adjust the margins.

8. At the right end of the **Page Setup** group's title bar, click the **Page Setup** dialog box launcher.

   The Page Setup dialog box opens.

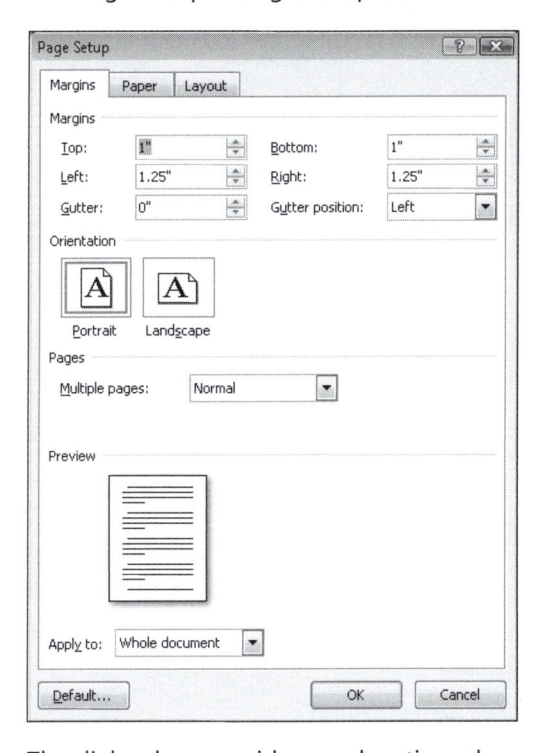

   The dialog box provides one location where you can set the margins and orientation, and specify the setup of a multi-page document. You can preview the results of your changes before applying them.

   See Also For information about setting up multi-page documents, see "Controlling What Appears on Each Page" in Chapter 4, "Changing the Look of a Document."

9. Click **Cancel** to close the dialog box.

10. In the **Themes** group, click the **Themes** button.

Working in the Word Environment   9

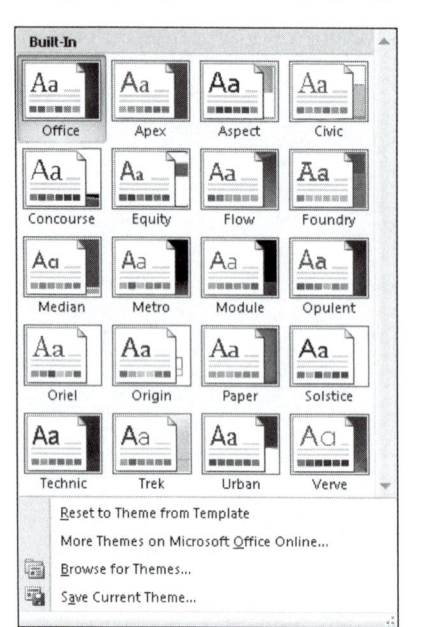

The group expands to display a gallery of the available themes.

11. Press Esc to close the gallery without making a selection.

12. In the **Page Background** group, click the **Page Color** button, and then in the top row of the **Theme Colors** palette, point to each box in turn.

The blank document page shows a live preview of what it will look like if you click the color you are pointing to. You can see the effect of the selection without actually applying it.

13. Press Esc to close the palette without making a selection.

14. Click the **References** tab, and then explore its buttons.

Buttons related to items you can add to long documents, such as reports, are organized on this tab in six groups: Table Of Contents, Footnotes, Citations & Bibliography, Captions, Index, and Table Of Authorities.

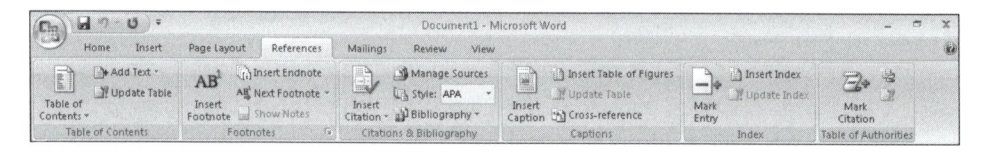

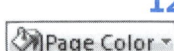

10 Chapter 1 Exploring Word 2007

15. Click the **Mailings** tab, and then explore its buttons.

    Buttons related to creating mass mailings are organized on this tab in five groups: Create, Start Mail Merge, Write & Insert Fields, Preview Results, and Finish.

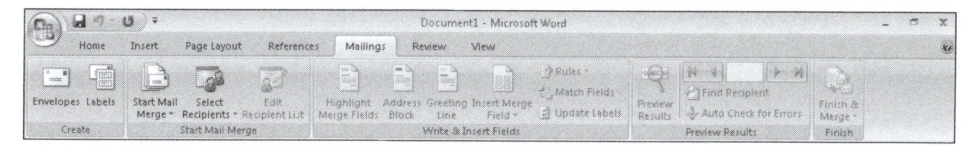

16. Click the **Review** tab, and then explore its buttons.

    Buttons related to proofing, commenting, and changing documents are organized on this tab in six groups: Proofing, Comments, Tracking, Changes, Compare, and Protect.

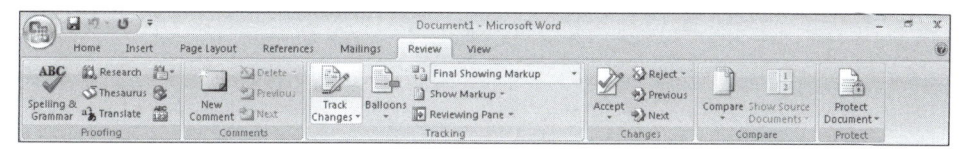

17. Click the **View** tab, and then explore its buttons.

    Buttons related to changing the view or the display of documents are organized on this tab in five groups: Document Views, Show/Hide, Zoom, Window, and Macros.

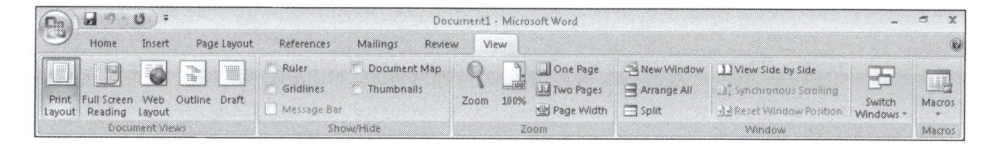

Opening, Moving Around in, and Closing a Document

To open an existing document, you click the Microsoft Office Button and then click Open to display the Open dialog box. The first time you use this command, the dialog box displays the contents of your *Documents* folder. If you display the dialog box again in the same Word session, it displays the contents of whatever folder you last used. To see the contents of a different folder, you use standard Windows techniques. After you locate the file you want to work with, you can double-click it to open it.

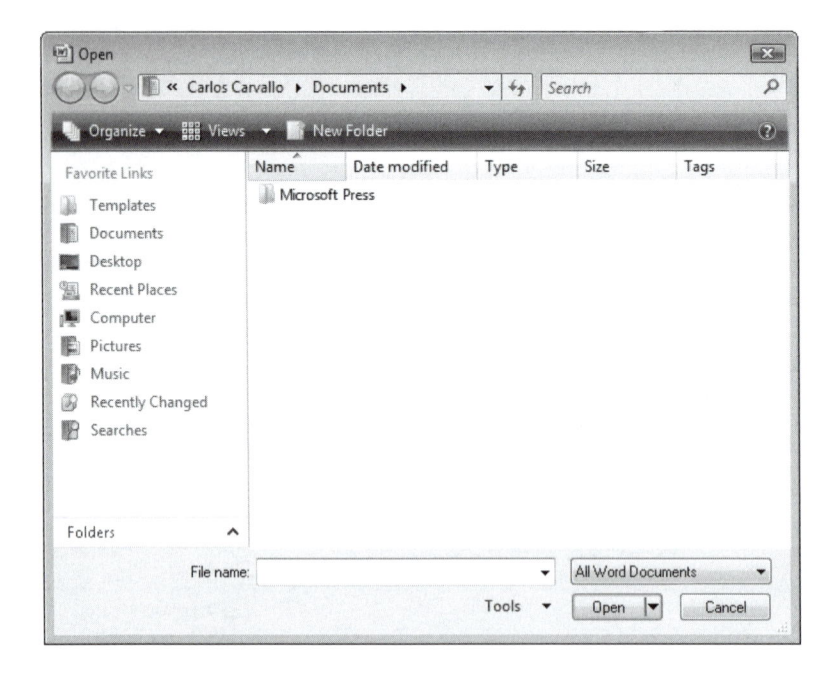

> **Tip** Clicking a file name and then clicking the Open arrow in the lower-right corner of the Open dialog box displays a list of alternative ways in which you can open the file. To look through the document without making any inadvertent changes, you can open the file as *read-only*, or you can open an independent copy of the file. You can open an file in a Web browser, or open an XML file with a transform (see Chapter 11). In the event of a computer crash or other similar incident, you can tell Word to open the file and attempt to repair any damage. And you can display earlier versions of the file.

To move around in an open document without changing the location of the insertion point, you can use the vertical and horizontal scroll bars in the following ways:

- Click the scroll arrows to move the document window up or down by a line, or left or right by a few characters.
- Click above or below the vertical scroll box to move up or down one windowful, or to the left or right of the horizontal scroll box to move left or right one windowful.
- Drag the scroll box on the scroll bar to display the part of the document corresponding to the location of the scroll box. For example, dragging the scroll box to the middle of the scroll bar displays the middle of the document.

You can also move around in a document in ways that do move the insertion point. To place the insertion point at a particular location, you simply click there. To move the insertion point back or forward a page, you can click the Previous Page and Next Page buttons below the vertical scroll bar.

You can also press a key or a *key combination* on the keyboard to move the insertion point. For example, you can press the Home key to move the insertion point to the left end of a line or press Ctrl+Home to move it to the beginning of the document.

> **Tip** The location of the insertion point is displayed on the status bar. By default, the status bar tells you which page the insertion point is on, but you can also display its location by section, line, and column, and in inches from the top of the page. Simply right-click the status bar, and then click the option you want to display.

This table lists ways to use your keyboard to move the insertion point.

To move the insertion point	Press
Left one character	Left Arrow
Right one character	Right Arrow
Down one line	Down Arrow
Up one line	Up Arrow
Left one word	Ctrl+Left Arrow
Right one word	Ctrl+Right Arrow
To the beginning of the current line	Home
To the end of the current line	End
To the beginning of the document	Ctrl+End
To the beginning of the previous page	Ctrl+Page Up
To the beginning of the next page	Ctrl+Page Down
Up one screen	Page Down
Down one screen	Page Up

In a long document, you might want to move quickly among elements of a certain type; for example, from graphic to graphic. You can click the Select Browse Object button at the bottom of the vertical scroll bar and then make a choice in the palette of browsing options that appears, such as Browse By Page or Browse By Graphic.

If more than one document is open, you can close it by clicking the Close button at the right end of the title bar. If only one document is open, clicking the Close button closes the document and also quits Word. If you want to close the document but leave Word open, you must click the Microsoft Office Button and then click Close.

In this exercise, you will open an existing document and explore various ways of moving around in it. Then you will close the document.

USE the *Opening* document. This practice file is located in the *Documents\Microsoft Press\Word2007SBS\ExploringWord* folder.

Microsoft Office Button

1. Click the **Microsoft Office Button**, and then click **Open**.

   The Open dialog box opens, showing the contents of the folder you used for your last open or save action.

2. If the contents of the *Documents* folder are not displayed, in the **Navigation Pane**, click **Documents**.

3. Double-click the *Microsoft Press* folder, double-click the *Word2007SBS* folder, and then double-click the *ExploringWord* folder.

4. Click the *Opening* document, and then click the **Open** button.

   The *Opening* document opens in the Word program window.

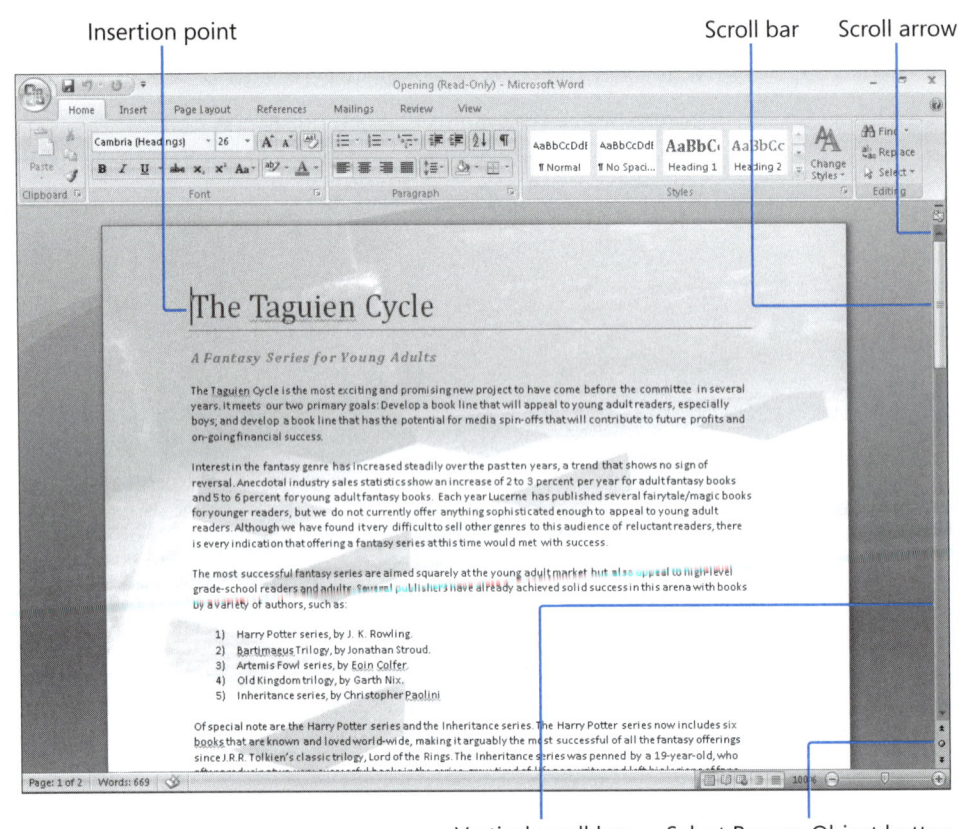

Insertion point — Scroll bar — Scroll arrow

Vertical scroll bar — Select Browse Object button

14 Chapter 1 Exploring Word 2007

5. In the second line of the document title, click at the end of the paragraph to position the insertion point.
6. Press the [Home] key to move the insertion point to the beginning of the line.
7. Press the [→] key two times to move the insertion point to the beginning of the word *Fantasy* in the heading.
8. Press the [End] key to move the insertion point to the end of the line.
9. Press [Ctrl]+[End] to move the insertion point to the end of the document.
10. Press [Ctrl]+[Home] to move the insertion point to the beginning of the document.

Next Page

11. At the bottom of the vertical scroll bar, click the **Next Page** button.
12. Click above the vertical scroll box to change the view of the document by one windowful.
13. Drag the vertical scroll box to the top of the vertical scroll bar.

    The beginning of the document comes into view. Note that the location of the insertion point has not changed—just the view of the document.

Select Browse Object

14. Click to the left of the title to place the insertion point at the top of the document, and then at the bottom of the vertical scroll bar, click the **Select Browse Object** button.

    A palette of browse choices opens.

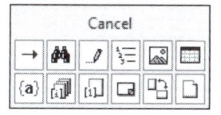

15. Move the pointer over the buttons representing the objects you can browse among.

    As you point to each button, the name of the object appears at the top of the palette.

Browse by Page

16. Click the **Browse by Page** button.

    The insertion point moves from the beginning of page 1 to the beginning of page 2.
17. Click the **Microsoft Office Button**, and then click **Close**.

> **Troubleshooting** If you click the Close button at the right end of the title bar instead of clicking the Microsoft Office Button and then clicking Close, you will close the open Word document and exit the Word program. To continue working, start Word again.

> **Compatibility with Earlier Versions**
>
> Word 2007 uses a different file format than previous versions of the program. You can open a document created with previous versions, but the new features of Word 2007 will not be available. The name of the document appears in the title bar with *[Compatibility Mode]* to its right. You can work in Compatibility Mode, or you can convert the document to the Word 2007 file format by clicking the Microsoft Office Button, and clicking Convert. You can then click the Save button on the Quick Access Toolbar to overwrite the existing document, or click Save As on the Office menu to save the document in the new format as a different file.
>
> You cannot open a Word 2007 document in a previous version of Word unless you install the Compatibility Pack for the 2007 Office system, which is available for free download from Microsoft Office Online. After installing the Compatibility Pack, you can open and work with Word 2007 documents, but you cannot open Word 2007 templates.

Displaying Different Views of a Document

In Word, you can view a document in a variety of ways:

- *Print Layout view.* This view displays a document on the screen the way it will look when printed. You can see elements such as margins, page breaks, headers and footers, and watermarks.

- *Full Screen Reading view.* This view displays as much of the content of the document as will fit on the screen at a size that is comfortable for reading. In this view, the Ribbon is replaced by one toolbar at the top of the screen with buttons that you can use to save and print the document, access references and other tools, highlight text, and make comments. You can also move from page to page and adjust the view.

- *Web Layout view.* This view displays a document on the screen the way it will look when viewed in a Web browser. You can see backgrounds, AutoShapes, and other effects. You can also see how text wraps to fit the window and how graphics are positioned.

    See Also For information about Web documents, see "Creating and Modifying a Web Document" in Chapter 11, "Creating Documents for Use Outside of Word."

- *Outline view.* This view displays the structure of a document as nested levels of headings and body text, and provides tools for viewing and changing its hierarchy.

See Also For information about outlining, see "Reorganizing a Document Outline" in Chapter 2, "Editing and Proofreading Documents."

- *Draft view*. This view displays the content of a document with a simplified layout so that you can type and edit quickly. You cannot see layout elements such as headers and footers.

You switch among views by using buttons in the Document Views group on the View tab or by using the buttons on the View toolbar in the lower-right corner of the window.

You can use other buttons on the View tab to do the following:

- Display rulers and gridlines to help you position and align elements.
- Display a separate pane containing the *Document Map*—a list of the headings that make up the structure of the document—while viewing and editing its text.
- Display a separate pane containing thumbnails of the document's pages.
- Arrange and work with windows.
- Change the magnification of the document.

You can also adjust the magnification of the document by using tools on the View toolbar at the right end of the status bar. You can click the Zoom button and then select or type a percentage; drag the slider to the left or right; or click the Zoom Out or Zoom In button at either end of the slider.

When you are creating more complex documents, it is easier to place elements exactly if you turn on the display of non-printing characters. These characters fall into two categories: those that control the layout of your document and those that provide the structure for behind-the-scenes processes such as indexing. You can turn the display of non-printing characters on and off by clicking the Show/Hide ¶ button in the Paragraph group on the Home tab.

> **Tip** You can hide any text by selecting it, clicking the Font dialog box launcher at the right end of the Font group's title bar on the Home tab, selecting the Hidden check box, and clicking OK. When the Show/Hide ¶ button is turned on, hidden text is visible and is identified in the document by a dotted underline.

In this exercise, you will first explore various ways that you can customize Print Layout view to make the work of developing documents more efficient. You will turn white space on and off, zoom in and out, display the rulers and Document Map, and view non-printing characters and text. Then you will switch to other views, noticing the differences

Displaying Different Views of a Document **17**

so that you have an idea of which one is most appropriate for which task. Finally, you will switch between open documents and view documents in more than one window at the same time.

> **USE** the *Viewing1* and *Viewing2* documents. These practice files are located in the *Documents\Microsoft Press\Word2007SBS\ExploringWord* folder.
> **OPEN** the *Viewing1* document.

1. In Print Layout view, scroll through the document.

   As you can see, on all pages but the first, the printed document will have the title in the header at the top of the page, the page number in the right margin, and the date in the footer at the bottom of each page.

   See Also For information about headers and footers, see "Adding Headers and Footers" in Chapter 4, "Changing the Look of a Document."

2. Point to the gap between any two pages, and when the pointer changes to two opposing arrows, double-click the mouse button. Then scroll through the document again.

   The white space at the top and bottom of each page and the gray space between pages is now hidden.

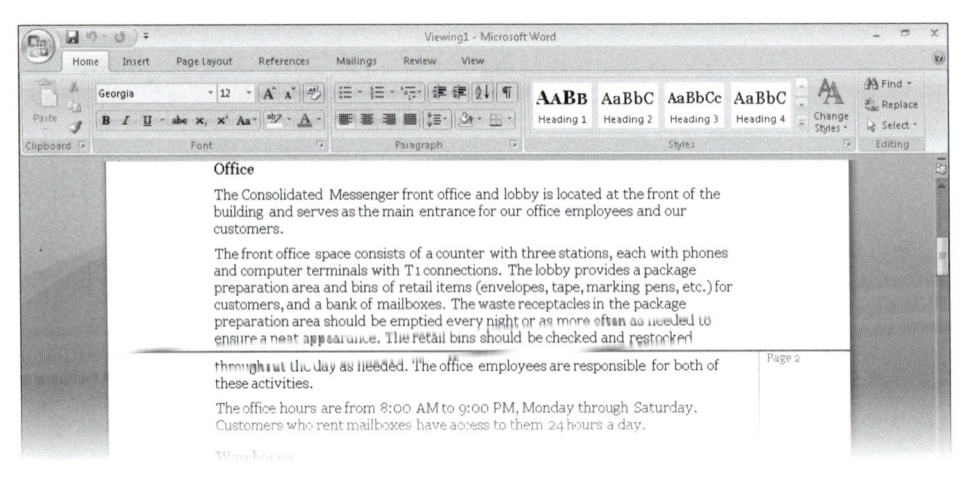

3. Restore the white space by pointing to the black line that separates one page from the next, double-clicking the mouse button.

4. Press Ctrl+Home to move to the top of the document, and then on the **View** toolbar, click the **Zoom** button.

   The Zoom dialog box opens.

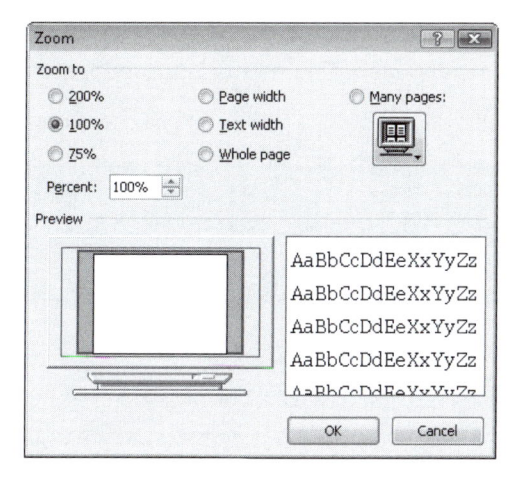

5. Under **Many pages**, click the monitor button, click the second page thumbnail in the top row, and then click **OK**.

   The magnification changes so that you can see two pages side by side.

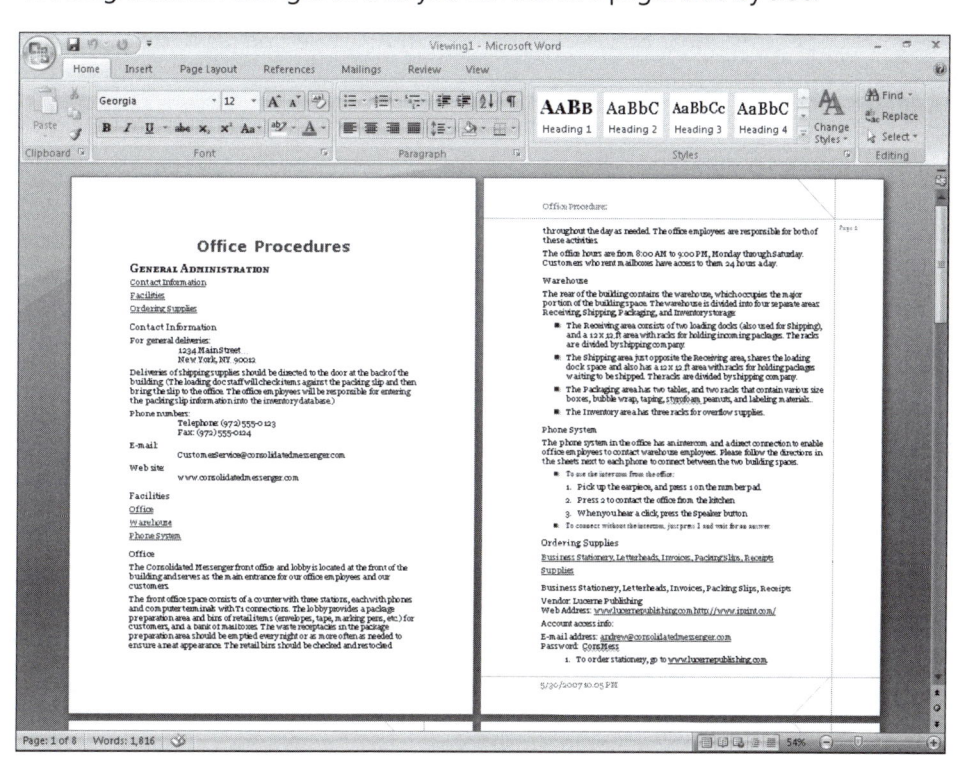

6. Below the vertical scroll bar, click the **Next Page** button to display the third and fourth pages of the document.

7. On the **View** toolbar, click the **Zoom** button. Then in the **Zoom** dialog box, click **75%**, and click **OK**.

   Notice that the Zoom slider position is adjusted to reflect the new setting.

8. At the left end of the **Zoom** slider, click the **Zoom Out** button a couple of times.

   As you click the button, the slider moves to the left and the Zoom percentage decreases.

9. At the right end of the **Zoom** slider, click the **Zoom In** button until the magnification is 100%.

10. On the **View** tab, in the **Show/Hide** group, select the **Ruler** check box.

    Horizontal and vertical rulers appear above and to the left of the page. On the rulers, the active area of the page is white and the margins are blue.

11. In the **Show/Hide** group, select the **Document Map** check box.

    A pane opens on the left side of the screen, displaying an outline of the headings in the document. The first heading on the active page is highlighted.

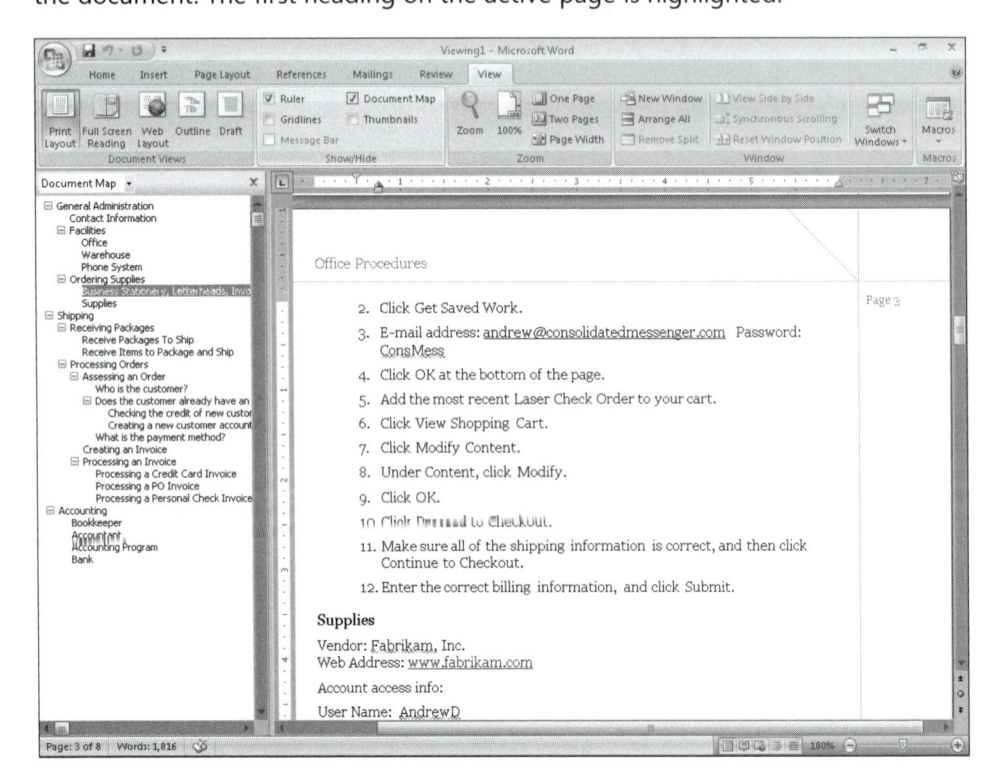

12. In the **Document Map**, click the **Shipping** heading.

    Word displays the page containing the selected heading.

13. In the **Show/Hide** group, click the **Thumbnails** check box, and then scroll the **Thumbnails** pane, and click Page **5**.

14. In the **Thumbnails** pane, click the **Close** button.

    The pane on the left closes.

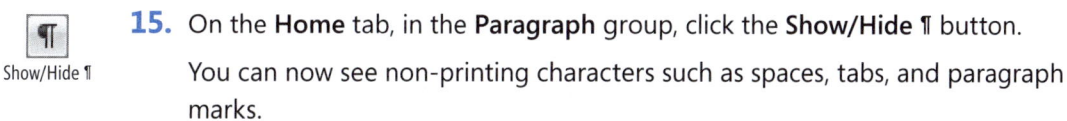

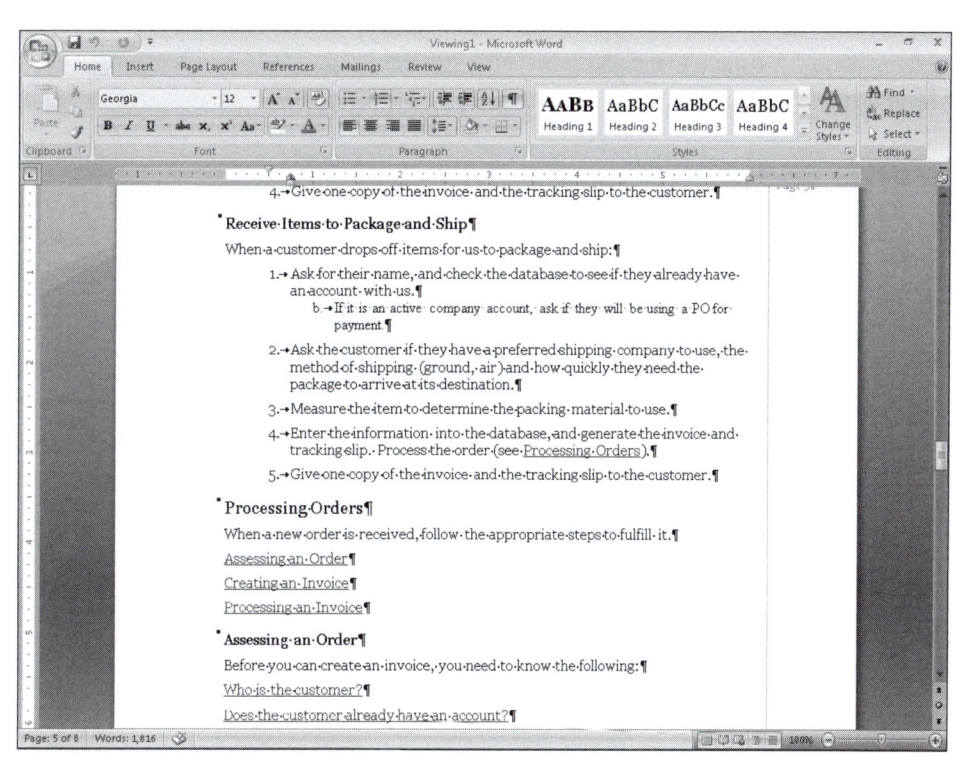

15. On the **Home** tab, in the **Paragraph** group, click the **Show/Hide ¶** button.

    You can now see non-printing characters such as spaces, tabs, and paragraph marks.

16. On the **View** tab, in the **Document Views** group, click the **Full Screen Reading** button.

    The screen changes to display the document in a format that makes it easy to read.

Displaying Different Views of a Document **21**

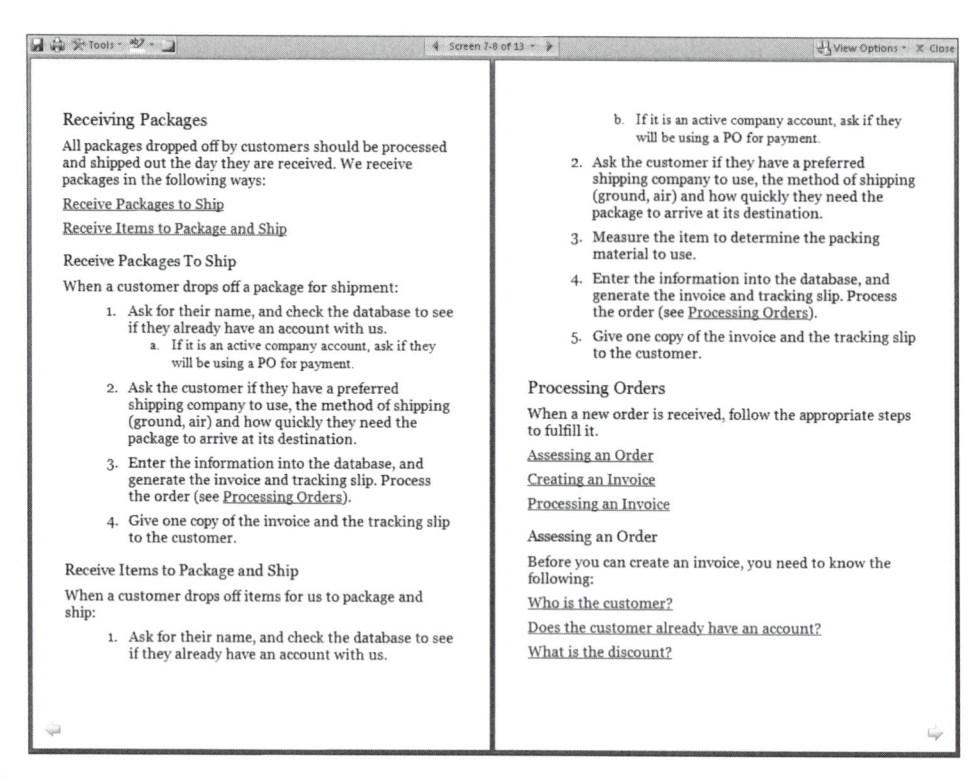

[screenshot of Full Screen Reading view showing two pages of a document about Receiving Packages and Processing Orders]

17. At the top of the screen, click the **Next Screen** button.

You move to the next two screens of information.

18. Explore the other buttons at the top of the Full Screen Reading view, and then click the **Close** button to return to Print Layout view.

19. Press [Ctrl]+[Home]. Then on the **View** toolbar, click the **Web Layout** button, and scroll through the document.

In a Web browser, the text column will fill the window and there will be no page breaks.

20. Press [Ctrl]+[Home], and then on the **View** toolbar, click the **Outline** button.

The screen changes to show the document's hierarchical structure, and the Outlining tab appears at the left end of the Ribbon.

21. On the **Outlining** tab, in the **Outline Tools** group, click the **Show Level** arrow, and in the list, click **Level 2**.

The document collapses to display only the Level 1 and Level 2 headings.

22 Chapter 1 Exploring Word 2007

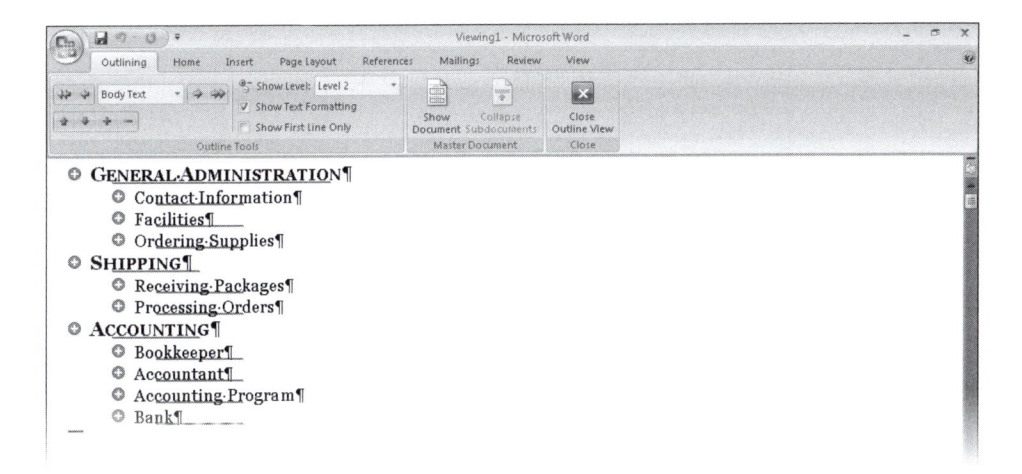

22. On the **View** toolbar, click the **Draft** button, and then scroll through the document.

    You can see the basic content of the document without any extraneous elements, such as margins and headers and footers. The active area on the ruler indicates the width of the text column, dotted lines indicate page breaks, and scrolling is quick and easy.

23. Click the **Microsoft Office Button**, click **Open**, and then in the **Open** dialog box, double-click *Viewing2*.

    The *Viewing2* document opens in Print Layout view in its own document window. Notice that the telephone number in the body of the memo has a dotted underline because it is formatted as hidden.

24. On the **Home** tab, in the **Paragraph** group, click the **Show/Hide ¶** button to turn it off.

    Non-printing characters and hidden text are no longer visible.

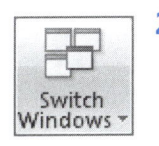

25. On the **View** tab, in the **Window** group, click **Switch Windows**, and then click *Viewing1*.

    The other open document is displayed in Draft view, with non-printing characters visible.

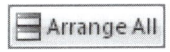

26. On the **View** tab, in the **Window** group, click the **Arrange All** button.

    The two document windows are sized and stacked one above the other. Each window has a Ribbon, so you can work with each document independently.

Creating and Saving a Document   23

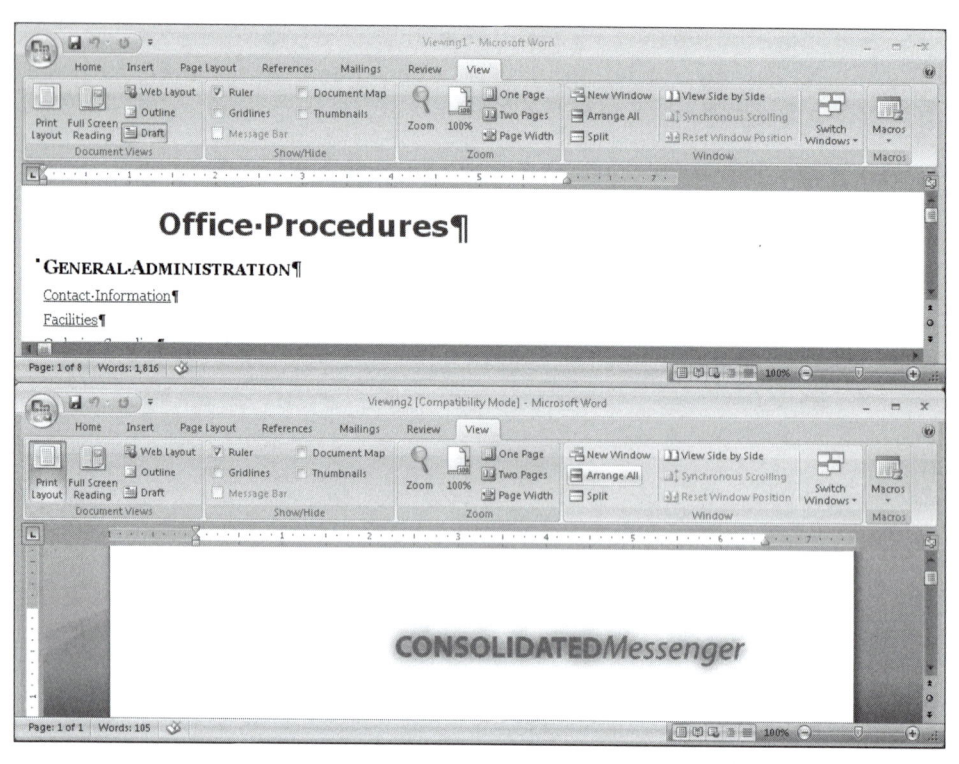

27. At the right end of the *Viewing1* window's title bar, click the **Close** button.

Close

Clicking the Close button does not exit Word because more than one document is open.

28. At the right end of the *Viewing2* window's title bar, click the **Maximize** button.

Maximize

The document window expands to fill the screen.

29. On the **View** tab, in the **Show/Hide** group, clear the **Ruler** check box to turn off the rulers.

> **CLOSE** the *Viewing2* document.

Creating and Saving a Document

To create a Word document, you simply open a new blank document and type your content. The blinking insertion point shows where the next character you type will appear. When the insertion point reaches the right margin, the word you are typing

24 Chapter 1 Exploring Word 2007

moves to the next line. Because of this *word wrap* feature, which is common in word-processing and desktop-publishing programs, you press Enter only to start a new paragraph, not a new line.

Each document you create is temporary unless you save it as a file with a unique name or location. To save a document for the first time, you click the Save button on the Quick Access Toolbar or click the Microsoft Office Button and then click Save. Either action displays the Save As dialog box, where you can assign the name and storage location.

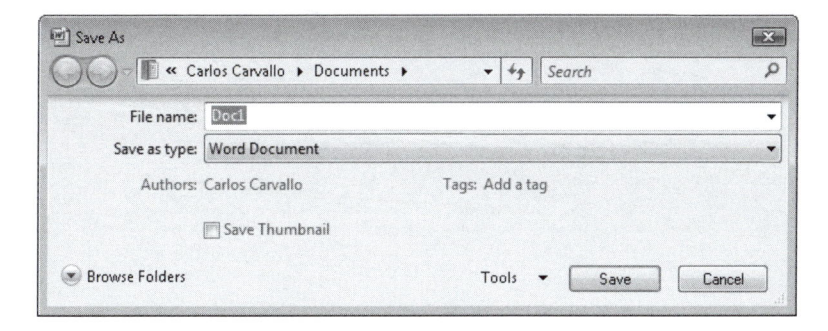

If you want to save the document in a folder other than the one shown in the Address bar, you can click the chevrons to the left of the current folder name and then navigate to the folder you want. You can also click Browse Folders to display the Navigation Pane and a toolbar. If you want to create a new folder in which to store the file, you can click the New Folder button on this toolbar.

After you save a document the first time, you can save changes simply by clicking the Save button. The new version of the document then overwrites the previous version. If you want to keep both the new version and the previous version, click Save As on the Office menu, and then save the new version with a different name in the same location or with the same name in a different location. (You cannot store two files of the same type with the same name in the same folder.)

In this exercise, you will enter text in a new document, and you will save the document in a folder that you create. There are no practice files for this exercise.

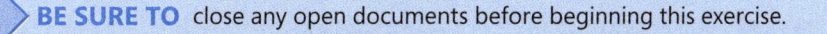

BE SURE TO close any open documents before beginning this exercise.

Microsoft Office Button

1. Click the **Microsoft Office Button**, click **New**. Then in the **New Document** window, double-click **Blank Document**.

A new document window opens, displaying a blank document in Print Layout view.

2. With the insertion point at the beginning of the new document, type **Decorators, Get Ready for Change!**, and then press `Enter`.

The text appears in the new document.

3. Type **With spring just around the corner, let's start making those home decor changes you've been thinking about all winter. Let's introduce fresh new color. Let's add some accessories. Let's come up with a great plan for a room to love.**

Notice that you did not need to press Enter when the insertion point reached the right margin because the text wrapped to the next line.

Decorators, Get Ready for Change!

With spring just around the corner, let's start making those home décor changes you've been thinking about all winter. Let's introduce fresh new color. Let's add some accessories. Let's come up with a great plan for a room to love.

> **Tip** If a red wavy line appears under a word or phrase, Word is flagging a possible error. For now, ignore any errors.

4. Press `Enter`, and then type **Here at Wide World Importers, we realize that you need to have the right tools to guarantee a successful room makeover. And with that in mind, we are proud to present the latest addition to our line of decorating tools, the Room Planner.**

5. On the **Quick Access Toolbar**, click the **Save** button.

   The Save As dialog box opens, displaying the contents of the *Documents* folder. In the File Name box, Word suggests *Decorators*, the first word in the document, as a possible name for this file.

6. In the lower-left corner of the dialog box, click **Browse Folders**.

   The dialog box expands to show the Navigation Pane and a toolbar.

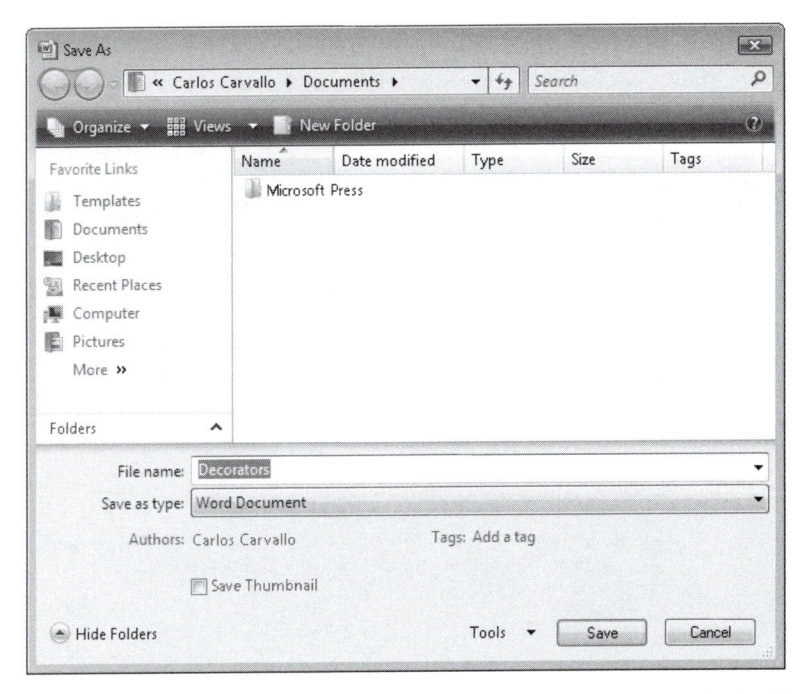

7. Double-click *Microsoft Press*, double-click *Word2007SBS*, and double-click *ExploringWord*.

8. On the dialog box's toolbar, click the **New Folder** button, type My New Documents as the name of the new folder, and then press Enter.

   My New Documents is now the current folder in the Save As dialog box.

9. In the **File name** box, double-click the existing entry, and then type My Announcement.

   > **Troubleshooting** Programs that run on the Windows operating systems use file name extensions to identify different types of files. For example, the extension *.docx* identifies Word 2007 documents. Windows Vista does not display these extensions by default, and you shouldn't type them in the Save As dialog box. When you save a file, Word automatically adds whatever extension is associated with the type of file selected in the Save As Type box.

10. Click **Save**.

    The Save As dialog box closes, Word saves the *My Announcement* file in the *My New Documents* folder, and the name of the document, *My Announcement*, appears on the program window's title bar.

11. Click the **Microsoft Office Button**, and then click **Save As**.

The Save As dialog box opens, displaying the contents of the *My New Documents* folder.

12. In the Address bar in the **Save As** dialog box, click the chevrons to the left of *My New Documents*, and then in the list, click **ExploringWord**.

    The dialog box now displays the contents of the *My New Documents* folder's *parent folder*, ExploringWord.

13. Click **Save**.

    Word saves the *My Announcement* file in the *ExploringWord* folder. You now have two versions of the document saved with the same name but in different folders.

CLOSE the *My Announcement* file.

> **Tip** By default, Word periodically saves the document you are working on in case the program stops responding or you lose electrical power. To adjust the time interval between saves, click the Microsoft Office Button, click Word Options, click Save in the left pane of the Word Options window, and specify the period of time in the box to the right of the Save AutoRecover Information Every check box. Then click OK.

Previewing and Printing a Document

When you are ready to print a document, you can click the Microsoft Office Button, point to Print, and then click Quick Print. Word then uses your computer's default printer and the settings specified in the Print dialog box. To use a different printer or change the print settings, you click the Microsoft Office Button, and then click Print to open the Print dialog box. You can then specify which printer to use, what to print, and how many copies, and you can make other changes to the settings.

Before you print a document, you almost always want to check how it will look on paper by previewing it. Previewing is essential for multi-page documents but is helpful even for one-page documents. To preview a document, you click the Microsoft Office Button, point to Print, and then click Print Preview. This view shows exactly how each page of the document will look when printed. Word displays a Print Preview tab on the Ribbon to provide tools for checking each page and making adjustments if you don't like what you see.

By using the buttons in the Page Setup group on the Print Preview tab, you can make the following changes:

- Change the margins of the document to fit more or less information on a page or to control where the information appears. You define the size of the top, bottom, left, and right margins by clicking the Margins button and making a selection from the Margins gallery, or by clicking Custom Margins and specifying settings on the Margins tab of the Page Setup dialog box.

- Switch the *orientation* (the direction in which a page is laid out on the paper). The default orientation is *portrait*, in which the page is taller than it is wide. You can set the orientation to *landscape*, in which the page is wider than it is tall, by clicking the Orientation button and selecting that option.

> **Tip** The pages of a document all have the same margins and are oriented the same way unless you divide your document into sections. Then each section can have independent margin and orientation settings.

See Also For more information about sections, see "Controlling What Appears on Each Page" in Chapter 4, "Changing the Look of a Document."

- Select the paper size you want to use by clicking the Size button and making a selection in the Paper Size gallery.

You can click buttons in other groups to change the printer options, change the view of the document, and change the mouse pointer so that you can edit the text.

In this exercise, you will preview a document, adjust the margins, change the orientation, and select a new printer before sending the document to be printed.

> **USE** the *Printing* document. This practice file is located in the *Documents\Microsoft Press\Word2007SBS\ExploringWord* folder.
> **BE SURE TO** install a printer and turn it on before starting this exercise.
> **OPEN** the *Printing* document.

1. Click the **Microsoft Office Button**, point to the **Print** arrow, and then click **Print Preview**.

   The window's title bar now indicates that you are viewing a preview of the document, and the Print Preview tab appears on the Ribbon.

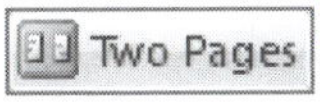

2. On the **Print Preview** tab, in the **Zoom** group, click the **Two Pages** button.

   Word displays the two pages of the document side by side.

Previewing and Printing a Document   29

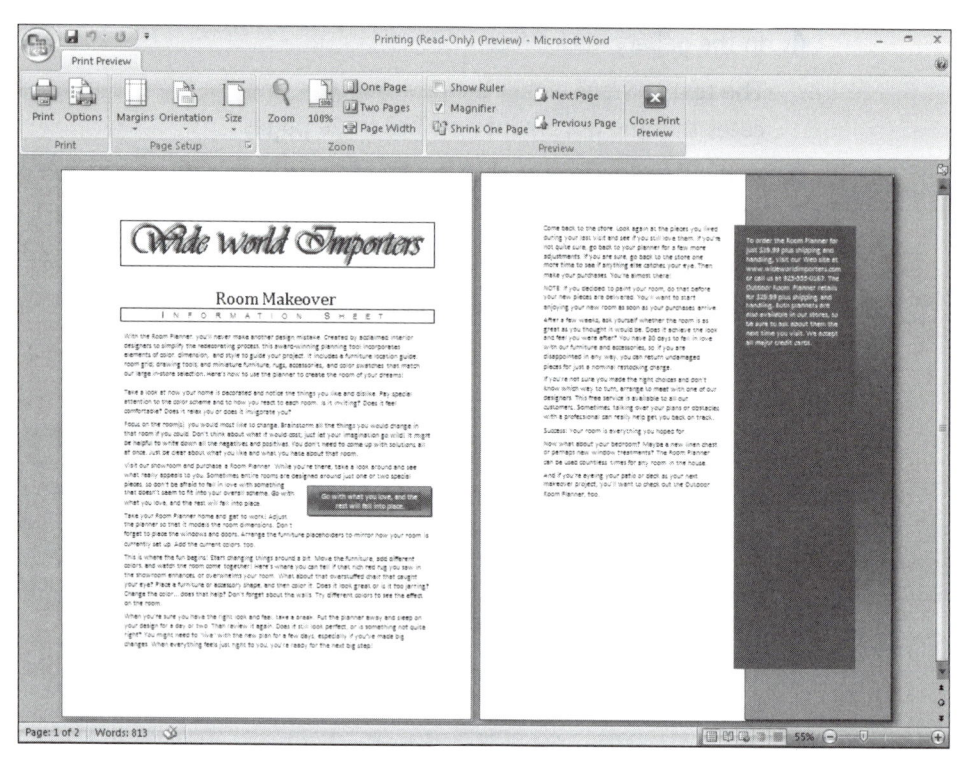

3. In the **Page Setup** group, click the **Margins** button.

The Margins gallery appears.

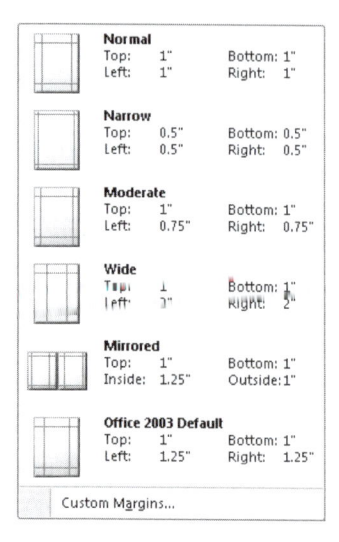

Chapter at a Glance

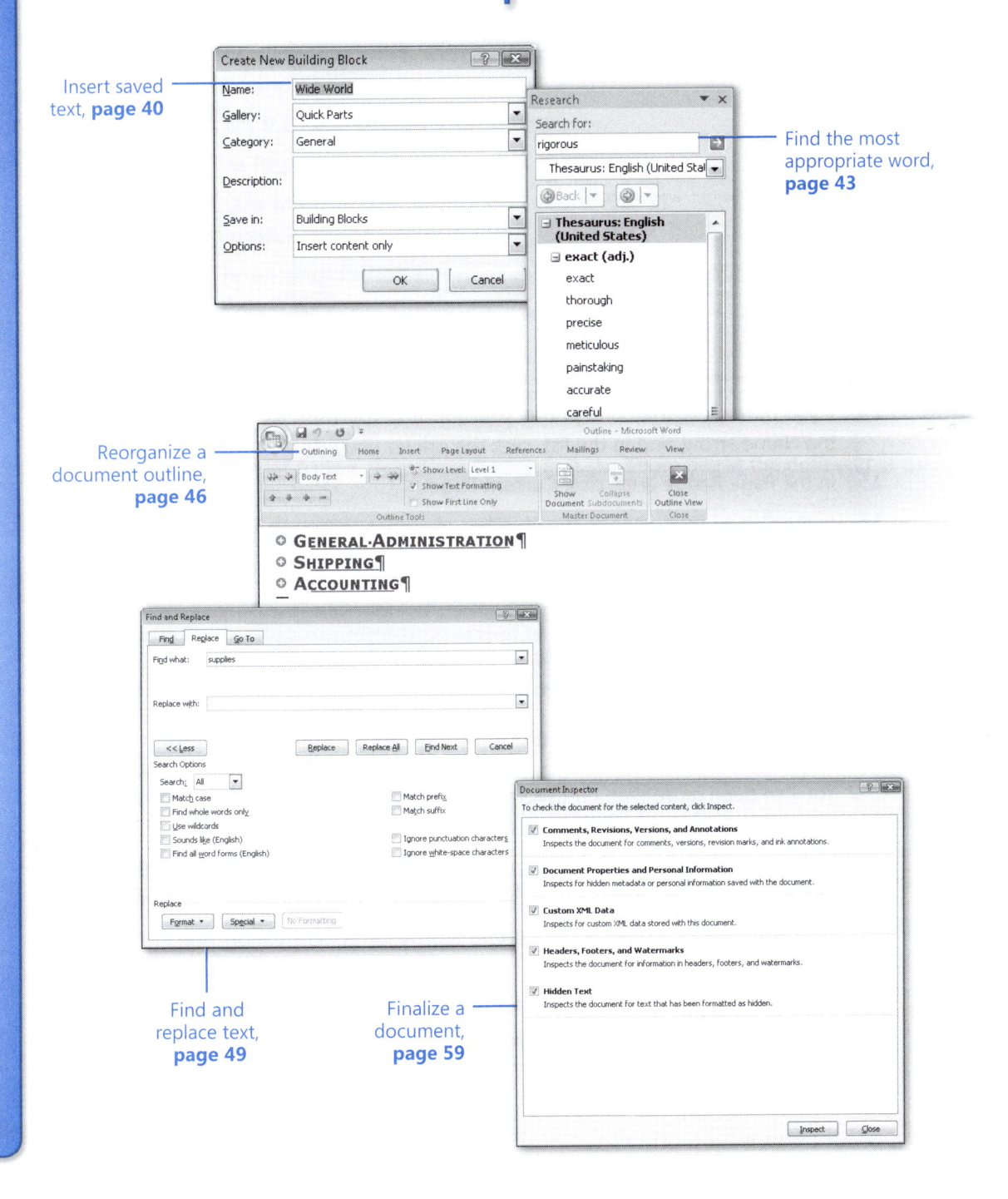

Insert saved text, **page 40**

Find the most appropriate word, **page 43**

Reorganize a document outline, **page 46**

Find and replace text, **page 49**

Finalize a document, **page 59**

2 Editing and Proofreading Documents

In this chapter, you will learn to:
- ✔ Make changes to a document.
- ✔ Insert saved text.
- ✔ Find the most appropriate word.
- ✔ Reorganize a document outline.
- ✔ Find and replace text.
- ✔ Correct spelling and grammatical errors.
- ✔ Finalize a document.

Unless the documents you create are intended for no one's eyes but your own, you need to ensure that they are correct, logical, and persuasive. Whether you are a novice writer or an experienced writer, Microsoft Office Word 2007 has several tools that make creating professional documents easy and efficient:

- Editing tools provide quick-selection techniques and drag-and-drop editing to make it easy to move and copy text anywhere you want it.
- The building blocks feature can be used to save and recall specialized terms or standard paragraphs.
- Reference and research tools include a thesaurus that makes it easy to track down synonyms and research services that provide access to a variety of Web-based reference materials.
- Outlining tools allow easy rearranging of headings and text to ensure that your argument is logical.

- Search tools can be used to locate and replace words and phrases, either one at a time or throughout a document.
- The AutoCorrect and Spelling And Grammar features make it easy to correct typographical and grammatical errors before you share a document with others.
- Finalizing tools ensure that a document is ready for distribution.

In this chapter, you will edit the text in a document by inserting and deleting text, copying and pasting a phrase, and moving a paragraph. You will save a couple of building blocks, and you'll rearrange a document in Outline view. You will find a phrase and replace one phrase with another throughout the entire document. You'll change an AutoCorrect setting and add a misspelled word to its list. You'll check the spelling and grammar in a document and add a term to the custom dictionary. Finally, you'll inspect a document for inappropriate information and mark it as final.

See Also Do you need only a quick refresher on the topics in this chapter? See the Quick Reference section at the beginning of this book.

Important Before you can use the practice files in this chapter, you need to install them from the book's companion CD to their default location. See "Using the Companion CD" at the beginning of this book for more information.

Troubleshooting Graphics and operating system–related instructions in this book reflect the Windows Vista user interface. If your computer is running Windows XP and you experience trouble following the instructions as written, please refer to the "Information for Readers Running Windows XP" section at the beginning of this book.

Making Changes to a Document

You will rarely write a perfect document that doesn't require any editing. You will almost always want to insert a word or two, change a phrase, or move text from one place to another. You can edit a document as you create it, or you can write it first and then revise it. Or you might want to edit a document that you created for one purpose so that it will serve a different purpose. For example, a letter from last year's marketing campaign might be edited to create a new letter for this year's campaign.

Inserting text is easy; you click to position the insertion point and simply begin typing. Any existing text to the right of the insertion point moves to make room for the new text.

> ### What Happened to Overtype?
>
> By default, Word 2007 is in Insert mode, so existing text moves to the right when you type new text before it. In previous versions of Word, it was possible to switch from Insert mode to Overtype mode by pressing the Insert key. In Overtype mode, each character you type replaces an existing character.
>
> In Word 2007, you must deliberately switch to Overtype mode if you want to use it. Here's how:
>
> 1. Right-click the status bar, and then click **Overtype** to display the Insert mode status at the left end of the status bar.
> 2. Click **Insert** on the status bar.
>
>   The word *Overtype* then replaces *Insert*. You can click the word to switch back to Insert mode when you have finished overtyping.
>
> By default, pressing the Insert key has no effect on the mode. If you want the Insert key to turn Overtype mode on and off, follow these steps:
>
> 1. Click the **Microsoft Office Button**, and then click **Word Options**.
> 2. In the **Word Options** dialog box, click **Advanced** in the left pane, and then in the **Editing options** area, select the **Use the Insert key to control overtype mode** check box.
> 3. Click **OK**.

Deleting text is equally easy. If you want to delete only one or a few characters, you can simply position the insertion point and then press the Backspace or Delete key until the characters are all gone. Pressing Backspace deletes the character to the left of the insertion point; pressing Delete deletes the character to the right of the insertion point

To delete more than a few characters efficiently, you need to know how to *select* the text. Selected text appears highlighted on the screen. You can select specific items as follows:

- To select a word, double-click it. Word selects the word and the space following it (but does not select punctuation following the word).
- To select a sentence, click anywhere in the sentence while holding down the Ctrl key. Word selects all the characters in the sentence, from the first character through the space following the ending punctuation mark.
- To select a paragraph, triple-click it. Word selects the text of the paragraph and the paragraph mark.

You can select adjacent words, lines, or paragraphs by positioning the insertion point at the beginning of the text you want to select, holding down the Shift key, and then pressing the Arrow keys or clicking at the end of the text that you want to select. If you want to select words, lines, or paragraphs that are not adjacent, you make the first selection and then hold down the Ctrl key while selecting the next block.

As an alternative, you can use the *selection area* to quickly select various items. This is an invisible area in the document's left margin, where the pointer becomes a hollow right-pointing arrow. You can use the selection area as follows:

- To select a line, click the selection area to the left of the line.
- To select a paragraph, double-click the selection area to the left of the paragraph.
- To select an entire document, triple-click the selection area.

Selection area

After selecting the text you want to delete, simply press either the Backspace key or the Delete key.

> **Tip** To deselect text, click anywhere in the document window except the selection area.

After selecting text, you can move or copy it in the following ways:

- Use the *Clipboard* when you need to move or copy text between two locations that you cannot see at the same time—for example, between pages or between documents. The Clipboard is a temporary storage area in your computer's memory. Select the text, and then click the Cut or Copy button in the Clipboard group on

the Home tab. Then reposition the insertion point and click the Paste button to insert the selection in its new location. When you cut text, it is removed from its original location, and when you copy it, it also remains in its original location.

See Also For more information, see the sidebar "About the Clipboard" later in this chapter.

● Use *drag-and-drop editing* (frequently referred to simply as *dragging*) when you need to move or copy text only a short distance—for example, within a paragraph or line. Dragging does not involve the Clipboard. Start by selecting the text. Then hold down the mouse button, drag the text to its new location, and release the mouse button. To copy the selection, hold down the Ctrl key while you drag.

If you make a change to a document and then realize that you made a mistake, you can easily reverse the change. You can undo your last editing action by clicking the Undo button on the Quick Access Toolbar. To undo an earlier action, click the Undo arrow and then click that actions in the list.

> **Tip** Selecting an action from the Undo list undoes that action and all the editing actions you performed after that one. You cannot undo one action except the last one you performed.

If you undo an action and then change your mind, you can click the Redo button on the Quick Access Toolbar. You can redo only the last action that you undid.

In this exercise, you will edit the text in a document. You'll insert and delete text, undo the deletion, copy and paste a phrase, and move a paragraph.

> **USE** the *Changes* document. This practice file is located in the *Documents\Microsoft Press\Word2007SBS\EditingText* folder.
> **BE SURE TO** start Word before beginning this exercise.
> **OPEN** the *Changes* document.

Show/Hide ¶

1. If non-printing characters are not visible in the document, on the **Home** tab, in the **Paragraph** group, click the **Show/Hide ¶** button.

2. In the third sentence of the first paragraph, click immediately to the left of the word *between*, hold down the [Shift] key, and then click immediately to the right of the word *fifteen* (and to the left of the comma that follows it).

   Word selects the text between the two clicks.

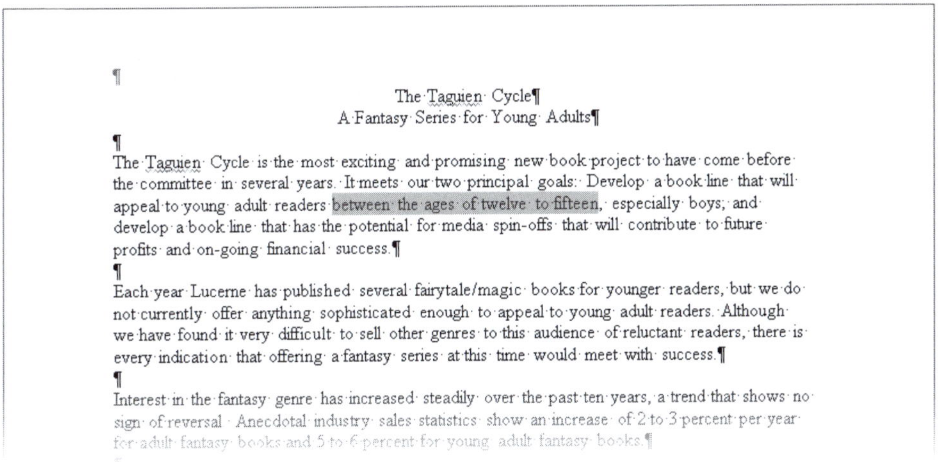

38 Chapter 2 Editing and Proofreading Documents

> ¶
> The Taguien Cycle¶
> A Fantasy Series for Young Adults¶
> ¶
> The Taguien Cycle is the most exciting and promising new book project to have come before the committee in several years. It meets our two principal goals: Develop a book line that will appeal to young adult readers between the ages of twelve to fifteen, especially boys; and develop a book line that has the potential for media spin-offs that will contribute to future profits and on-going financial success.¶
> ¶
> Each year Lucerne has published several fairytale/magic books for younger readers, but we do not currently offer anything sophisticated enough to appeal to young adult readers. Although we have found it very difficult to sell other genres to this audience of reluctant readers, there is every indication that offering a fantasy series at this time would meet with success.¶
> ¶
> Interest in the fantasy genre has increased steadily over the past ten years, a trend that shows no sign of reversal. Anecdotal industry sales statistics show an increase of 2 to 3 percent per year for adult fantasy books and 5 to 6 percent for young adult fantasy books.¶

3. Press the **Del** key to delete the selection.

   Word also deletes the space before the selection.

4. Select the word **book** in the first sentence of the first paragraph by double-clicking it, and then press the **Backspace** key.

5. Double-click the word **principal** in the same paragraph, and then replace it by typing **primary**.

   Notice that you don't have to type a space after *primary*. Word inserts the space for you.

   > **Tip** Word inserts and deletes spaces because the Use Smart Cut And Paste check box is selected on the Advanced page of the Word Options dialog box. If you want to be able to control the spacing yourself, click the Microsoft Office Button, click Word Options, click Advanced, clear this check box, and click OK.

6. Position the mouse pointer in the selection area to the left of the phrase *A Fantasy Series for Young Adults*, and then click once to select the entire line of text.

7. On the **Home** tab, in the **Clipboard** group, click the **Copy** button.

   The selection is copied to the Clipboard.

8. Click the **Next Page** button below the vertical scroll bar to move to the beginning of the next page, press the **↓** key, and then in the **Clipboard** group, click the **Paste** button (not its arrow).

   The Paste Options button appears below and to the right of the insertion. You can click this button if you want to change Word's default way of pasting, but in this case, you can just ignore it.

Making Changes to a Document   39

9. Return to page 1, and then in the numbered list, triple-click anywhere in the *Bartimaeus Trilogy* paragraph to select the entire paragraph.

10. In the **Clipboard** group, click the **Cut** button.

11. Press the ↑ key to move to the beginning of the *Harry Potter series* paragraph, and then in the **Clipboard** group, click the **Paste** button.

   The two paragraphs have effectively switched places and the list has been renumbered.

   See Also For more information about numbered lists, see "Creating and Modifying Lists" in Chapter 3, "Changing the Look of Text."

12. On the **Quick Access Toolbar**, click the **Undo** arrow, and in the list, click the third action (**Paste**).

   Word undoes the previous cut-and-paste operation and the pasting of the copied text.

13. Press Ctrl+Home to move to the top of the document. Then move the pointer into the selection area adjacent to the paragraph that begins *Interest in the fantasy genre*, and double-click to select the paragraph.

14. Point to the selection, hold down the mouse button, and then drag the paragraph up to the beginning of the paragraph above it.

   When you release the mouse, the text appears in its new location.

15. With the text still selected, press the End key.

   Word releases the selection and moves the insertion point to the end of the paragraph.

16. Press Space, and then press Del.

   Word deletes the paragraph mark, and the two paragraphs are now one paragraph.

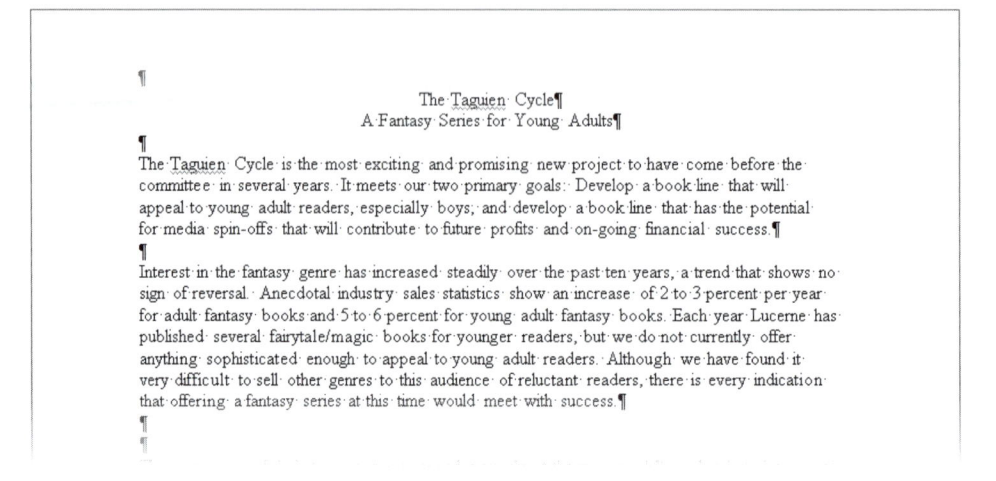

¶
                            The Taguien Cycle¶
                        A Fantasy Series for Young Adults¶
¶
The Taguien Cycle is the most exciting and promising new project to have come before the committee in several years. It meets our two primary goals: Develop a book line that will appeal to young adult readers, especially boys; and develop a book line that has the potential for media spin-offs that will contribute to future profits and on-going financial success.¶
¶
Interest in the fantasy genre has increased steadily over the past ten years, a trend that shows no sign of reversal. Anecdotal industry sales statistics show an increase of 2 to 3 percent per year for adult fantasy books and 5 to 6 percent for young adult fantasy books. Each year Lucerne has published several fairytale/magic books for younger readers, but we do not currently offer anything sophisticated enough to appeal to young adult readers. Although we have found it very difficult to sell other genres to this audience of reluctant readers, there is every indication that offering a fantasy series at this time would meet with success.¶
¶
¶

17. In the selection area, click adjacent to the paragraph mark below the combined paragraph, and then press [Del].

> **CLOSE** the *Changes* document without saving your changes.

About the Clipboard

You can view the items that have been cut and copied to the Clipboard by clicking the Clipboard dialog box launcher to open the Clipboard task pane, which displays up to 24 cut or copied items.

To paste an individual item at the insertion point, you simply click the item. To paste all the items, click the Paste All button. You can point to an item, click the arrow that appears, and then click Delete to remove it from the Clipboard, or you can remove all the items by clicking the Clear All button.

You can control the behavior of the Clipboard task pane by clicking Options at the bottom of the pane. You can choose to have the Clipboard task pane appear when you cut or copy one item or multiple items. You can also choose to display the Clipboard icon in the status area of the taskbar when the Clipboard task pane is displayed.

To close the Clipboard task pane, click the Close button at the right end of its title bar.

Inserting Saved Text

To save time and ensure consistency in your documents, you can save any text you use frequently as a *building block*. You do this by selecting the text, clicking Quick Parts in the Text group on the Insert tab, clicking Save Selection To Quick Part Gallery, and assigning the text a name. It then appears under its assigned name in the Quick Parts gallery.

See Also For information about the many different kinds of pre-defined building blocks that you can use to enhance your documents, see "Inserting Ready-Made Document Parts" in Chapter 8, "Working with Longer Documents."

After you have saved the text, you can insert it at any time by clicking Quick Parts to display its gallery and then clicking the building block you want.

> **Tip** You can also type the name of the building block and then press the F3 key to insert it at the insertion point.

Inserting Saved Text 41

In this exercise, you will save the names of a company and a product as building blocks so that you can insert them elsewhere in a document.

> **USE** the *SavedText* document. This practice file is located in the *Documents\Microsoft Press\Word2007SBS\EditingText* folder.
> **OPEN** the *SavedText* document.

1. Toward the end of the first paragraph of the document, select **Wide World Importers**.

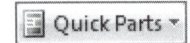

   ![Quick Parts]

2. On the **Insert** tab, in the **Text** group, click the **Quick Parts** button, and then click **Save Selection to Quick Part Gallery**.

   The Create New Building Block dialog box opens.

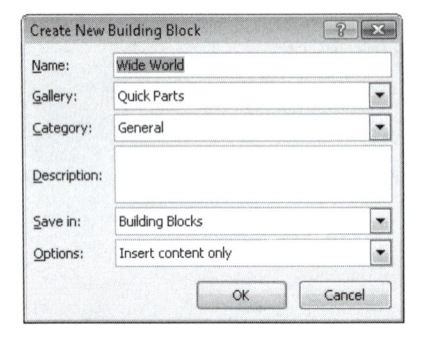

3. In the **Name** box, type **www**, and then click **OK**.

   Word saves the selection in the Quick Parts gallery.

4. In the third paragraph of the document, select **chimonobambusa marmorea**, and then in the **Text** group, click the **Quick Parts** button.

   Notice that the company name now appears as a building block in the Quick Parts gallery.

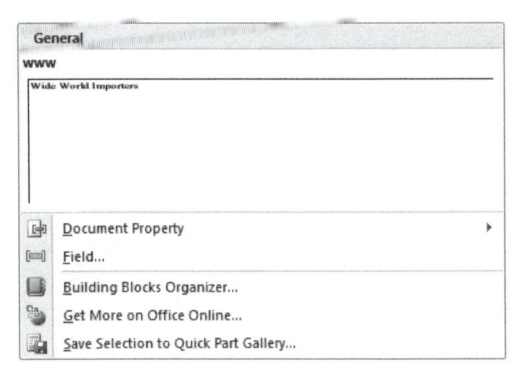

5. Click **Save Selection to Quick Part Gallery**, and save the selected text with the name **cm**.
6. Press `Ctrl`+`End` to move the insertion point to the end of the document, and then press `Space`.
7. Type **In particular** and a space. Then in the **Text** group, click the **Quick Parts** button, and in the gallery, click the **www** entry.

   The company name appears at the insertion point.
8. Type a space followed by **recommends cm**.
9. Press the `F3` key, and then type a period.

   Word replaces *cm* with its building block, *chimonobambusa marmorea*.

www   cm

> **Troubleshooting** Pressing the F3 key substitutes the corresponding building block only if the name you type contains no spaces. There must be a space to its left, and the insertion point must be to its right.

✕ **CLOSE** the *SavedText* document without saving your changes.

> **Important** When you exit Word, you will be asked whether you want to save the Building Blocks template, which by default is where your custom building blocks are saved. If you want to discard the building blocks you have created in this Word session, click No. If you want to save them, click Yes.

Inserting the Date and Time

One of the easiest ways to insert today's date or the current time in a document is to use the Insert Date And Time button in the Text group on the Insert tab. After you specify the format you want to use, Word retrieves the date or time from your computer's internal calendar or clock. You can insert the information as regular text or as a *field*. A field is a placeholder that tells Word to supply the specified information in the specified way. The advantage of using a field is that it can be updated with the click of a button.

Here are the steps for inserting the date or time:

1. With the insertion point located where you want the date or time to appear, on the **Insert** tab, in the **Text** group, click the **Date & Time** button.

   The Date And Time dialog box opens.

2. Under **Available formats**, click the date and/or time format you want.

3. If you want to insert a date or time field, select the **Update automatically** check box.

4. Click **OK**.

If you selected Update Automatically, Word inserts a Date or Time field depending on the format you selected. When you point to the field, it is highlighted as a unit. You can click the field to select it, and you can click the Update button that appears above it to update the field with the most current information. If you right-click the field, you can click Toggle Field Codes to see the codes that control the field; click the command again to redisplay the date or time information.

You can insert other types of date and time fields, such as a PrintDate field or an EditTime field. Insert a Date or Time field in the usual way, right-click the field, and then click Edit Field. In the Field dialog box, change the setting in the Categories box to Date And Time, and in the Field Names list, click the field you want. When you click OK, the information corresponding to the field type you specified is shown in the document.

Finding the Most Appropriate Word

Language is often contextual—you use different words and phrases in a marketing brochure, in a letter requesting immediate payment of an invoice, and in an informal memo about a social gathering after work. To help you ensure that you are using the words

that best convey your meaning in any given context, Word provides a *Thesaurus* where you can look up synonyms (alternative words) for a selected word. The Thesaurus is one of a set of Research services provided by Word.

To look up alternatives for a word in the Thesaurus, you select the word and then click the Thesaurus button in the Proofing group on the Review tab. The Research task pane opens, displaying a list of synonyms. You then click the synonym that you want to replace the selected word.

In this exercise, you will use the Thesaurus to replace one word with another.

> **USE** the *FindingWord* document. This practice file is located in the *Documents\Microsoft Press\Word2007SBS\EditingText* folder.
> **OPEN** the *FindingWord* document.

1. Double-click the word **rigorous** in the last line of the first paragraph of the letter.
2. On the **Review** tab, in the **Proofing** group, click the **Thesaurus** button.

   The Research task pane opens, listing synonyms for the word *rigorous*.

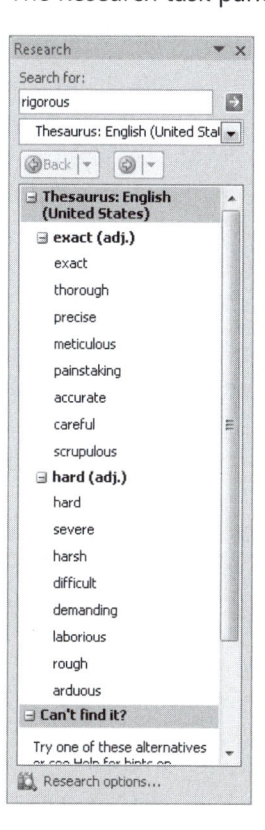

3. In the task pane, under **exact**, click **meticulous**.

   The word *meticulous* replaces *rigorous* in the Search For box at the top of the task pane, and synonyms for *meticulous* are now listed in the task pane.

4. Point to the word **thorough**, click the arrow that appears, and then click **Insert**.

   The word *thorough* replaces *rigorous* in the document.

5. Close the **Research** task pane.

> **CLOSE** the *FindingWord* document without saving your changes.

Researching Information

In addition to the Thesaurus, the Research task pane provides access to a variety of informational resources from within Word. You can enter a topic in the Search For box and specify in the box below which resource Word should use to look for information about that topic. By clicking Research Options at the bottom of the Research task pane, you can specify which of a predefined list of reference materials, such as Microsoft Encarta and various Internet resources, will be available from a list, and you can add your own reference-material sources.

To research information:

1. On the **Review** tab, in the **Proofing** group, click the **Research** button to display the Research task pane.

2. In the **Search for** box, type the topic you are interested in researching.

   For example, you might type *bamboo*.

3. Click the arrow to the right of the box below the Search For box, and then in the list, click the resource you want to use to search for information.

   For example, you might click MSN Search. When you have made your selection, the Start Searching button to the right of the Search For box flashes, and seconds later, the search results are displayed in the task pane.

4. Click any information sources that interest you.

   You can click a hyperlink to a Web address to go to the Web to track down further information. You can also select part of a topic, right-click the selection, click Copy, and then paste the selection into your document. Or you can click right-click the selection and click Look Up to research information about the selection.

> **Translating Text**
>
> Word now comes with built-in dictionaries for many common languages, so you can easily translate words and phrases from one language to another.
>
> To translate a word into another language:
>
> 1. Select the word, and then on the **Review** tab, in the **Proofing** group, click the **Translate** button.
>
>   The Research task pane opens with boxes in which you can specify the source language and the translation language.
>
> 2. Under **Translation** in the **Research** task pane, change the settings in the **From** and **To** boxes as necessary.
>
>   The translated text appears under Bilingual Dictionary.
>
> To translate a different word or phrase, you can type it in the Search For box and then click the Start Searching button to the right.
>
> To view the translation of any word you point to, click the Translation ScreenTip button in the Proofing group on the Review tab, and then select the language you want to see. You can then point to any word in a document to display the equivalent word in the language you selected. Click the button again, and then click Turn Off Translation ScreenTip to turn off the translation display.

Reorganizing a Document Outline

If you are creating a document that contains headings, you can format it with built-in heading styles that include outline levels. Then it is easy to view and organize the document in Outline view. In this view, you can hide all the body text and display only the headings at and above a particular level. You can then rearrange the sections of a document by moving their headings.

See Also For more information about formatting with styles, see "Working with Templates" in Chapter 4, "Changing the Look of a Document."

To view a document in Outline view, click the Outline button in the Document Views group on the View tab, or click the Outline button on the View toolbar. The document is then displayed with a hierarchical structure, and the Outlining tab appears on the Ribbon.

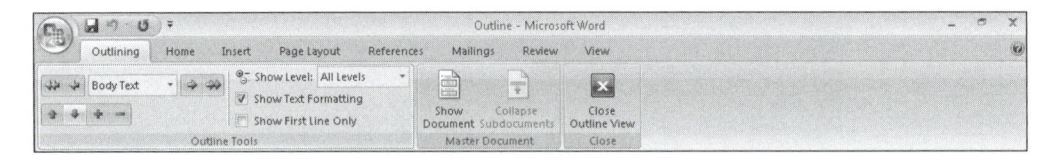

The Outline Tools group on this tab includes buttons you can click to display only the headings at a specific level and above, to *promote* or *demote* headings or body text by changing their level, and to move headings and their text up or down in the document. The indentations and symbols used in Outline view to indicate the level of a heading or paragraph in the document's structure do not appear in the document in other views or when you print it.

> **Tip** You can click the buttons in the Master Document group to create a master document with subdocuments that you can then display and hide. The topic of master documents and subdocuments is beyond the scope of this book. For information, see Word Help.

In this exercise, you'll switch to Outline view, promote and demote headings, move headings, and expand and collapse the outline.

> **USE** the *Outline* document. This practice file is located in the *Documents\Microsoft Press\Word2007SBS\EditingText* folder.
> **OPEN** the *Outline* document.

1. In the lower-right corner of the window, on the **View** toolbar, click the **Outline** button.

   The screen changes to display the document in Outline view, and the Outlining tab appears at the left end of the Ribbon.

2. On the **Outlining** tab, in the **Outline Tools** group, click the **Show Level** arrow, and in the list, click **Level 1**.

   The document collapses to display only level-1 headings.

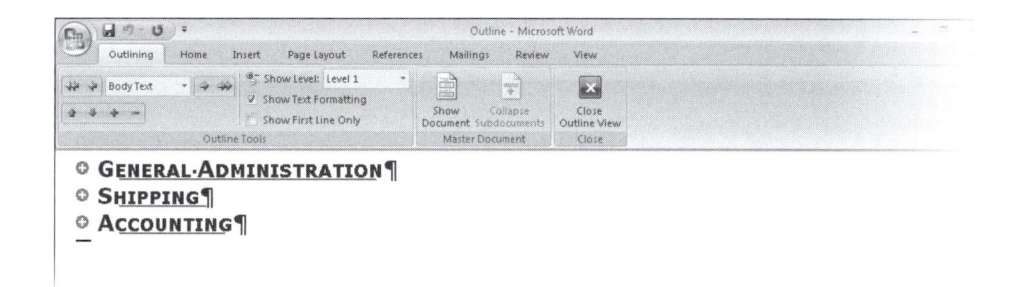

48 Chapter 2 Editing and Proofreading Documents

⊕ **GENERAL ADMINISTRATION**¶
⊕ **SHIPPING**¶
⊕ **ACCOUNTING**¶

3. Click anywhere in the **Accounting** heading.

4. In the **Outline Tools** group, click the **Expand** button.

   Word expands the *Accounting* section to display its level-2 headings.

5. In the **Outline Tools** group, click the **Demote** button.

   The *Accounting* heading changes to a level-2 heading.

6. On the **Quick Access Toolbar**, click the **Undo** button.

   The *Accounting* heading changes back to a level-1 heading.

7. In the **Outline Tools** group, click the **Collapse** button.

8. Click the **Demote** button.

   Again, the *Accounting* heading changes to a level-2 heading.

9. Click the **Expand** button.

   Because the subheadings were hidden under *Accounting* when you demoted the heading, all the subheadings have been demoted to level 3 to maintain the hierarchy of the section.

10. Click the **Collapse** button, and then in the **Outline Tools** group, click the **Promote** button.

    The *Accounting* heading is now a level-1 heading again.

11. Press **Ctrl**+**Home** to move to the top of the document, and then in the **Outline Tools** group, in the **Show Level** list, click **Level 2**.

    The outline shows all the level-1 and level-2 headings.

12. Click the plus sign to the left of the *Accounting* heading, and then in the **Outline Tools** group, click the **Move Up** button three times.

The *Accounting* heading and all its subheadings move above the *Shipping* heading.

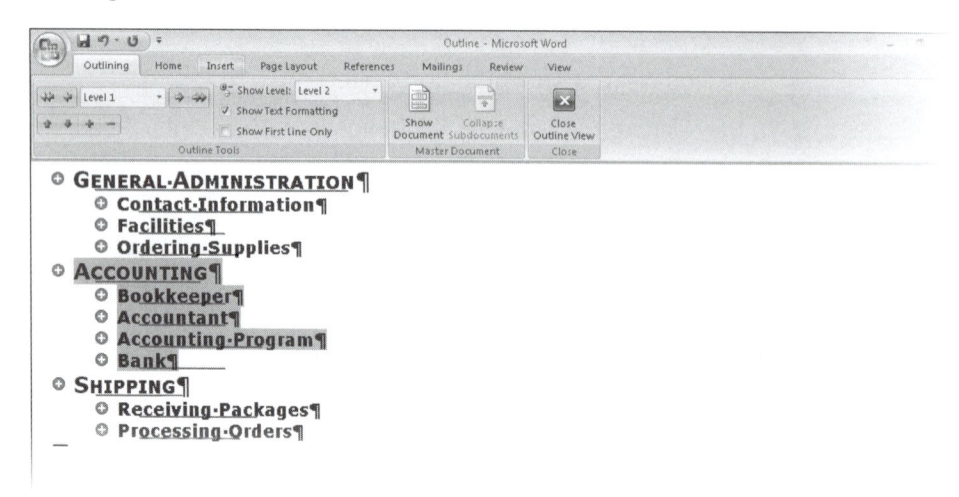

13. In the **Outline Tools** group, in the **Show Level** list, click **All Levels**.

    You can now scroll through the document to see the effects of the reorganization.

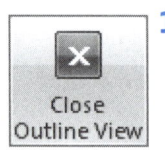

14. In the **Close** group, click the **Close Outline View** button.

    Word displays the reorganized document in Print Layout view.

> **CLOSE** the *Outline* document without saving your changes.

Finding and Replacing Text

One way to ensure that the text in your documents is consistent and accurate is to use the Find feature of Word to search for every instance of a particular word or phrase. For example, if you were responsible for advertising a trademarked product, you would probably want to search your marketing materials to check that every instance of the product's name was correctly identified as a trademark.

Clicking the Find button in the Editing group on the Home tab displays the Find tab of the Find And Replace dialog box. After you enter the text you want to find in the Find What box, you can do the following:

- Click Find Next to select the first occurrence of that text.
- In the Reading Highlight list, click Highlight All to highlight all occurrences.

If you find an error in the document while conducting a search, you can make editing changes on the fly without closing the Find And Replace dialog box. Simply click the document, make the change, and then click the Find And Replace dialog box to make it active again.

If you know that you want to substitute one word or phrase for another, you can use the Replace feature to find each occurrence of the text you want to change and replace it with different text. Clicking the Replace button in the Editing group displays the Replace tab of the Find And Replace dialog box, which is similar to the Find tab. On the Replace tab, you can do the following:

- Click Replace to replace the selected occurrence with the text in the Replace With box and move to the next occurrence.
- Click Replace All to replace all occurrences with the text in the Replace With box.
- Click Find Next to leave the selected occurrence as it is and locate the next one.

You can use other options in the Find And Replace dialog box to carry out more complicated searches and replaces. Clicking More expands the box to make these additional options available.

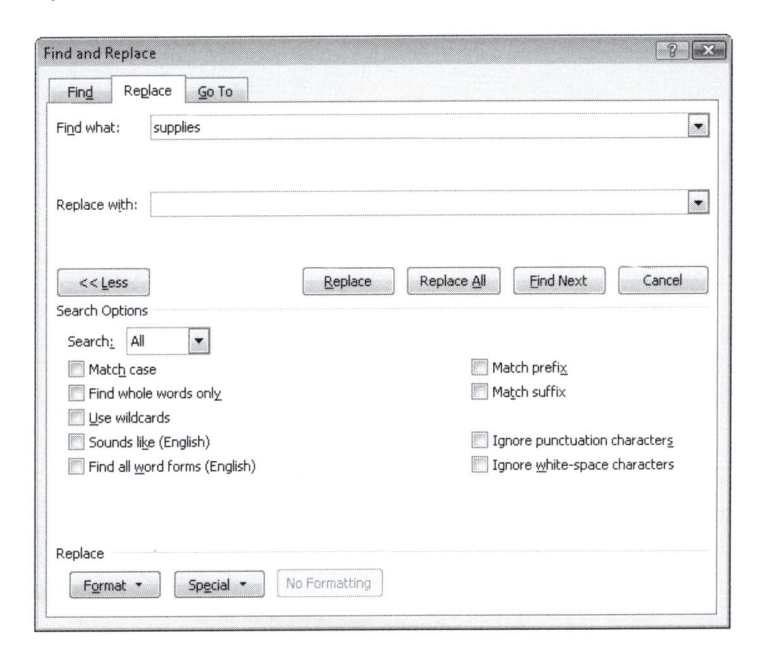

You can make a selection from the Search list to guide the direction of the search. You can select the Match Case check box to match capitalization and select the Find Whole Words Only check box to find only whole-word occurrences of the Find What text. If you want to check that your usage of two similar words, such as *effect* and *affect*, is correct, you can select the Use Wildcards check box and then enter a *wildcard character* in the Find What box to locate variable information. The two most common wildcard characters are:

- The ? wildcard stands for any single character in this location in the Find What text.
- The * wildcard stands for any number of characters in this location in the Find What text.

> **Tip** To see a list of the other available wildcards, use Help to search for wildcards.

Selecting the Sounds Like check box finds occurrences of the search text that sound the same but are spelled differently, such as *there* and *their*. Selecting the Find All Word Forms check box finds occurrences of a particular word in any form, such as *plan*, *planned*, and *planning*. You can match a prefix or a suffix, and you can ignore punctuation and white space. Finally, you can locate formatting, such as bold, or special characters, such as tabs, by selecting them from the Format or Special list.

In this exercise, you will find a phrase and make a correction to the document. Then you'll replace one phrase with another throughout the entire document.

> **USE** the *FindingText* document. This practice file is located in the *Documents\Microsoft Press\Word2007SBS\EditingText* folder.
> **OPEN** the *FindingText* document.

1. With the insertion point at the beginning of the document, on the **Home** tab, in the **Editing** group, click the **Find** button.

   The Find And Replace dialog box opens, displaying the Find tab.

2. In the **Find what** box, type The Taguien Cycle, click **Reading Highlight**, and then in the list, click **Highlight All**.

3. Scroll to page 2.

   Word has found and selected all the occurrences of *The Taguien Cycle* in the document. (We dragged the title bar of the dialog box to move it to the side.)

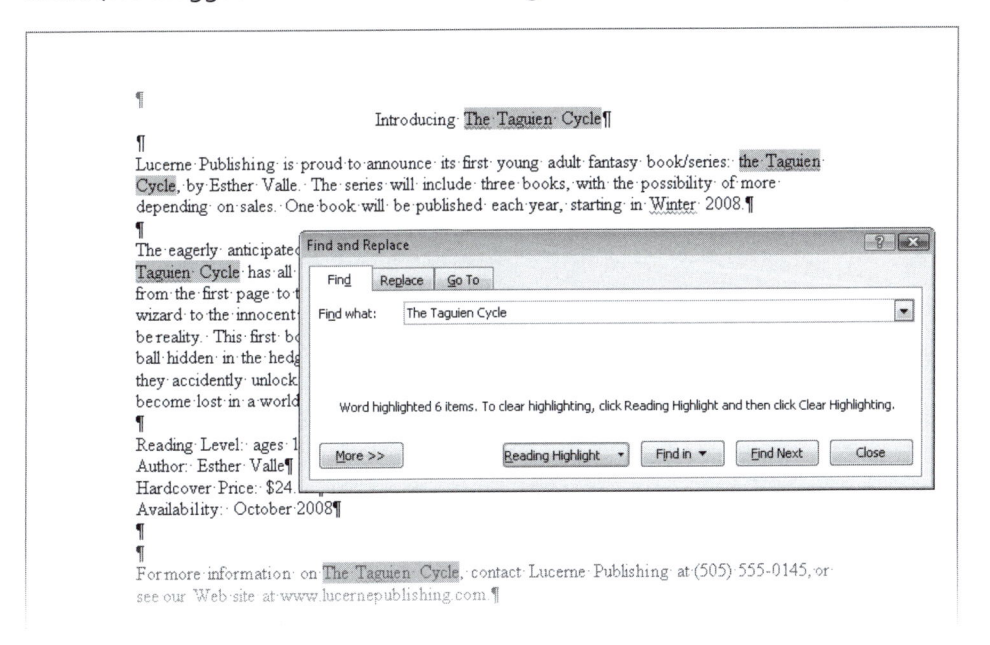

4. Click the document behind the **Find and Replace** dialog box, double-click the word **the** in *the Taguien Cycle* in the first paragraph (not the title) on page 2, and then type **The** to correct the capitalization.

5. Press Ctrl+Home to move the insertion point to the beginning of the document.

6. Click the title bar of the **Find and Replace** dialog box, and then click the **Replace** tab.

   The Find What box retains the entry from the previous search.

7. Click the **Replace with** box, type The Taguien Cycle, and then click the **More** button.

8. At the bottom of the expanded dialog box, click the **Format** button, and then click **Font**.

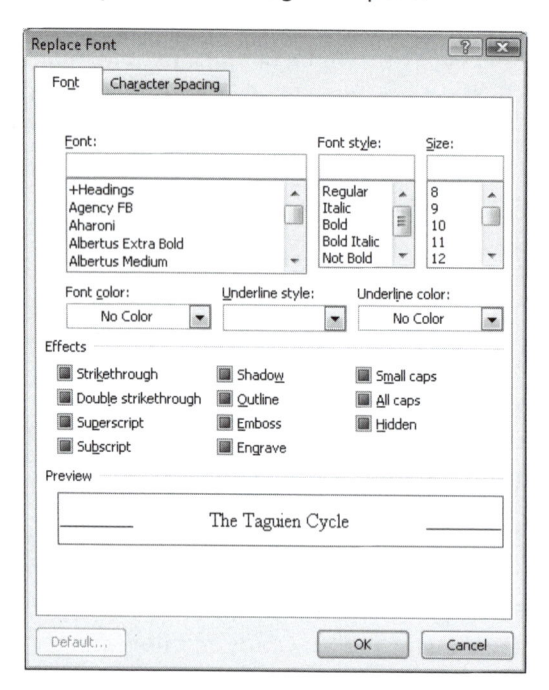

The Replace Font dialog box opens.

9. Under **Font Style**, click **Italic**, and then click **OK**.
10. Click **Find Next**, and then click **Replace**.

    The selected plain text title is replaced with italicized text, and the next occurrence of *The Taguien Cycle* is selected.

11. Click **Replace All**.

    Word displays a message box indicating that six replacements were made.

12. Click **OK** to close the message box, and then in the **Find and Replace** dialog box, click the **Find** tab.
13. In the **Find what** box, click **Reading Highlight**, and then in the list, click **Highlight All**.

    Word highlights six occurrences of the Find What text.

14. Click **Reading Highlight**, and then in the list, click **Clear Highlighting**.

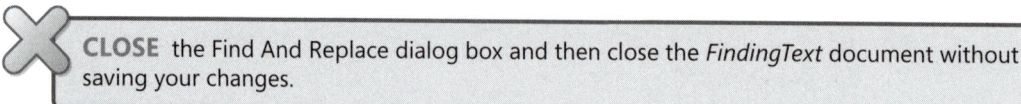

> **CLOSE** the Find And Replace dialog box and then close the *FindingText* document without saving your changes.

Correcting Spelling and Grammatical Errors

In the days of handwritten and typewritten documents, people might have tolerated a typographical or grammatical error or two because correcting such errors without creating a mess was difficult. Word processors like Word have built-in spelling and grammar checkers, so now documents that contain these types of errors are likely to reflect badly on their creators.

> **Tip** Although Word can help you eliminate misspellings and grammatical errors, its tools are not infallible. You should always read through your documents to catch the problems that the Word tools can't detect.

Word provides two tools to help you with the chore of eliminating spelling and grammar errors: the AutoCorrect and Spelling And Grammar features.

Have you noticed that Word automatically corrects some misspellings as you type them? This is the work of the AutoCorrect feature. AutoCorrect corrects commonly misspelled words, such as *adn* to *and*, so that you don't have to correct them yourself. AutoCorrect comes with a long list of frequently misspelled words and their correct spellings. If you frequently misspell a word that AutoCorrect doesn't change, you can add it to the list in the AutoCorrect dialog box.

If you deliberately mistype a word and don't want to accept the AutoCorrect change, you can reverse it by clicking the Undo button on the Quick Access Toolbar before you type anything else.

Although AutoCorrect ensures that your documents are free of common misspellings, it doesn't detect random typographical and grammatical errors. For those types of errors, you can turn to the Spelling And Grammar feature for help. You might have noticed that as you type, Word underlines potential spelling errors with red wavy underlines and grammatical errors with green wavy underlines. You can right-click an underlined word or phrase to display suggested corrections.

If you want to check the spelling or grammar of the entire document, it is easier to click the Spelling & Grammar button in the Proofing group on the Review tab than to deal with underlined words and phrases individually. Word then works its way through the document from the insertion point and displays the Spelling And Grammar dialog box if it encounters a potential error. If the error is a misspelling, the Spelling And Grammar dialog box suggests corrections; if the error is a breach of grammar, the Spelling And Grammar dialog box tells you which rule you have broken as well as suggesting corrections. The buttons available in the Spelling And Grammar dialog box are dynamic and change to those most appropriate for fixing the error. For example, for a grammatical error, you are given the opportunity to ignore the rule you have broken throughout the document.

In this exercise, you'll change an AutoCorrect setting and add a misspelled word to its list. You'll check the spelling in the document and add terms to the custom dictionary, and you'll find, review, and correct a grammatical error.

> **USE** the *Spelling* document. This practice file is located in the *Documents\Microsoft Press\Word2007SBS\EditingText* folder.
> **OPEN** the *Spelling* document.

1. Click at the end of the first paragraph in the letter, press [Space], and then type **in your reserch**, followed by a period.

   As soon as you type the period, AutoCorrect changes *reserch* to *research*.

2. Click the **Microsoft Office Button**, and then click **Word Options**.

3. In the left pane of the **Word Options** window, click **Proofing**, and then on the Proofing page, click **AutoCorrect Options**.

   The AutoCorrect dialog box opens, displaying the AutoCorrect tab.

Microsoft Office Button

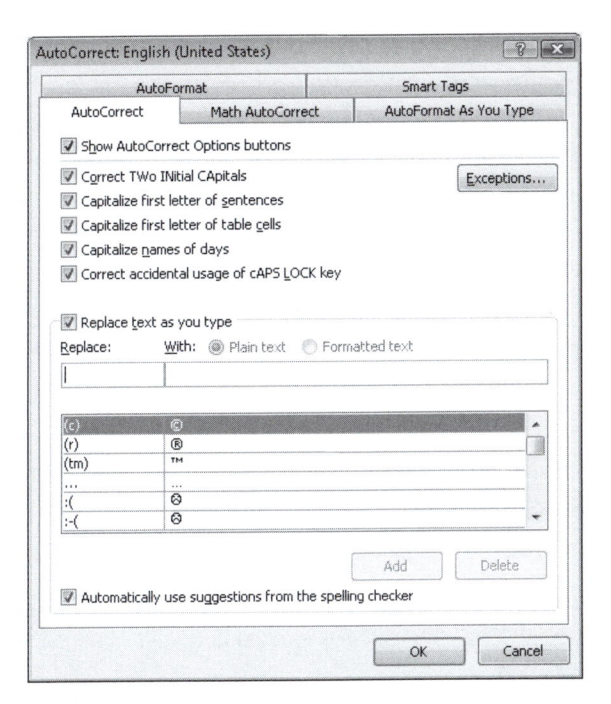

Notice the corrections that AutoCorrect will make. You can clear the check box of any item you don't want corrected. For example, if you don't want AutoCorrect to capitalize a lowercase letter or word that follows a period, clear the Capitalize First Letter Of Sentences check box.

4. Click in the **Replace** box, and then type avalable.

   Word scrolls the list below to show the entry that is closest to what you typed.

5. Press the Tab key to move the insertion point to the **With** box, and then type available.

6. Click **Add** to add the entry to the correction list, and then click **OK**.

7. Click **OK** to close the Word Options window.

8. Press Ctrl+End to move to the end of the document, and then in the paragraph that begins *Thank you for your* interest, position the insertion point to the right of the period at the end of the third sentence.

9. Press Space, and then type Shelly will not be avalable May 10-15 followed by a period.

   The word *avalable* changes to *available*.

10. Press Ctrl+Home to move to the top of the document, and then right-click *sorces*, the first word with a red wavy underline.

Word lists possible correct spellings for this word, as well as actions you might want to carry out.

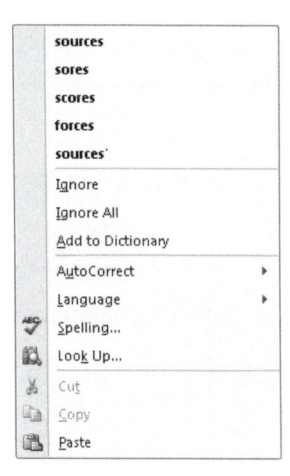

> sources
> sores
> scores
> forces
> sources
> Ignore
> Ignore All
> Add to Dictionary
> AutoCorrect
> Language
> Spelling...
> Look Up...
> Cut
> Copy
> Paste

11. In the list, click **sources**.

Word removes the red wavy underline and inserts the correction.

12. Press Ctrl+Home again, and then on the **Review** tab, in the **Proofing** group, click the **Spelling & Grammar** button.

The Spelling And Grammar dialog box opens, with the first word that Word does not recognize, *commited*, displayed in red in the Not In Dictionary box.

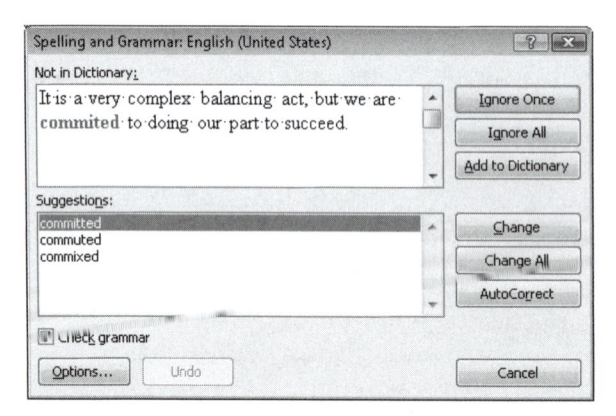

13. With **committed** selected in the **Suggestions** box, click **AutoCorrect**.

Word adds the misspelling and the selected correction to the AutoCorrect list, so that the next time you type *commited* by mistake, the spelling will be corrected for you as you type. Word then flags *Dyck* as the next possible misspelling.

> **Troubleshooting** If the errors we mention don't appear to be in the practice file, click Options at the bottom of the Spelling And Grammar dialog box. Then in the Word Options window, under When Correcting Spelling And Grammar In Word, click Recheck Document, click Yes to reset the checkers, and then click OK.

14. Click **Ignore All**.

    Word will now skip over this and any other occurrences of this proper noun. It moves on to highlight the duplicate word *for*.

15. Click **Delete**.

    Word deletes the second *for* and then flags a possible grammatical error.

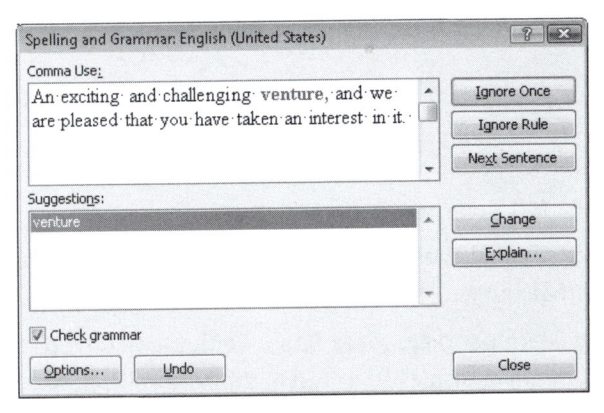

    This grammatical error is identified as incorrect use of a comma. You need to read the sentence and then decide whether and how to correct it. In this case, the error is not related to the comma after *venture* but to the fact that there is no verb in the first half of the sentence.

    > **Tip** Word's grammar checker helps identify phrases and clauses that do not follow traditional grammatical rules, but it is not always accurate. It is easy to get in the habit of ignoring green wavy underlines. However, it is wise to scrutinize them all to be sure that your documents don't contain any embarrassing mistakes.

16. Behind the **Spelling and Grammar** dialog box, click the document, double-click the word **An** at the beginning of the sentence with the error, and then type **The import business is an**.

17. Click the title bar of the **Spelling and Grammar** dialog box, and then click **Resume**.

Word flags *Florian* as a word that it doesn't recognize. *Florian* is a proper noun and is spelled correctly. By adding words like this one to the custom dictionary, you can prevent Word from continuing to flag them.

18. Click **Add to Dictionary**.

    Word displays a message, indicating that it has finished checking the spelling and grammar of the document.

19. Click **OK** to close the message box.

> **CLOSE** the *Spelling* document without saving your changes.

Viewing Document Statistics

As you type, Word keeps track of the number of pages and words in your document, displaying this information at the left end of the status bar. To see the number of words in only part of the document, such as a few paragraphs, simply select that part. The status bar then displays the number of words in the selection, expressed as a fraction of the total, such as 250/800.

To see more statistics, you can open the Word Count dialog box by clicking the Word Count button in the Proofing group on the Review tab. In addition to the count of pages and words, the Word Count dialog box displays the number of characters, paragraphs, and lines. It also gives you the option of including or excluding words in text boxes, footnotes, and endnotes.

Finalizing a Document

When a document is complete and ready for distribution, you typically perform several final tasks. These might include inspecting the document for any remaining private or inappropriate information, restricting access, or adding a digital signature.

Many documents go through several revisions, and some are scrutinized by multiple reviewers. During this development process, documents can accumulate information that you might not want in the final version, such as the names of people who worked on the document, comments that reviewers have added to the file, or hidden text about status and assumptions. This extraneous information is not a concern if the final version is to be delivered as a printout. However, these days more and more files are delivered electronically, making this information available to anyone who wants to read it.

Word 2007 includes a tool called the Document Inspector, which finds and removes all extraneous and potentially confidential information. You can instruct the Document Inspector to look for comments, revisions, and annotations; for any personal information saved with the document; and for hidden text. The Document Inspector displays a summary of its findings and gives you the option of removing anything it finds.

Word also includes another finalizing tool called the Compatibility Checker, which checks for the use of features not supported in previous versions of Word.

After you have handled extraneous information and compatibility issues, you can mark a document as final and make its file read-only, so that other people know that they should not make changes to this released document.

In this exercise, you will inspect a document for inappropriate information and mark it as final.

> **USE** the *Finalizing* document. This practice file is located in the *Documents\Microsoft Press\Word2007SBS\EditingText* folder.
>
> **OPEN** the *Finalizing* document.

Microsoft Office Button

1. Click the **Microsoft Office Button**, point to **Prepare**, and then click **Properties**.

   The Document Information Panel opens above the document, showing that identifying information has been saved with the file. Some of the information, including the name of the author, was attached to the file by Word. Other information was added by a user.

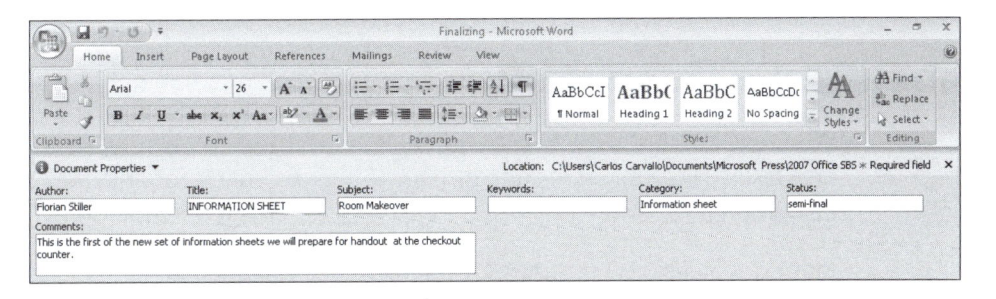

2. In the upper-left corner of the **Document Information Panel**, click the **Document Properties** arrow, and then in the list, click **Advanced Properties**.

The Properties dialog box opens.

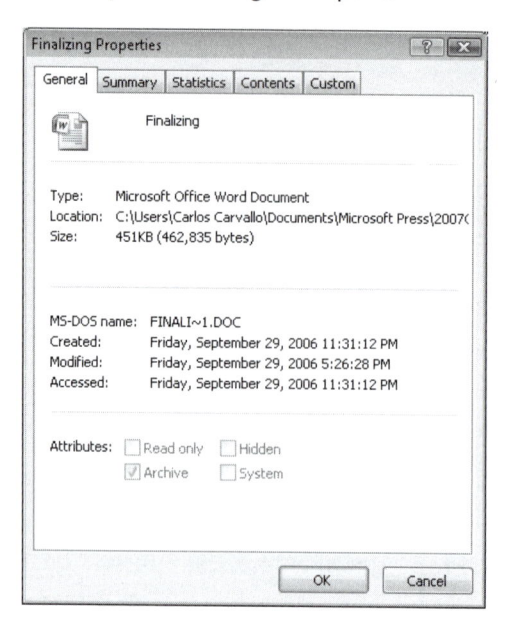

3. In turn, click the **Summary** and **Statistics** tabs, noticing that additional identifying information is displayed there.

4. Click **Cancel** to close the **Properties** dialog box, and then in the upper-right corner of the **Document Information Panel**, click the **Close** button.

Close

5. Save the document in the *EditingText* folder with the name My Information Sheet.

6. Click the **Microsoft Office Button**, point to **Prepare**, and then click **Inspect Document**.

The Document Inspector dialog box opens, listing the items that will be checked.

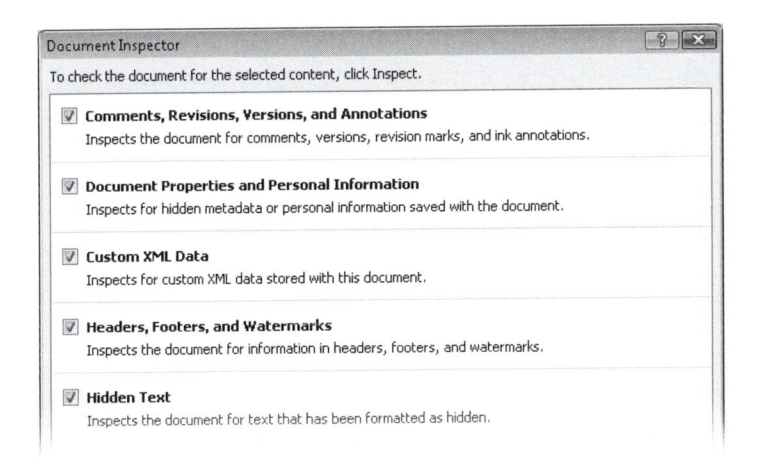

Document Inspector dialog box showing checked options: Comments, Revisions, Versions, and Annotations; Document Properties and Personal Information; Custom XML Data; Headers, Footers, and Watermarks; Hidden Text.

7. Without changing the default selections in the **Document Inspector** dialog box, click **Inspect**.

   The Document Inspector reports the presence of the document properties and personal information that you viewed earlier in this exercise, as well as some custom XML data.

8. To the right of **Document Properties and Personal Information**, click **Remove All**.

   Word removes the document properties and personal information.

9. To the right of **Custom XML Data**, click **Remove All**.

   See Also For information about XML, see "Creating an XML Document" in Chapter 11, "Creating Documents for Use Outside of Word."

10. In the **Document Inspector** dialog box, click **Close**.

11. Click the **Microsoft Office Button**, point to **Prepare**, and then click **Mark As Final**.

    A message tells you that the document will be marked as final and then saved.

12. Click **OK** to complete the process.

    A message tells you that the document has been marked as final and that typing, editing commands, and proofing marks are turned off.

13. Click **OK** to close the message, and then click the **Insert** tab.

    Most of the buttons are inactive, indicating that you cannot make changes.

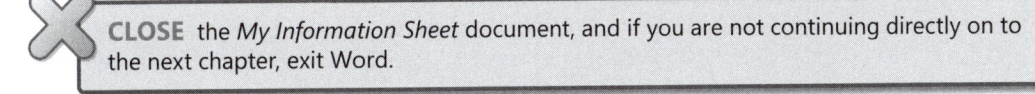

> **CLOSE** the *My Information Sheet* document, and if you are not continuing directly on to the next chapter, exit Word.

> **Adding a Digital Signature**
>
> When you create a document that will be circulated to other people via e-mail or the Web, you might want to attach a *digital signature*, which is an electronic stamp of authentication. The digital signature confirms the origin of the document and indicates that no one has tampered with the document since it was signed.
>
> To add a digital signature to a Word document, you must first obtain a digital ID from a company such as IntelliSafe Technologies or Comodo Inc. You can obtain the ID and attach it to a document by clicking the Microsoft Office Button, pointing to Prepare, clicking Add A Digital Signature, and then following the instructions.
>
> When preparing a document that will be digitally signed, you can insert a digital signature line in the document, which, when signed, will display a text version of the digital signature. To insert a digital signature line, click Signature Line in the Text group on the Insert tab.

Key Points

- You can cut or copy text and paste it elsewhere in the same document or in a different document. Cut and copied text is stored on the Clipboard.
- Made a mistake? No problem! You can undo one action or the last several actions you performed by clicking the Undo button (or its arrow) on the Quick Access Toolbar. You can even redo an action if you change you mind again.
- You don't have to type the same text over and over again. Instead, save the text as a Quick Part and insert it with a few mouse clicks.
- Need a more precise word to get your point across? You can use the Thesaurus to look up synonyms for a selected word, and use the Research service to access specialized reference materials and online resources.
- If you take the time to apply heading styles to a document, you can use the outline to rearrange the document.
- You can find each occurrence of a word or phrase and replace it with another.
- You can rely on AutoCorrect to correct common misspellings. Correct other spelling and grammatical errors individually as you type or by checking the entire document in one pass.
- Before you distribute an electronic document, you can remove any information you don't want people to be able to see.

Chapter at a Glance

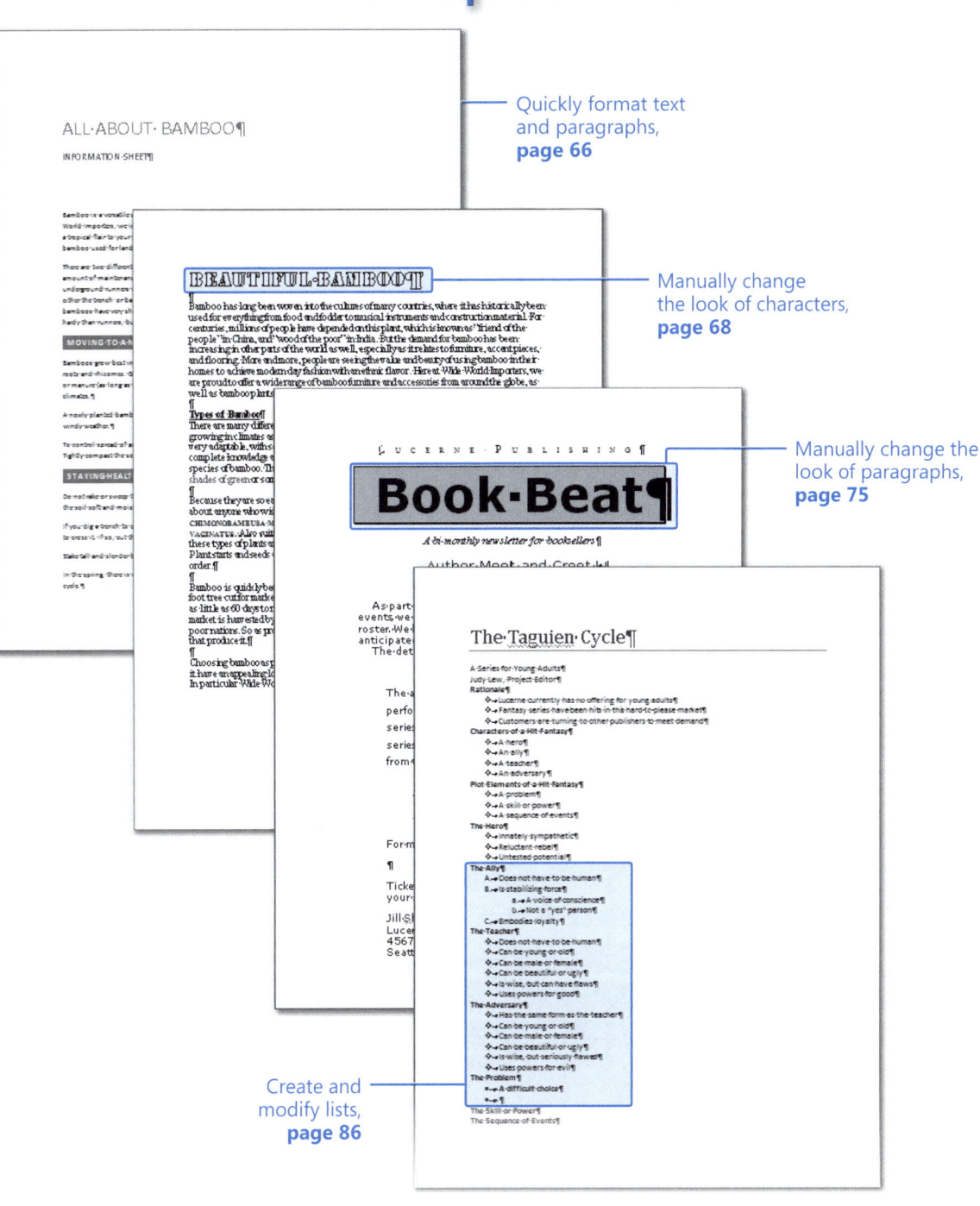

Quickly format text and paragraphs, **page 66**

Manually change the look of characters, **page 68**

Manually change the look of paragraphs, **page 75**

Create and modify lists, **page 86**

3 Changing the Look of Text

In this chapter, you will learn to:
- ✔ Quickly format text and paragraphs.
- ✔ Manually change the look of characters.
- ✔ Manually change the look of paragraphs.
- ✔ Create and modify lists.

The appearance of your documents helps to convey their message. Microsoft Office Word 2007 can help you develop professional-looking documents whose appearance is appropriate to their contents. You can easily format your text so that key points stand out and your arguments are easy to grasp.

In this chapter, you will experiment with Quick Styles and then change the look of individual words. Then you'll indent paragraphs, change paragraph alignment and spacing, set tab stops, modify line spacing, and add borders and shading. Finally you'll create and format both bulleted and numbered lists.

See Also Do you need only a quick refresher on the topics in this chapter? See the Quick Reference section at the beginning of this book.

Important Before you can use the practice files in this chapter, you need to install them from the book's companion CD to their default location. See "Using the Companion CD" at the beginning of this book for more information.

Troubleshooting Graphics and operating system–related instructions in this book reflect the Windows Vista user interface. If your computer is running Windows XP and you experience trouble following the instructions as written, please refer to the "Information for Readers Running Windows XP" section at the beginning of this book.

65

Quickly Formatting Text and Paragraphs

Word 2007 includes a number of new features, as well as enhancements to existing features, that make the process of formatting content effortless. For example, buttons for changing the font size, color, and other character attributes have been gathered in the Font group on the Home tab so that they are all easily accessible. And many common formatting buttons are available on the Mini toolbar that appears when you point to selected text.

See Also For information about changing character attributes, see "Manually Changing the Look of Characters" later in this chapter.

However, you don't have to apply attributes one at a time. You can easily change several attributes at once with a couple of mouse clicks by using *Quick Styles*. This powerful tool is available in the Styles group on the Home tab. Quick Styles are galleries consisting of the following:

- *Paragraph styles.* You can use these styles to apply a consistent look to different types of paragraphs, such as headings, body text, captions, quotations, and list paragraphs.
- *Character styles.* You can use these styles to change the appearance of selected words.

All of the Quick Styles in a particular gallery coordinate with each other, lending a clean, consistent, professional look to your documents. You can switch from one set of styles to another by selecting from Quick Styles galleries with names like Traditional, Distinctive, Modern, and Elegant. To help you choose the style you want, you can point to the name of the set to see a live preview of how your document will look with a particular set of Quick Styles applied to it. After you have applied one set of Quick Styles, you can easily change the look of the entire document by selecting a different set of Quick Styles from the Change Styles list.

In this exercise, you will experiment with Quick Styles.

> **USE** the *QuickFormatting* document. This practice file is located in the *Documents\Microsoft Press\Word2007SBS\FormattingText* folder.
> **BE SURE TO** start Word before beginning this exercise.
> **OPEN** the *QuickFormatting* document.

1. With the insertion point at the top of the document, on the **Home** tab, in the **Styles** group, point to each thumbnail in the displayed row of the **Quick Styles** gallery.

Quickly Formatting Text and Paragraphs **67**

The formatting of the heading changes to show you a live preview of how the heading will look if you click the style you are pointing to. You don't have to actually apply the formatting to see its effect.

Down

2. Without making a selection, click the **Down** arrow to the right of the gallery.

> **Tip** This arrow has a dynamic ScreenTip that currently reads *Row 1 of 5*.

The next row of the Quick Styles gallery scrolls into view.

3. Move the pointer over each thumbnail in this row of the **Quick Styles** gallery.

More

4. In the **Styles** group, click the **More** button.

Word displays the entire Quick Styles gallery. The style applied to the paragraph containing the insertion point is surrounded by a border.

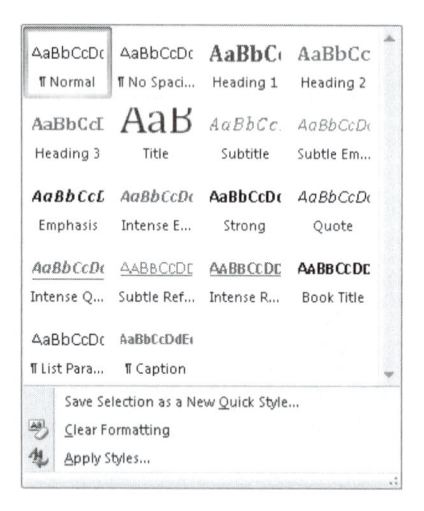

5. In the gallery, click the **Title** thumbnail to apply that style to the paragraph containing the insertion point.

6. Click anywhere in the **Information Sheet** heading, and then in the **Styles** group, click the **Subtitle** thumbnail.

> **Troubleshooting** If you select text and then apply a paragraph style, only the selected text takes on the formatting of the style. You can simply click again in the paragraph and reapply the style.

Up

7. Click anywhere in the **Moving to a New Home** heading, and then in the **Styles** group, click the **Up** arrow, and click the **Heading 1** thumbnail.

8. Apply the **Heading 1** style to the **Staying Healthy** and **Keeping Bugs at Bay** headings.
9. Apply the **Heading 3** style to the **Mites** and **Mealy Bugs** headings. 
10. In the **Styles** group, click the **Change Styles** button, click **Style Set**, and then point to each set name in turn, watching the effect on the document.
11. When you have finished exploring, click **Modern**.

   The formatting of the document changes and the headings and text take on the look assigned to this set of styles.

> **CLOSE** the *QuickFormatting* document without saving your changes.

Manually Changing the Look of Characters

When you type text in a document, it is displayed in a particular font. Each *font* consists of 256 alphabetic characters, numbers, and symbols that share a common design. By default the font used for text in a new Word document is Calibri, but you can change the font at any time. The available fonts vary from one computer to another, depending on the programs installed. Common fonts include Arial, Verdana, and Times New Roman.

You can vary the look of a font by changing the following *attributes*:

- Almost every font comes in a range of *font sizes*, which are measured in *points* from the top of letters that have parts that stick up (ascenders), such as *h*, to the bottom of letters that have parts that drop down (descenders), such as *p*. A point is approximately 1/72 of an inch.
- Almost every font comes in a range of *font styles*. The most common are regular (or plain), italic, bold, and bold italic.
- Fonts can be enhanced by applying *font effects*, such as underlining, small capital letters (small caps), or shadows.
- A palette of harmonious *font colors* is available, and you can also specify custom colors.
- You can alter the *character spacing* by pushing characters apart or squeezing them together.

After you have selected an appropriate font for a document, you can use these attributes to achieve different effects. Although some attributes might cancel each other out, they are usually cumulative. For example, you might use a bold font in various sizes and various shades of green to make different heading levels stand out in a newsletter. Collectively, the font and its attributes are called *character formatting*.

In this exercise, you will format the text in a document by changing its font, font style, size, color, and character spacing.

> **USE** the *Characters* document. This practice file is located in the *Documents\Microsoft Press\Word2007SBS\FormattingText* folder.
>
> **OPEN** the *Characters* document.

1. In the *Beautiful Bamboo* heading, click anywhere in the word **Beautiful**.
2. On the **Home** tab, in the **Font** group, click the **Underline** button.

   > **Tip** If you click the Underline arrow, you can choose a style from the Underline gallery. You can also change the underline color.

   The word containing the insertion point is now underlined. Notice that you did not have to select the entire word.

3. In the same heading, click anywhere in the word **Bamboo**, and then on the **Quick Access Toolbar**, click the **Repeat** button.

   The last formatting command is repeated. Again, although you did not select the entire word, it is now underlined.

4. In the selection area, click adjacent to *Beautiful Bamboo* to select the entire heading.

   Word displays a Mini toolbar of buttons that you can use to quickly change the look of the selection.

5. On the **Mini toolbar**, click the **Bold** button.

   The heading is now bold. The active buttons on the Mini toolbar and in the Font group on the Home tab indicate the attributes that you applied to the selection.

70 Chapter 3 Changing the Look of Text

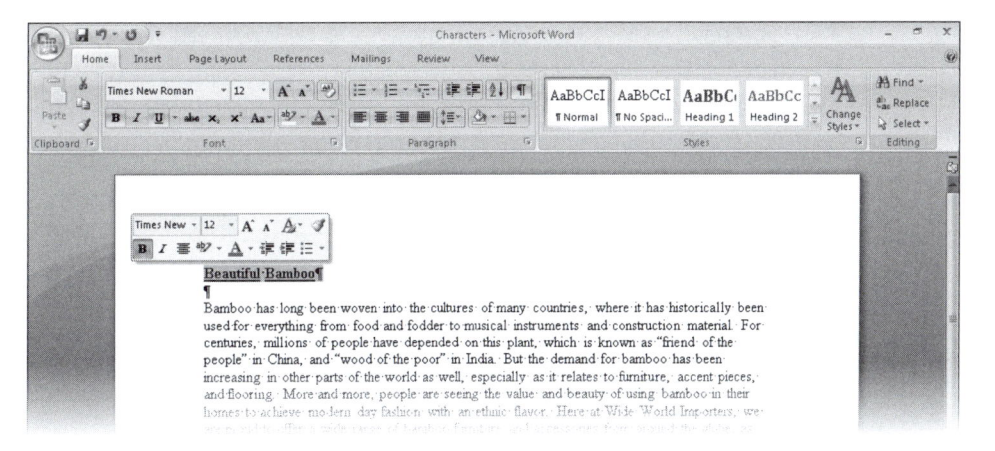

![Screenshot of Microsoft Word showing a document with "Beautiful Bamboo" heading and the Mini toolbar displayed above the text.]

See Also For information about the use of character formatting, see the sidebar "More About Case and Character Formatting" later in this chapter.

[Format Painter icon]
Format Painter

6. On the **Mini toolbar**, click the **Format Painter** button, and then click in the selection area adjacent to the *Types of Bamboo* heading.

   Word applies the formatting of *Beautiful Bamboo* to *Types of Bamboo*.

   > **Tip** The Format Painter button is also available in the Clipboard group on the Home tab.

7. Select **Beautiful Bamboo**, and then on the **Home** tab, in the **Font** group, click the **Font** arrow, scroll the list of available fonts, and then click **Stencil**.

   > **Troubleshooting** If Stencil is not available, select any heavy font that catches your attention.

   The heading at the top of the document now appears in the new font.

[Font Size icon]
Font Size

8. In the **Font** group, click the **Font Size** arrow, and then in the list, click **26**.

   The size of the heading text increases to 26 points.

   > **Tip** You can increase or decrease the font size in set increments by clicking the Grow Font and Shrink Font buttons in the Font group, or by clicking the same buttons on the Mini toolbar that appears when you select text.

[Dialog Box Launcher icon]
Dialog Box Launcher

9. Click the **Font** dialog box launcher.

   The Font dialog box opens.

Manually Changing the Look of Characters   71

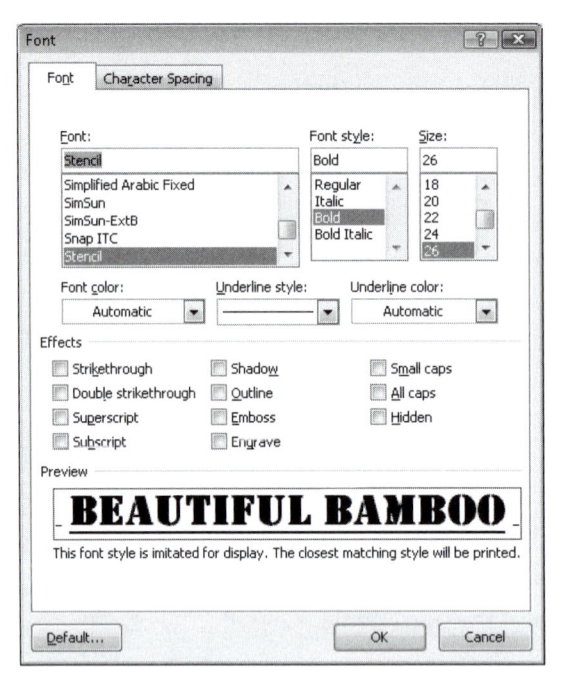

10. Click the **Underline style** arrow, and then in the list, click **(none)**.
11. In the **Effects** area, select the **Outline** check box.
12. Click the **Character Spacing** tab.

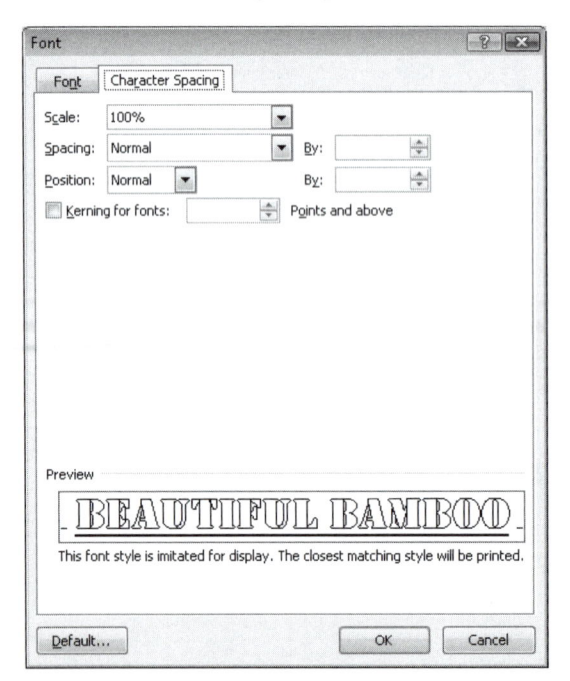

13. Click the **Spacing** arrow, and then in the list, click **Expanded**.
14. To the right, click the **By** up arrow until the spacing is expanded by **2 pt** (points), and then click **OK**.

    The selected text appears with an outline effect and with the spacing between the characters expanded by 2 points.

15. On the **Home** tab, in the **Font** group, click the **Clear Formatting** button.

    Clear Formatting

    The formatting of the selected text is removed.

16. On the **Quick Access Toolbar**, click the **Undo** button.

    Undo

    The formatting of the selected text is restored.

17. In the last sentence of the second paragraph, select the words **light green**.
18. On the **Home** tab, in the **Font** group, click the **Font Color** arrow, and then under **Standard Colors** in the palette, click the light green box.

    Font Color

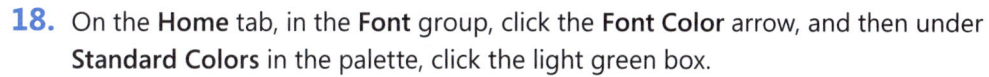

    The selected words are now light green. (To see the color, clear the selection by clicking a blank area of the document.)

    > **Tip** If you want to apply the Font Color button's current color, you can simply click the button (not the arrow).

19. In the same sentence, select **dark, rich shades of green**, click the **Font Color** arrow, and then below the palette, click **More Colors**.

    The Colors dialog box opens.

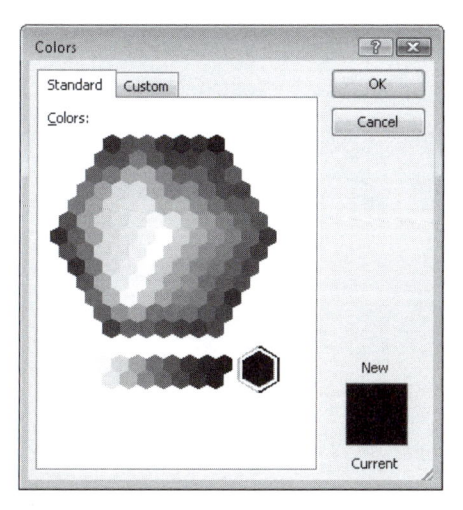

20. In the **Colors** wheel on the **Standard** tab, click one of the dark green shades on the left, and then click **OK**.

    The selection is now dark green.

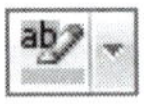

21. Select the phrase **supports the environment** in the second sentence of the last paragraph. Then in the **Font** group, click the **Highlight** arrow, and under **Recent Colors** in the palette, click the green box.

    This is the same green that you selected in step 20. After you select a custom color in one palette, it is available in all the palettes. The highlighted phrase now stands out from the rest of the text.

    > **Tip** If you click the Highlight button without first making a selection, the mouse pointer becomes a highlighter that you can drag across text. Click the Highlight button again or press Esc to turn off the highlighter.

22. In the paragraph that begins *Because they are so easy to grow*, select the bamboo species name **chimonobambusa marmorea**. Then hold down the Ctrl key while selecting **indocalamus tessellatus**, **pleioblastus chino vaginatus**, **bambusa glaucophylla**, and **otatea acuminata aztectorum**.

23. Click the **Font** dialog box launcher.

24. In the **Font** dialog box, click the **Font** tab, and in the **Effects** area, select the **Small caps** check box. Then click **OK**.

    The lowercase letters in the species names now appear in small capital letters, making those names easy to find in the text.

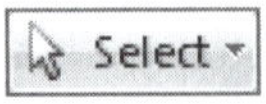

25. Click anywhere in the first species name. Then on the **Home** tab, in the **Editing** group, click the **Select** button, and click **Select Text with Similar Formatting**.

    All the species names that have been formatted in small caps are selected.

26. In the **Font** group, click the **Bold** button, and then click away from the selection.

    The species names are now both small caps and bold.

> Types of Bamboo
>
> There are many different sizes and varieties of bamboo. It is both tropical and subtropical, growing in climates as diverse as jungles and mountainsides. Actually giant, woody grasses, it is very adaptable, with some species deciduous and others evergreen. Although there isn't yet a complete knowledge about this plant, there are believed to be between 1100 and 1500 different species of bamboo. The color range is from light green leaves and culms (stems) to dark, rich shades of green or some combination thereof.
>
> Because they are so easy to grow in such a variety of climates, there is a plant available for just about anyone who wishes to grow one in their backyard. Some dwarf species include **CHIMONOBAMBUSA MARMOREA**, **INDOCALAMUS TESSELLATUS**, and **PLEIOBLASTUS CHINO VAGINATUS**. Also suitable for the personal garden are those categorized as mid-size. Examples of these types of plants are **BAMBUSA GLAUCOPHYLLA** and **OTATEA ACUMINATA AZTECTORUM** Plant starts and seeds are easier to find than ever, being available at nurseries and through mail order.
>
> Bamboo is quickly becoming an important economic factor in many developing nations. A 60-foot tree cut for marketing can take up to 60 years to replace, whereas a 60-foot bamboo can take as little as 60 days to reach marketability. And the majority of bamboo destined for the world market is harvested by women and children, most of who live at or below subsistence levels in poor nations. So as production increases, so does support for the economies of those countries that produce it.
>
> Choosing bamboo as part of home or garden design makes sense on many levels. Not only does it have an appealing look, but it supports the environment as well as the countries that produce it. In particular Wide World Importers recommends chimonobambusa marmoreal.

CLOSE the *Characters* document without saving your changes.

More About Case and Character Formatting

The way you use case and character formatting in a document can influence its visual impact on your readers. Used judiciously, case and character formatting can make a plain document look attractive and professional, but excessive use can make it look amateurish and detract from the message. For example, using too many fonts in the same document is the mark of inexperience, so don't use more than two or three.

Bear in mind that lowercase letters tend to recede, so using all uppercase (capital) letters can be useful for titles and headings or for certain kinds of emphasis. However, large blocks of uppercase letters are tiring to the eye.

Where do the terms uppercase and lowercase come from? Until the advent of computers, individual characters were assembled to form the words that would appear on a printed page. The characters were stored alphabetically in cases, with the capital letters in the upper case and the small letters in the lower case.

> **Tip** If you want to see a summary of the formatting applied to a selection, you can display the Style Inspector pane by clicking the Styles dialog box launcher and then clicking the Style Inspector button (the middle button at the bottom of the Styles task pane). You can then click anywhere in the document to see a formatting summary of the word containing the insertion point. To see details about the formatting, you can click the Reveal Formatting button at the bottom of the Style Inspector pane to open the Reveal Formatting task pane.

Manually Changing the Look of Paragraphs

As you know, you create a *paragraph* by typing text and then pressing the Enter key. The paragraph can be one word, one sentence, or multiple sentences. You can change the look of a paragraph by changing its alignment, its line spacing, and the space before and after it. You can also put borders around it and shade its background. Collectively, the settings you use to vary the look of a paragraph are called *paragraph formatting*.

In Word, you don't define the width of paragraphs and the length of pages by defining the area occupied by the text; instead you define the size of the white space—the left, right, top, and bottom *margins*—around the text. You use the Margins button in the Page Setup group on the Page Layout tab to define these margins, either for the whole document or for sections of the document.

See Also For information about setting margins, see "Previewing and Printing a Document" in Chapter 1, "Exploring Word 2007." For information about sections, see "Controlling What Appears on Each Page" in Chapter 4, "Changing the Look of a Document."

Although the left and right margins are set for a whole document or section, you can vary the position of the text between the margins. The easiest way to do this is by moving controls on the horizontal ruler. You can indent paragraphs from the left and right margins, as well as specify where the first line of a paragraph begins and where the second and subsequent lines begin.

Setting a right indent indicates where all the lines in a paragraph should end, but sometimes you might want to specify where only one line should end. For example, you might want to break a title after a particular word to make it look balanced on the page. You can end an individual line by inserting a *text wrapping break* or *line break*. After positioning the insertion point where you want the break to occur, you click the Breaks button in the Page Setup group on the Page Layout tab, and then click Text Wrapping. Word indicates the line break with a bent arrow. Inserting a line break does not start a new paragraph, so when you apply paragraph formatting to a line of text that ends with a line break, the formatting is applied to the entire paragraph, not just that line.

> **Tip** You can also press Shift+Enter to insert a line break.

You can align lines of text in different locations across the page by using *tab stops*. The easiest way to set tab stops is to use the horizontal ruler. By default, Word sets left-aligned tab stops every 0.5 inch, as indicated by gray marks below this ruler. To set a custom tab stop, you start by clicking the Tab button located at the left end of the ruler until the type of tab stop you want appears. You have the following options:

- **Left Tab.** Aligns the left end of the text with the stop.
- **Center Tab.** Aligns the center of the text with the stop.
- **Right Tab.** Aligns the right end of the text with the stop.
- **Decimal Tab.** Aligns the decimal point in the text with the stop.
- **Bar Tab.** Draws a vertical bar aligned with the stop down the paragraph containing the insertion point.

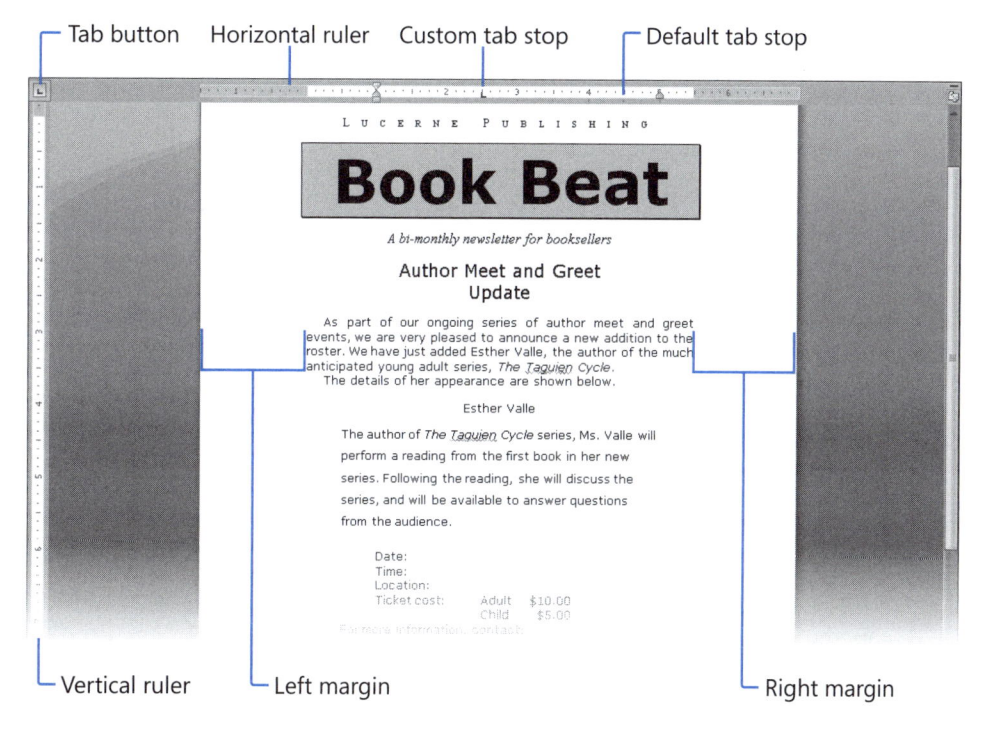

After selecting the type of tab stop, you simply click the ruler where you want the tab stop to be. Word then removes any default tab stops to the left of the one you set. To change the position of an existing custom tab stop, you drag it to the left or right on the ruler. To delete a custom tab stop, you drag it away from the ruler.

To move the text to the right of the insertion point to the next tab stop, you press the Tab key. The text is then aligned on the tab stop according to its type. For example, if you set a center tab stop, pressing Tab moves the text so that its center is aligned with the tab stop.

> **Tip** When you want to fine-tune the position of tab stops, click the Paragraph dialog box launcher on either the Home or Page Layout tab. In the Paragraph dialog box, click the Tabs button to display the Tabs dialog box. You might also open this dialog box if you want to use *tab leaders*—visible marks such as dots or dashes connecting the text before the tab with the text after it. For example, tab leaders are useful in a table of contents to carry the eye from the text to the page number.

In addition to tab stops, the horizontal ruler also displays *indent markers* that are used to control where each line of text starts and ends. You use these markers to indent text from the left or right margins as follows:

- **First Line Indent.** Begins a paragraph's first line of text at this marker.
- **Hanging Indent.** Begins a paragraph's second and subsequent lines of text at this marker.
- **Left Indent.** Indents the text to this marker.
- **Right Indent.** Wraps the text when it reaches this marker.

You can also determine the positioning of a paragraph between the left and right margins by changing its alignment. You can click buttons in the Paragraph group on the Home tab to align paragraphs as follows:

- **Align Left.** Aligns each line of the paragraph at the left margin, with a ragged right edge.
- **Align Right.** Aligns each line of the paragraph at the right margin, with a ragged left edge.
- **Center.** Aligns the center of each line in the paragraph between the left and right margins, with ragged left and right edges.
- **Justify.** Aligns each line between the margins, creating even left and right edges.

> **Tip** If you know that you want to type a centered paragraph, you don't have to type it and then format it as centered. You can use the *Click and Type* feature to create appropriately aligned text. Move the pointer to the center of a blank area of the page, and when the pointer's shape changes to an I-beam with centered text attached, double-click to create an insertion point that is ready to enter centered text. Similarly, you can double-click at the left edge of the page to enter left-aligned text and at the right edge to enter right-aligned text.

To make it obvious where one paragraph ends and another begins, you can add space between them by adjusting the Spacing After and Spacing Before settings in the Paragraph group on the Page Layout tab. You can adjust the spacing between the lines in a paragraph by clicking the Line Spacing button in the Paragraph group on the Home tab.

When you want to make several adjustments to the alignment, indentation, and spacing of selected paragraphs, it is sometimes quicker to use the Paragraph dialog box than to click buttons and drag markers. Click the Paragraph dialog box launcher on either the Home or Page Layout tab to open the Paragraph dialog box.

To make a paragraph really stand out, you can put a border around it or shade its background. For real drama, you can do both.

> **Tip** A paragraph's formatting is stored in its paragraph mark. If you delete the paragraph mark, thereby making it part of the following paragraph, its text takes on the formatting of that paragraph. If you position the insertion point anywhere in the paragraph and press Enter to create a new one, the new paragraph takes on the existing paragraph's formatting.

In this exercise, you'll change text alignment and indentation, insert and modify tab stops, modify paragraph and line spacing, and add borders and shading around paragraphs to change their appearance.

> **USE** the *Paragraphs* document. This practice file is located in the *Documents\Microsoft Press\Word2007SBS\FormattingText* folder.
> **BE SURE TO** turn on the display of non-printing characters for this exercise. Also display the rulers.
> **OPEN** the *Paragraphs* document.

1. In the lower-right corner of the document window, click the **Zoom Out** button twice to set the zoom percentage to 80%.

   You can now see all the text of the document.

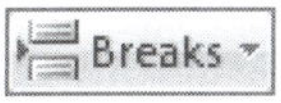

2. In the fourth line of the document, click to the left of *Update*, and then on the **Page Layout** tab, in the **Page Setup** group, click the **Breaks** button, and then click **Text Wrapping**.

   Word inserts a line break character and moves the part of the paragraph that follows that character to the next line.

Manually Changing the Look of Paragraphs   79

See Also For information about page and section breaks, see "Controlling What Appears on Each Page" in Chapter 4, "Changing the Look of a Document." For information about column breaks, see "Presenting Information in Columns" in Chapter 5, "Presenting Information in Columns and Tables."

[Center]

3. Select the first four lines of the document, and then on the **Home** tab, in the **Paragraph** group, click the **Center** button.

   The lines are now centered between the margins. Notice that even though you did not select the fifth line, it is also centered because it is part of the *Author Meet and Greet* paragraph.

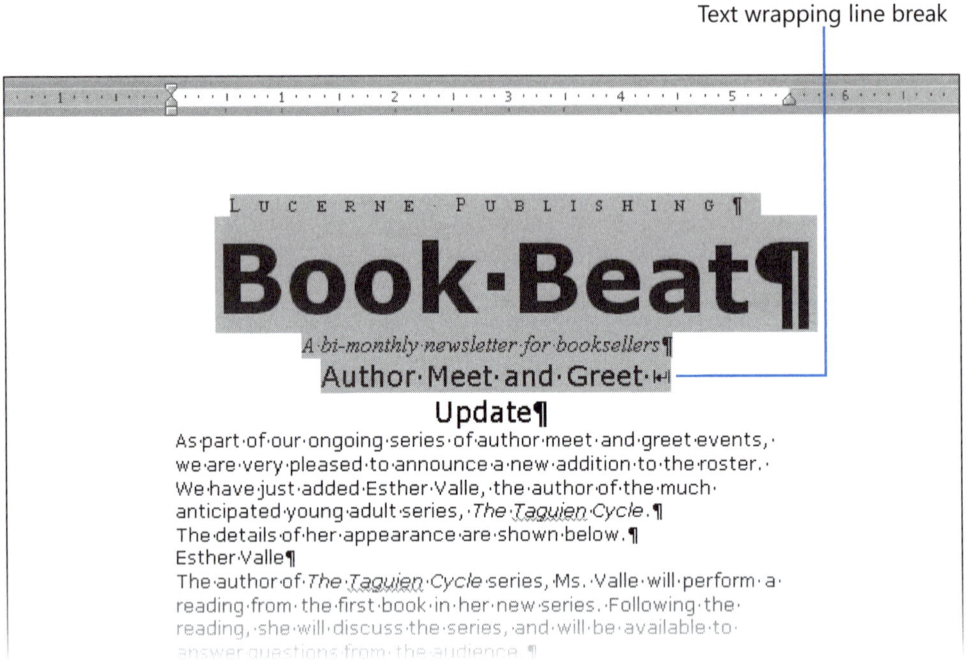

   Text wrapping line break

   [Screenshot of document showing "LUCERNE PUBLISHING / Book·Beat / A bi-monthly newsletter for booksellers / Author·Meet·and·Greet / Update" followed by body text about an author meet and greet event featuring Esther Valle, author of The Taquien Cycle.]

[Justify]

4. Select the next two paragraphs, and then in the **Paragraph** group, click the **Justify** button.

   The edges of the first paragraph are now flush against both the left and right margins. The second paragraph doesn't change because it is less than a line long.

[First Line Indent]

5. With both paragraphs still selected, on the horizontal ruler, drag the **First Line Indent** marker to the 0.25-inch mark.

   The first line of each paragraph is now indented 0.25 inch from the left margin.

First Line Indent marker

LUCERNE · PUBLISHING ¶

Book·Beat¶

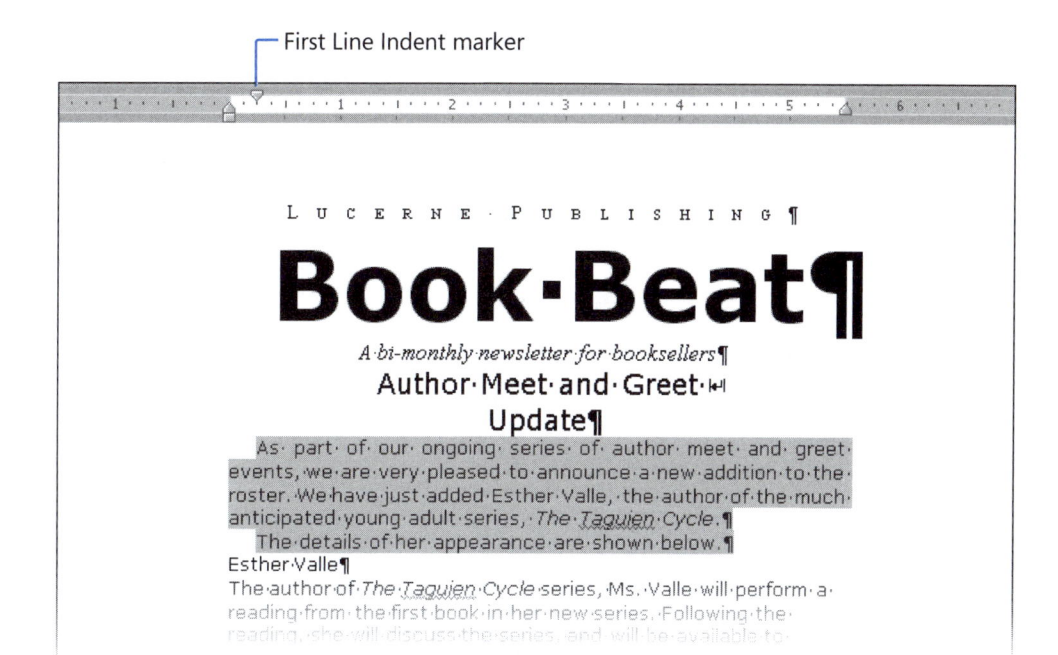

A bi-monthly newsletter for booksellers ¶
Author·Meet·and·Greet·↵
Update¶

As·part·of·our·ongoing·series·of·author·meet·and·greet·events,·we·are·very·pleased·to·announce·a·new·addition·to·the·roster.·We·have·just·added·Esther·Valle,·the·author·of·the·much·anticipated·young·adult·series,·*The·Taguien·Cycle.*¶
The·details·of·her·appearance·are·shown·below.¶
Esther·Valle¶
The·author·of·*The·Taguien·Cycle*·series,·Ms.·Valle·will·perform·a·reading·from·the·first·book·in·her·new·series.·Following·the·reading,·she·will·discuss·the·series,·and·will·be·available·to·

6. Click anywhere in the *Esther Valle* paragraph, and then in the **Paragraph** group, click the **Center** button.

> **Tip** When applying paragraph formatting, you don't have to select the entire paragraph.

Left Indent

7. Select all the paragraphs below *Esther Valle*, and then on the horizontal ruler, drag the **Left Indent** marker to the 0.5-inch mark.

   The First Line Indent and Hanging Indent markers move with the Left Indent marker, and all the selected paragraphs are now indented 0.5 inch from the left margin.

Right Indent

8. Drag the **Right Indent** marker to the 5-inch mark.

   The paragraphs are now indented from the right margin as well.

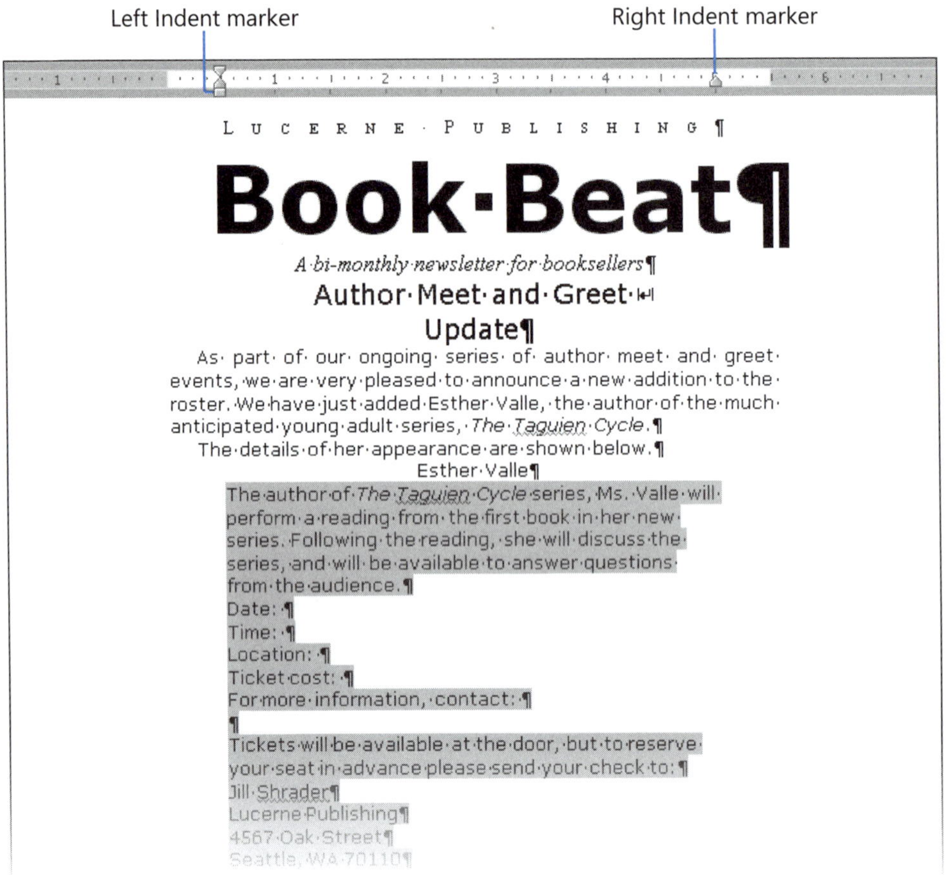

> **Tip** Left and right margin indents are frequently used to draw attention to special paragraphs, such as quotations.

9. Select the **Date**, **Time**, **Location**, and **Ticket cost** paragraphs, and then in the **Paragraph** group, click the **Increase Indent** button.

   These four paragraphs are now indented to the 1-inch mark.

10. Without changing the selection, make sure the **Left Tab** button at the junction of the horizontal and vertical rulers is active, and then click the ruler at the 2.5-inch mark to set a left tab stop.

82 Chapter 3 Changing the Look of Text

11. Click at the right end of the **Date** paragraph to position the insertion point before the paragraph mark, and then press the [Tab] key.

   Word will left-align any text you type after the tab character at the new tab stop.

12. Press the [↓] key, and then press [Tab].

13. Repeat step 12 for the *Location* and *Ticket cost* paragraphs.

   All four paragraphs now have tabs that are aligned with the tab stop at the 2.5-inch mark.

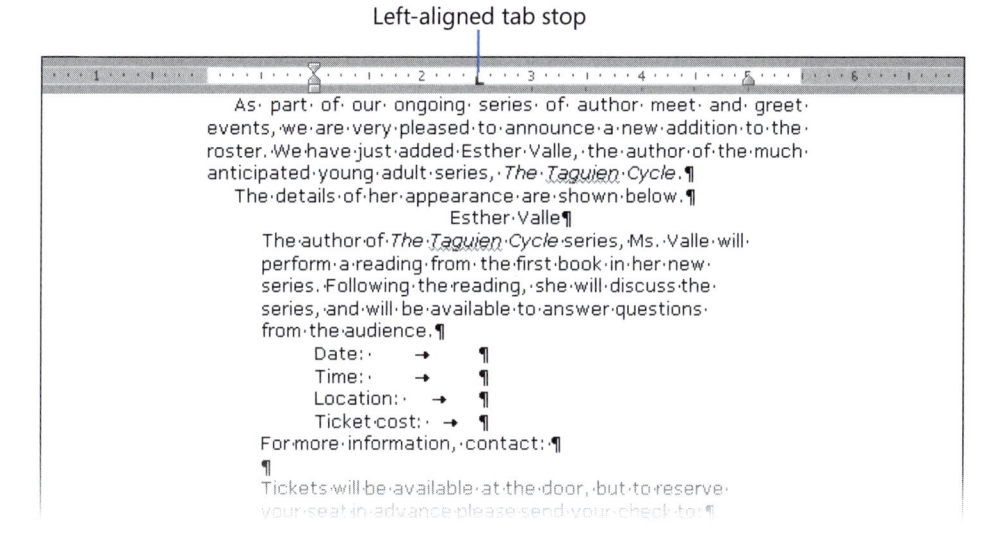

   Left-aligned tab stop

   As part of our ongoing series of author meet and greet events, we are very pleased to announce a new addition to the roster. We have just added Esther Valle, the author of the much anticipated young adult series, *The Taguien Cycle*.¶
   The details of her appearance are shown below.¶
   Esther Valle¶
   The author of *The Taguien Cycle* series, Ms. Valle will perform a reading from the first book in her new series. Following the reading, she will discuss the series, and will be available to answer questions from the audience.¶
   Date: → ¶
   Time: → ¶
   Location: → ¶
   Ticket cost: → ¶
   For more information, contact: ¶
   ¶
   Tickets will be available at the door, but to reserve your seat in advance please send your check to ¶

14. Without moving the insertion point, type **Adult**, and then press [Tab].

   Decimal Tab

15. Click the **Tab** button three times to activate a decimal tab, and then click the 4-inch mark on the horizontal ruler.

16. Type **$10.00**, press [Enter], press [Tab] type **Child**, press [Tab] again, and then type **$5.00**.

   The new paragraph takes on the same paragraph formatting as the *Ticket cost* paragraph, and the dollar amounts are aligned on their decimal points.

Manually Changing the Look of Paragraphs   83

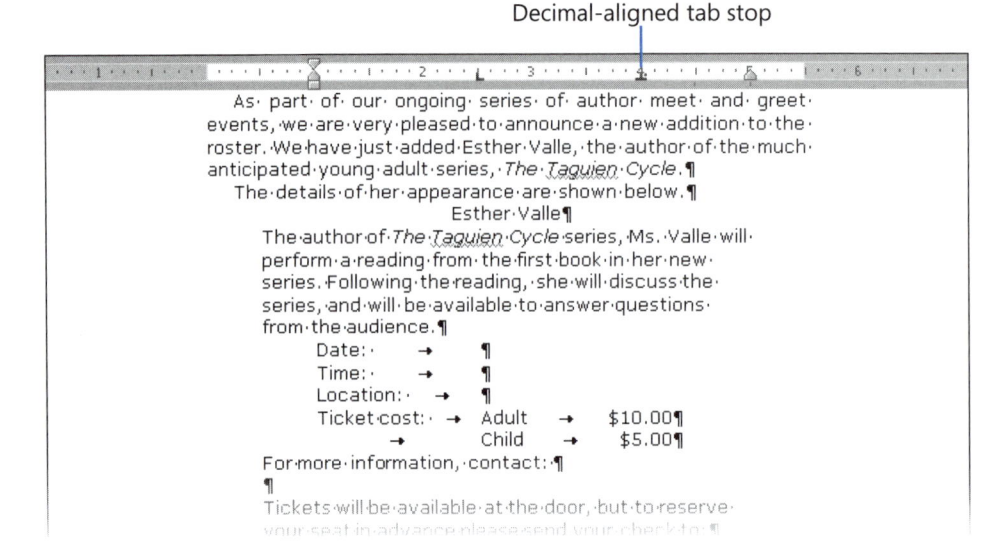

Decimal-aligned tab stop

[Screenshot of document with ruler showing decimal-aligned tab stop, containing text about Esther Valle, The Taguien Cycle series, with Date, Time, Location, Ticket cost (Adult $10.00, Child $5.00) entries]

17. Drag through any part of the two paragraphs with dollar amounts, and then on the horizontal ruler, drag the decimal tab stop from the 4-inch mark to the 3.5-inch mark.

18. On the **Home** tab, in the **Editing** group, click the **Select** button, and then click **Select All**.

19. On the **Page Layout** tab, in the **Paragraph** group, change the **Spacing After** setting to **12 pt**.

    Word inserts 12 points of space after every paragraph in the document.

20. Click anywhere in the paragraph that begins *As part of*, and then on the **Home** tab, in the **Paragraph** group, click the **Line Spacing** button, and then click **Remove Space After Paragraph**.

21. Select the **Date**, **Time**, **Location**, and **Ticket cost** paragraphs, and then repeat step 20.

22. Select the **Jill Shrader**, **Lucerne Publishing**, and **4567 Oak Street** paragraphs, and then repeat step 20 again.

23. Click anywhere in the paragraph that begins *The author of*, click the **Line Spacing** button again, and then click **1.5**.

    You have adjusted both the paragraph and line spacing of the document.

24. Click the *Book Beat* paragraph. Then on the **Home** tab, in the **Paragraph** group, click the **Borders** arrow, and at the bottom of the list, click **Borders and Shading**.

    The Borders And Shading dialog box opens.

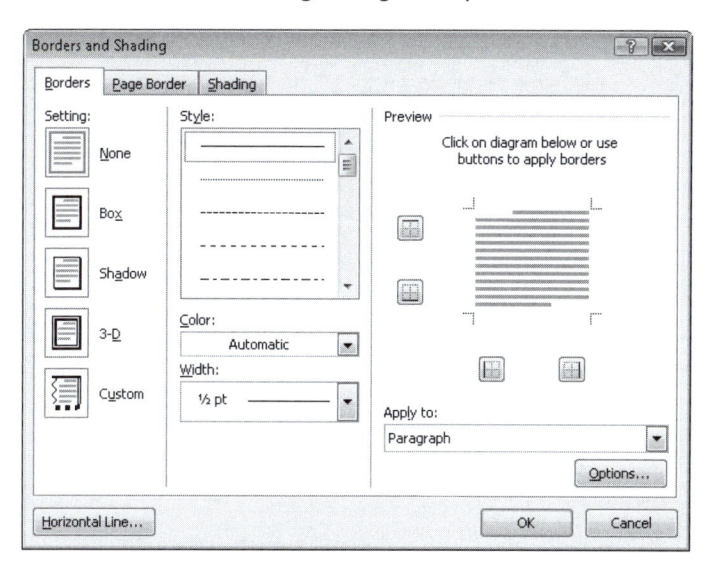

25. Under **Setting**, click the **Shadow** icon to select that border style.

    > **Tip** You can change the settings in the Style, Color, and Width boxes to create the kind of border you want. If you want only one, two, or three sides of the selected paragraphs to have a border, click the buttons surrounding the image in the Preview area.

26. Click the **Shading** tab.

    You can use the options on this tab to format the background of the selected paragraph.

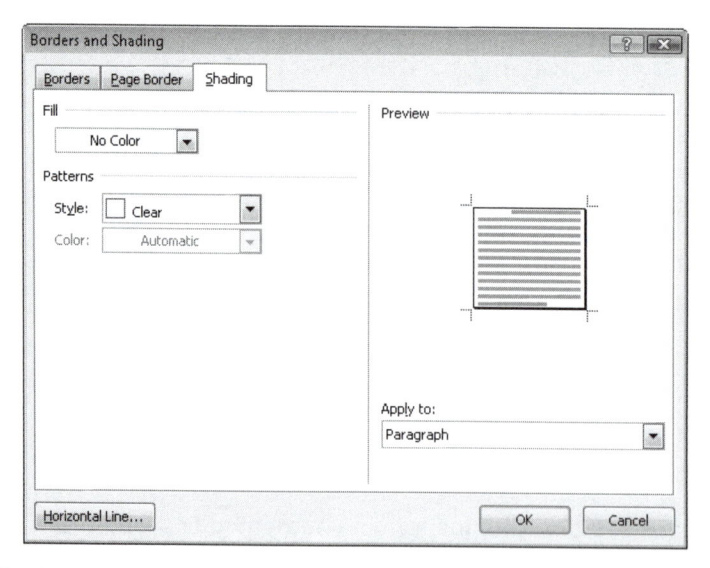

27. Click the **Fill** arrow, and under **Theme Colors**, in the column of purple boxes, click the second box from the bottom (**Purple, Accent 4, Lighter 60%**). Then click **OK** to close the **Borders and Shading** dialog box.

A border with a shadow surrounds the text, and the background color is light purple.

> **BE SURE TO** change the Zoom percentage back to 100% before moving on to the next exercise, and if you want, turn off the rulers.
>
> **CLOSE** the *Paragraphs* document without saving your changes.

> **Finding and Replacing Formatting**
>
> In addition to searching for words and phrases, you can use the Find And Replace dialog box to search for a specific format and replace it with a different format.
>
> To search for a specific format and replace it with a different format:
>
> 1. On the **Home** tab, in the **Editing** group, click the **Replace** button.
>
>   The Find And Replace dialog box opens, displaying the Replace tab.
>
> 2. Click **More** to expand the dialog box, click **Format**, and then click **Font** or **Paragraph**. (You can also click Style to search for paragraph styles or character styles.)
>
>   The Find Font or Find Paragraph dialog box opens.
>
> 3. In the dialog box, click the format you want to find, and then click **OK**.
>
> 4. Click the **Replace with** text box, click **Format**, click **Font** or **Paragraph**, click the format you want to substitute for the Find What format, and then click **OK**.
>
> 5. Click **Find Next** to search for the first occurrence of the format, and then click **Replace** to replace that one instance or **Replace All** to replace every instance.

Creating and Modifying Lists

When you want to present a list of items in a document, you will usually want to put each item on its own line rather than burying the items in a paragraph. When the order of items is not important—for example, for a list of items needed to carry out a task—use a bulleted list. When the order is important—for example, for the steps in a procedure—use a numbered list.

In a Word document, you can start a bulleted or numbered list as follows:

- To create a bulleted list, type * (an asterisk) at the beginning of a paragraph, and then press the Spacebar or the Tab key.
- To create a numbered list, type 1. (the numeral 1 followed by a period) at the beginning of a paragraph, and then press the Spacebar or the Tab key.

In either case, you then type the first item in the list and press Enter. Word starts the new paragraph with a bullet character or the number 2 followed by a period, and formats the first and second paragraphs as bulleted or numbered list items. Typing items and pressing Enter adds subsequent bulleted or numbered items. To end the list, press Enter twice, or press Enter and then Backspace.

> **Troubleshooting** If you want to start a paragraph with an asterisk or number but don't want the paragraph to be formatted as a bulleted or numbered list, click the AutoCorrect Options button that appears after Word changes the formatting, and then click Undo.

After you create a list, you can modify, format, and customize the list as follows:

- You can move items around in a list, insert new items, or delete unwanted items. If the list is numbered, Word automatically updates the numbers.

- You can sort items in a bulleted list into ascending or descending order by clicking the Sort button in the Paragraph group on the Home tab.

- For a bulleted list, you can change the bullet symbol by clicking the Bullets arrow in the Paragraph group and making a selection from the Bullet Library. You can also define a custom bullet by clicking the Bullets arrow and then clicking Define New Bullet.

- For a numbered list, you can change the number style by clicking the Numbering arrow in the Paragraph group and making a selection from the Numbering Library. You can also define a custom style by clicking the Numbering arrow and then clicking Define New Number Format.

- You can create a multilevel bulleted list, numbered list, or outline by clicking the Multilevel List button in the Paragraph group, selecting a style from the List Library, and then typing the list. You press Enter to create a new item at the same level, the Tab key to move down a level, and the Backspace key to move up a level.

    See Also For information about another way to create an outline, see "Reorganizing a Document Outline" in Chapter 2, "Editing and Proofreading Documents."

- You can modify the indentation of the list by dragging the indent markers on the horizontal ruler. Lists are set up with the first line "outdented" to the left from the other lines, and you can change both the overall indentation of the list and the relationship of the first line to the other lines.

88 Chapter 3 Changing the Look of Text

In this exercise, you will create a bulleted list and a numbered list and then modify lists in various ways. You will then create a multilevel list with letters instead of numbers.

> **USE** the *Lists* document. This practice file is located in the *Documents\Microsoft Press\Word2007SBS\FormattingText* folder.
> **OPEN** the *Lists* document.

Bullets

1. Select the three paragraphs under *Rationale*, and then on the **Home** tab, in the **Paragraph** group, click the **Bullets** button.

   The selected paragraphs are reformatted as a bulleted list.

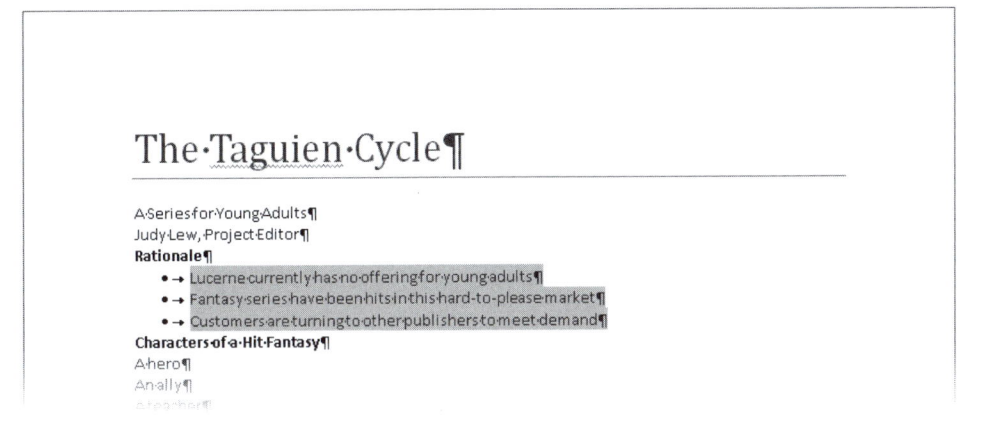

   The Taguien Cycle

   A Series for Young Adults
   Judy Lew, Project Editor
   Rationale
   • Lucerne currently has no offering for young adults
   • Fantasy series have been hits in this hard-to-please market
   • Customers are turning to other publishers to meet demand
   Characters of a Hit Fantasy
   A hero
   An ally
   A teacher

2. With the three paragraphs still selected, in the **Paragraph** group, click the **Bullets** arrow.

   The Bullet Library appears.

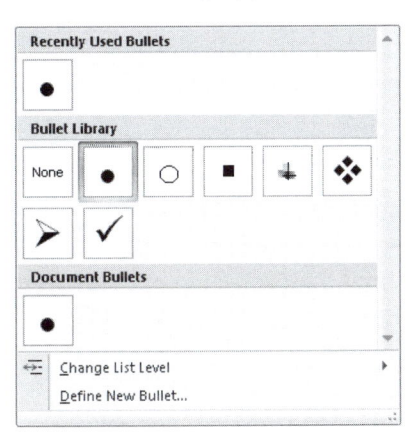

Creating and Modifying Lists 89

3. In the gallery, click the bullet composed of four diamonds.

   The bullet character in the selected list changes.

4. Select the four paragraphs under *Characters of a Hit Fantasy*, and then in the **Paragraph** group, click the **Bullets** button.

   The new list has the bullet character you selected for the previous list. This character will be the default until you change it.

5. Select the paragraphs under each of the bold headings, and then in the **Paragraph** group, click the **Bullets** button.

6. Scroll to the bottom of the page, select the four paragraphs under *The Sequence of Events*, and then in the **Paragraph** group, in the **Bullets Library**, click **None**.

   The bulleted paragraphs revert to normal paragraphs.

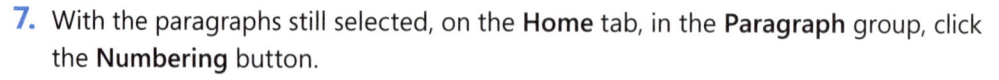

7. With the paragraphs still selected, on the **Home** tab, in the **Paragraph** group, click the **Numbering** button.

   The selected paragraphs are reformatted as a numbered list.

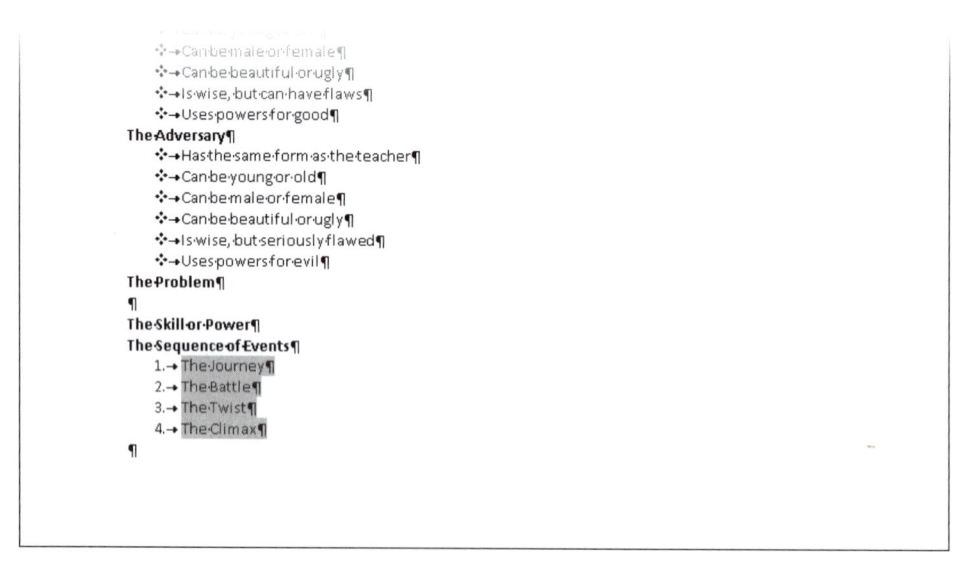

8. In the **Paragraph** group, click the **Numbering** arrow.

   The Numbering Library appears.

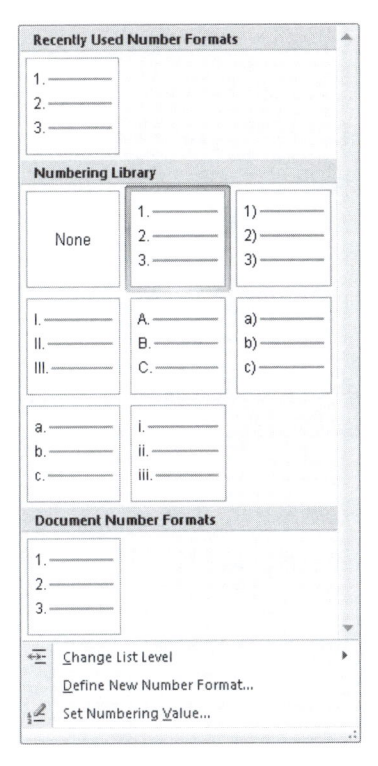

9. In the gallery, click the **A. B. C.** box.

   The numbers change to capital letters.

   Decrease Indent

10. With the numbered paragraphs still selected, in the **Paragraph** group, click the **Decrease Indent** button.

    The numbered list moves to the left margin.

    Increase Indent

11. In the **Paragraph** group, click the **Increase Indent** button to move the list back to its original indent.

    > **Tip** You can also adjust the indent level of a bulleted list by selecting its paragraphs, and on the horizontal ruler, dragging the Left Indent marker to the left or right. The First Line Indent and Hanging Indent markers move with the Left Indent marker. You can move just the Hanging Indent marker to adjust the space between the bullets and their text.

    Sort

12. Scroll the document until you can see the bulleted list under *The Hero*, select the three bulleted paragraphs, and then on the **Home** tab, in the **Paragraph** group, click the **Sort** button.

    The Sort Text dialog box opens.

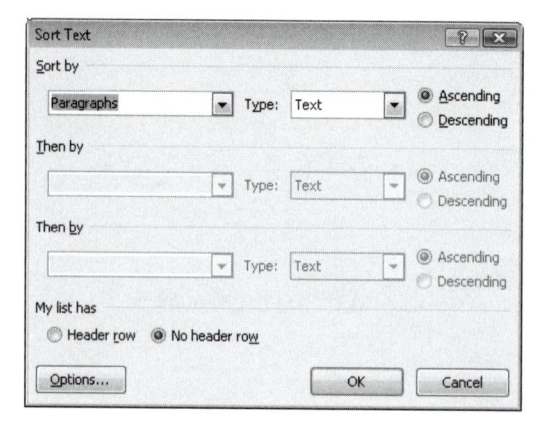

13. With the **Ascending** option selected, click **OK**.

    The order of the bulleted items changes to ascending alphabetical order.

14. Click the blank paragraph under *The Ally*, and then on the **Home** tab, in the **Paragraph** group, click the **Multilevel List** button.

    The List Library appears.

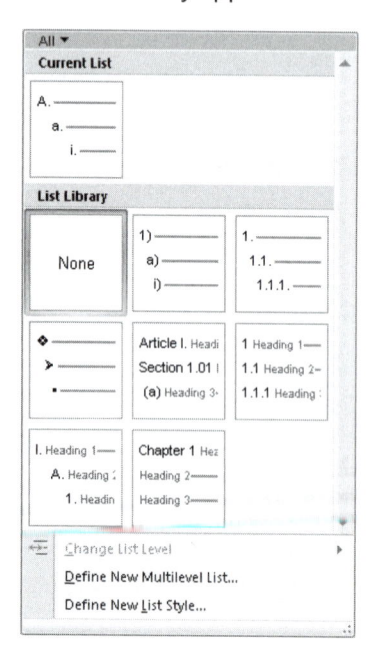

15. In the gallery, click the thumbnail under **Current List**.

    The first item in the new numbered list will have a capital letter as its numbering style.

92 Chapter 3 Changing the Look of Text

16. Type **Does not have to be human**, press `Enter`, type **Is a stabilizing force**, press `Enter`, and then press `Tab`.

    The new item is indented to the next level and assigned a different number style.

17. Type **A voice of conscience**, press `Enter`, type **Not a "yes" person**, press `Enter`, and then press `Shift`+`Tab`.

18. Type **Embodies loyalty**.

    Word takes care of all the formatting of the multilevel list.

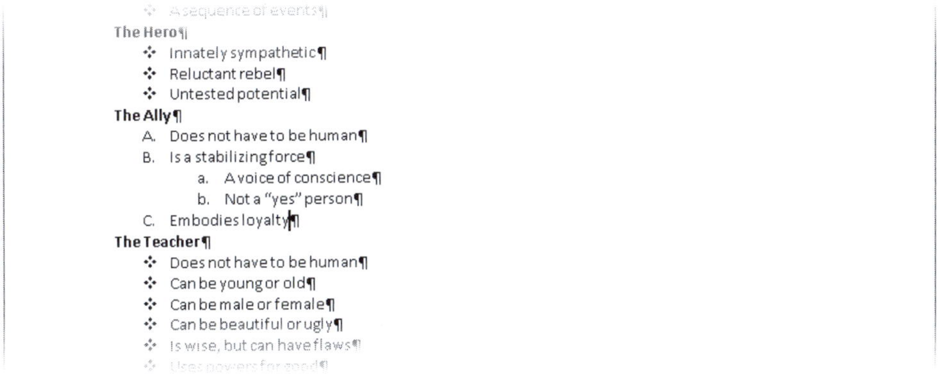

    ❖ A sequence of events¶
    The Hero¶
       ❖ Innately sympathetic¶
       ❖ Reluctant rebel¶
       ❖ Untested potential¶
    The Ally¶
       A. Does not have to be human¶
       B. Is a stabilizing force¶
          a. A voice of conscience¶
          b. Not a "yes" person¶
       C. Embodies loyalty¶
    The Teacher¶
       ❖ Does not have to be human¶
       ❖ Can be young or old¶
       ❖ Can be male or female¶
       ❖ Can be beautiful or ugly¶
       ❖ Is wise, but can have flaws¶
       ❖ Uses powers for good¶

19. Under *The Problem*, click to the left of the blank paragraph mark, type * (an asterisk), press `Tab`, type **A difficult choice**, and then press `Enter`.

    Word converts the asterisk into a bullet and formats the next paragraph as a bulleted item.

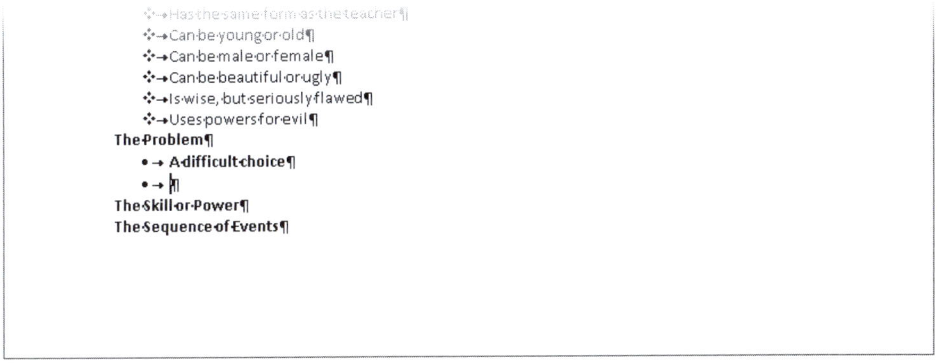

    ❖→Has the same form as the teacher¶
    ❖→Can be young or old¶
    ❖→Can be male or female¶
    ❖→Can be beautiful or ugly¶
    ❖→Is wise, but seriously flawed¶
    ❖→Uses powers for evil¶
    The Problem¶
       •→ A difficult choice¶
       •→ ¶
    The Skill or Power¶
    The Sequence of Events¶

20. Type **An injustice**, press `Enter`, and then type **A quest**.

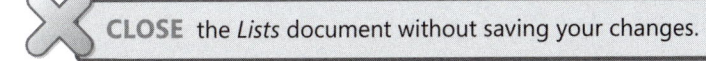

✖ **CLOSE** the *Lists* document without saving your changes.

> **Formatting Text as You Type**
>
> The Word list formatting capabilities are just one example of the program's ability to intuit how you want to format an element based on what you type. You can learn more about these and other AutoFormatting options by exploring the AutoCorrect dialog box. To open this dialog box, click the Microsoft Office Button, click Word Options, click Proofing in the left pane of the Word Options window, and then click AutoCorrect Options in the right pane.
>
> On the AutoFormat As You Type tab, you can see the options that Word implements by default, including bulleted and numbered lists. You can select and clear options to control Word's AutoFormatting behavior.
>
> One interesting option is Border Lines. When this check box is selected, you can type three consecutive hyphens (-) and press Enter to have Word draw one line across the page. Or you can type three consecutive equal signs (=) and press Enter to have Word draw a double line.

Key Points

- Quick Styles are a great way to apply combinations of formatting to give your documents a professional look.
- You can format characters with an almost limitless number of combinations of font, size, style, and effect—but for best results, resist the temptation to use more than a handful of combinations.
- You can change the look of paragraphs by varying their indentation, spacing, and alignment and by setting tab stops. Use these formatting options judiciously to create documents with a balanced, uncluttered look.
- Bulleted and numbered lists are a great way to present information in an easy to read, easy to understand format. If the built-in bulleted and numbered list styles don't provide what you need, you can define your own styles.

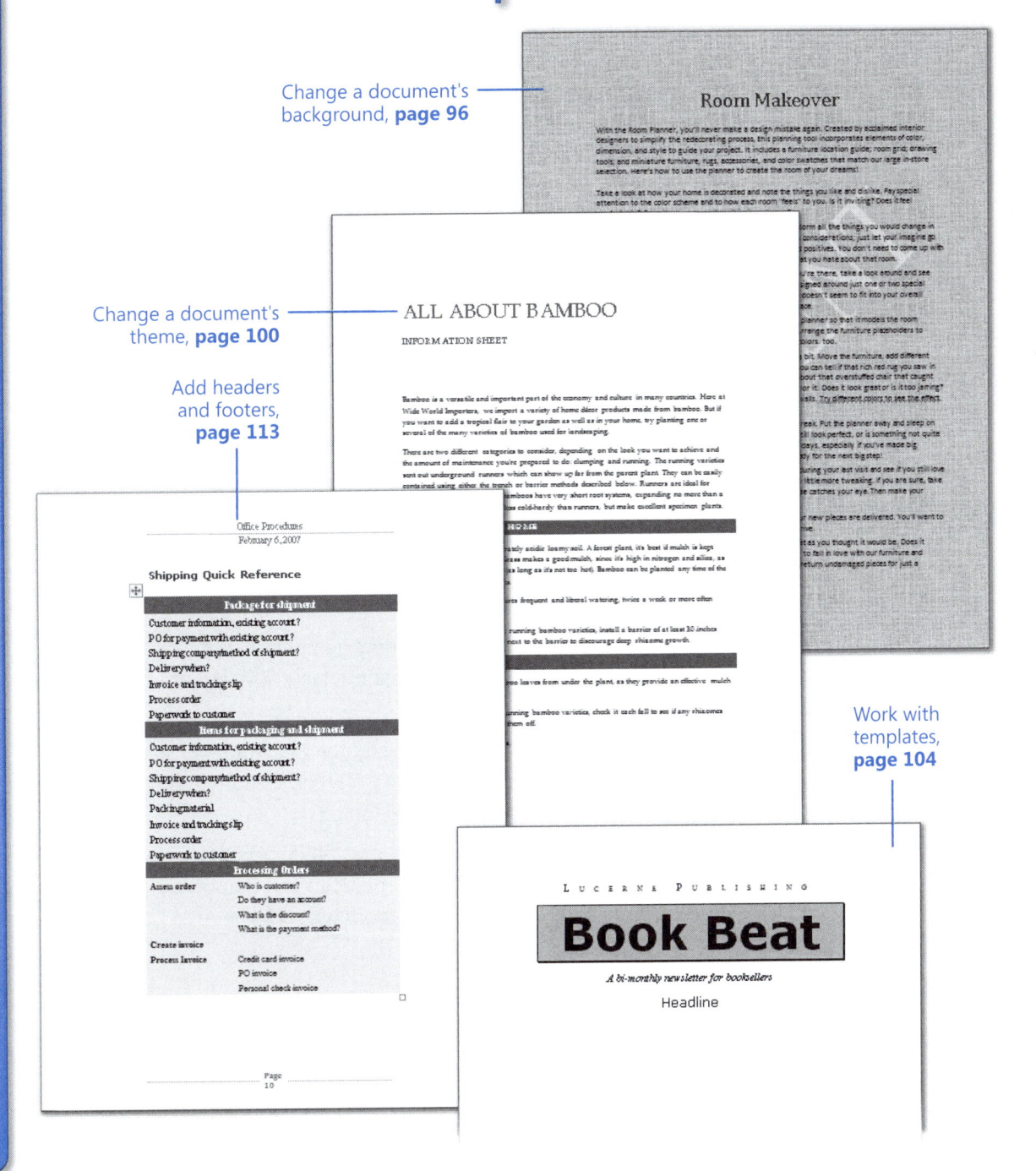

Chapter at a Glance

Change a document's background, **page 96**

Change a document's theme, **page 100**

Add headers and footers, **page 113**

Work with templates, **page 104**

4 Changing the Look of a Document

In this chapter, you will learn to:
- ✔ Change a document's background.
- ✔ Change a document's theme.
- ✔ Work with templates.
- ✔ Add headers and footers.
- ✔ Control what appears on each page.

Microsoft Office Word 2007 comes with formatting tools that you can use to ensure the consistent presentation of an entire document. To give a document a polished look, you can specify a background for its pages and a theme for its major elements. You can control the look of a document by basing it on one of the predefined business or personal templates that are installed with Word or that are available for download from the Microsoft Office Online Web site. You can also create your own templates and use them as the basis for new documents.

Word gives you control of the layout of the pages in a document that will be printed. For example, if you want the same information to be repeated on every page, you can set up the information in headers and footers. You can control how the text in the document appears on each page by specifying page and section breaks.

In this chapter, you will apply a background pattern and color, and then you'll add a text watermark. You'll apply a theme to an existing document, change the colors and the fonts, and save a custom theme. You will use a predefined Word template to create a document, modify the document, and then save it as a new template. You will also create a custom template. Finally, you will add headers and footers to a document, and you'll learn how to use page and section breaks to keep information together in logical units.

See Also Do you need only a quick refresher on the topics in this chapter? See the Quick Reference section at the beginning of this book.

Important Before you can use the practice files in this chapter, you need to install them from the book's companion CD to their default location. See "Using the Companion CD" at the beginning of this book for more information.

Troubleshooting Graphics and operating system–related instructions in this book reflect the Windows Vista user interface. If your computer is running Windows XP and you experience trouble following the instructions as written, please refer to the "Information for Readers Running Windows XP" section at the beginning of this book.

Changing a Document's Background

Whether you are creating a document that will be printed, viewed on a computer, or published on the Internet and viewed in a Web browser, you can make your document stand out by adding a background color or pattern.

See Also For information about creating documents for the Web, see "Creating and Modifying a Web Document" in Chapter 11, "Creating Documents for Use Outside of Word."

There might be times when you want words or a graphic to appear behind the text of a printed or online document. For example, you might want the word *CONFIDENTIAL* to appear faintly behind the text in a contract, or you might want a graphic to appear faintly behind the text in a press release. These faint background images are called *watermarks*. Watermarks are visible in a document, but because they are faint, they don't interfere with the readers' ability to view the document's main text.

Background colors, patterns, and watermarks are applied by clicking buttons in the Page Background group on the Page Layout tab.

In this exercise, you will apply a background color and pattern, and then you'll add a text watermark.

USE the *Background* document. This practice file is located in the *Documents\Microsoft Press\Word2007SBS\FormattingDocs* folder.
BE SURE TO start Word before beginning this exercise.
OPEN the *Background* document.

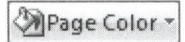

1. On the **Page Layout** tab, in the **Page Background** group, click the **Page Color** button, and then under **Theme Colors**, in the column of green boxes, click the second box from the bottom (**Olive Green, Accent 3, Lighter 60%**).

   The background of the document changes to the selected color.

2. In the **Page Background** group, click the **Page Color** button, and then click **Fill Effects**.

   The Fill Effects dialog box opens.

3. Click the **Texture** tab.

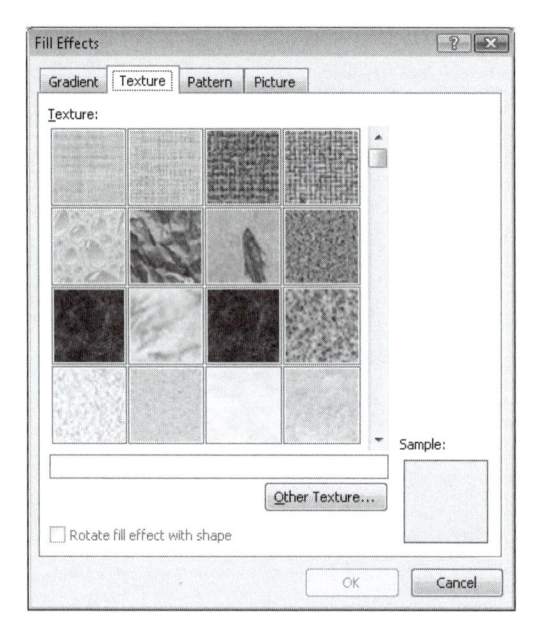

4. Click the effect in the second column of the first row, and then click **OK**.

   The background changes to display the effect rather than the color.

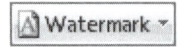

5. On the **Page Layout** tab, in the **Page Background** group, click the **Watermark** button.

   The Watermark gallery opens.

6. Scroll to the bottom of the gallery, noticing the available options.

   Clicking any of these options will insert the specified watermark in pale blue on every page of the current document.

7. Below the gallery, click **Custom Watermark**.

   The Printed Watermark dialog box opens. Notice that you can insert a picture or text as a watermark.

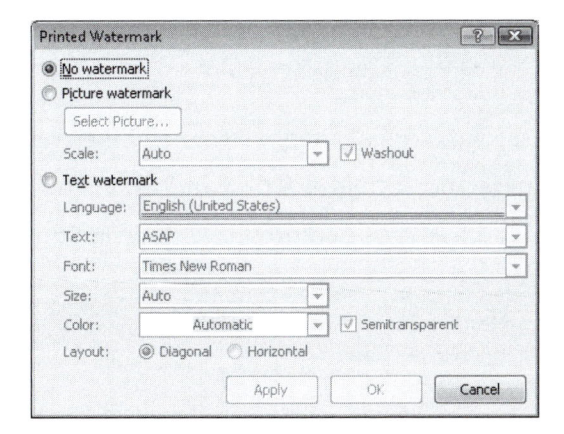

8. Click **Text watermark**, click the **Text** arrow, scroll down the list, and then click **URGENT**.

9. Click the **Color** arrow, and under **Theme Colors**, click the white box.

10. With the **Semitransparent** check box and **Diagonal** option selected, click **OK**.

    The specified text is inserted diagonally across the page.

11. At the right end of the status bar, click the **Zoom** button. Then in the **Zoom** dialog box, click **Whole Page**, and click **OK**.

    The document displays the texture and watermark you specified.

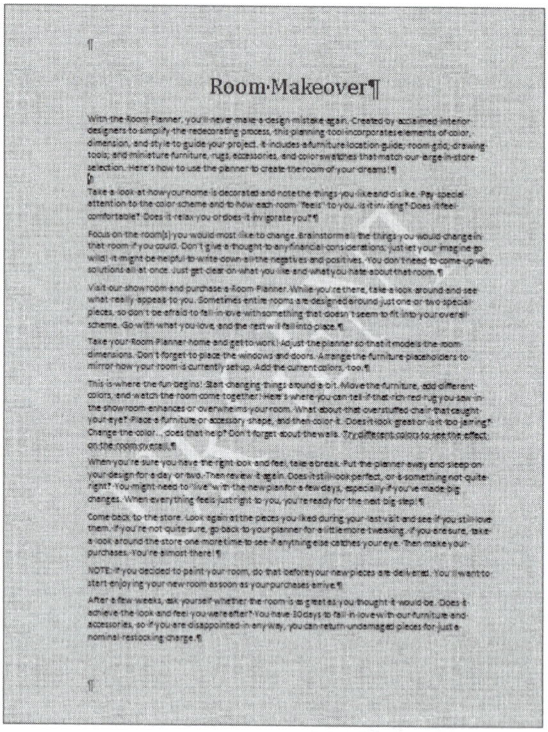

CLOSE the *Background* document without saving your changes.

> **Using a Picture as a Watermark**
>
> When you want to dress up the pages of your document without distracting attention from the main text, you might consider adding a graphic watermark.
>
> Here's how to add a graphic watermark to every page of a document:
>
> 1. On the **Page Layout** tab, in the **Page Background** group, click the **Watermark** button, and then click **Custom Watermark**.
> 2. In the **Printed Watermark** dialog box, click **Picture watermark**, and then click **Select Picture**.
> 3. In the **Insert Picture** dialog box, navigate to the folder where the picture you want to use is stored, and double-click the name of the picture.
> 4. Click the **Scale** arrow, and choose how big or small you want the watermark picture to appear in the document.
> 5. For a more vibrant picture, clear the **Washout** check box.
> 6. Click **OK**.
>
>   The picture is inserted as a watermark at the size you specified.

Changing a Document's Theme

You can enhance the look of a document by applying one of Word's pre-defined themes. A *theme* is a combination of colors, fonts, and effects that project a certain feeling or tone. For example, the Flow theme uses a palette of blues and greens, the Calabri and Constantia fonts, and understated effects.

You apply a theme to the entire document by clicking the Themes button in the Themes group on the Page Layout tab, and then making a selection from the Themes gallery. If you like the colors of one theme and the fonts of another, you can mix and match theme elements. First find the theme that most closely resembles the look you want, and then in the Themes group, change the colors by clicking the Theme Colors button or the fonts by clicking the Theme Fonts button.

If you create a combination of colors and fonts that you would like to be able to use with other documents, you can save the combination as a new theme. By saving the theme in the default *Document Themes* folder, you make the theme available in the Themes

gallery. However, you don't have to store custom themes in the *Document Themes* folder; you can store them anywhere on your hard disk, on removable media, or in a network location. To use a theme that is stored in a different location, you can click the Themes button, and then click Browse For Themes at the bottom of the gallery. Locate the theme you want in the Choose Theme Or Themed Document dialog box, and then click Open to apply that theme to the current document.

> **Tip** Click Search Office Online at the bottom of the Themes gallery to display the Templates page of the Microsoft Office Online Web site, where you can find more information about themes and download themes and templates created by other people.

In this exercise, you'll apply a theme to an existing document and then change the colors and the fonts. You will then save the custom theme.

> **USE** the *Theme* document. This practice file is located in the *Documents\Microsoft Press\Word2007SBS\FormattingDocs* folder.
> **OPEN** the *Theme* document.

1. On the **Page Layout** tab, in the **Themes** group, click the **Themes** button.

   The Themes gallery opens.

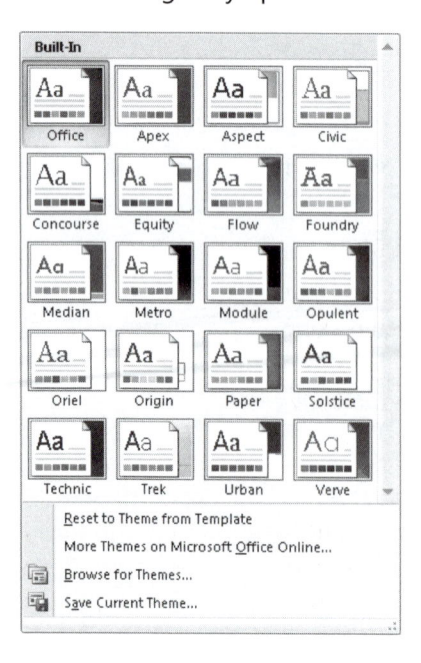

102 Chapter 4 Changing the Look of a Document

2. Point to each thumbnail in turn to display a live preview of the theme.
3. In the **Themes** gallery, click **Aspect**.

    The colors and fonts change to those defined for the selected theme.

Theme Colors

4. In the **Themes** group, click the **Theme Colors** button.

    The Theme Colors gallery opens. The currently selected colors have a border around them.

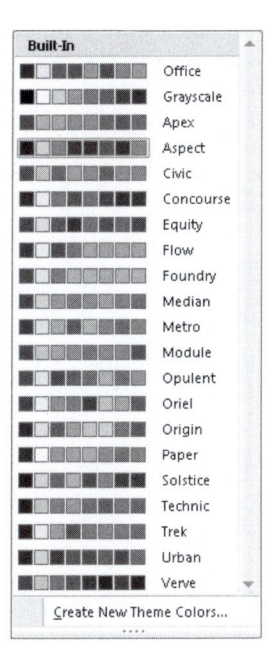

    Built-In
    - Office
    - Grayscale
    - Apex
    - Aspect
    - Civic
    - Concourse
    - Equity
    - Flow
    - Foundry
    - Median
    - Metro
    - Module
    - Opulent
    - Oriel
    - Origin
    - Paper
    - Solstice
    - Technic
    - Trek
    - Urban
    - Verve

    Create New Theme Colors...

5. Display a live preview of any set of colors that interests you, and then in the gallery, click **Opulent**.

    The Opulent colors replace the Aspect colors, but nothing else in the document changes.

Theme Fonts

6. In the **Themes** group, click the **Theme Fonts** button.

    The Theme Fonts gallery opens. The currently selected fonts are highlighted. Each built-in option includes a set of two fonts—the first is used for headings and the second for text.

Built-In

Aa	**Office** Cambria Calibri
Aa	**Office 2** Calibri Cambria
Aa	**Office Classic** Arial Times New Roman
Aa	**Office Classic 2** Arial Arial
Aa	**Apex** Lucida Sans Book Antiqua
Aa	**Aspect** Verdana Verdana
Aa	**Civic** Georgia Georgia

Create New Theme Fonts...

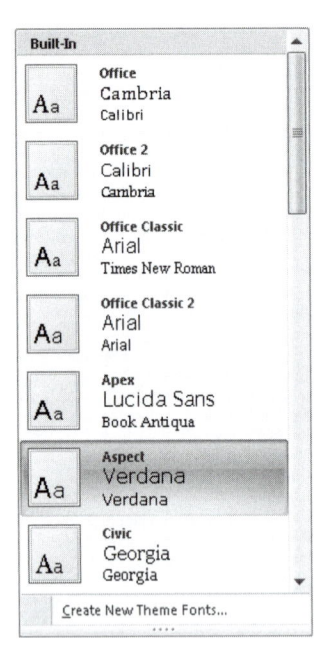

7. Display a live preview of any set of fonts that interests you, and then in the gallery, click **Apex**.

The Apex fonts replace the Aspect fonts, but the colors remain the same.

8. In the **Themes** group, click the **Themes** button, and then below the gallery, click **Save Current Theme**.

The Save Current Theme dialog box opens, displaying the *Document Themes* folder in the Address bar. This dialog box resembles the Save As dialog box. The *Document Themes* folder is the default location for saving any new themes you create.

9. In the **File name** box, replace the suggested name with My Theme, and then click **Save**.

10. In the **Themes** group, click the **Themes** button to display the gallery.

Your new theme appears at the top of the gallery, under Custom. You can now apply this theme to any document.

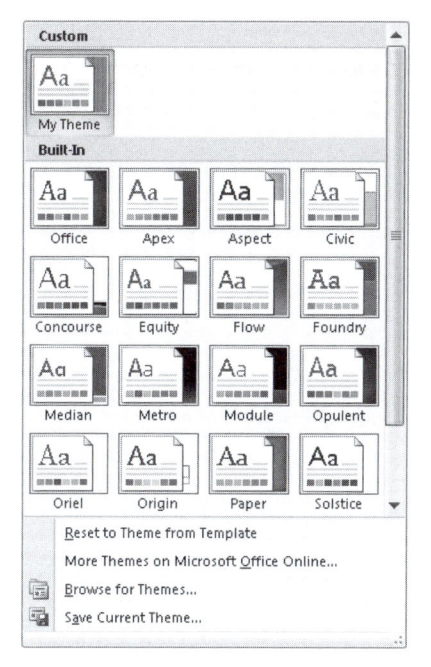

11. Press [Esc] to close the gallery without making a selection.

CLOSE the *Theme* document without saving your changes.

Working with Templates

When you want to quickly create an effective, visually attractive document, one of the most efficient methods is to leverage the design work of other people. With Word 2007, you have access to many ready made, professionally designed templates. A *template* is a file that stores text, character and paragraph styles, page formatting, and elements such as graphics for use as a pattern in creating other documents.

Unless you specify otherwise, all new documents are based on the Normal document template, which defines a few fairly plain styles, such as paragraph styles for regular text paragraphs, a title, and different levels of headings; and a few character styles that change the look of selected text. The styles from the Normal template appear in the

Styles gallery on the Home tab when you create a new blank document. If you create a document based on a different template, the styles defined in that template appear in the Styles gallery, and you can apply those styles to quickly format the text in the document.

> **Tip** Templates are stored with the .dotx file name extension.

See Also For more information about applying styles, see "Quickly Formatting Text and Paragraphs" in Chapter 3, "Changing the Look of Text."

In addition to the Normal document template, Word comes with a variety of templates for a variety of documents. To create a document based on one of these templates, you start by displaying the New Document window. Then in the left pane, under Templates, you click Installed Templates, and in the list that appears in the center pane, you click the template you want.

If none of the built-in templates meets your needs, you can look for templates on the Office Online Web site. To create a document based on one of these templates, you start by displaying the New Document window. Then in the left pane, under Microsoft Office Online, you click a category (such as Brochures or Newsletters), and in the list that appears in the center pane, you click first the subcategory and then the template you want.

Templates such as Normal contain only formatting information, which in addition to styles can include backgrounds, themes, and so on. These types of templates define the look of the document, and you add your own content. Templates can also contain content that you customize for your own purposes. For example, if you base a new document on a form template from Microsoft Office Online, the text of the form is already in place, and all you have to do is customize it for your organization.

Sometimes, a document based on a Word template displays formatted placeholders surrounded by square brackets—for example, *[Company Name]*. You replace a placeholder with your own text by clicking it and then typing the replacement. If you don't need a placeholder, you simply delete it. After you have entered all the text you need for the document, you save it in the usual way.

The changes you have made affect the document, not the template it is based on, which remains available to help create other documents.

In addition to using the templates that come with Word or that you download from Office Online, you can create your own templates. If you routinely create the same type of document, such as a monthly financial report, you can create and format the document once and then save it as a template on which to base future versions of that type of document. You can save your new template with text in it, which is handy if you create many documents with only slight variations. Or you can delete the text so that a document based on it will open as a new, blank document with the styles already defined and ready to apply to whatever content you enter.

> **Tip** If the designation *(Compatibility Mode)* appears in the title bar when you create a document based on a template, it indicates that the template was created in an earlier version of Word. Usually this will have no effect on your use of the template, but bear in mind that sometimes compatibility can have an impact on functionality.

To save even more time, you can create a document based on one of the Word templates, modify it—for example, by adding your own name and address—and then save the document as a new template with a different name. The next time you need to create this type of document, you can use your modified version of the template instead of the one provided by Word.

In this exercise, you will create a new template based on a predefined Word template, and then you'll create a new document based on the custom template. You will also convert a document to a template, and you'll modify the template by creating a new style. Finally, you'll create a document based on the template, and you'll apply the new style.

> **USE** the *Template* document. This practice file is located in the *Documents\Microsoft Press\Word2007SBS\FormattingDocs* folder.
> **BE SURE TO** close all open documents before beginning this exercise.

1. Click the **Microsoft Office Button**, click **New**, and then under **Templates** in the **New Document** window, click **Installed Templates**.

   The center pane of the New Document window displays thumbnails of the installed templates.

Working with Templates   **107**

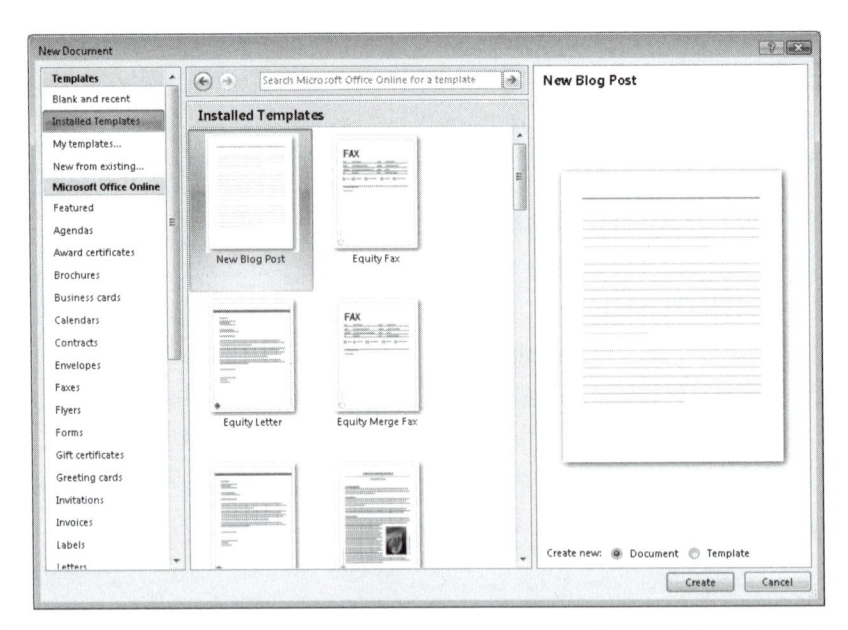

[Screenshot of the New Document dialog showing Installed Templates including New Blog Post, Equity Fax, Equity Letter, and Equity Merge Fax, with a preview of New Blog Post on the right.]

2. In the center pane, scroll the **Installed Templates** list, and double-click the **Oriel Fax** template.

Word opens a new fax cover document based on the selected template, with placeholders for the text you need to supply.

[Screenshot of a fax cover document template with placeholders: [Pick the date], TO: [TYPE THE RECIPIENT NAME], FAX: [Type the recipient fax number], PHONE: [Type the recipient phone number], FROM: Judy Lew, FAX: [Type the sender fax number], PHONE: [Type the sender phone number], PAGES: [Type the number of pages], RE: [Type text], CC: [Type text], COMMENTS: [Type comments]. A vertical "FAX" banner appears on the right side with [Type the sender company name] [Type the company address].]

3. On the right side of the page, click the **[company name]** placeholder, and type Lucerne Publishing.

4. Click the **[address]** placeholder, type 4567 Oak Street, Seattle, WA 70110.

5. Scroll the page, click the **[phone number]** placeholder, type (505) 555-0145, and then click outside the placeholder.

6. Under **Judy Lew**, click the **[fax number]** placeholder, and then type (505) 555-0146.

7. Click the **[phone number]** placeholder, and then type (505) 555-0145.

8. On the right side of the page, click **Lucerne Publishing**, drag across it to select it, and then on the **Home** tab, in the **Styles** group, click the **Strong** style.

9. In turn, select the address and phone number, and apply the **Emphasis** style.

10. Click the **Microsoft Office Button**, and then click **Save As**.

    The Save As dialog box opens.

11. In the **File name** box, type My Fax Template.

12. Click the **Save as type** arrow, and then in the list, click **Word Template**.

    > **Tip** If you want users who have older versions of Word to be able to use the template, click Word 97-2003 Template instead.

13. In the **Navigation Pane**, click **Templates**.

    Word displays your *Templates* folder.

    > **Troubleshooting** Word expects templates to be stored in your default *Templates* folder. If you do not store the templates you create in this folder, Word will not display them in your My Templates list.

    See Also For information about changing default file locations, see "Changing Default Program Options" in Chapter 12, "Customizing Word."

14. Click **Save**, and then close the template.

15. Display the **New Document** window, and under **Templates**, click **My templates**.

    The New dialog box opens.

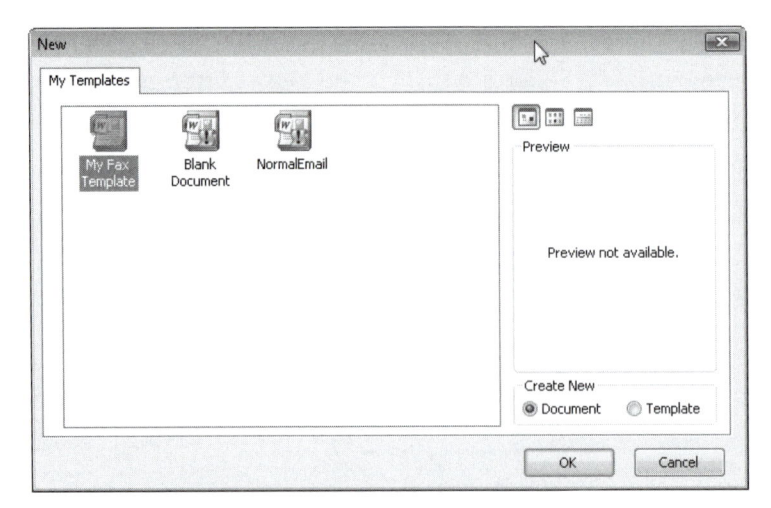

16. On the **My Templates** tab, check that **My Fax Template** is highlighted, and then with the **Document** option selected in the **Create New** area, click **OK**.

    Word opens a new document based on the Lucerne Publishing fax cover template. The name on the From line is the name of your Windows user account.

17. Customize the fax cover page in any way you want, save it in the *FormattingDocs* folder with the name My Fax, and then close the document.

> **Troubleshooting** Be sure to navigate to the *Documents\Microsoft Press\Word2007SBS\FormattingDocs* folder before clicking Save.

18. Click the **Microsoft Office Button**, click **Open**, and then open the *Template* document from the *FormattingDocs* folder.

19. Display the **Save As** dialog box, and in the **File name** box, type My Newsletter. Change the **Save as type** setting to **Word Template**, change the save location to the **Templates** folder, and then click **Save**.

    Word saves the document as a template.

110 Chapter 4 Changing the Look of a Document

▭ More

20. Click anywhere in the *Author Meet and Greet Update* heading, and then on the **Home** tab, in the **Styles** group, click the **More** button, and below the gallery, click **Save Selection as a New Quick Style**.

    The Create New Style From Formatting dialog box opens. Notice that the style in the Paragraph Style Preview box reflects the formatting of the paragraph containing the insertion point.

21. In the **Name** box, replace **Style1** with Headline, and then click **Modify**.

    The dialog box expands to display options for modifying the new style.

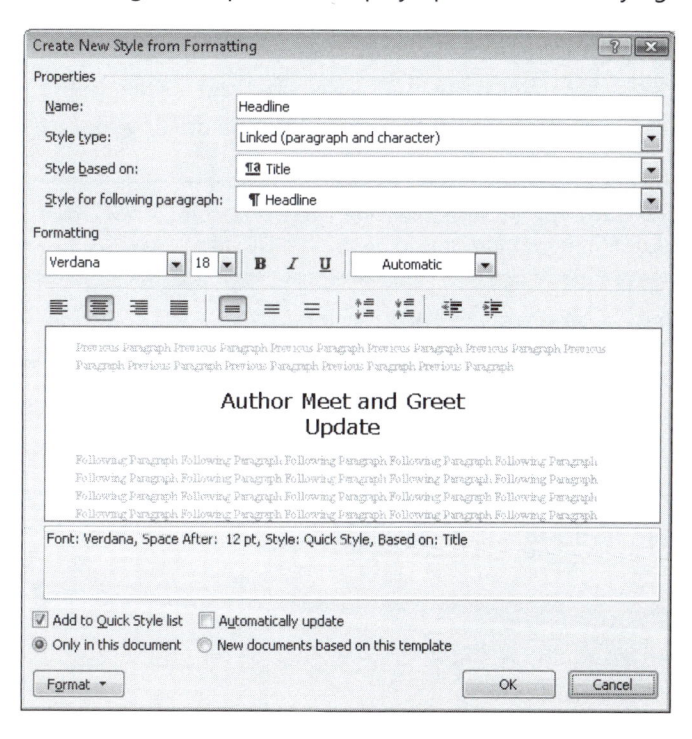

22. At the bottom of the expanded dialog box, click **New documents based on this template**, and then click **OK**.
23. Back in the template, replace **Author Meet and Greet Update** with Headline, and then select all the text below the headline paragraph and press Backspace.
24. On the **Quick Access Toolbar**, click the **Save** button, and then close the template.

Save

25. Display the **New Document** window, click **My templates**, and from the **New** dialog box, create a new document based on the **My Newsletter** template.

   Word opens a new document with the template's title and headline already in place. First you need to customize the headline.

26. Select the word **Headline**, and type Fantasy Author Starts Book Tour.

   You can then add the text of the newsletter below the headline.

   L U C E R N E   P U B L I S H I N G

   Book Beat

   A bi-monthly newsletter for booksellers

   Fantasy Author Starts Book Tour

CLOSE the document without saving your changes.

> **Tip** If you want to change an existing template, you can open the template by displaying the Open dialog box, setting the file type to Word Templates, navigating to your *Templates* folder, and double-clicking the template.

Applying a Different Template to an Existing Document

A quick and easy way to change the look of an existing document is to apply a new template to it. For this to work smoothly, the new template must use the same paragraph and character style names as the existing template. For example, if the existing template uses the name Heading 1 for top-level headings, the new template must also use the name Heading 1. If the style names do not match, you can still apply a new template to a document and then use the Styles task pane to find all instances of each particular style and replace them with one of the new template's corresponding styles.

To apply a new template to an open document:

1. Click the **Microsoft Office Button**, click **Word Options**, and in the left pane, click **Add-Ins**.
2. At the bottom of the right pane, click the **Manage** arrow, and in the list, click **Templates**. Then click **Go**.

    The Templates And Add-ins dialog box opens.
3. In the **Document Template** area, click **Attach**.

    The Attach Template dialog box opens.
4. Locate and double-click the template you want to attach.
5. In the **Templates and Add-ins** dialog box, select the **Automatically update document styles** check box, and then click **OK**.

    The new template is attached and the styles used in the document change to reflect their definitions in the new template.

To replace all instances of one style with another style:

1. On the **Home** tab, in the **Styles** group, click the **Styles** dialog box launcher.
2. In the **Styles** list, point to a style you want to replace, click the arrow that appears, and then click **Select All Instance(s)**.

    Word selects all the text to which that style has been applied.
3. In the **Styles** list, click the style you want to apply.
4. Repeat steps 2 and 3 for each style that needs to be replaced.

Adding Headers and Footers

You can display page numbers and other information on every page of your document by creating *headers* and *footers*—regions at the top and bottom of a page that can be created and formatted independently. You can have a different header and footer on the first page of a document, and you can have different headers and footers on odd and even pages.

> **Tip** If your document contains section breaks, each successive section inherits the headers and footers of the preceding section unless you break the link between the two sections. You can then create a different header and footer for the current section. For information about sections, see "Controlling What Appears on Each Page" later in this chapter.

When you create a header or footer, you can select the style you want from a gallery. Word applies the specified style to the document, indicates the header and footer areas by displaying dotted borders, and displays a contextual Design tab on the Ribbon. You can enter information in the header and footer areas the same way you enter ordinary text. You can use the buttons on the Design tab to enter and format items such as page numbers and to move from one header or footer to another.

In this exercise, you will add a header and footer to a document. You will then create a different header and footer for the first page.

> **USE** the *Header* document. This practice file is located in the *Documents\Microsoft Press\Word2007SBS\FormattingDocs* folder.
> **OPEN** the *Header* document.

1. With the insertion point at the beginning of the document, on the **Insert** tab, in the **Header & Footer** group, click the **Header** button.

   The Header gallery opens.

114 Chapter 4 Changing the Look of a Document

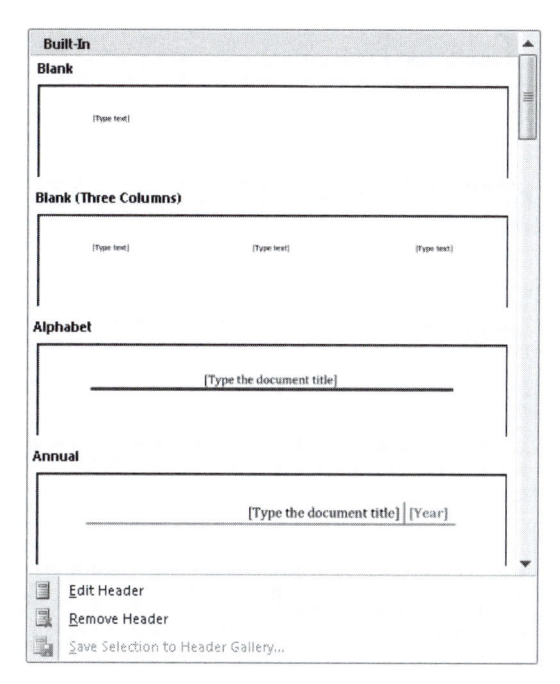

2. Scroll through the gallery, noticing the variety of headers that are available, and then click **Motion (Even Page)**.

   Word displays a Header & Footer Tools contextual tab called *Design* on the Ribbon. It dims the text of the document, outlines the header area at the top of the first page, and adds the formatting defined for this header to the document.

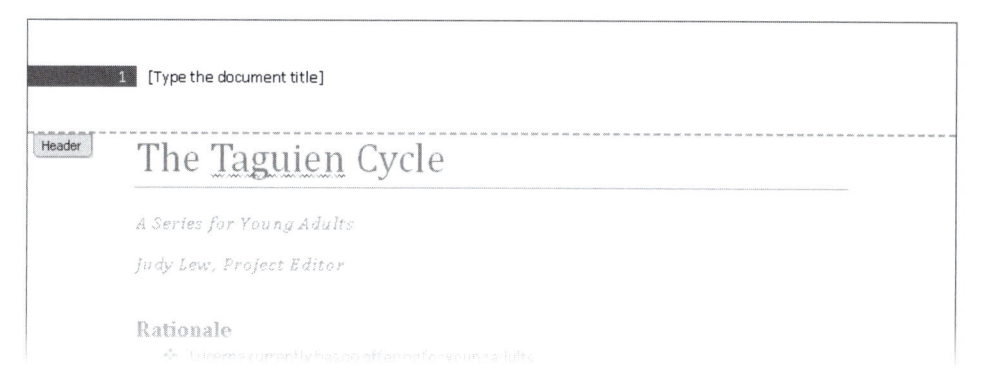

3. On the **Design** tab, in the **Options** group, click the **Different First Page** check box.

   Word replaces the header area with an area labeled *First Page Header*.

4. On the **Design** tab, in the **Navigation** group, click the **Next Section** button.

   Word moves to page 2 of the document, which still has the original header.

5. In the header, click the **[Type the document title]** placeholder, and then type **The Taguien Cycle**.

> **Tip** While the header or footer is active, you can edit and format its content just as you would ordinary text.

6. On the **Design** tab, in the **Navigation** group, click the **Go to Footer** button.

   Word displays the footer area at the bottom of the page.

7. In the **Header & Footer** group, click the **Footer** button, and then in the **Footer** gallery, click **Motion (Even Page)**.

   Because the page number and document name are included in the header, you want only the date to appear in the footer.

8. Click the **Pick the date** placeholder, click the arrow to the right, and then in the date navigator, click today's date.

   Word inserts the current date in the footer on page 2.

9. In the **Navigation** group, click the **Previous Section** button.

   Although you specified that page 1 should be different, you do want the footer with the date to appear on this page.

10. In the **Header & Footer** group, click the **Footer** button, and then click **Motion (Even Page)** in the gallery.

    The date is now shown on page 1.

11. On the **Design** tab, in the **Close** group, click the **Close Header and Footer** button.

12. At the right end of the status bar, click the **Zoom** button. In the **Zoom** dialog box, click **Whole page**, and then click **OK** to display the header and footer at the same time.

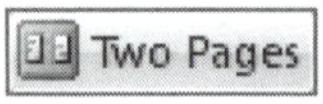

13. On the **View** tab, in the **Zoom** group, click the **Two Pages** button to display the headers and footers on both pages.

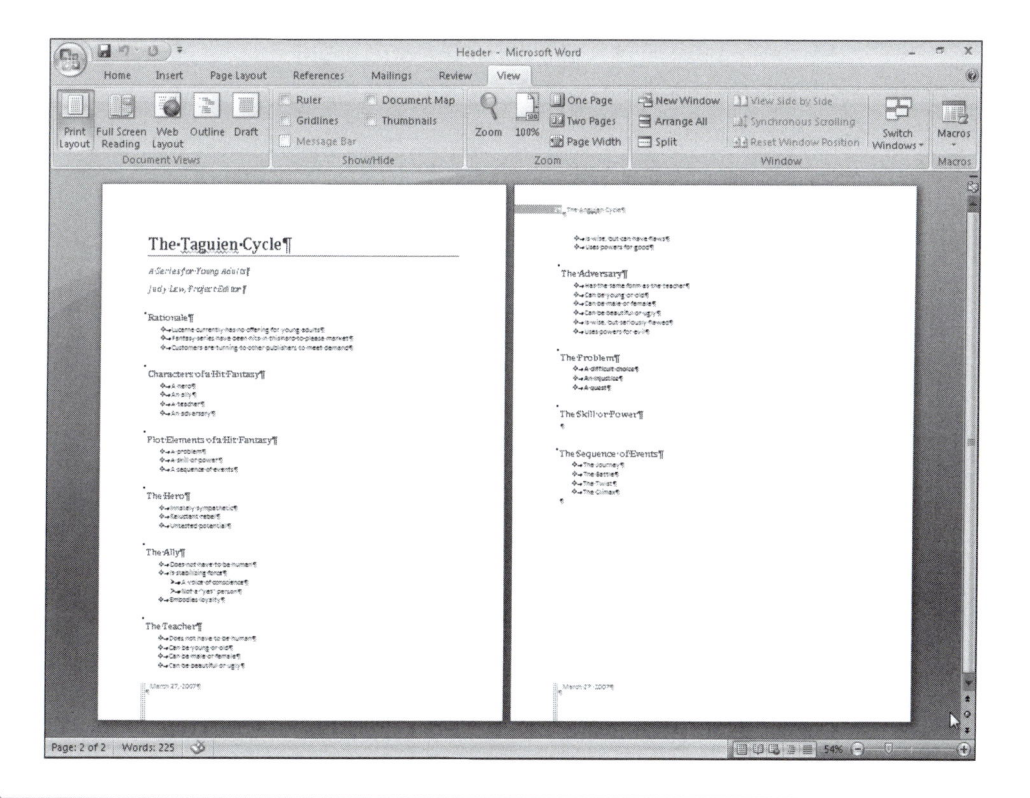

CLOSE the *Header* document without saving your changes.

Controlling What Appears on Each Page

When you add more content than will fit within the document's top and bottom margins, Word creates a new page by inserting a soft page break. A *soft page break* produces separate pages in Print Layout view and is displayed as a dotted line in Draft view.

If you want to control how pages break, you can insert a manual page break in one of three ways:

- Click Page Break in the Pages group on the Insert tab.
- Click Breaks in the Page Setup group on the Page Layout tab, and then click Page.
- Press Ctrl+Enter.

A *manual page break* produces separate pages in Print Layout view, and appears as a dotted line with the words *Page Break* in the middle in Draft view.

> ### Inserting and Formatting Page Numbers
>
> If the only information you want to appear in a header or footer is the page number, you can insert it by clicking the Page Number button in the Header & Footer group on the Insert tab. In the Page Number gallery, you can select a page number that is positioned at the top or bottom of the page and aligned in various ways with formatting that ranges from simple to fairly fancy. You can also position the page number in the margin at the side of the page.
>
> If you want to change the style of existing page numbers, you can do so by clicking the Page Number button again and making a different selection from the Top Of Page, Bottom Of Page, or Page Margins options.
>
> If you want to use a numbering scheme other than Arabic numerals, number pages by chapter, or control the starting number, you can do so by following these steps:
>
> 1. On the **Insert** tab, in the **Header & Footer** group, click the **Page Number** button, and then click **Format Page Numbers**.
>
>   The Page Number Format dialog box opens.
>
> 2. Click the **Number format** arrow, and then in the list, click the number format you want.
>
> 3. Select any other options you want to apply, and then click **OK**.

> **Tip** As you edit the text in a document, Word changes the location of the soft page breaks but not of any manual page breaks you might have inserted.

You can control whether page breaks leave widows and orphans—individual lines that appear on a different page from their paragraphs. A *widow* is the last line of a paragraph at the top of a page, and an *orphan* as the first line of a paragraph at the bottom of a page. These single lines of text can make a document hard to read, so by default Word specifies a two-line minimum. You can change the following options on the Line And Page Breaks tab of the Paragraph dialog box displayed when you click the Paragraph dialog box launcher:

- **Widow/Orphan Control.** This option controls whether Word will break a page with the last line of a paragraph by itself at the top of a page or the first line of a paragraph by itself at the bottom of a page. This option is turned on by default for all new documents.

- **Keep With Next.** This option controls whether Word will break a page between the selected paragraph and the following paragraph.
- **Keep Lines Together.** This option controls whether Word will break a page within a paragraph.
- **Page Break Before.** This option controls whether Word will break a page before the selected paragraph.

> **Tip** You can apply the options in the Paragraph dialog box to individual paragraphs, or you can incorporate them into the styles you define for document elements such as headings. For more information about styles, see "Working with Templates" earlier in this chapter.

In addition to page breaks, you can insert section breaks in your documents. A *section break* identifies a part of the document to which you can apply page settings, such as orientation or margins, that are different from those of the rest of the document. For example, you might want to turn a large table sideways.

You insert a section break by clicking Breaks in the Page Setup group on the Page Layout tab. The following types of section breaks are available:

- **Next Page.** This break starts the following section on the next page.
- **Continuous.** This break creates a new section without affecting page breaks.
- **Even Page.** This break starts the following section on the next even-numbered page.
- **Odd Page.** This break starts the following section on the next odd-numbered page.

A section break is not displayed in Print Layout view unless non-printing characters are turned on, in which case it appears as a double-dotted line from the preceding paragraph mark to the margin. In Draft view, a section break appears as a double-dotted line across the page. In both cases, the words *Section Break* and the type of section break appear in the middle of the line.

> **Tip** To remove a page or section break, click to the left of the break and then press the Delete key.

In this exercise, you will insert page and section breaks, and ensure that the pages break in logical places.

> **USE** the *ControllingPage* document. This practice file is located in the *Documents\Microsoft Press\Word2007SBS\FormattingDocs* folder.
> **OPEN** the *ControllingPage* document.

Controlling What Appears on Each Page   119

1. Scroll through the document, noticing any awkward page breaks, such as a section or list that starts close to the bottom of a page.

2. On the **Home** tab, in the **Editing** group, click the **Select** button, and then click **Select All**.

3. Click the **Paragraph** dialog box launcher, and then in the **Paragraph** dialog box, click the **Line and Page Breaks** tab.

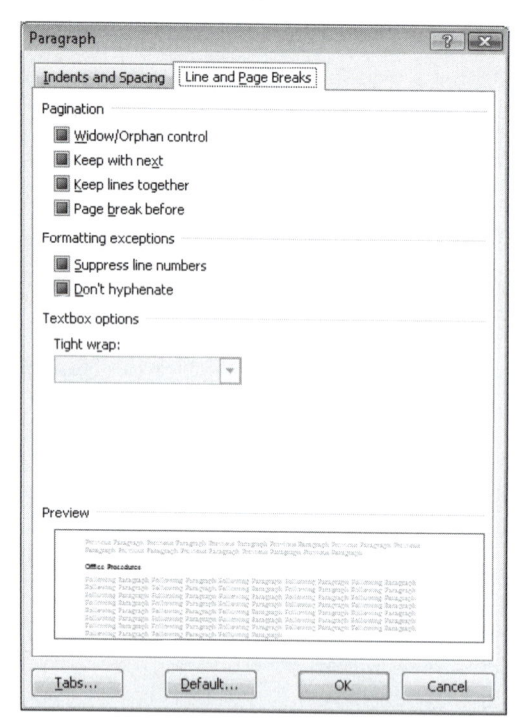

Dialog Box Launcher

4. Select the **Widow/Orphan control** and **Keep lines together** check boxes.

5. Clear all the other check boxes by clicking them twice, and then click **OK**.

   These settings ensure that all the lines of text in each paragraph appear on the same page.

6. Scroll the document, and click to the left of the *Facilities* heading.

7. On the **Insert** tab, in the **Pages** group, click the **Page Break** button.

   Word breaks the page and moves the *Facilities* heading and the following text to the next page.

8. Scroll down the document, select the **To use the intercom from the office** heading and the following two steps, and then on the **Home** tab, click the **Paragraph** dialog box launcher.

9. On the **Line and Page Breaks** tab of the **Paragraph** dialog box, select the **Keep with next** check box, and then click **OK**.

   Word moves the procedure to the next page.

10. Click to the left of the *Shipping Quick Reference* heading toward the end of the document.

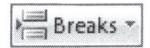

11. On the **Page Layout** tab, in the **Page Setup** group, click the **Breaks** button, and then under **Section Breaks**, click **Next Page**.

    A double dotted line with the words *Section Break (Next Page)* appears on the page before the section break.

12. Click anywhere in the heading of the newly defined section, and on the **Page Layout** tab, in the **Page Setup** group, click the **Margins** button. Then in the **Margins** gallery, click **Wide**.

    The text in the new section moves to the right between margins that are wider than the rest of the document.

13. On the **Insert** tab, in the **Header & Footer** group, click the **Header** button, and then click **Edit Header**.

    Because the Link To Previous and Different First Page options are turned on, the header for the first page of the new section is the same as the first page of the document.

14. On the **Design** tab, in the **Options** group, clear the **Different First Page** check box.

    Now the Link To Previous option causes the header text from pages 2 through 9 of the document to be repeated for this section.

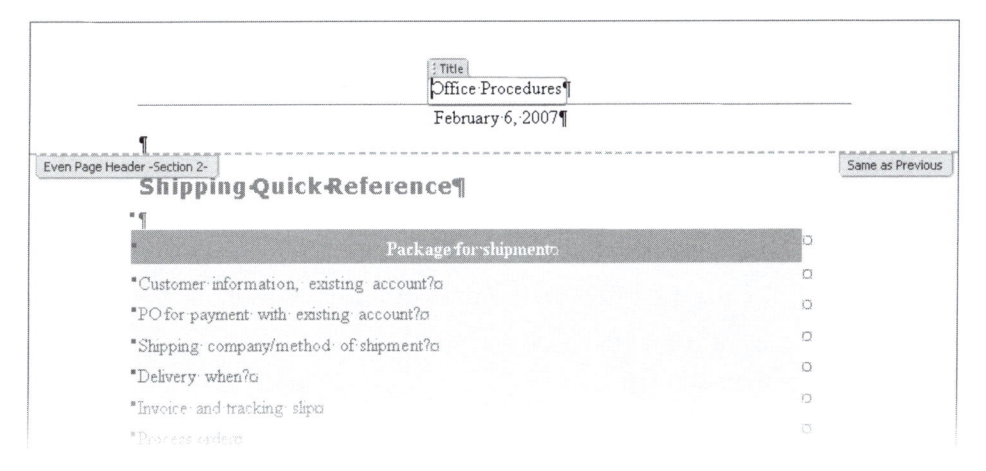

CLOSE the *ControllingPage* document without saving your changes.

Key Points

- A background color or pattern can really give a document pizzazz, but be careful that it doesn't overwhelm the text. The same is true for text or picture watermarks.
- The same document can look and feel very different depending on the theme applied to it. Colors, fonts, and effects can be combined to create just the look you want.
- Take the effort out of creating sophisticated documents by using one of Word's predefined templates as a starting point. You can also create your own templates.
- Headers and footers provide useful information and add a professional touch to any document that is longer than one page.
- You can control which elements should be kept together on a page, and you can divide a document into sections, each with its own margins and formatting.

Chapter at a Glance

Present information in columns, **page 124**

Present information in a table, **page 130**

Perform calculations in a table, **page 142**

Use a table to control page layout, **page 150**

5 Presenting Information in Columns and Tables

In this chapter, you will learn to:
- ✔ Present information in columns.
- ✔ Create a tabular list.
- ✔ Present information in a table.
- ✔ Format table information.
- ✔ Perform calculations in a table.
- ✔ Use a table to control page layout.

When creating a Microsoft Office Word 2007 document, you might find it useful to organize certain information into columns or tables. Flowing text in multiple columns is common practice in newsletters, flyers, and brochures. After you specify the number of columns, Word flows the text from one column to the next. You can also manually end one column and move subsequent text to the next column.

It is often more efficient to present numeric data in a table than to explain it in a paragraph of text. Tables make the data easier to read and understand. Small amounts of data can be displayed in simple columns separated by left, right, centered, or decimal tab stops to create a tabular list. Larger amounts or more complex data is better presented in a Word table that includes a structure of rows and columns, frequently with row and column headings.

A Word table is useful not only for presenting data but also for providing the structure for complex document layouts. For example, you can set up a table with two columns and two rows to present a set of four paragraphs, four bulleted lists, or four tables in a format in which they can be easily compared.

In this chapter, you will create and modify columns of text, create a simple tabular list, create tables from scratch and from existing text, format a table in various ways, and perform calculations within a table. You will copy and paste worksheet data, link to worksheet data, and create a Microsoft Office Excel object. And finally, you will create a table for the purpose of displaying two other tables side by side.

See Also Do you need only a quick refresher on the topics in this chapter? See the Quick Reference section at the beginning of this book.

> **Important** Before you can use the practice files in this chapter, you need to install them from the book's companion CD to their default location. See "Using the Companion CD" at the beginning of this book for more information.

> **Troubleshooting** Graphics and operating system–related instructions in this book reflect the Windows Vista user interface. If your computer is running Windows XP and you experience trouble following the instructions as written, please refer to the "Information for Readers Running Windows XP" section at the beginning of this book.

Presenting Information in Columns

By default, Word displays text in one *column*, but you can specify that text be displayed in two, three, or more columns to create layouts like those used in newspapers and magazines. When you format text to *flow* in columns, the text fills the first column and then moves to the top of the next column. You can insert a *column break* to move to the next column before the current column is full.

Word provides several standard options for dividing text into columns. You have the choice of one, two, or three equal columns, or two other two-column formats: one with a narrow left column and the other with a narrow right column. No matter how you set up the columns initially, you can change the layout or column widths at any time.

You can format the text in columns the same way you would any text. If you *justify* the columns for a neater look, you might want to have Word hyphenate the text to ensure that there are no large gaps between words.

In this exercise, you will divide part of a document into three columns. You will then justify the columns, change the column spacing, hyphenate the text, and indent a couple of paragraphs. You'll also break a column at a specific location instead of allowing the text to flow naturally from one column to the next.

USE the *Columns* document. This practice file is located in the *Documents\Microsoft Press\Word2007SBS\CreatingTables* folder.

BE SURE TO start Word and display the rulers and non-printing characters before starting this exercise.

OPEN the *Columns* document.

1. Click just to the left of the paragraph that begins *Take a look* (do not click in the selection area). Then scroll the end of the document into view, hold down the Shift key, and click just to the right of the period after *credit cards*.

   Word selects the text from the *Take a look* paragraph through the end of the document.

   Tip If you want to format an entire document with the same number of columns, you can simply click anywhere in the document—you don't have to select the text.

2. On the **Page Layout** tab, in the **Page Setup** group, click the **Columns** button, and then click **Three**.

3. Press Ctrl+Home to move to the top of the document.

   Word has inserted a section break above the selection and formatted the text after the section break into three columns.

See Also For information about sections, see "Controlling What Appears on Each Page" in Chapter 4, "Changing the Look of a Document."

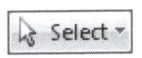

4. On the **Home** tab, in the **Editing** group, click the **Select** button, and then click **Select All**.

5. In the **Paragraph** group, click the **Justify** button.

   The spacing of the text within the paragraphs changes so the right edge of the paragraph is straight.

6. Press Ctrl+Home to deselect the text and move to the top of the document, and then in the **Paragraph** group, click the **Center** button to center the title.

7. At the right end of the status bar, click the **Zoom** button. Then in the **Zoom** dialog box, click **75%**, and click **OK**.

   You can now see about two-thirds of the first page of the document.

8. Click anywhere in the first column.

   On the horizontal ruler, Word indicates the margins of the columns.

9. On the **Page Layout** tab, in the **Page Setup** group, click the **Columns** button, and then click **More Columns**.

   The Columns dialog box opens. Because the Equal Column Width check box is selected, you can adjust the width and spacing of only the first column.

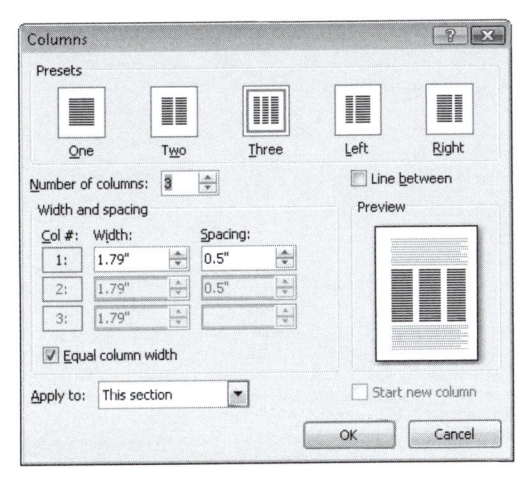

10. Under **Width and spacing**, in the **Spacing** column, click the down arrow until the setting is **0.2"**.

    Word changes the measurement in the box below and widens all the columns to reflect the new setting.

11. Click **OK**.

Word reflows the columns to fit their new margins.

Room Makeover

With the Room Planner, you'll never make a design mistake again. Created by acclaimed interior designers to simplify the redecorating process, this planning tool incorporates elements of color, dimension, and style to guide your project. It includes a furniture location guide; room grid; drawing tools; and miniature furniture, rugs, accessories, and color swatches that match our large in-store selection. Here's how to use the planner to create the room of your dreams!

———————————————————— Section Break (Continuous) ————————————————————

Take a look at how your home is decorated and note the things you like and dislike. Pay special attention to the color scheme and to how each room "feels" to you. Is it inviting? Does it feel comfortable? Does it relax you or does it invigorate you?

Focus on the room(s) you would most like to change. Brainstorm all the things you would change in that room if you could. Don't give a thought to any financial considerations; just let your imagine go wild! It might be helpful to write down all the negatives and positives. You don't need to come up with

planner so that it models the room dimensions. Don't forget to place the windows and doors. Arrange the furniture placeholders to mirror how your room is currently set up. Add the current colors, too.

This is where the fun begins! Start changing things around a bit. Move the furniture, add different colors, and watch the room come together! Here's where you can tell if that rich red rug you saw in the showroom enhances or overwhelms your room. What about that overstuffed chair that caught your eye? Place a furniture or accessory shape,

just right to you, you're ready for the next big step!

Come back to the store. Look again at the pieces you liked during your last visit and see if you still love them. If you're not quite sure, go back to your planner for a little more tweaking. If you are sure, take a look around the store one more time to see if anything else catches your eye. Then make your purchases. You're almost there!

NOTE: If you decided to paint your room, do that before your new pieces are delivered. You'll want to start enjoying your new room as soon as your purchases

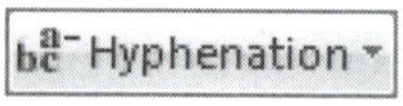

12. Click immediately to the left of *Take a look*. Then in the **Page Setup** group, click the **Hyphenation** button, and click **Automatic**.

Word hyphenates the text of the document, which fills in some of the large gaps between words.

13. Click anywhere in the *NOTE* paragraph in the third column.

14. On the horizontal ruler, in the third column, drag the **Hanging Indent** marker 0.25 inch (two marks) to the right.

All the lines in the *NOTE* paragraph except the first are now indented, offsetting the note from the paragraphs above and below it.

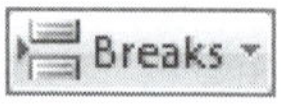

15. Click just to the left of *Take your Room Planner home* at the bottom of the first column on page 1. Then in the **Page Setup** group, click the **Breaks** button, and click **Column**.

The text that follows the column break moves to the top of the second column.

16. Click just to the left of *If you're not sure* at the bottom of the third column on page 1, and then on the **Quick Access Toolbar**, click the **Repeat Insertion** button to insert another column break.

Repeat

The text that follows the column break moves to the top of the first column on page 2.

> **CLOSE** the *Columns* document without saving your changes.

Creating a Tabular List

If you have a relatively small amount of data to present in a table, you might choose to display it in a *tabular list*, which arranges text in simple columns separated by left, right, centered, or decimal tab stops.

See Also For more information about setting tab stops, see "Manually Changing the Look of Paragraphs" in Chapter 3, "Changing the Look of Text."

When entering text in a tabular list, people have a tendency to press the Tab key multiple times to align the columns of the list. If you do this, you have no control over the column widths. To be able to fine-tune the columns, you need to set custom tab stops rather than relying on the default ones. When you want to set up a tabular list, you should press Tab only once between the items that you want to appear in separate columns. You can then apply any necessary formatting and set the tabs in order from left to right so that you can see how everything lines up.

> **Tip** In addition to left, right, centered, and decimal tabs, you can set a bar tab. This type of tab does not align text like the others, but instead adds a vertical line to selected paragraphs. This bar can be used to further distinguish the columns in a tabular list.

In this exercise, you will create a tabular list. First you'll enter text separated by tabs, and then you'll format the text and set custom tab stops.

> **USE** the *TabularList* document. This practice file is located in the *Documents\Microsoft Press\Word2007SBS\CreatingTables* folder.
> **BE SURE TO** display the rulers and non-printing characters before starting this exercise.
> **OPEN** the *TabularList* document.

1. Scroll down to the bottom of the document, click to the left of the paragraph mark at the end of *The Skill or Power*, and then press `Enter`.

Creating a Tabular List **129**

2. Type **Self**, press `Tab`, type **Other People**, press `Tab`, type **Nature**, and then press `Enter`.

3. Add three more lines to the list by typing the following text, pressing the `Tab` and `Enter` keys where indicated.

   Transformation `Tab` **Life/death** `Tab` **Weather** `Enter`

   Time travel `Tab` **Telepathy** `Tab` **Oceans** `Enter`

   Visible/invisible `Tab` **Mind control** `Tab` **Animals**

   The tab characters push the items to the next default tab stop, but because some items are longer than others, they do not line up.

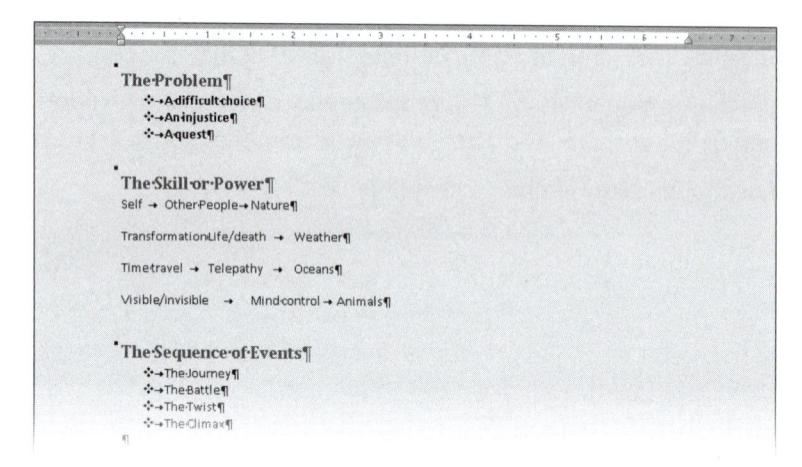

   ```
   The Problem¶
       ❖→A difficult choice¶
       ❖→An injustice¶
       ❖→A quest¶

   The Skill or Power¶
   Self  →  Other People→Nature¶
   Transformation Life/death  →  Weather¶
   Time travel  →  Telepathy  →  Oceans¶
   Visible/invisible  →    Mind control → Animals¶

   The Sequence of Events¶
       ❖→The Journey¶
       ❖→The Battle¶
       ❖→The Twist¶
       ❖→The Climax¶
   ¶
   ```

   See Also For information about tab stops, see "Manually Changing the Look of Paragraphs" in Chapter 3, "Changing the Look of Text."

   [B] Bold

4. Select the first line of the tabular list, and then on the **Mini toolbar** that appears, click the **Bold** button.

   > **Troubleshooting** If the Mini toolbar doesn't appear, click the Bold button in the Font group on the Home tab.

   Increase Indent

5. Select all four lines of the tabular list, and then on the **Mini toolbar**, click the **Increase Indent** button.

6. With the lines still selected, on the **Page Layout** tab, in the **Paragraph** group, under **Spacing**, change the **After** setting to **0 pt**.

Left Tab

7. Without changing the selection, verify that the **Tab** button at the junction of the horizontal and vertical rulers shows a left tab stop (an L), and then click the 2-inch mark on the horizontal ruler.

   Word displays a left tab stop on the ruler, and the items in the second column of all the selected lines left-align themselves at that position.

8. Click the **Left Tab** button twice.

   The icon on the button changes to a right tab stop (a backward L), indicating that clicking the ruler now will set a right-aligned tab.

9. Click the horizontal ruler at the 4-inch mark.

   Word displays a right tab stop on the ruler, and the items in the third column of the selected lines jump to right-align themselves at that position.

10. On the **Home** tab, in the **Paragraph** group, click the **Show/Hide ¶** button to hide non-printing characters. Then click away from the tabular list to see the results.

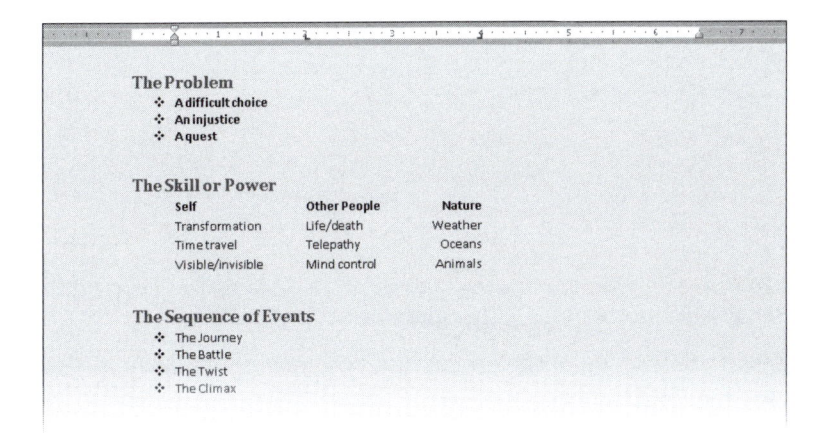

    The tabular list resembles a simple table.

The Problem
- A difficult choice
- An injustice
- A quest

The Skill or Power

Self	Other People	Nature
Transformation	Life/death	Weather
Time travel	Telepathy	Oceans
Visible/invisible	Mind control	Animals

The Sequence of Events
- The Journey
- The Battle
- The Twist
- The Climax

CLOSE the *TabularList* document without saving your changes.

Presenting Information in a Table

Creating a Word table is a simple matter of clicking the Table button and selecting the number of rows and columns you want from a grid. You can then enter text, numbers, and graphics into the table's *cells*, which are the boxes at the intersections of a row and a column. At any time, you can change the table's size; insert and delete columns, rows,

and cells; and format individual entries or the entire table. You can sort the information in a logical order and perform calculations on the numbers in a column or row.

Clicking the Table button creates a table with the number of columns and rows you select from the grid, with all the cells of equal size. You can click Insert Table below the grid to open the Insert Table dialog box, where you can specify the number of rows and columns as well as their sizes. You can also create a table by drawing cells the size you want. If the text you want to appear in a table already exists in the document, you can convert the text to a table.

See Also For information about drawing tables, see "Using a Table to Control Page Layout" later in this chapter.

A new table appears in the document as a set of blank cells surrounded by *gridlines*. Each cell has an end-of-cell marker, and each row has an end-of-row marker. When the pointer is over the table, the table has a move handle in its upper-left corner and a size handle in its lower-right corner. While the insertion point is in the table, Word displays two Table Tools contextual tabs, Design and Layout.

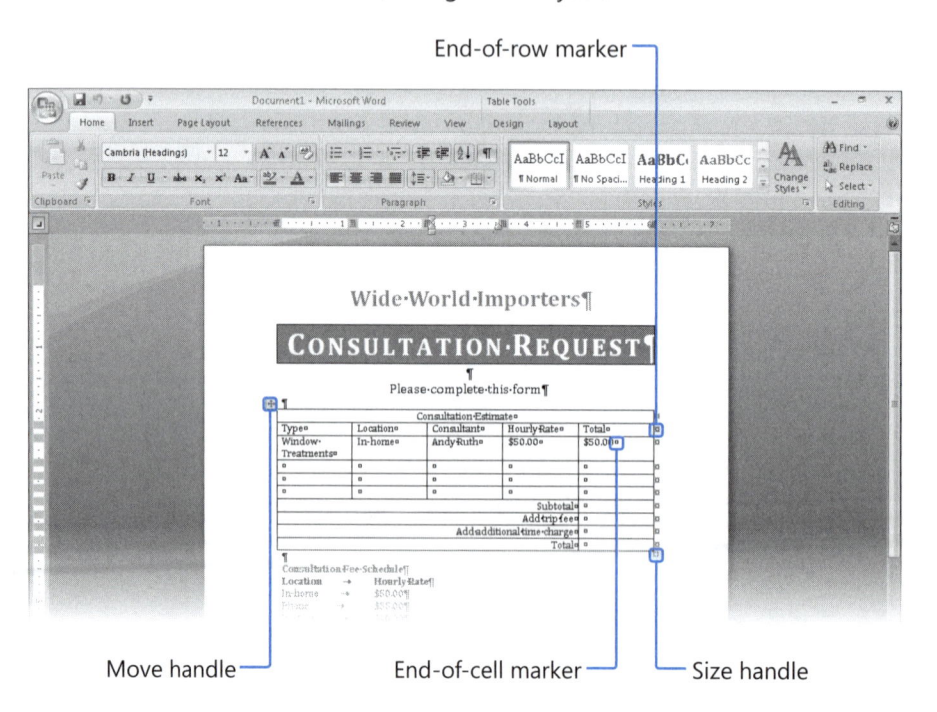

Tip You cannot see the move handle and size handle in Draft view.

After you create a table, you can type text or numbers into cells and press the Tab key to move the insertion point from cell to cell. Pressing Tab when the insertion point is in the last cell in the last row adds a new row to the bottom of the table. In addition to the Tab key, you can use the Arrow keys to position the insertion point, or you can simply click any cell.

You can modify a table's structure at any time. To change the structure, you often need to select the entire table or specific rows or columns, by using the following methods:

- **Select a table.** Click anywhere in the table. Then on the Layout contextual tab, in the Table group, click the Select button, and click Select Table.
- **Select a column.** Point to the top border of the column. When the pointer changes to a black, down-pointing arrow, click once.
- **Select a row.** Point to the left border of the row. When the pointer changes to a white, right-pointing arrow, click once.
- **Select a cell.** Triple-click the cell or click its left border.
- **Select multiple cells.** Click the first cell, hold down the Shift key, and press the arrow keys to select adjacent cells in a column or row.

The basic methods for manipulating tables are as follows:

- **Insert a row or column.** Click anywhere in a row or column adjacent to where you want to make the insertion. Then on the Layout tab, in the Rows & Columns group, click the Insert Above, Insert Below, Insert Left, or Insert Right button. Selecting more than one row or column before you click an Insert button inserts that number of rows or columns in the table.

  > **Tip** You can insert cells by clicking the Rows & Columns dialog box launcher and specifying in the Insert Cells dialog box how adjacent cells should be moved to accommodate the new cells.

- **Delete a row or column.** Click anywhere in the row or column, and in the Rows & Columns group, click the Delete button. Then click Delete Cells, Delete Columns, Delete Rows, or Delete Table.
- **Size an entire table.** Drag the size handle.
- **Size a single column or row.** Drag a column's right border to the left or right. Drag a row's bottom border up or down.
- **Merge cells.** Create cells that span columns by selecting the cells you want to merge and clicking the Merge Cells button in the Merge group on the Layout tab. For example, to center a title in the first row of a table, you can create one merged cell that spans the table's width.

● **Split cells.** Divide a merged cell into its component cells by clicking Split Cells in the Merge group on the Layout tab.

● **Move a table.** Point to the table, and then drag the move handle that appears in its upper-left corner to a new location. Or use the Cut and Paste buttons in the Clipboard group on the Home tab to move the table.

● **Sort information.** Use the Sort button in the Data group on the Layout tab to sort the rows in ascending or descending order by the data in any column. For example, you can sort a table that has the column headings Name, Address, ZIP Code, and Phone Number on any one of those columns to arrange the information in alphabetical or numerical order.

In this exercise, you will work with two tables. First you'll create a table, enter text, align text in the cells, add rows, and merge cells. Then you'll create a second table by converting existing tabbed text, you'll size a column, and you'll size the entire table.

> **USE** the *Table* document. This practice file is located in the *Documents\Microsoft Press\Word2007SBS\CreatingTables* folder.
>
> **OPEN** the *Table* document.

1. Click in the second blank line below *Please complete this form*.
2. On the **Insert** tab, in the **Tables** group, click the **Table** button, point to the upper-left cell, and move the pointer across five columns and down five rows.

   Word highlights the cells as you drag across them and creates a temporary table in the document to show you what the selection will look like.

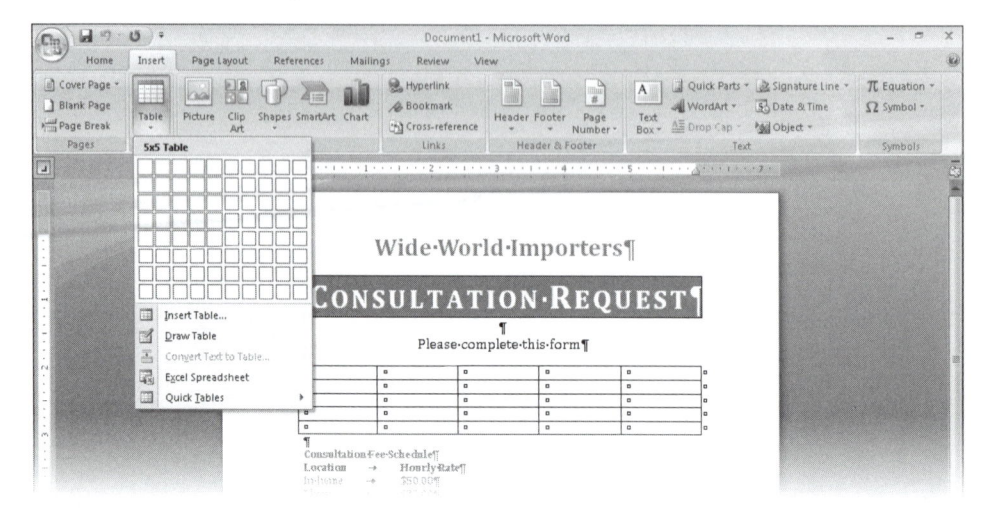

3. Click the lower-right cell in the selection.

   Word creates a blank table with five columns and five rows. The insertion point is located in the first cell. Because the table is active, Word displays the Table Tools Design and Layout contextual tabs.

4. In the selection area, point to the first row, and then click to select the row.

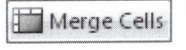

5. On the **Layout** contextual tab, in the **Merge** group, click the **Merge Cells** button.

   Word combines the five cells in the first row into one cell.

6. With the merged cell selected, in the **Alignment** group, click the **Align Center** button.

   The end-of-cell marker moves to the center of the merged cell to indicate that anything you type there will be centered.

7. Type **Consultation Estimate**.

   The table now has a title.

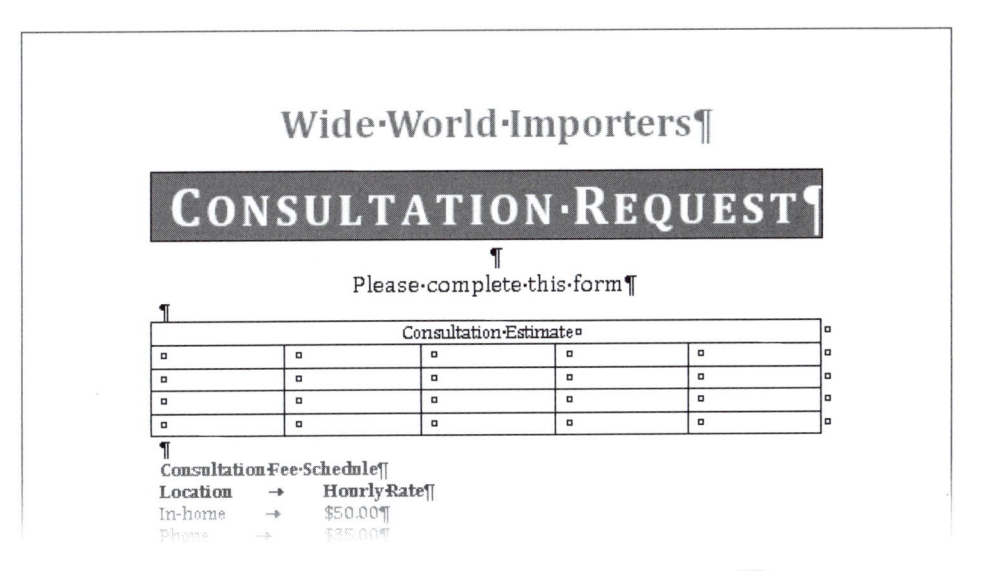

8. Click the first cell in the second row, type **Type**, and then press Tab.

9. Type **Location**, **Consultant**, **Hourly Rate**, and **Total**, pressing Tab after each entry.

   The table now has a row of column headings. Pressing Tab after the *Total* heading moves the insertion point to the first cell of the third row.

10. Type **Window Treatments**, **In-home**, **Andy Ruth**, **$50.00**, and **$50.00**, pressing Tab after each entry.

    You have entered a complete row of data.

11. Select the last two rows, and then on the **Layout** tab, in the **Rows & Columns** group, click the **Insert Below** button.

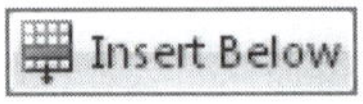

    Word adds two new rows and selects them.

12. In the last row, click the first cell, hold down the Shift key, and then press the → key four times to select the first four cells in the row.

13. In the **Merge** group, click the **Merge Cells** button.

    Word combines the selected cells into one cell.

14. In the **Alignment** group, click the **Align Center Right** button.

15. Type **Subtotal**, and then press Tab twice.

    Word adds a new row with the same structure to the bottom of the table.

16. Type **Add trip fee**, press [Tab] twice to add a new row, and then type **Add additional time charge**.

17. Press [Tab] twice to add a new row, and then type **Total**.

18. Scroll to the bottom of the document, and select the rows of the tabular list beginning with *Distance* and ending with *$20.00*.

19. On the **Insert** tab, in the **Tables** group, click the **Table** button, and then click **Convert Text to Table**.

    The Convert Text To Table dialog box opens.

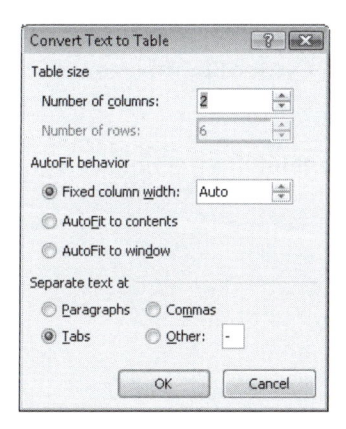

> **Tip** To convert a table to text, select the table, and then click the Convert To Text button in the Data group on the Layout tab.

20. Verify that the **Number of columns** box displays **2**, and then click **OK**.

    The selected text appears in a table with two columns and six rows.

21. Click anywhere in the table to release the selection, and point to the right border of the table. When the pointer changes to two opposing arrows, double-click the right border.

    Word adjusts the width of the right column so that it is exactly wide enough to contain its longest line of text.

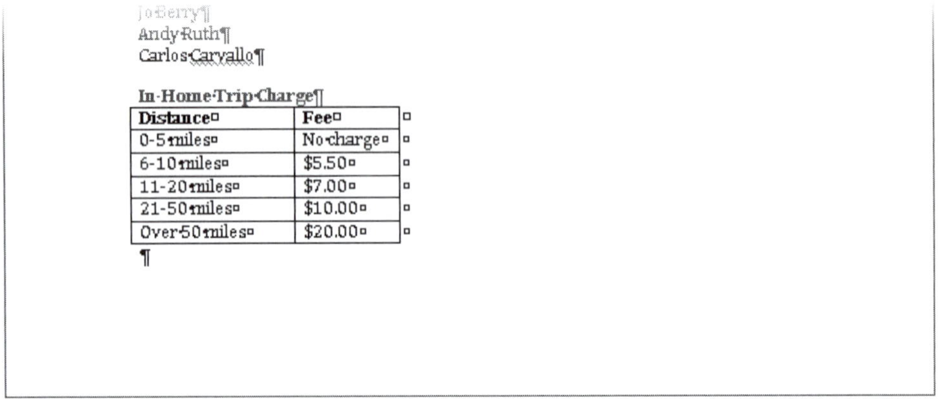

22. Point to the In-Home Trip Charge table.

    Word displays the move handle in the upper-left corner and the size handle in the lower-right corner.

23. Drag the size handle to the right, releasing the mouse button when the right edge of the table aligns approximately with the 4-inch mark on the horizontal ruler.

CLOSE the *Table* document without saving your changes.

Other Layout Options

You can control many aspects of a table by clicking Properties in the Table group on the Layout tab to display the Table Properties dialog box. You can then set the following options:

- On the Table tab, you can specify the preferred width of the entire table, as well as the way it interacts with the surrounding text.
- On the Row tab, you can specify the height of each row, whether a row is allowed to break across pages, and whether a row of column headings should be repeated at the top of each page.

> **Tip** The Repeat As Header Row option is available only if the insertion point is in the top row of the table.

- On the Column tab, you can set the width of each column.
- On the Cell tab, you can set the preferred width of cells and the vertical alignment of text within them.

> **Tip** You can also control the widths of selected cells by using the buttons in the Cell Size group on the Layout contextual tab.

- You can control the margins of cells (how close text comes to the cell border) by clicking the Options button on either the Table or Cell tab.

> **Tip** You can also control the margins by clicking the Cell Margins button in the Alignment group on the Layout contextual tab.

If the first row of your table has several long headings that make it difficult to fit the table on one page, you can turn the headings sideways. Simply select the heading row and click the Text Direction button in the Alignment group on the Layout tab.

Formatting Table Information

Formatting a table to best convey its data is often a process of trial and error. With Word 2007, you can quickly get started by creating a *Quick Table*, a preformatted table with sample data that you can customize. You can then apply one of the *table styles* available on the Design contextual tab, which include a variety of borders, colors, and other attributes to give the table a professional look.

To customize the appearance of a Quick Table or a table you have created from scratch, you can use the buttons on the Design and Layout contextual tabs. You can also use buttons in the Paragraph group on the Home tab to change alignment and spacing. You can format the text by using the buttons in the Font group, just as you would to format any text in a Word document. You can also apply character formatting from the Styles gallery.

In this exercise, you will create a Quick Table and then apply a table style to it. You will then change some of the text attributes and modify the borders and shading in various cells to make the formatting suit the table's data. There are no practice files for this exercise.

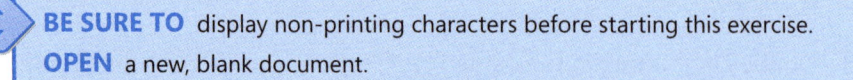

> **BE SURE TO** display non-printing characters before starting this exercise.
>
> **OPEN** a new, blank document.

1. With the Zoom level at 100%, on the **Insert** tab, in the **Tables** group, click the **Table** button, and then point to **Quick Tables**.

   The Quick Tables gallery opens.

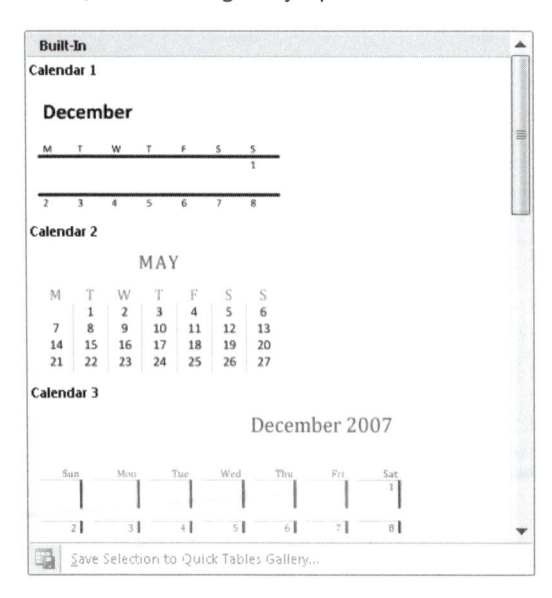

2. Scroll through the gallery, noticing the types of tables that are available, and then click **Matrix**.

   Word inserts the selected table and displays the Design contextual tab. Notice that the table data includes headings across the top and down the left column. Some of the cells are blank, and obviously have less importance than the cells that contain numbers. The table does not include summary data, such as totals.

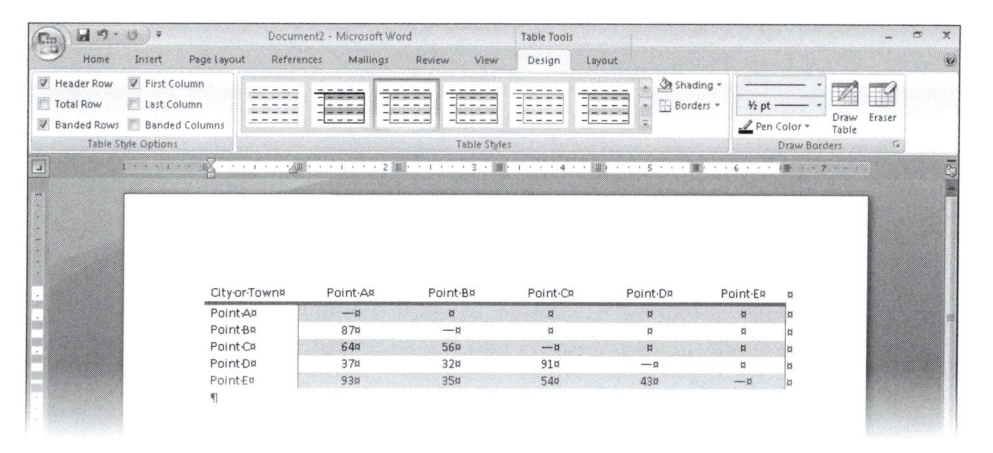

3. On the **Design** tab, in the **Table Style Options** group, clear the **Banded Rows** check box.

4. In the **Table Styles** group, point to each style in turn to see its live preview, and then click the **More** button to display the Table Styles gallery.

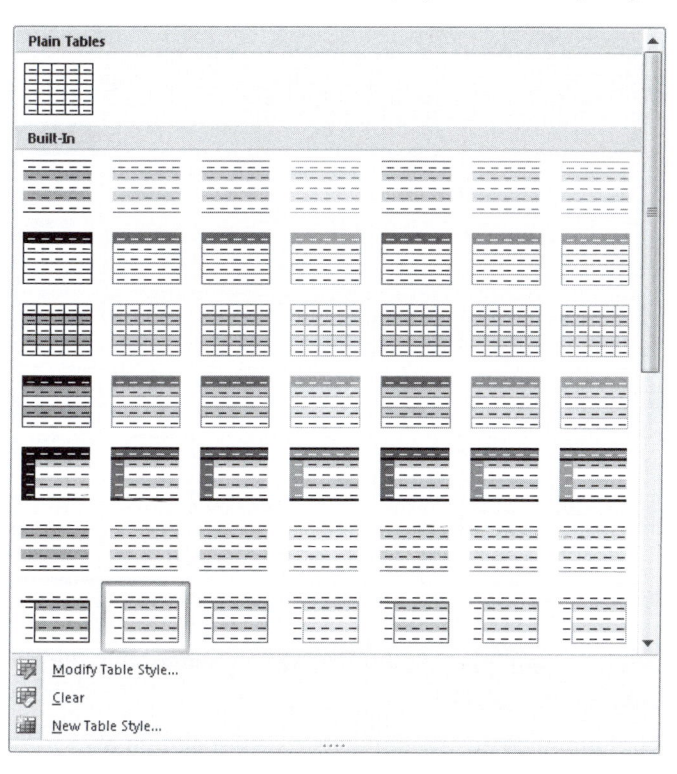

5. Explore all the styles in the gallery. When you finish exploring, click the **Medium Shading 2 – Accent 2** thumbnail.

You need to modify this style a bit, but it is a good starting point.

6. Select all the white cells by dragging through them. Then in the **Table Styles** group, click the **Borders** arrow, and in the list, click **All Borders**.

7. Select all the cells in the last row (*Point E*) by clicking to its left, and in the **Table Styles** group, in the **Borders** list, click **Borders and Shading**.

The Borders And Shading dialog box opens, displaying the borders applied to the selected cells. The thick gray borders in the Preview area indicate that different borders are applied to different cells in the selection.

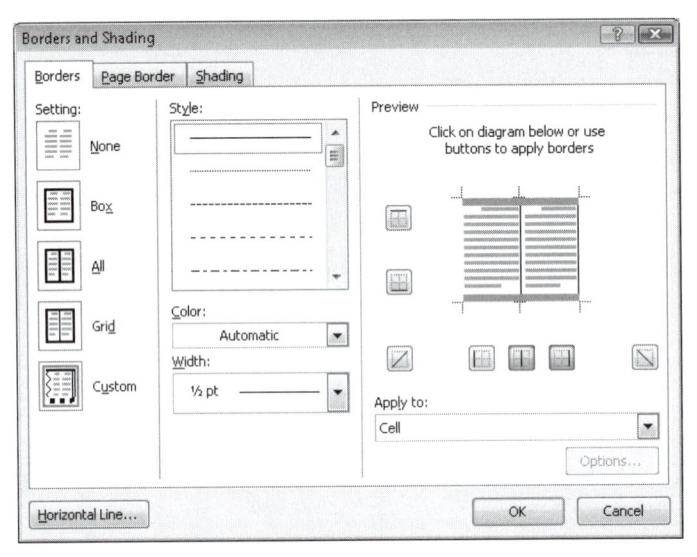

8. In the **Preview** area, click the bottom border of the diagram twice to remove all bottom borders.

9. Click the **Color** arrow, and then under **Theme Colors**, click the black box (**Black, Text 1**).

10. Click the **Width** arrow, and then in the list, click **2 1/4 pt**.

11. In the **Preview** area, click the bottom border of the diagram, and then click **OK**.

The table now has the same border at the top and bottom.

12. Select the empty cells in the *Point A* row. In the **Table Styles** group, click the **Shading** arrow, and then under **Theme Colors**, click the lightest burgundy box (**Red, Accent 2, Lighter 80%**).

13. Repeat step 12 for all the remaining blank cells in the table.

14. Select the dash in the cell at the junction of the *Point A* column and the *Point A* row, hold down the [Ctrl] key, and select the other four dashes.

15. On the **Mini toolbar**, click the **Font Color** arrow, and then under **Standard Colors** in the palette, click the bright **Red** box.

> **Troubleshooting** If the Mini toolbar doesn't appear, click the Font Color arrow in the Font group on the Home tab.

16. Click outside the table to release the selection, and then in the **Paragraph** group, click the **Show/Hide ¶** button to hide non-printing characters.

    You can now judge how well the table displays its data.

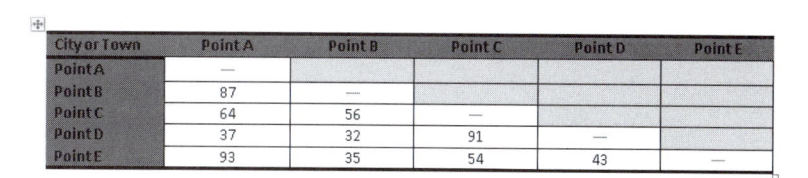

City or Town	Point A	Point B	Point C	Point D	Point E
Point A	—				
Point B	87	—			
Point C	64	56	—		
Point D	37	32	91	—	
Point E	93	35	54	43	—

✖ **CLOSE** the document without saving your changes.

Performing Calculations in a Table

When you want to perform a calculation on numbers in a Word table, you can create a *formula* that uses a built-in mathematical function. You construct a formula by using the tools in the Formula dialog box, which you can access by clicking Formula in the Data group on the Layout contextual tab. A formula consists of an equal sign (=), followed by a function name (such as SUM), followed by parentheses containing the location of the cells on which you want to perform the calculation. For example, the formula =SUM(Left) totals the cells to the left of the cell containing the formula.

To use a function other than SUM in the Formula dialog box, you click the function you want in the Paste Function list. You can use built-in functions to perform a number of calculations, including averaging (AVERAGE) a set of values, counting (COUNT) the number of values in a column or row, or finding the maximum (MAX) or minimum (MIN) value in a series of cells.

> **Creating Table Styles**
>
> If none of the predefined table styles meets your needs, you can create your own styles for tables in much the same way you create styles for regular text.
>
> To create a table style:
>
> 1. On the **Design** tab, in the **Table Styles** group, click the **More** button, and then click **New Table Style**.
>
>   The Create New Style From Formatting dialog box opens.
>
> 2. In the **Name** box, type a name for the new style.
>
> 3. Click the **Apply formatting to** arrow, and in the list, select the table element for which you are creating the new style.
>
> 4. Select the formatting options you want, until the table shown in the Preview area looks the way you want it.
>
> 5. If you want the style to be available to tables in other documents based on this template, select that option, and then click **OK**.
>
> To apply a custom table style:
>
> 1. Select the table element to which you want to apply the new style.
>
> 2. On the **Design** tab, in the **Table Styles** group, click the **More** button, and under **Custom**, click the thumbnail for your custom style.

Although formulas commonly refer to the cells above or to the left of the active cell, you can also use the contents of specified cells or constant values in formulas. To use the contents of a cell, you type the *cell address* in the parentheses following the function name. The cell address is a combination of the column letter and the row number—for example, A1 is the cell at the intersection of the first column and the first row. A series of cells in a row can be addressed as a range consisting of the first cell and the last cell separated by a colon, such as A1:D1. For example, the formula =SUM(A1:D1) totals the values in row 1 of columns A through D. A series of cells in a column can be addressed in the same way. For example, the formula =SUM(A1:A4) totals the values in column A of rows 1 through 4.

When the built-in functions don't meet your needs, you can insert an Excel worksheet in a Word document. Part of the Microsoft Office system, Excel includes sophisticated functions for performing mathematical, accounting, and statistical calculations. For example,

you can use an Excel worksheet to calculate loan payments at various interest rates. You can insert Excel worksheet data into a Word document in the following ways:

- **By copying and pasting.** You can open Excel, enter the data and formulas, and then copy and paste the data as a table in a Word document. The data is pasted as regular text, with the formulas converted to their results.

- **By linking.** While pasting Excel worksheet data into a Word document, you can link the version in the document to the original source worksheet. You can then double-click the linked object in the document to open the source worksheet in Excel for editing. After you edit and save the worksheet, you can return to the document, right-click the linked object, and then click Update Link to display the edited version of the data.

- **By embedding.** You can create an Excel worksheet directly in a Word document by clicking the Table button in the Tables group on the Insert tab, and then clicking Excel Spreadsheet. The worksheet is created as an object with Excel row and column headers, and the Excel tabs and groups replace those of Word so that you can enter data and manipulate it using Excel.

> **Tip** If you change a value in a Word table, you must recalculate formulas manually. If you change a value in an Excel worksheet, the formulas are automatically recalculated.

In this exercise, you will perform a few calculations in a Word table. Then you'll copy and paste worksheet data, link the same data, and enter the same data in an Excel object so that you can see the three different ways of working with Excel data.

USE the *Calculations* document and the *LoanData* workbook. These practice files are located in the *Documents\Microsoft Press\Word2007SBS\CreatingTables* folder.

OPEN the *LoanData* workbook in Excel, and then open the *Calculations* document in Word.

1. Save the practice file in the *CreatingTables* folder with the name My Calculations.

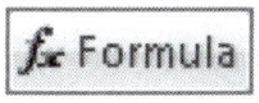

2. In the table displayed in the document, click the cell below the *Total* column heading, and on the **Layout** contextual tab, in the **Data** group, click the **Formula** button.

   The Formula dialog box opens.

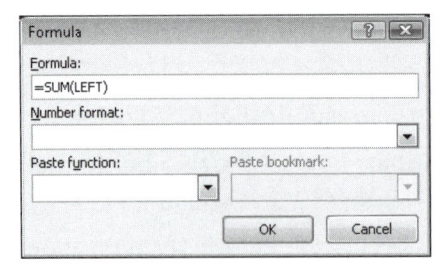

3. Select the contents of the **Formula** box, and then type =C2*B2.
4. Click the **Number format** arrow, and in the list, click $#,##0.00;($#,##0.00).
5. In the **Number format** box, delete .00 from both the positive and negative portions of the format, and then click **OK**.

   You have told Word to multiply the first dollar amount under *Unit Price* by the quantity on the same row and to display the result as a whole dollar amount. Word enters the result, $60,000, in the cell containing the formula.

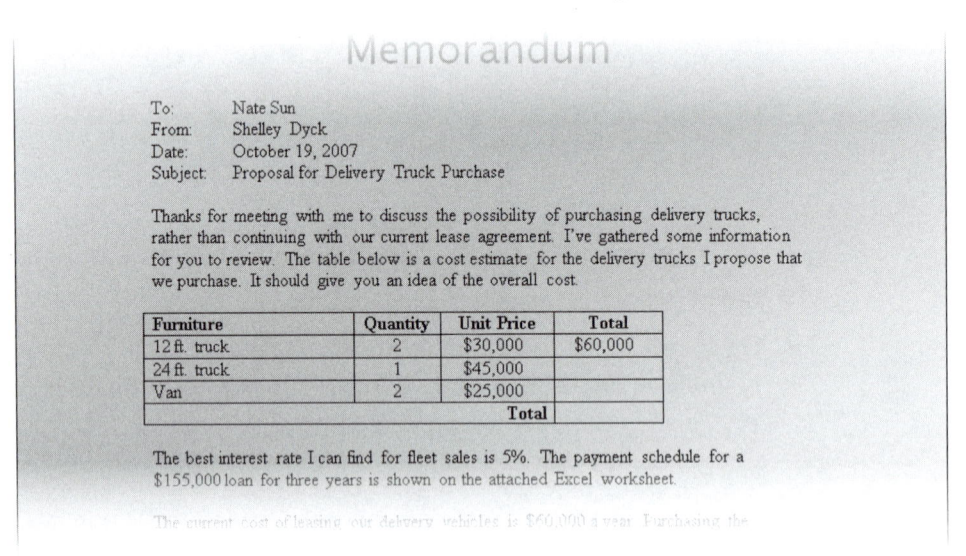

6. Repeat steps 2 through 5 for the next two cells under *Total*, adjusting the cell addresses appropriately.
7. In cell **B4**, change 2 to 3, right-click the formula in cell **D4**, and then click **Update Field**.

   Word recalculates the formula and enters the new result, $75,000, in the cell.

146 Chapter 5 Presenting Information in Columns and Tables

8. Change the **Unit Price** of the **24 ft. truck** to **$42,500**, and then update the corresponding total.

9. Click cell **D5**, and in the **Data** group, click the **Formula** button.

10. With **=SUM(ABOVE)** in the **Formula** box, set the **Number format** to whole dollar amounts (following the method in steps 3 and 4), and then click **OK**.

    You have told Word to add the amounts in the *Total* column. Word enters the result, $177,500, in the cell containing the formula.

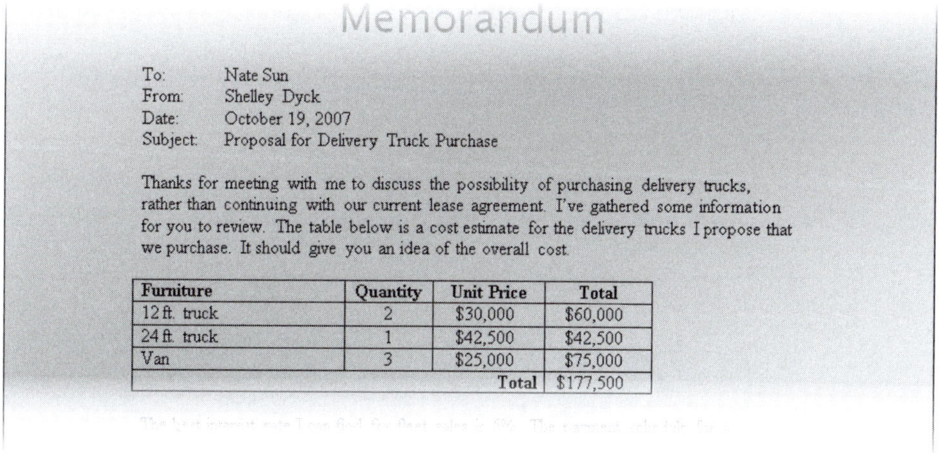

11. Press Ctrl+End to move to the end of the document, and then on the Windows taskbar, click the **Microsoft Excel** button.

12. On **Sheet1** in the *LoanData* workbook, select cells **A1:B8** by dragging through them. Then on the **Home** tab, in the **Clipboard** group, click the **Copy** button.

    The worksheet data is copied to the Clipboard. From there it can be pasted into any Microsoft Office program.

13. Redisplay the *My Calculations* document. Then on the **Home** tab, in the **Clipboard** group, click the **Paste** button.

    Word pastes a copy of the worksheet data in the document as a table.

Performing Calculations in a Table 147

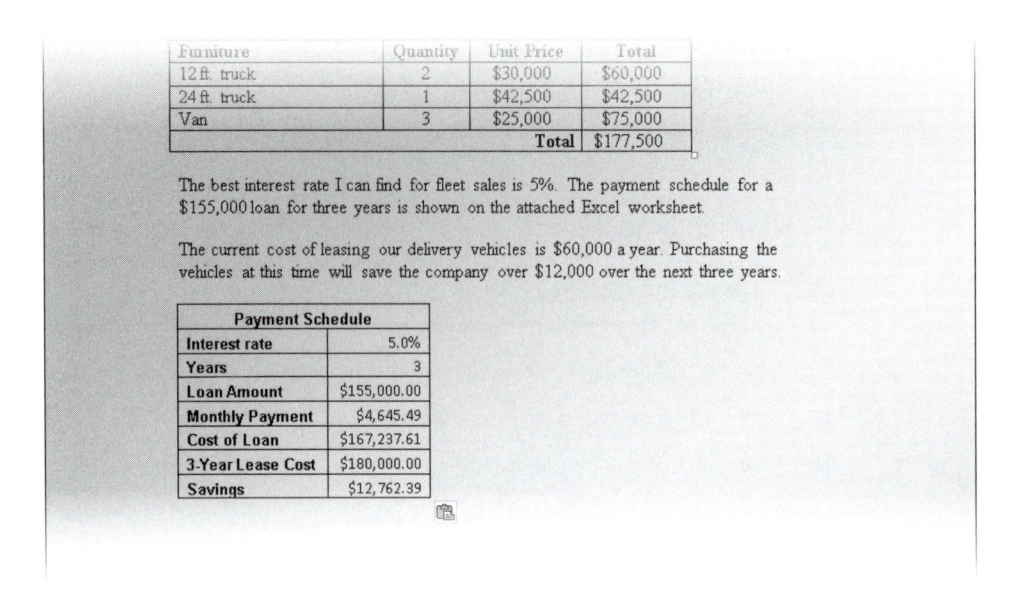

Furniture	Quantity	Unit Price	Total
12 ft. truck	2	$30,000	$60,000
24 ft. truck	1	$42,500	$42,500
Van	3	$25,000	$75,000
		Total	$177,500

The best interest rate I can find for fleet sales is 5%. The payment schedule for a $155,000 loan for three years is shown on the attached Excel worksheet.

The current cost of leasing our delivery vehicles is $60,000 a year. Purchasing the vehicles at this time will save the company over $12,000 over the next three years.

Payment Schedule	
Interest rate	5.0%
Years	3
Loan Amount	$155,000.00
Monthly Payment	$4,645.49
Cost of Loan	$167,237.61
3-Year Lease Cost	$180,000.00
Savings	$12,762.39

14. Press **Enter**, and then in the **Clipboard** group, click the **Paste** arrow, and click **Paste Special**.

The Paste Special dialog box opens.

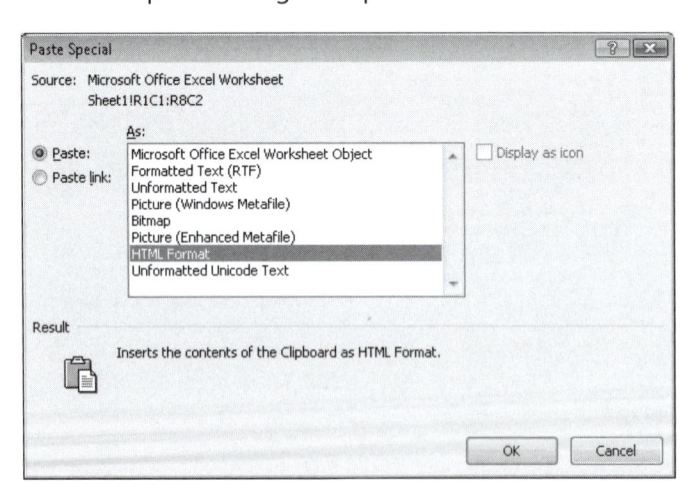

15. In the **As** list, click **Microsoft Office Excel Worksheet Object**, click **Paste link**, and then click **OK**.

Word pastes a second copy of the worksheet data as a linked table on a new page.

148 Chapter 5   Presenting Information in Columns and Tables

16. Double-click the new table.

    The linked worksheet opens in Excel.

17. Click cell **B2**, type **6**, and then press Enter.

    > **Troubleshooting** If someone has already worked through this exercise using the practice files on your computer, 6.0% might already appear in cell B2. In that case, change the value to 5.0%.

    Excel recalculates the formulas in the worksheet to reflect the new interest rate.

18. Save and close the workbook, and exit Excel.

19. In Word, right-click the linked table, and then click **Update Link**.

    Word updates the table to reflect the change you made to the worksheet data.

20. Press Ctrl+End to move to the end of the document, press Enter twice to add some space, and then save the document.

21. On the **Insert** tab, in the **Tables** group, click the **Table** button, and then click **Excel Spreadsheet**.

    Word inserts an Excel object in the document.

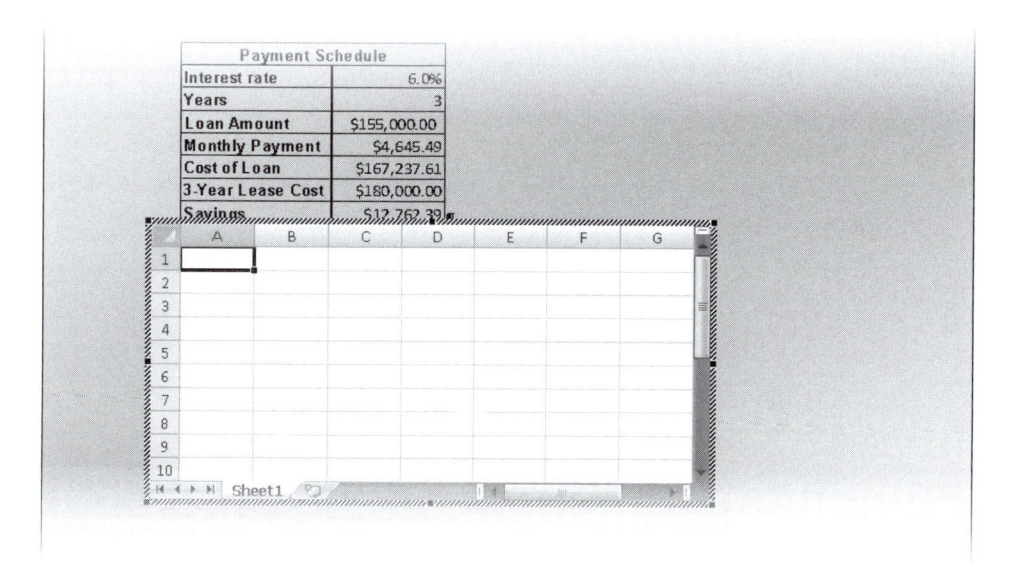

Payment Schedule	
Interest rate	6.0%
Years	3
Loan Amount	$155,000.00
Monthly Payment	$4,645.49
Cost of Loan	$167,237.61
3-Year Lease Cost	$180,000.00
Savings	$12,762.39

22. In row **1**, type **Rate**, press Tab, and then type **5%**.

23. Type the following in rows **2**, **3**, and **4**:

   2   Years [Tab] 3
   3   Amount [Tab] $155,000
   4   Payment [Tab]

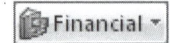

24. With cell **B4** active, on the **Formulas** tab, in the **Function Library** group, click the **Financial** button, scroll the list, and then click **PMT**.

   Excel enters =PMT() in cell B4 and then opens the Function Arguments dialog box so that you can enter the information needed to calculate the monthly payment on a loan of $155,000 at 5% interest for three years.

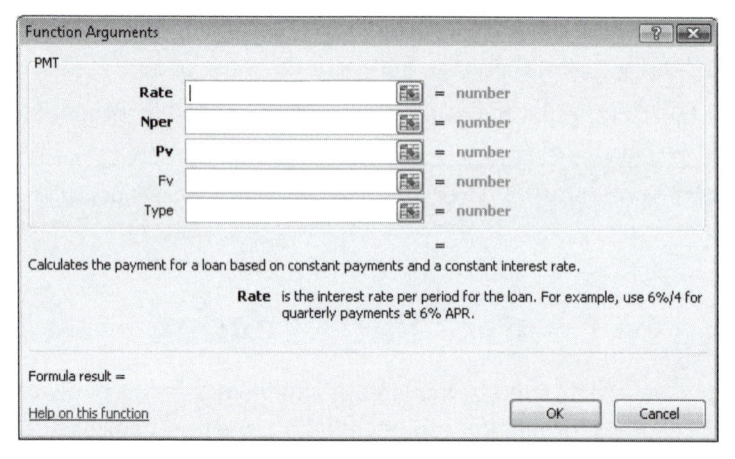

25. In the **Rate** box, type **B1/12** (the annual rate per month), in the **Nper** box, type **B2*12** (the number of years expressed as months), and in the **Pv** box, type **B3**. Then click **OK**.

   Excel calculates the formula and enters the result, $4,645.49, expressed as a negative because it is money you are paying out.

   > **Tip** To express the payment as a positive, you can insert a minus sign between the equal sign and PMT in the formula.

26. Drag the black handle in the lower-right corner of the Excel object up and to the left, until the frame of the object is just big enough to enclose the cells with data in them. Then click a blank area of the page to deactivate the object.

   The object appears on the page as a table with barely visible borders around its cells.

150   Chapter 5   Presenting Information in Columns and Tables

Payment Schedule	
Interest rate	6.0%
Years	3
Loan Amount	$155,000.00
Monthly Payment	$4,645.49
Cost of Loan	$167,237.61
3-Year Lease Cost	$180,000.00
Savings	$12,762.39

Rate	5%
Years	3
Amount	$155,000
Payment	($4,645.49)

27. Double-click the object to activate it in Excel again, change the entry in cell **B1** to **7%**, press Enter, and then click a blank area of the page.

The object's formulas have updated the monthly payment to reflect the change.

> **CLOSE** the *My Calculations* document without saving your changes.

Using a Table to Control Page Layout

Most people are accustomed to thinking of a table as a means of displaying data in a quick, easy-to-grasp format. But tables can also serve to organize your pages in creative ways. For example, suppose you want to display two tables next to each other. The simplest way to do this is to first create a table with one tall row and two wide columns and no gridlines. You can then insert one table in the first cell and the other table in the second cell. These *nested tables* then appear to be arranged side by side.

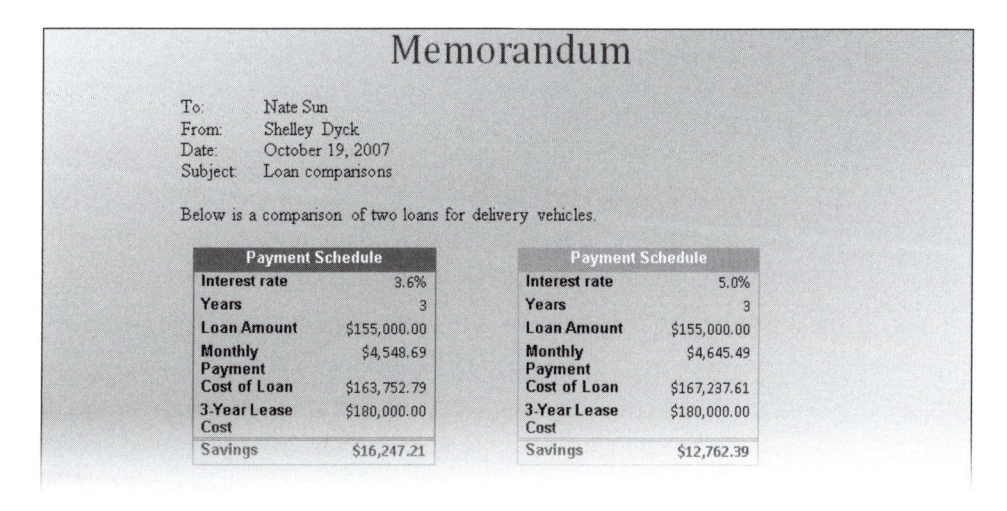

Memorandum

To: Nate Sun
From: Shelley Dyck
Date: October 19, 2007
Subject: Loan comparisons

Below is a comparison of two loans for delivery vehicles.

Payment Schedule	
Interest rate	3.6%
Years	3
Loan Amount	$155,000.00
Monthly Payment	$4,548.69
Cost of Loan	$163,752.79
3-Year Lease Cost	$180,000.00
Savings	$16,247.21

Payment Schedule	
Interest rate	5.0%
Years	3
Loan Amount	$155,000.00
Monthly Payment	$4,645.49
Cost of Loan	$167,237.61
3-Year Lease Cost	$180,000.00
Savings	$12,762.39

Deciding How to Insert Excel Data

To decide how to insert Excel data in a Word document, you need to understand how Microsoft Office system programs integrate data from outside sources. Understanding this will enable you to decide how to use information created in any other Office program, not just Excel.

If you don't need to maintain a connection with the source Excel worksheet and the data is simple enough to be edited in Word, you can copy and paste the data.

If you do need to maintain a connection with the source Excel worksheet, or if you need to be able to manipulate the data in Excel after it is incorporated into the Word document, you can use the Microsoft linking and embedding technology to insert an *object* (a file or part of a file) created in Excel into a document created in Word. The object is sometimes called the *source file*, and the document into which you are inserting the information is called the *destination file*. The difference between linking and embedding is the type of connection that is maintained between the source and destination files, as follows:

- A *linked object* is displayed in the destination file, but its data is stored in the source file. If you want to change the data, you do it in the source file. Then when you open the destination file, the linked object is updated to reflect the change.

- An *embedded object* is displayed in the destination file and its data is stored there. If you want to update the data, you do it in the destination file using the source program.

Whether an object should be linked or embedded depends on whether you need the information in the destination file to always be the same as the information in the source file. If you do, it is best to link the object so that you don't have to manually update the data in two places.

As with regular tables, you can create a nested table from scratch, by formatting existing information, or by inserting Excel data. And just like other tables, you can format a nested table either manually or using one of Word's ready-made table styles.

> **Tip** Tables can be used to organize a mixture of elements such as text, tables, charts, and diagrams. For more information, you might want to consult *Advanced Microsoft Office Documents 2007 Edition Inside Out* by Stephanie Krieger (Microsoft Press, 2007).

When creating a table to contain other elements, you might want to take advantage of the Word table-drawing feature. If you click Draw Table below the grid displayed when you click the Table button, the pointer changes to a pencil with which you can draw cells on the page. You can set up the container table visually, without having to fuss with dialog boxes and precise dimensions while you are designing the layout. Then after everything is set up the way you want it, you can use the Table Properties dialog box to fine-tune the table specifications.

In this exercise, you will draw a table to contain two other tables. You will then insert and format the nested tables.

> **USE** the *Loan* workbook and the *Memo* and *TableAsLayout* documents. These practice files are located in the *Documents\Microsoft Press\Word2007SBS\CreatingTables* folder.
> **BE SURE TO** display non-printing characters before starting this exercise.
> **OPEN** the *Loan* workbook in Excel, and then open the *Memo* document and the *TableAsLayout* document in Word.

1. Before you begin, save a copy of the *TableAsLayout* document in the *CreatingTables* folder as My Nested Tables.

   > **Troubleshooting** The operations you perform in this exercise use a lot of your computer's resources. You will have better results if you save the *My Nested Tables* document regularly.

2. In the *My Nested Tables* document, on the **Insert** tab, in the **Tables** group, click the **Table** button, and then click **Draw Table**.

   The pointer becomes a pencil.

3. Point below the last paragraph mark in the document, and drag across and down to create a cell about 3 inches wide and 1.5 inches tall.

   > **Tip** The location of the pencil is marked with guides on the horizontal and vertical rulers. You can use these guides to help you draw cells of specific dimensions.

4. Point to the upper-right corner of the cell (you don't have to be precise), and drag to create another cell about the same size as the first.

   When you release the mouse button, Word joins the two cells to create the structure of a table.

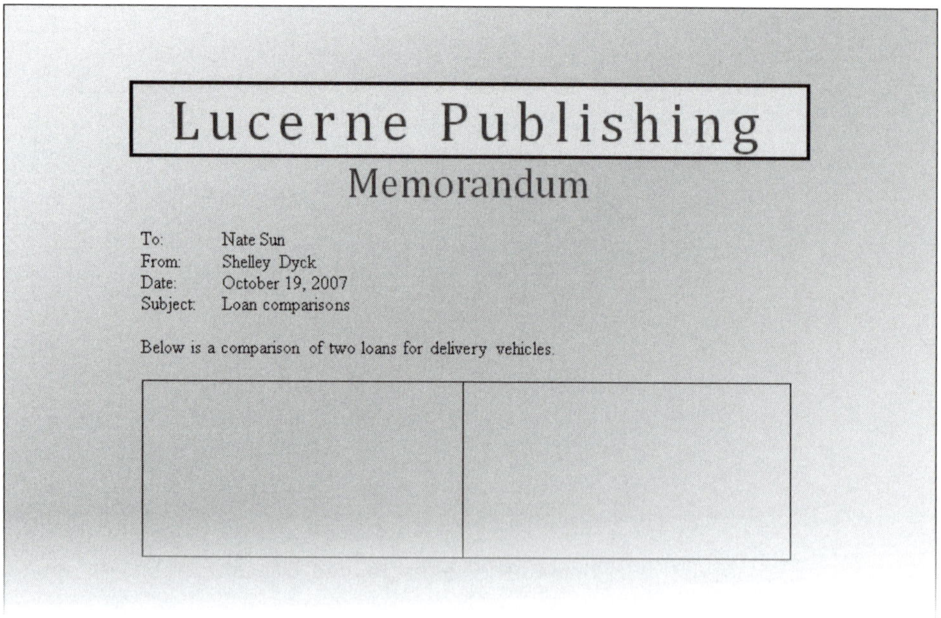

Using a Table to Control Page Layout   153

> **Lucerne Publishing**
> Memorandum
>
> To: Nate Sun
> From: Shelley Dyck
> Date: October 19, 2007
> Subject: Loan comparisons
>
> Below is a comparison of two loans for delivery vehicles.

Switch Windows

5. On the **View** tab, in the **Window** group, click the **Switch Windows** button, and then click *Memo*.

6. Scroll to the bottom of the page, click anywhere in the *Payment Schedule* table, and on the **Layout** tab, in the **Table** group, click **Select**, and then click **Select Table**.

Copy

7. On the **Home** tab, in the **Clipboard** group, click the **Copy** button.

8. Switch to the *My Nested Tables* document, right-click the first cell in the table, and then click **Paste as Nested Table**.

   Word inserts the table you copied into the cell and adjusts the size of the container table to fit the size of the nested table.

9. On the Windows taskbar, click the **Microsoft Excel** button to activate Sheet1 of the *Loan* workbook, select cells **A1:B8**, and then on the **Home** tab, in the **Clipboard** group, click the **Copy** button.

Paste

10. Switch back to the *My Nested Tables* document, click the second cell in the table, and then on the **Home** tab, in the **Clipboard** group, click the **Paste** button.

    Word inserts the worksheet data as a nested table in the cell.

> **Troubleshooting** If the pasted table doesn't appear in the container table, minimize the document window and then maximize it.

154 Chapter 5   Presenting Information in Columns and Tables

> **Memorandum**
>
> To: Nate Sun
> From: Shelley Dyck
> Date: October 19, 2007
> Subject: Loan comparisons
>
> Below is a comparison of two loans for delivery vehicles.
>
> | Payment Schedule | |
> |---|---|
> | Interest rate | 3.6% |
> | Years | 3 |
> | Loan Amount | $155,000.00 |
> | Monthly Payment | $4,548.69 |
> | Cost of Loan | $163,752.79 |
> | 3-Year Lease Cost | $180,000.00 |
> | Savings | $16,247.21 |
>
> | Payment Schedule | |
> |---|---|
> | Interest rate | 5.0% |
> | Years | 3 |
> | Loan Amount | $155,000.00 |
> | Monthly Payment | $4,645.49 |
> | Cost of Loan | $167,237.61 |
> | 3-Year Lease Cost | $180,000.00 |
> | Savings | $12,762.39 |

11. Move the pointer to the selection area adjacent to the container table, and then click to select its two cells.

12. On the **Home** tab, in the **Paragraph** group, click the **Borders** arrow, and then in the list, click **No Border**.

Borders

Word removes the borders from the container cells.

13. Click anywhere in the left table, and on the **Design** contextual tab, in the **Table Style Options** group, select the **Header Row** and **Total Row** check boxes, and clear all the other check boxes.

14. In the **Table Styles** group, display the **Table Styles** gallery, and click the thumbnail of a table style that you want to apply to the nested table.

We used Light List – Accent 4.

15. Repeat steps 13 and 14 to format the right table, perhaps using a similar table style with a different color.

We used Light List – Accent 6.

16. Turn off non-printing characters to see the results.

The nested tables now look as shown at the beginning of this topic.

> **CLOSE** the *My Nested Tables* document, saving your changes. Then close the *Memo* document, and if you are not proceeding directly to the next chapter, exit Word. Finally, close the *Loan* workbook without saving changes, and exit Excel.

Key Points

- To vary the layout of a document, you can divide text into columns.
- If your data is simple, you can create the look of a table by using tabs to set up the data as a tabular list.
- Word comes with quick tables that you can use as a starting point for creating professional, easy-to-read table formats.
- If you have already created a table, you can format it quickly by applying a table style. You can enhance the style by applying text attributes, borders, and shading.
- Formulas that perform simple calculations are easy to build in Word. For more complex calculations, you can create an Excel worksheet and then insert the worksheet data as a table in the Word document.
- Tables are great tools for organizing different types of information on the page. By using tables in creative ways, you can place information in non-linear arrangements for easy comparison or analysis.

Chapter at a Glance

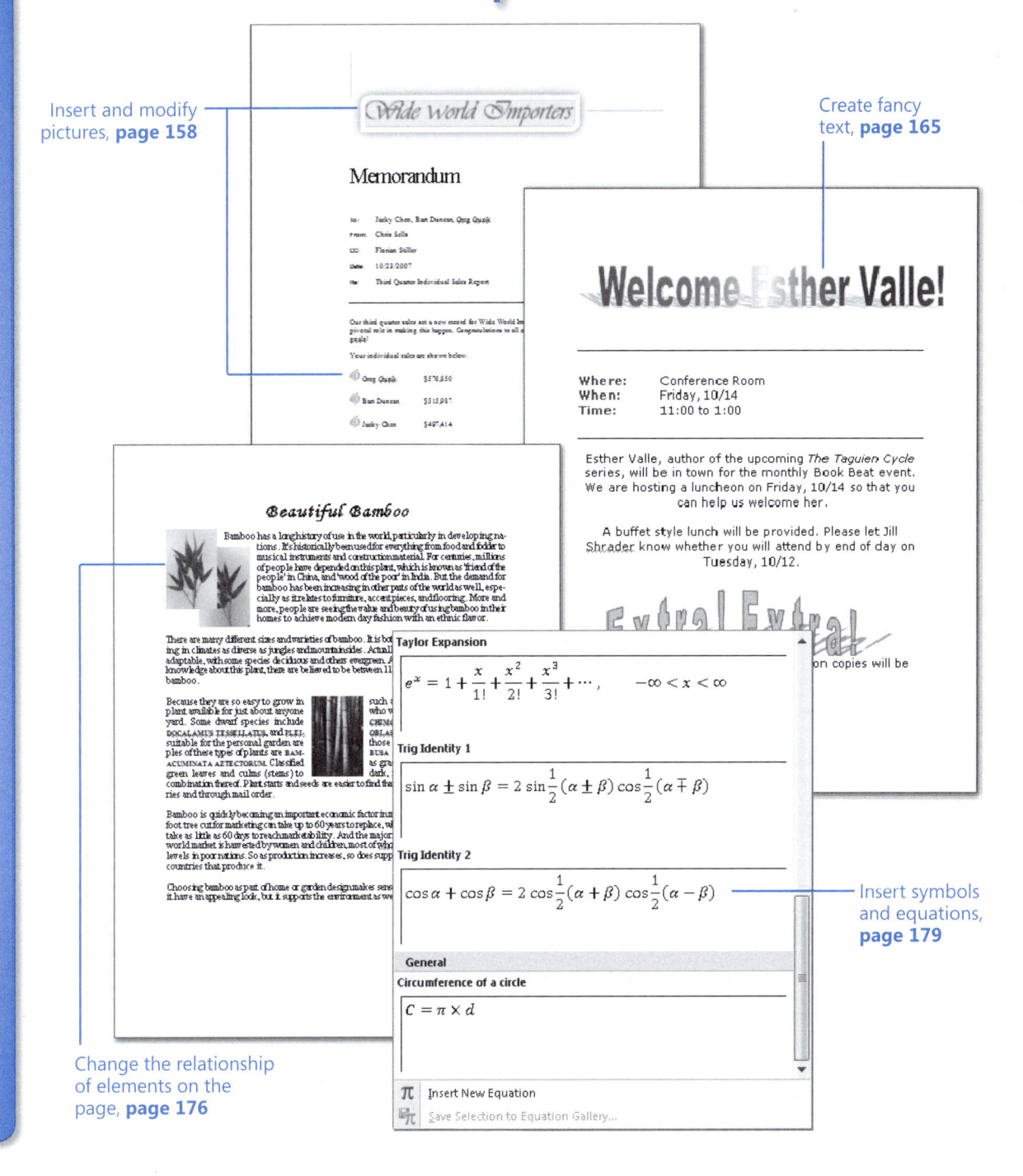

Insert and modify pictures, **page 158**

Create fancy text, **page 165**

Change the relationship of elements on the page, **page 176**

Insert symbols and equations, **page 179**

6 Working with Graphics, Symbols, and Equations

In this chapter, you will learn to:
- ✔ Insert and modify pictures.
- ✔ Create fancy text.
- ✔ Draw and modify shapes.
- ✔ Change the relationship of elements on the page.
- ✔ Insert symbols and equations.

Some documents are straightforward communications of information that require nothing more than words. Others might benefit from the addition of graphics, either to reinforce their concepts or to make them more attention grabbing or visually appealing.

Graphics can include a wide variety of images, including pictures and drawing objects. *Pictures* are graphics that have been created outside of Microsoft Office Word 2007—a scanned photograph, clip art, or a file created on a computer with a graphics program. *Drawing objects* are graphics that are created within Word—a shape, a diagram, a line, or WordArt text. You can use the buttons on the Insert tab to insert pictures and draw different kinds of objects. No matter what the origin of the graphic, you can change its position and how it relates to other elements on the page.

Like other graphics, symbols can add visual information or eye-appeal to a document. However, they are different from other graphics in that they are characters associated with a particular font. Equations are not graphics—they are accurately rendered mathematical formulas; however, they are similar to graphics in that they can be displayed inline with the surrounding text or in their own space with text above and below them.

In this chapter, you will insert and modify pictures, create WordArt objects, and draw shapes to create a simple picture. You will modify the text-wrapping, position, and stacking order of pictures in a document. Finally, you will also insert a symbol and build a simple equation.

See Also Do you need only a quick refresher on the topics in this chapter? See the Quick Reference section at the beginning of this book.

> **Important** Before you can use the practice files in this chapter, you need to install them from the book's companion CD to their default location. See "Using the Companion CD" at the beginning of this book for more information.

> **Troubleshooting** Graphics and operating system–related instructions in this book reflect the Windows Vista user interface. If your computer is running Windows XP and you experience trouble following the instructions as written, please refer to the "Information for Readers Running Windows XP" section at the beginning of this book.

Inserting and Modifying Pictures

You can insert scanned photographs or pictures created in almost any program into a Word document. Two buttons in the Illustrations group on the Insert tab can be used to specify the source of the picture, as follows:

- **Picture.** Click this button to insert a picture from a file. If a digital camera is connected to your computer, you can also insert a picture directly from the camera.

- **Clip Art.** Click this button to insert one of the hundreds of clip art images that come with Word, such as photos and drawings of people, places, and things.

    See Also For information about organizing clip art, see the sidebar "Organizing Clips" later in this chapter.

After you insert a picture in a document, you can modify the image by using buttons on the Format contextual tab, which is displayed only when a picture or drawing object is selected. For example, you can use buttons in the Adjust group to change the picture's brightness and contrast, recolor it, and compress it to reduce the size of the document containing it. The Picture Styles group offers a wide range of picture styles that you can apply to a picture to change its shape and orientation, as well as add borders and picture effects. The Arrange group has buttons for moving and grouping pictures on the page. And finally, you can use the buttons in the Size group for cropping and resizing pictures.

Inserting and Modifying Pictures **159**

In this exercise, you will insert and modify a picture. You will then insert, size, move, and copy a clip art image.

> **USE** the *Picture* document and the *Logo* graphic. These practice files are located in the *Documents\Microsoft Press\Word2007SBS\CreatingGraphics* folder.
>
> **BE SURE TO** start Word and display the rulers and non-printing characters before starting this exercise.
>
> **OPEN** the *Picture* document.

Picture

1. With the insertion point at the top of the page, on the **Insert** tab, in the **Illustrations** group, click the **Picture** button.

   The Insert Picture dialog box opens, displaying the contents of your *Pictures* folder.

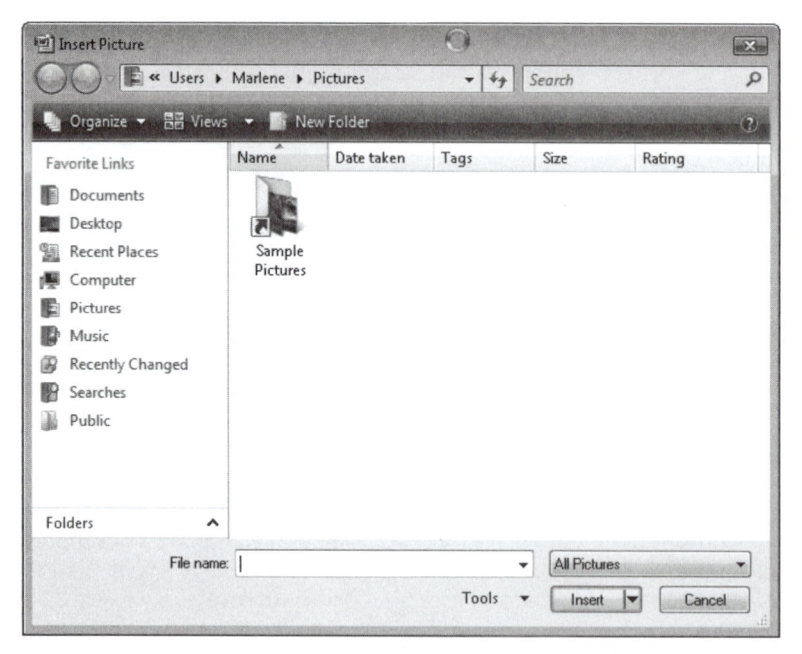

2. In the **Favorite Links** pane, click **Documents**. Then double-click *Microsoft Press*, double-click *Word2007SBS*, double-click *CreatingGraphics*, and double-click *Logo*.

   Word inserts the picture at the insertion point and displays the Format contextual tab on the Ribbon.

3. On the lower-right corner of the graphic, point to the handle (the circle), and when it changes to a double arrow, click and drag up and to the left until the graphic's shadow frame is about at the 4.5-inch mark on the horizontal ruler.

160   Chapter 6   Working with Graphics, Symbols, and Equations

---

Wide World Importers

Memorandum

To:	Jacky Chen, Bart Duncan, Greg Guzik
From:	Chris Sells
CC:	Florian Stiller
Date:	10/23/2007
Re:	Third Quarter Individual Sales Report

Recolor

4. On the **Format** contextual tab, in the **Adjust** group, click the **Recolor** button.

5. In the **Recolor** gallery, under **Light Variations**, click the second thumbnail (**Accent color 1 Light**).

   The picture's colors change.

Brightness

6. In the **Adjust** group, click the **Brightness** button.

7. In the **Brightness** gallery, point to each option to preview its effect, and then click **+10%**.

Contrast

8. In the **Adjust** group, click the **Contrast** button, and then in the **Contrast** gallery, click **-30%**.

> **Tip** You can fine-tune the brightness and contrast of a picture by clicking Picture Corrections Options at the bottom of either the Brightness or Contrast gallery. The Format Picture dialog box opens with the Picture page active. Drag the slider or change the percentage by clicking the up or down arrow. To restore the original picture, click Reset Picture to discard any changes you made.

More

9. On the **Format** tab, in the **Picture Styles** group, click the **More** button.

   The Picture Styles gallery opens.

> **Tip** Similar galleries of preformatted styles (referred to as Quick Styles) are available for charts, illustrations, SmartArt graphics, tables, and text. Quick Styles are available from the Styles group on the Format tab or contextual tab, when the item you want to format is selected. Point to any Quick Style to display a preview of its effect; click the Quick Style to apply it.

Inserting and Modifying Pictures **161**

10. In the gallery, point to each thumbnail in turn to see its effects. Then click the fourth thumbnail in the third row (**Rounded Diagonal Corner, White**), and click away from the graphic.

    The logo now has a three-dimensional perspective.

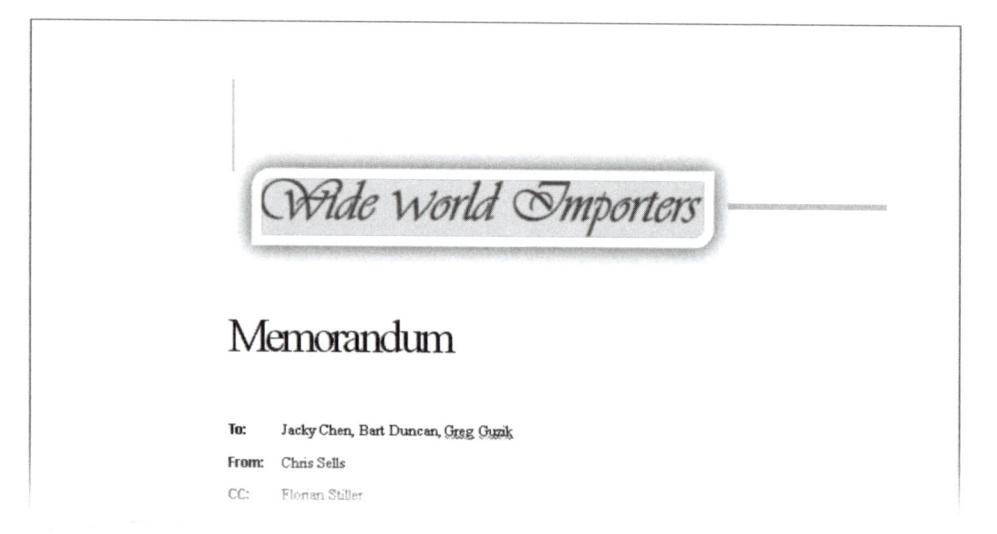

11. Scroll down the document until you see the tabular list, and click at the end of the *Greg Guzik* paragraph.

12. On the **Insert** tab, in the **Illustrations** group, click the **Clip Art** button.

13. In the **Clip Art** task pane, select the current entry in the **Search for** box (or click in the box if there is no entry), type **symbols**, and then click **Go**.

> **Troubleshooting** If you see a message asking whether you want to search the clip art available from Microsoft Office Online, click No.

The task pane displays graphics representing common symbols.

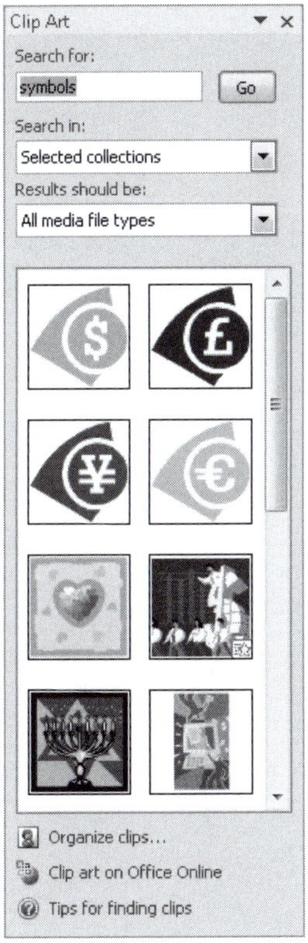

14. In the task pane, click the stylized dollar sign ($) to insert it in the document, and then click the task pane's **Close** button.

    The inserted image is selected in the document, as indicated by the circular handles surrounding its frame.

15. Point to the lower-right handle of the image, and when the pointer changes to a double arrow, drag up and to the left until the image is about 0.25 inch square.

Inserting and Modifying Pictures **163**

> **Tip** You can also change the size of a picture or clip art image by adjusting the Shape Height and Shape Width settings in the Size group on the Format tab.

16. Point to the dollar sign image, and when the pointer changes to a four-headed arrow, drag the image to the beginning of the *Greg Guzik* paragraph.

17. If the image is no longer selected, click it to select it.

> **Troubleshooting** If you have trouble selecting the image, press the Esc key, and then try again.

18. Point to the image, hold down the mouse button, hold down the Ctrl key, and drag a copy of the image to the left of *Bart Duncan*, releasing first the mouse button and then the Ctrl key.

A copy of the graphic is inserted in front of *Bart Duncan*.

> **Tip** If you release the Ctrl key first, Word will move the image from the second paragraph to the third instead of being copied.

19. Repeat step 18 to drag a copy to the left of *Jacky Chen*.

The images preceding each paragraph resemble bullets.

> Our third quarter sales set a new record for Wide World Importers, and our strong sales staff played a pivotal role in making this happen. Congratulations to all of you for exceeding your target sales goals!
>
> Your individual sales are shown below:
>
> Greg Guzik $576,850
>
> Bart Duncan $515,987
>
> Jacky Chen $497,414

✕ CLOSE the *Picture* document without saving your changes.

Organizing Clips

To make clip art images, pictures, sounds, and movie clips conveniently available regardless of where they are actually stored, you can use the *Microsoft Clip Organizer* to arrange them in collections. You can arrange clips from Microsoft Office, from the Web, or from other sources into existing collections or new ones.

To experiment with the Clip Organizer, follow these steps:

1. Display the **Clip Art** task pane, and at the bottom of the pane, click **Organize clips**.

   The Favorites - Microsoft Clip Organizer window opens.

2. In the **Collection List**, under **My Collections**, click **Favorites**.

3. On the window's **File** menu, point to **Add Clips to Organizer,** and then click **On My Own**.

   The Favorites - Add Clips To Organizer dialog box opens.

4. Navigate to the folder where the file you want to add to the Favorites collection is stored, click the file name, and then click **Add**.

   To place images in a different collection, click Add To in the Add To Clips Organizer dialog box. Then in the Import To Collection dialog box, select the collection, and click OK. (You can click New in the Import To Collection dialog box to create a new collection.)

5. Point to the thumbnail of the file you just added, click the arrow that appears, and then click **Edit Keywords**.

   The Keywords dialog box opens.

6. In the **Keyword** box, type the word or words that you want to associate with this file, and then click **Add**.

   The keyword is added to the Keywords For Current Clip list.

7. Click **OK** to close the **Edit Keywords** dialog box, and then close the **Microsoft Clip Organizer** window.

   You can now search for the file by that keyword in the Clip Art task pane.

To delete a clip from the Clip Organizer, in the Microsoft Clip Organizer window, click the clip's arrow, click Delete From Clip Organizer, and then click OK to confirm the deletion.

Creating Fancy Text

When you want a text banner that is fancier than one you can create by applying font attributes, you can use *WordArt*. WordArt text can swirl, grow bigger from one end to the other or in the middle, take on a three-dimensional shape, and change color from one letter to another.

To insert WordArt text, you click the WordArt button in the Text group on the Insert tab, and click a style in the WordArt gallery. Then in the Edit WordArt Text dialog box, you can enter the text. You can also adjust the font, font size, and font style. Clicking OK inserts the WordArt object in the document at the insertion point.

> **Tip** You can also select existing text before clicking the WordArt button to convert that text into a WordArt object.

Selecting a WordArt object displays the Format contextual tab, which you can use to edit and format a WordArt object to meet your needs. From the Format tab, you can add special effects such as shadows and 3-D effects; position the WordArt object on the page; change the fill color; and change the text spacing, alignment, and orientation.

In this exercise, you will insert a new WordArt object. Then you'll turn existing text into a WordArt object and modify the object to look the way you want it.

> **USE** the *WordArt* document. This practice file is located in the *Documents\Microsoft Press\Word2007SBS\CreatingGraphics* folder.
> **BE SURE TO** display non-printing characters before starting this exercise.
> **OPEN** the *WordArt* document.

1. Press the [↓] key twice to move the insertion point to the third blank paragraph of the document.

2. On the **Insert** tab, in the **Text** group, click the **WordArt** button.

   The WordArt gallery opens, displaying a list of styles.

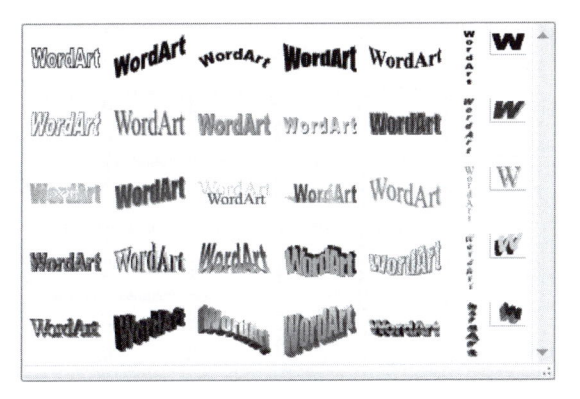

3. Click the fourth thumbnail in the third row (**WordArt style 16**).

   The Edit WordArt Text dialog box opens, displaying the words *Your Text Here* as a placeholder.

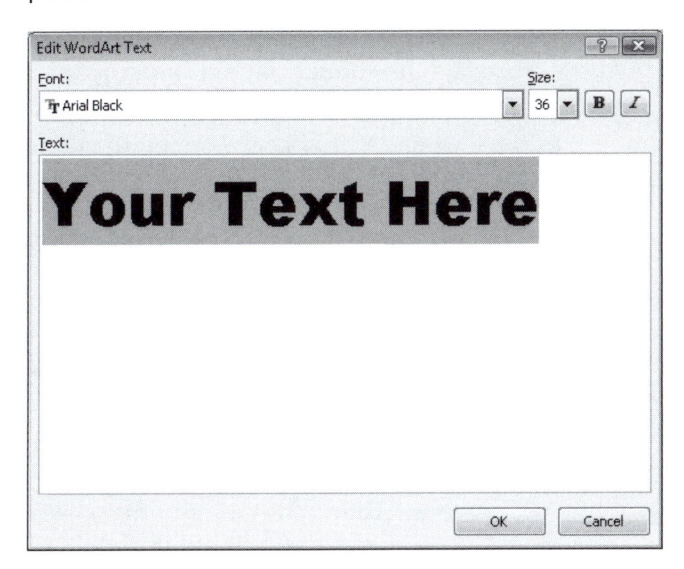

4. In the **Text** box, type Welcome Esther Valle!.
5. Click the **Size** arrow, and in the list, click **44**. Then click **OK**.

   The text is inserted as an object at the insertion point, and the Format contextual tab appears on the Ribbon.

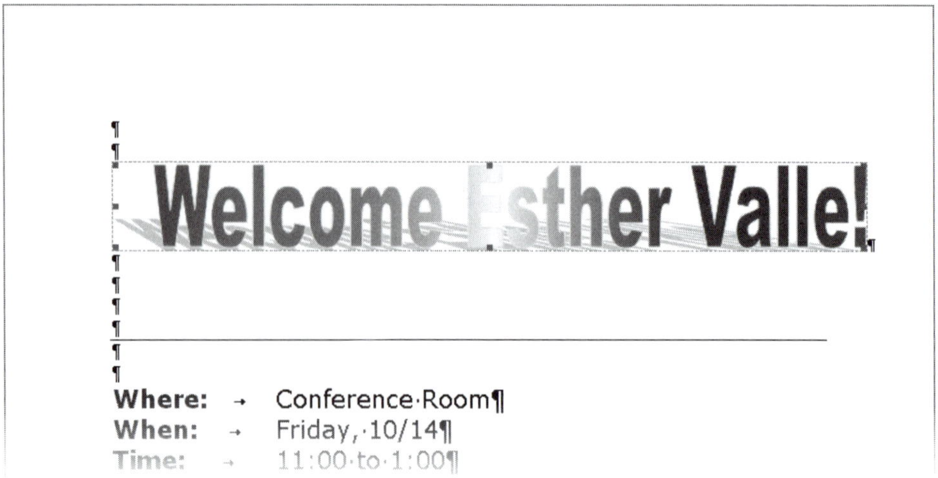

6. Scroll down the document, and select the words **Extra! Extra!**.
 7. On the **Insert** tab, in the **Text** group, click the **WordArt** button, and then click the third thumbnail in the fourth row of the gallery (**WordArt style 21**).
 8. In the **Edit WordArt Text** dialog box, click **OK**.

 The text you selected is converted into a WordArt object and the Format contextual tab appears on the Ribbon.

 9. Click the WordArt object, and on the **Format** tab, in the **WordArt Styles** group, click the **Shape Fill** arrow.
 10. Under **Standard Colors** in the palette, click the **Orange** box.

 The color of the WordArt object changes to orange. Notice that the Shape Fill button's color is now orange.

 11. In the **Text** group, click the **Spacing** button, and then click **Very Loose**.

 The spacing between the letters increases.

 12. In the **WordArt Styles** group, click the **Shape Outline** arrow, and then under **Standard Colors** in the palette, click the **Red** box.

 The letters are now outlined in red.

 13. Point to the WordArt object's middle-right handle, and when the pointer changes to a double arrow, drag to the right for an inch or two to stretch the object's frame.

When you release the mouse button, the stretched object snaps to the horizontal center of the page.

Esther Valle, author of the upcoming *The Taguien Cycle* series, will be in town for the monthly Book Beat event. We are hosting a luncheon on Friday, 10/14 so that you can help us welcome her.

A buffet style lunch will be provided. Please let Jill Shrader know whether you will attend by end of day on Tuesday, 10/12.

Extra! Extra!

A limited number of signed first edition copies will be available!

Change Shape

14. In the **WordArt Styles** group, click the **Change WordArt Shape** button.

The Change Shape gallery opens.

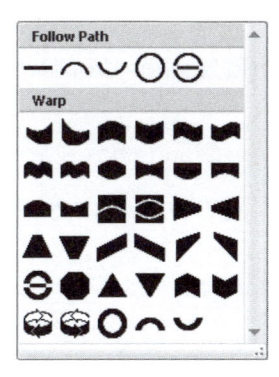

15. In the gallery, click the first thumbnail in the third row (**Inflate Top**).

The WordArt shape changes to an arch.

16. Drag the upper-middle handle upward to exaggerate the curve.

17. In the **Shadow Effects** group, click the **Shadow Effects** button, and in the **Shadow Effects** gallery, under **Perspective Shadow**, click the second thumbnail in the first row (**Shadow Style 7**).

   The new shadow effect is applied to the letters.

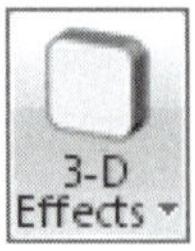

18. On the **Format** tab, in the **3-D Effects** group, click the **3-D Effects** button.

   > **Troubleshooting** If you see a 3-D Effects button but not a group, click the button to display the group, and then click the 3-D Effects button in the group to open the gallery.

19. In the **3-D Effects** gallery, point to each thumbnail in turn to observe its effects.

20. Press the Esc key to close the gallery without making a selection, and then if necessary, click Esc again to close the 3-D Effects group.

21. Turn off non-printing characters, and then click away from the WordArt object to see the results.

CLOSE the *WordArt* document without saving your changes.

> ### Formatting the First Letter of a Paragraph
>
> Many books, magazines, and reports begin the first paragraph of a section or chapter by using an enlarged, decorative capital letter. Called a *dropped capital*, or simply a *drop cap*, this effect can be an easy way to give a document a finished, professional look.
>
> To apply a drop cap, follow these steps:
>
> 1. Click anywhere in a paragraph of text, and then on the **Insert** tab, in the **Text** group, click the **Drop Cap** button.
>
>   The Drop Cap gallery opens, providing two basic drop-cap styles: Dropped, which displaces some of the paragraph text, and In Margin, which hangs in the margin adjacent to the paragraph text. In either case, the drop cap is as tall as three lines of text and uses the same font as the rest of the paragraph.
>
> 2. Point to each thumbnail to display its live preview, and then click the one you want.
>
>   Word converts the first letter of the paragraph into a graphic. If you selected Dropped, it wraps the text to the right of the graphic.
>
> For more options, click Drop Cap Options at the bottom of the Drop Cap gallery to open the Drop Cap dialog box. There, you can choose a font for the drop cap that is different from the rest of the paragraph and make adjustments to the drop cap's height and distance from the text.

Drawing and Modifying Shapes

If you want to add visual interest and impact to a document but you don't need anything as fancy as a picture or a clip art image, you can draw a shape, also called a *drawing object*. Shapes can be simple, such as lines, circles, or squares, or more complex, such as stars, hearts, and arrows.

To draw a shape directly on the page (Word's default setting), you click the Shapes button in the Illustrations group on the Insert tab, click the shape you want in the Shapes gallery, and then do one of the following:

- Click the document where you want a drawing object of the default size and shape to be placed.
- Drag the pointer across the page to create a drawing object the size and shape you want.

If you want to assemble a group of shapes to create a drawing, you might want to draw the shapes on a drawing canvas instead of directly on the page. The drawing canvas keeps the parts of the drawing together, helps you position the drawing, and provides a frame-like boundary between your drawing and the text on the page. To open a drawing canvas, you click New Drawing Canvas at the bottom of the Shapes gallery. You can then draw shapes on the canvas in the usual ways. At any time, you can size and move the drawing canvas and the objects it contains as one unit.

> **Tip** If you prefer to always use the drawing canvas when creating drawing objects, click the Microsoft Office Button, click Word Options, and click Advanced. Then under Editing Options, select the Automatically Create Drawing Canvas When Inserting AutoShapes check box, and click OK.

> **Tip** To make a drawing canvas stand out on the page, but you can put a border around it and shade it. You can use the tools on the Format contextual tab to size and position it precisely and to specify how text should wrap around it.

When you finish drawing a shape, it is automatically selected. Later you can select the shape by clicking it. While the shape is selected, you can move and size it, and you can modify it by using the buttons on the Format contextual tab. The attributes you can change include the following:

- The fill color inside the object
- The color, thickness, and style of the border around the object
- The shadow effect behind the object
- The three-dimensional aspect, or perspective, from which you are observing the object
- The angle of rotation, or orientation, of the object
- The alignment of the object in relation to the page
- The way text wraps around the object
- The order of the object in a stack of objects
- The size of the object

You can also change the size and shape of an object by dragging its handles. You can reposition it by dragging it, or by pressing the Arrow keys on your keyboard to move the object in small increments.

Tip If you change the attributes of a shape—for example, its fill color and border weight—and you want all the shapes you draw from now on in this document to have those attributes, right-click the shape, and then click Set AutoShape Defaults.

If you want to move or size more than one related graphic, you can ensure that they retain their positions in relation to each other by *grouping* them. They then act as one object. To break the bond, you can ungroup the objects.

In this exercise, you will draw and manipulate a few shapes on a drawing canvas, and you will then size and position the canvas.

USE the *Shapes* document. This practice file is located in the *Documents\Microsoft Press\Word2007SBS\CreatingGraphics* folder.
BE SURE TO display the rulers before starting this exercise.
OPEN the *Shapes* document.

1. Press **Ctrl**+**End** to position the insertion point at the end of the document.

2. On the **Insert** tab, in the **Illustrations** group, click the **Shapes** button, and then at the bottom of the **Shapes** gallery, click **New Drawing Canvas**.

   Word adds a page to the document, inserts a drawing canvas, and displays the Format contextual tab on the Ribbon.

3. On the **Format** contextual tab, in the **Insert Shapes** group, click the **Oval** button, and then move position the pointer in the upper-left corner of the drawing canvas.

4. Hold down the **Shift** key, and then drag down and to the right to draw a circle about 1.5 inches in diameter.

   Tip To draw a shape with equal height and width, such as a square or circle, hold down the Shift key while you draw, and then release the mouse button before releasing the Shift key.

   When you finish drawing, the circle is selected, as indicated by the handles around it.

Drawing and Modifying Shapes   **173**

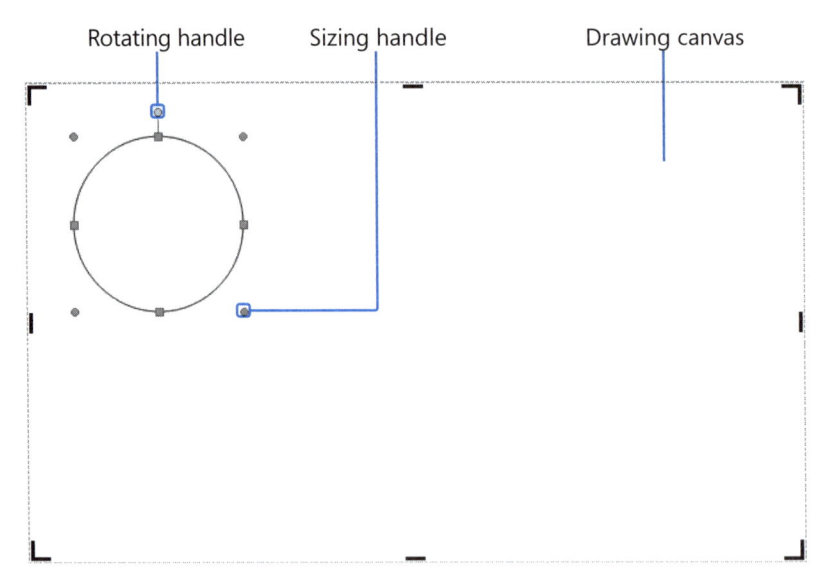

Rotating handle   Sizing handle   Drawing canvas

5. Hold down the Ctrl key, and drag the shadow outline of the circle to the upper middle of the drawing canvas. Be sure to release the mouse button before releasing the Ctrl key.

   Word creates a copy of the circle in the location where you release the mouse button.

6. Create a copy of the second circle in the upper-right corner of the drawing canvas.

   Shape Fill

7. Click the left circle. Then on the **Format** tab, in the **Shape Styles** group, click the **Shape Fill** arrow, and under **Standard Colors** in the palette, click the **Yellow** box.

8. Click the middle circle, and repeat step 7 to fill it with the **Light Green** color.

9. Click the right circle, and repeat step 7 to fill it with the **Purple** color.

   All the circles are now filled with color so that they resemble balloons.

   Curve

10. In the **Insert Shapes** group, click the third button in the third row (**Curve**).

11. Point to the bottom of the left balloon, drag down and to the left about an inch, click the canvas, drag down and to the right about an inch, and then double-click the canvas.

    A curved line resembling a string appears below the left balloon.

12. Hold down Ctrl, point to the curved line, and drag a copy of it to the bottom of the middle balloon. Then drag another curved line to the bottom of the right balloon.

    All the balloons now have strings, and the one on the right is still selected.

174 Chapter 6   Working with Graphics, Symbols, and Equations

13. Hold down Ctrl, and click the purple balloon.

    Both the balloon and its string are selected.

14. In the **Arrange** group, click the **Group** button, and then click **Group**.

    One set of handles now appears around the balloon and its string, indicating that the two shapes are grouped as one object.

15. In the **Arrange** group, click the **Rotate** button, and then click **Flip Horizontal**.

    The balloon and its string are now facing the other way.

16. Press the ↑ key five times.

    The balloon and its string are now positioned slightly higher on the drawing canvas than the other two balloons.

17. Click a blank area of the drawing canvas to release the selection.

18. In the **Size** group, click the **Shape Height** down arrow until the height of the drawing canvas is 2".

    Word moves the drawing canvas to the bottom of the first page of the document, where it now fits. The balloons have shrunk in proportion to the canvas.

19. In the **Arrange** group, click the **Text Wrapping** button, and then click **In Front of Text**.

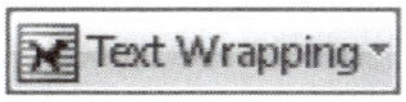

    You can now move the drawing canvas independently of the text around it.

    See Also For information about text wrapping, see "Changing the Relationships of Elements on the Page" later in this chapter.

20. In the **Arrange** group, click the **Position** button.

    The Position gallery opens.

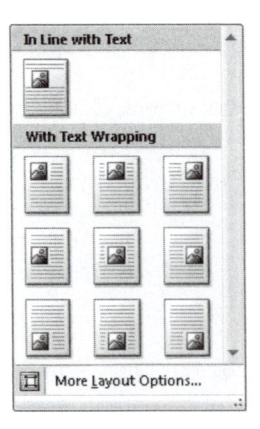

21. In the gallery, click the second thumbnail in the third row (**Position in Bottom Center with Square Text Wrapping**).

    The drawing canvas moves with the objects it contains to the center of the page, below the document's last paragraph.

22. Click outside of the drawing canvas.

    If non-printing characters are turned on, you might want to turn them off to get a better view of the results.

CLOSE the *Shapes* document without saving your changes.

Changing the Relationship of Elements on the Page

When you insert an object such as a picture into a document, it moves any associated text out of the way. You can change the way text wraps around objects and the relationship of overlapping objects by using the buttons in the Arrange group on the Format contextual tab.

When you choose any text wrapping option other than Behind Text or In Line With Text, you can specify that a picture be positioned in one of two ways:

- **Absolutely.** This option positions the picture at a distance you set from a margin, page, paragraph, or line.
- **Relatively.** This type of positioning is determined by the relationship of the picture to a margin or page.

After you position a picture, adding text might upset the arrangement of text and graphics on the page. You can specify whether a picture should remain anchored in its position on the page or should move with its related text. You can also specify whether the picture should be allowed to overlap text.

When graphics overlap each other, they are *stacked*. The stacking order (which graphic appears on top) is initially determined by the order in which you inserted the graphics. You can change the order by selecting a graphic and clicking the Bring To Front or Send To Back button in the Arrange group to move the graphic to the top or bottom of the stack. If you click either button's arrow and then click Bring Forward or Send Backward, the graphic moves forward or backward in the stack one position at a time.

In this exercise, you will modify the text-wrapping, position, and stacking order of pictures that have already been inserted into a document.

> **USE** the *Relationships* document. This practice file is located in the *Documents\Microsoft Press\Word2007SBS\CreatingGraphics* folder.
> **BE SURE TO** display non-printing characters before starting this exercise.
> **OPEN** the *Relationships* document.

1. Scroll to the bottom of the first page, and drag the picture of a bamboo grove up to the beginning of the word *TESSELLATUS* in the middle of the paragraph that begins *Because they are so easy*.

   The picture is positioned wherever you dropped it, and the surrounding text is moved to make room.

2. On the **Format** contextual tab, in the **Arrange** group, click the **Text Wrapping** button, and then click **More Layout Options**.

The Advanced Layout dialog box opens, with the In Line With Text option selected.

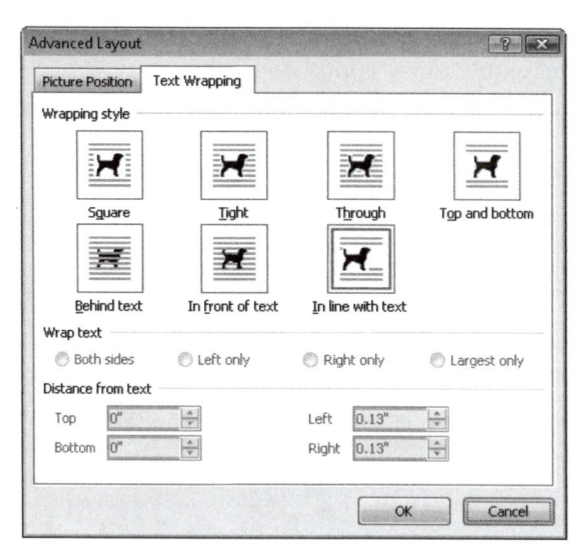

3. Click the **Square** wrapping style, and in the **Wrap text** area, click **Both sides**. Then click the **Picture Position** tab.

The options on this tab control the location of the picture on the page and whether it moves when you make changes to the text.

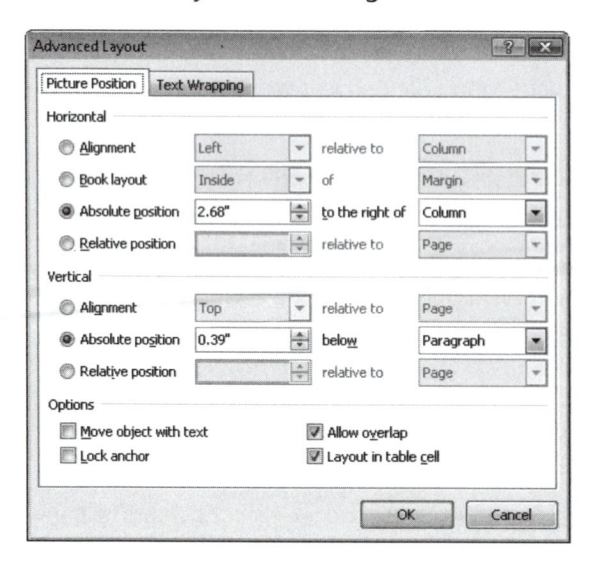

4. In the **Horizontal** area, click **Alignment**, click the **Alignment** arrow, and then click **Centered**. Then in the **Vertical** area, change the **Absolute position** setting to **0"**.

5. Click **OK**.

   The picture is repositioned so that it is aligned with the top and center of the paragraph, with the paragraph text wrapped on either side.

6. Click to the left of the word *Because* at the beginning of the paragraph, and press Enter.

   The picture moves with the paragraph.

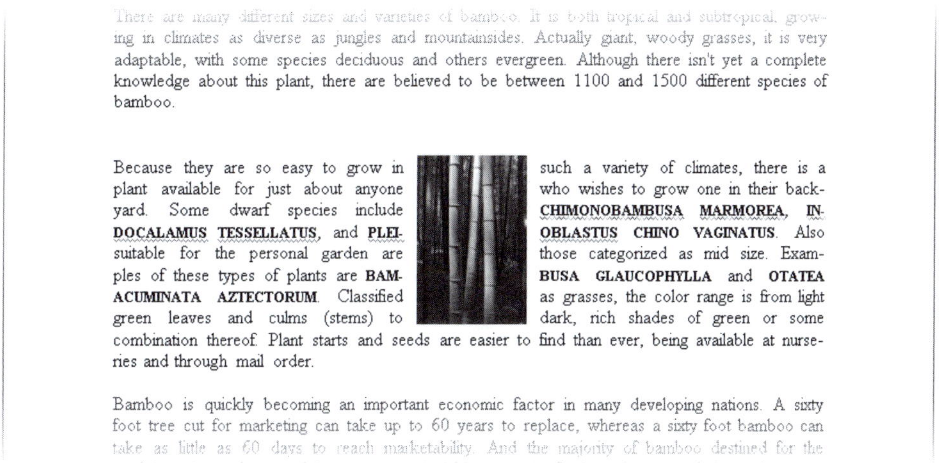

7. On the **Quick Access Toolbar**, click the **Undo** button to remove the extra blank paragraph.

8. Scroll to the next page, and change the text wrapping style of the two pictures on that page from **In line with text** to **Tight**.

   The relationship of the pictures with the text is broken, and because they are now essentially floating over the text, they both move to the first page.

9. Scroll to the top of the document, and drag the selected picture down and to the right, releasing the mouse button while the pictures are still overlapped.

10. In the **Arrange** group, click the **Text Wrapping** button, and then click **More Layout Options**.

11. In the **Advanced Layout** dialog box, on the **Text Wrapping** tab, in the **Wrap text** area, click the **Right only** option, and then click **OK**.

12. On the **Format** tab, in the **Arrange** group, click the **Send to Back** button.

    The lower picture moves behind the upper picture.

13. Hold down [Shift], and click the upper picture to add it to the selection. Then press the [↓] key to nudge the pictures down until the text is neatly aligned to the right of the pictures.

14. Click a blank area of the page to release the selection.

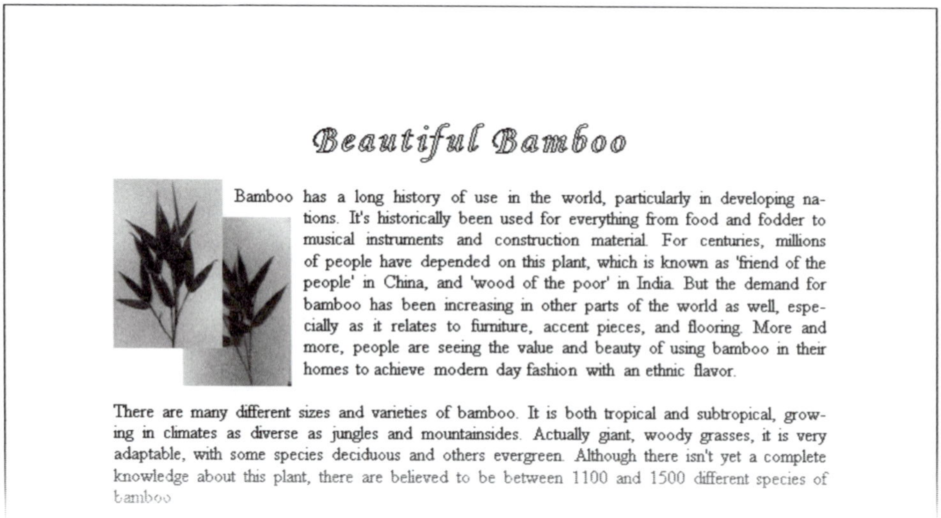

CLOSE the *Relationships* document without saving your changes.

Inserting Symbols and Equations

Some documents require characters not found on a standard keyboard. These characters might include the copyright (©) or registered trademark (®) symbols, currency symbols (such as € or £), Greek letters, or letters with accent marks. Or you might want to add arrows (such as ↗ or ↖) or graphic icons (such as ☂ or ✈). Word gives you easy access to a huge array of symbols that you can easily insert into any document.

> **Tip** You can insert some common symbols by typing a keyboard combination. For example, if you type two consecutive dashes followed by a word and a space, Word changes the two dashes to a professional-looking em-dash—like this one. (This symbol gets its name from the fact that it was originally the width of the character *m*.) To use these features, click the Microsoft Office Button, click Word Options, and in the Proofing panel, click AutoCorrect Options. On the AutoCorrect tab of the AutoCorrect dialog box, make sure the Replace Text As You Type check box is selected, and select any check boxes you like on the AutoFormat As You Type tab.

You can insert mathematical symbols such as π (pi) or ∑ (sigma, or summation) the same way you would insert any other symbol. But you can also create entire mathematical equations in a document. You can drop some equations, including the Quadratic Formula, the Binomial Theorem, and the Pythagorean Theorem, into a document with a few clicks. If you need something other than the standard equations that are pre-defined in Word, you can build your own equations using a library of mathematical symbols.

The buttons for inserting symbols and equations are in the Symbols group on the Insert tab:

- Clicking the Symbol button displays a Symbol gallery of commonly used symbols. From this gallery, you can also open the Symbol dialog box, where you can select from hundreds of symbols and special characters in a variety of fonts.
- Clicking the Equation arrow displays the Equation gallery of commonly used equations that you can click to insert in your document.
- Clicking the Equation button inserts a blank area where you can type an equation and also adds the Design contextual tab to the Ribbon. This tab provides access to mathematical symbols, structures such as fractions and radicals, and the Equation Options dialog box. After building your equation, you can add it to the Equation gallery so that it is readily available the next time you need it.

An equation appears in the document as a field. It resembles a graphic in that you can choose whether to display it inline with the surrounding text or displayed in its own space, with the surrounding text flowing above and below it.

In this exercise, you will insert a graphical icon into a document, and then you will build a simple equation and add it to the Equation gallery.

> **USE** the *Symbols* document. This practice file is located in the *Documents\Microsoft Press\Word2007SBS\CreatingGraphics* folder.
> **OPEN** the *Symbols* document.

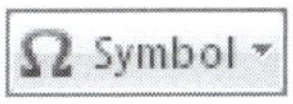

1. With the insertion point to the left of the document's title, on the **Insert** tab, in the **Symbols** group, click the **Symbol** button, and then click **More Symbols**.

   The Symbol dialog box opens.

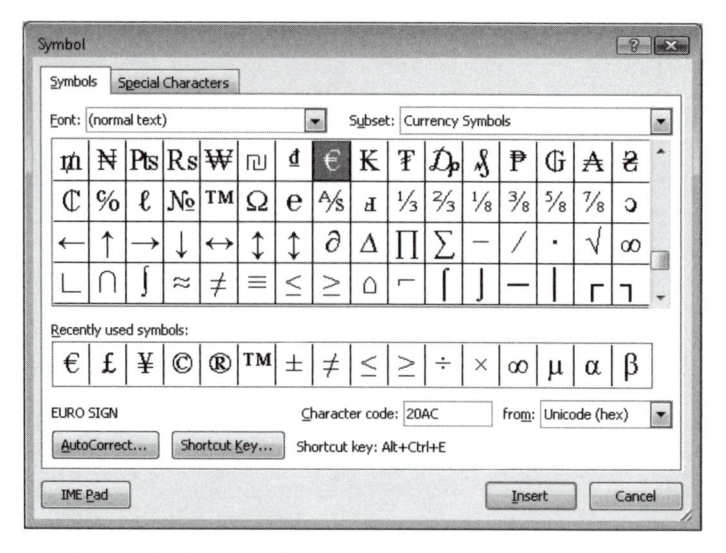

2. On the **Symbols** tab of the dialog box, click the **Font** arrow, and then in the list, click **Webdings**.

3. In the list of symbols, click the ninth icon in the third row (the house), click **Insert**, and then click **Close**.

   Word inserts the house icon at the insertion point.

4. Press End, and in the **Symbols** group, click the **Symbol** button.

   The Symbol gallery opens, with the icon you just inserted at the top.

5. Click the house icon.

   The house icon now appears at both ends of the title.

182 Chapter 6 Working with Graphics, Symbols, and Equations

Home Decorator Fabric Special

Dear Wide World Importers Friend:

We're so excited about the recent arrival of a fabulous group of decorator fabrics purchased from one of Asia's finest mills. Our selection includes solid dupioni, prints, plaids, stripes, jacquards, and more, in colors ranging from subtle to eye-popping. Whether used for a single pillow or an elaborate window treatment, these fabrics will add an elegant touch to any room in your home.

6. Display non-printing characters, scroll the document, and then in the second step in the numbered list, click between the two spaces to the left of the word *where* in the third line.

7. On the **Insert** tab, in the **Symbols** group, click the **Equation** button.

   The Equation Builder inserts an area where you can type the equation, and the Design contextual tab is added to the Ribbon.

8. Type **C** and then on the **Design** contextual tab, in the **Symbols** group, click the **Equal** button.

9. In the **Symbols** group, click the **More** button.

   The Basic Math gallery opens.

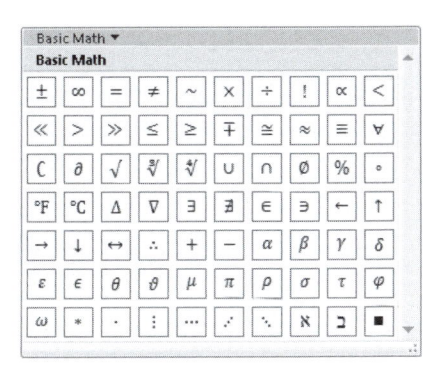

10. In the **Basic Math** gallery, click the sixth symbol in the sixth row (π).

    Notice that the row containing the pi symbol is now visible in the Symbols group.

11. In the **Symbols** group, click the up arrow until the top of the gallery scrolls into view, click the **Multiplication Sign** button, and then type **d**.

Inserting Symbols and Equations **183**

As you add to the equation, the Equation Builder adjusts the spacing and formatting of the formula.

12. Click outside the equation to see how it looks.

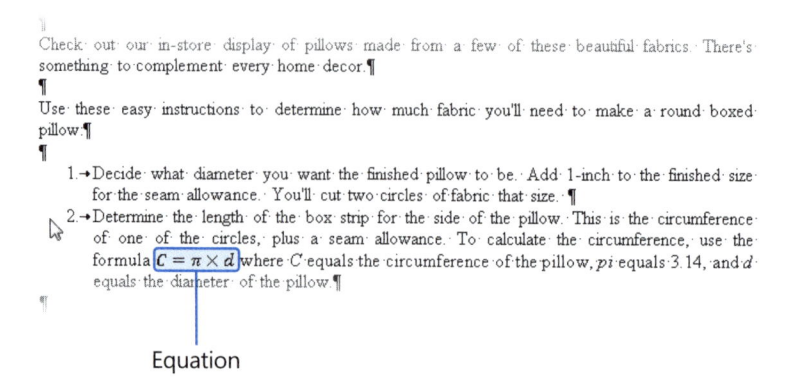

Equation

13. Click the equation, click the arrow that appears to the right, and then click **Save as New Equation**.

The Create New Building Block dialog box opens.

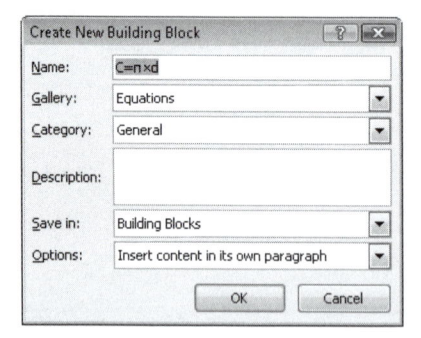

See Also For more information about building blocks, see "Inserting Ready-Made Document Parts" in Chapter 8, "Working with Longer Documents."

14. In the **Name** box, type Circumference of a circle, and then click **OK**.

15. Press the ↓ to release the selection. Then on the **Insert** tab, in the **Symbols** group, click the **Equation** arrow, and scroll the **Equation** gallery.

Your custom equation is now available in the Equation gallery.

Taylor Expansion

$$e^x = 1 + \frac{x}{1!} + \frac{x^2}{2!} + \frac{x^3}{3!} + \cdots, \quad -\infty < x < \infty$$

Trig Identity 1

$$\sin \alpha \pm \sin \beta = 2 \sin\frac{1}{2}(\alpha \pm \beta) \cos\frac{1}{2}(\alpha \mp \beta)$$

Trig Identity 2

$$\cos \alpha + \cos \beta = 2 \cos\frac{1}{2}(\alpha + \beta) \cos\frac{1}{2}(\alpha - \beta)$$

General

Circumference of a circle

$$C = \pi \times d$$

π Insert New Equation
    Save Selection to Equation Gallery...

16. Press the **Esc** key to close the gallery without making a selection.

17. Click the equation, click its arrow, and then click **Change to Display**.

    Word inserts a line break before and after the equation and positions it in the center of the page.

18. Click the equation's arrow, point to **Justification**, and then click **Left**.

19. Click the equation's arrow, click **Change to Inline**, and then click a blank area of the document.

> **CLOSE** the *Symbols* document without saving your changes. If you are not continuing directly on to the next chapter, exit Word.

> **Important** When you exit Word, you will be asked whether you want to save the addition you have made to the Building Blocks template. Click No if you want to discard the equation you added in this exercise.

Key Points

- You can insert artwork created with most graphics programs, as well as scanned photographs and images, into a Word document.
- When character formatting doesn't produce the dramatic effect you need for a document, create fancy text banners for your documents by using WordArt.
- You can dress up a document with simple shapes. You can also group shapes on a drawing canvas to create simple pictures.
- You can position a graphic in relation to the text that surrounds it or to other objects in the document.
- The Symbols dialog box provides access not only to the kinds of symbols you might need in a professional document but also to little icons that add pizzazz.
- The Equation Builder can help construct and display complex formulas.

Chapter at a Glance

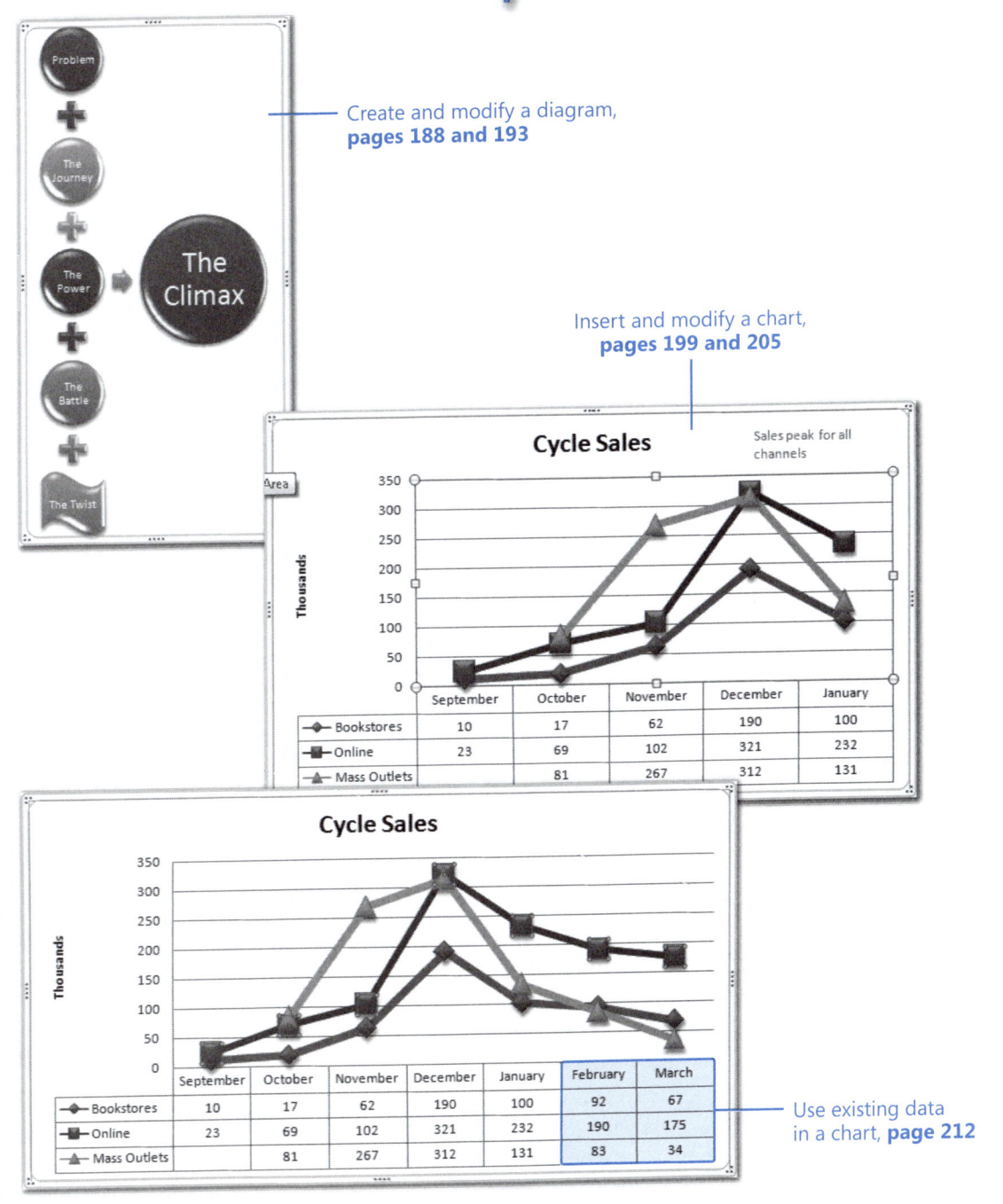

Create and modify a diagram, **pages 188 and 193**

Insert and modify a chart, **pages 199 and 205**

Use existing data in a chart, **page 212**

7 Working with Diagrams and Charts

In this chapter, you will learn to:
- ✔ Create a diagram.
- ✔ Modify a diagram.
- ✔ Insert a chart.
- ✔ Modify a chart.
- ✔ Use existing data in a chart.

You will often find it helpful to reinforce the argument you are making in a document with facts and figures that are best presented in a diagram or chart. These graphic objects serve the following purposes:

- *Diagrams.* These objects depict hierarchies or processes.
- *Charts.* These objects present numerical information in visual ways when it is more important for your audience to understand trends than identify precise values.

In this chapter, you will add a diagram to a document and specify the position of the diagram in relation to the document text and margins. You will add shapes to the diagram, edit and add text, and change the layout, visual style, and color theme. Then you will add a chart to a document and modify its appearance by changing its chart type, style, and layout as well as the color of various elements. Finally, you will create a chart from data stored in a Microsoft Office Excel worksheet.

See Also Do you need only a quick refresher on the topics in this chapter? See the Quick Reference section at the beginning of this book.

Important Before you can use the practice files in this chapter, you need to install them from the book's companion CD to their default location. See "Using the Companion CD" at the beginning of this book for more information.

> **Troubleshooting** Graphics and operating system–related instructions in this book reflect the Windows Vista user interface. If your computer is running Windows XP and you experience trouble following the instructions as written, please refer to the "Information for Readers Running Windows XP" section at the beginning of this book.

Creating a Diagram

When you need your document to clearly illustrate a concept such as a process, cycle, hierarchy, or relationship, you can create a dynamic, visually appealing diagram by using *SmartArt graphics*, a powerful new tool available in Microsoft Office Word 2007, Microsoft Office PowerPoint 2007, and Microsoft Office Outlook 2007. By using predefined sets of sophisticated formatting, you can almost effortlessly put together any of the following diagrams:

- *List diagrams*. These diagrams visually represent lists of related or independent information—for example, a list of items needed to complete a task, including pictures of the items.
- *Process diagrams*. These diagrams visually describe the ordered set of steps required to complete a task—for example, the steps you take to process an order.
- *Cycle diagrams*. These diagrams represent a circular sequence of steps, tasks, or events; or the relationship of a set of steps, tasks, or events to a central, core element—for example, the importance of introducing the basic elements of a story in order to build up to an exciting ending.
- *Hierarchy diagrams*. These diagrams illustrate the structure of an organization or entity—for example, the top-level management structure of a company.
- *Relationship diagrams*. These diagrams show convergent, divergent, overlapping, merging, or containment elements—for example, how using similar methods to organize your e-mail, calendar, and contacts can improve your productivity.
- *Matrix diagrams*. These diagrams show the relationship of components to a whole—for example, the product teams in a department.
- *Pyramid diagrams*. These diagrams illustrate proportional or interconnected relationships—for example, the amount of time that should ideally be spent on different phases of a project.

The categories are not mutually exclusive, meaning that some diagrams appear in more than one category.

You create a diagram by clicking the SmartArt button in the Illustrations group on the Insert tab. Then you select the type of diagram you want to create and insert it into the document. You add text to the diagram either directly or from its text pane.

In this exercise, you will add a diagram to a document, add text to the diagram, and then specify the position of the diagram in relation to the document text and page margins.

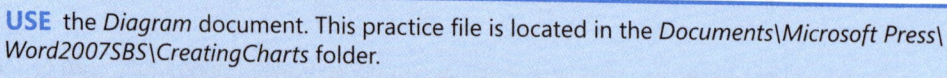

> **USE** the *Diagram* document. This practice file is located in the *Documents\Microsoft Press\Word2007SBS\CreatingCharts* folder.
> **BE SURE TO** start Word before beginning this exercise.
> **OPEN** the *Diagram* document.

1. Click at the end of the third bulleted item under *Rationale*, press Enter, and then on the **Insert** tab, in the **Illustrations** group, click the **SmartArt** button.

   The Choose A SmartArt Graphic dialog box opens, displaying all the available graphics.

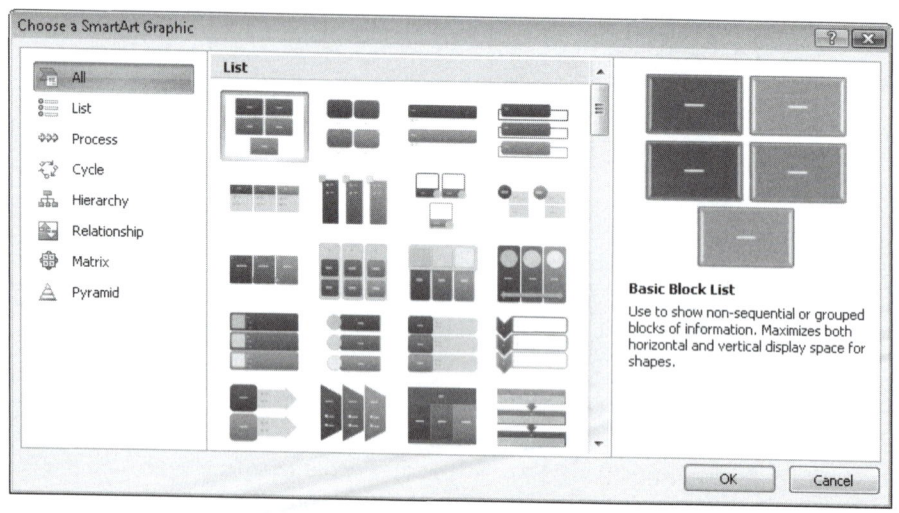

2. In the left pane, click each diagram category in turn to display only the available layouts of that type in the center pane.

3. In the left pane, click **Process**. Then in the center pane, click each process diagram layout in turn to view an example, along with a description of what the diagram best conveys, in the right pane.

4. When you finish exploring, click the first thumbnail in the fourth row (**Vertical Process**), and then click **OK**.

The process diagram is inserted at the insertion point. Text placeholders appear in the diagram shapes and in the adjacent text pane, where they are formatted as a bulleted list. The Design and Format contextual tabs appear on the Ribbon.

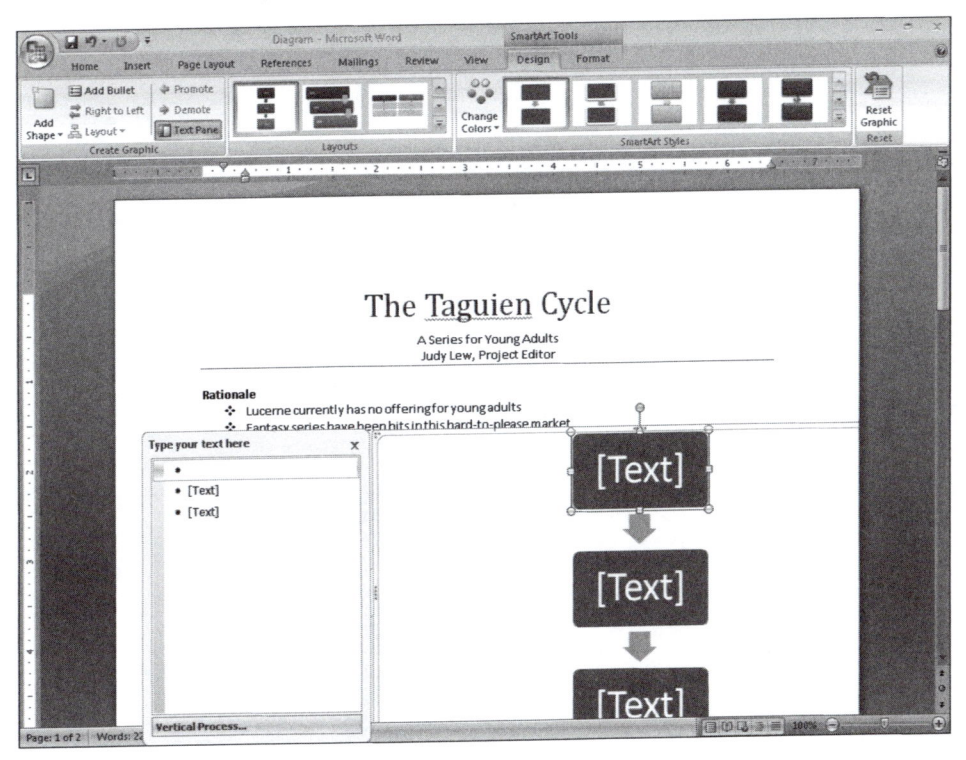

> **Troubleshooting** If the text pane is not visible, click the tab on the left side of the diagram's frame. You can also display the text pane by clicking the Text Pane button in the Create Graphic group on the Design contextual tab.

5. With the first bullet selected in the text pane, type **The Journey**, and then press the ↓ key to move the insertion point to the next placeholder.

As you type in the text pane, the words also appear in the shapes of the diagram.

6. Repeat step 5 for the remaining two placeholders, entering **The Battle** and **The Twist**.

7. With the insertion point at the end of the third bulleted item in the text pane, press **Enter** to extend the bulleted list and add a new box to the chart. Then type **The Climax**.

Creating a Diagram **191**

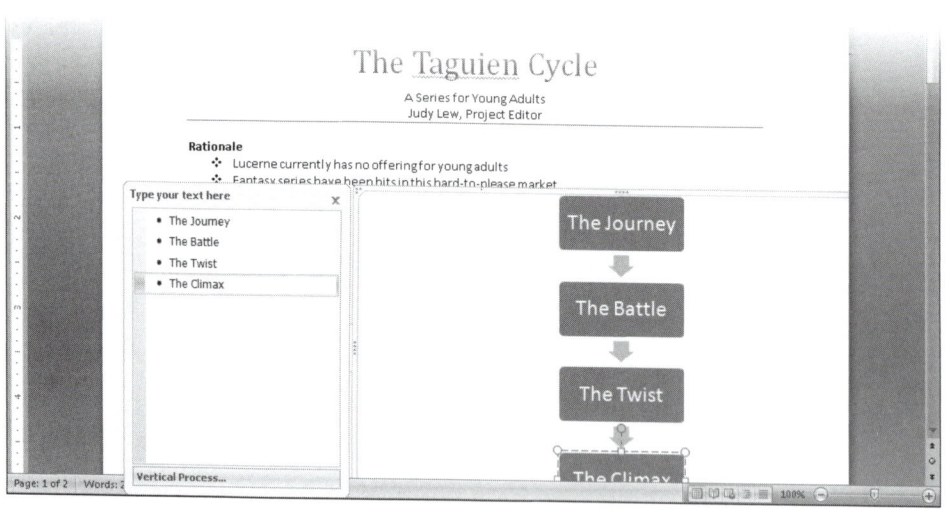

[screenshot of Word document showing "The Taguien Cycle" with a vertical process diagram containing The Journey, The Battle, The Twist, The Climax, alongside a text pane]

8. In the text pane, click the **Close** button.

9. Drag the left center *sizing handle* of the diagram pane to the right until the pane is approximately as wide as the shapes within the diagram.

> **Troubleshooting** Be sure to point to the set of dots (the sizing handle) on the diagram's frame, not to a blank part of the frame.

You can ignore the diagram while you drag. When you release the mouse button, the diagram pane moves to the left margin of the document, with the diagram centered within it.

> **Tip** You can precisely resize the diagram pane by clicking the Size button on the Format contextual tab and then adjusting the Shape Height or Shape Width setting.

10. On the **Format** contextual tab, in the **Arrange** group, click the **Text Wrapping** button, and then in the list, click **More Layout Options**.

> **Troubleshooting** Depending on your window size and screen resolution, you might need to click the Arrange button to display the Arrange group.

The Advanced Layout dialog box opens, with the Text Wrapping tab active.

See Also For more information about text wrapping, see "Changing the Relationship of Elements on the Page" in Chapter 6, "Working with Graphics, Symbols, and Equations."

11. In the **Wrapping style** area, click **Tight**, and in the **Wrap text** area, click **Both sides**.
12. Click the **Picture Position** tab.

    On this tab are options for controlling where the diagram appears relative to other elements of the document.
13. In the **Horizontal** area, click **Alignment**.
14. Click the **Alignment** arrow, and then in the list, click **Right**.
15. Click the **relative to** arrow, and then in the list, click **Margin**.
16. In the **Vertical** area, with the **Absolute position** option selected, click the **below** arrow, and then in the list, click **Page**.
17. Click **OK**. Then click a blank area of the document to see the results of your changes.

    Instead of sitting at the left margin with text before and after it, the diagram now sits to the right of the text, without interrupting its flow.

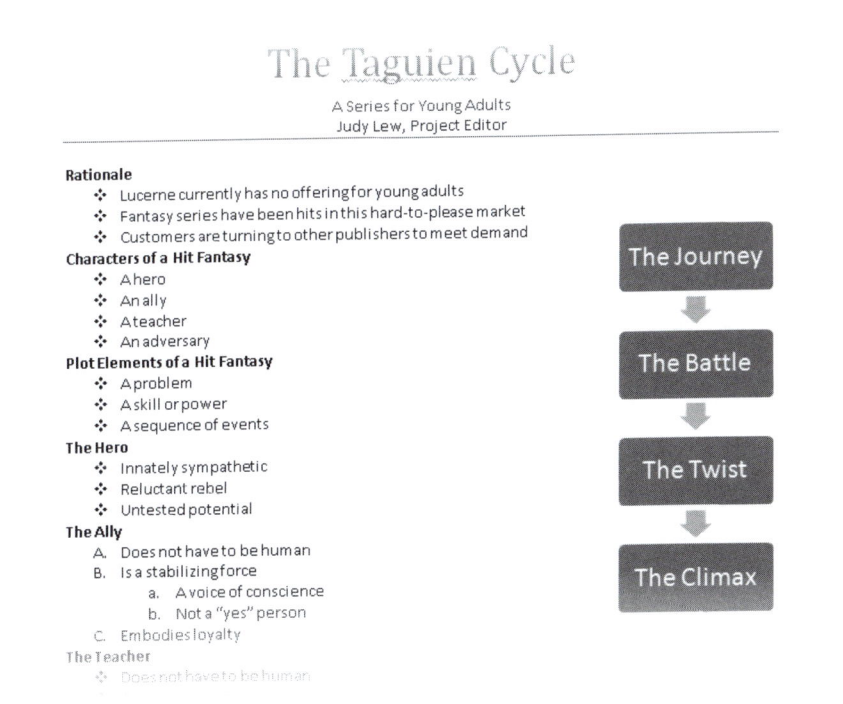

CLOSE the *Diagram* document without saving your changes.

Modifying a Diagram

After you create a diagram, you can add and remove shapes and edit its text by making changes in the text pane. If you scroll the document while the text pane is open, the text pane remains visible so that you can easily copy text from the document into the text pane rather than retyping it.

You can also customize a diagram by using the options on the SmartArt Tools contextual tabs. You can make changes such as the following by using the buttons on the Design contextual tab:

- Switch to a different layout of the same type or of a different type.

> **Tip** If you have entered more text than will fit in the new layout, the text is not shown, but it is retained so that you don't have to retype it if you switch the layout again.

- Add shading and three-dimensional effects to all the shapes in a diagram.
- Change the color scheme.
- Add and change the hierarchy of shapes.

> **Tip** You can remove a shape by selecting it and then pressing the Delete key. You can also rearrange shapes by dragging them.

You can customize individual shapes in the following ways by using the buttons on the Format contextual tab:

- Change an individual shape—for example, you can change a square into a star to make it stand out.
- Apply a built-in shape style.
- Change the color, outline, or effect of a shape.

> **Tip** You can use Live Preview to display the effects of these changes before you apply them. If you apply a change and then decide you preferred the original version, you can click the Reset Graphic button in the Reset group on the Design tab.

In this exercise, you will add shapes to a diagram; add and edit text; and then change the diagram layout, its visual style and color theme, and the shape of one of its elements.

> **USE** the *ModifyingDiagram* document. This practice file is located in the *Documents\Microsoft Press\Word2007SBS\CreatingCharts* folder.
>
> **OPEN** the *ModifyingDiagram* document.

1. Click the diagram to activate it, and then click the **Text Pane** tab to open the text pane.

   Note that the type of layout used for the diagram (Vertical Process) is described at the bottom of the text pane.

2. Position the insertion point to the left of *The Journey*, and then press [Enter].

   A blank placeholder is added at the beginning of the bulleted list, and a new shape is added to the top of the diagram.

3. Press the [↑] key to move to the new bullet, type **The Problem**, and then close the text pane.

4. Click the second shape in the diagram (*The Journey*). Then on the **Design** contextual tab, in the **Create Graphic** group, click the **Add Shape** arrow, and in the list, click **Add Shape After**.

   A new shape is added and selected.

5. With the new shape selected, type **The Power**.

6. Double-click the word *The* in the first shape.

   A box appears around the selection, and the Mini toolbar appears.

7. Press the [Del] key, and then remove *The* from the remaining shapes in the diagram.

   After you remove the word from the final shape, all the shapes in the diagram become narrower.

8. Click a blank area inside the diagram pane to activate the diagram as a whole.

   > **Troubleshooting** If any of the shapes in the diagram is surrounded by a dotted line and white handles, that shape is selected instead of the diagram as a whole.

9. On the **Design** contextual tab, in the **Layouts** group, click the **More** button.

   The Layouts gallery opens.

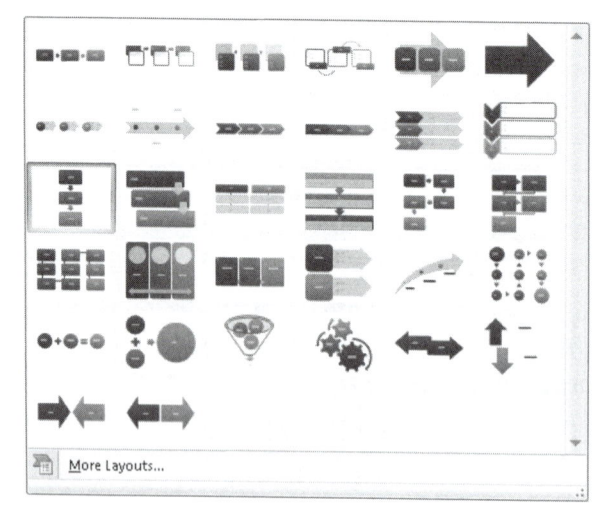

10. In the **Layouts** gallery, point to other diagram options to preview the diagram with those layouts.

   Because changing the layout does not change the width of the diagram, the horizontal layouts create a very small diagram.

11. In the **Layouts** gallery, click the second thumbnail in the fifth row (**Vertical Equation**).

   The diagram changes to a series of circles arranged in an equation.

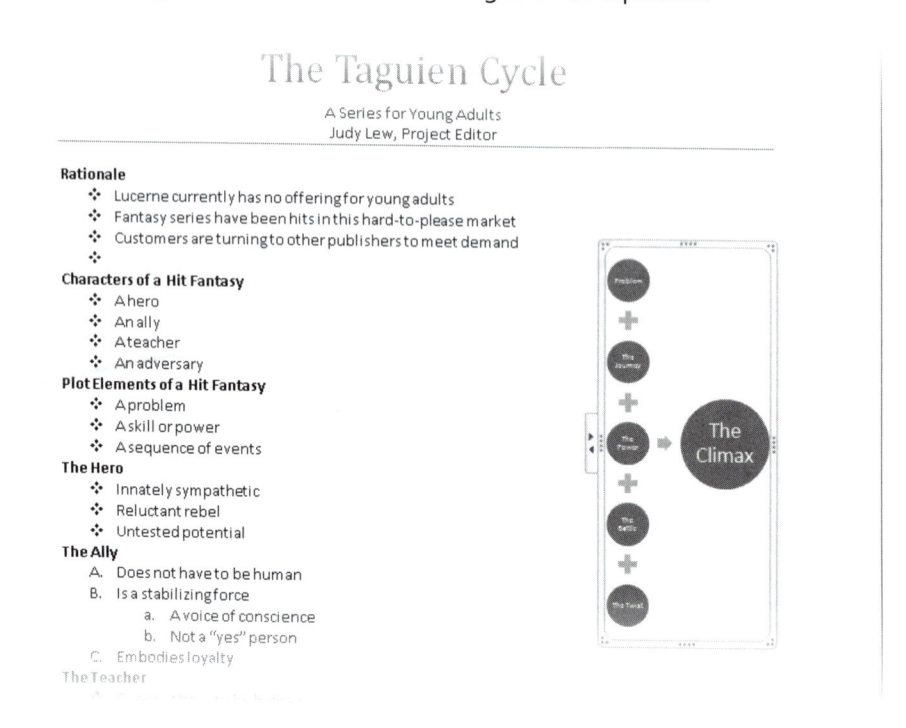

12. Point to the diagram's frame, and when the pointer changes to a four-headed arrow, drag the frame down until its top edge is aligned with the third heading (*Plot Elements of a Hit Fantasy*).

> **Troubleshooting** Be sure to point to a blank part of the frame, not to the sizing handles (the sets of dots on the diagram's frame).

13. Scroll the document, and then drag the sizing handle in the lower-left corner of the diagram's frame drag down and to the left until the frame is about an inch wider and an inch taller than its original size.

   When you release the mouse button, the shapes in the diagram expand to fill the resized frame.

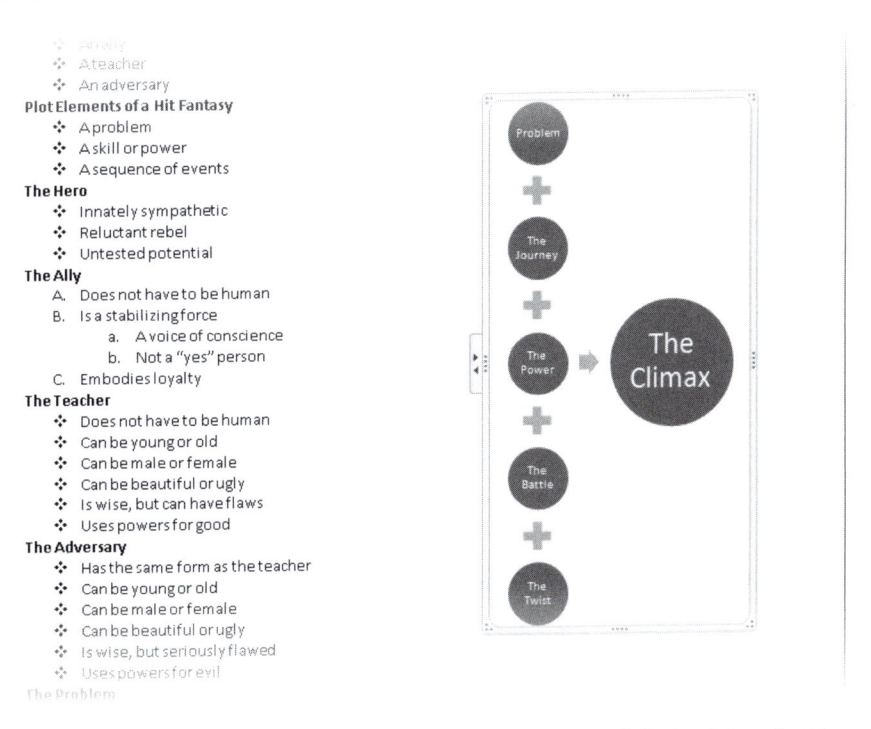

14. On the **Design** contextual tab, in the **SmartArt Styles** group, click the **More** button.

   The SmartArt Styles gallery opens.

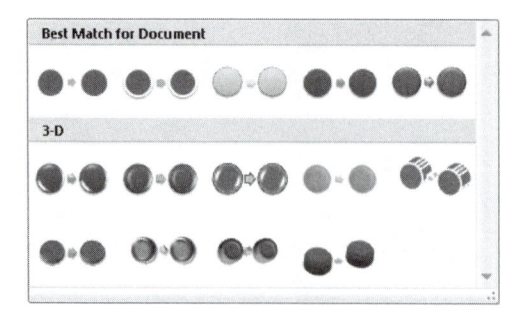

15. In the gallery, point to each style, noticing the changes to your diagram. Then under **3-D**, click the first thumbnail in the first row (**Polished**).

> **Troubleshooting** The live preview from this gallery might be slower than from other galleries. Just be patient; you will soon see the effects of the style on your diagram.

The diagram takes on the effects of the new style.

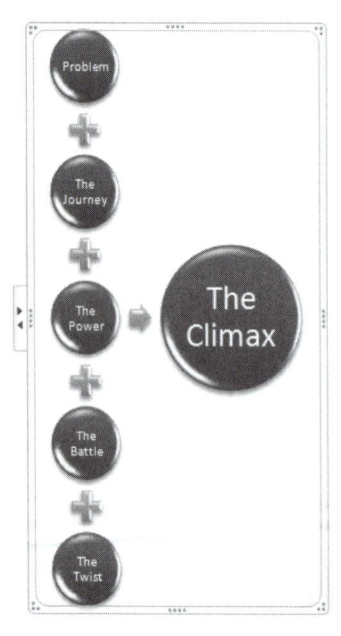

16. In the **SmartArt Styles** group, click the **Change Colors** button.

    The Theme Colors gallery opens.

198 Chapter 7 Working with Diagrams and Charts

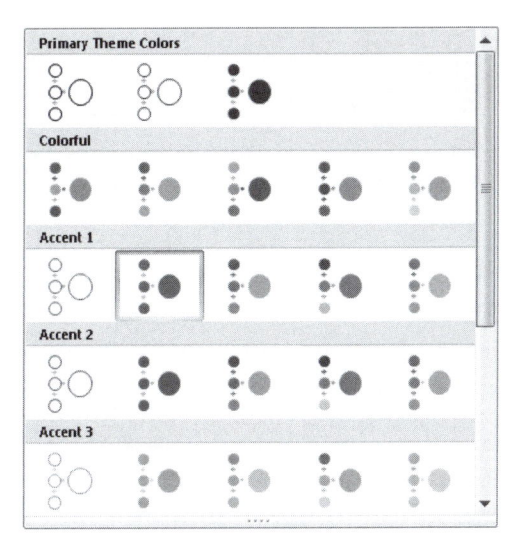

17. Display the live preview of a few color combinations, and then under **Colorful**, click the first thumbnail (**Colorful – Accent Colors**).

18. On the left side of the diagram, click the bottom shape (*Twist*), and then on the **Format** contextual tab, in the **Shapes** group, click the **Change Shape** button.

19. Under **Stars and Banners**, click the seventh shape in the second row (**Wave**).

CLOSE the *ModifyingDiagram* document without saving your changes.

Inserting a Chart

When you add a chart to a document created in Word 2007, a sample chart is embedded in the document. The data used to plot the sample chart is stored in an Excel 2007 worksheet that is incorporated into the Word file. (You don't have to maintain a separate Excel file.)

> **Tip** You can't see charts in Draft or Outline view.

To customize the chart, you replace the sample data in the Excel worksheet with your own data, in much the same way you would enter information in a table. Because the Excel worksheet is linked to the chart, when you change the values in the worksheet, the chart changes as well.

The Excel worksheet is composed of rows and columns of cells that contain values, or *data points*, that make up a *data series*. To enter data in an individual cell—the intersection of a row and column—you click the cell to select it, and start typing. You can select an entire column by clicking the *column heading*—the shaded box containing a letter at the top of each column—and an entire row by clicking the *row heading*—the shaded box containing a number to the left of each row. You can select the entire worksheet by clicking the Select All button—the darker box at the junction of the column headings and row headings.

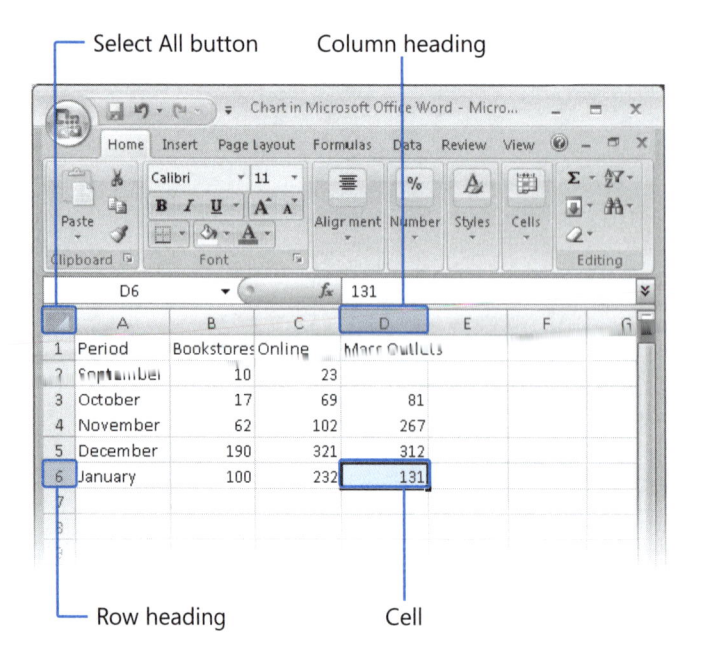

Tip If you create a chart and later want to edit its data, you can open the associated worksheet by clicking the chart and then clicking the Edit Data button in the Data group on the Design contextual tab.

In this exercise, you will add a chart to a document and then replace the sample data in the worksheet with your own data.

Troubleshooting If you open a document created in Word 2003 in Word 2007 and then add a chart to it, Word uses Microsoft Graph to create the chart. This Word 2003 charting technology has been retained to maintain compatibility with earlier versions of the program. The steps in this exercise will work only with a document created in Word 2007.

USE the *Chart* document. This practice file is located in the *Documents\Microsoft Press\Word2007SBS\CreatingCharts* folder.
OPEN the *Chart* document.

1. Press Ctrl+End to move the insertion point to the end of the document.
2. On the **Insert** tab, in the **Illustrations** group, click the **Chart** button.

   The Insert Chart dialog box opens.

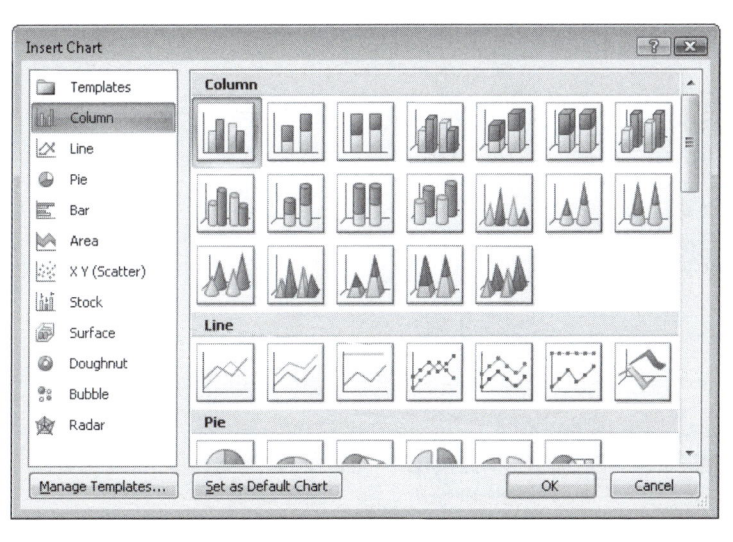

3. In the gallery on the right, under **Column**, click the fourth thumbnail in the first row (**3-D Clustered Column**). Then click **OK**.

   A sample column chart is inserted in the document on the left and an Excel worksheet containing the plotted sample data opens on the right.

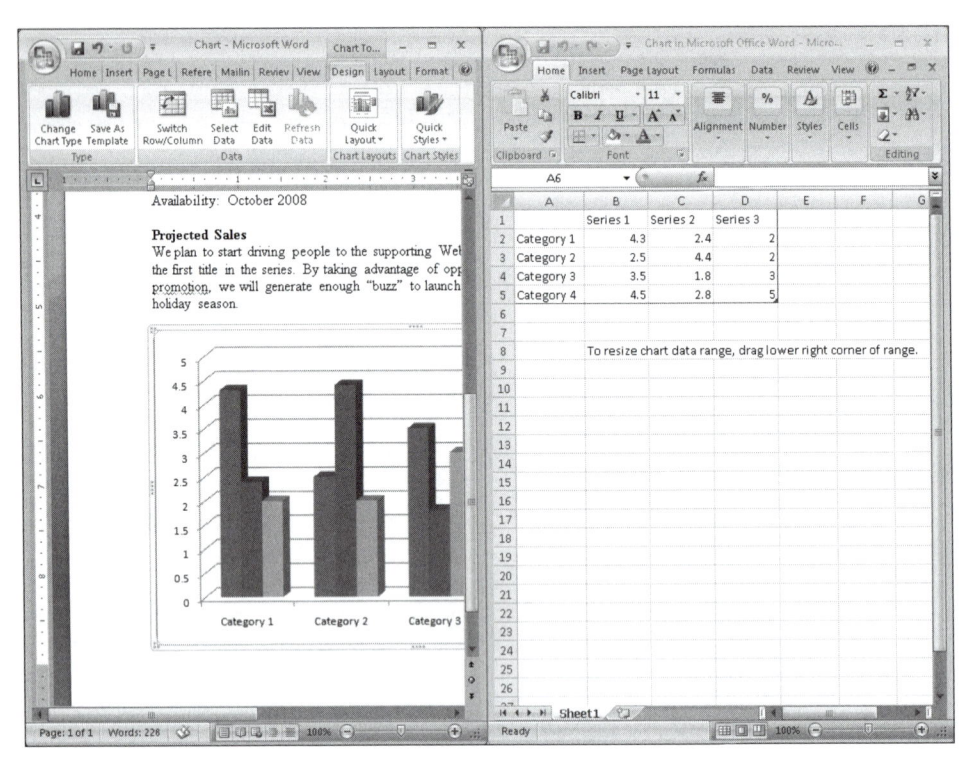

4. Click the **Select All** button in the upper-left corner of the Excel worksheet, and then press the Del key.

   The sample data in the worksheet is deleted, leaving a blank worksheet. The columns in the sample chart in the document disappear, leaving a blank chart area.

5. In the first cell in row 1 (cell **A1**), type **Period**, and then press the Tab key.

   > **Tip** As with Word tables, each worksheet cell is identified by an address consisting of its column letter and row number—for example, A2. A range of cells is identified by the address of the cell in the upper-left corner and the address of the cell in the lower-right corner, separated by a colon—for example, A2:D5.

   Excel enters the heading and activates the next cell in the same row.

6. In cells **B1** through **D1**, type **Bookstores**, **Online**, and **Mass Outlets**, pressing Tab after each to move to the next cell.

7. Point to the border between any two columns, and when the pointer changes to a double-headed arrow, double-click.

   Excel adjusts the width of the columns to fit their entries.

8. In cells **A2** through **C2**, type **September**, **10**, and **23**. (There is no data in D2.)

Tip You can use the keyboard to move around the worksheet. Press Enter to move down in the same column or Shift+Enter to move up; and press Tab to move to the right in the same row or Shift+Tab to move to the left. You can also press the Arrow keys to move up, down, left, or right one cell at a time.

9. Type the following data into the cells of the Excel worksheet:

	A	B	C	D
3	October	17	69	81
4	November	62	102	167
5	December	190	321	312
6	January	100	232	131

As you enter data, the chart changes to reflect what you type. (We've scrolled the Word window to display more of the chart.)

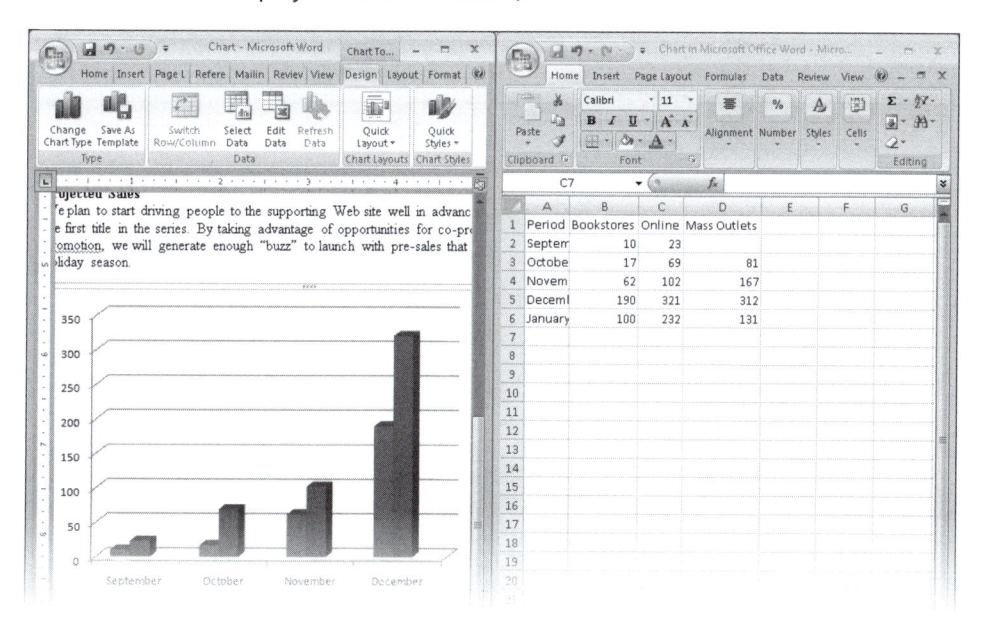

Something is wrong. You entered data for September through January, but January is not shown. This is because the original sample chart plotted only the cells in the range A1:D5, and you have entered data in A1:D6. You need to specify the new range.

10. In the Word document, click the chart to activate it. Then on the **Design** contextual tab, in the **Data** group, click the **Select Data** button.

Inserting a Chart   203

In the Excel worksheet, the plotted data range is surrounded by a blinking dotted border, and the Select Data Source dialog box opens so that you can make any necessary adjustments.

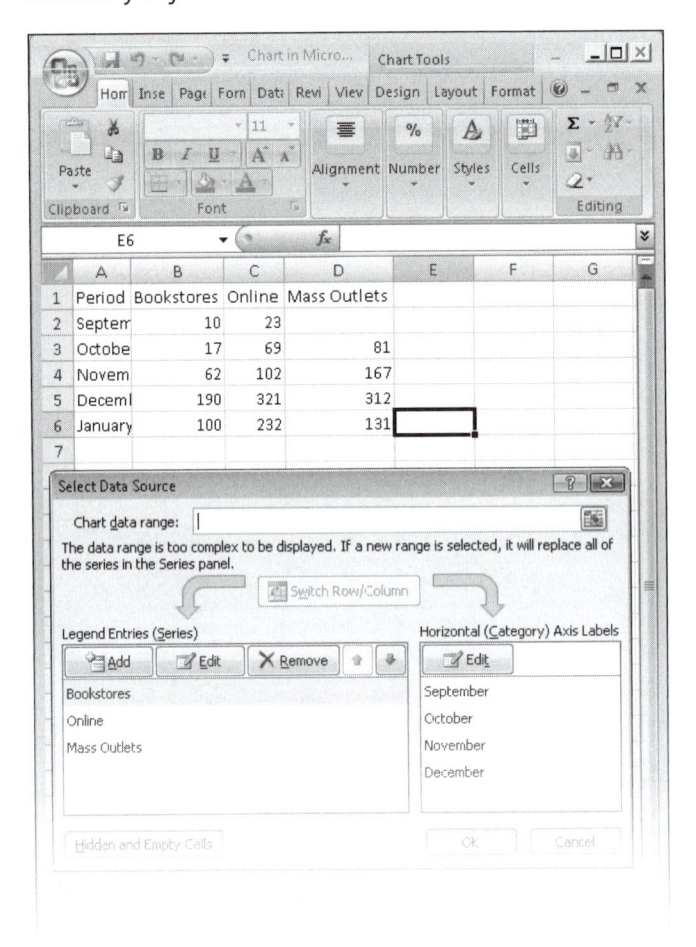

Collapse Dialog

11. At the right end of the **Chart data range** box, click the **Collapse Dialog** button to shrink the **Select Data Source** dialog box.

Expand

12. In the Excel worksheet, point to cell **A1**, and drag down and to the right to cell **D6**. Then in the **Select Data Source** dialog box, click the **Expand Dialog** button.

In the Select Data Source dialog box, the Chart Data Range box now contains the new range and the Horizontal (Category) Axis Labels list now includes January.

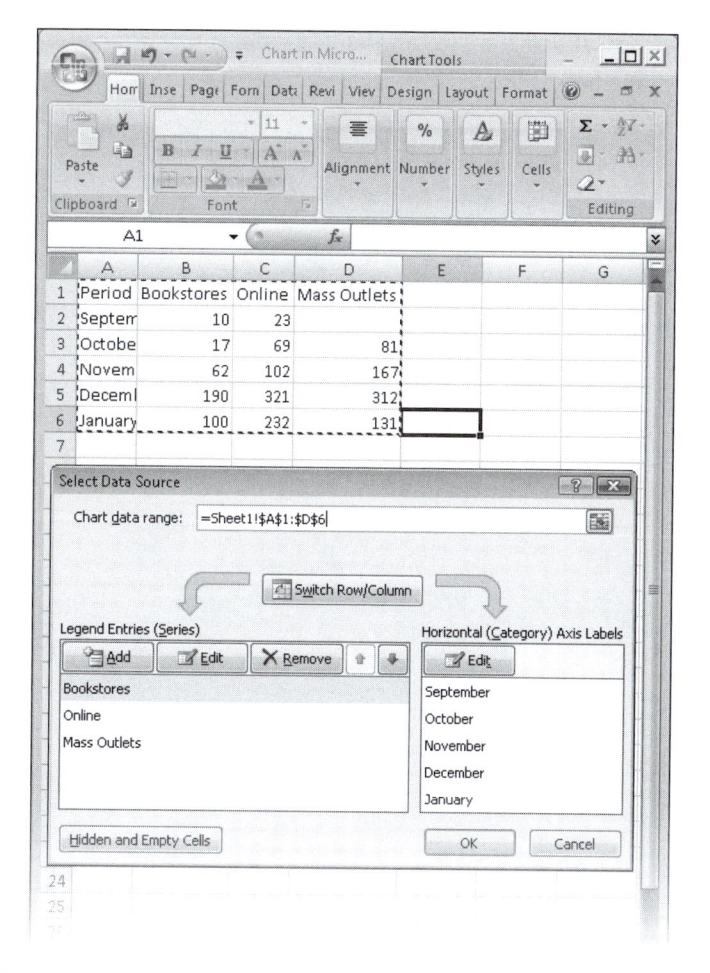

13. Click **OK** to close the dialog box, and then in the upper-right corner of the Excel window, click the **Close** button to close the worksheet.

    The Word window expands to fill the screen. The data for January now appears in the chart. Suppose you realize that you made an error when typing the data for mass outlets.

14. On the **Design** tab, in the **Data** group, click the **Edit Data** button to open the Excel worksheet.

15. In the Excel worksheet, click cell **D4**, type 267 to change the data, press Enter, and then close the Excel window.

    In the chart, the Mass Outlets column for November becomes taller to represent the new value.

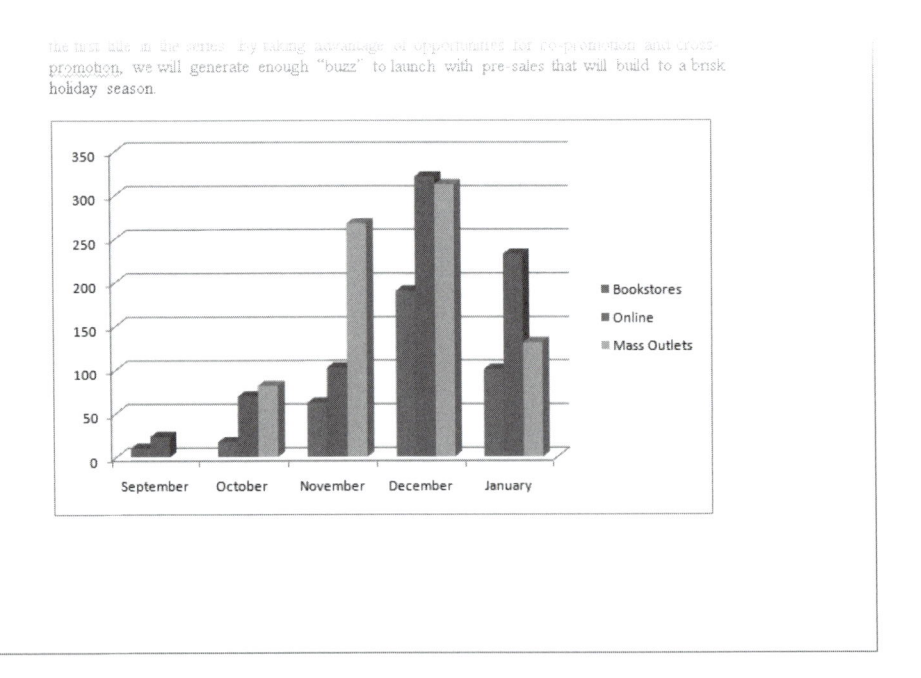

CLOSE the *Chart* document without saving your changes.

Modifying a Chart

If you decide that the chart you created doesn't adequately depict the most important characteristics of your data, you can change the chart type at any time. Word provides 11 types of charts, each with two-dimensional and three-dimensional variations. Common chart types include the following:

- *Column charts*. These are good for showing how values change over time.
- *Bar charts*. These are good for showing the values of several items at one point in time.
- *Line graphs*. These are good for showing erratic changes in values over time.
- *Pie charts*. These are good for showing how parts relate to the whole.

Having settled on the most appropriate chart type, you can modify the chart as a whole or any of its elements, which include the following:

- *Chart area*. This is the entire area within the frame displayed when you click a chart.
- *Plot area*. This is the rectangular area bordered by the axes.

- **X-axis and y-axis.** The data is plotted against an x-axis—also called the *category axis*—and a y-axis—also called the *value axis*. (Three-dimensional charts also have a *z-axis*.)
- **Tick-mark labels.** Along each axis are labels that identify the data.
- **Data markers.** Each data point in a data series is represented graphically in the chart by a *data marker*.
- **Legend.** This key identifies the data series.

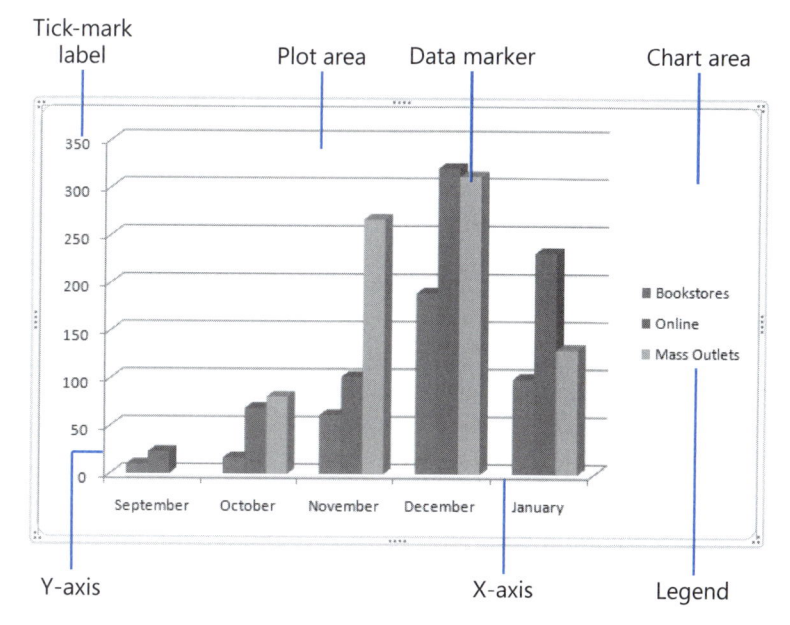

You can modify the elements by using the buttons on the Layout contextual tab. To modify a specific element, you first select it by clicking it, or by clicking its name in the Chart Elements box in the Current Selection group on the Format contextual tab. You can then use the buttons on the Format contextual tab. If you make extensive modifications, you might want to save the customized chart as a template so that you can use it for plotting similar data in the future without having to repeat all the changes.

In this exercise, you will modify the appearance of a chart by changing its chart type and style. You will change the color of the plot area and the color and weight of a data series. You will then hide gridlines and change the layout to display titles and a datasheet. After adding an annotation in a text box, you will save the chart as a template.

> **USE** the *ModifyingChart* document. This practice file is located in the *Documents\Microsoft Press\Word2007SBS\CreatingCharts* folder.
> **OPEN** the *ModifyingChart* presentation.

1. Scroll the document to display the chart, and click anywhere in the chart to activate it.

   Word displays the Design, Layout, and Format contextual tabs.

2. On the **Design** contextual tab, in the **Type** group, click the **Change Chart Type** button.

   The Change Chart Type dialog box opens.

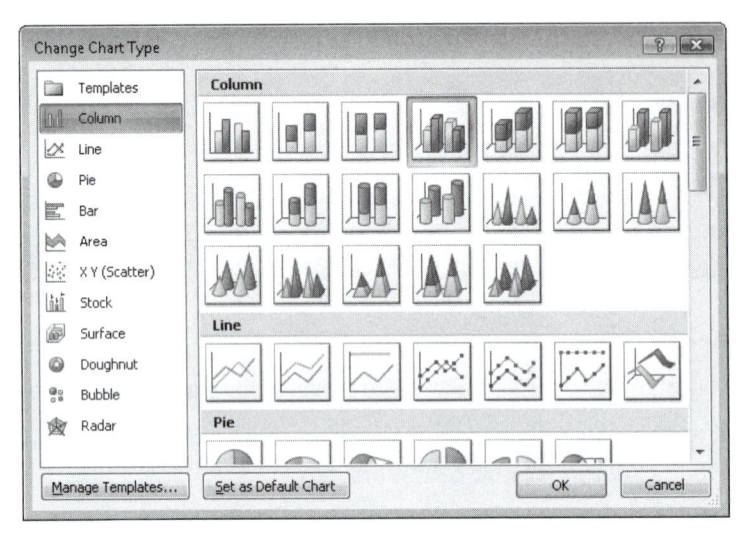

3. In the gallery on the right, under **Line**, double-click the fourth thumbnail (**Line with Markers**).

   The column chart changes to a line chart, which depicts data by using colored lines instead of columns.

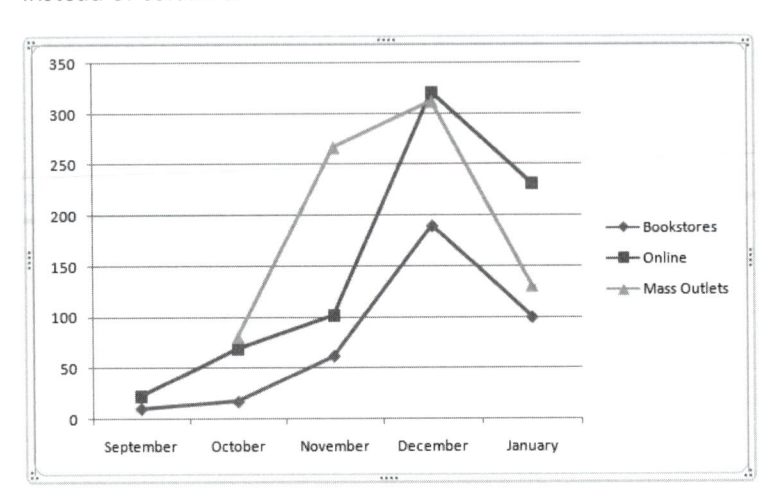

4. On the **Design** tab, in the **Chart Styles** group, click the **More** button.

The **Chart Styles** gallery opens.

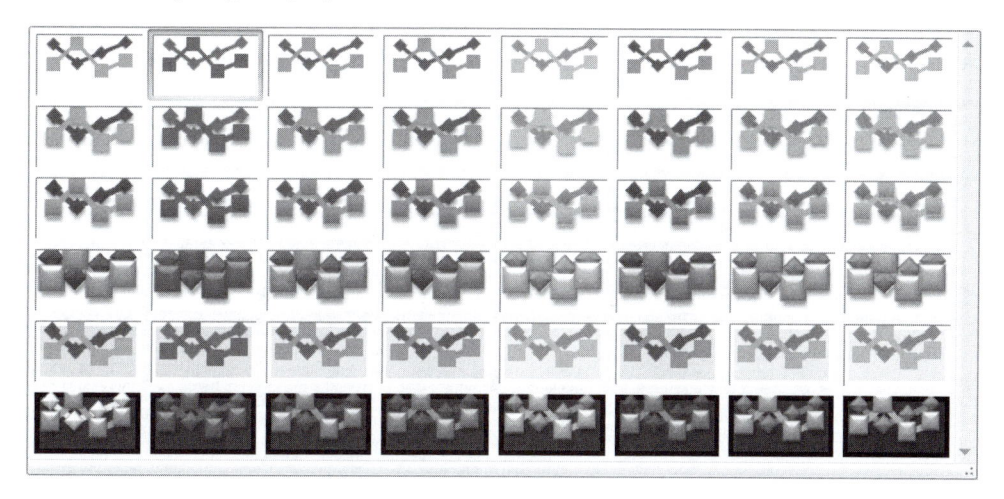

5. In the gallery, click the second thumbnail in the fourth row (**Style 26**).

The lines are now thicker, and the data points are three-dimentional.

6. Click the plot area—the area of the chart containing the data markers—to select it, and then click the **Format** contextual tab.

The Chart Elements box in the Current Selection group on the Format tab displays the name of the selected chart element.

7. On the **Format** tab, in the **Shape Styles** group, click the **Shape Fill** button, and then in the list, click **More Fill Colors**.

The Colors dialog box opens.

8. On the **Standard** tab of the **Colors** dialog box, click the color to the lower left of the center (the palest yellow), and then click **OK**.

The plot area is now shaded a pale yellow to distinguish it from the rest of the chart.

> **Tip** To change several aspects of the plot area, right-click the area and then click Format Plot Area to open the Format Plot Area dialog box. You can then change the fill, border, shadow, and 3-D format in one location.

9. In the **Current Selection** group, click the **Chart Elements** arrow, and then in the list, click **Series "Online"**.

Small blue circles appear around the data points of the selected series.

10. In the **Current Selection** group, click the **Format Selection** button.

   The Format Data Series dialog box opens.

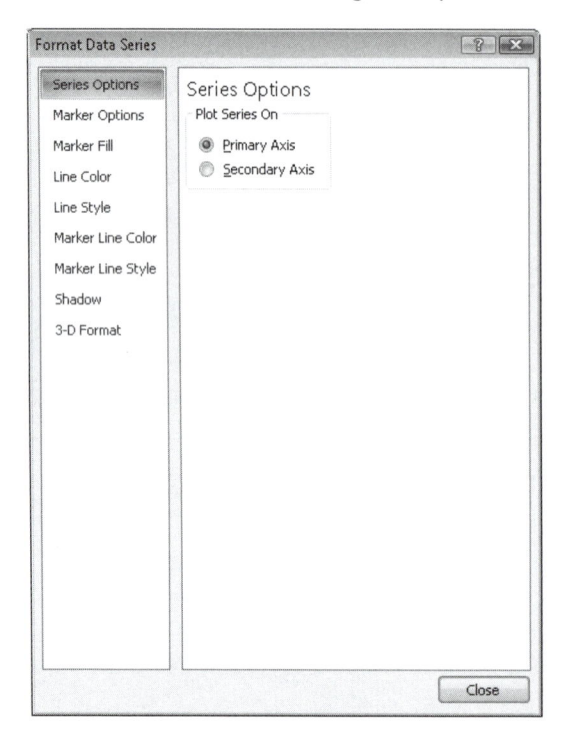

11. In the left pane, click **Line Color**. Then on the **Line Color** page, click **Solid Line**, click the **Color** button that appears, and under **Standard Colors**, click the **Purple** box.

12. In the left pane, click **Line Style**. Then on the **Line Style** page, in the **Width** box, type or select **3 pt**. Then click **Close**.

   The Online data series is now represented by a thin purple line.

13. On the **Layout** contextual tab, in the **Axes** group, click the **Gridlines** button, point to **Primary Horizontal Gridlines**, and then click **None** to remove the horizontal gridlines from the chart.

14. On the **Design** contextual tab, in the **Chart Layouts** group, click the **More** button.

   The Chart Layouts gallery opens.

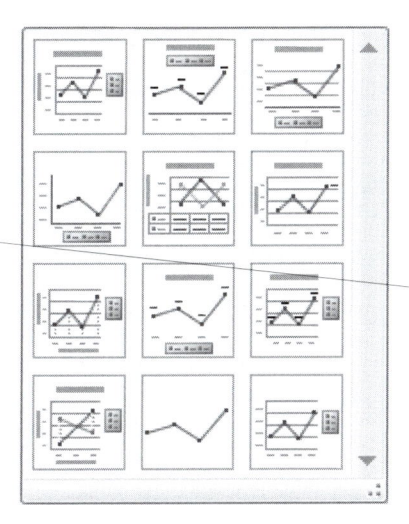

15. In the gallery, click the second thumbnail in the second row (**Layout 5**).

    The legend now appears below the chart with a datasheet, gridlines have been turned back on, and placeholders for a chart title and axis title have been added to the top of the chart.

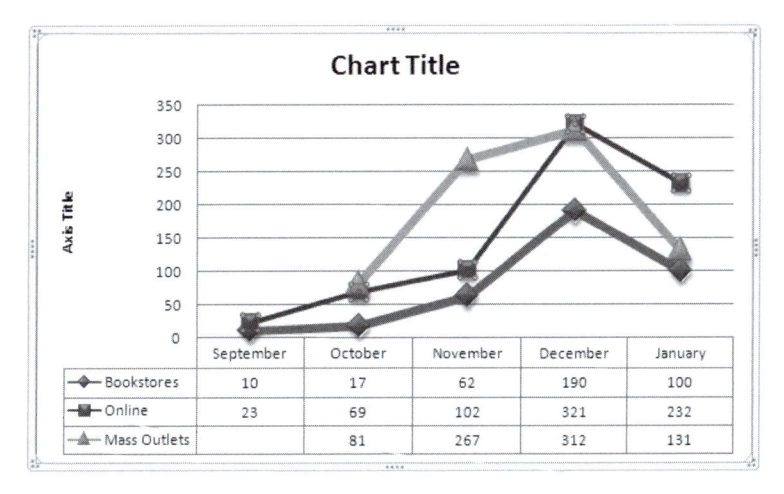

16. In the chart, replace the **Chart Title** placeholder at the top with Cycle Sales and the **Axis Title** placeholder on the left with Thousands.

17. On the **Layout** contextual tab, in the **Insert** group, click the **Draw Text Box** button.

18. In the chart, point to a spot above the December peak sales, and then drag diagonally down and to the right until the text box fills the space to the right of the title.

19. Type **Sales peak for all channels**. Then select the text, and on the **Home** tab, in the **Font** group, change the size to **10** points and the color to **Red**.

20. Click outside the chart to see the results of your changes.

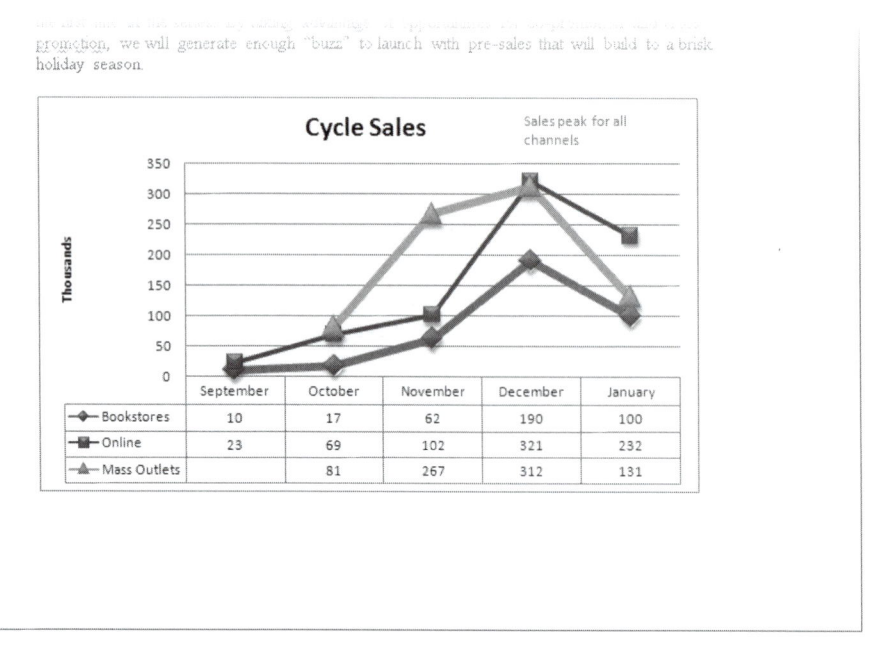

21. Click the chart area to activate the chart. Then on the **Design** tab, in the **Type** group, click the **Save As Template** button.

    The Save Chart Template dialog box opens and displays the contents of your *Charts* folder, which is a subfolder of your *Templates* folder.

    > **Troubleshooting** If the *Charts* folder is not displayed in the Address bar, navigate to the *AppData\Roaming\Microsoft\Templates\Charts* folder under your user profile.

22. With the *Charts* folder displayed in the Address bar, type **My Sales Chart** in the **File name** box, and then click **Save**.

23. In the **Type** group, click the **Change Chart Type** button, and then in the left pane of the **Change Chart Type** dialog box, click **Templates**.

    The folder contains an unidentified template with a line chart icon.

212 Chapter 7 Working with Diagrams and Charts

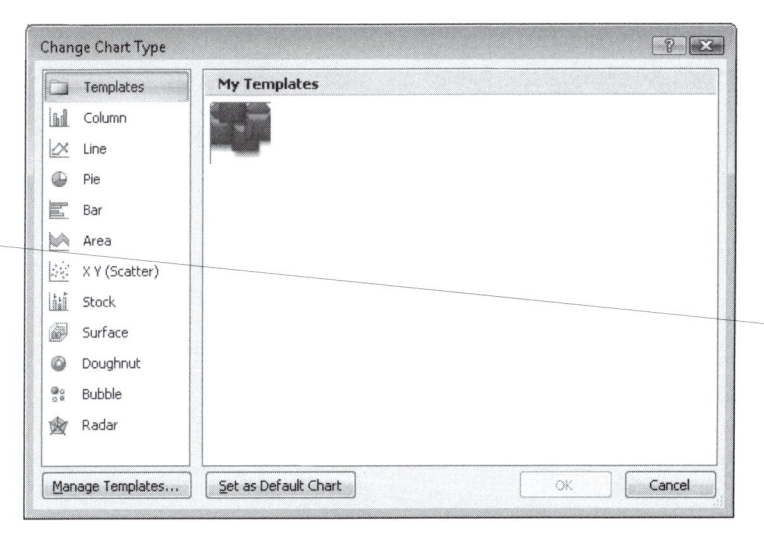

24. Verify that this template is the one you just saved by pointing to it to view the ScreenTip, and then click **Cancel** to close the dialog box.

CLOSE the *ModifyingChart* document without saving your changes.

Using Existing Data in a Chart

If the data you want to plot as a chart already exists in a Microsoft Office Access database, an Excel worksheet, or a Word table, you don't have to retype it in the chart's worksheet. You can copy the data from its source program and paste it into the worksheet.

In this exercise, you will copy data stored in a range of cells in an Excel worksheet into a chart's worksheet and then expand the plotted data range so that the new data appears in the chart.

USE the *ExistingData* document and the *Sales* workbook. These practice files are located in the *Documents\Microsoft Press\Word2007SBS\CreatingCharts* folder.
OPEN the *ExistingData* document.

1. Press [Ctrl]+[End] to move to the end of the document, right-click the chart, and then click **Edit Data** to open the associated Excel worksheet.

2. In the Excel window, click the **Microsoft Office Button**, and then click **Open**. In the **Open** dialog box, navigate to your *Documents\Microsoft Press\Word2007SBS\ CreatingCharts* folder, and double-click the *Sales* workbook.

Microsoft Office Button

Using Existing Data in a Chart   213

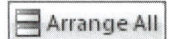

3. On the Excel **View** tab, in the **Window** group, click the **Arrange All** button.
4. In the **Arrange Windows** dialog box, click **Horizontal**, and click **OK**.

   Excel arranges one of the open worksheets above the other, so that both are visible at the same time.

5. Scroll the *Sales* worksheet, point to cell **A10**, and drag down and to the right to select the range **A10:D11**.
6. On the Excel **Home** tab, in the **Clipboard** group, click the **Copy** button.
7. Click the **Chart in Microsoft Office Word** worksheet to activate it, click cell **A7**, and then on the Excel **Home** tab, in the **Clipboard** group, click the **Paste** button.

   The data from the *Sales* worksheet is pasted into the chart's worksheet.

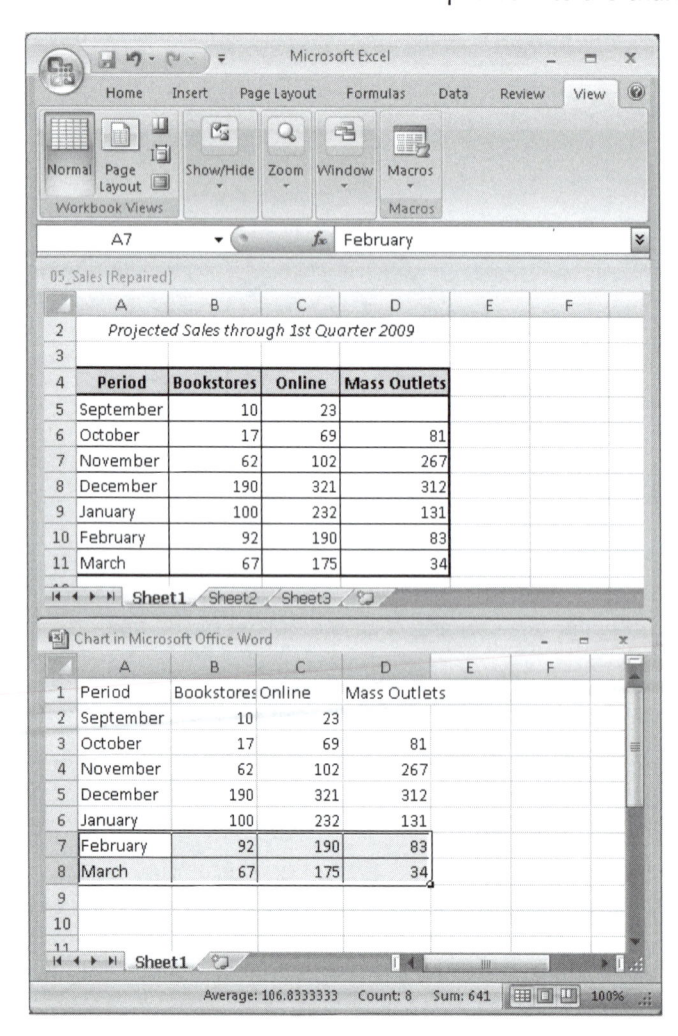

214 Chapter 7 Working with Diagrams and Charts

8. Close the *Sales* workbook.

   The top window closes, but the bottom window does not expand to take its place.

   Maximize

9. Click the chart worksheet's **Maximize** button.

   Now you need to specify that the new data should be included in the chart.

   Select Data

10. Click the chart in the document to activate it, and then on the **Design** contextual tab, in the **Data** group, click the **Select Data** button.

    The Select Data Source dialog box opens.

11. Move the dialog box so that all of the data in the Excel window is visible.

12. Click at the right end of the **Chart data range** box, change the cell range to read =Sheet1!$A$1:$D$8, and then click **OK**.

13. Close the Excel window.

    The chart now contains two more months of data.

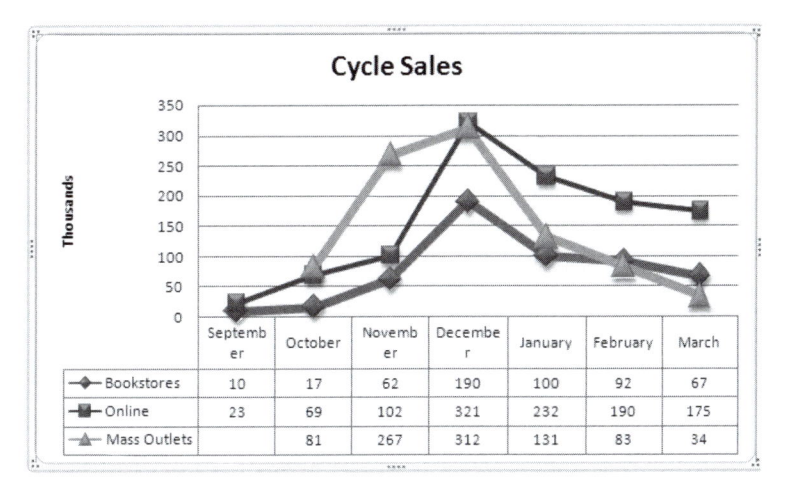

    Cycle Sales

	September	October	November	December	January	February	March
Bookstores	10	17	62	190	100	92	67
Online	23	69	102	321	232	190	175
Mass Outlets			81	267	312	131	83	34

14. Click *Sales peak for all channels*, click the border of the text box, and then press [Del].

15. In the middle of the frame's right border, drag the dotted handle to the right until all the month labels in the datasheet appear on one line.

CLOSE the *ExistingData* document without saving your changes.

Tip You can also import data into your chart from a text file, Web page, or other external source, such as Microsoft SQL Server. To import data, first activate the linked Excel worksheet. Then on the Excel Data tab, in the Get External Data group, click the button for your data source, and navigate to the source. For more information see Microsoft Office Online Help.

Key Points

- You can easily create a sophisticated diagram to convey a process or the relationship between hierarchical elements.
- Diagrams are dynamic illustrations that you can customize to produce precisely the effect you are looking for.
- A chart is often the most efficient way to present numeric data with at-a-glance clarity.
- You can select the type of chart and change the appearance of its component elements until it clearly conveys key information.
- Existing data in a Word table, Excel workbook, Access database, or other structured source can easily be copied and pasted into a chart's worksheet, eliminating time-consuming typing.

Chapter at a Glance

Create and modify a table of contents, **page 226**

Insert ready-made document parts, **page 218**

Add hyperlinks, **page 242**

Add sources and compile a bibliography, **page 246**

8 Working with Longer Documents

In this chapter, you will learn to:
- ✔ Insert ready-made document parts.
- ✔ Create and modify a table of contents.
- ✔ Create and modify an index.
- ✔ Add bookmarks and cross-references.
- ✔ Add hyperlinks.
- ✔ Add sources and compile a bibliography.

If you create long, complex documents and are concerned about helping your readers find the information they are looking for, you can rely on the following Microsoft Office Word 2007 tools to do the job:

- **Building blocks.** You can draw attention to specific information and add visual interest to a document by incorporating these preformatted document parts (such as cover pages, pull quotes, and sidebars) into a document. You can choose from a variety of elements and formatting styles, as well as create your own building blocks.

- **Table of contents.** You can provide an overview of the information contained in a document and help readers locate topics by compiling a table of contents from the document headings. Depending on the intended delivery format (printed or electronic) you can choose to include page numbers or hyperlinks to each heading.

- **Index.** You can help readers locate specific information by inserting index entry fields within a document and compiling an index of keywords and concepts that directs the reader to the corresponding page numbers.

- **Bookmarks.** You can quickly return to a specific location in a document by inserting a bookmark (also called an *anchor*). You can go to a bookmarked location by selecting it from the Bookmarks dialog box; you can also help readers find information by inserting hyperlinks or cross-references to bookmarks.

- **Cross-references.** To help a reader move to a related location in a document, you can insert a cross-reference.
- **Hyperlinks.** To help a reader move to a location in the same file, in another file, or on a Web page, you can add links from text or graphics to the target location.
- **Information sources and a bibliography.** You can appropriately attribute information to its source by inserting citations within a document; Word will compile a professional bibliography from the citations.

In this chapter, you will insert several preformatted building blocks in a document, and save an element of the document as a custom building block. After creating and updating both a table of contents and an index, you will experiment with bookmarks, cross-references, and hyperlinks. Finally, you will use the Source Manager to enter source information, insert a few citations, and compile a bibliography.

See Also Do you need only a quick refresher on the topics in this chapter? See the Quick Reference section at the beginning of this book.

Important Before you can use the practice files in this chapter, you need to install them from the book's companion CD to their default location. See "Using the Companion CD" at the beginning of this book for more information.

Troubleshooting Graphics and operating system–related instructions in this book reflect the Windows Vista user interface. If your computer is running Windows XP and you experience trouble following the instructions as written, please refer to the "Information for Readers Running Windows XP" section at the beginning of this book.

Inserting Ready-Made Document Parts

Longer documents typically include elements such as a cover page and headers and footers to provide identifying and organizing information. To reinforce key concepts and also alleviate the monotony of page after page of plain text, they might also include elements such as sidebars and quotations pulled from the text.

To simplify the creation of professional visual text elements, Word 2007 comes with ready-made *building blocks*, which are available from the Building Blocks Organizer.

See Also For information about saving frequently used text as custom building blocks, see "Inserting Saved Text" in Chapter 2, "Editing and Proofreading Documents."

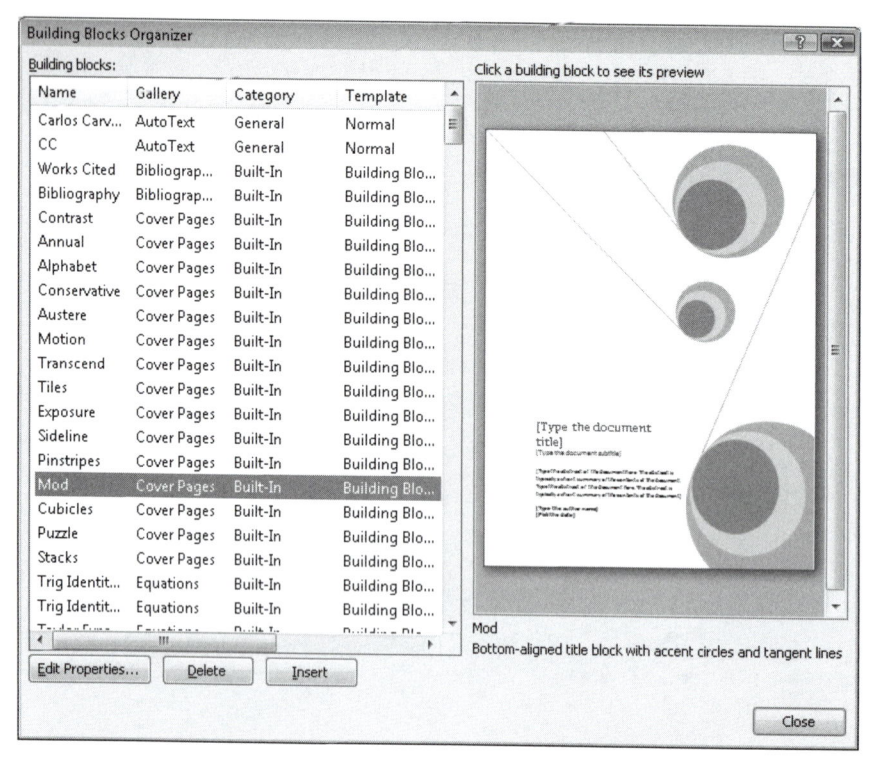

The names of the building blocks that come with Word indicate the graphic theme of the element—in most cases, an entire family of building blocks is available in a theme, including page elements such as:

- Cover pages
- Page headers
- Page footers
- Page numbers
- Quotes
- Sidebars

Other page elements, such as bibliographies, tables, equations, and watermarks, aren't specific to a theme.

The Gallery column indicates the page element created by the building block. More information about each building block is available by scrolling the Building Blocks list to the right.

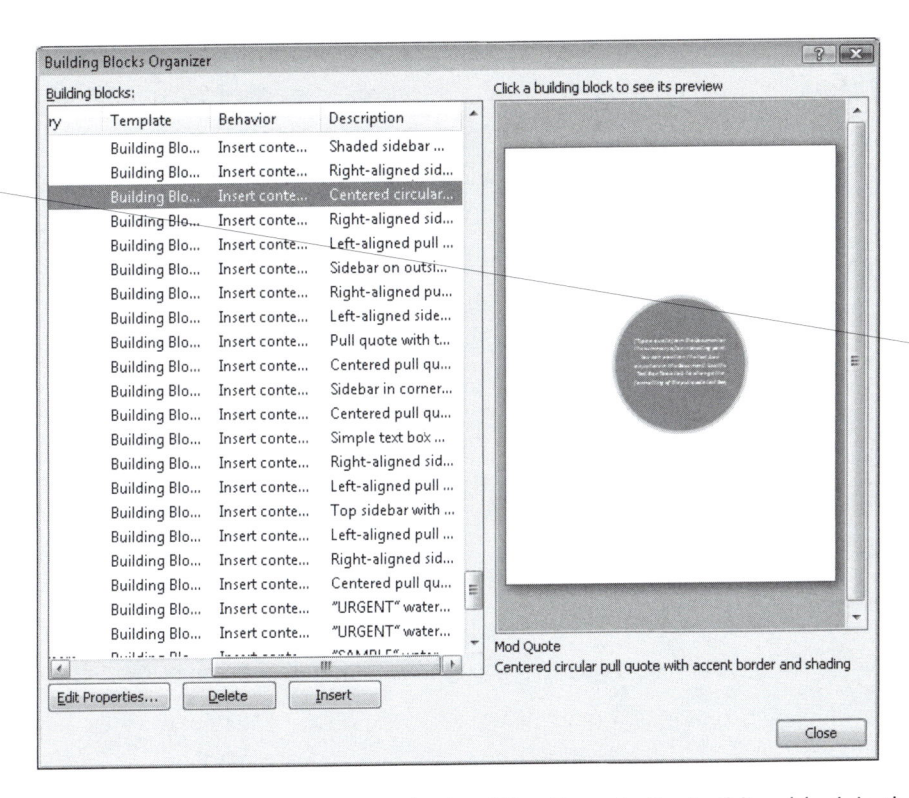

The Behavior column indicates whether Word inserts the building block in the existing text, in its own paragraph, or on its own page. The Description column includes information about the building block, and in some cases, recommendations for its use.

> **Tip** You can display the entire contents of a column by pointing to the right column header border and then, when the pointer changes to a double-headed arrow, dragging to the right, into the preview pane. (In the case of the Description column, you drag into the preview pane.)

Some building blocks are also available from the Ribbon—for example, you can add headers and footers from the Header & Footer group on the Insert tab. If you frequently use a specific element in your documents, such as a formatted title-subtitle-author arrangement at the beginning of reports, you can define it as a custom building block. It is then available from the Building Blocks Organizer.

In this exercise, you will insert several ready-made building blocks in a document. You will also save an element of the document as a custom building block.

> **USE** the *Parts* document. This practice file is located in the *Documents\Microsoft Press\Word2007SBS\Organizing* folder.
> **OPEN** the *Parts* document.

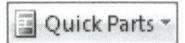

1. With the insertion point at the beginning of the document, on the **Insert** tab, in the **Text** group, click the **Quick Parts** button, and then click **Building Blocks Organizer**.

   > **Troubleshooting** If you or your organization have made custom building blocks available from your computer, clicking the Quick Parts button displays them in the Quick Parts gallery. If no custom building blocks are available, clicking the Quick Parts button displays a list of building block-related commands.

   The Building Blocks Organizer opens. The left pane displays a complete list of all the building blocks available on your computer; clicking a building block in the left pane displays a preview in the right pane.

   > **Tip** The Building Blocks list you see on your computer includes AutoText entries for your user name and initials. To change either of these entries, click the Microsoft Office Button, click Word Options, and then on the Popular page of the Word Options window, update your information and click OK.

2. Scroll through the **Building blocks** list, and preview a few of the building blocks.

   Notice that page elements of the same theme are coordinated and that page elements with different themes contain similar information.

3. If the **Gallery** column of the **Building blocks** list is not sorted alphabetically, double-click the **Gallery** column heading. Then in the list of **Cover Pages**, click the **Pinstripes** cover page, and click **Insert**.

   Word inserts the cover page at the beginning of the document, adds the title, company name, and user name that are attached as properties to the document, and indicates with placeholders where you should type the subtitle and date.

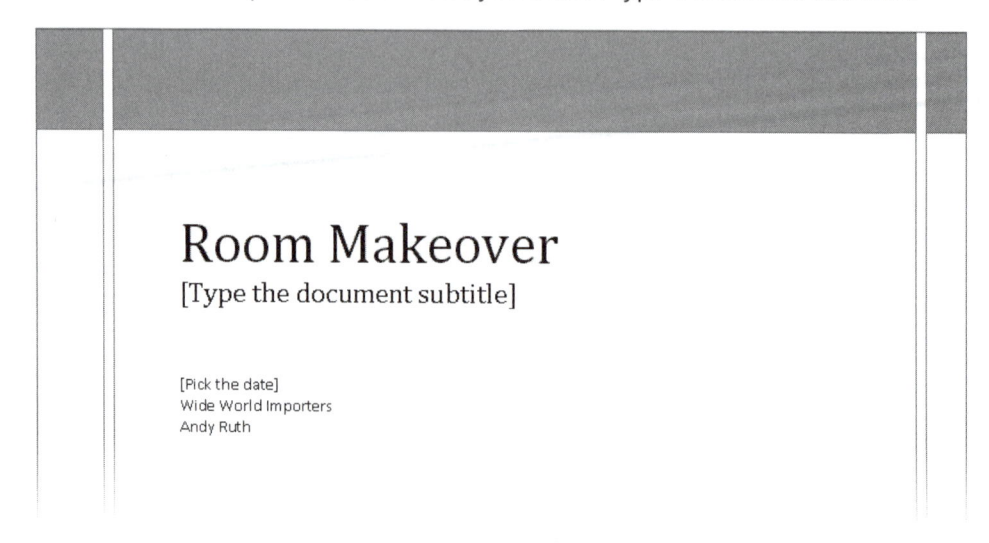

   # Room Makeover
   [Type the document subtitle]

   [Pick the date]
   Wide World Importers
   Andy Ruth

4. Click anywhere in the subtitle placeholder, and type **Information Sheet**. Then click the date placeholder, click the arrow that appears, and in the calendar, click today's date (indicated by a red box).

5. Move to page **2** (which was originally the first page of the document), and click anywhere on the page. Then display the **Building Blocks Organizer**, scroll to the list of **Text Boxes**, click **Pinstripes Quote**, and click **Insert**.

   Word inserts the quote box half way down the right side of the page. Placeholder text in the quote box tells you how to insert your own text and format the block.

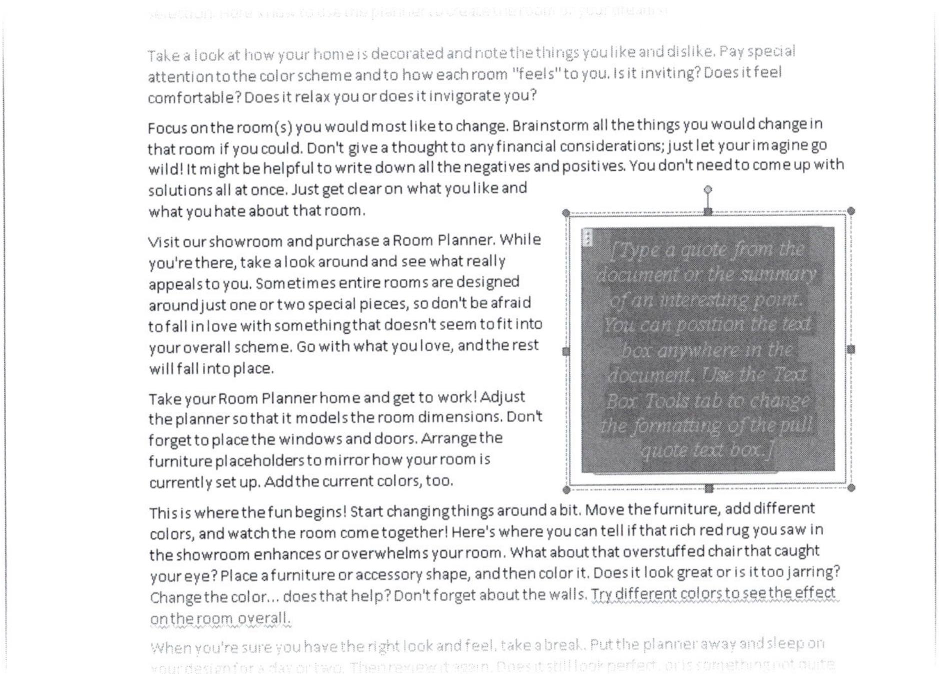

6. Select and copy the last sentence of the fourth paragraph (*Go with what you love...*), and then click the quote box to select the placeholder text.

7. On the **Home** tab, in the **Clipboard** group, click the **Paste** arrow, and in the list, click **Paste Special**. Then in the **Paste Special** dialog box, click **Unformatted Text**, and click **OK**.

   The copied text replaces the placeholder, and because it was pasted as unformatted text, it retains the formatting of the placeholder text. The quote box automatically resizes to fit its new contents.

> **Tip** You can reposition a text box by dragging it to another location in the document. You can change the outline and fill colors by using the commands in the Text Box Styles group on the Format contextual tab.
>
> You can link text boxes so that text flows from one to the next. To do so, click the first text box and then in the Text group on the Format contextual tab, click Link. The mouse pointer changes to a small pitcher. Point to the second text box, and then when the mouse pointer changes to a pouring pitcher, click once. Note that you cannot link to a text box that contains a placeholder.

8. Move to page **3**, and click anywhere on the page. Then display the **Building Blocks Organizer**, scroll to the list of **Text Boxes**, click **Pinstripes Sidebar**, and click **Insert**.

   Word inserts the sidebar on the right third of the page.

9. Delete **NOTE:** (including the colon and following space) from the beginning of the last paragraph of the document, select the paragraph, and then in the **Clipboard** group, click the **Cut** button.

10. Click the sidebar to select the placeholder text, and then in the **Clipboard** group, click the **Paste** arrow, and in the list, click **Paste Special**. Then in the **Paste Special** dialog box, click **Unformatted Text**, and click **OK**.

    The sidebar is too narrow to completely hold the Web site address, so you need to widen it.

accessories, so if you are disappointed in any way, you can return undamaged pieces for just a nominal restocking charge.

If you're not sure you made the right choices and don't know which way to turn, arrange to meet with one of our designers. This free service is available to all our customers. Sometimes talking over your plans or obstacles with a professional can really help get you back on track.

Success! Your room is everything you hoped for. Now what about your bedroom? Maybe a new linen chest or perhaps new window treatments? The Room Planner can be used countless times for any room in the house. And if you're eyeing your patio or deck as your next makeover project, you'll want to check out the Outdoor Room Planner, too.

To order the Room Planner for just $39.99 plus shipping and handling, visit our Web site at www.wideworldimporters.com or call us at 925-555-0167. The Outdoor Room Planner retails for $29.99 plus shipping and handling. Both planners are also available in our stores, so be sure to ask about them the next time you visit. We accept all major credit cards.

11. Drag the blue handle on the left edge of the white sidebar placeholder to the left, until it sits slightly to the left of the frame of the text block.

12. On the **Insert** tab, in the **Text** group, click the **Quick Parts** button, and then click **Save Selection to Quick Part Gallery**.

> **Troubleshooting** If you click the text in the sidebar or elsewhere in the document after resizing the sidebar, it will no longer be selected and the Save Selection To Quick Part Gallery command will not be available. If this happens, click the sidebar's sizing handle to reselect the sidebar, and then repeat step 12.

The Create New Building Block dialog box opens.

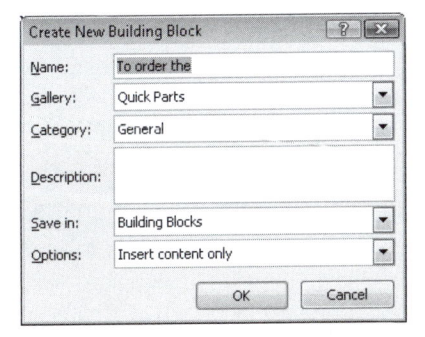

The options in this dialog box correspond to the columns of information displayed in the Building Blocks Organizer. You can save this building block in the Building Blocks template or the Normal template.

13. Replace the text in the **Name** box with **Order Sidebar**, and then click **OK**.

    You can now insert this custom sidebar from the Quick Parts gallery into other documents.

14. In the **Text** group, click the **Quick Parts** button.

    The Order Sidebar custom building block appears at the top of the Quick Parts gallery.

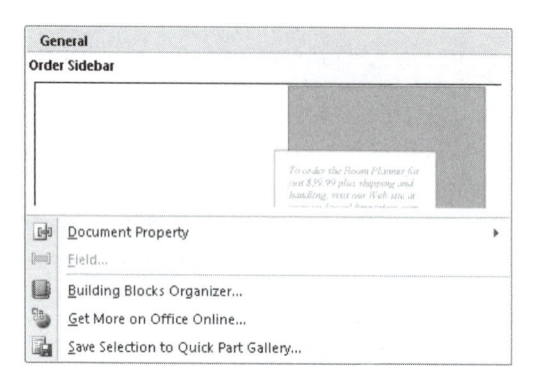

15. Display the **Building Blocks Organizer**, and click the **Category** column heading to sort the **Building blocks** list by that column. Then scroll to the **General** category.

    The General category includes your custom building block and the AutoText entries.

16. In the list, click **Order Sidebar** once.

    In the preview pane, Word displays the building block you just created.

    > **Tip** To delete a building block from your computer, select it in the Building Blocks Organizer, and then click Delete.

17. Close the **Building Blocks Organizer** dialog box.

CLOSE the *Parts* document without saving your changes.

> **Important** When you exit Word after saving a custom building block, you will be asked whether you want to save changes to the template in which you stored the building block. If you want the building block to be available for future documents, click Yes; otherwise, click No.

> **Tip** You can insert a blank page anywhere in a document—even in the middle of a paragraph—by positioning the insertion point and then clicking the Blank Page button in the Pages group on the Insert tab.

Creating and Modifying a Table of Contents

If you create a long document with headings and subheadings, such as an annual report or a catalog that has several sections, you might want to add a *table of contents* to the beginning of the document to give your readers an overview of and the document's contents and to help them navigate to specific sections. In a document that will be printed, you can indicate with a page number the starting page of each section; if the document will be distributed electronically, you can link each heading and subheading in the table of contents to the section in the document, so that readers can jump directly there with a click of the mouse.

By default, Word expects to create a table of contents based on paragraphs within the document that you have formatted with the standard heading styles (Heading 1, Heading 2, and so on). (Word can also create a table of contents based on outline levels or on fields that you have inserted in the document.) When you tell Word to create the table, Word identifies the table of contents entries and inserts the table at the insertion point as a single field. You can modify the elements on which Word bases the table at any time.

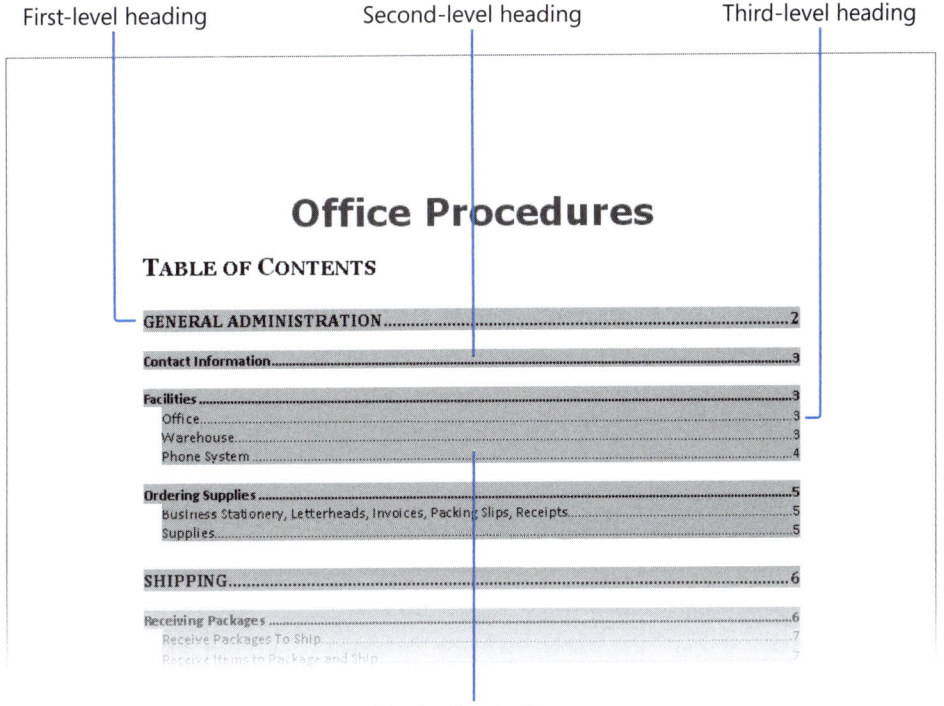

First-level heading   Second-level heading   Third-level heading

Office Procedures

TABLE OF CONTENTS

GENERAL ADMINISTRATION..2
Contact Information..3
Facilities...3
    Office...3
    Warehouse...3
    Phone System...4
Ordering Supplies..5
    Business Stationery, Letterheads, Invoices, Packing Slips, Receipts..........5
    Supplies..5

SHIPPING...6

Receiving Packages..6
    Receive Packages To Ship...7
    Receive Items to Package and Ship

This shading indicates that the table of contents is a single field.

See Also For information about applying styles, see "Working with Templates" in Chapter 4, "Changing the Look of a Document."

The Table Of Contents gallery (available from the References tab) offers three standard table options:

- **Automatic Table 1.** This option inserts a table of contents with the heading Contents.
- **Automatic Table 2.** This option inserts a table of contents with the heading Table of Contents.
- **Manual Table.** This option inserts a table of contents with placeholders that you replace manually.

The formatting of the entries in a table of contents is controlled by nine levels of built-in TOC styles (TOC 1, TOC 2, and so on). By default, Word uses the styles that are assigned in the template attached to the document. If you want to use a different style, instead of clicking one of the standard options in the Table Of Contents gallery, you can click Insert Table Of Contents below the gallery to display the Table Of Contents dialog box, where you can choose from several variations, such as Classic, Fancy, and Simple.

> **Tip** If you create a table of contents based on the document's template, you can customize the TOC styles during the creation process. On the References tab, in the Table Of Contents group, click the Tables Of Contents button, and then in the list, click Insert Table Of Contents. In the Table Of Contents dialog box, click Modify. The Style dialog box opens, displaying the nine TOC styles. You can modify the font, paragraph, tabs, border, and other formatting of these styles the same way you change any other style.

After you create a table of contents, you can format it manually by selecting text and then applying character or paragraph formatting or styles.

You can edit the text of a table of contents, but it is much easier to click the Update Table button and have Word do the work for you. You have the option of updating only the page numbers, or if you have changed, added, or deleted headings, you can update (re-create) the entire table.

In this exercise, you will create a table of contents for a document based on heading styles. Then you will alter the document by inserting page breaks, and update the table of contents to reflect your changes.

> **USE** the *Contents* document. This practice file is located in the *Documents\Microsoft Press\Word2007SBS\Organizing* folder.
> **OPEN** the *Contents* document.

1. Position the insertion point to the left of *GENERAL ADMINISTRATION*, and then on the **References** tab, in the **Table of Contents** group, click the **Table of Contents** button.

2. In the **Table of Contents** gallery, click **Automatic Table 1**. Then press Ctrl+Home to return to the beginning of the document.

   Word inserts a table of contents with predefined styles at the insertion point.

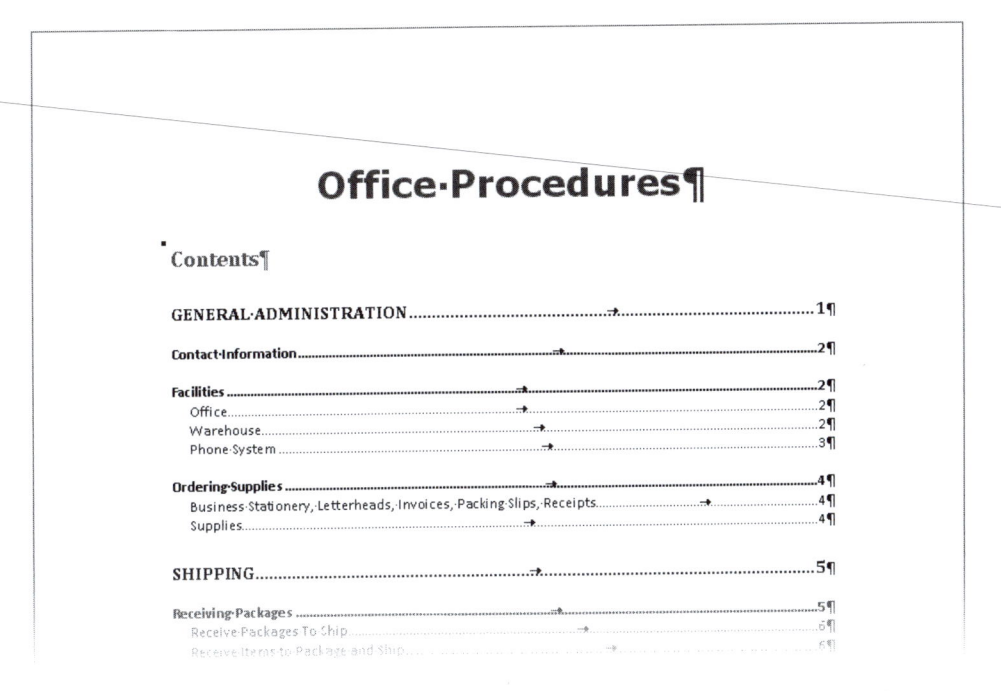

   Office Procedures¶

   Contents¶

   GENERAL ADMINISTRATION .... 1¶
   Contact Information .... 2¶
   Facilities .... 2¶
       Office .... 2¶
       Warehouse .... 2¶
       Phone System .... 3¶
   Ordering Supplies .... 4¶
       Business Stationery, Letterheads, Invoices, Packing Slips, Receipts ... 4¶
       Supplies .... 4¶

   SHIPPING .... 5¶
   Receiving Packages .... 5¶
       Receive Packages To Ship .... 6¶
       Receive Items to Package and Ship .... 6¶

3. In the **Table of Contents** group, click the **Table of Contents** button, and then below the gallery, click **Remove Table of Contents**.

4. Position the insertion point to the left of *GENERAL ADMINISTRATION*, type Table of Contents, press the Enter key, and then on the **Insert** tab, in the **Pages** group, click the **Page Break** button.

5. Press the ↑ key to position the insertion point in the empty page break paragraph.

   > **Tip** If you want to see this paragraph, display non-printing characters.

6. On the **References** tab, in the **Table of Contents** group, click the **Table of Contents** button, and then below the gallery, click **Insert Table of Contents**.

   The Table Of Contents dialog box opens.

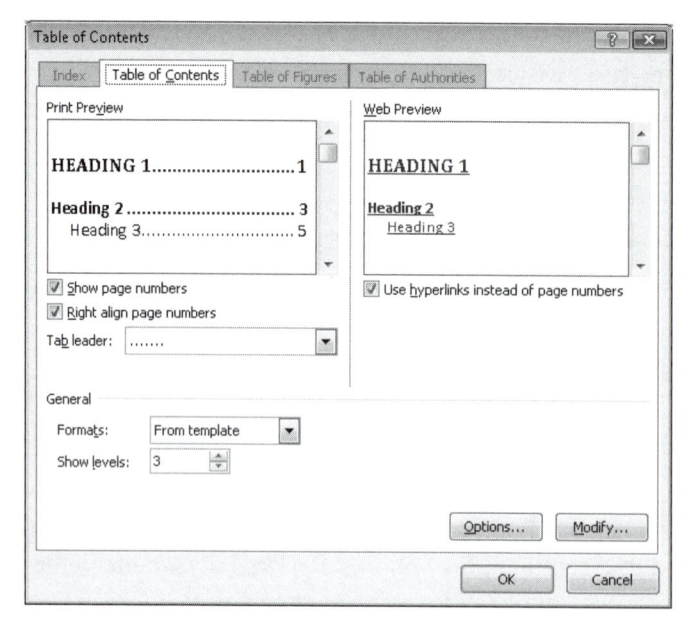

7. On the **Table of Contents** tab, in the **General** area, click the **Formats** arrow, and then in the list, click **Classic**.

   Examples of the Classic table of contents format appears in the preview boxes.

8. Click the **Tab leader** arrow, and then in the list, click the dotted line.

   The Print Preview box changes to display dotted tab leaders.

9. Click **OK** to insert the table of contents, and then press Ctrl+Home to return to the beginning of the document.

10. Point to any entry in the table.

    A ScreenTip appears, notifying you that you can hold down the Ctrl key and click any entry in the table of contents to jump to that heading in the document.

11. Click anywhere in the table.

    The entire table is selected, because it consists of only one field.

12. Move to the top of the third page, click at the beginning of the *Contact Information* heading, and then press Ctrl+Enter to insert a page break.

    The *Contact Information* heading is now on page 4.

13. Scroll down to the *Ordering Supplies* heading, and insert a page break before that heading.

14. On the **References** tab, in the **Table of Contents** group, click the **Update Table** button.

    The Update Table Of Contents dialog box opens.

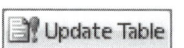

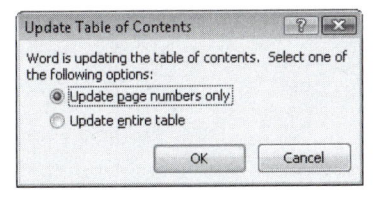

15. Click **Update entire table**, and click **OK**. Then press Ctrl + Home.

Word has updated the table of contents to reflect the new page numbers.

CLOSE the *Contents* document without saving your changes.

Creating Other Types of Tables

If a document includes figures or tables that have descriptions, or *captions*, you can tell Word to create a *table of figures*. If a legal document contains items such as regulations, cases, and statutes that are identified as legal citations, you can tell Word to create a *table of authorities*. Word uses the captions or citations to create these types of tables the same way it uses headings to create a table of contents.

To insert a caption:

1. Position the insertion point where you want the caption to appear (usually directly after the figure), and then on the **References** tab, in the **Captions** group, click the **Insert Caption** button.

    The Caption dialog box opens.

2. If you want to change the designator shown in the **Caption** box (the default is *Figure*), click **New Label**, type the caption you want, and then click **OK**.

3. In the **Caption** box, click to the right of the default text and number, press Space, type the caption, and then click **OK**.

    Word adds the caption to the document.

To create a table of figures:

1. Position the insertion point where you want to insert the table of figures, and then on the **References** tab, in the **Captions** group, click **Insert Table of Figures**.

    The Table Of Figures dialog box opens.

2. If you want to change the default type of caption to be included in the table, in the **General** area, click the **Caption label** arrow, and then in the list, click the type of caption you want.

Creating and Modifying an Index

To help readers find specific concepts and terms that might not be readily located by looking at a table of contents, you can include an *index* at the end of a document. Word creates an index by compiling an alphabetical listing with page numbers based on *index entry fields* that you have marked in the document. As with a table of contents, an index is inserted at the insertion point as one field.

> 3. If you want to change the default table format, click the **Formats** arrow, and then in the list, click the format you want.
>
> 4. Select any additional options you want, and then click **OK**.
>
>   Word inserts the table in the specified format above the insertion point.
>
> To insert a legal citation:
>
> 1. Select the first legal reference that you want to mark with a citation.
>
> 2. On the **References** tab, in the **Table of Authorities** group, click the **Mark Citation** button.
>
>   The Mark Citation dialog box opens.
>
> 3. In the **Selected text** box and the **Short citation** box, edit the citation to reflect the way you want it to appear in the table.
>
> 4. If you want to change the category, click the **Category** arrow, and then in the list, click the category that applies to the citation.
>
> 5. To mark one citation, click **Mark**. To mark all citations that match the selected citation, click **Mark All**.
>
> To create a table of authorities:
>
> 1. Position the insertion point where you want the table of authorities to appear, and then on the **References** tab, in the **Table of Authorities** group, click the **Insert Table of Authorities** button.
>
>   The Table Of Authorities dialog box opens.
>
> 2. In the **Category** list, click the category of citations that you want to appear in the table, or click **All** to include all categories.
>
> 3. Select formatting options for the table, and then click **OK**.
>
>   Word inserts the table in the specified format before the insertion point.

> **Tip** You don't need to create indexes for documents that will be distributed electronically because readers can use the Find feature or Windows Desktop Search to go directly to search terms.
>
> To make a document easier to locate through a Find or Search operation, enter keywords and other properties in the Document Information Panel. To display the Document Information Panel, click the Microsoft Office Button, point to Prepare, and then click Properties.

In the index, an *index entry* might apply to a word or phrase that appears on one page or is discussed for several pages. The entry might have related *subentries*. For example, the main index entry *shipping* might have below it the subentries *supplies*, *procedures*, and *packing*. An index might also include *cross-reference entries* that direct readers to related entries. For example, the main index entry *shipping* might have below it a cross-reference to *warehouse*.

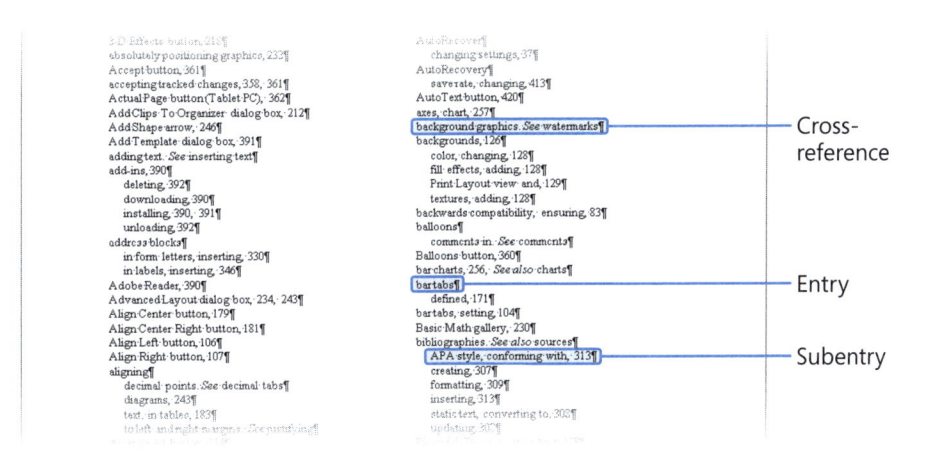

To insert an index entry field in the document, you select the text you want to mark, and click Mark Entry in the Index group on the References tab to open the Mark Index Entry dialog box, where you can do the following:

- Use the selected text as is, modify the entry, and add a subentry.
- Format the entry—for example, to make it appear bold or italic in the index—by right-clicking it, clicking Font, and selecting the options you want.
- Designate the entry as a cross-reference, one-page entry, or a page-range entry.

> **Tip** Cross-references appear in the index in the following format:
>
> intercom. *See* phones
>
> In this manner, you can direct readers to index terms they might not think of when looking for specific information.

- Specify the formatting of this entry's page number.

After you have set the options in the dialog box the way you want them, you can insert an index entry field adjacent to the selected text by clicking Mark, or adjacent to every occurrence of the selected text in the document by clicking Mark All. The Mark Index Entry dialog box remains open to simplify the process of inserting multiple index entry fields—you don't have to click the Mark Entry button for each new entry. You can move the dialog box off to the side so that it doesn't block the text you're working with.

> **Tip** When building an index, you should choose the text you mark carefully, bearing in mind what terms readers are likely to look up. One reader might expect to find information about *cell phones* by looking under *cell*, whereas another might look under *mobile*, another under *phones*, and another under *telephones*. A good index will include all four entries.

Index entry fields are formatted as hidden; you cannot see them unless you click the Show/Hide ¶ button in the Paragraph group on the Home tab. When the field is visible, it appears in the document enclosed in quotation marks within a set of braces, with the designator *XE* and a dotted underline.

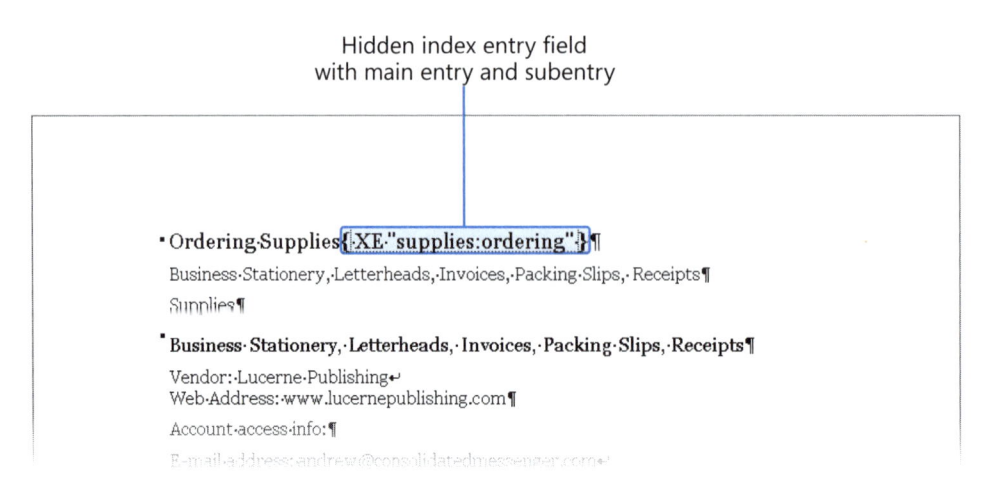

Hidden index entry field
with main entry and subentry

- Ordering Supplies { XE "supplies:ordering" } ¶
  Business Stationery, Letterheads, Invoices, Packing Slips, Receipts ¶
  Supplies ¶
- Business Stationery, Letterheads, Invoices, Packing Slips, Receipts ¶
  Vendor: Lucerne Publishing
  Web Address: www.lucernepublishing.com ¶
  Account access info: ¶
  E-mail address: andrew@consolidatedmessenger.com

> **Tip** You can hide any text in a document by selecting it, clicking the Font dialog box launcher on the Home tab, selecting the Hidden check box, and clicking OK. When you print the document, Word will not include the hidden text unless you click Options in the Print dialog box and then under Printing Options, select the Print Hidden Text check box.

You can change the text of an index entry by editing the text within the quotation marks in the index entry field as you would any other. (You could also edit the text of the index generated from the entries, but that change would not be permanent; regenerating the index would restore the original entry.) To delete an index entry, you select the entire hidden field and then press the Delete key. You can also move and copy index entries using the techniques you would use for regular text.

> **Tip** Dragging through any part of an index entry field that includes one of the enclosing braces selects the entire field.

To create an index in a document based on the index entries in that document, you position the insertion point where you want the index to appear and then click the Insert Index button in the Index group on the Reference tab to open the Index dialog box, where you can specify the following:

- Whether the index formatting should use styles from the current template or be based on one of six predefined formats that you can preview in the Print Preview box.
- Whether page numbers should be right-aligned, and if so whether they should have dotted, dashed, or solid tab leaders.
- Whether the index should be indented, with each subentry on a separate line below the main entries, or run-in, with subentries on the same line as the main entries.

When you click OK in the Index dialog box, Word calculates the page numbers of all the entries and subentries, consolidates them, and inserts the index as one field in the specified format at the specified location in the document.

> **Tip** If you make changes to the document that affect its index entries or page numbering, you can update the index by clicking it and then clicking the Update Index button in the Index group on the References tab. You can also update the index by right-clicking it and then clicking Update Field.

In this exercise, you will first mark a few index entries and a cross-reference entry. Then you'll create and format an index, delete an index entry from the document, and update the index.

Creating and Modifying an Index   235

> **USE** the *Index* document. This practice file is located in the *Documents\Microsoft Press\Word2007SBS\Organizing* folder.
> **BE SURE TO** display non-printing characters before starting this exercise.
> **OPEN** the *Index* document.

1. In the table of contents, point to the **Warehouse** heading, hold down the Ctrl key, and then click the heading to move to the bottom of page 3.

2. In the paragraph below the heading, select the word **Receiving**. Then on the **References** tab, in the **Index** group, click the **Mark Entry** button.

   The Mark Index Entry dialog box opens.

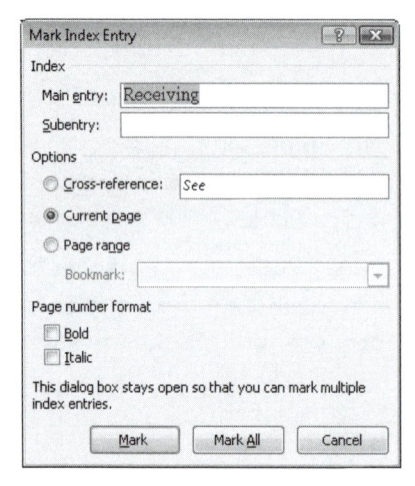

3. In the **Main entry** box, change *Receiving* to *receiving* (with a lowercase *r*).

   > **Tip** Index entries will appear in the index exactly as they appear in the Mark Index Entry dialog box. For consistency, make all entries lowercase except those for proper nouns.

4. Click **Mark All**.

   Word inserts hidden index entry fields adjacent to every occurrence of the word *Receiving* in the document.

   > **Tip** If this document contained instances of the word *receiving*, those would not be marked because their capitalization does not match the selected word.

5. In the same paragraph, select the word **Shipping**, and click the title bar of the **Mark Index Entry** dialog box to activate it and enter the selected text. Then change the first letter in the **Main entry** box from uppercase to lowercase, and click **Mark All**.

6. Repeat step 5 for the words **Packaging** and **Inventory** in the same paragraph.

> **Troubleshooting** You might have to move the dialog box to see and select the words you want to mark.

7. On the next page, in the paragraph under the *Phone System* heading, select the word **phone**, and then in the **Mark Index Entry** dialog box, change the entry to **phones**, and click **Mark All**.

8. In the same paragraph, select the word **intercom**, and then in the **Mark Index Entry** dialog box, in the **Options** area, click **Cross-reference**.

   The insertion point moves to the space after the word *See* in the adjacent box.

9. Without moving the insertion point, type **phones**, and then click **Mark**.

   A cross-reference to the *phones* index entry appears adjacent to the word *intercom*.

10. Move to page 5, and select the word **Supplies** in *Ordering Supplies*. Then in the **Mark Index Entry** dialog box, change word in the **Main entry** box to **supplies**, type **ordering** in the **Subentry** box, and click **Mark**.

11. Move to the bottom of page 6, and select the word **Packages** in the second *Receiving Packages* heading. Then in the **Mark Index Entry** dialog box, replace the word *Packages* in the **Main entry** box with **supplies**, type **receiving** in the **Subentry** box, and click **Mark**.

12. Close the **Mark Index Entry** dialog box.

13. Press `Ctrl`+`End` to move to the end of the document, and then press `Ctrl`+`Enter` to insert a page break.

    The insertion point moves to the top of the new page.

14. Type **Index**, press `Enter`, apply the **Heading 1** style to the new heading, press `Enter`, and then press `Enter` again.

15. On the **Home** tab, in the **Paragraph** group, click the **Show/Hide ¶** button to hide non-printing characters.

> **Troubleshooting** When hidden text is visible, the document might not be paginated correctly. Always turn off the display of non-printing characters before creating an index.

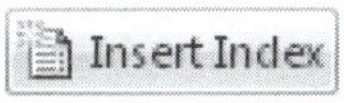

16. On the **References** tab, in the **Index** group, click the **Insert Index** button.

    The Index dialog box opens.

Creating and Modifying an Index   **237**

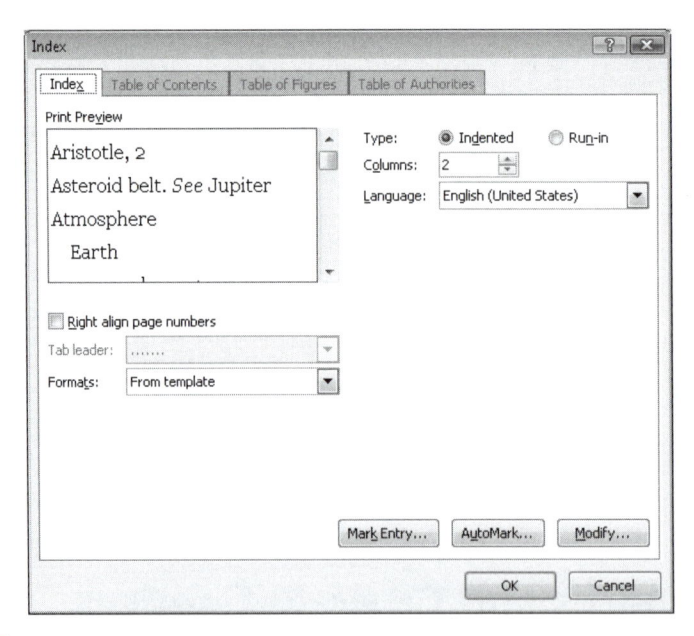

17. In the **Columns** box, change the setting to **1**.
18. Click the **Formats** arrow, and in the list, click **Formal**.
19. Clear the **Right align page numbers** check box. Then click **OK**.

    Word compiles a short index based on the index entries you just marked. The index is formatted in one column with the page numbers adjacent to their index entries.

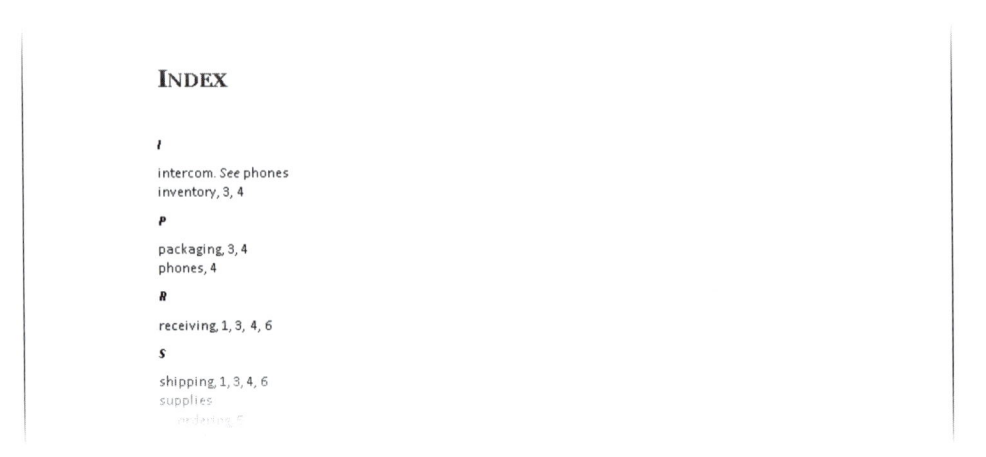

20. Display non-printing characters so that you can see the index entry fields in the document, and move to the *Phone System* heading on page 4.
21. Select the entire cross-reference entry following *intercom*, and press the Del key.

> **Troubleshooting** If you find it hard to select just this entry, try pointing to the right of the closing brace (}) and dragging slightly to the left.

The cross-reference entry is deleted from the document.

22. Press **Ctrl**+**End** to move to the end of the document, and click anywhere in the index to select it.

23. Hide the non-printing characters. Then on the **References** tab, in the **Index** group, click the **Update Index** button.

The index is updated to reflect that you have deleted the cross-reference.

CLOSE the *Index* document without saving your changes.

Adding Bookmarks and Cross-References

Word provides several tools for navigating long documents, two of which—bookmarks and cross-references—enable you to jump easily to designated places within the same document. Both tools require you to mark locations in the document and name them.

See Also For information about using hyperlinks to jump to other locations, see "Adding Hyperlinks" later in this chapter. For information about using the Document Map to jump to any paragraph styled as a heading, see "Displaying Different Views of a Document" in Chapter 1, "Exploring Word 2007."

Whether the document you are reading was created by you or by someone else, you can insert bookmarks to flag information to which you might want to return later. Like a physical bookmark, a Word bookmark marks a specific place in a document. After inserting a bookmark, you can quickly jump to it by displaying the Bookmark dialog box, clicking the bookmark you want to locate, and then clicking Go To.

> **Tip** Alternatively, you can display the Go To tab of the Find And Replace dialog box, click Bookmark in the Go To What list, and then select the bookmark you want from the Enter Bookmark Name list.

If you are developing a long document, you can create cross-references to quickly move readers to associated information elsewhere in the document. You can create cross-references to two types of elements:

- Headings, figures, and tables, for which Word automatically creates pointers
- Manually created bookmarks

Adding Bookmarks and Cross-References 239

If you later delete an item you have designated as the target of a cross-reference, you will need to update the cross-reference.

In this exercise, you will insert a bookmark and then jump to it. You will also create a cross-reference, edit the referenced item, and then update the cross-reference.

> **USE** the *Bookmarks* document. This practice file is located in the *Documents\Microsoft Press\Word2007SBS\Organizing* folder.
> **OPEN** the *Bookmarks* document.

1. On the **Home** tab, in the **Editing** group, click the **Find** arrow, and in the list, click **Go To**.

   The Find And Replace dialog box opens, with the Go To tab active.

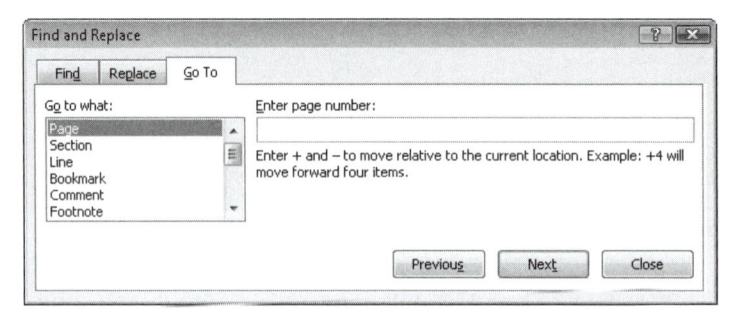

2. With **Page** selected in the **Go to what** list, in the **Enter page number** box, type 8. Then click **Go To**, and click **Close**.

3. On page 8, position the insertion point to the left of the *Checking the credit of new customers* heading, and then on the **Insert** tab, in the **Links** group, click the **Bookmark** button.

   The Bookmark dialog box opens.

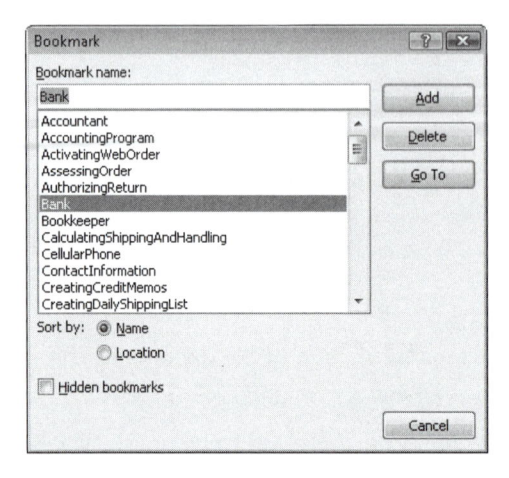

4. Move the dialog box to the right side of the screen, and then scroll the list of pre-defined bookmarks.

    Word has already created bookmarks for headings down to the fourth level by removing articles (*a* and *the*), spaces, and punctuation and initial capping words. For example, notice the *DoesCustomerAlreadyHaveAccount* bookmark for the fourth-level *Does the customer already have an account?* heading on this page.

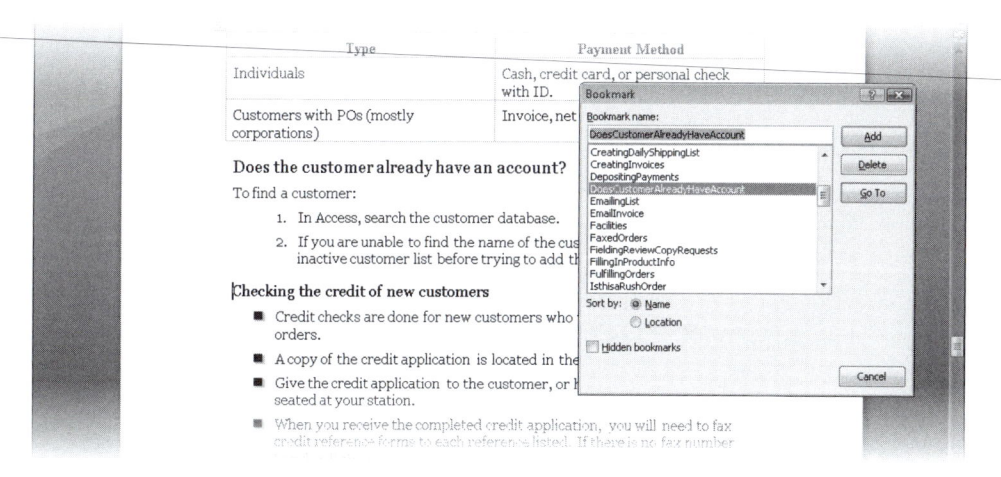

    The name that already appears in the Bookmark Name box is the name of the bookmark selected in the list below, not a suggested name for your new bookmark. Replacing it will not delete that existing bookmark.

5. In the **Bookmark name** box, type **CreditCheck**, and then click **Add**.

    > **Troubleshooting** Bookmark names cannot contain spaces. If you enter a space and then type a character, the Add button becomes inactive. To name bookmarks with multiple words, either run the words together and capitalize each word or replace the spaces with underscores for readability.

    The Bookmark dialog box closes, and although you can't see it, a bookmark named CreditCheck is inserted into the document.

    > **Tip** To know whether a document contains bookmarks, display the Bookmark dialog box. You can sort the bookmarks alphabetically or in the order in which they are located.

6. Press **Ctrl**+**Home** to move to the beginning of the document. Then on the **Home** tab, in the **Editing** group, click the **Find** arrow, and click **Go To**.

7. In the **Find and Replace** dialog box, in the **Go to what** list, click **Bookmark**.

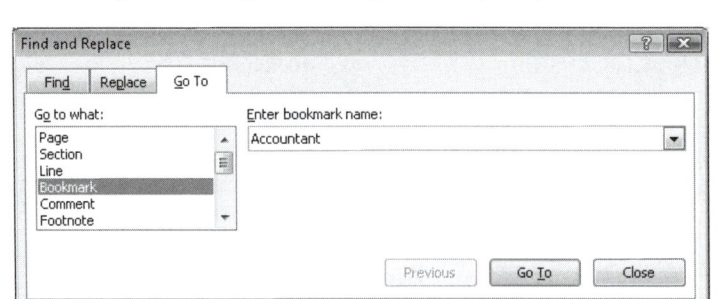

The dialog box changes so that you can specify the bookmark you want to jump to.

8. Click the **Enter bookmark name** arrow, and in the list, click **CreditCheck**. Then click **Go To**.

   The insertion point moves to the location of the bookmark. The dialog box remains open in case you want to move somewhere else.

9. Close the **Find and Replace** dialog box.

   > **Tip** To delete a bookmark, click Bookmark in the Links group on the Insert tab, click the bookmark's name, and then click Delete.

10. At the top of page 7, position the insertion point at the right end of the step 1 paragraph, press [Space], type For more information, see, and then press [Space] again.

11. On the **Insert** tab, in the **Links** group, click the **Cross-reference** button.

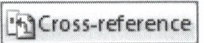

    The Cross-Reference dialog box opens.

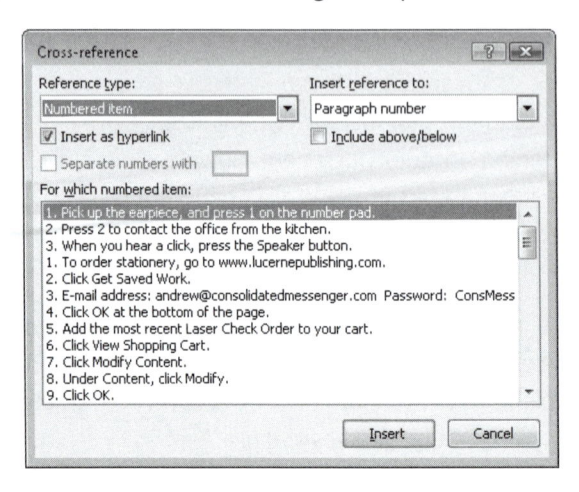

12. Click the **Reference type** arrow, and in the list, click **Heading**. Then with **Heading text** selected in the **Insert reference to** box, scroll the **For which heading** list, and click **Does the customer already have an account?**.

13. Click **Insert**, and then click **Close**.

    The text *Does the customer already have an account?* appears in the document at the insertion point. Although it is not obvious, the text is inserted as one field and formatted as a cross-reference.

14. Hold down the Ctrl key, and then click the cross-reference to move to that heading.

15. In the heading, click to position the insertion point after the word *account* (before the question mark), press Space, and then type **with us**.

16. Move back to the top of page 7, and at the end of the step 1 paragraph, click **Does the customer have an account?** to select the cross-reference field.

> **Troubleshooting** Don't select the *For more information, see* introductory text.

17. Right-click the selected cross-reference, and then click **Update Field**.

    Word inserts the words *with us* at the end of the cross-reference to reflect the change you made to the heading.

18. Hold down Ctrl, and click the cross-reference to return to the associated heading.

✘ **CLOSE** the *Bookmarks* document without saving your changes.

Adding Hyperlinks

Like Web pages, Word documents can include hyperlinks that provide a quick way to perform tasks such as opening another document, downloading a file, or sending an e-mail message. You insert hyperlinks into a Word document by displaying the Insert Hyperlink dialog box, specifying the type of link you want to create, and then entering an appropriate target for that type of link.

While creating a hyperlink to a target in the same document, in another document, or on a Web page, you can specify whether the target information should appear in the same window or frame as the document or in a new window or frame. You can also make a particular setting the default for all hyperlinks.

Tip When the target is a Web page, you specify its location by using its *Uniform Resource Locator (URL)*, such as *www.microsoft.com*.

Within a document, hyperlinks appear underlined and in the color specified for hyperlinks by the document's theme. You can jump to the target of the hyperlink by holding down the Ctrl key and clicking the link. After you click the hyperlink, it appears in the color specified for followed hyperlinks.

To edit or remove a hyperlink, you can select it and click Hyperlink in the Links group on the Insert tab or you can right-click the selection and then click the appropriate command.

In this exercise, you will insert, test, and modify a hyperlink.

> **USE** the *Hyperlinks* and *OtherLogos* documents. These practice files are located in the *Documents\Microsoft Press\Word2007SBS\Organizing* folder.
>
> **OPEN** the *Hyperlinks* document.

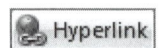

1. Click the **Wide World Importers** logo graphic at the top of the page. Then on the **Insert** tab, in the **Links** group, click the **Hyperlink** button.

   The Insert Hyperlink dialog box opens. On the Link To bar, Existing File Or Web Page is selected, and the dialog box shows the contents of the *Organizing* practice file folder.

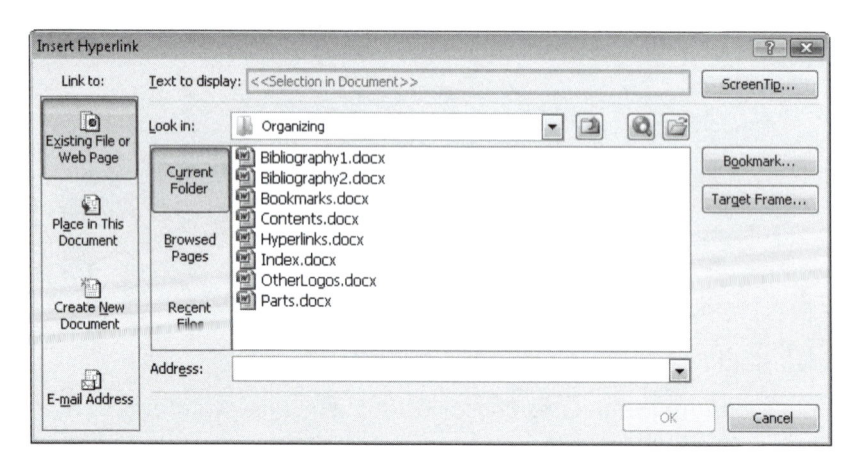

   > **Troubleshooting** If you don't see the contents of the *Organizing* folder, click Existing File Or Web Page on the Link To bar, and then navigate to your *Documents\ Microsoft Press\Word2007SBS\Organizing* folder.

2. In the list of file names, click (don't double-click) the *OtherLogos* document, and then click **Target Frame**.

   The Set Target Frame dialog box opens with Page Default (none) selected as the frame in which the document will open.

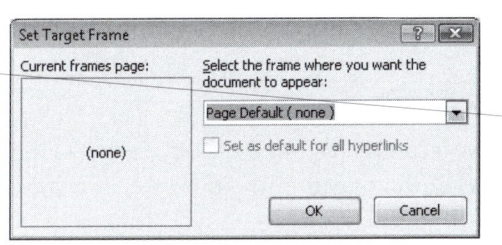

3. Click the **Select the frame** arrow, and in the list, click **New window**. Then click **OK**.

4. Click **OK** to insert a hyperlink from the logo graphic to the specified document, and then click a blank area of the document to release the selection.

   > **Troubleshooting** When a hyperlinked word or object (such as the logo) is selected, the hyperlink might not work correctly.

5. Point to the logo.

   Word displays a ScreenTip that shows the path to the *OtherLogos* document and instructions for following the link.

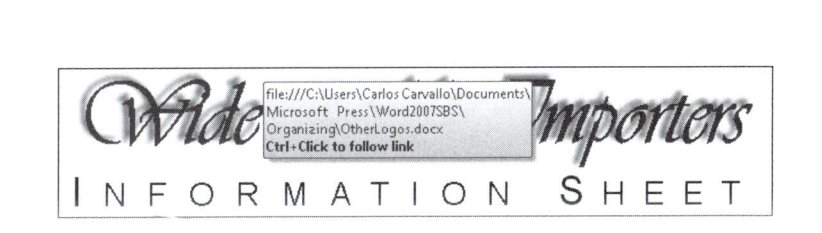

6. Hold down Ctrl, and then click the logo.

   Word opens the *OtherLogos* document in a new window.

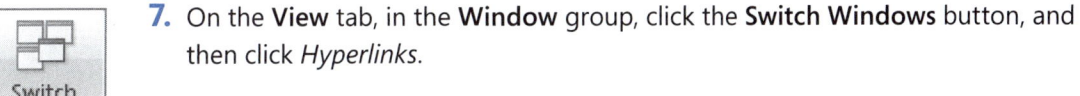

7. On the **View** tab, in the **Window** group, click the **Switch Windows** button, and then click *Hyperlinks*.

8. Move to page 2, click at the end of the paragraph in the sidebar, and press Enter twice.

9. Type Please contact us if you need more information, and then select the text.

10. On the **Insert** tab, in the **Links** group, click the **Hyperlink** button, and then on the **Link to** bar of the **Insert Hyperlink** dialog box, click **E-mail Address**.

   The dialog box changes so that you can enter the information appropriate for an e-mail hyperlink.

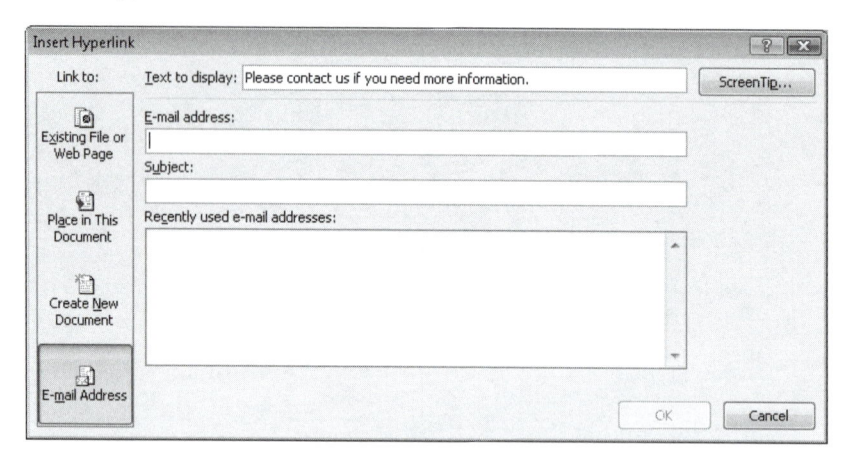

11. In the **E-mail address** box, type Kelly@wideworldimporters.com.

   > **Tip** When you begin typing the e-mail address, Word inserts *mailto:* in front of it.

   When a person clicks the link, Word will start his or her default e-mail program and open a new e-mail message window.

12. In the **Subject** box, type Room Planner inquiry.

   This text will be automatically entered in the Subject box of the new message.

13. Click **OK**.

   The hyperlinked text is indicated by an underline and its assigned theme color. Pointing to it displays a ScreenTip with the hyperlink's target.

14. Right-click the **Please contact us** hyperlink, and then click **Edit Hyperlink**.

   The Edit Hyperlink dialog box opens with the current destination for this link in the E-Mail Address box.

15. In the upper-right corner of the dialog box, click **ScreenTip**.

   The Set Hyperlink ScreenTip dialog box opens.

16. In the **ScreenTip** box, type Send e-mail message to Wide World Importers, and then click **OK**.

17. In the **E-mail address** box, replace *Kelly* with Carlos, and click **OK**.

18. Point to the hyperlink to see the new ScreenTip. Then hold down Ctrl, and click the hyperlink.

    Your e-mail program opens, with the specified e-mail address in the To box and the specified description in the Subject box.

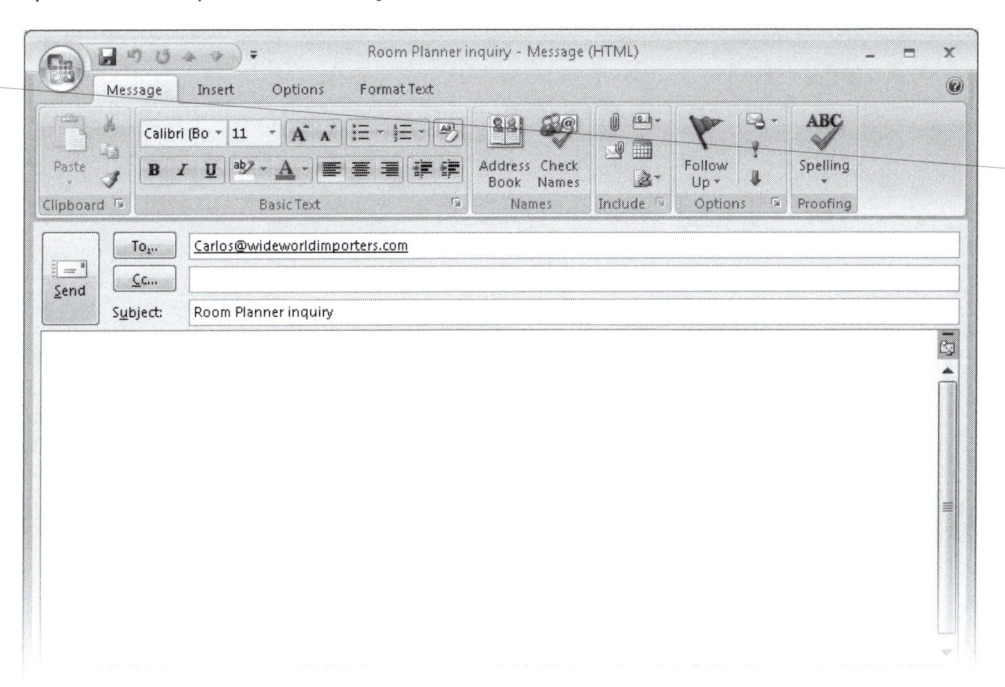

19. Close the message window, clicking **No** when asked whether you want to save the changes.

    The hyperlinked text is now displayed in the color assigned to followed hyperlinks.

CLOSE the *OtherLogos* and *Hyperlinks* documents without saving your changes.

Adding Sources and Compiling a Bibliography

Word 2007 includes the new Source Manager feature, which keeps track of the sources you use while researching a document and helps you reference them in the proper format. Whether your sources are books, periodicals, Web pages, or interviews, you can record details about them and then select a common style guide, such as the *Chicago Manual of Style*, to have Word automatically list your sources in that style guide's standard format.

Adding Footnotes and Endnotes

When you want to make a comment about a statement in a document—for example, to explain an assumption or cite the source for a different opinion—you can enter the comment as a footnote or an endnote. Doing so inserts a number or symbol called a *reference mark*, and your associated comment appears with the same number or symbol either as a *footnote* at the bottom of the page or as an *endnote* at the end of the document or document section. In most views, footnotes or endnotes are divided from the main text by a *note separator* line.

To create a footnote or endnote:

1. With the insertion point where you want the reference mark to appear, on the **References** tab, in the **Footnotes** group, click either the **Insert Footnote** or the **Insert Endnote** button.

   Word inserts the reference mark in the document and creates a linked area at the bottom of the page or end of the section.

2. Type the note text.

Word applies default styles to the reference marks for footnotes and endnotes. By default, footnote reference marks use the 1, 2, 3 format, and endnote reference marks use the i, ii, iii style. To change the number format of existing footnotes or endnotes:

1. On the **References** tab, click the **Footnotes** dialog box launcher.
2. In the **Footnote and Endnote** dialog box, click **Footnotes** or **Endnotes**.
3. Under **Format**, click the **Number format** arrow, and then in the list, click the number format you want.
4. With **Whole document** shown in the **Apply changes to** box, click **Apply**.

   All footnotes or endnotes change to the new number format.

To change the formatting applied to footnote or endnote reference marks:

1. In the document text, select the reference mark for any footnote or endnote.
2. On the **Home** tab, in the **Editing** group, click the **Select** button, and then click **Select Text with Similar Formatting**.

   All the footnote or endnote reference marks are selected.

3. On the **Home** tab, apply the character formatting you want the reference marks to have.

   All the reference marks in the body of the document now appear with the character formatting you applied.

There are two ways to enter a new source:

- You can open the Source Manager dialog box and enter all the sources you know you will need to cite in the document.
- You can open the Create Source dialog box and enter the information for one specific source. When you click OK, the citation is entered in parentheses at the insertion point.

No matter which method you use to enter the source information, Word stores the sources in a separate file on your computer's hard disk so that you can cite them in any document you create. You can view this Master List and select which sources are available to the current document from the Source Manager dialog box. After you copy a source from the Master List to the Current List, you can cite it anywhere in the current document.

After you enter sources, you can easily compile them into a bibliography or list of works cited. The Bibliography gallery (available from the Citations & Bibliography group on the References tab) includes two options:

- **Bibliography.** This option builds the source list at the insertion point with a Bibliography heading.
- **Works Cited.** This option builds the source list at the insertion point with a Works Cited heading.

You can also click Insert Bibliography at the bottom of the gallery to insert a list of sources without a heading.

When you compile a bibliography, Word inserts it at the insertion point as one field. You can edit the text of a bibliography, but if the source information might change, it is much easier to update it in the same way you would a table of contents or index.

> **Tip** You can update a bibliography by clicking the bibliography, and then clicking the Update Citations and Bibliography button that appears above the field. If you used the Insert Bibliography command to compile the source list, the Update Citations and Bibliography button does not appear when you click the field. In that case, you can update the bibliography by right-clicking anywhere in the field and then clicking Update Field.

In this exercise, you will enter information for a couple of sources, insert citations for existing sources, add a new source, compile a bibliography, and then change its format.

> **USE** the *Bibliography1* and *Bibliography2* documents. These practice files are located in the *Documents\Microsoft Press\Word2007SBS\Organizing* folder.
> **OPEN** the *Bibliography1* document.

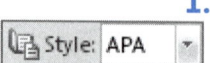

Adding Sources and Compiling a Bibliography 249

1. On the **References** tab, in the **Citations & Bibliography** group, click the **Style** arrow, and then click **Chicago**.

   Any sources you create and citations you insert will be formatted according to the *Chicago Manual of Style* rules.

2. In the **Citations & Bibliography** group, click the **Manage Sources** button.

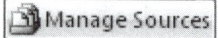

   The Source Manager dialog box opens.

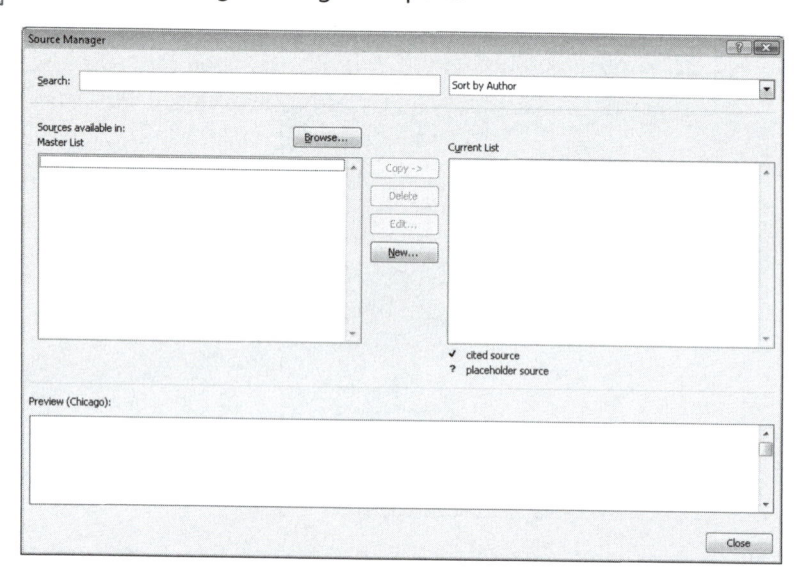

> **Troubleshooting** Don't worry if your dialog box already contains sources. If other documents on your hard disk contain citations, their source information might appear.

3. In the **Source Manager** dialog box, click **New**.

   The Create Source dialog box opens.

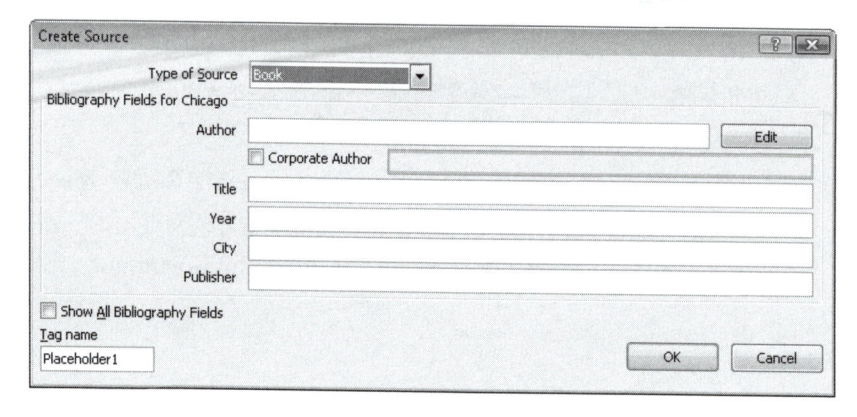

4. With **Book** selected in the **Type of Source** list, in the **Bibliography Fields for Chicago** area, type Goldberg, Gale Beth in the **Author** box, Bamboo in the **Title** box, 2004 in the **Year** box, Gibbs Smith in the **Publisher** box, and then click **OK**.

   The new source is added not only to the Master List but also to the Current List, which is the list of sources that can be used in this document.

5. In the **Source Manager** dialog box, click **New**, and then in the **Create Source** dialog box, click **Edit**.

   The Edit Name dialog box opens.

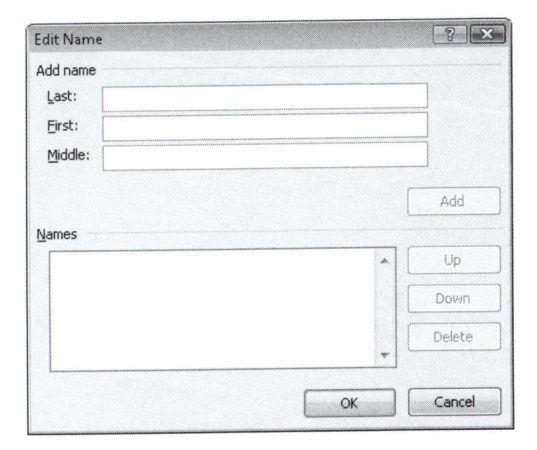

6. Under **Add name**, type Cusack in the **Last** box, type Victor in the **First** box, and then click **Add**.

   Cusack, Victor appears in the Names box.

   The new source is added not only to the Master List but also to the Current List, which is the list of sources that can be used in this document.

7. To enter a second author for the same book, type Stewart in the **Last** box, type Deirdre in the **First** box, click **Add**, and then click **OK**.

8. In the **Create Source** dialog box, type Bamboo World in the **Title** box, 2000 in the **Year** box, and Simon & Schuster Australia in the **Publisher** box. Then click **OK**.

9. Close the **Source Manager** dialog box.

10. Open the *Bibliography2* document, and then open the **Source Manager** dialog box.

    The two sources you just entered appear in the Master List but not in the Current List, meaning they are not available for use in this document.

Adding Sources and Compiling a Bibliography **251**

[Source Manager dialog box screenshot]

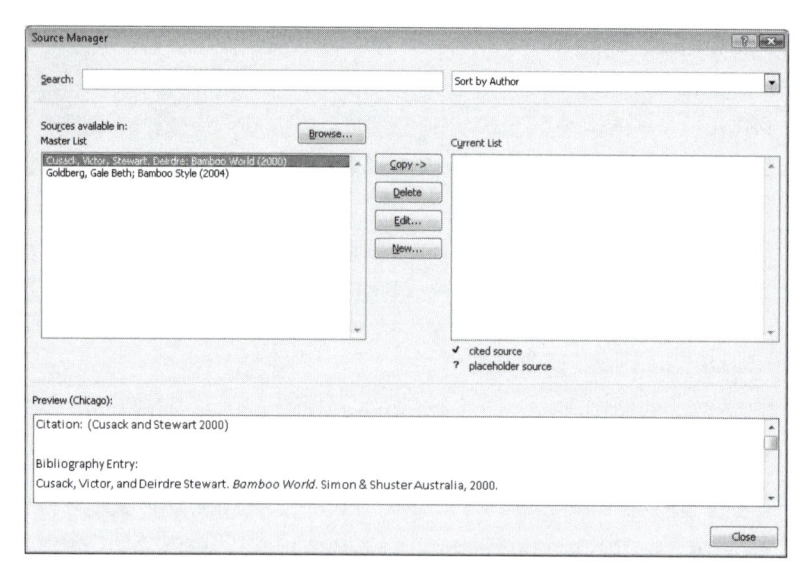

11. With the **Cusack** source selected in the **Master List** box, click **Copy** to make that source available in this document. Then copy the **Goldberg** source to the **Current List** box, and click **Close**.

12. In the document, position the insertion point to the right of *Bamboo Style* on the last line of the first paragraph. Then on the **References** tab, in the **Citations & Bibliography** group, click the **Insert Citation** button, and in the list of citations, click **Goldberg, Gale Beth**.

   Word inserts the source in parentheses.

Beautiful Bamboo

Bamboo has a long history of use in the world, particularly in developing nations. It's historically been used for everything from food and fodder to musical instruments and construction material. For centuries, millions of people have depended on this plant, which is known as 'friend of the people' in China, and 'wood of the poor' in India. But the demand for bamboo has been increasing in other parts of the world as well, especially as it relates to furniture, accent pieces, and flooring. More and more, people are seeing the value and beauty of using bamboo in their homes to achieve modern day fashion with an ethnic flavor. Entire books have been written on the subject, including *Bamboo Style* (Goldberg 2004) and *Bamboo World*.

There are many different sizes and varieties of bamboo. It is both tropical and subtropical, growing in climates as diverse as jungles and mountainsides. Actually giant, woody grasses, it is very

Citation

13. Insert a **Cusack, Victor** citation to the right of *Bamboo World* (but before the period) at the end of the same paragraph.

14. Position the insertion point to the right of *Entire books*, and then in the **Citations & Bibliography** group, click the **Insert Citation** button, and in the list, click **Add New Source**.

15. In the **Create Source** dialog box, click the **Type of Source** arrow, and then click **Web site**. Then type American Bamboo Society in the **Name of Web Page** box, 2006 in the **Year** box, and www.americanbamboo.org/BooksOnBamboo.html in the **URL** box, and click **OK**.

    Word inserts the source in parentheses at the insertion point.

16. In the **Citations & Bibliography** group, click the **Manage Sources** button.

    In the Source Manager dialog box, the new citation appears in both the Master List and the Current List. Because the sources in the Current List are actually cited in the document, they have a check mark beside them.

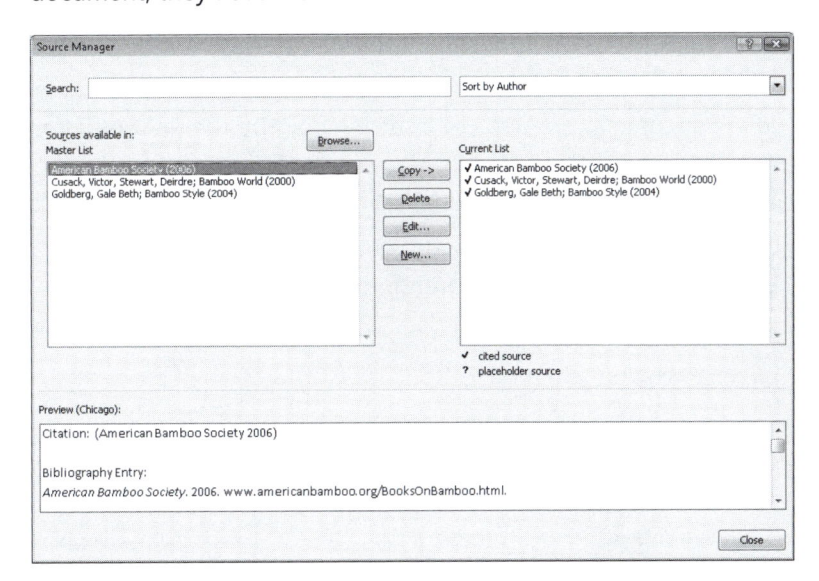

17. Close the **Source Manager** dialog box, and then press Ctrl+End to move to the end of the document.

18. In the **Citations & Bibliography** group, click **Bibliography**, and then in the gallery, click **Bibliography**.

    Word inserts a bibliography of all the citations in the document in alphabetical order and formatted according to the *Chicago* style.

> **Bibliography**
> *American Bamboo Society*. 2006. www.americanbamboo.org/BooksOnBamboo.html.
> Cusack, Victor, and Deirdre Stewart. *Bamboo World*. Simon & Shuster Australia, 2000.
> Goldberg, Gale Beth. *Bamboo Style*. Gibbs Smith, 2004.

19. In the **Citations & Bibliography** group, click the **Style** arrow, and in the list, click **APA**.

> **Tip** You don't have to select the bibliography to apply this change; you can do it from anywhere in the document.

The format of the bibliography and of the citations changes to bring it in line with the *Associated Press* style.

CLOSE the *Bibliography1* and *Bibliography2* documents without saving your changes.

Key Points

- Word comes with predefined building blocks you can use to quickly create a specific type of document or to add an element to an existing document.
- You can quickly navigate to specific points in a document by using bookmarks to flag information you might want to look up later, and cross-references to quickly jump to related information.
- A table of contents provides an overview of the topics covered in a document and lets readers navigate quickly to a topic. You can format the table of contents by selecting a predefined format or by changing individual table of content styles.
- After marking index entries for key concepts, words, and phrases, you can use the Insert Index command to tell Word to compile the index.
- Documents can contain hyperlinks to Web pages, files, bookmarks, or e-mail addresses.

Chapter at a Glance

Prepare data for mail merge, **page 257**

Prepare a form letter, **page 263**

Send a personalized e-mail message to multiple recipients, **page 270**

Create and print labels, **page 274**

9 Creating Form Letters, E-Mail Messages, and Labels

In this chapter, you will learn to:
- ✔ Understand mail merge.
- ✔ Prepare data for mail merge.
- ✔ Prepare a form letter.
- ✔ Merge a form letter with its data source.
- ✔ Send a personalized e-mail message to multiple recipients.
- ✔ Create and print labels.

Many businesses and other organizations communicate with their customers or members by means of letters, newsletters, and promotional pieces that are sent to everyone on a mailing list. The easiest way to generate a set of documents that are identical except for certain information—such as the name, address, and greeting of a letter—is to use a process called *mail merge*. If you have a list of potential recipients stored in a consistent format, you can use the mail merge process to easily produce a set of personalized documents and mailing labels.

In this chapter, you will use the Mail Merge wizard to guide you through the process of creating a form letter. You will select a data source, add a record to it, sort it, and filter it. You will then add merge fields for an address and greeting line to an existing form letter, preview the merged data, exclude recipients from the merge, merge the letters into a new document, and then save the merged file. You will also set up and send a merged e-mail message. Finally, you will create and print mailing labels.

See Also Do you need only a quick refresher on the topics in this chapter? See the Quick Reference section at the beginning of this book.

> **Important** Before you can use the practice files in this chapter, you need to install them from the book's companion CD to their default location. See "Using the Companion CD" at the beginning of this book for more information.

> **Troubleshooting** Graphics and operating system–related instructions in this book reflect the Windows Vista user interface. If your computer is running Windows XP and you experience trouble following the instructions as written, please refer to the "Information for Readers Running Windows XP" section at the beginning of this book.

Understanding Mail Merge

The mail merge process combines the static information from one document with variable information from another document, as follows:

- *Main document.* This is a document, such as a letter or e-mail message, that contains the static text that will appear in all the merged documents, plus place-holders—called *merge fields*—that tell Microsoft Office Word 2007 where to insert the variable information.

- *Data source.* This is a structured document, such as customer list stored in a Word table, a Microsoft Office Excel worksheet, or a Microsoft Office Access database table, or a Microsoft Office Outlook contacts list, that contains sets—called *records*—of information in a predictable format. You can use an existing data source, or you can create a new one as part of the mail merge process.

You can use the Mail Merge wizard in Word to merge a main document with a data source in easy steps. The first step is to select from a list of document types that includes letters, e-mail messages, envelopes, labels, and a directory. The type you select determines the subsequent steps. The end result is one copy of the merged document for every record in the data source.

You can merge the main document and data source into a new document, with each merged document separated from the next by a page break. You can then personalize the merged documents before printing, and you can save the document for later use. If you don't need to edit or save the merged documents, you can merge the main document and data source directly to the printer or to an e-mail message.

> **Tip** When you have some experience with mail merge, you might want to use the buttons on the Mailings tab to create and merge documents, instead of the Mail Merge wizard.

Preparing Data for Mail Merge

Before you can merge documents, you need to either specify an existing data source or create one. The data source consists of a matrix of rows and columns, with each row containing one record, such as the complete name and address of a customer, and each column containing a particular type of information—called a *field*—such as the first name of a customer. Each field is identified in the data source by the column heading—called a *field name*—in the first row of the data source.

> **Tip** Because the field names are also used as the merge fields in the main document, they cannot contain spaces. To make the field names readable with no spaces, capitalize each word, as in *PostalCode*, or replace the spaces with underscores, as in *Last_Name*.

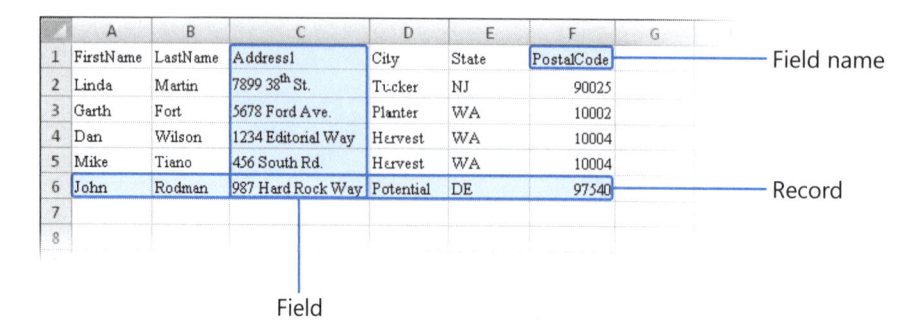

	A	B	C	D	E	F	G
1	FirstName	LastName	Address1	City	State	PostalCode	
2	Linda	Martin	7899 38th St.	Tucker	NJ	90025	
3	Garth	Fort	5678 Ford Ave.	Planter	WA	10002	
4	Dan	Wilson	1234 Editorial Way	Harvest	WA	10004	
5	Mike	Tiano	456 South Rd.	Harvest	WA	10004	
6	John	Rodman	987 Hard Rock Way	Potential	DE	97540	
7							
8							

— Field name (row 1)
— Record (row 6)
— Field (column C)

If the data source contains many records and it changes frequently, you might want to create it in a program designed for working with large amounts of data, such as Excel or Access. You can also use the contacts list from Outlook, Windows Mail, or Microsoft Outlook Express (if your computer is running Windows XP). If the data source contains only a few records and it won't be updated often, you can create it in Word, either as a table or as a list with each field separated by a tab. Or you can create it as part of the mail merge process.

What if you want to create merge documents for only a subset of the data in the data source? For example, you might have mail-order customers from all over the United States, but want to target a bulk mailing about a store sale to only customers with addresses in your state. After you specify the data source and create the main document, you can do the following:

- *Filter* the data source to create merged documents for only some of its data.
- Create a *query* (a set of selection criteria) to extract only the information you are interested in—for example, all the postal codes for your state.
- Sort the data source—for example, in postal code order for a bulk mailing.

When you use a filter or a query, all the data remains in the data source, but only the data that meets your specifications is used for the mail merge.

In this exercise, you will open a main document and use the Mail Merge Wizard to select the data source. You will then add a record to the data source, sort it, and filter it.

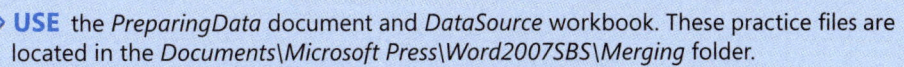

> **USE** the *PreparingData* document and *DataSource* workbook. These practice files are located in the *Documents\Microsoft Press\Word2007SBS\Merging* folder.
> **BE SURE TO** start Word before beginning this exercise.
> **OPEN** the *PreparingData* document.

1. On the **Mailings** tab, in the **Start Mail Merge** group, click the **Start Mail Merge** button, and then click **Step by Step Mail Merge Wizard**.

   The Mail Merge task pane opens, showing step 1 of the wizard's six steps.

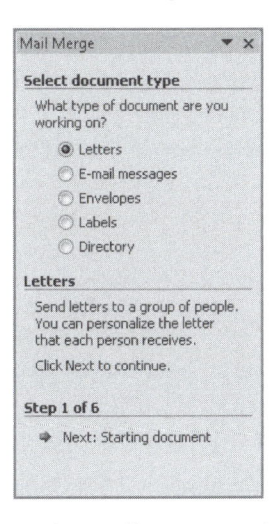

2. In the **Mail Merge** task pane, with the **Letters** option selected, at the bottom of the pane, click **Next: Starting document**.

   Step 2 appears in the Mail Merge task pane.

3. In the **Mail Merge** task pane, with the **Use the current document** option selected, click **Next: Select recipients**.

4. In the step 3 pane, with the **Use an existing list** option selected, click **Browse**.

   The Select Data Source dialog box opens so that you can navigate to and select the file in which your recipient information is stored.

5. In the **Favorite Links** list, click **Documents**, browse to the *Microsoft Press\ Word2007SBS\Merging* folder, and double-click the *DataSource* workbook.

   The Select Table dialog box opens.

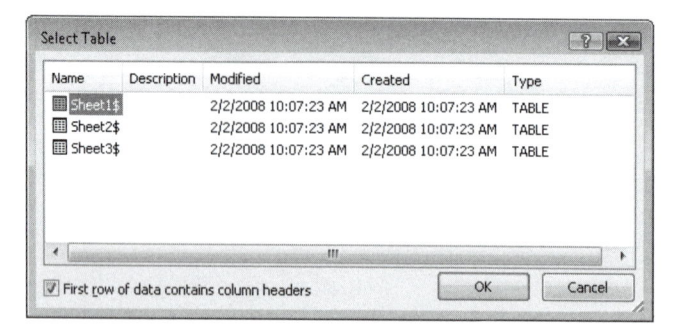

6. In the **Select Table** dialog box, with **Sheet1$** selected, click **OK**.

   The Mail Merge Recipients dialog box opens, displaying the records contained in the data source.

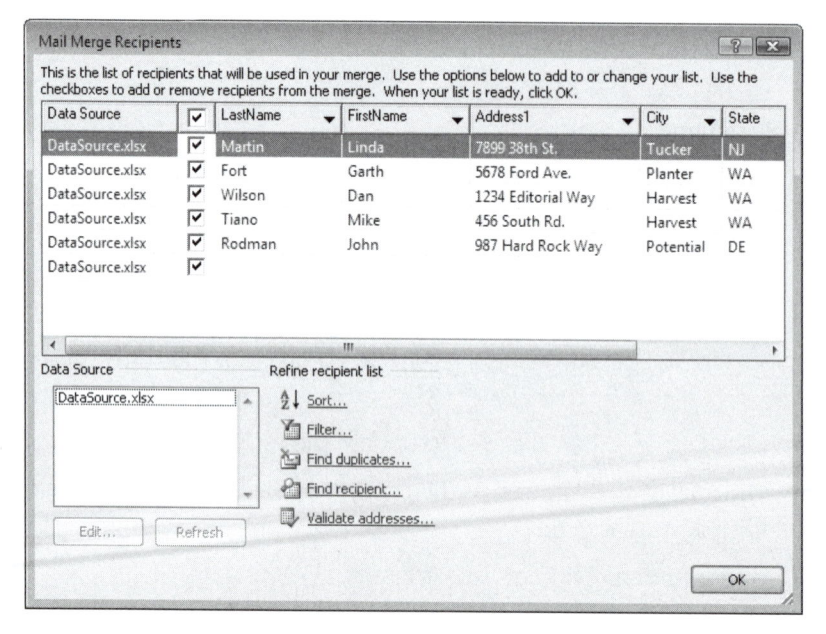

7. Below the list of recipients in the top half of the dialog box, in the **Data Source** box, click *DataSource.xlsx*, and then click **Edit**.

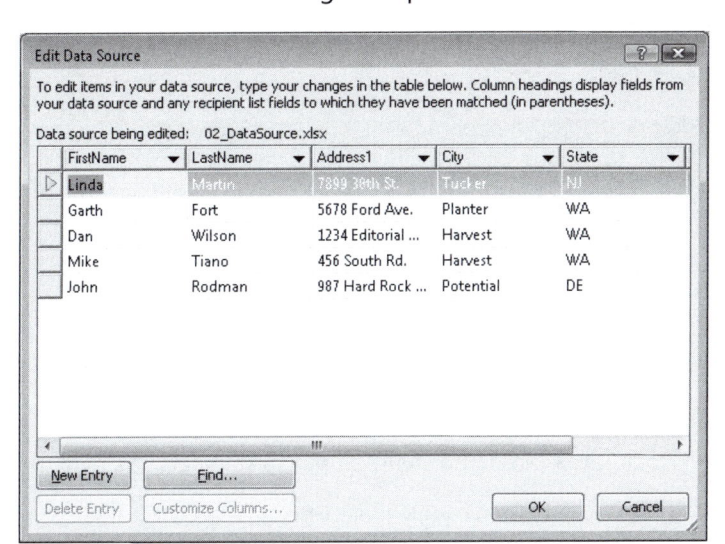

The Edit Data Source dialog box opens.

8. Click **New Entry**, and then in the cell below *John*, type the following, pressing [Tab] to move from box to box:

FirstName	Heidi
LastName	Steen
Address1	678 Pine St.
City	Agriculture
State	WA
PostalCode	10003

   > **Tip** You can add multiple records by clicking New Entry after you enter each record.

9. Click **OK**, and then click **Yes** to update the recipient list.

   The new record appears at the bottom of the list of recipients in the Mail Merge Recipients dialog box.

10. Under **Refine recipient list**, click **Sort**.

    The Filter And Sort dialog box opens, showing the Sort Records tab.

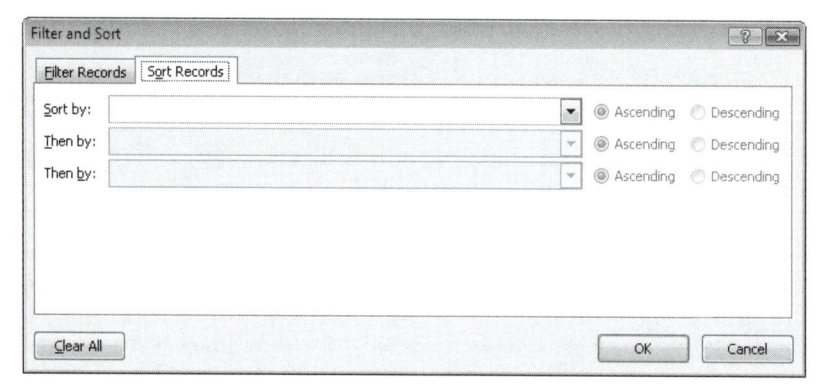

11. Click the **Sort by** arrow, click **PostalCode** in the list, and then click **OK**.

> **Tip** You can also sort data by clicking the arrow to the right of the field you want to sort on, and then clicking Sort Ascending or Sort Descending.

12. Scroll the recipient list to the right, and verify that the records are sorted in ascending order by the PostalCode field. Then under **Refine recipient list**, click **Filter**.

    The Filter And Sort dialog box opens, showing the Filter Records tab.

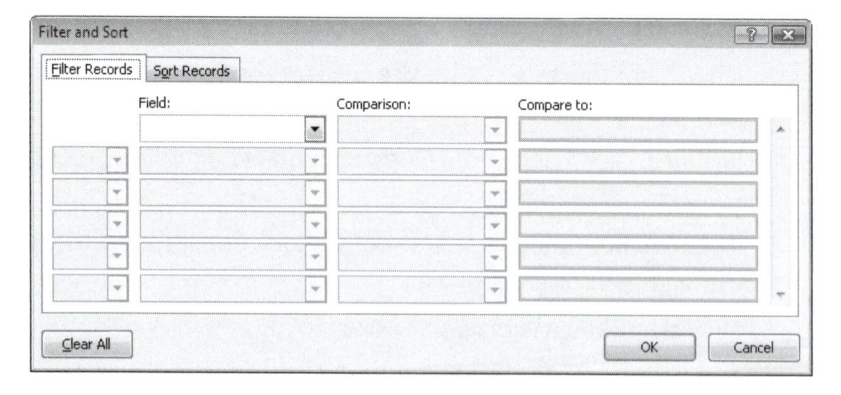

> **Tip** You can also open the Filter And Sort dialog box by clicking the arrow to the right of any field name and then clicking Advanced.

13. Click the **Field** arrow, and then in the list, click **State**.

    The Comparison box displays the default Equal To criterion.

14. In the **Compare to** box, type **WA**, and then click **OK**.

    The Filter And Sort dialog box closes, and the Mail Merge Recipients dialog box is updated to show only Washington State residents in ascending PostalCode order. The other records are hidden and will be excluded from the merge process.

15. Click **OK** to close the **Mail Merge Recipients** dialog box.

> **CLOSE** the *PreparingData* document without saving your changes to the document or to the data source.

Using an Outlook Contacts List as a Data Source

Using information from an Outlook contacts list as the data source for the merge process requires a few extra steps in the Mail Merge Wizard.

To use Outlook information as the data source for a form letter:

1. On the **Mailings** tab, in the **Start Mail Merge** group, click **Start Mail Merge**, and then click **Step by Step Mail Merge Wizard**.

2. In the **Mail Merge** task pane, click **Letters**, and then click **Next: Starting document**.

3. In step 2 of the wizard, click **Use the current document**, and then click **Next: Select recipients**.

4. In step 3, click **Select from Outlook contacts**, and then click **Choose Contacts Folder**.

5. If you are prompted to select your Outlook profile, select the one you want to use, and then click **OK**.

    The Select Contacts dialog box opens.

6. Click a contacts list, and then click **OK**.

7. In the **Mail Merge Recipients** dialog box displaying your Outlook contacts, clear the check boxes of any contacts you want to exclude from the merge process. Then click **OK**.

8. In the **Mail Merge** task pane, click **Next: Write your letter**.

You can then continue with the next steps in the merge process, as explained in later topics in this chapter.

Preparing a Form Letter

One common type of main document used in the mail merge process is a form letter. This type of document typically contains merge fields for the name and address of each recipient along with text that is the same in all the letters. In the form letter, each merge field is enclosed in *guillemet characters*, also called *chevrons* (« and »)—for example, «AddressBlock».

Merge field

If you have already written the letter, you can insert the merge fields during the merge process; if you haven't written the letter, you can write it as part of the process. Either way, you first enter the text that will be common to all the letters and then insert the merge fields that will be replaced by the variable information from the data source.

> **Tip** If you need to stop before you finish the merge process, you can save the form letter to retain the work you have done so far. You can then open the form letter and resume from where you left off.

You can insert merge fields in two ways:

- From the Mail Merge task pane in step 4 of the Mail Merge wizard.
- By clicking buttons in the Write & Insert Fields group on the Mailings tab.

Either way, clicking Address Block or Greeting Line opens a dialog box in which you can refine the fields' settings, whereas clicking individual fields inserts them with their default settings.

Tip To save the form letter without any mail merge information, click Start Mail Merge in the Start Mail Merge group on the Mailings tab, and then click Normal Word Document.

In this exercise, you will modify an existing form letter by adding merge fields for a standard inside address, an informal greeting line, and the recipient's first name.

USE the *FormLetter* document and *DataSource* workbook. These practice files are located in the *Documents\Microsoft Press\Word2007SBS\Merging* folder.
BE SURE TO display non-printing characters before starting this exercise.
OPEN the *Documents\Microsoft Press\Word2007SBS\Merging* folder in Windows Explorer.

1. In the *Merging* folder, double-click the *FormLetter* document.

   Before the document opens, a message box appears, informing you that Word will run a SQL command.

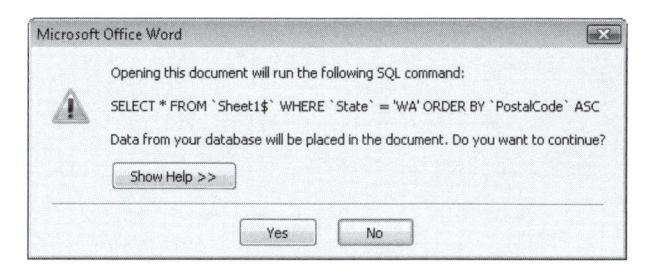

2. In the **Microsoft Office Word** message box, click **Yes**.

   The Select Data source dialog box opens.

   Troubleshooting You are prompted to attach the data source to the main document because the data source was not originally attached to the main document from your computer. When you are working with your own documents, you will not be prompted to attach the data source when you reopen your main document.

3. In the **Favorite Links** list, click **Documents**, and then browse to the *Microsoft Press\Word2007SBS\Merging* folder. Double-click the *DataSource* workbook. If the **Select Table** dialog box opens, click **OK**.

   The main document opens with the *DataSource* workbook attached to it.

4. On the **Mailings** tab, in the **Start Mail Merge** group, click the **Start Mail Merge** button, and then click **Step by Step Mail Merge Wizard**.

5. In the **Mail Merge** task pane, click **Next: Write your letter**.

6. In the document, position the insertion point in the second empty paragraph below the date, and then in the **Mail Merge** task pane, click **Address block**.

> **Tip** To position the insertion point without displaying non-printing characters, click at the right end of the date and then press the Down Arrow key twice.

The Insert Address Block dialog box opens. From this dialog box, you can refine the format of the fields that make up the Address Block merge field.

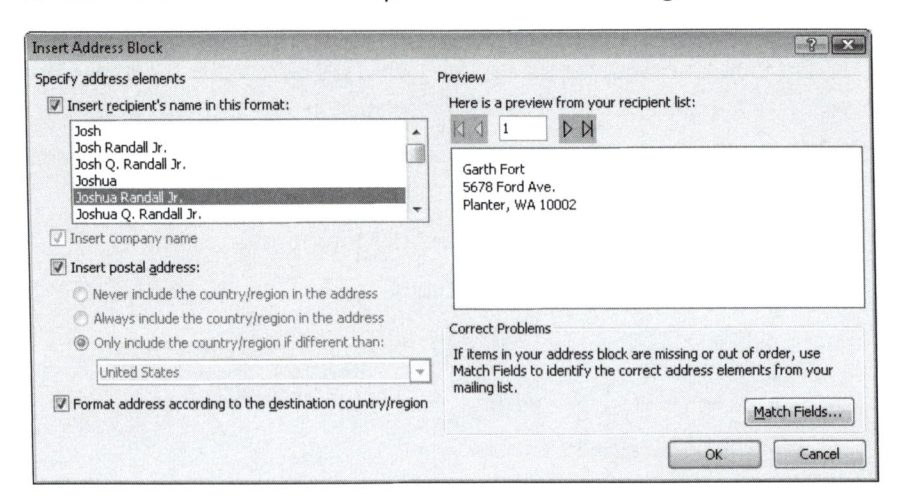

7. Click **OK** to accept the default settings.

   Word inserts the «AddressBlock» merge field into the document. When you merge the form letter with the data source, Word will substitute the component name and address information for this merge field.

8. Press the [Enter] key twice, and then in the **Mail Merge** task pane, click **Greeting line**.

   The Insert Greeting Line dialog box opens so that you can specify how the greeting line should appear in the merged letters.

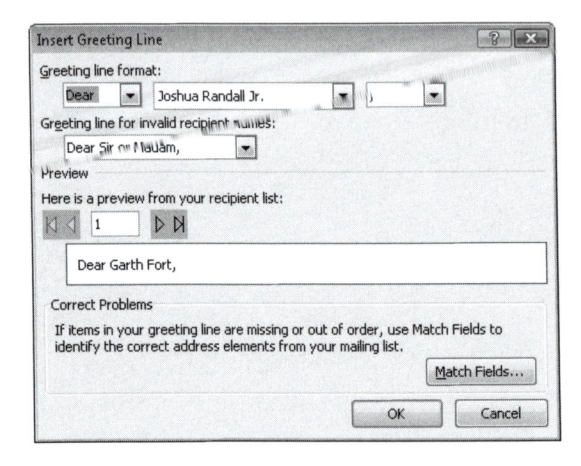

9. Under **Greeting line format**, click the arrow to the right of the second box, and then in the list, click **Joshua**.

10. In the **Preview** area, click the **Next** button three times to view the greeting line for each of the recipients in the linked data source. Then click **OK** to close the Insert Greeting Line dialog box.

   Word inserts the «GreetingLine» merge field into the document. When you merge the form letter with the data source, Word will replace this merge field with the word *Dear* and a space, followed by the information in the FirstName field, followed by a comma.

11. Position the insertion point at the beginning of the third paragraph of the letter (*For even greater savings...*).

12. In the **Mail Merge** task pane, click **More items**.

   The Insert Merge Field dialog box opens.

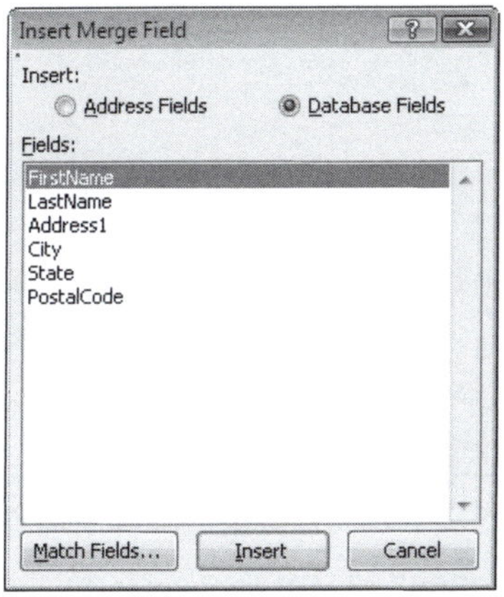

13. With the **Database Fields** option selected and **FirstName** highlighted in the **Fields** box, click **Insert**, and then click **Close**.

   The «FirstName» merge field appears at the beginning of the third paragraph.

14. Without moving the insertion point, type a comma and press [Space]. Then change *For* to *for*.

   The form letter is now ready for merging.

February 18, 2007

«AddressBlock»

«GreetingLine»

I want to take a moment to thank you for your continued support of Wide World Importers. Because loyal customers like you come back year after year, we are growing rapidly.

As you know, we will celebrate our 10th anniversary on March 15. In honor of that occasion, we are holding a special *March Madness* sale! Everything in the store will be 10% off throughout the month, and selected specials at higher discounts will be offered each day. Please pick up one of our promotional flyers the next time you visit the store for a complete schedule of these special offerings.

«FirstName», for even greater savings, be sure to bring this letter with you when you shop. Identify yourself as a VIP Customer by presenting the letter to your salesperson at the time of your purchase, and you will receive an additional 5% off your total bill.

Discounts and savings are our way of thanking you for your continued patronage of Wide World Importers. Remember, we are the one-stop design center for all of your home decor needs!

CLOSE the *FormLetter* document without saving your changes.

Merging a Form Letter with Its Data Source

After you specify the data source you want to use and enter merge fields in the form letter, you can preview the merged letters before performing the actual merge. You can exclude recipients during this preview. When you are ready, you can either send the merged letters directly to the printer or you can merge them one after the other into a new document, separated by page breaks. If you merge to a new document, you have another chance to review and, if necessary, edit the merged letters before sending them to the printer.

In this exercise, you will preview merged letters, exclude recipients from the merge, merge the letters into a new document, and then save the merged file.

USE the *MergingData* document and *DataSource* workbook. These practice files are located in the *Documents\Microsoft Press\Word2007SBS\Merging* folder.

OPEN the *MergingData* document. When Word asks you to confirm that you want to run a command that will attach data from the *DataSource* file to the document, click Yes, and then in the Select Data Source dialog box, browse to the *Merging* folder, and double-click the *DataSource* file.

1. On the **Mailings** tab, in the **Start Mail Merge** group, click the **Start Mail Merge** button, and then click **Step by Step Mail Merge Wizard**.

2. At the bottom of the **Mail Merge** task pane, click **Next** twice to move to step 5.

3. Scroll the letter until you can see the address block, the greeting line, and the third paragraph.

   Word displays a preview of how the first personalized letter will look when merged with the data source.

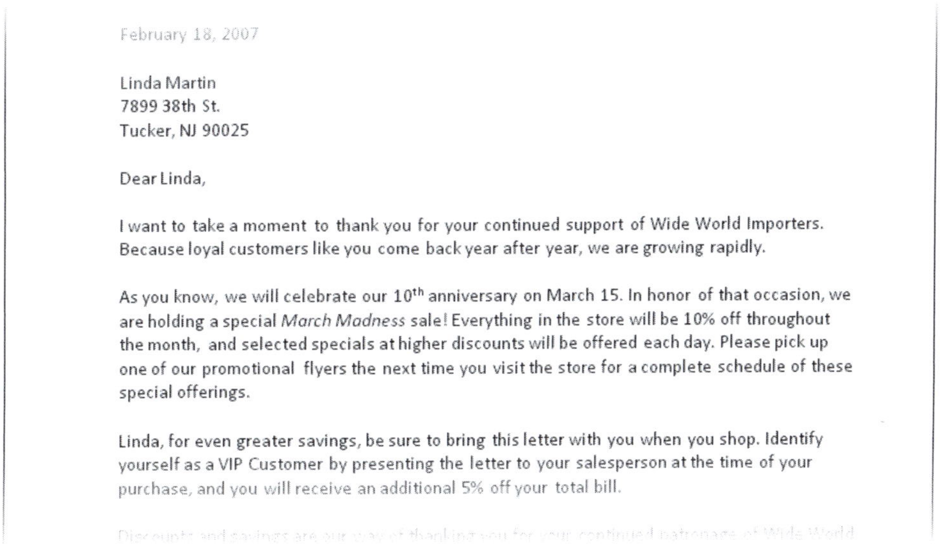

   February 18, 2007

   Linda Martin
   7899 38th St.
   Tucker, NJ 90025

   Dear Linda,

   I want to take a moment to thank you for your continued support of Wide World Importers. Because loyal customers like you come back year after year, we are growing rapidly.

   As you know, we will celebrate our 10th anniversary on March 15. In honor of that occasion, we are holding a special *March Madness* sale! Everything in the store will be 10% off throughout the month, and selected specials at higher discounts will be offered each day. Please pick up one of our promotional flyers the next time you visit the store for a complete schedule of these special offerings.

   Linda, for even greater savings, be sure to bring this letter with you when you shop. Identify yourself as a VIP Customer by presenting the letter to your salesperson at the time of your purchase, and you will receive an additional 5% off your total bill.

4. Under **Preview your letters** in the **Mail Merge** task pane, click the **Next Record** button four times to preview all the letters.

   Tip You can also preview the next or previous documents by clicking the Next Record or Previous Record button in the Preview Results group on the Mailings tab.

5. On the **Mailings** tab, in the **Preview Results** group, click the **First Record** button.

6. To exclude this recipient (*Linda Martin*) from the merge, under **Make changes** in the **Mail Merge** task pane, click **Exclude this recipient**.

7. Preview the letters again. Then at the bottom of the **Mail Merge** task pane, click **Next: Complete the merge**.

8. In the **Mail Merge** task pane, click **Edit individual letters**.

The Merge To New Document dialog box opens.

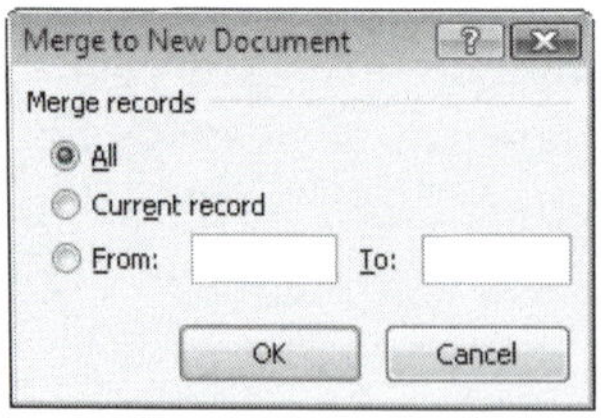

9. With the **All** option selected, click **OK**.

Word creates a document called *Letters1* that contains a personalized copy of the form letter for each of the selected records.

> **Troubleshooting** If the Wide World Importers logo graphic is not visible in the header of the merged form letter, view the letter in Print Preview.

10. On the **Quick Access Toolbar**, click the **Save** button.

The Save As dialog box opens so that you can save the new document with a more specific name.

11. With the contents of the *Merging* folder displayed, type **My Merged Letters** in the **File name** box, and then click **Save**.

Word saves the new document in the specified folder with the name *My Merged Letters*.

CLOSE the *My Merged Letters* document, and then close the *MergingData* document without saving your changes.

> **Printing Envelopes**
>
> You can print an envelope based on an address in a document. To do this:
>
> 1. Select the lines of the address. (Do not select any blank lines above or below the address.)
> 2. On the **Mailings** tab, in the **Create** group, click the **Envelopes** button.
>
>   The Envelopes And Labels dialog box opens. You can edit the address directly in the Delivery Address box, and you can enter a return address in the Return Address box. If you have electronic postage software installed on your computer, you can include electronic postage. You can click Options and then specify the envelope size, the feed method (horizontally or vertically), and the font and font size of both the address and the return address.
>
> > **Tip** You can have Word supply the return address by clicking the Microsoft Office Button, clicking Word Options, and then in the Word Options window, clicking the Advanced tab. Toward the bottom of the page, under General, in the Mailing Address box, enter your address, and click OK. The address then appears by default as the Return Address in the Envelopes And Labels dialog box. If you want to use envelopes with a preprinted return address, you must select the Omit check box to avoid duplication.
>
> 3. Size 10 is the default envelope size. If you want to select a different envelope size, click **Options**, make your selection, and then click **OK**.
> 4. Insert an envelope in the printer, and then click **Print**.

Sending a Personalized E-Mail Message to Multiple Recipients

When you want to send the same information to all the people on a list—for example, all your customers, or all the members of a club or your family—you don't have to print letters and physically mail them. Instead, you can use mail merge to create a message that can be sent to a list of e-mail addresses. As with a form letter that will be printed, you can either use the Mail Merge wizard or use the buttons on the Mailings tab to insert merge fields into the document containing the text of the message, which we call the *form message*. These merge fields will be replaced with information from a data source such as a table or contacts list.

If you are using the wizard, be sure to click E-Mail Messages in step 1. If you are not using the wizard, you can specify the list of e-mail addresses you want to send the message to by clicking the Select Recipients button in the Start Mail Merge group on the Mailings tab. You then have three options:

- Type an entirely new list of recipients.
- Use an existing list of recipients.
- Select recipients from an Outlook contacts list.

You can quickly add merge fields to a form message by using the buttons in the Write & Insert Fields group. Many e-mail messages need only a greeting line. Because e-mail messages tend to be less formal than printed letters, you might want to start the messages with something other than the predefined options (*Dear* and *To:*) by typing a custom greeting.

In this exercise, you will open an existing form message, use the buttons on the Mailings tab to create a short mailing list, add a custom greeting line merge field, and then complete the merge.

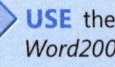

> **USE** the *E-mail* document. This practice file is located in the *Documents\Microsoft Press\Word2007SBS\Merging* folder.
> **OPEN** the *E-mail* document.

1. On the **Mailings** tab, in the **Start Mail Merge** group, click the **Select Recipients** button, and then in the list, click **Type New List**.

    The New Address List dialog box opens.

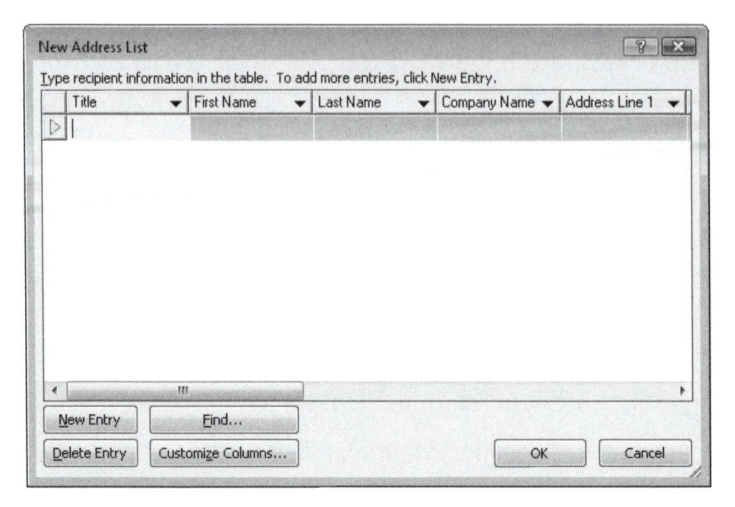

2. Skipping over the **Title** field, type **Andrea** in the **First Name** field, type **Dunker** in the **Last Name** field, press the Tab key until you reach the **E-mail Address** field (the last field in the table), and then type **andrea@consolidatedmessenger.com**.

3. Click **New Entry**, and then add **Judy Lew**, whose e-mail address is **judy@lucernepublishing.com**.

> **Tip** If you have several e-mail addresses to add to the list, you can press Tab in the last field of the last entry, instead of clicking New Entry each time.

4. Repeat step 3 to add **Ben Miller**, whose e-mail address is **ben@wingtiptoys.com**, and then click **OK**.

   The Save Address List dialog box opens, with the contents of your *My Data Sources* folder displayed. This dialog box is very similar to the Save As dialog box.

5. In the **Favorite Links** list, click **Documents**, navigate to the *Microsoft Press\Word2007SBS\Merging* folder, type **My E-Mail Data Source** in the **File name** box, and then click **Save**.

   Word saves the data source in the specified location as an Access database.

> **Tip** If you look in the *Merging* folder at this point in the exercise, you will see two like-named database files. The smaller one is locking the database because Word is accessing it as the data source for this exercise. The locking file will disappear when you close the form message.

6. With the insertion point at the beginning of the document, press Enter twice, and then press the ↑ key twice.

7. On the **Mailings** tab, in the **Write & Insert Fields** group, click the **Greeting Line** button.

   The Insert Greeting Line dialog box opens.

8. In the first box under **Greeting line format**, replace *Dear* with **Hello** followed by a space. Then click the arrow to the right of the second box, and in the list, click **Joshua**.

9. In the **Preview** area, click the **Next** button twice to preview the greetings as they will appear in the e-mail messages.

10. Click the **First** button to return to the first record, and then click **OK**.

    Word inserts the «GreetingLine» merge field at the top of the form message.

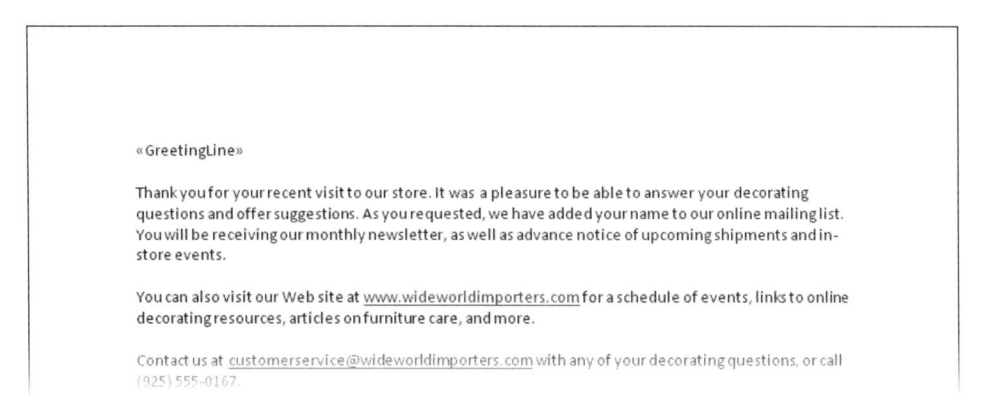

Sending a Personalized E-Mail Message to Multiple Recipients   **273**

> «GreetingLine»
>
> Thank you for your recent visit to our store. It was a pleasure to be able to answer your decorating questions and offer suggestions. As you requested, we have added your name to our online mailing list. You will be receiving our monthly newsletter, as well as advance notice of upcoming shipments and in-store events.
>
> You can also visit our Web site at www.wideworldimporters.com for a schedule of events, links to online decorating resources, articles on furniture care, and more.
>
> Contact us at customerservice@wideworldimporters.com with any of your decorating questions, or call (925) 555-0167.

11. On the **Mailings** tab, in the **Preview Results** group, click the **Preview Results** button.

    Word shows a preview of the first message. You can click the Next Record button in the Preview Results group to preview the messages for other recipients. Clicking the Preview Results button again turns off the preview.

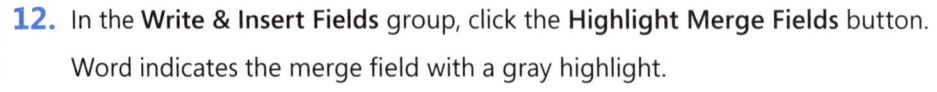

12. In the **Write & Insert Fields** group, click the **Highlight Merge Fields** button.

    Word indicates the merge field with a gray highlight.

13. In the **Finish** group, click the **Finish & Merge** button, and then in the list, click **Send E-mail Messages**.

    The Merge To E-Mail dialog box opens.

14. In the **Message options** area, verify that **Email_Address** is selected in the **To** box, type Welcome to Wide World Importers! in the **Subject line** box, and verify that **HTML** is selected in the **Mail format** box.

15. With the **All** option selected in the **Send records** area, click **OK**.

Word converts the form message to an e-mail message and transmits it to your default e-mail program, which then sends the message to each of the selected addresses in the data source.

> **Tip** Your e-mail program might require that you log in or manually send the messages (they will be held in the outbox until sent). If you are using Outlook, a copy of each sent message appears in your Outlook *Sent Items* folder. If you plan to send a very large number of messages, you might want to turn off the saving of sent messages.

CLOSE the *E-mail* document without saving your changes.

Creating and Printing Labels

Most organizations keep information about their customers or clients in a worksheet or database that can be used for several purposes. For example, the address information might be used to send billing statements, form letters, and brochures. It might also be used to print sheets of mailing labels that can be attached to items such as packages and catalogs.

To create sheets of mailing labels, you first prepare the data source and then prepare the main document by selecting the brand and style of labels you plan to use. Word creates cells the size of the labels, set within a page the size of the label sheet, so that each record will print on one label in a sheet. You insert merge fields into one cell as a template for all the other cells. When you merge the main document and the data source, you can print the labels or create a new label document that you can use whenever you want to send something to the same set of recipients.

In this exercise, you will use the Mail Merge wizard to create mailing labels. You will then print the labels on standard paper to proofread them.

USE the *DataSource* workbook. This practice file is located in the *Documents\Microsoft Press\Word2007SBS\Merging* folder.

BE SURE TO display non-printing characters and turn on the printer you will be using before starting this exercise. If you don't want to print the labels, you can proof them on-screen.

1. Click the **Microsoft Office Button**, click **New**, and then in the **New Document** window, double-click **Blank document**.

A new blank document opens.

2. On the **Mailings** tab, in the **Start Mail Merge** group, click the **Start Mail Merge** button, and then click **Step by Step Mail Merge Wizard**.

3. In the **Mail Merge** task pane, click **Labels**, and then click **Next: Starting document**.

4. With the **Change document layout** option selected, click **Label options**.

   The Label Options dialog box opens.

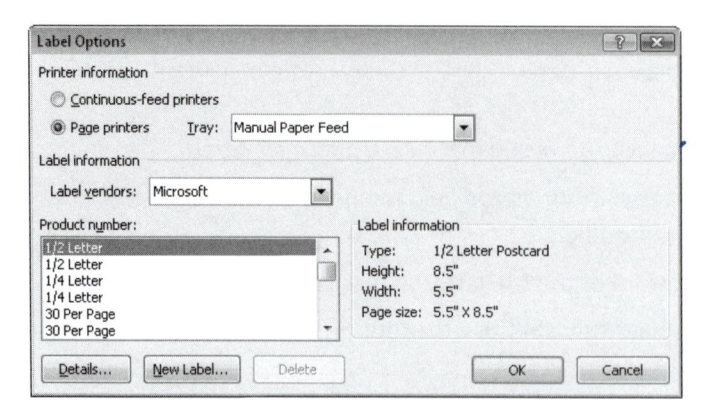

5. In the **Label information** area, click the **Label vendors** arrow, and in the list, click **Avery US Letter**.

6. In the **Product number** list, click **5159**, and then click **OK**.

   Word inserts a table that fills the first page of the main document.

7. At the bottom of the **Mail Merge** task pane, click **Next: Select recipients**.

8. With the **Use an existing list** option selected, click **Browse**, navigate to your *Documents\Microsoft Press\Word2007SBS\Merging* folder, double-click the *DataSource* workbook, and then in the **Select Table** dialog box, click **OK**.

9. In the **Mail Merge Recipients** dialog box, clear the check boxes of the two recipients whose addresses are not in Washington State (WA), and then click **OK**.

   Word inserts a «Next Record» merge field in all the cells in the main document except the first.

10. At the bottom of the **Mail Merge** task pane, click **Next: Arrange your labels**, and then scroll the main document so that you can see its left edge.

11. With the insertion point positioned in the first cell, in the **Mail Merge** task pane, click **Address block**.

12. In the **Insert Address Block** dialog box, click **OK** to accept the default settings.

    Word inserts an «AddressBlock» merge field into the first cell.

13. In the **Mail Merge** task pane, click **Update all labels**.

    The «AddressBlock» merge field is copied to the other cells, after the «Next Record» merge field.

14. At the bottom of the **Mail Merge** task pane, click **Next: Preview your labels**.

    Word displays the labels for the four recipients as they will appear after the merge.

> **Troubleshooting** If you see only one label for the last record in the data source, under Preview Your Labels in the Mail Merge task pane, click the Previous Record button three times.

15. At the bottom of the **Mail Merge** task pane, click **Next: Complete the merge**. Then in the **Mail Merge** task pane, click **Print**.

    The Merge To Printer dialog box opens.

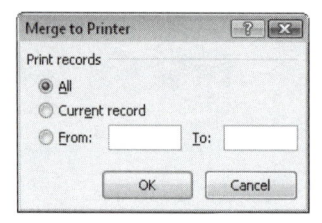

16. With the **All** option selected, click **OK**.

17. In the **Print** dialog box, verify that the name of the printer you want to use appears in the **Name** box, and then click **OK** to print the labels.

    The labels are printed on regular paper on the printer you selected. If you want to print on label sheets, insert them in the printer's paper tray before clicking OK in the Print dialog box.

> **CLOSE** the label document without saving your changes.

Key Points

- To become familiar with the mail-merge process, you can use the Mail Merge wizard to create letters, e-mail messages, envelopes, labels, and directories. When you are comfortable with the process, you can use the individual buttons on the Mailings tab to create and modify mail-merge documents.

- The mail-merge process works by combining static information from one document with variable information from another document. The static information is stored in a main document, such as a form letter. You insert merge fields into this document to tell Word where to merge items of variable information. The variable information is stored in a data source. This file is organized into sets of information, called records, with each record containing the same items, called fields.

- You can use a structured file created in another program, such as an Excel worksheet, an Access database, or a contacts list from Outlook, Windows Mail, or Outlook Express, as a data source.

- You don't have to use all the records in a data source in the mail-merge process. You can filter the data and exclude specific records.

- You can merge the main document and the data source into a new document that you can edit and save, or you can merge the document and data source directly to your printer.

Chapter at a Glance

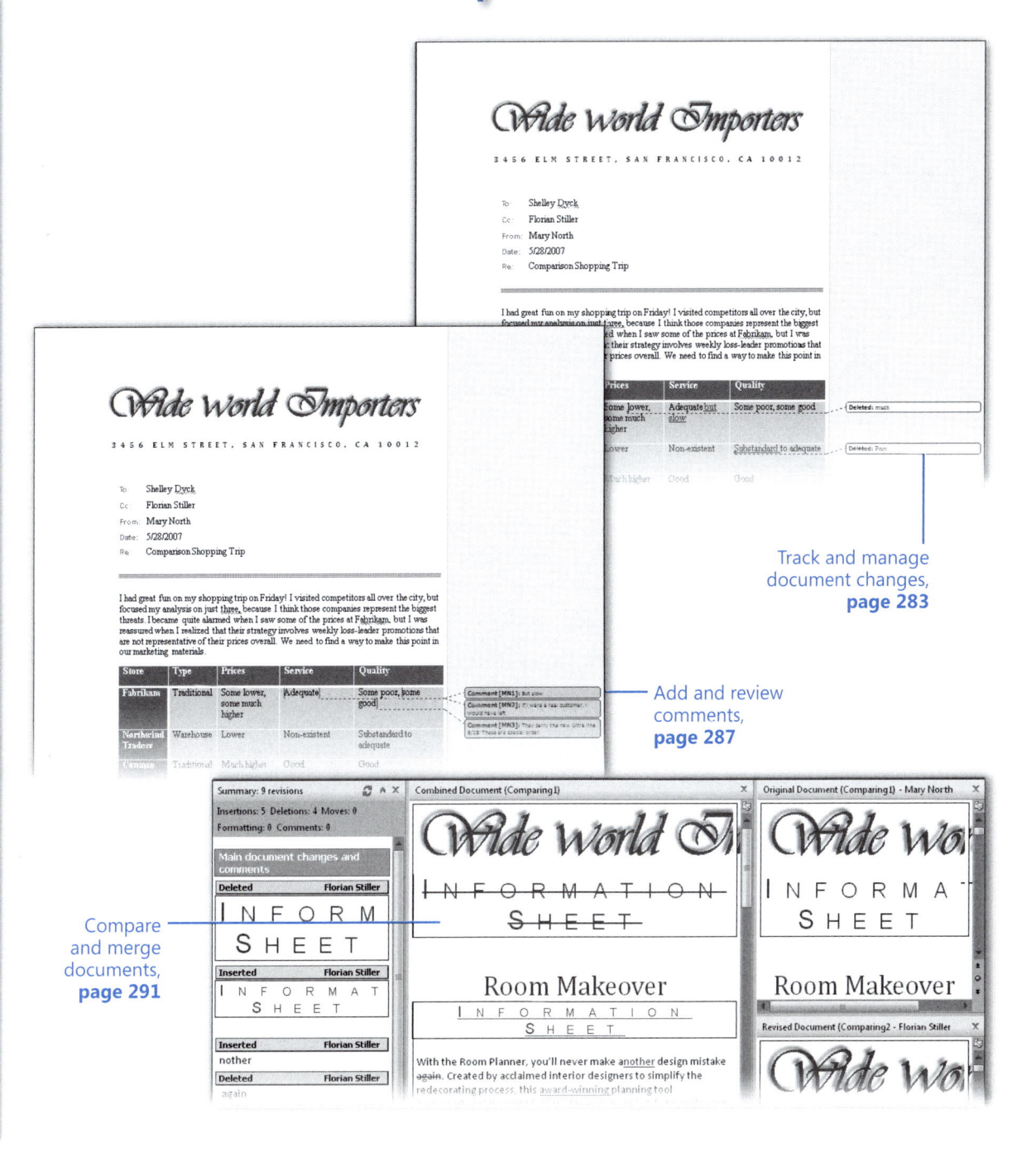

Track and manage document changes, **page 283**

Add and review comments, **page 287**

Compare and merge documents, **page 291**

10 Collaborating with Others

In this chapter, you will learn to:
- ✔ Send a document directly from Word.
- ✔ Track and manage document changes.
- ✔ Add and review comments.
- ✔ Compare and merge documents.
- ✔ Password-protect a document.
- ✔ Prevent changes.
- ✔ Use document workspaces.

In today's workplace, many documents are developed collaboratively by a team of people. You might be the lead author of some documents that will be reviewed by your colleagues and managers, and you might be a reviewer of other documents. These days, most documents are reviewed on the screen rather than on printouts. In Microsoft Office Word 2007, it is easy to edit documents without losing track of the original test, make comments and ask questions, and accept or reject changes and respond to comments made by others.

Sometimes you will want other people to review a document but not change it. You can prevent other people from making changes to a document by assigning a password to it. You can also specify that only certain people are allowed to make changes, and what types of formatting and content changes are allowed.

If you send a document out for review and then receive several copies with changes and suggestions back from different people, you can merge the different versions into one file to simplify the process of reviewing and accepting or rejecting changes. If your organization uses a collaboration site built with Microsoft SharePoint products and technologies, you can store the document in a document workspace on the site so that only one person can actively work on the document at a time.

In this chapter, you will send documents for review by other people by attaching them to an e-mail message. You will track changes that you make to a document, and then accept and reject changes. You will review, add, delete, and hide comments, and merge three versions of the same document. Finally, after setting and removing a password and setting up editing and formatting restrictions, you will see how to create a document workspace on a SharePoint site.

See Also Do you need only a quick refresher on the topics in this chapter? See the Quick Reference section at the beginning of this book.

Important Before you can use the practice files in this chapter, you need to install them from the book's companion CD to their default location. See "Using the Companion CD" at the beginning of this book for more information.

Troubleshooting Graphics and operating system–related instructions in this book reflect the Windows Vista user interface. If your computer is running Windows XP and you experience trouble following the instructions as written, please refer to the "Information for Readers Running Windows XP" section at the beginning of this book.

Sending a Document Directly from Word

After you create a document, you can quickly send it via e-mail from within Word, without starting your e-mail program. You simply point to Send on the Office menu, and click E-mail to display a message window. The current document is already attached to the message, so all you have to do is enter the e-mail addresses of anyone you want to receive the message and its attachment. If you want, you can modify the subject line, which contains the name of the document you are sending.

Tip If your organization uses SharePoint products and technologies to enhance collaboration and you have permission to create workspaces on a SharePoint site, you can create a document workspace when sending a document in e-mail by using Microsoft Office Outlook 2007. Before you send your message, in the message window, click the Attachment File button in the Include group on the Message tab, and then click Attachments Options. In the Attachment Options task pane, click Shared Attachments, and specify the URL for the site. For more information about document workspaces, see "Using Document Workspaces" later in this chapter.

In this exercise, you will attach three documents to an e-mail message so that you can send them for review.

Sending a Document Directly from Word **281**

> **USE** the *Sending1*, *Sending2*, and *Sending3* documents. These practice files are located in the *Documents\Microsoft Press\Word2007SBS\Collaborating* folder.
>
> **BE SURE TO** have an e-mail program installed on your computer and an e-mail account set up before beginning this exercise. Microsoft Office Outlook 2007 is recommended. You can use another e-mail program, but the steps for attaching and sending a message might vary from those given in this exercise.
>
> **OPEN** the *Sending1* document.

Microsoft Office Button

1. Click the **Microsoft Office Button**, point to **Send**, and then click **E-mail**.
2. If the **Choose Profile** dialog box prompts you for a mail profile, select the profile you want, and then click **OK**.

   A message window opens with the name of the document in the Subject line and the document attached.

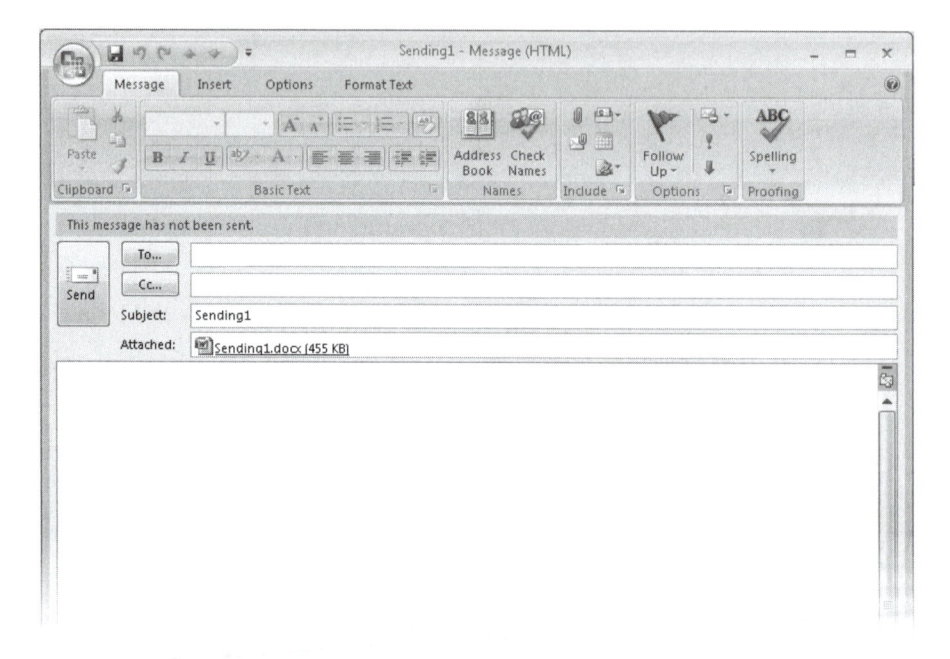

3. In the **To** box, type your own e-mail address.

Attach File

4. On the **Insert** tab of the message window, in the **Include** group, click the **Attach File** button.

   The Insert File dialog box opens.

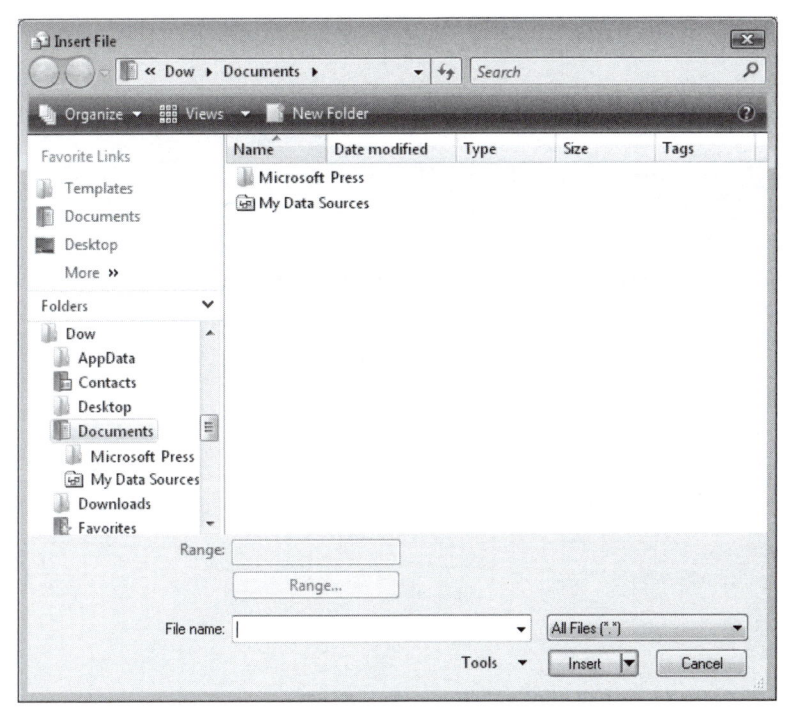

5. From your Documents folder, navigate to the *Microsoft Press\Word2007SBS\Collaborating* folder.

6. Click *Sending2*, hold down the Ctrl key, click *Sending3*, and then click **Insert**.

   In the message window, the Attach box shows that three files are attached to the message.

7. On the **Message** tab of the message window, in the **Options** group, click the **High Importance** button.

   If the message recipient is using Outlook, the message header will display a red exclamation mark to indicate that it is important.

8. In the message content pane, type Please review the attached documents.

   You can format the text of the message in the same way you would the text of a document.

9. In the message header, click the **Send** button.

   Outlook moves the e-mail message with the attached documents to the Outbox. You will receive the sent e-mail message the next time Outlook connects to your mail server.

CLOSE the *Sending1* document without saving your changes.

> **Faxing a Document**
>
> In addition to sending a document as an e-mail attachment from within Word, if you have signed up with an Internet fax service provider, you can send it as a fax. Although the exact terms vary from one provider to another, these services let you send and receive faxes from your computer without needing a fax machine or dedicated fax line.
>
> After establishing Internet fax service, you can send the current document to the fax service by clicking the Microsoft Office Button, pointing to Send, and then clicking Internet Fax. You then follow the procedure specified by your fax service provider.
>
> If you have not yet signed up with an Internet fax service provider, when you click Internet Fax, a message box appears. Clicking OK opens a Web page where you can choose a fax service provider.

Tracking and Managing Document Changes

When two or more people collaborate on a document, one person usually creates and "owns" the document and the others review it, adding or revising content to make it more accurate, logical, or readable. In Word, reviewers can turn on the Track Changes feature so that the revisions they make to the active document are recorded without the original text being lost. (Note that Track Changes affects only the active document, not any other documents that might also be open.) To turn on Track Changes, you click the Track Changes button in the Tracking group on the Review tab. You then edit the text as usual.

> **Tip** If you want to know whether Track Changes is turned on when you're working from a tab other than the Review tab, right-click the status bar and then click Track Changes on the Customize Status Bar menu. Word adds a Track Changes button to the status bar.

By default, your *revisions* appear in a different color from the original text, as follows:

- Insertions and deletions are marked in the text, in your assigned color. Insertions are underlined, and deletions are crossed out.
- In Print Layout view, you can display deletions in balloons rather than in the text. Simply click the Balloons button in the Tracking group on the Review tab, and then click Show Revisions In Balloons.
- In Print Layout view, formatting changes appear in *balloons* in the right margin.
- All changes are marked in the left margin by a vertical line.

> **Tip** The colors used for revisions are controlled by the settings in the Track Changes Options dialog box, which you can display by clicking the Track Changes arrow and then clicking Change Tracking Options.

You can display a ScreenTip identifying the name of the reviewer who made a specific change and when the change was made by pointing to a revision or balloon. The reviewer name is taken from the user information stored with the computer. If you are working on someone else's computer, you might want to change the name by clicking the Track Changes arrow, clicking Change User Name, typing the name and initials you want in the Word Options window, and then clicking OK.

You can work with revisions in the following ways by using the commands available from the Review tab:

- If you want to track changes without showing them on the screen, you can hide the revisions by clicking Final in the Display For review list in the Tracking group. To display the revisions again, click Final Showing Markup in the Display For Review list. You can also display the original version, with or without revisions.
- When revisions are visible in the document, you can select the types of revisions that are displayed, from the Show Markup list in the Tracking group—for example, you can display only comments or only insertions and deletions. You can also display or hide the revisions of specific reviewers from this list.
- You can move forward or backward from one revision mark or comment to another by clicking the Next or Previous button in the Changes group.
- You can incorporate a highlighted change into the document and move to the next change by clicking the Accept button in the Changes group. You can click the Reject button to remove the highlighted change, restore the original text, and move to the next change.
- You can accept all the changes at once by clicking the Accept arrow and then clicking Accept All Changes In Document. To reject all the changes at once, click the Reject arrow and then click Reject All Changes In Document.
- You can accept or reject selected changes by selecting the text containing changes you want to process and then clicking the Accept or Reject button, or by right-clicking the change and then clicking Accept Change or Reject Change.
- You can accept or reject only certain types of changes or changes from specific reviewers by displaying only the changes you want to accept or reject, clicking the Accept or Reject arrow, and then clicking All Changes Shown in the list.

In this exercise, you will open a document, turn on change tracking, make changes to the document, and accept and reject changes.

Tracking and Managing Document Changes   **285**

> **USE** the *TrackChanges* document. This practice file is located in the *Documents\Microsoft Press\Word2007SBS\Collaborating* folder.
>
> **OPEN** the *TrackChanges* document in Print Layout view.

1. On the **Review** tab, in the **Tracking** group, click the **Track Changes** button.

   The active (orange) button indicates that Track Changes is turned on. Any changes that you make now will be indicated in the document in revisions.

2. In the table at the end of the document, in *Some much lower* in the third column, double-click **much**, and press the [Del] key.

   Word changes the font color of the word *much* and indicates with strikethrough formatting that you deleted it. A vertical bar appears adjacent to the change in the left margin.

   > **Troubleshooting** Results may vary depending on your Balloons setting. To display changes the same way we do here, click the Balloons button and then click Show All Revisions Inline.

3. In the fourth column of the same row, position the insertion point at the right end of *Adequate*, press [Space], and then type **but slow**.

   Word inserts the new text in the same color as the deletion, and indicates with an underline that you inserted it.

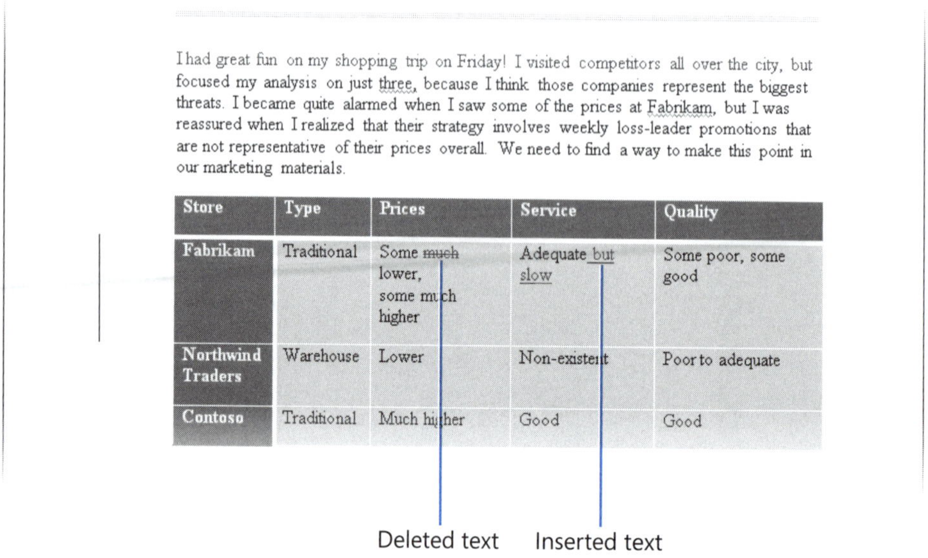

   I had great fun on my shopping trip on Friday! I visited competitors all over the city, but focused my analysis on just three, because I think those companies represent the biggest threats. I became quite alarmed when I saw some of the prices at Fabrikam, but I was reassured when I realized that their strategy involves weekly loss-leader promotions that are not representative of their prices overall. We need to find a way to make this point in our marketing materials.

Store	Type	Prices	Service	Quality
Fabrikam	Traditional	Some ~~much~~ lower, some much higher	Adequate <u>but slow</u>	Some poor, some good
Northwind Traders	Warehouse	Lower	Non-existent	Poor to adequate
Contoso	Traditional	Much higher	Good	Good

   Deleted text   Inserted text

4. In the fifth column of the *Northwind Traders* row, select the word **Poor**, and then type **Substandard**.

   Word interprets this one change as both a deletion and an insertion.

5. Point to **Substandard**.

   A ScreenTip displays your user name, the date and time you made the change, the type of change, and the affected text.

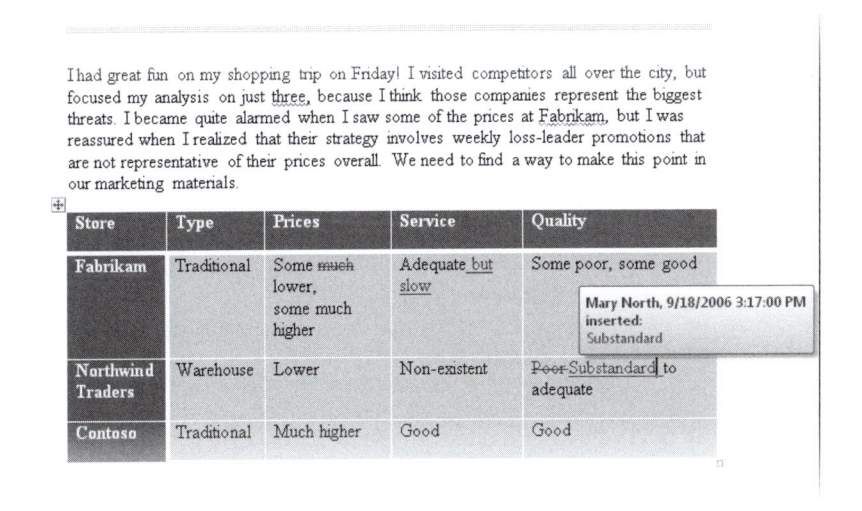

6. In the **Tracking** group, click the **Balloons** button, and then in the list, click **Show Revisions in Balloons**.

   Word removes the deletions from the text and displays them in balloons in the right margin.

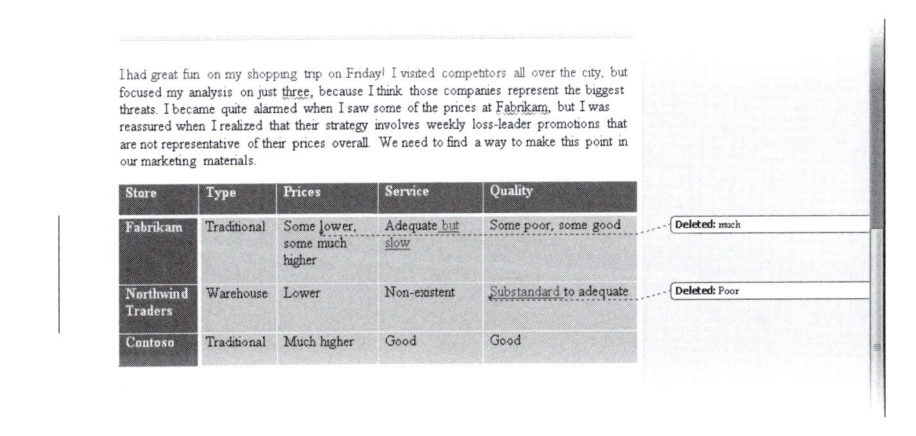

7. In the **Tracking** group, in the **Display for Review** list, click **Final**.

Word hides the revisions, displaying the document as it would appear if all the changes are accepted.

8. In the **Display for Review** list, click **Final Showing Markup** to make the revisions visible again.

9. Press Ctrl+Home to move to the beginning of the document.

10. In the **Changes** group, click the **Next** button.

    Word selects the first change in the document—the deleted word *much*.

11. In the **Changes** group, click the **Accept** button.

    Word accepts the change, removes the markup formatting and associated balloon, and moves to the next change (*but slow*).

12. In the **Changes** group, click the **Reject** button.

    Word removes the inserted text, and because there are no more changes in this row of the table, it also removes the vertical bar from the left margin. It then moves to the next change (*Substandard*).

13. In the **Changes** group, click the **Accept** button to implement the deletion, and then click the same button again to implement the insertion.

    A message box tells you that there are no more changes in the document.

14. Click **OK** to close the message box.

15. In the **Tracking** group, click the **Track Changes** button to stop tracking changes made to the active document.

CLOSE the *TrackChanges* document without saving your changes.

Adding and Reviewing Comments

In addition to tracking the changes made to a document, you can insert notes, or *comments*, to ask questions, make suggestions, or explain edits. To insert a comment, you select the text to which the comment refers, click the New Comment button in the Comments group on the Review tab, and type what you want to say in the balloon that appears. In Print Layout view, Word highlights the associated text in the document in the same color as the balloon and adds your initials and a sequential number to the balloon itself.

You can work with comments in the following ways:

- To display the reviewer's name and the date and time the comment was inserted, you point to either the commented text or the balloon.

- To review comments, you can scroll through the document, or in the case of long documents, you might want to click the Next or Previous button in the Comments group to jump from balloon to balloon.
- To edit a comment, you simply click the balloon and use normal editing techniques.
- To delete a comment, you click its balloon and then click the Delete button in the Comments group, or right-click the balloon and then click Delete Comment.
- To respond to a comment, you can add text to an existing balloon. You can also click the existing balloon and then click the New Comment button to attach a new balloon to the same text in the document.
- If the complete text of a comment isn't visible in its balloon, you can view it in its entirety by clicking the Reviewing Pane button in the Tracking group on the Review tab. (Clicking the Reviewing Pane arrow gives you the option of opening either a vertical or horizontal reviewing pane.) In addition to displaying comments, the reviewing pane displays all the editing and formatting changes you have made to a document, with the number of each type of change summarized at the top of the pane. To close the reviewing pane, click its Close button, or click the Reviewing Pane button again.

> **Tip** To change the size of the reviewing pane, point to its border, and when the pointer changes to a double-headed arrow, drag the border.

- You can turn off the display of comment balloons by clicking the Show Markup button in the Tracking group and then clicking Comments.

If multiple people have reviewed a document and you want to see only the comments of a specific person, you can click the Show Markup button, click Reviewers, and then click the check boxes of the reviewers whose comments you don't want to see.

In this exercise, you will show and review comments in a document, add a comment, delete one that is no longer needed, and then hide the remaining comments.

> **USE** the *Comments* document. This practice file is located in the *Documents\Microsoft Press\Word2007SBS\Collaborating* folder.
> **OPEN** the *Comments* document in Print Layout view.

Display for Review

1. If comments are not visible in the document, display the **Review** tab. Then in the **Tracking** group, in the **Display for Review** list, click **Final Showing Markup**.

2. On the **Review** tab, in the **Comments** group, click the **Next** button.

   In the document, Word highlights in the first instance of commented text. It also positions the insertion point in the associated comment balloon.

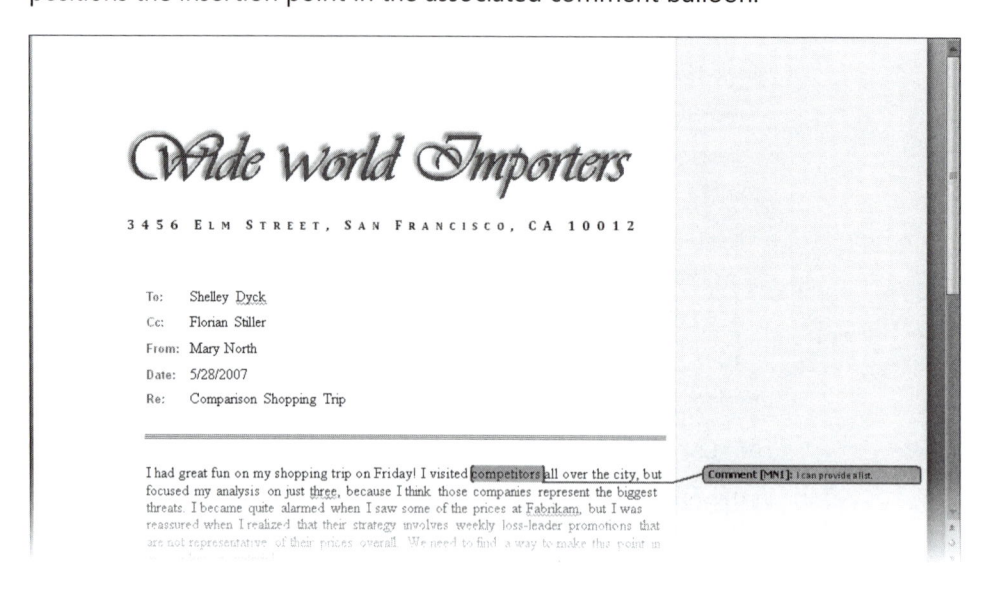

   Tip If a document contains both comments and tracked changes, clicking the Next or Previous button moves sequentially among both elements.

3. In the **Comments** group, click the **Next** button.

   Word moves to the next comment.

4. Point to **Adequate**.

   A ScreenTip displays information about who inserted the comment and when.

5. In the fifth column of the same row, select the words **some good**, and then in the **Comments** group, click the **New Comment** button.

   Word highlights the selection and displays a new balloon in the right margin.

6. In the comment balloon, type They carry the new Ultra line.

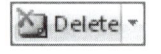

7. Click the comment balloon associated with the word *competitors*, and in the **Comments** group, click the **Delete** button.

   Word deletes the comment and its balloon.

8. In the **Tracking** group, click the **Reviewing Pane** button.

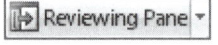

   The reviewing pane opens to the left of the Word window, showing the two remaining comments.

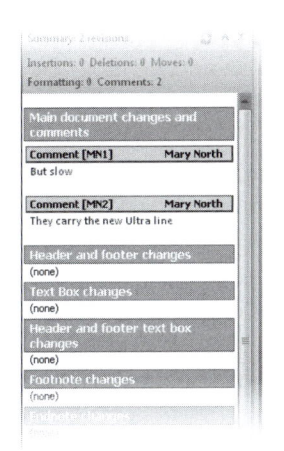

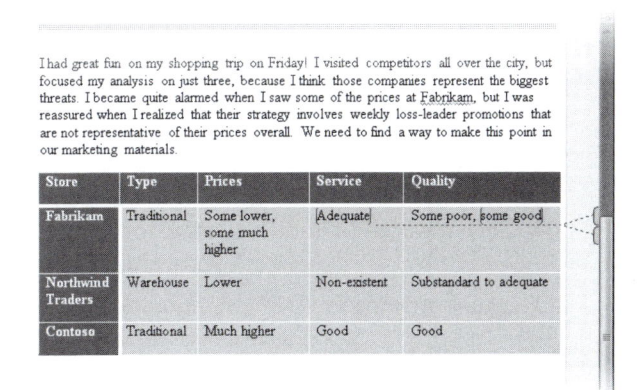

9. In the reviewing pane, click at the right end of the second comment, press [Enter], type the date and a colon (:), press [Space], and then type These are special order.

    The new text is added to the same comment in the reviewing pane.

10. In the **Tracking** group, click the **Reviewing Pane** button to close the pane, and then scroll the document so that you can see its text.

11. Click anywhere in the comment balloon associated with *Adequate*, and then in the **Comments** group, click the **New Comment** button.

    Word attaches a response comment to the same text in the document.

12. In the response comment balloon, type If I were a real customer, I would have left.

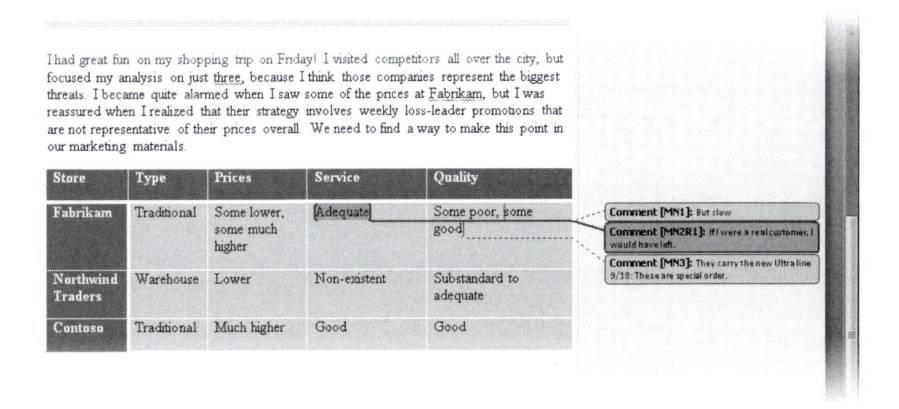

13. In the **Review** group, click the **Show Markup** button, and then click **Comments** to hide them.

CLOSE the *Comments* document without saving your changes.

> ### Entering Handwritten Changes
>
> With Word 2007 running on a computer or device with ink input capability, such as a Tablet PC, you can make handwritten changes to a document. You can make handwritten comments, circle words or paragraphs, cross things out, draw arrows, and sketch diagrams to make your point. To add a handwritten comment to a document on a Tablet PC:
>
> 1. In Print Layout view, select the text to be commented.
> 2. On the **Review** tab, in the **Comments** group, tap the **Ink Comment** button.
> 3. Write your comment.
>
> To annotate a document:
> 1. On the **Review** tab, in the **Ink** group, tap the **Start Inking** button.
>
>   The Pens contextual tab is added to the Ribbon.
>
> 2. On the **Pens** tab, select the type of pen, color, and weight you want, and then make your annotations in the document.
>
> 3. When you are done, in the **Close** group, click the **Close Ink Tools** button.
>
> To remove individual annotations, use the Eraser tool. To remove all annotations, in the Select group, click the Delete All Ink button.
>
> Other people don't need ink input capability to see your handwritten notes. Your annotations appear as objects in the Word document, where they can be moved and sized, or deleted when they are no longer necessary.

Comparing and Merging Documents

Sometimes you might want to compare several versions of the same document. For example, if you have sent a document out for review by colleagues, you might want to compare their edited versions with the original document.

Instead of comparing multiple open documents visually, you can tell Word to compare the documents and merge the changes into one document. Even if the changes were not made with Track Changes turned on, they are recorded in the merged document as revisions. From within that one document, you can view all the changes from all the reviewers or view only those from a specific reviewer.

In this exercise, you merge three versions of the same document and then evaluate and handle the revisions that indicate the differences between the versions.

USE the *Comparing1*, *Comparing2*, and *Comparing3* documents. These practice files are located in the *Documents\Microsoft Press\Word2007SBS\Collaborating* folder.

OPEN the *Comparing1* document.

1. On the **Review** tab, in the **Compare** group, click the **Compare** button, and then click **Combine**.

   Tip Click Compare to compare two documents and display the differences between them in a third document. The documents being compared are not changed.

   The Combine Documents dialog box opens.

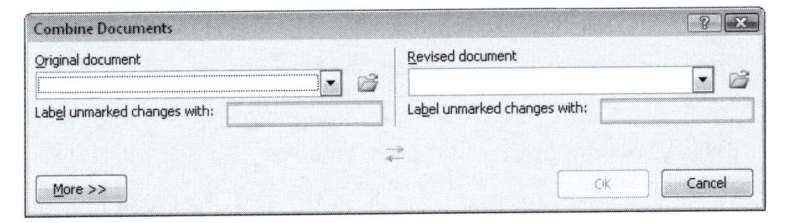

2. In the **Original document** list, click *Comparing1*.
3. In the **Revised document** list, click **Browse**, navigate to the *Documents\Microsoft Press\Word2007SBS\Collaborating* folder, and then double-click *Comparing2*.

   Under both documents, Word indicates to whom any revisions will be attributed.

4. In the lower-left corner of the dialog box, click **More**, and then in the **Comparison settings** area, verify that all the check boxes are selected.
5. In the **Show changes in** area, under **Show changes in**, click **Original document**, and then click **OK**.

   Troubleshooting If the documents contain conflicting formatting, you will see a message box asking you to confirm which document's formatting should be used.

   Word compares the two documents and marks the differences in the document displayed in the center pane, *Comparing1*. To the left it displays the reviewing pane, and to the right, it displays the two documents being compared.

   Troubleshooting If the reviewing pane is not open, click the Reviewing Pane button in the Tracking group on the Review tab.

6. On the **Review** tab, in the **Compare** group, click the **Compare** button, and then click **Combine** to display the **Combine Documents** dialog box.

7. In the **Original document** list, click *Comparing 1*, and in the **Revised document** list, click *Comparing3*. Then click **OK**.

   The changes from the *Comparing3* version of the document are added to those of the other two versions.

8. In the center pane, scroll through the document to see all the revisions, and then in the reviewing pane, scroll through the individual revisions.

9. On the **Review** tab, in the **Tracking** group, click the **Show Markup** button, point to **Reviewers**, and then click **Florian Stiller**.

   The revisions made by Florian Stiller are hidden.

10. In the **Tracking** group, click the **Show Markup** button, point to **Reviewers**, and then click **All Reviewers** to redisplay all the revisions.

11. Press $Ctrl$+$Home$ to move to the top of the document. Then in the **Changes** group, click the **Accept** arrow, and in the list, click **Accept All Changes in Document**.

    All the changes are accepted.

12. Close the reviewing pane, and close the two windows on the right side of the screen.

CLOSE the *Comparing1* document without saving your changes.

Password-Protecting a Document

Sometimes, you might want only certain people to be able to open and change a document. The easiest way to exercise this control is to assign a password to protect the document. Word then requires that the password be entered correctly before it will allow the document to be opened and changed. Anyone who doesn't know the password has no choice but to open a *read-only* version.

In this exercise, you will set a password for a document and then test the document's security by entering an incorrect password. You will open a read-only version of the document and then reopen it with the correct password. Finally, you'll remove the password-protection from the document.

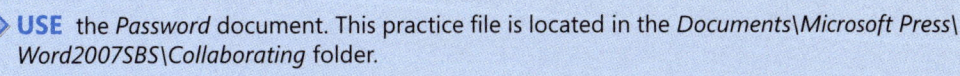

> **USE** the *Password* document. This practice file is located in the *Documents\Microsoft Press\Word2007SBS\Collaborating* folder.
>
> **OPEN** the *Password* document.

Microsoft Office Button

1. Click the **Microsoft Office Button**, and then click **Save As**.
2. With the *Collaborating* folder displayed in the **Save As** dialog box, type **My Password** in the **File name** box.
3. At the bottom of the dialog box, click **Tools**, and then in the list, click **General Options**.

   The General Options dialog box opens.

> **Tip** If you want people to be able to read the document's contents but you don't expect them to change the document, you can select the Read-Only Recommended check box to tell Word to display a message suggesting that the document be opened as read-only. Then click OK to close the General Options dialog box without assigning a password.

4. In the **Password to modify** box, type P@ssword.

   As you type the password, dots appear instead of the characters to keep the password confidential.

   > **Important** Don't use common words or phrases as passwords, and don't use the same password for multiple documents. After assigning a password, make a note of it in a safe place. If you forget it, you will not be able to open the password-protected document.

5. Click **OK**.

   The Confirm Password dialog box opens.

6. In the **Reenter password to modify** box, type P@ssword, and then click **OK** to set the password.

7. In the **Save As** dialog box, click **Save**.

   Word protects the document by assigning the selected password, and then saves it in the *Collaborating* folder.

8. Close the *My Password* document.

9. Click the **Microsoft Office Button**, and then in the **Recent Documents** pane, click the **My Password** document.

   Because this document is protected by the password you just set, the Password dialog box opens.

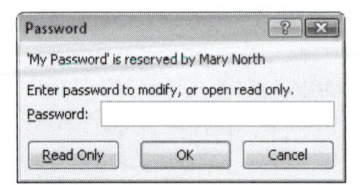

10. In the **Password** box, type password, and click **OK**.

    A message tells you that you typed an incorrect password.

11. In the message box, click **OK**.

12. In the **Password** dialog box, click **Read Only**.

    The *My Password* document opens as a read-only document, as indicated by *(Read-Only)* in its title bar.

13. Close the document, and then reopen it.

    A message reminds you that you previously opened this document as read-only and asks whether you want to do the same thing again.

14. In the message box, click **No**.

15. In the **Password** dialog box, type P@ssword, and then click **OK**.

    Because you typed the correct password, the document opens.

16. Click the **Microsoft Office Button**, click **Save As**, click **Tools**, and then click **General Options**.

17. In the **General Options** dialog box, select the contents of the **Password to modify** box, press [Del], click **OK**, and then click **Save**.

    The document is no longer protected by a password.

> **CLOSE** the *My Password* document.

> **Tip** If you have signed up for the Microsoft Information Rights Management (IRM) Service, or if your organization is running its own rights management server, you can control who can see and work with your documents by granting permission to perform such tasks as opening, printing, saving, or copying a file to specific people. For more information, on the Review tab, in the Protect group, click the Protect Document button, and then click Restricted Access.

Preventing Changes

Sometimes you will want people to be able to open and view a document but not make changes to it. Sometimes you will want to allow changes, but only of certain types. For example, you can specify that other people can insert comments in the document but not make changes, or you can require that people track their changes. To prevent anyone from introducing inconsistent formatting into a document, you can limit the styles that can be applied. You can select the styles individually, or you can implement the recommended minimum set, which consists of all the styles needed by Word for features such as tables of contents. (The recommended minimum set doesn't necessarily include all the styles used in the document.)

To protect a document from unauthorized changes, you click the Protect Document button in the Protect group on the Review tab to display the Protect Document task pane, in which you specify the types of changes that are allowed.

In this exercise, you'll set editing and formatting restrictions to selectively allow modifications to a document.

> **USE** the *PreventingChanges* document. This practice file is located in the *Documents\Microsoft Press\Word2007SBS\Collaborating* folder.
> **OPEN** the *PreventingChanges* document.

1. On the **Review** tab, in the **Protect** group, click the **Protect Document** button, and then in the list, click **Restrict Formatting and Editing**.

   The Restrict Formatting And Editing task pane opens.

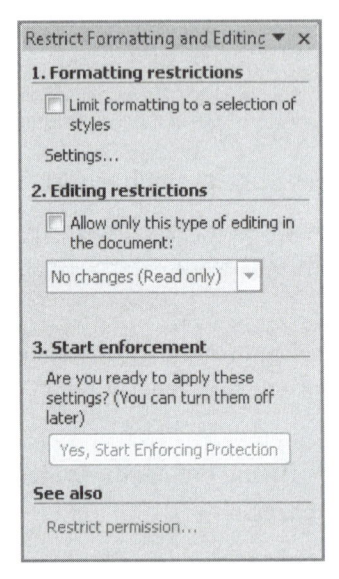

2. Under **Formatting restrictions** in the task pane, select the **Limit formatting to a selection of styles** check box, and then click **Settings**.

   The Formatting Restrictions dialog box opens.

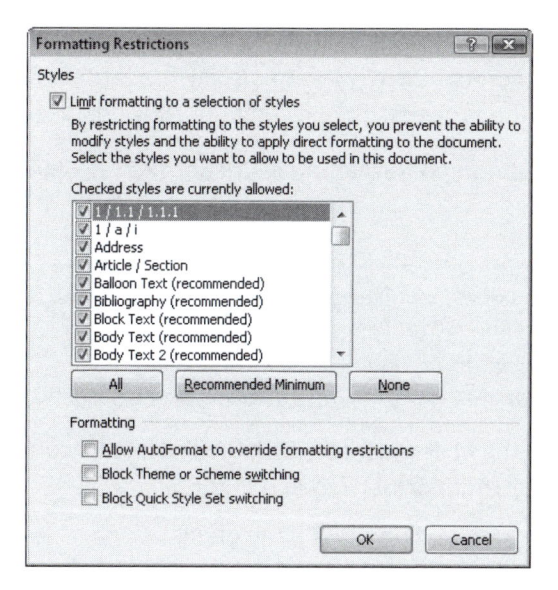

3. Scroll through the **Checked styles are currently allowed** list.

   The styles reflect those in the template attached to the open document, including styles that are available but not currently in use.

4. Click **Recommended Minimum**, and then scroll through the list again.

   All the selected styles are designated by the word *recommended*. The recommended set does not include some of the styles used in the document, so you need to add them.

5. In the list, select the **Address** check box. Then scroll the list, and select the **BulletList1**, **BulletList2**, **NumList1**, **NumList2**, and **Proch1** (meaning *Procedural heading*) check boxes.

6. In the **Formatting** area, select the **Block Theme or Scheme switching** and the **Block Quick Style Set switching** check boxes.

7. Click **OK** to implement the restricted set of styles.

   Word displays a message stating that the document might contain formatting that has been applied directly rather than through styles and restricted styles, and asking if you want it removed.

8. In the message box, click **Yes**.

9. Under **Editing restrictions** in the task pane, select the **Allow only this type of editing in the document** check box. Then click the arrow to the right of the box below, and in the list, click **Tracked changes**.

10. Under **Start enforcement** in the task pane, click **Yes, Start Enforcing Protection**.

 The Start Enforcing Protection dialog box opens.

 You enter a password if you want only those people who know the password to be able to turn off document protection.

 11. Without entering a password, click **OK**.

 The Restrict Formatting And Editing task pane indicates that formatting and editing in this document is now restricted.

 12. Close the task pane, and then display the **Home** tab.

 The buttons in the Font and Paragraph groups are now unavailable.

 13. Display the **Review** tab, and notice that the Track Changes button is not active.

 14. In the document title, double-click the word **Office**, and type Operations.

 Although Track Changes is not active, your change is marked as a revision.

> **CLOSE** the *PreventingChanges* document without saving your changes.

Using Document Workspaces

If your organization is running a collaboration site built with SharePoint products and technologies, you and your colleagues can develop documents from within a *document workspace*. The document workspace provides a forum in which multiple people in different locations can work on one document. The document can be checked out by any member of the team. While the document is checked out, other people can view it but they cannot edit it. After the document is declared final, you can move it to a more permanent storage location and delete the document workspace.

To create and use a document workspace from within Word, you publish the document to the SharePoint site. The process of publishing creates the workspace and stores a copy of the document there so that other people can work on it. When you open the copy of the document stored on your computer, Word asks whether you want to download updates from the document workspace and provides a Document Management task pane with tools that enable you to keep your copy synchronized with the copy stored in the document workspace.

> **Tip** You don't have to publish a document to a document workspace to be able to work with it on a SharePoint site. If you upload the document to the site, you and your colleagues can work with it from there. Working with documents from within a SharePoint site is beyond the scope of this book. For information, refer to *Microsoft Windows SharePoint Services Step By Step* by Olga Londer, Todd Bleeker, Penelope Coventry, and James Edelen (Microsoft Press, 2005).

In this exercise, you will publish a document to a document workspace. You will explore the Document Management task pane, view the document workspace, and then delete it.

> **Important** The steps for this exercise assume that you have access to a site created with Microsoft Office SharePoint Server 2007. If you have access to a site created with a different version of SharePoint, the steps will be different.

> **USE** the *Workspace* document. This practice file is located in the *Documents\Microsoft Press\Word2007SBS\Collaborating* folder.
> **BE SURE TO** have the user name and password for the SharePoint site available.
> **OPEN** the *Workspace* document.

1. Save the open document in the *Collaborating* folder with the name My Workspace.

2. Click the **Microsoft Office Button**, point to **Publish**, and then click **Create Document Workspace**.

   The Document Management task pane opens, with the name of the current document entered in the Document Workspace Name box.

Microsoft Office Button

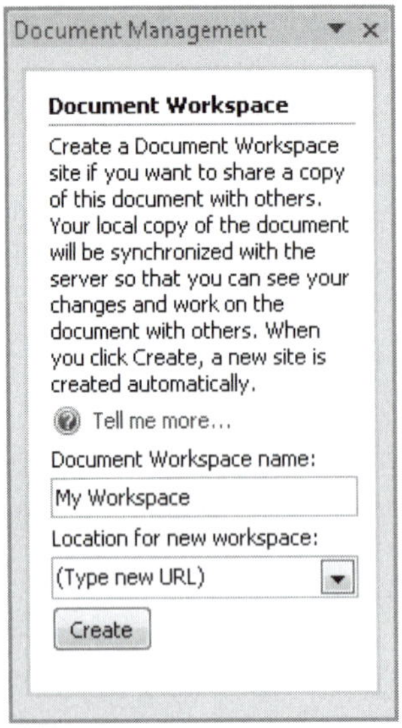

3. In the **Location for new workspace** box, type the URL of the SharePoint site where you want to create the document workspace (or if you've previously connected to the site, select it from the list).

4. Click **Create**.

> **Troubleshooting** A message might appear saying that the URL you have typed is a restricted or non-trusted site. If you trust the site, open your Web browser and add the URL to your list of trusted sites. Then click Create again.
>
> To add a site to your list of trusted sites in Internet Explorer, click Internet Options on the Tools menu, click the Security tab, click Trusted Sites, and then click the Sites button. In the Trusted Sites dialog box, enter the Web site address in the Add This Website To The Zone box, click Add, and then click Close. Click OK in the Internet Options dialog box to complete the process.

Word displays a couple of message boxes to let you know how the process is progressing.

5. If you are asked to supply your user name and password to connect to the site, provide your SharePoint site credentials in the **User name** and **Password** boxes, and then click **OK**.

When the document workspace is created and the document has been saved in the space, the Document Management task pane reappears with the name of the workspace at the top and five tabs that show information from the workspace.

You can download changes that have been made to a document stored in a workspace by clicking Get Updates. You can view or set options associated with the site by clicking Options.

6. In the task pane, click the **Members** tab.

   The task pane now shows the members of this workspace (currently just you). To add a new member, click Add New Members below the list box, and then complete the Add New Member dialog box. You can also send an e-mail message directly to members from the task pane.

7. In the task pane, click the **Tasks** tab.

   If there are any outstanding tasks associated with the document, they are listed on this tab. To add a new task, click Add New Task below the list box. If you click Alert Me About Tasks, you are taken to the New Alert page of the document workspace, where you can specify that you should be alerted when the tasks associated with the document change.

   > **Tip** If your organization uses workflow technology and a workflow has been set up for this document, you can click View Workflow Tasks to get information about your tasks.

8. In the task pane, click the **Documents** tab.

   The task pane now shows the names of any documents in this workspace (currently just *My Workspace*). To add a new document, click Add New Document below the list box. To create a new folder in which to store documents, click Add New Folder, and to be alerted when documents are added or changed, click Alert Me About Documents.

9. In the task pane, click the **Links** tab.

   If there are any links associated with the document, they are listed on this tab. To add a new link, click Add New Link below the list box, and to be alerted when links are added or changed, click Alert Me About Links.

10. Below the workspace name at the top of the **Document Management** task pane, click **Open site in browser**, and if necessary, enter your site credentials.

Your Web browser starts and opens the document workspace on the SharePoint site. You can add members, tasks, documents, and links in the workspace, and they will be reflected in the Document Management task pane in Word.

11. Close your Web browser without making any changes to the document workspace.
12. In the **Document Management** task pane, point to the name of the workspace, and click the arrow that appears.

    A list of workspace commands appears.
13. In the list, click **Delete Workspace**, and then click **Yes** to confirm the deletion.
14. Close the **Document Management** task pane.

> **CLOSE** the *My Workspace* document without saving your changes, and if you are not continuing directly to the next chapter, exit Word.

Key Points

- You can send a document for review via e-mail, and then when you receive the reviewed versions, you can merge them so that all the changes are recorded in one document.
- When you collaborate on a document, you can record the revisions you make to the document without losing the original text.
- You can insert comments in a document to ask questions or explain suggested edits. You can view comments individually in balloons in the right margin of the document or collectively in a reviewing pane.
- If you want only specific people to be able to work on a document, you can protect it with a password. If you want to allow only specific types of changes, you can restrict how people can edit and format the document.
- If you have access to a SharePoint site, creating a document workspace is a great way to collaborate with your colleagues on a document.

Chapter at a Glance

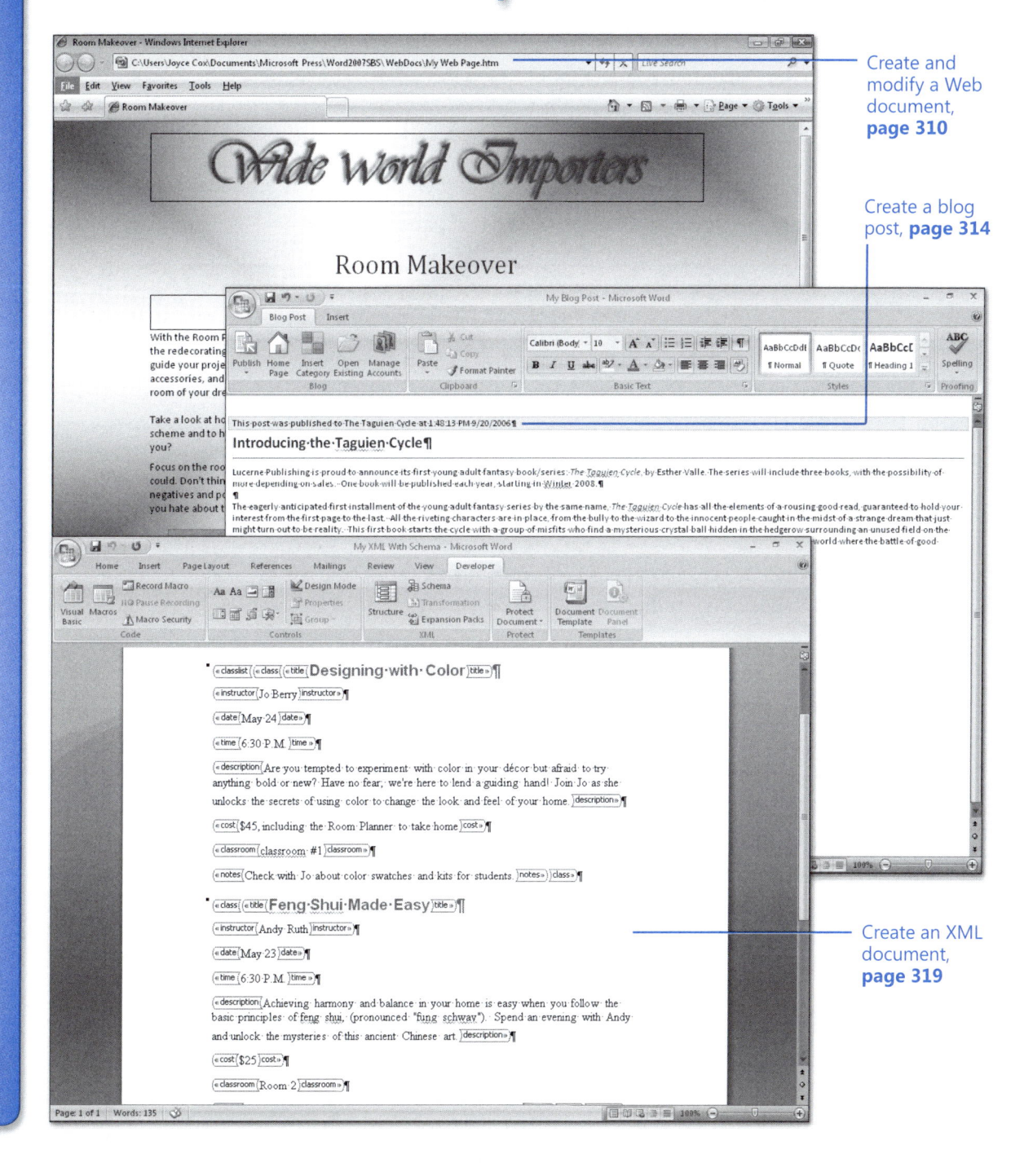

Create and modify a Web document, **page 310**

Create a blog post, **page 314**

Create an XML document, **page 319**

11 Creating Documents for Use Outside of Word

In this chapter, you will learn to:
- ✔ Save a file in a different format.
- ✔ Create and modify a Web document.
- ✔ Create a blog post.
- ✔ Create an XML document.

Sometimes you will create a document in Microsoft Office Word 2007 and then want to send it to someone who does not have Word 2007 installed on his or her computer. Word comes with several conversion utilities that you can use to save documents in other *file formats* so that you can distribute documents that your colleagues can read and use no matter what programs they work with.

One way of distributing the information in your documents is by converting them to *Web pages* so that people can read them on the Web. The Web has become a major part of our everyday lives. We use it to shop, check the news, find out how our favorite sports team is doing, and research topics. It's also a great publishing tool if you are trying to reach a broad audience. For example, your organization might want to publish a Web newsletter to provide information while advertising its goods or services. Or you might want to use built-in Word tools to create and post articles to a *blog* (short for *Web log*) about a particular topic.

In addition to converting documents into Web pages, you can convert them into *Extensible Markup Language (XML)* documents. The XML format distinguishes different parts of a document, giving it a structure that enables you to identify and extract

items of information. For example, if you write a training document including procedures whose numbered steps are uniquely identified with a Procedure style, and then convert the document to XML format, all the procedures can be extracted into a different file for a different purpose—perhaps as a frequently asked questions (FAQ) page for your organization's Web site.

In this chapter, you will first learn about saving documents in other file formats. You will then preview a document in Web Layout view, save the document as a Web page, and make adjustments necessary for optimum presentation on the Web. You will create a blog post, register an existing blog account, and then publish the blog post. Finally, you will save a document as an XML file and view its XML tags, and then attach a schema containing custom tags to it.

See Also Do you need only a quick refresher on the topics in this chapter? See the Quick Reference section at the beginning of this book.

Important Before you can use the practice files in this chapter, you need to install them from the book's companion CD to their default location. See "Using the Companion CD" at the beginning of this book for more information.

Troubleshooting Graphics and operating system–related instructions in this book reflect the Windows Vista user interface. If your computer is running Windows XP and you experience trouble following the instructions as written, please refer to the "Information for Readers Running Windows XP" section at the beginning of this book.

Saving a File in a Different Format

When you save a Word document, the default file save format is the Microsoft Office Word 2007 .docx format. If you want to be able to use the file with an earlier version of Word or with a different program, you can save it in a different file format.

See Also For information about the .docx format, see the sidebar "The DOCX Format" later in this chapter.

To save a document in a different file format, display the Save As dialog box, and then change the Save As Type setting to the format you want to use. If you want to save a Word document in a format that can be opened by the widest variety of programs, use one of the following formats:

- **Rich Text Format (*.rtf).** Save the document in this format if you want to preserve its formatting.
- **Text Only (*.txt).** Save the document in this format if you want to preserve only its text.

If you want someone to be able to view a document but not change it, you can save the document as a Portable Document Format (PDF) file. In recent years, PDF has become a common standard for distributing information. The text and graphics in a PDF file are essentially static, and because a PDF file breaks a document into discrete pages, it mimics the way information appears on a printed page. Unlike a printed document, however, a PDF file can be sent by e-mail to many recipients, or it can be made available on a Web page for download to anyone who wants it. Using a PDF file can also help guarantee the quality of your document when you print it because it sets exact page breaks, which ensures that the pages are printed as you intended them to be.

You can open and read PDF files by using a PDF reader such as Adobe Acrobat Reader, which is available as a free download from the Adobe Web site as well as from many Web sites that distribute PDF files. You can create PDF files from Word documents by purchasing the full version of Adobe Acrobat.

> **Important** The PDF file is no longer a Word document, and it cannot be opened, viewed, and edited in Word. To view the document, you must have a PDF reader, such as Adobe Reader (available free from *www.adobe.com*), installed on your computer.

Saving Files for Electronic Distribution

From the Microsoft Downloads Web site at *www.microsoft.com/downloads/*, you can install a free add-in that enables you to save Word documents in the more securely distributable Portable Document Format (PDF) and XML Paper Specification (XPS) file formats. (XPS is the reasonably new Microsoft XML-based format for delivering documents as electronic representations of the way they look when printed.)

When saving a Word document as a PDF or XPS file, there are several ways in which you can optimize the document to suit your purposes. You can optimize the file size for your intended distribution method, or click Options to fine-tune the PDF output by selecting only certain pages of the document, including or excluding comments and tracked changes, creating electronic bookmarks, and so on.

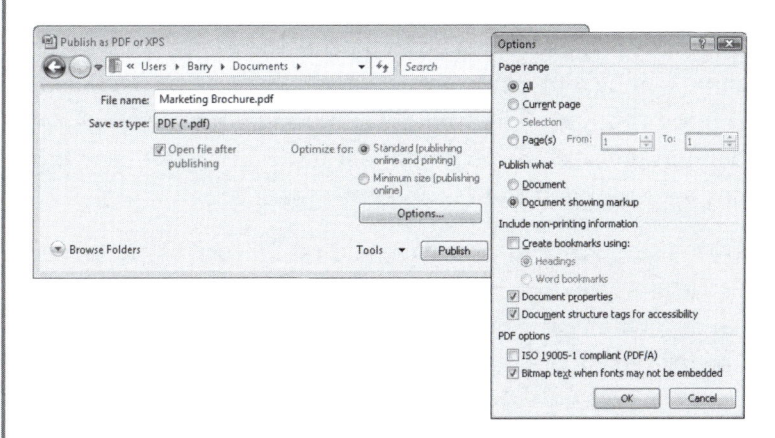

To save a document as a PDF or XPS file after installing the Save As PDF Or XPS add-in:

1. Click the **Microsoft Office Button**, point to **Save As**, and then click **PDF or XPS**.
2. In the **Publish as PDF Or XPS** dialog box, browse to the location where you want to save the file (if necessary, click **Browse Folders** to display the **Folders** list). If you want to, enter a new name for the converted document in the **File name** box. (Changing the file name here does not change the name of the original Word document.)
3. In the **Save as type** list, choose **PDF** or **XPS Document**.
4. If you will be distributing the file online, click **Minimum size (publishing online)**.
5. If you want to make additional changes as discussed above, click **Options**, make the changes you want, and then click **OK**.
6. In the **Publish as PDF or XPS** dialog box, click **Publish**.

Using Add-Ins

Add-ins are utilities that add specialized functionality to a program (but aren't full-fledged programs themselves). There are several sources of add-ins:

- You can purchase add-ins from third-party vendors—for example, you can purchase an add-in that tracks the entire print history of a document.
- You can download free add-ins from the Microsoft Web site or other Web sites.
- When installing a third-party program, you might install an add-in to allow it to interface with a 2007 Microsoft Office system program. For example, you can install an add-in to capture screens from within an Office document.

> **Important** Be careful when downloading add-ins from Web sites other than those you trust. Add-ins are executable files that can easily be used to spread viruses and otherwise wreak havoc on your computer. For this reason, default settings in the Trust Center intervene when you attempt to download or run add-ins.

To use some add-ins, you must first install them on your computer and then load them into your computer's memory, as follows:

1. Click the **Microsoft Office Button**, and then in the lower-right corner, click **Word Options**.
2. In the page list in the left pane of the **Word Options** window, click **Add-Ins**.
3. At the bottom of the page, click the **Manage** arrow, and in the list, click the type of add-in you want to install. Then click **Go**.

    A dialog box corresponding to the type of add-in you selected opens. For example, if you select COM Add-Ins, the COM Add-Ins dialog box opens; if you select Templates, the Templates And Add-Ins dialog box opens.

4. In the dialog box, click **Add**.
5. In the **Add** dialog box, navigate to the folder where the add-in you want to install is stored, and double-click its name.

    The new add-in appears in the list of those that are available for use.

6. In the **Checked items are currently loaded** list, select the check box of the new add-in, and then click **OK**.

    The add-in is now available for use in Word.

To unload an add-in, display the Add-Ins dialog box and clear the add-in's check box to remove the add-in from memory but keep its name in the list. To remove the add-in from the list entirely, click the add-in name, and then click Remove.

Creating and Modifying a Web Document

You don't need to be a Web designer to create a Web page. From within Word 2007, you can view a document in Web Layout view, make any necessary adjustments in Word, and then save the document as a Web page, as easily as you would save it in any other format.

When you save a document as a Web page, Word converts the styles and formatting in the document to *Hypertext Markup Language (HTML)* codes, which are called *tags*. These tags tell your Web browser how to display the document. During the conversion, some of the formatting might be changed or ignored because it is not supported by all Web browsers. If that is the case, Word alerts you and gives you the option of stopping the conversion process so that you can make adjustments to the formatting to make it more compatible.

> **Tip** In the Web Options dialog box, you can specify which browsers you anticipate will be used to view your Web pages. You can also have Word disable any features that are incompatible with the specified browsers.

After you save a document as a Web page, it is no longer a Word document. It is saved in HTML format with the *.htm* or *.html* file name extension. However, you can still open, view, and edit the Web page in Word, just as you would a normal document. (You can also open and edit HTML-format Web pages created in other programs.) Making changes can be as basic as replacing text and adjusting alignment, or as advanced as moving and inserting graphics. When you finish modifying the Web page, you can resave it as a Web page, or save it as a regular Word document.

In this exercise, you will check that your computer is optimized for displaying documents as Web pages as they will appear in Microsoft Internet Explorer 6 or later. You will then preview a document in Web Layout view and make any adjustments necessary for this medium. Finally, you will save the document as a Web page, open the Web page in Word to make some modifications, and then save and view your changes.

> **USE** the *Web* document. This practice file is located in the *Documents\Microsoft Press\Word2007SBS\WebDocs* folder.
>
> **BE SURE TO** install a Web browser on your computer before beginning this exercise. Windows Internet Explorer 7 or later is recommended; the steps might be different for other browsers and versions.
>
> **OPEN** the *Web* document.

Microsoft Office Button

1. Click the **Microsoft Office Button**, and then click **Word Options**.

   The Word Options window opens.

2. In the page list in the left pane, click **Advanced**. Then at the bottom of the **Advanced** page, in the **General** section, click **Web Options**.

   The Web Options dialog box opens.

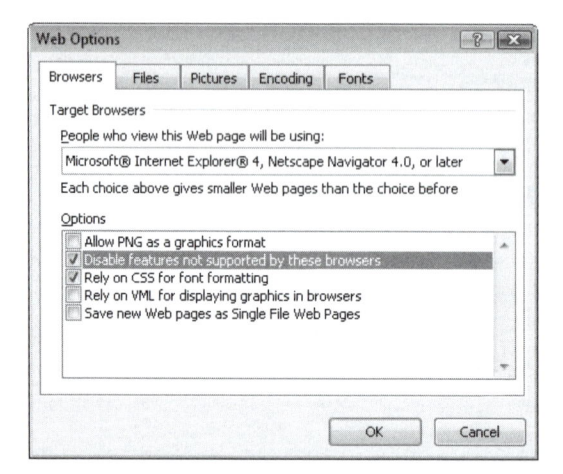

3. On the **Browsers** tab, verify that the **People who view this Web page will be using** option is set to **Microsoft Internet Explorer 6 or later**.

4. Under **Options**, select all five check boxes, and then click **OK** in each of the open dialog boxes.

Web Layout

5. On the status bar at the bottom of the program window, click the **Web Layout** button on the **View** toolbar, and then if the **Zoom** level is not set to **100%**, use the slider to adjust the magnification to that percentage.

Word displays the page as it will appear in your Web browser. As you can see, you need to increase the page margins and adjust the size of the quote box.

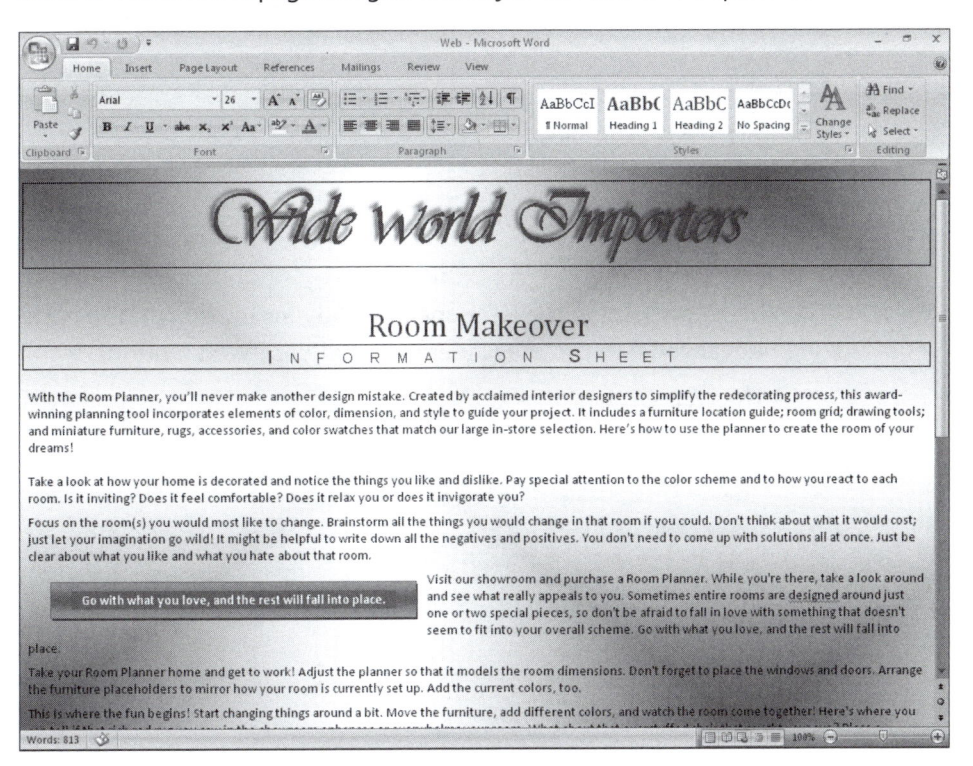

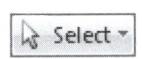

6. On the **Home** tab, in the **Editing** group, click the **Select** button, and then in the list, click **Select All**.

7. With all the text of the document selected, click the **Paragraph** dialog box launcher.

8. In the **Paragraph** dialog box, in the **Indentation** area, change the **Left** and **Right** settings to 1.25", and then click **OK**.

   The text is now indented from the left and right edges of the window.

9. Click the quote box to select it, drag its middle-right handle to the left until its box is half its original width and the quote wraps to two lines.

   The Web document is now more readable.

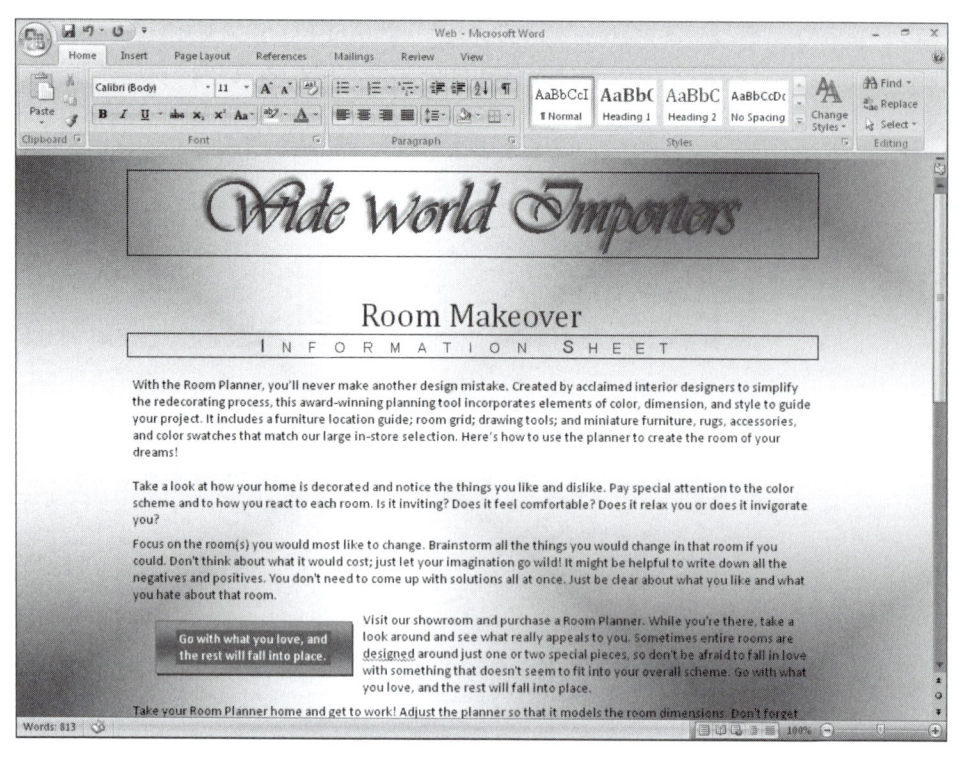

10. Click the **Microsoft Office Button**, and then click **Save As**.
11. With the contents of the *WebDocs* folder displayed in the **Save As** dialog box, type My Web Page in the **File name** box.
12. Click the **Save as type** arrow, and then in the list, click **Web Page**.
13. Click **Change Title**. Then in the **Set Page Title** dialog box, type Room Makeover in the **Page title** box, and click **OK**.

    This title will appear in the title bar of the Web browser window.
14. In the **Save As** dialog box, click **Save**.

    The Microsoft Office Word Compatibility Checker tells you that the Small Caps effect used for the *Information Sheet* subtitle is not supported by Web browsers and will be changed to all capital letters.
15. In the **Compatibility Checker**, click **Continue**.

    Word saves the document as an HTML file called *My Web Page*.
16. Press [Ctrl]+[End] to move to the end of the document, and then type Looking for free advice? Check our schedule of decorating mini-seminars!
17. If you want, format the text to make it stand out. Then save the Web page.

18. Click the **Start** button, and in the right pane, click **Documents**. Then in the **Documents** window, navigate to the *Microsoft Press\Word2007SBS\WebDocs* folder.

    The *WebDocs* folder contains *My Web Page* and a folder named *My Web Page_files*, which contains supporting files for the Web page.

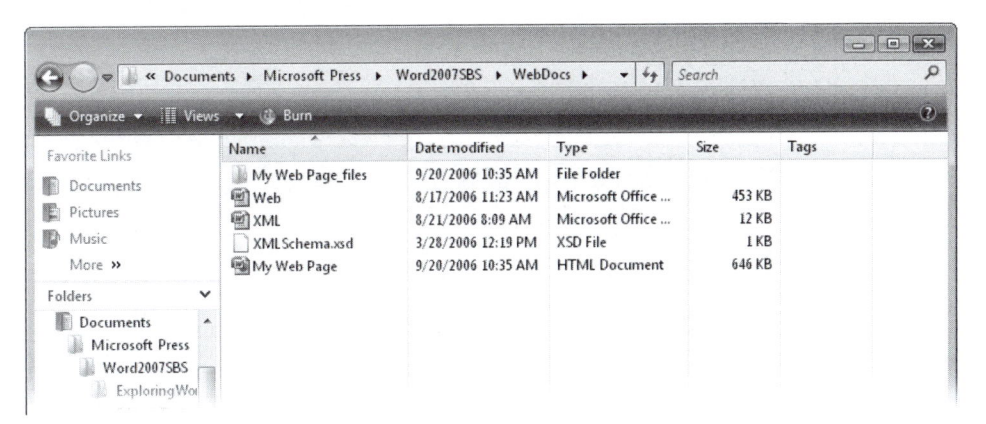

19. Double-click **My Web Page**.

    Your Web browser starts, and the Web page opens. You can scroll to the bottom of the page to see the changes you made to the HTML file in Word.

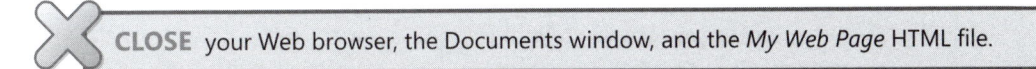

CLOSE your Web browser, the Documents window, and the *My Web Page* HTML file.

Creating a Blog Post

A blog is a personal Web site. It might be a personal online diary, or it might provide commentary, news, or information about a specific subject, such as a genre of music, a political point of view, a medical condition, or local news. A blog consists of *posts* that can include text, images, and links to related blogs, Web pages, and other media.

Word 2007 makes it easy to create posts that you can upload to your blog. If you have already set up a blog space with a blog service provider, you can register your blog space with Word the first time you create a blog post. If you haven't yet set up the blog space, you will need to register with a service provider before you can publish your first post. Thereafter, Word uses your registered blog account information when you create or publish a post.

Setting Up a Blog Account

To set up a blog, you must first decide which blog service provider you want to use. Many service providers, such as Windows Live Spaces (*spaces.live.com*) and Blogger (*www.blogger.com*), offer blog space free of charge. If your organization is running Microsoft Office SharePoint Server 2007, the site manager can set up a blog space for you.

To open a Windows Live Spaces account and create a blog space:

1. Start your Web browser, and then in the **Address** bar, type http://spaces.live.com.
2. On the **Windows Live Spaces** home page, click **Create your space**.
3. On the **Sign in** page, type your Windows Live ID and password, and click **Sign In**.
4. On the **Create your Windows Live Space** page, type a title for your space and the Web address you want, and then click **Check availability**.
5. If Windows Live Spaces reports that the Web address is available, click **Create**; if it is not available, repeat step 4 with another name.
6. On the **You've created your space** page, click **Go to your space**.

You can then enter information about yourself (your profile), give access to friends, and add content directly on your blog's home page. If you want to publish to your blog from Word, you need to first turn on e-mail publishing.

To turn on e-mail publishing:

1. In the upper-right corner of your blog page header, click **Options**.
2. On the left side of the page, in the **Options** pane, click **E-mail publishing**.
3. On the **E-mail Publishing** page, select the **Turn on e-mail publishing** check box, type up to three e-mail addresses you will use to publish blog posts, type a secret word (the password you will use to register your blog account in Word), choose whether to publish e-mail submissions immediately or review them online before publishing, and then click **Save**.

> **Tip** You can register multiple blog accounts, and then choose the account you want to use for each blog post you create.

In this exercise, you will register your existing blog space in Word, create a blog post, publish it to your blog, and then view the published blog post.

> **USE** the *Blog* document. This practice file is located in the *Documents\Microsoft Press\Word2007SBS\WebDocs* folder.
> **BE SURE TO** set up an account with Windows Live Spaces or another blog service provider, and turn on e-mail publishing or the equivalent if necessary, before beginning this exercise.

1. Start Word, if it is not already running. Click the **Microsoft Office Button**, and then click **New**.

2. In the **Blank and recent** pane of the **New Document** window, click **New blog post**. Then click **Create**.

   Word creates a document and the Register A Blog Account dialog box opens. If you already have a blog account, you can click Register Now, and follow the instructions to register your existing account. If you don't have a blog account, you can click the Office Online link for information about getting an account.

   > **Important** It's not essential to have a blog account before creating a blog post. You can click Register Later and skip to step 8. Word will prompt you again to register your account the first time you publish a blog post or the next time you create a blog post.

   The following steps are for registering a blog account created on Windows Live Spaces.

3. Click **Register Now**.

   The New Blog Account dialog box opens.

Creating an XML Document **321**

4. Click the **Start** button, click **Documents**, and then in the **Documents** window, navigate to the *Microsoft Press\Word2007SBS\WebDocs* folder.

5. Right-click the **My XML** file, point to **Open With**, and then click **Notepad**.

   The Notepad plain text editor opens, displaying the contents of the XML file.

   This "simple" method of creating XML files turns out to be not so simple after all! Hundreds of tags enclosed in greater than (>) and less than (<) signs make it possible for this plain text document to be displayed exactly as it appears in Word.

6. Close the Notepad window, and then in the **WebDocs** window, double-click the *XML* document to reopen it in Word.

7. Click the **Microsoft Office Button**, and click **Word Options**. Then on the **Popular** page of the **Word Options** window, under **Top options for working with Word**, select the **Show Developer tab in the Ribbon** check box, and click **OK**.

   The Developer tab appears on the Ribbon.

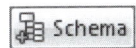

Chapter 11 Creating Documents for Use Outside of Word

![Schema icon]

8. On the **Developer** tab, in the **XML** group, click the **Schema** button.

   The Templates And Add-Ins dialog box opens.

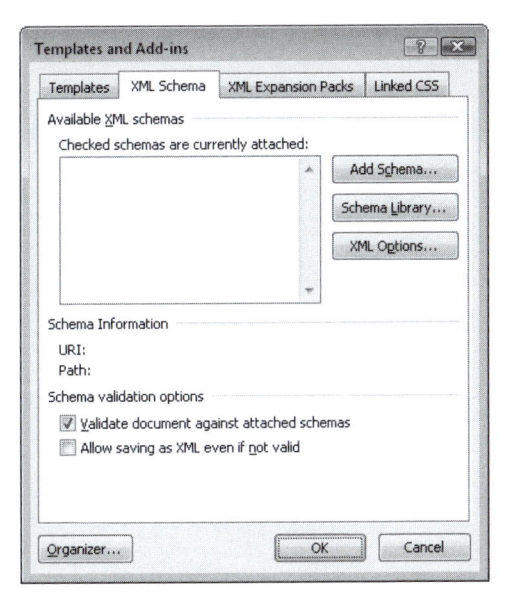

9. On the **XML Schema** tab of the dialog box, click **Add Schema**.

10. In the **Add Schema** dialog box, navigate to the *Documents\Microsoft Press\ Word2007SBS\WebDocs* folder, and then double-click *XMLSchema*.

    The Schema Settings dialog box opens.

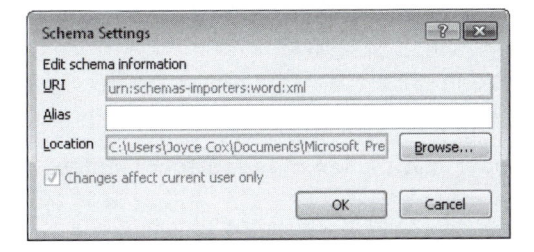

11. In the **Alias** box, type XMLSchema, and then click **OK**.

    Word adds the schema to the list of available schemas and attaches it to the document.

12. In the **Templates and Add-ins** dialog box, click **XML Options**.

    The XML Options dialog box opens.

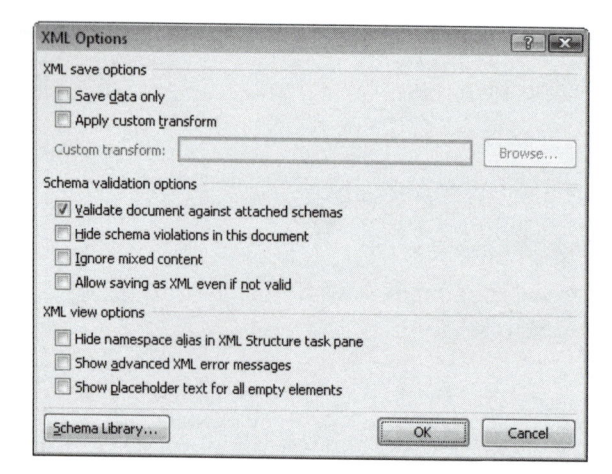

13. In the **Schema validation options** area, verify that the **Validate document against attached schemas** check box is selected and the **Hide schema violations in this document** check box is cleared.

14. In the **XML view options** area, verify that the **Hide namespace alias in XML Structure task pane** check box is cleared, and then select the **Show advanced XML error messages** check box.

15. Click **OK** to close the **XML Options** dialog box, and then close the **Templates and Add-ins** dialog box.

    The XML Structure task pane opens.

16. In the **XML Structure** task pane, verify that the **Show XML tags in the document** check box is selected.

    > **Tip** When you don't need to see XML tags in a document, you can hide them by clearing the Show XML Tags In The Document check box.

17. Click anywhere in the document window. Then at the bottom of the **XML Structure** task pane, in the **Choose an element to apply to your current selection** list, click **classlist {XMLSchema}**.

18. In the message box asking how you want to apply the selected element, click **Apply to Entire Document**.

    Word selects all the text in the document, adds an opening XML tag and a closing XML tag at either end of the document to indicate that the entire document is now a classlist element, and lists the element in the Elements In The Document box in the XML Structure task pane.

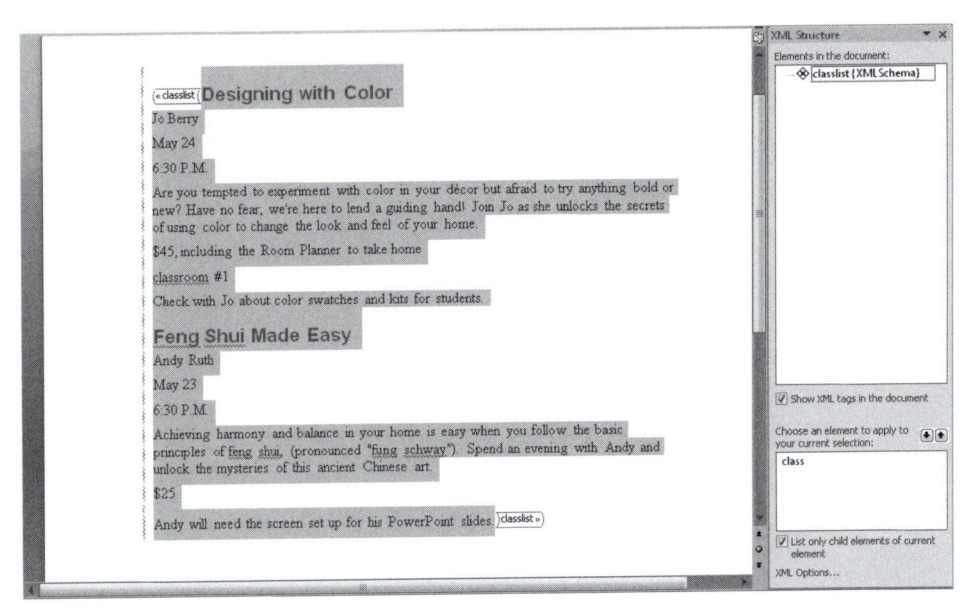

[Screenshot of Word document showing XML tagging with classlist element containing class information for "Designing with Color" and "Feng Shui Made Easy" courses, with XML Structure pane on the right]

19. Select all the text from *Designing with Color* down through *Check with Jo about color swatches and kits for students*. Then in the **Choose an element to apply to your current selection** box, click **class**.

    Word tags the selection as a class element. All the information between the two class tags belongs to one particular class.

    > **Tip** By default, the List Only Child Elements Of Current Element check box is selected. This simplifies the list of elements by showing only the ones that are valid in the current location. If you want to see a complete list of elements allowed in this schema, clear this check box. Invalid elements are then flagged with a slash inside a circle (the "not allowed" symbol).

20. Select the *Designing with Color* heading, and tag it as **title**. Then select each of the next six paragraphs one at a time, and tag them in turn as **instructor**, **date**, **time**, **description**, **cost**, and **classroom**.

    > **Tip** It is helpful to have non-printing characters displayed when you are selecting paragraphs for tagging.

    As you tag each element, it appears in the Elements In The Document box. An X next to the classlist and class elements indicates that the structure is not valid according to the schema rules, and three dots under the classroom element and at the end of the class element tell you that an element is missing.

21. Point to the **X** beside *class*.

    A ScreenTip tells you that untagged text is not allowed in the class element; all text must be enclosed in valid start and end element tags.

22. Select the sentence that begins *Check with Jo* (the only remaining untagged text in the class element). Then in the **Choose an element to apply to your current selection** list, click **notes**.

    Word tags the element, and the X next to *class* disappears.

23. Select all the text from *Feng Shui Made Easy* down to *Andy will need the screen set up for his PowerPoint slides*. In the **Choose an element to apply to your current selection** box, click **class**.

    Word tags the element and the X next to *classlist* disappears.

24. Select each of the paragraphs in this class in turn, and tag them as **title**, **instructor**, **date**, **time**, **description**, **cost**, and **notes**.

    In the Elements In The Document box, a question mark appears next to the second class element, and a wavy purple line appears in the left margin of the document to show you the section with invalid structure.

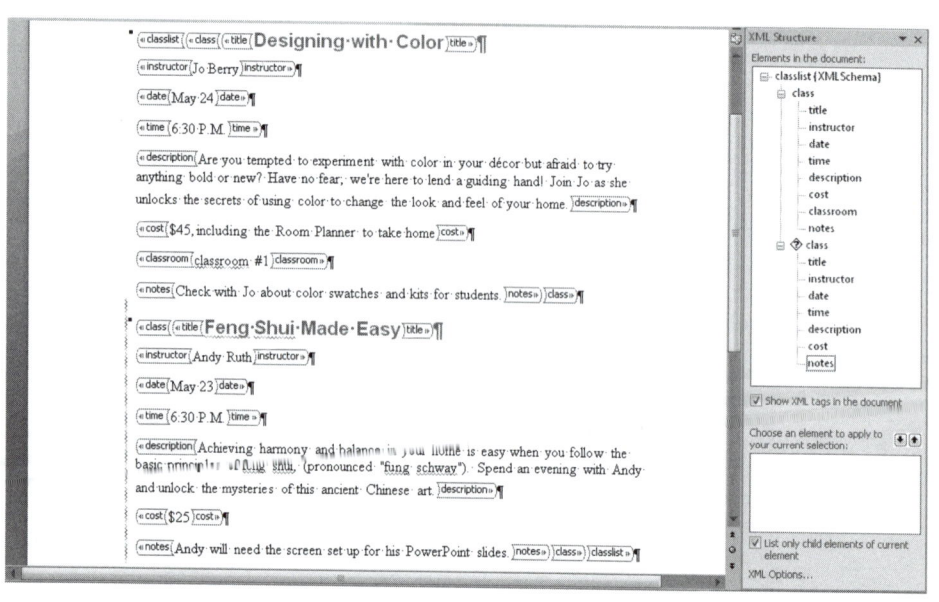

25. Point to the question mark.

    Word tells you that according to the rules laid out by the schema, the class element is incomplete.

26. In the *Feng Shui Made Easy* class in the document, click to the right of the **cost** end tag, press the [Enter] key, type **Room 2**, select the text, and tag it as **classroom**.

    The document's structure is now fully valid, and you're ready to save the document as an XML file.

    > **Troubleshooting** If the Allow Saving As XML Even If Not Valid check box is cleared in the XML Options dialog box, Word will not allow you to save a document as XML unless the structure is valid. If Word tells you that it cannot save your document as XML because its structure violates the rules set by the schema, you have three choices: save the file as a Word document; click Cancel and change the option in the XML Options dialog box; or click Cancel and go back to the Elements In The Document box of the XML Structure task pane to correct the structure of marked elements.

27. Click the **Microsoft Office Button**, click **Save As**, name the file **My XML With Schema**, change the **Save as type** setting to **Word XML Document**, and then click **Save**.

28. Close the **XML Structure** task pane, and then close the **My XML With Schema** document.

29. Click the **Microsoft Office Button**, and then in the **Recent Documents** pane, click **My XML With Schema**.

    The XML file opens in Word, where you can edit it like a normal document.

> ✕ **BE SURE TO** hide the Developer tab by displaying the Word Options window and clearing the Show Developer Tab In The Ribbon check box.
>
> **CLOSE** the *My XML With Schema* file, and if you are not continuing directly on to the next chapter, exit Word.

> **Tip** The power of XML lies in its flexibility. After you create an XML file, you can apply a *transform* (also called a *translation*) to it to pull only the data you need and put it in the format you want. For example, you could apply one transform to the list of classes that extracts the title, description, instructor, cost, date, and time of the class and then formats that information as a Web page for customers. You could also apply a different transform that extracts the date, classroom, and notes and then formats that information as a memo for setup staff. The subject of transforms is beyond the scope of this book. For more information, see *Microsoft Office Word 2007 Inside Out*, by Katherine Murray, Mary Millhollon, and Beth Melton (Microsoft Press, 2007).

> **The DOCX Format**
>
> The Microsoft Office 2007 system introduces a new file format based on XML, called Microsoft Office Open XML Formats. By default, Word 2007 files are saved in the .docx format, which is the Word variation of this new file format.
>
> The .docx format provides the following benefits:
>
> - File size is smaller because files are compressed when saved, decreasing the amount of disk space needed to store the file, and the amount of bandwidth needed to send files in e-mail, over a network, or across the Internet.
> - Recovering at least some of the content of damaged files is possible because XML files can be opened in a text program such as Notepad.
> - Security is greater because .docx files cannot contain macros, and personal data can be detected and removed from the file. (Word 2007 provides a different file format—.docm—for files that contain macros.)

Key Points

- If you want to send a document to people who might not have Word installed on their computers, you can save the document in a more universal file format so that it can be opened in other programs.
- Word documents can easily be converted to Web pages. In Web Layout view, you can see how a document will look in a Web browser, and you can make adjustments to the layout from within Word.
- The XML format stores information in such a way that it can be extracted and manipulated in a variety of ways in a variety of programs. With Word, you can convert a document to XML with a straightforward save process, or you can use a schema to ensure the validity of the document's structure before saving it as an XML file.

Chapter at a Glance

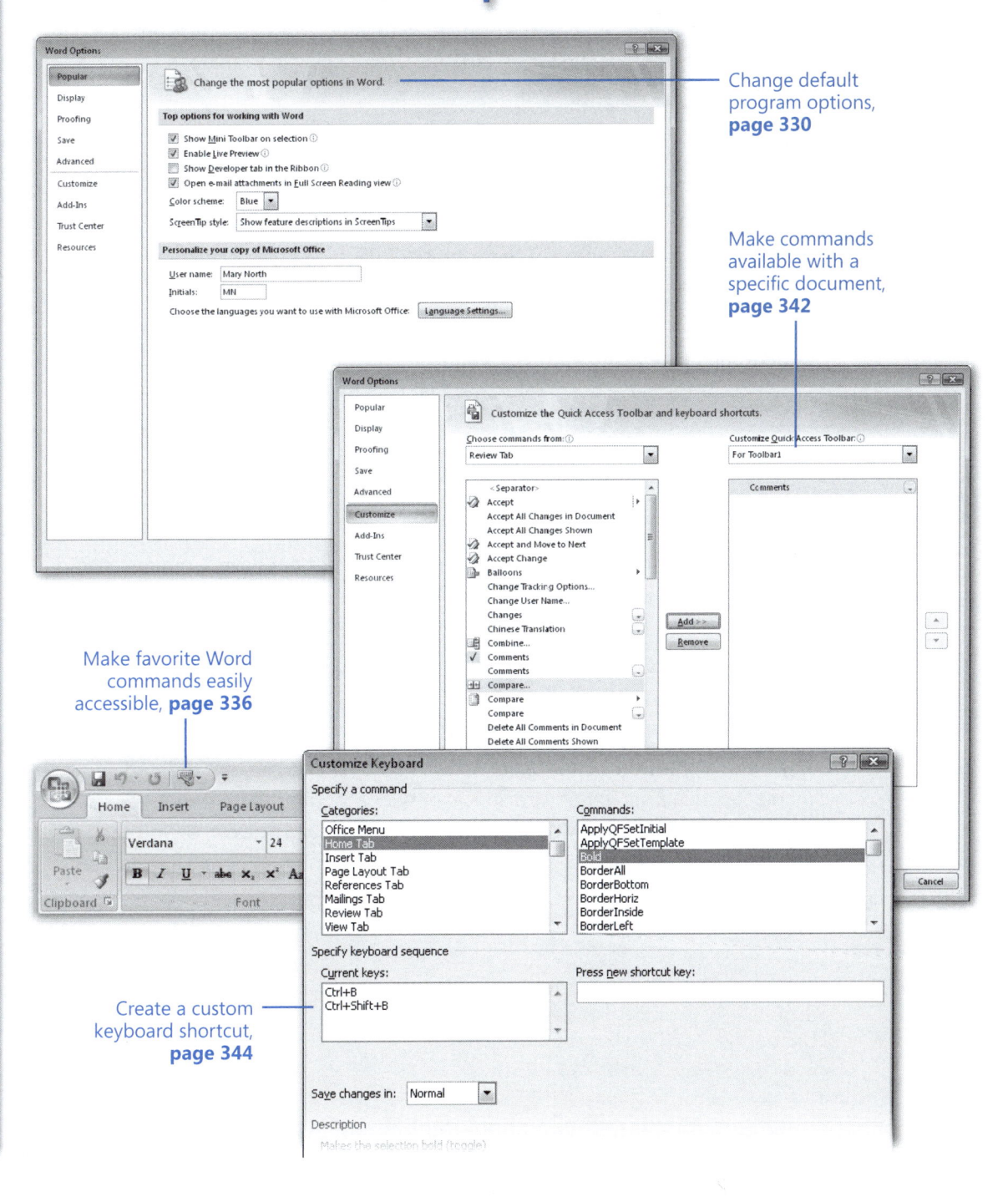

Change default program options, **page 330**

Make commands available with a specific document, **page 342**

Make favorite Word commands easily accessible, **page 336**

Create a custom keyboard shortcut, **page 344**

12 Customizing Word

In this chapter, you will learn to:
- ✔ Change default program options.
- ✔ Make favorite Word commands easily accessible.
- ✔ Make commands available with a specific document.
- ✔ Create a custom keyboard shortcut.

If you use Microsoft Office Word 2007 only occasionally, you might be perfectly happy with the default environment options and behind-the-scenes settings. However, if you create a lot of documents, you might find yourself wishing that you could change aspects of the program to customize it for the kinds of documents you create.

In this chapter, you will explore the pages of the Word Options window to understand the ways in which you can customize the program. Then you will add buttons to the Word 2007 Quick Access Toolbar, and to a document's custom toolbar. Finally, you will create a keyboard shortcut for a command so that you can invoke it without using your mouse.

See Also Do you need only a quick refresher on the topics in this chapter? See the Quick Reference section at the beginning of this book.

Important Before you can use the practice files in this chapter, you need to install them from the book's companion CD to their default location. See "Using the Companion CD" at the beginning of this book for more information.

Troubleshooting Graphics and operating system–related instructions in this book reflect the Windows Vista user interface. If your computer is running Windows XP and you experience trouble following the instructions as written, please refer to the "Information for Readers Running Windows XP" section at the beginning of this book.

329

Changing Default Program Options

In earlier chapters, we mentioned that you can change settings in the Word Options window to customize the Word environment in various ways. For example, you can create new AutoCorrect entries, adjust the save period for AutoRecover information, and determine the Print setting to use. Knowing which settings are where in the Word Options window will make the customizing process more efficient.

In this exercise, you will open the Word Options window and explore several of the available pages. There are no practice files for this exercise.

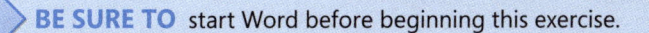

> **BE SURE TO** start Word before beginning this exercise.

Bold

1. On the **Home** tab, in the **Font** group, point to the **Bold** button.

   Word displays a ScreenTip that includes the button name, its keyboard shortcut, and a description of its purpose.

   See Also For information about keyboard shortcuts, see "Creating a Custom Keyboard Shortcut" later in this chapter.

Microsoft Office Button

2. Click the **Microsoft Office Button**, and then at the bottom of the Office menu, click **Word Options**.

   The Word Options window opens, displaying the Popular page.

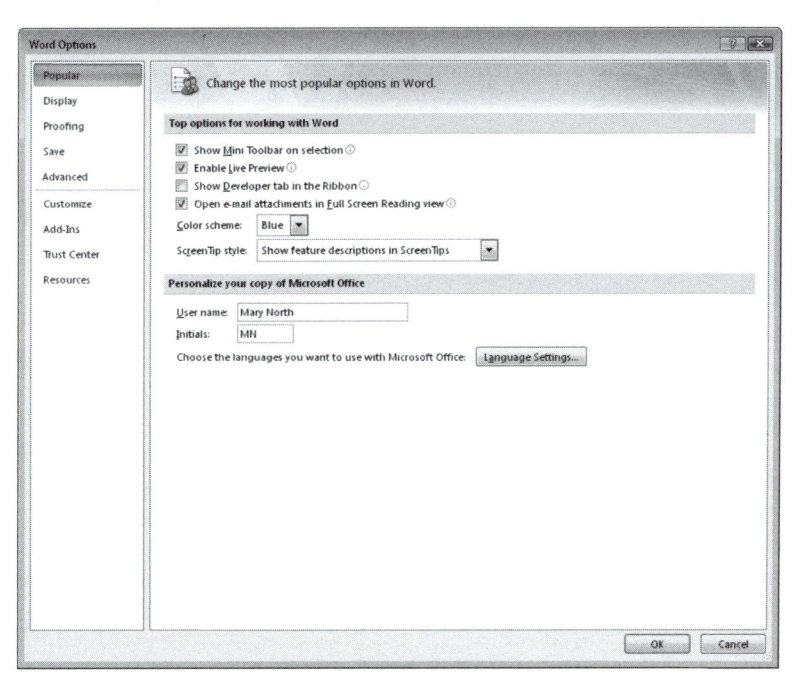

Changing Default Program Options   **331**

3. Under **Top options for working with Word**, click the **Color scheme** arrow, and then in the list, click **Silver**.

> **Tip** If having the Mini toolbar appear when you select text is more of a hindrance than a help, you can disable that feature by clearing the Show Mini Toolbar On Selection check box. Similarly, you could disable the live preview of styles and formatting by clearing the Enable Live Preview check box. If you create documents for international audiences, you can make additional editing languages available by clicking Language Settings, choosing the languages you want to have available, and then clicking OK.

4. Click the **ScreenTip style** arrow, and then in the list, click **Don't show feature descriptions in ScreenTips**.

5. Under **Personalize your copy of Microsoft Office**, verify that the **User Name** and **Initials** are correct, or change them to the way you want them to appear.

6. Click **OK** to close the Word Options window.

   The program window elements are now silver.

7. In the **Font** group, point to the **Bold** button.

   The ScreenTip now includes only the button name and its keyboard shortcut.

8. Display the **Word Options** window, and in the page list in the left pane, click **Display**.

   On this page, you can adjust how documents look on the screen and when printed.

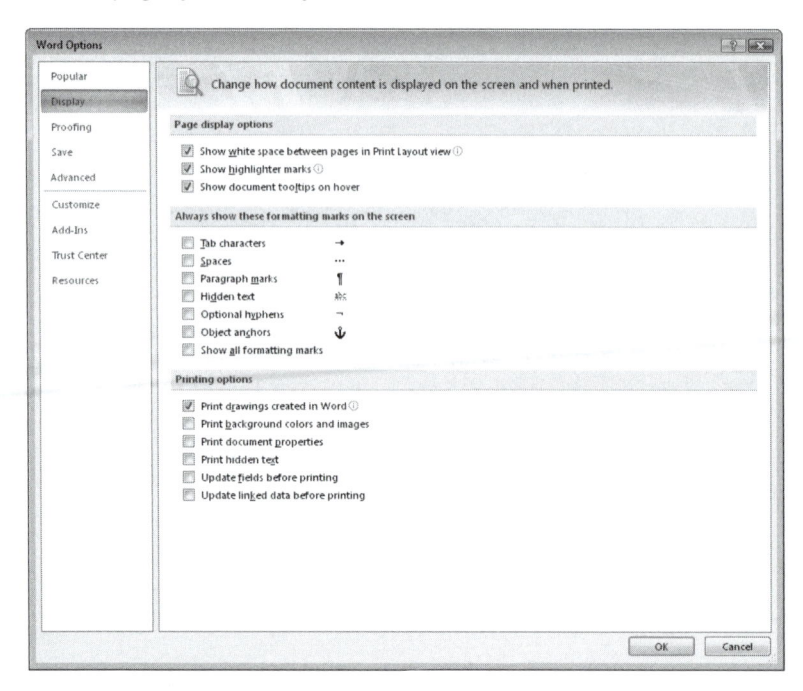

9. In the page list, click **Proofing**.

   This page provides options for adjusting the AutoCorrect settings and for refining the spell-checking process.

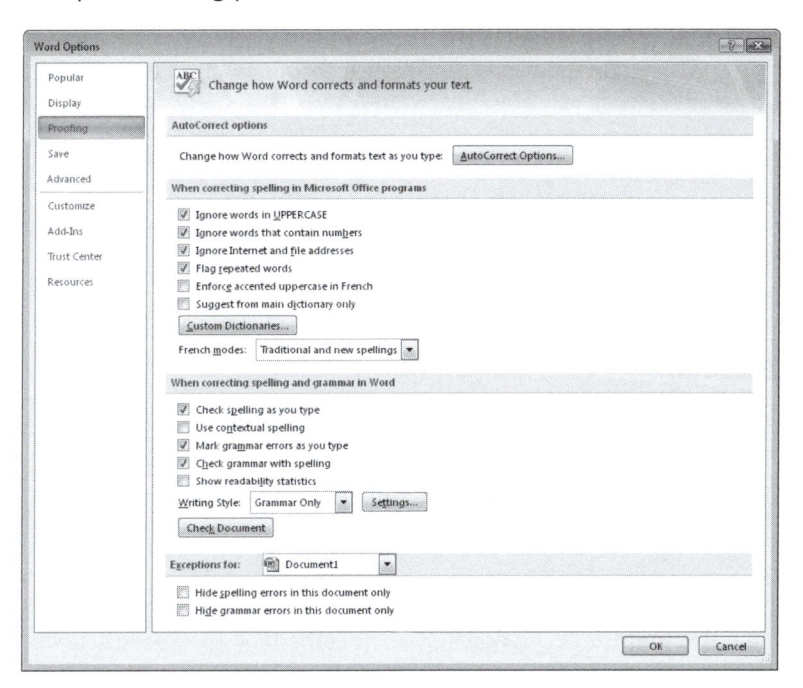

   See Also For information about AutoCorrect and checking spelling, see "Correcting Spelling and Grammatical Errors" in Chapter 2, "Editing and Proofreading Documents."

10. Display the **Save** page.

    On this page, you can change the default document format; the AutoRecover file save rate and location; the default location to which Word saves new files you create; and the default location for files you check out from document management servers (such as Microsoft Office SharePoint Server 2007) and drafts of those files saved while you are working offline. You can also specify whether you want the fonts used within the current document to be embedded in the document, in the event that someone who opens the document doesn't have those fonts on his or her computer.

[Screenshot of Word Options dialog, Save page]

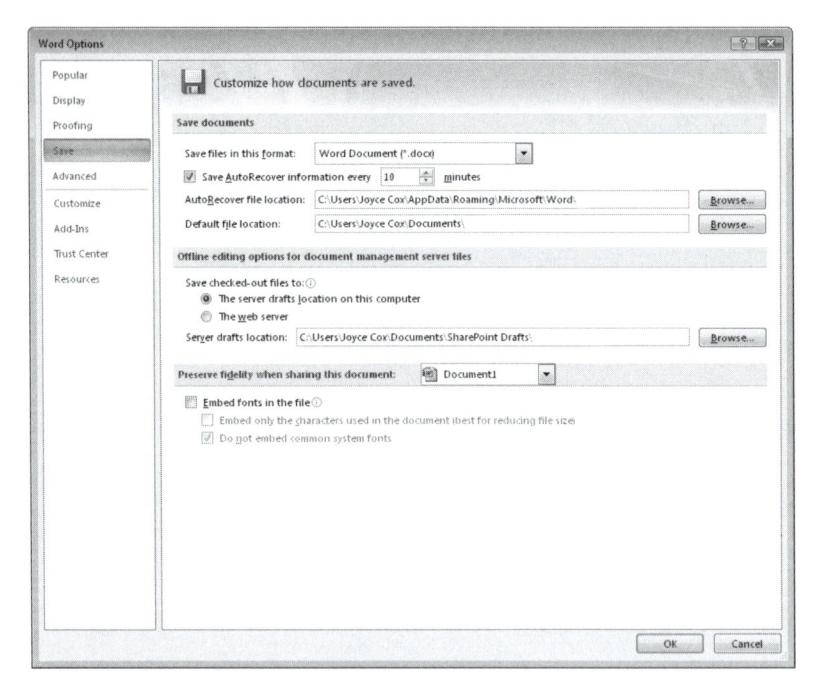

11. Under **Save documents**, click the **Save files in this format** arrow.

   In the list, notice the many formats in which you can save files. One of these is the Word 97-2003 Document format that creates .doc files compatible with earlier versions of Word. If you have upgraded to Word 2007 but your colleagues are still working in an earlier version of the program, you might want to select this option so that they will be able to view and work with any document you create.

   > **Tip** If you want to save just one document in a format that is compatible with earlier versions of the program, you can point to the Save As arrow on the Office menu, and then click Word 97-2003 to display the Save As dialog box with this format already selected as the Save As Type setting.

12. Click away from the list to close it, and then display the **Advanced** page.

   This page includes options related to editing document content; displaying documents on-screen; printing, saving, and sharing documents; and a variety of other options.

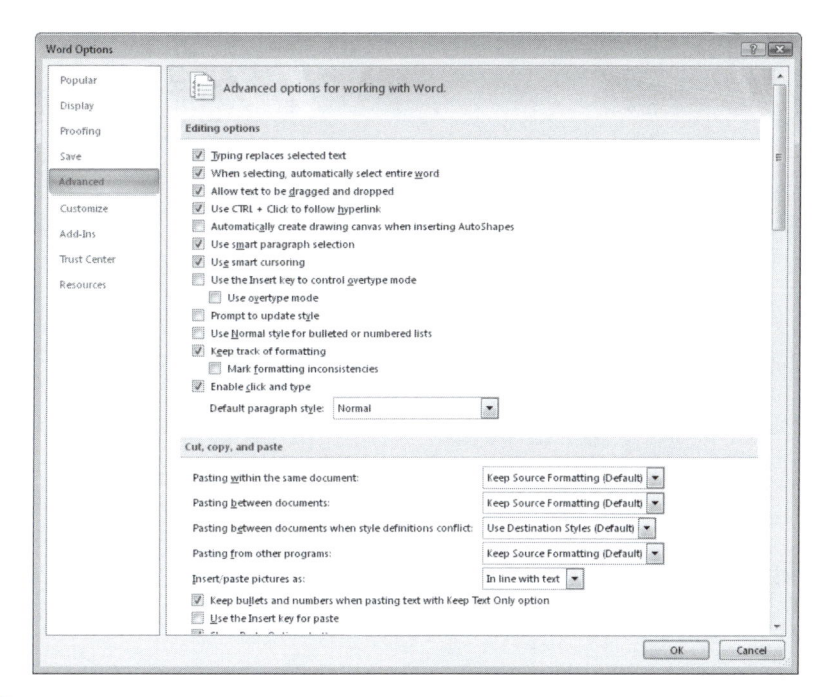

13. Take a few minutes to explore all the options on this page.

    Although these options are labeled advanced, they are the ones you are most likely to want to adjust to fit the way you work. At the bottom of the page are the following buttons:

    - File Locations, which you click to change the default locations of various types of files associated with Word and its documents.
    - Web Options, which you click to adjust settings for converting a document to a Web page.
    - Service Options, which you click to adjust settings related to working with documents stored on SharePoint sites.

    See Also For information about converting a Word document to a Web page, see "Creating and Modifying a Web Document" in Chapter 11, "Creating Documents for Use Outside of Word." For information about storing documents on SharePoint sites, see "Using Document Workspaces" in Chapter 10, "Collaborating with Others."

14. Display the **Trust Center** page.

    This page provides links to information about privacy and security. It also provides links to the Trust Center settings that control the actions Word takes in response to documents that are provided by certain people or companies, that are saved in certain locations, or that contain ActiveX controls or macros.

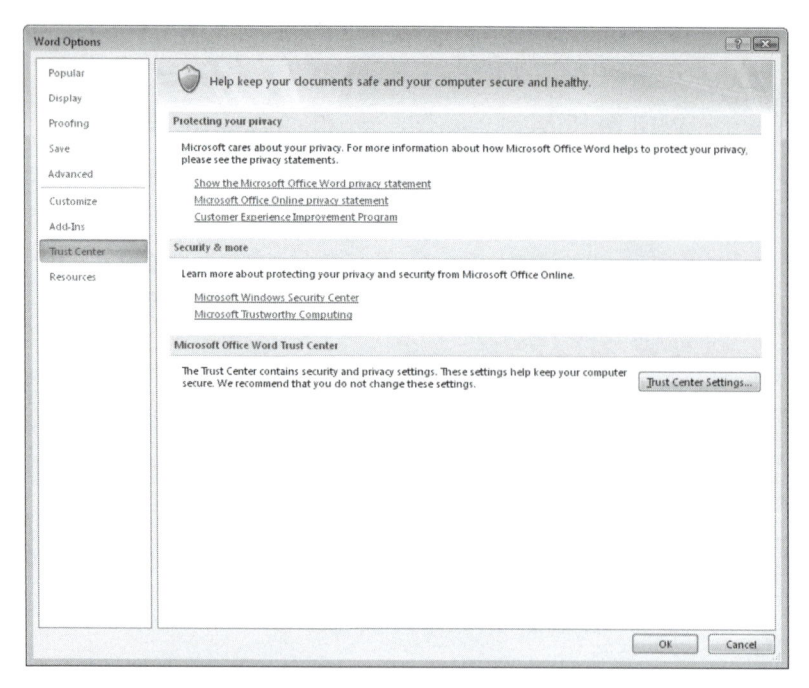

15. Under **Microsoft Office Word Trust Center**, click **Trust Center Settings**, and then in the page list in the left pane of the **Trust Center** window, click **Trusted Locations**.

   On this page, you can specify the locations from which Word will not block content.

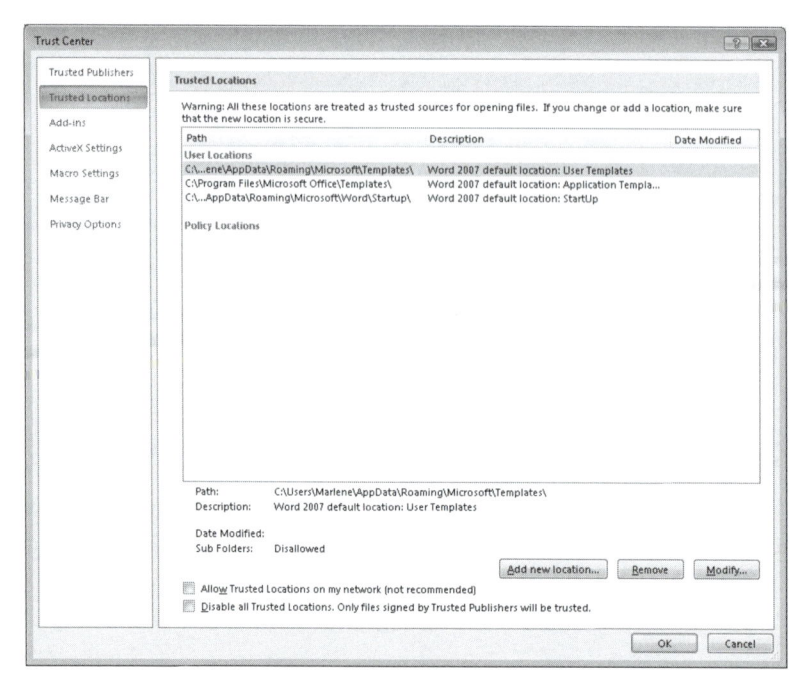

16. Explore the other pages of the Trust Center window, and then click **Cancel** to return to the Word Options window.

17. In the **Word Options** window, display the **Resources** page.

    On this page are links for activating, updating, and maintaining your Office programs. Most of these links require that you have Internet access.

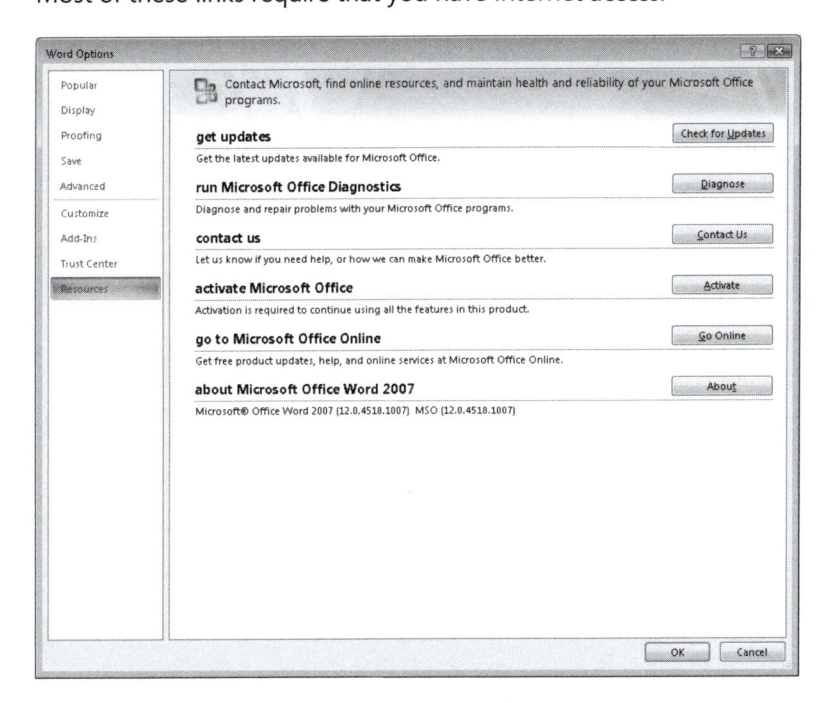

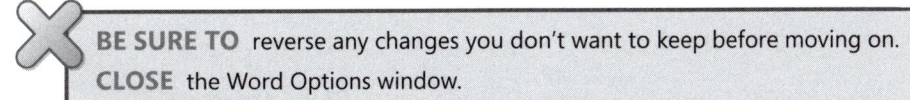

> **BE SURE TO** reverse any changes you don't want to keep before moving on.
>
> **CLOSE** the Word Options window.

See Also For information about using the settings available on the Customize page, see the topics that follow. For information about working with add-ins, see the sidebar "Using Add-Ins" in Chapter 11, "Creating Documents for Use Outside of Word."

Making Favorite Word Commands Easily Accessible

If Word 2007 is the first version of the program you have ever worked with, you will by now have become accustomed to working with commands represented as buttons on the Ribbon. However, if you have upgraded from an earlier version, you might have identified a few commands that no longer seem to be available.

> **Tip** You can find out where a favorite Word 2003 command appears on the Office menu or Ribbon by searching Word Help for *2003 commands*, and then displaying the *Reference: Locations Of Word 2003 Commands In Word 2007* topic. Scroll to the bottom of the topic and click the Word Ribbon Mapping Workbook link under New Locations Of Familiar Commands.
>
> You can find a list of all the commands that do not appear on the Ribbon but are still available in Word by displaying the Customize page of the Word Options window and then clicking Commands Not In The Ribbon in the Choose Commands From list.

For the 2007 Microsoft Office release, Microsoft conducted extensive research to find out how people actually use the programs in the Office suite. As a result, a few Word features that seemed superfluous have been abandoned, and a few others that were used very rarely have been pushed off to one side. If you sorely miss one of these sidelined features, you can make it a part of your Word environment by adding it to the Quick Access Toolbar.

You might also want to customize the Quick Access Toolbar if you regularly use buttons that are scattered on various tabs of the Ribbon and don't want to switch between tabs to access the buttons. If you use only a few buttons, you can add them to the Quick Access Toolbar and then hide the Ribbon by double-clicking the active tab—the Quick Access Toolbar and tab names remain visible. (You can temporarily redisplay the Ribbon by clicking the tab you want to view, or permanently redisplay it by double-clicking any tab.)

> **Tip** As you add buttons to the Quick Access Toolbar, it expands to accommodate them. If you add many buttons, it might become difficult to view the text in the title bar, or all the buttons might not be visible. To resolve this problem, you can move the Quick Access Toolbar below the Ribbon by clicking the Customize Quick Access Toolbar button and then clicking Show Below The Ribbon.

In this exercise, you will add a button to the Word 2007 Quick Access Toolbar.

> **USE** the *Commands* document. This practice file is located in the *Documents\Microsoft Press\Word2007SBS\CustomizingWord* folder.
>
> **OPEN** the *Commands* document.

Customize Quick Access Toolbar

1. At the right end of the **Quick Access Toolbar**, click the **Customize Quick Access Toolbar** button.

   By default, the Save, Undo, and Repeat buttons appear on the Quick Access Toolbar.

You can add a button to the toolbar for any of the common commands that appear in the Customize Quick Access Toolbar list by clicking the command in the list.

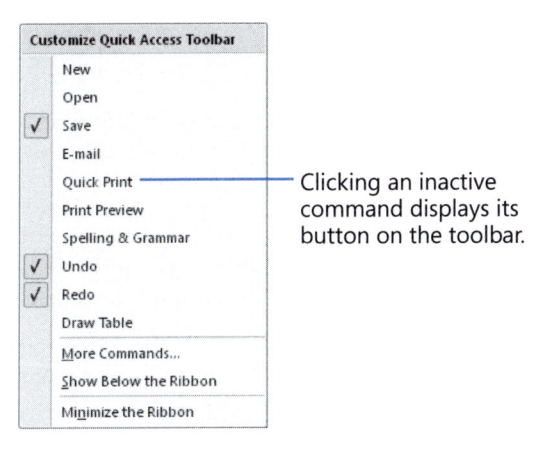

Clicking an inactive command displays its button on the toolbar.

2. In the **Customize Quick Access Toolbar** list, click **More Commands**.

   The Word Options window opens, displaying the Customize page.

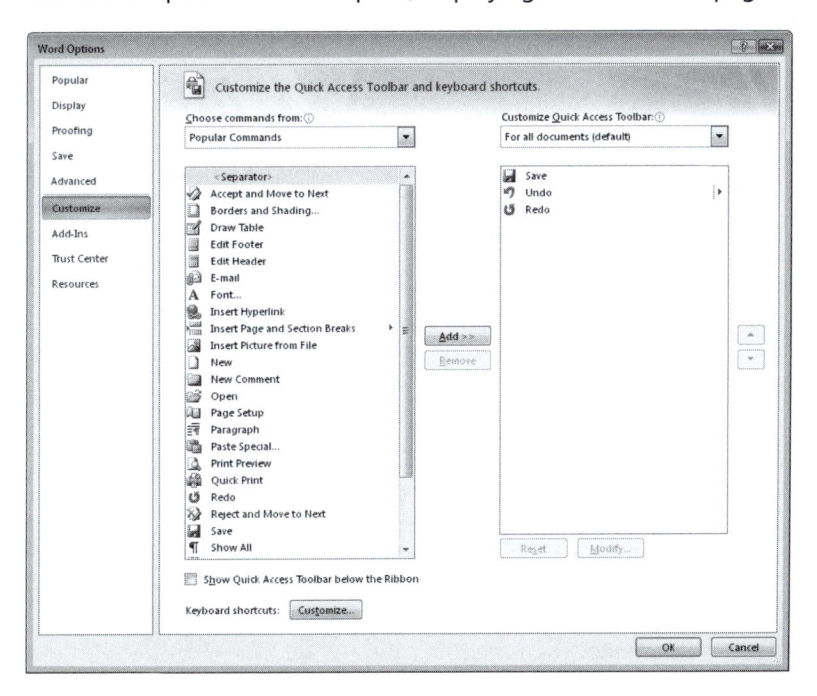

You can add a less common command to the Quick Access Toolbar by selecting it in the list of available commands on the left side of the page, and then clicking Add (or double-clicking the command) to copy it to the list of toolbar commands on the right side of the page.

3. Click the **Choose commands from** arrow, and then in the list, click **Commands Not in the Ribbon**.

   The available commands list changes to include only the commands that are available in Word 2007 but do not appear on any tab of the Ribbon.

4. In the available commands list, click **AutoText**, and then click **Add** to add the command to the global Quick Access Toolbar.

   The arrow to the right of the command indicates that clicking the AutoText button will display a list of options. In this case, clicking the AutoText button will display a gallery from which you can insert a saved text item in a document.

5. At the top of the available commands list, click **<Separator>**, and then click **Add**.

   The separator—a horizontal line indicating the beginning or end of a group of commands—appears at the bottom of the toolbar commands list.

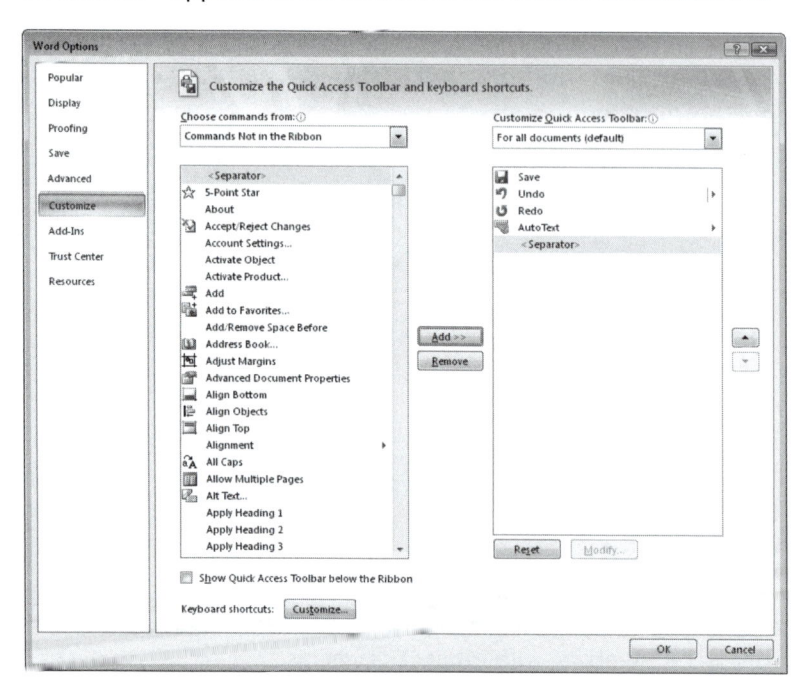

6. In the toolbar commands list, click **<Separator>**, and then click the **Move Up** button.

   Move Up

   The separator moves up one position to separate the three default commands from the AutoText command. Buttons appear from left to right on the Quick Access Toolbar in the same order that they appear from top to bottom in the toolbar commands list.

7. In the **Word Options** window, click **OK**.

   The Quick Access Toolbar expands to accommodate the separator bar and button you added.

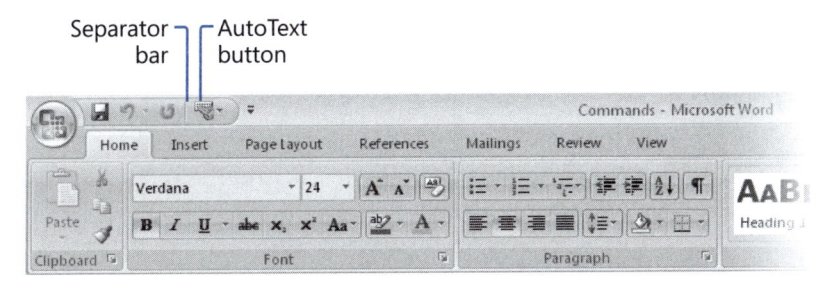

   Separator bar — AutoText button

8. On the first page of the document, position the insertion point to the right of *For general deliveries* and to the left of the colon, press `Space`, and then type **to Consolidated Messenger**.

   AutoText

9. Select the words **Consolidated Messenger**, and on the **Quick Access Toolbar**, click the **AutoText** button.

10. In the **AutoText** gallery, click **Save Selection to AutoText Gallery**.

    The Create New Building Block dialog box opens.

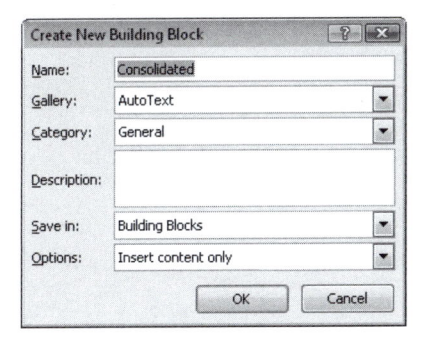

    See Also For information about building blocks, see "Inserting Saved Text" in Chapter 2, "Editing and Proofreading Documents," and "Inserting Ready-Made Document Parts" in Chapter 8, "Working with Longer Documents."

11. Type **cm** in the **Name** box, and then click **OK**.

12. Position the insertion point at the left end of the *Phone numbers* paragraph, press `Enter`, press the `↑` key, type **Urgent deliveries should be taken directly to the** and then press `Space`.

13. On the **Quick Access Toolbar**, click the **AutoText** button.

    The AutoText gallery now includes the *Consolidated Messenger* entry you just added.

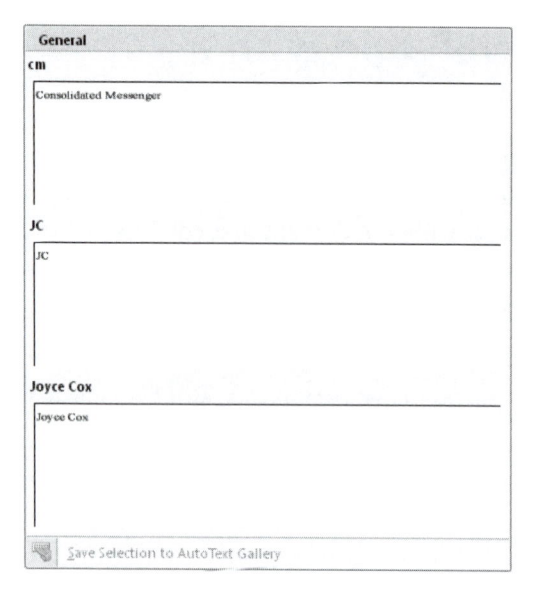

14. In the **AutoText** gallery, click **cm** to insert the saved text in the document.

> **Tip** You can also replace an AutoText name with its corresponding entry by typing the name and then pressing the F3 key.

15. Press [Space], and then type employee to whom they are addressed.
16. At the right end of the **Quick Access Toolbar**, click the **Customize Quick Access Toolbar** button, and then in the list, click **More Commands**.
17. In the **Word Options** window, click **Reset**. Then in the message box asking you to confirm that you want to restore the Quick Access Toolbar to its default command set, click **Yes**.
18. Close the **Word Options** window.

    The AutoText button and separator no longer appear on the Quick Access Toolbar.

CLOSE the *Commands* document without saving your changes.

> **Important** When you exit Word, you will be asked whether you want to save the Building Blocks template, which is where AutoText entries are saved. To discard the AutoText entry you created in this exercise, click No.

Making Commands Available with a Specific Document

In addition to customizing the global Quick Access Toolbar to make a set of buttons available for all documents, you can customize the Quick Access Toolbar for a specific document. For example, to work with a document that contains a complex table-based layout, you might want to increase your efficiency by providing one-click access to commands that allow you to turn the rulers and gridlines on or off without switching to the View tab.

See Also For information about table-based layouts, see "Using a Table to Control Page Layout" in Chapter 5, "Presenting Information in Columns and Tables."

In this exercise, you will add a button to a document-specific Quick Access Toolbar. Then after testing the button, you will remove it from the toolbar.

> **USE** the *Toolbar1* and *Toolbar2* documents. These practice files are located in the *Documents\Microsoft Press\Word2007SBS\CustomizingWord* folder.
> **OPEN** the *Toolbar1* document.

Customize Quick Access Toolbar

1. At the right end of the **Quick Access Toolbar**, click the **Customize Quick Access Toolbar** button, and then in the list, click **More Commands**.

   The Word Options window opens, displaying the Customize page. A list of available commands appears on the left side of the page, and a list of the commands available from the global Quick Access Toolbar appears on the right.

2. Click the **Customize Quick Access Toolbar** arrow, and then in the list, click **For Toolbar1**.

   > **Troubleshooting** If the current document is read-only, the only option available in the list is For All Documents (Default). You cannot customize the Quick Access Toolbar for a read-only document.

   The toolbar command list is now empty, ready for you to specify which commands should appear on this document-specific toolbar.

3. Click the **Choose commands from** arrow, and then in the list, click **Review Tab**.

   The available commands list now contains all the commands that are available from the Review tab on the Ribbon, including several that are related to adding, editing, and deleting comments.

4. In the available commands list, click the second **Comments** command (the one with the arrow button to its right). Then click **Add**.

   The Comments command appears in the toolbar commands list. The arrow button to the right of the command indicates that clicking this button on the Quick Access Toolbar will display a menu of options.

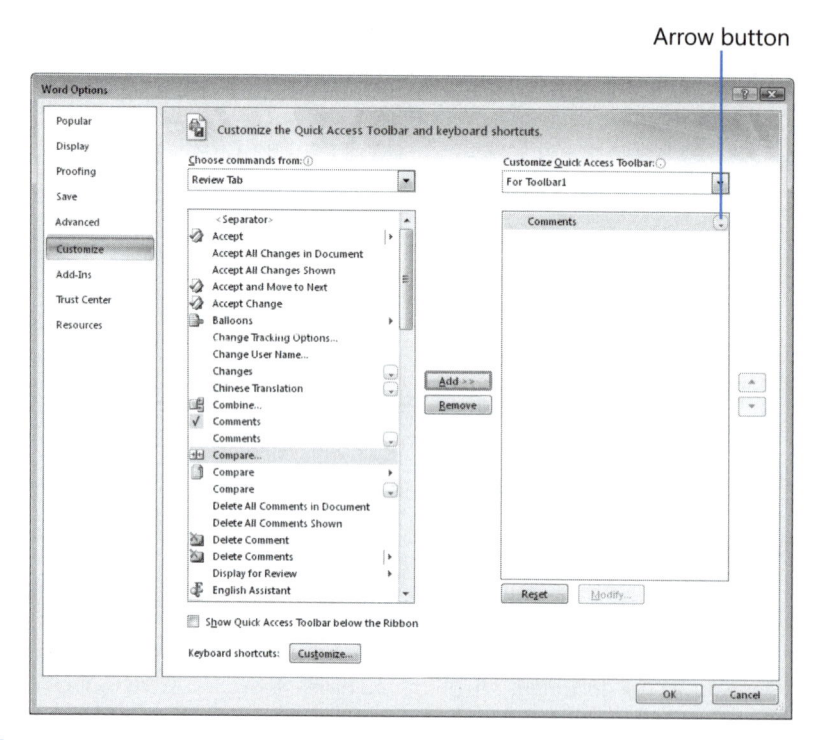

   Arrow button

5. Click **OK**.

   The Quick Access Toolbar now includes the Save, Undo, and Repeat buttons from the default toolbar and the Comments button from the custom toolbar. The custom toolbar appears within a separate box on the Quick Access Toolbar.

6. Open the *Toolbar2* document from the *CustomizingWord* folder, notice that the custom toolbar is not available for this document, and then close it.

7. Scroll the *Toolbar1* document, and at the end of the paragraph below the numbered list, select **thirsting for more**.

8. On the **Quick Access Toolbar**, click the **Comments** button.

   Although no arrow appears next to the button, a group of comment options appears.

Comments

Comments group

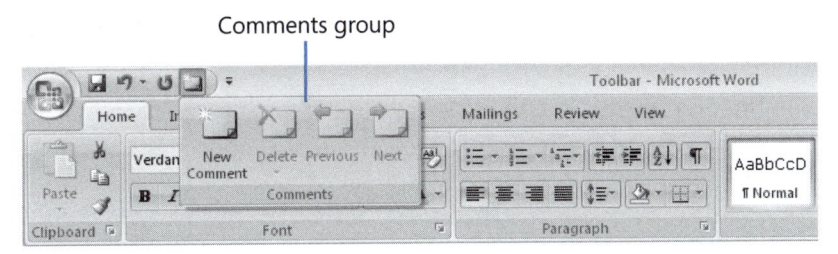

9. In the **Comments** group, click **New Comment**, and in the comment balloon, type *Paolini now says he is "finally making good headway" on the third book*. Then click anywhere in the text of the document (not the balloon).

10. Click the **Customize Quick Access Toolbar** button, and then click **More Commands**.

11. On the **Customize** page of the Word Options window, click **For Toolbar1** in the **Customize Quick Access Toolbar** list to display the list of buttons on the custom toolbar. Then click **Reset**.

12. In the **Reset Customizations** message box, click **Yes** to return the document-specific toolbar to its default contents (empty). Then click **OK**.

    Now only the buttons assigned to the default Quick Access Toolbar are visible.

CLOSE the *Toolbar1* document without saving your changes.

Tip If you send a document for which you have created a custom toolbar to someone else, or if you make the document available for collaborative development in a document workspace, the custom toolbar is available to anyone who opens the document in Word 2007.

Creating a Custom Keyboard Shortcut

Another way to access commands quickly is to use *keyboard shortcuts*—combinations of two or more keys that invoke a command. Keyboard shortcuts are particularly efficient if your hands are already on the keyboard typing document text. Word has a large variety of built-in keyboard shortcuts. For example, to format text as bold, you can simply select it and then press Ctrl+B.

If a command you use frequently doesn't have a built-in keyboard shortcut, you can create one from the Customize page of the Word Options window. Clicking Customize

at the bottom of this page opens the Customize Keyboard dialog box, where you can choose the categories and commands you want and assign keyboard shortcuts.

In this exercise, you will assign keyboard shortcuts to two commands, and then test the keyboard shortcuts. There are no practice files for this exercise.

> **OPEN** a new blank document.

Customize Quick Access Toolbar

1. At the right end of the **Quick Access Toolbar**, click the **Customize Quick Access Toolbar** button, and then in the list, click **More Commands**.

   The Word Options window opens, displaying the Customize page.

2. At the bottom of the window, to the right of **Keyboard shortcuts**, click **Customize**.

   The Customize Keyboard dialog box opens. The Ribbon tabs are listed in the Categories box on the left, and the commands available for the selected category are listed in the Commands box on the right.

3. In the **Categories** list, click **Home Tab**, and then in the **Commands** list, click **Bold**.

   In the Current Keys box, Word displays the keyboard shortcuts already assigned to the Bold command.

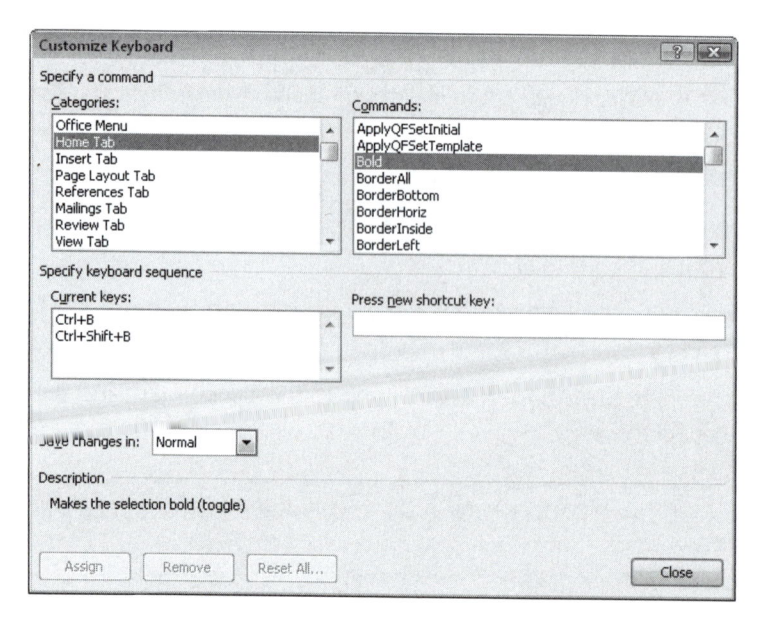

> **Tip** To delete an existing keyboard shortcut to make it available for reassignment, select it in the Current Keys box, and then click Remove.

4. In the **Commands** list, click **DecreaseIndent**.
5. Click to position the insertion point in the **Press new shortcut key** box, and then press `Ctrl`+`D`.

    Under the Current Keys box, Word tells you that this keyboard shortcut is already assigned to the FormatFont command.

6. Press the `Backspace` key (not `Del`) to clear the **Press new shortcut key** box, and then press `Alt`+`D`.

    Under the Current Keys box, Word tells you that this keyboard shortcut is currently unassigned (unless you have already assigned it to a different command).

7. Click **Assign**.
8. Repeat steps 4, 5, and 7 to assign the keyboard combination `Alt`+`I` to the **IncreaseIndent** command.
9. Close the **Customize Keyboard** dialog box and the **Word Options** window.

> **Tip** Using the options in the Save Changes In list, you can save new keyboard shortcuts either in a template to make them available to all documents using that template, or in a specific document to make them available only within that document.

Now let's test the new keyboard shortcut.

10. On the **View** tab, in the **Show/Hide** group, select the **Ruler** check box to display the horizontal and vertical rulers.
11. Press `Alt`+`I` twice to indent the paragraph, and then press `Alt`+`D` once to decrease the indent.

    On the ruler, the indent markers jump to the 1-inch mark and then jump back to the 0.5-inch mark.

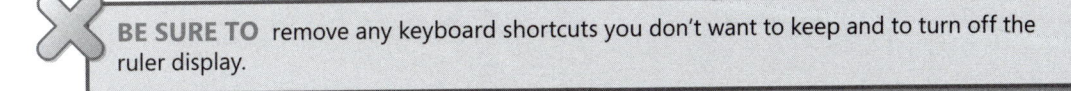

BE SURE TO remove any keyboard shortcuts you don't want to keep and to turn off the ruler display.

> **Tracking Down Built-In Keyboard Shortcuts**
>
> The list of built-in Word keyboard shortcuts is extensive and too long to reproduce here. To print a list of these shortcuts:
>
> 1. At the right end of the Ribbon, click the **Help** button.
> 2. In the **Search** box, type keyboard shortcuts, and then click **Search**.
> 3. In the results list, click **Keyboard shortcuts for Microsoft Office Word**.
> 4. Click the **Show All** link at the beginning of the topic to display all the text, and then on the toolbar, click the **Print** button.

Key Points

- The Word environment is flexible and can be customized to meet your needs.
- Most of the environment settings are gathered on the pages of the Word Options window.
- You can provide one-click access to any Word 2007 command by adding a button for it to the Quick Access Toolbar, either for all documents or for one document.
- When the major work in a document involves typing, you can increase efficiency by using keyboard shortcuts, because you don't have to take your hands off the keyboard to use your mouse.
- It's worth taking the time to memorize common built-in keyboard shortcuts and to create custom shortcuts for favorite commands that don't already have them.

Glossary

add-in A utility that adds specialized functionality to a program.

attribute Individual items of character formatting, such as style or color, which determine how text looks.

balloon A box containing a comment, deletion, or formatting change that appears to the right of a document when Track Changes is turned on.

bar chart A chart in which data is plotted in rows to illustrate comparisons among individual items.

blog A personal Web site.

bookmark A location in a document that marks text so that it can be found quickly.

building blocks Frequently used text saved in a gallery, from which it can be inserted quickly into a document.

bullet A small graphic to the left of each item in a bulleted list.

caption A description of a graphic or figure.

cell A box at the intersection of a column and row in a table or worksheet.

cell address The location of a cell, expressed as its column letter and row number, as in A1.

character formatting The collection of attributes applied to text.

character spacing The space between characters, which can be expanded or contracted so that characters are pushed apart or pulled together.

character style A variation of a font, such as bold or italic.

chart A visual representation of numeric data.

chart area The entire area occupied by a chart, including the legend and any titles.

chevron The « or » characters that surround each merge field in a main document; also known as *guillemet* characters.

Click and Type A feature that allows you to double-click a blank area of a document to position the insertion point in that location, with the appropriate paragraph alignment already in place.

Clipboard A storage area shared by all Office programs where cut or copied items are stored.

column In a chart, a vertical representation of plotted data from a table or worksheet. In page layout, the area between margins where text is allowed to flow. (Pages can have a single column or multiple columns.)

column break A break inserted in the text of a column to force the text below it to move to the next column.

column chart A chart in which data is plotted in columns to illustrate comparisons among individual items or changes over time.

column headings The gray boxes at the top of the columns in a worksheet. See also *row headings*.

comment A note inserted in a document and displayed either in a balloon or the reviewing pane.

cross-reference entry An entry in an index that refers readers to a related entry.

cycle diagram A type of diagram used to represent a circular sequence of steps, tasks, or events; or the relationship of a set of steps, tasks, or events to a central, core element.

data marker A graphic representation of a plotted value, such as a bar or column.

data point A plotted value in a table or worksheet.

349

data series A set of related data points in a table or worksheet.

data source A file that provides the variable information used in the mail-merge process.

demote In an outline, the process of changing a heading to a lower-level heading or body text.

desktop publishing A process that creates pages by combining text and objects such as tables and graphics in a visually appealing way.

destination file A file into which you insert an object created in another program.

diagram A visual representation of information, such as a process or a relationship.

dialog box launcher A button located in the lower-right corner of selected command groups, labeled with an arrow, that displays a related dialog box or task pane containing options for refining a command.

digital signature A security mechanism used on the Internet that relies on two keys, one public and one private, that are used to encrypt messages before transmission and to decrypt them on receipt.

Document Map A pane that displays a linked outline of a document's headings and allows you to jump to a heading in the document by clicking it in the Document Map.

document window The window that provides a workspace for an open document.

document workspace A space on a SharePoint site, created to facilitate the collaborative development of a single document.

Draft view A view that displays the content of a document with a simplified layout.

drag-and-drop editing A way of moving or copying selected text by dragging it with the mouse pointer.

dragging A way of moving objects by pointing to them, holding down the mouse button, moving the mouse pointer to the desired location, and releasing the button.

drawing canvas A graphical object on which you can draw shapes and objects to create a compound graphic, which moves and changes size with the canvas.

drawing object An object created with Word, such as a shape, a diagram, or WordArt text.

drop cap An enlarged, decorative capital letter that appears at the beginning of a paragraph.

embedded object An object that is created in a different program but that is incorporated into a Word document.

endnote A note that appears at the end of a section or the document to add tangential information to a discussion or report. See also *footnote*.

Extensible Markup Language (XML) A system for coding the structure of text documents and other forms of data so that they can be used in a variety of environments.

field A placeholder that tells Word to supply the specified information in the specified way. Also, the set of information of a specific type in a data source, such as all the last names in a contacts list.

field name A first-row cell in a data source that identifies data in the column below.

file A named set of information, such as a program or data created with that program.

file format The system used to code a file so that the program that created it, or other programs, can open and work with it.

filter To extract records from a data source, excluding records that don't match the filtering criteria.

flow The way text continues from the bottom of one column to the top of the next column.

font A complete set of characters that all have the same design.

font color One of a range of colors that can be applied to text.

font effect An attribute, such as superscript, small capital letters, or shadow, that can be applied to a font.

font size The size of the characters in a font, in points.

font style An attribute that changes the look of text. The most common font styles are regular (or plain), italic, bold, and bold italic.

footer A region at the bottom of a page whose text can be applied to all or some of the pages in a document.

footnote A note or citation that appears at the bottom of a page to explain, comment on, or provide references for text in a document. See also *endnote*.

formula A mathematical equation that performs a calculation, such as addition.

Full Screen Reading view A view that displays as much of the content of the document as will fit in the screen at a size that is comfortable for reading.

gallery A grouping of thumbnails that display options visually.

graphic Any piece of art used to illustrate or convey information or to add visual interest to a document.

gridlines Lines that visually clarify the information in a chart.

group A category of buttons on a tab.

grouping Assembling several objects, such as graphics, into a single unit so they act as one object and can easily be moved and sized.

guillemet characters The « and » characters that surround each merge field in a main document; also known as *chevrons*.

header A region at the top of a page whose text can be repeated on all or some of the pages in a document.

hierarchy diagram A diagram that illustrates the structure of an organization or entity.

hover To pause the pointer over an object, such as a menu name or button, for a second or two to display more information, such as a submenu or ScreenTip.

Hypertext Markup Language (HTML) A tagging system used to code documents so that they can be viewed as pages in a Web browser.

indent marker A marker on the horizontal ruler that controls the indentation of text from the left or right side of a document.

index An alphabetical list of concepts and terms and the page numbers where they are found.

index entry An entry in the body of a document that tags terms to be included in Word's automated construction of an index.

index entry field The XE field, including the braces ({}), that defines an index entry.

justify To make all lines of text in a paragraph or column fit the width of the document or column, with even margins on each side.

keyboard shortcut A combination of two or more keys that perform an action when pressed together.

landscape The orientation of a horizontal page whose width is larger that its height.

legend A key that identifies the series in a chart.

line break A manual break that forces the text that follows it to the next line. Also called a *text wrapping break*.

line graph A graph in which lines are used to show changes in values over time.

linked object An object that exists in a source file and that is inserted in a document with a link to that source file.

list diagram A diagram in which lists of related or independent information are visually represented.

live preview A feature of a thumbnail that displays what an option will look like if applied to a document.

mail merge A process used to personalize individual documents based on information in a data source.

main document The mail merge document that contains the information that doesn't change.

manual page break A page break inserted to force subsequent information to appear on the next page.

margin Blank space around the column in which text can flow on the page.

matrix diagram A diagram used to show the relationship of components to a whole.

merge field Fields in a main document that tell Word where to insert corresponding information from a data source.

Microsoft Clip Organizer A tool that lets you arrange clip art images, pictures, sounds, and movie clips into collections.

Microsoft Office Button A button located at the left end of the Ribbon, labeled with the Office logo, that provides access to a menu of commands for managing Word and Word documents as a whole (rather than document content).

Microsoft Office Word Help button A button located at the right end of the Ribbon, labeled with a question mark (?), that provides access to the Word Help system.

nested table A table that is positioned inside another table.

note separator A line that separates footnotes or endnotes from regular text.

object An item, such as a graphic, video clip, sound file, or worksheet, that can be inserted in a Word document and then selected and modified.

Office menu A menu that contains commands related to managing documents (such as creating, saving, and printing). This menu takes the place of the File menu that appeared in previous versions of Word.

orientation The direction—horizontal or vertical—in which a page is laid out.

orphan At the bottom of a page, a single line of a paragraph that continues on the next page.

Outline view A view that shows headings and body text and can be used to evaluate and reorganize the structure of a document.

paragraph In word processing, a block of text of any length that ends when you press the Enter key.

paragraph formatting Collectively, the settings used to vary the look of paragraphs.

paragraph style A set of formatting that can be applied to the paragraph containing the insertion point by selecting the style from a list.

parent folder The folder in which another folder is contained.

permissions Authorization that allows access to designated documents or programs.

picture A scanned photograph, clip art, or another type of image created with a program other than Word.

pie chart A chart used to show how parts relate to the whole.

plot area The area bordered by the category (x) and value (y) axes in a chart.

point The unit of measure for expressing the size of characters in a font, where 72 points equals 1 inch.

portrait The orientation of a vertical page whose width is smaller that its height.

post Content published to a blog.

Print Layout view A view that shows how a document will look when printed.

process diagram A diagram used to visually represent the ordered set of steps required to complete a task.

promote In an outline, to change body text to a heading, or to change a heading to a higher-level heading.

pyramid diagram A diagram used to illustrate proportional or interconnected relationships.

query Selection criteria for extracting information from a data source for use in the mail merge process.

Quick Access Toolbar A toolbar that displays the Save, Undo, and Repeat buttons by default, but can be customized to show other commands.

quick table A table with sample data that you can customize.

read-only Available for viewing but protected from alterations.

record A set of fields of information about a single item in a data source, often structured in a row.

reference mark An indicator in the text of a document that further information is available in a corresponding footnote or endnote.

relationship diagram A diagram used to show convergent, divergent, overlapping, merging, or containment elements.

revision marks Underlines, strike-through marks, and colored text that distinguishes revised text from original text.

revisions Changes in a document that are marked with revision marks when Word's Track Changes feature is turned on.

Ribbon An area across the top of the screen that makes almost all the capabilities of Word available in a single area.

row headings The gray boxes at the left end of the rows in a worksheet. See also *column headings*.

ScreenTip Information displayed in a small window when you rest the pointer over a button or window element.

section break A break inserted so that subsequent information can have different page formatting (such as different orientation) than preceding information.

select To highlight an item in preparation for making some change to it.

selection area An area in a document's left margin in which you can click and drag to select blocks of text.

sizing handle Small circles, squares, or sets of dots that appear at the corners and sides of a selected object. These handles can be dragged to change the shape of an object.

smart tag A flag that identifies information of a certain type, such as an address. Click the button associated with the tag to quickly perform common tasks related to that type of information.

SmartArt graphic A predefined set of formatting for creating and formatting a diagram.

soft page break A page break that Word inserts when the text reaches the bottom margin of a page.

source file A file containing an object that is inserted in a destination file.

stacked graphics Graphics that overlap each other.

Standard Generalized Markup Language (SGML) A system for coding the structure of text and other data so that it can be used in a variety of environments.

status bar An area across the bottom of the program window that gives information about the current document.

Styles A gallery of text formatting that can be applied quickly to paragraphs and characters.

subentry In an index, a subordinate entry.

tab An area on the Ribbon that contains buttons organized in groups.

tab leader A repeating character (usually a dot or dash) that separates text before the tab from text or a number after it.

tab stop A location in the text column where text will align after you press the Tab key to insert a tab character.

table of authorities A table used in legal papers and other types of official documents that lists statutes, citations, case numbers, and similar information.

table of contents A sequential list of the headings in a document and the page numbers where they are found.

table of figures A list of graphics, pictures, or figures and their corresponding captions.

tabular list A list that arranges text in simple columns separated by left, right, centered, or decimal tab stops.

tag A command inserted in a document that specifies how the document, or a portion of the document, should be formatted.

template A predefined set of text, formatting, and graphics, stored in a special type of document that can be used as the basis for other documents.

text wrapping break A manual break that forces the text that follows it to the next line. Also called a *line break*.

theme A predefined set of font and color specifications that can be applied to any document.

Thesaurus A tool that supplies synonyms for a selected word.

thumbnail A picture representation of choices available in a gallery; or of pages in a document.

tick-mark label The labels along each axis in a chart, identifying the data.

title bar An area at the top of the program window that displays the name of the active document.

transform A command that extracts specified information from an XML file.

View toolbar A toolbar on the right end of the status bar that contains tools for adjusting the view of document content.

watermark Faint text or a graphic that appears in the background of all the pages of a document.

Web Layout view A view that shows how a document will look when viewed in a Web browser.

Web page An HTML document that can be viewed in a Web browser.

widow At the top of a page, a single line of a paragraph that continues from the previous page.

wildcard characters When using the Find and Replace dialog box, characters that serve as placeholders for a single character, such as *?ffect* for *affect* and *effect*, or for multiple characters.

word processing The writing, editing, and formatting of documents in a word processor.

word wrap The automatic breaking of a line of text when it reaches the page margin.

WordArt A gallery of text styles that you can use to create text with special effects.

x-axis Also called a *category axis*, the vertical aspect of a chart, representing the categories of the data.

XML schema A description of a document's structure.

y-axis Also called a *value axis*, the horizontal aspect of a chart, showing the values of the data.

z-axis Also called a *series axis*, the depth aspect of a 3-D chart, showing a series of data.

Index

Numbers
3-D Effects button, 169
3-D Effects gallery, 169

A
absolutely positioning graphics, 176
Accept button, 287
accepting tracked changes, lix, lx, 284, 287
Actual Page button (Tablet PC), 291
add-ins
    defined, 309, 349
    deleting, 309
    downloading, 309
    installed, viewing, 309
    installing, 309
    Save As PDF Or XPS, 308
    unloading, 309
Add Clips To Organizer dialog box, 164
adding. See inserting
address blocks
    in form letters, 264
    in labels, 275
Add Shape arrow, 194
Adobe Reader, 307
Advanced Layout dialog box, 177, 191
Align Center button, 134
Align Center Right button, 135
aligning
    decimal points, 82
    diagrams, 192
    to left and right margins (see justifying text)
    paragraphs, xlv
    table text, 138
Align Left button, 77
Align Right button, 77
anchors, 217, 238, 349
    deleting, 241
    displaying, 240
    inserting, lv, 238, 239
    jumping to, 240
    predefined, 240
Arrange All button, 213

Arrange Windows dialog box, 213
Attach button, 281
Attach Template dialog box, 112
attachments, e-mail, lix, 280
attributes, 349
authenticating documents. See digital signatures
AutoCorrect
    adding items to, 54
    defined, 54
    deleting items from, 56
    demonstration of, 55
    rejecting changes made by, 54
    settings, changing, 332
AutoCorrect dialog box, 55, 93
AutoFormat, 93
automatic hyphenation, turning on, 127
automatic save, 27
automatically correcting spelling. See AutoCorrect
AutoRecover, 27, 332
AutoText, 221. See also building blocks
AutoText button, 340
AutoText gallery, 340
axes, chart, 206, 354

B
background graphics
    adding, xlvi, 97
    adding, as graphics, 100
    adding, as text, 99
    color, adding, 99
    defined, 96, 354
    graphics as, xlvii, 100
backgrounds, 96
    color, changing, xlvi, 97
    fill effects, xlvi, 97
    textures, adding, 97
backwards compatibility, 60
balloons
    comments in (see comments)
    defined, 349
    tracked changes, displaying in, lix
Balloons button, 286
bar charts, 205, 349. See also charts

355

bar tabs, 128
Basic Math gallery, 182
bibliographies. See also sources
  APA style, conforming with, 253
  creating, lvi, 248
  formatting, 249
  inserting, 252
  sources, adding to Source Manager, lvi
  updating, 248
Bibliography gallery, 248
binomial theorem, inserting, 180
blank documents, opening, xl
blank pages, inserting, 225
blocks, selecting, xli
Blogger service, 315
blog posts, 314
  creating, 316
  defined, 352
  editing, 319
  naming, 318
  publishing, 318, 319
  titles, creating, 318
blog space, registering, lxii
blogs, 305, 314, 349
  accounts, setting up, 315
  picture upload ability, enabling, 317
  publishing, lxii, 315
  recent entries, displaying, 319
  registering, 314, 316
  setting up, 315
  SharePoint and, 315
  text, formatting, 318
Bold button, 69, 129
bolding text, 69, 73, 129
Bookmark dialog box, 239
bookmarks, 217, 238, 349
  deleting, 241
  displaying, 240
  inserting, lv, 238, 239
  jumping to, 240
  predefined, 240
border lines, inserting, 93
borders
  applying to tables, 141
  around paragraphs, xlv, 84
  settings, changing, 84
Borders And Shading dialog box, 141
Borders button, 84
breaks
  column, xlix, 124, 127, 349

line, xliv, 75–78, 351
page, deleting, 118
page, inserting, xlix, 116, 118–19
page, manual, 116, 352
page, options for, 117
page, preventing, 118, 120
page, repagination of, 117
page, soft, 116, 353
page, in tables of contents, 228, 229
section, creating, without breaking pages, 118
section, defined, 118, 353
section, deleting, 118
section, display of, 118
section, to even or odd-numbered pages, 118
section, headers and footers and, 113
section, inserting, xlix, 118, 120
Breaks button, 120, 127
Brightness button, 160
Brightness gallery, 160
Browse By Page button, 14
browsers, Web
  home page, opening to, 319
  viewing documents as displayed in (see Web Layout view)
  Web documents, opening in, 314
browsing through documents quickly, 12
building blocks. See also AutoText
  creating, 224
  custom, 224
  defined, 217–18
  deleting, liv
  inserting, 221
  placeholders, replacing, 222
  text boxes, 222
Building Blocks Organizer, 218, 221
Building Blocks template, 42, 341
bulleted lists. See also lists; numbered lists
  creating, 86
  ending, 87
  formatting bullets in, 87
  numbered lists, converting into, xlv
  paragraphs, converting into, 88
  sorting, 91
  when to use, 86
bullets, 349
Bullets button, 88
Bullets gallery, 88
Business Tools tab, 3
button arrows, 4

C

calculating in tables. See formulas
calendar date, 43
Caption dialog box, 230
captions, 349
   inserting, 230
   table of, creating (see tables of figures)
categories for citations, changing, 231
cell addresses, 143, 349
Cell Margins button, 138
cells, table, 130, 349
   aligning text in, 138
   borders, applying, 141
   centering text in, 134
   deleting, 132
   formatting, 141
   in formulas, 143
   inserting, 132
   margins, setting, 138
   merging, l, 132, 134
   selecting, 132
   shading, 141
   splitting, 133
   width, specifying, 138
Center button, 77, 79, 126
centering
   paragraphs, 77, 79
   table text, 134
   text, 126
Change Chart Type button, 207, 211
Change Chart Type dialog box, 207
Change Colors button, 197
Change Shape button, 168, 198
Change Shape gallery, 168
Change Styles button, 68
changes, tracking. See also revisions
   accepting/rejecting, lix, 284, 287
   accepting all, lx
   balloons, showing in, lix, 283, 286
   editors, viewing names of, 286
   turning on/off, lix, 283, 285
changing documents. See editing
character attributes, changing multiple at once. See Quick Styles
character formatting, xliv, 69, 349
character spacing, 68, 72, 349
character styles, 66, 349. See also Quick Styles

characters
   deleting, 35
   non-printing, 16, 22
   non-standard (see symbols)
chart area, 349
Chart Layouts gallery, 209
Chart Styles gallery, 208
charts. See also diagrams
   activating, 207
   axes, 206, 354
   bar, 205
   colors, 208
   columns, 205
   columns, fitting to longest entry, liv
   creating, 199, 200
   data, editing, 200
   data, entering, liv
   data markers, 206, 349
   data series, 350
   data series, formatting, 209
   data source, selecting, 203
   defined, 187, 349
   editing, liv
   elements, modifying, 205
   elements, selecting, 208
   Excel worksheets in (see Excel worksheets)
   gridlines, turning on/off, liv, 209
   inserting, liv
   legends, 206
   line, 205
   pie, 205, 352
   plot area, defined, 352
   plot area, formatting, 208
   saving as templates, 211
   styles, applying, liv, 208
   tick-mark labels, 206, 354
   types, liv, 205, 207
checking documents out. See document workspaces
checking spelling, xliii
   automatically (see AutoCorrect)
   dictionary, adding words to, 59
   of entire document, 55
   ignoring errors during, 58
   settings, changing, 332
chevrons, 263, 349
Choose A SmartArt Graphic dialog box, 189
Choose Profile dialog box, 281

citations. See also bibliographies
   APA style, conforming with, 253
   categories, changing, 231
   citing, 248
   creating, 249
   editing, 250
   entering in Source Manager, 248
   formatting, 249
   inserting, lvi, 231, 251
   making available in current document, 251
   storage of, 248
   table of, creating (see tables of authorities)
   tracking, 246
Clear All button, 40
Clear Formatting button, 72
clearing formatting, xliv, 72
Click And Type, 77, 349
clip art
   inserting, li, 158, 162
   keywords, adding, 164
   in Microsoft Clip Organizer, 164
   organizing, 164
   resizing, 163
Clip Art button, 158, 161
Clipboard, 36, 40, 349
Close button, 3, 12, 23, 162
Close Header and Footer button, 115
Close Outline View button, 49
Close Print Preview button, 30
closing
   Clipboard task pane, 40
   documents, 12
   headers and footers, 115
   menus, 7
   Word, 12
collapsing Outline view, xlii, 21, 47
Color button, 142
color schemes. See themes
colors
   applying to page elements, 9
   applying to table cells, 141
   background (see backgrounds)
   default, changing, 331
   font, 68, 72, 350
   in graphics, adjusting, 160
   in themes, replacing, 102
Colors dialog box, 72, 208
column breaks, xlix, 124, 127, 349
column charts, 205, 349. See also charts

columns, 124, 349
   appearance of, 125
   applying to entire document, 125
   formatting text as, xlix, 125
   formatting text in, 124
   hanging indent, changing, 127
   justifying, 124, 126
   layout options for, 124
   margins, 126
   separated by tab stops (see tabular lists)
   spacing, adjusting, 126
   tabular lists in (see tabular lists)
   text flow in, 124, 350
   usefulness of, 123
   width, changing, xlix, 126
columns, table
   deleting, 132
   selecting, 132
   totaling, l
   width, changing, 132, 137, 138
columns, worksheet, 199, 349
Columns button, 125
Columns dialog box, 126
COM Add-Ins dialog box, 309
Combine Documents dialog box, 292
combining
   compared documents, 291–92
   paragraphs, 39
   table cells, l, 132, 134
commands
   previewing effects of (see live preview)
   Word 2003, missing in current version, 336
comments, 349
   deleting, lix, 288, 289
   displaying, 288
   editing, lix, 288
   hiding, lx, 288, 290
   inserting, lix, 287, 289
   navigating through, lix, 288, 289
   responding to, lix, 288, 290
   ScreenTips for, 287, 289
   text, viewing all, 288
Comments button, 343
Compare button, 292
comparing and merging documents, lx, 291–92
Compatibility Checker, 60
Compatibility Mode, 15, 106
confidential information, finding/removing, 60, 62
Confirm Password dialog box, 295

deleting 359

Connect To Your Space dialog box, 318
contacts, Outlook, as mail merge data source, 262
Continuous break, 118
contrast, picture, 160
Contrast button, 160
Contrast gallery, 160
Convert Text To Table dialog box, 136
converting
    documents, to earlier versions of Word, xxxix
    text into tables, 136
Copy button, 38, 146, 153, 213, 318
copying and pasting
    automatic space insertion, turning on/off, 38
    from Clipboard, 40
    drawing objects, lii, 173
    Excel worksheets, as links, 147
    Excel worksheets, into Word documents, 144, 146
    formatting, xliv, 70, 128
    graphics, 163
    index entries, 234
    vs. linking or embedding, 151
    text, xli, 36–38
    text, unformatted, 222
correcting spelling, xliii
    automatically (see AutoCorrect)
    dictionary, adding words to, 59
    of entire document, 55
    ignoring errors during, 58
    settings, changing, 332
cover pages, 221. See also building blocks
Create New Building Block dialog box, 41, 183, 224, 340
Create New Folder button, 24, 26
Create New Style From Formatting dialog box, 110, 143
Create Source dialog box, 248, 249
Cross-Reference button, 241
Cross-Reference dialog box, 241
cross-references, 218, 238, 349
    inserting, 241
    jumping to, 242
    updating, 242
cross-references in indexes
    appearance of, 233
    marking, lv, 236
cursor. See insertion point
Curve button, 173
curved text. See WordArt
curves. See drawing objects
custom dictionary, 59

custom styles, 143
Customize Keyboard dialog box, 345
Customize Quick Access Toolbar button, 337, 342, 345
Cut button, 39, 223
cutting and pasting tables, 133
cutting text, xli, 39, 223
cycle diagrams, 188, 349

D

data markers, 206, 349
data points in worksheets, 199, 349
data source for mail merge, 256, 257, 350
    creating, 257
    data, adding, 259
    fields in, 257
    filtering, lvii, 261
    merging data from, 257
    Outlook contacts list as, 262
    records, 256
    records, adding, lvii
    saving, 272
    sorting, lvii
database files, 272
Date & Time button, 43
date and time, 43
Date And Time dialog box, 43
decimal tabs, 82
default options, changing, lxiii
Delete button, 289
deleting
    add-ins, 309
    AutoCorrect items, 56
    bookmarks, 241
    building blocks, liv
    characters, 35
    clip art, from Microsoft Clip Organizer, 161
    Clipboard items, 40
    comments, lix, 288, 289
    confidential information, 60, 62
    document workspaces, 303
    Excel worksheet data, 201
    gridlines, from charts, 209
    hyperlinks, 243
    index entries, 234, 237
    keyboard shortcuts, 346
    page breaks, 118
    paragraph marks, 39
    personal information, xliii

deleting (continued)
    Quick Parts, from Building Blocks Organizer, 225
    section breaks, 118
    selected text, 38
    shapes, in diagrams, 193
    table cells, 132
    table columns, 132
    table rows, 132
    tables of contents, 228
    tab stops, 76
    text, xli, 35
Demote button, 48
demoting headings, xlii, 48, 350
deselecting text, 36
Design tab, 139
desktop publishing, 3, 350
destination file, 350
Developer tab, lxii
diagrams. See also charts; SmartArt graphics
    aligning, 192
    colors, changing, 198
    creating, 189
    cycle, 188
    defined, 187–88, 350
    frame, resizing, 196
    hierarchy, 188, 351
    inserting, liii
    layout, switching, liii, 189, 193, 194
    list, 188
    matrix, 188
    modifying, 193
    moving, liii
    pane, resizing, 191
    placeholders, 190
    positioning, 192
    process, 188, 190, 352
    pyramid, 188
    relationship, 188, 353
    resetting to original version, 193
    resizing, 196
    selecting, 194
    shapes (see shapes, diagram)
    styles, applying, liii, 197
    text, adding, liii
    text pane, displaying, 190, 194
    text wrapping, 191
Dialog Box Launcher, 4, 8, 350
dialog boxes
    Add Clips To Organizer, 164
    Advanced Layout, 177, 191

Arrange Windows, 213
AutoCorrect, 55
Bookmark, 239
Building Blocks Organizer, 221
Caption, 230
Change Chart Type, 207
Choose A SmartArt Graphic, 189
Choose Profile, 281
Colors, 208
COM Add-Ins, 309
Combine Documents, 292
Confirm Password, 295
Connect To Your Space, 318
Create New Building Block, 41, 183, 224, 340
Create Source, 248, 249
Cross-Reference, 241
Customize Keyboard, 345
Date And Time, 43
Document Inspector, 61
Drop Cap, 170
Edit Data Source, 260
Edit Hyperlink, 245
Edit Name, 250
Edit WordArt Text, 165, 166
Envelopes And Labels, 270
Equation Options, 180
Filter And Sort, 260, 261
Find And Replace, 51, 239
Footnote And Endnote, 247
Format Data Series, 209
Format Picture, 160
Formatting Restrictions, 297
General Options, 294
help for, accessing, xxxiii
Import To Collection, 164
Index, 234, 236
Insert Address Block, 265, 275
Insert Chart, 200
Insert File, 281
Insert Greeting Line, 265, 272
Insert Hyperlink, 243
Insert Merge Field, 266
Insert Picture, 159
Keywords, 164
Label Options, 275
Mail Merge Recipients, 259, 275
Mark Citation, 231
Mark Index Entry, 232, 235
Merge To E-Mail, 273
Merge To New Document, 269
Merge To Printer, 276
New Address List, 271

documents   **361**

   New Blog Account, 316
   New Windows Live Spaces Account, 317
   Open, 10, 13
   Page Setup, 8, 30
   Paragraph, 312
   Paste Special, 222
   Picture Options, 317
   Print, 27, 30, 277
   Properties, 61
   Publish As PDF Or XPS, 308
   Save Address List, 272
   Save As, 24, 25, 269, 313, 318
   Save Chart Template, 211
   Schema Settings, 322
   Select Contacts, 262
   Select Data Source, 203, 214, 258
   Set Hyperlink ScreenTip, 245
   Set Page Title, 313
   Set Target Frame, 244
   Source Manager, 248, 249
   Spelling And Grammar, 55, 57
   Start Enforcing Protection, 299
   Symbol, 180
   Table Of Authorities, 231
   Table Of Contents, 227, 228
   Table Of Figures, 230
   Templates And Add-Ins, 309, 322
   Update Table Of Contents, 229
   Web Options, 310, 311
   Word Count, 59
   Word Options, 35
   XML Options, 322
   Zoom, 17
digital IDs, 63
digital signatures, 63, 250
digital signature line, inserting, 63
disallowing
   editing, lxi, 298
   styles, 297
Display For Review arrow, 286
distributing. See publishing
document format, 332
Document Information Panel, displaying, 232
Document Inspector, 60
Document Inspector dialog box, 61
Document Management task pane, 302
Document Map
   defined, 16, 350
   displaying, xxxix, 19
   hiding, 19
   navigating in, 20

document window, 4, 11, 350
document workspaces
   creating, lxi, 300
   defined, 299, 350
   deleting, 303
   documents, adding, 302
   folders, creating, 302
   links, displaying, 302
   members, displaying, 302
   tasks, displaying, 302
   updating, 302
documents
   backgrounds for (see backgrounds)
   checking spelling of (see checking spelling)
   closing, 12
   comparing and merging, lx, 291–92
   converting to earlier versions of Word, xxxix
   e-mailing, 280
   faxing, 283
   final, displaying, 286
   finalizing, 59
   fonts, default, 68
   freezing graphics and layout (see PDF files)
   full screen, 15, 20, 351
   jumping to specific point in (see bookmarks)
   layout direction, 28, 30, 352
   magnification, adjusting (see zooming)
   marking as final, xliii, 62
   multiple, viewing, xl
   navigating, 11–12
   number of pages, viewing, 59
   opening, xl, 10–11, 13
   organizing, with headings, 46
   orientation, 28, 30, 352
   outline, viewing, 15
   password-protecting, 294–96
   PDF files, saving as, 307
   pre-designed (see templates)
   preventing changes to, 296 (see also passwords; read-only documents)
   previewing, before printing, 27
   printing, 27
   Quick Access Toolbar, customizing for specific, 342
   read-only (see read-only documents)
   renaming, 24
   saving, xl, 24, 109, 306, 308
   selecting, xli, 36
   simplified layout, viewing (see Draft view)
   statistics, viewing, 59
   switching between, xl

362   Documents folder

documents (continued)
  templates (see templates)
  text-only, 307
  thumbnails of, displaying, xxxix
  title bar, 3, 354
  tracking changes (see tracking changes)
  viewing, as displayed in Web browser, 15, 21, 354
  viewing, as printed, 15, 17, 352
  viewing two pages at once, 18
  Web pages, saving as, lxii (see Web documents)
  window displayed in, 4, 11, 350
  word count, displaying, 59
  XML format, saving in, lxi
Documents folder, 13
.docx file format, 306, 327
downloading
  add-ins, 309
  templates, 105
Draft button, 22
Draft view, 16, 350
  switching to, 22
  table items not visible in, 131
drag-and-drop editing, 37, 350
dragging text, xli, 37, 39
Draw Text Box button, 210
drawing
  lines, across the page, 93
  tables, li, 152
drawing canvases, 350
  formatting, 171
  moving independently of text, 174
  opening, 171
  resizing, 174
  setting as default, 171
  wrapping text around, 174
drawing objects, 157, 350, 352. See also graphics; pictures
  attributes of, 171–72
  automatic selection of, 171
  colors, changing, 173
  commonly used, 170
  copying, lii, 173
  drawing canvases (see drawing canvases)
  grouping, lii, 172, 174
  height and width, creating equal, 172
  inserting, 170, 172
  moving, li, 174
  resizing, li
  rotating, 174
  selecting multiple, 174

Drop Cap button, 170
Drop Cap dialog box, 170
Drop Cap gallery, 170
drop caps, 170, 350
drop shadow, 169

E

e-mail attachments, lix, 280
e-mail hyperlinks, 245. See also hyperlinks
e-mail messages
  documents, attaching to, 280
  importance, setting, 282
  personalizing, lviii
  sending, 282
  sending to multiple recipients (see mail merge e-mail messages)
Edit Data button, 200, 204
Edit Data Source dialog box, 260
Edit Hyperlink dialog box, 245
Edit Name dialog box, 250
Edit WordArt Text dialog box, 165, 166
editing, 34
  blog posts, 319
  chart data, 200
  charts, liv
  comments, lix, 288
  Excel worksheets, 204
  hyperlinks, lvi, 243, 245
  index entries, 234
  restricting, lxi, 298
  sources, 250
  tables of contents, 227
  text, with Find And Replace dialog box, 50
editing, highlighting. See tracking changes
embedded objects, 350
embedding
  Excel worksheets, in Word documents, 144
  vs. linking, 151
em dashes, 179. See also symbols
ending lists, 87
endnotes and footnotes, 247, 350–51
enlarging windows to fill screen, 23
envelopes, 270. See also labels
Envelopes And Labels dialog box, 270
Envelopes button, 270
environment, 3, 9
Equal button, 182
Equation button, 180, 182
Equation gallery, 180, 183

Equation Options dialog box, 180
equations
    custom, creating, 183
    defined, 351
    inserting, liii, 180, 182
Even Page break, 118
Excel worksheets
    cell ranges in, 201
    columns, resizing, 201
    copying and pasting into Word documents, 144, 146
    copying data to, 212
    data, deleting, 201
    data, editing, 204
    data, entering, 201
    embedding in Word documents, 144
    inserting, l, 143
    keyboard commands for, 202
    linking to, 144, 147
    methods of inserting, 151
    navigating in, 202
    range for data source, editing, 203
    selecting, 199
    structure of, 199
    updating, 199
Expand button, 48
expanding headings in Outline view, xlii, 48
expanding windows to fill screen, 23
Extensible Markup Language (XML), 319, 324–25
Extensible Markup Language (XML) documents
    class elements, applying, 324
    creating, 320
    defined, 305, 350
    invalid structure, saving with, 326
    saving, lxii, 326
    tags, 323
    transforms, 326, 354
extensions, file name, 26

F

fancy text (WordArt)
    3-D effects, adding, 169
    color, changing, 167
    contextual tabs for, 165
    converting text into, 167
    creating, 165
    defined, 354
    inserting, lii, 165
    outline, adding to text, 167

resizing, 167
shadow effect, applying, 169
shape, changing, 168
spacing between letters, changing, 167
faxing documents, 283
field names, 350
fields. See also bibliographies; cross-references; indexes; tables of authorities; tables of contents
    codes, toggling display of, 43
    defined, 43, 350
    inserting date and time as, 43
    in mail merge data source, 257
    selecting, 43
    updating, 43
figures, table of, 230, 354
file formats, 305, 350
    compatibility with earlier versions, 15
    default, 306
    .docx, 306, 327
    HTML, 310
    saving documents in different, 306
    for Web documents, 310
file locations, changing, 334
File menu. See Office menu
file name extensions, 26
files, 350. See also documents
    locking, 11, 353
    opening, xxxix, 11
    preventing changes to, 11, 353
    renaming, 26
fill effects, adding to backgrounds, 97
Fill Effects dialog box, 97
Filter And Sort dialog box, 260, 261
filtering, 261, 350
finalizing documents, xliii, 59
Find And Replace dialog box, 50–51, 86, 239
Find button, 51
finding
    confidential information, and removing, 60, 62
    formatting, 86
    styles, and replacing, 112
finding text, xliii, 49
    all forms of word, 51
    homonyms and, 51
    matching case when, 51
    options for, 50
    selecting results of, 52
    whole words only, 51
    using wildcard characters when, 51
    with certain formatting, 51

Finish & Merge button, 273
first letter of paragraph, formatting, 170, 350
first line indent, 79
first page, different header on, 114
First Record button, 269
flashing bar. See insertion point
flipping drawing objects, 174
flow, 350
folders, creating, xl, 24
font attributes, 68, 73–74
Font button, 70
Font Color button, 72
font colors, xliv, 68, 72, 350
Font dialog box, 70
font effects, 68, 351
font size, 68, 70, 351
Font Size button, 70
font style, 68, 351
fonts, 68, 350. See also text
   changing, xliv, 70
   commonly available, 68
   default for new documents, 68
   in themes, changing, 102
Footer button, 115
footers. See building blocks; headers and footers
Footnote And Endnote dialog box, 247
footnotes and endnotes, 247, 351
foreign languages, 46
form document for mail merge, 256
form letters, 263
   address blocks, inserting, 264
   creating, 264
   greeting lines, inserting, 265, 272
   saving without mail merge information, 264
Format Data Series dialog box, 209
Format Painter button, 70
Format Picture dialog box, 160
Format Selection button, 209
formatting
   applying to consecutive paragraphs, 78
   as you type, 93
   bullets, in bulleted lists, 87
   clearing, xliv
   copying, xliv, 70, 128
   creating styles from, 143 (see Quick Styles)
   finding, 86
   removing, 72
   repeating, 128
   restricting, lxi

   searching for, 51
   selected text, with Mini toolbar, 69
   selecting text with similar, xliv, 73
   in tables, 139
Formatting Restrictions dialog box, 297
Formula button, 144
Formula dialog box, 144
formulas, 142, 180
   creating, 142, 145
   defined, 351
   functions in, 142
   recalculating, 145
   referencing cells in, 143
Full Screen Reading button, 20
Full Screen Reading view, 15, 20, 351
Function Arguments dialog box, 149
functions, 142

G

galleries, 5, 351
   3-D Effects, 169
   AutoText, 340
   Basic Math, 182
   Bibliography, 248
   Brightness, 160
   Change Shape, 168
   Chart Layouts, 209
   Chart Styles, 208
   Contrast, 160
   Drop Cap, 170
   Equation, 180, 183
   Layout, 194
   Margins, 29
   Paper Size, 28
   Picture Styles, 160
   Position, 174
   Quick Parts, 40, 221
   Recolor, 160
   ShadowEffects, 169
   Shapes, 170
   SmartArt Styles, 196
   Symbol, 180, 181
   Table Of Contents, 227
   Theme Colors, 197
   Themes, 9
   WordArt, 165
General Options dialog box, 294
Go To Footer button, 115

graphic watermarks, xlvii, 100. See also watermarks
   adding, xlvi, 97, 100
   color, adding, 99
   defined, 96, 354
graphics. See also drawing objects; pictures
   arranging text around, 176
   background (see watermarks)
   brightness, 160
   color, 160
   copying, 163
   created within Word (see drawing objects)
   defined, 351
   inserting, li, 159
   modifying, 158
   moving, li, lii, 163
   overlapping, 176
   positioning absolutely, vs. relatively, 176
   resizing, li, 159
   stacked, 176, 353
   wrapping text around, lii, 176
graphs. See charts
green underlined words. See checking spelling
greeting lines in form letters, 265, 272
gridlines, liv, 209, 351
Gridlines button, 209
Group button, 174
grouping drawing objects, lii, 172–74, 351
groups, in tabs, 4
Grow Font button, 70
guillemet characters, 263, 351

H

handwritten changes, 291
hanging indent, 77, 127
Hanging Indent marker, 127
Header button, 113
Header gallery, 113
headers and footers, 113, 351. See also building blocks
   changing for first page only, 114
   closing, 115
   creating, 113
   inserting, xlviii, 114, 120
   moving to, 114, 115
   page numbers in, 117
   placeholders in, 115
   section breaks and, 113

headings
   built-in styles for, 46
   demoting, 48
   moving, in Outline view, 48
   organizing documents around, 46
   promoting, 48
   selecting, 69
   tables of contents and, 226
headings, column, 349
headings, row, 353
Help, for dialog boxes, accessing, xxxiii
hidden characters, 16, 22
hiding
   comments, lx, 290
   Document Map, 19
   field codes, 43
   margins, in Print Layout view, 17
   non-printing characters, xxxix, 22
   paragraph marks, 20, 142
   revisions, lx, 284, 286
   ruler, 19
   status bar items, 4
   text, 16, 234
   white space (top and bottom margins), 17
   XML tags, 323
hierarchy diagrams, 188, 351
High Importance button, 282
Highlight button, 73
Highlight Merge Fields button, 273
highlighting. See selecting
Home Page button, 319
home pages, opening Web browsers to, 319
Home tab, 3, 7
homonyms, finding, 51
hovering, 4, 351
HTML documents
   defined, 351
   file formats, 310
   formatting, 312
   indentation, changing, 312
   Internet Explorer compatibility, 311
   naming, 313
   opening in Web browsers, 314
   previewing, 311
   saving Web pages as, lxii
   settings, changing, 334
   text, adding, 314
HTML tags, 310

hyperlinks, 218, 242
    appearance of, 243
    deleting, 243
    e-mail, 245
    editing, lvi, 243, 245
    inserting, lvi, 242, 243, 245
    jumping to, lvi, 243, 244
    new windows, opening in, 244
    ScreenTips, adding to, 245
    target frame, setting, 242, 244
    to URLs, 243
Hypertext Markup Language (HTML). See HTML tags; Web documents
hyphenating automatically, xlix, 127
Hyphenation button, 127

I

ignoring spelling errors, 58. See also checking spelling
images. See drawing objects; graphics; pictures
importance, setting in e-mail messages, 282
Import To Collection dialog box, 164
Increase Indent button, 90, 129
indent
    hanging, 77, 127t
    increasing, 81
    of lists, changing, 90
indent markers, 77
indenting paragraphs, xlv
Index dialog box, 234, 236
index entries, 231, 351
    copying, 234
    deleting, 234, 237
    editing, 234
    formatting, 232
    marking, lv, 232, 235
    page ranges, 232
    selecting, 238
    subentries, 232, 236, 353
indexes, 217, 231, 351
    columns in, formatting, 237
    cross-references, lv, 233, 236
    electronically distributed documents and, 232
    fields, 233
    formatting, 234, 237
    inserting, lv, 234, 236
    tab leaders, formatting, 234
    term selection, 233
    updating, 234, 238

initial letter of paragraph, formatting, 170, 350
initials
    AutoText entry for, changing, 221
    changing, 331
ink changes, 291
Insert Address Block dialog box, 265, 275
Insert Below button, 135
Insert Caption button, 230
Insert Chart dialog box, 200
Insert Citation button, 251, 252
Insert Date And Time button, 43
Insert File dialog box, 281
Insert Greeting Line dialog box, 265, 272
Insert Hyperlink dialog box, 243
Insert Index button, 234
Insert Ink Annotations button, 291
Insert key, 35
Insert Merge Field dialog box, 266
Insert mode, 35
Insert Picture dialog box, 100, 159
Insert tab, 7
Insert Table of Authorities button, 231
inserting
    bibliographies, 252
    bookmarks, 239
    border lines, 93
    captions, 230
    citations, 231
    clip art, 158, 162
    column breaks, 127
    comments, 287, 289
    cross-references, 241
    date and time, 43
    date and time, as fields, 43
    drawing objects, 170, 172
    e-mail hyperlinks, 245
    em dashes, 179
    endnotes, 247
    Excel worksheets, 143, 151
    footnotes, 247
    graphics, 159
    headers and footers, 114, 120
    hyperlinks, 242, 243
    indexes, 234, 236
    line breaks, 76, 78
    mathematical equations, 180, 182
    merge fields, 263, 271
    page breaks, 116, 119
    page numbers, 117
    pictures, 158, 159

Quick Parts, 40
quick tables, 139
saved text (see Quick Parts)
section breaks, 118, 120
sidebars, 223
sources, 251
symbols, 180
table cells, 132
table rows, 132, 135
tables, 130, 133
text, 34
WordArt, 165
insertion point
   location display on status bar, 12
   moving, 11
   moving, to beginning of document, xxxix
   moving, to beginning of line, 14
   moving, to end of document, xxxix, 12, 14
   moving, to end of line, 12, 14
   moving, keyboard shortcuts for, 12
   moving, to next page, 14
   moving, one character, 14
   moving, from tab stop to tab stop, 77
   placing at specific point, 11
   scroll bars and, 11
installing add-ins, 309
invisible text, 16, 234

J

Justify button, 77, 79, 126
justifying text, 77, 79, 124, 126, 351

K

keyboard shortcuts, 344
   creating, lxiii, 344
   customizing, 345
   defined, 351
   deleting, 346
   displaying all, 347
   for moving insertion point, 12
   printing list of, 347
   saving to specific template, 346
   for symbols, 179
keywords
   clip art, 164
   inserting, 232
Keywords dialog box, 164

L

Label Options dialog box, 275
labels, 274
   address block, inserting, 275
   creating, lviii
   printing, 276
   type, selecting, 275
landscape orientation, 28, 30, 351
languages, translating text into, 46
Layouts gallery, 194
left indent, 77, 80
Left Tab stop, 130
legal citations, 231. See also tables of authorities
legends, 206, 351
letters. See also characters
   form (see form letters)
   greeting lines, 272
line breaks, xliv, 75–78, 351
line charts, 205. See also charts
line graphs, 205, 351
line spacing, 78
lines
   drawing (see drawing objects)
   drawing across the page, 93
   ending (see line breaks)
   selecting, xli, 36, 38
linked objects, 351
linking, 151
   vs. embedding, 151
   Excel worksheets, 147
   to Excel worksheets, 144
links, 218, 242
   appearance of, 243
   deleting, 243
   e-mail, 245
   editing, lvi, 243, 245
   inserting, lvi, 242, 243, 245
   jumping to, lvi, 243, 244
   new windows, opening in, 244
   ScreenTips, adding to, 245
   target frame, setting, 242, 244
   to URLs, 243
list diagrams, 188, 351
list of works cited, 248
lists, 86. See also bulleted lists; numbered lists
   automatic renumbering of, 87
   ending, 87
   indent, changing, 90
   indent level, changing, xlvi

lists (continued)
   multilevel, creating, xlvi, 87, 91
   nested, creating, xlvi, 87
   paragraphs, formatting as, xlv
   sorting, xlvi, 87
   tabular (see tabular lists)
   type, changing, xlv
live preview, 5
   defined, 351
   for styles, 66
   for theme colors, 9
locking files, 11, 272, 353
looking up information in reference material, xlii, 45. See also thesaurus
lowercase, 74

M

macros. See Quick Parts
magnification, xxxix, 16
   to exact percentage, 19, 126
   in Print Preview, 30
   to view two pages at once, 18
   zooming out, 78
mail merge, 255, 256. See also merge fields
   address blocks, inserting, 264
   defined, 352
   with e-mail messages, 270
   form document, 256
   for form letters (see form letters)
   for labels (see labels)
   main document, defined, 352
   previewing, 268, 273
   printing, lviii
   recipient list, 259–60, 269, 271
   recipients, selecting, 258
   records, 353
   saving while in process, 263
mail merge data source, lvii, 256–57, 350
   adding data to, lvii, 259
   creating, 257
   fields in, 257
   filtering, lvii, 261
   merging selected data from, 257
   Outlook contacts list as, 262
   records in, 256
   sorting, lvii
Mail Merge Recipients dialog box, 258, 275
Mail Merge task pane, 258
Mail Merge Wizard, 256

mailing labels, 274
   address block, inserting, 275
   creating, lviii
   printing, 276
   type, selecting, 275
Mailings tab, 10
mailto links, 245. See also hyperlinks
manual page breaks, 116, 352. See also page breaks
margins
   changing, xlix, 28, 29
   of columns, 126
   defined, 352
   hiding, in Print Layout view, 17
   settings for, 75
   setting to default, 120
   in table cells, setting, 138
Margins button, 8, 120
Margins gallery, 29
Mark Citation button, 231
Mark Citation dialog box, 231
Mark Entry button, 235
Mark Index Entry dialog box, 232, 235
marking citations. See sources
marking documents as final, 62
marking index entries. See indexes
mass e-mails. See mail merge
mathematical equations, 180, 182
mathematical expressions in tables, 142
   creating, 142, 145
   defined, 351
   functions in, 142
   recalculating, 145
   referencing cells in, 143
matrix diagrams, 188, 352. See also diagrams
Maximize button, 23, 214
maximizing windows, 23
menus, closing, 7
Merge Cells button, 134
merge fields, 256. See also mail merge
   address blocks as, 264
   defined, 352
   greeting lines as, 265
   highlighting, 273
   inserting, lvii, 263, 271
Merge To E-Mail dialog box, 273
Merge To New Document dialog box, 269
Merge To Printer dialog box, 276
merging
   compared documents, 291–92
   mail (see mail merge)

paragraphs, 39
table cells, l, 132, 134
Microsoft Clip Art collections, 164
Microsoft Clip Organizer, 164, 352
Microsoft Excel button, 146
Microsoft Office 2007 SharePoint Services. See document workspaces
Microsoft Office Button, 3, 6, 13, 24, 106, 352
Microsoft Office Excel worksheets
   cell ranges in, 201
   columns, resizing, 201
   copying and pasting into Word documents, 144, 146
   copying data to, 212
   data, deleting, 201
   data, editing, 204
   data, entering, 201
   embedding in Word documents, 144
   inserting, l, 143
   keyboard commands for, 202
   linking to, 144, 147
   methods of inserting, 151
   navigating in, 202
   range for data source, editing, 203
   selecting, 199
   structure of, 199
   updating, 199
Microsoft Office Word Help button, 352
Microsoft Office Word
   closing, 12
   importing data to Excel worksheet, 212
   starting, xxxix, 6
Microsoft Office Word 2003, 336
Mini toolbar, 69, 331
Minimize button, 3
minimizing Ribbon, 337
More button, 110
mouse pointer, 4
Move Up button, 48
moving
   drawing objects, 174
   graphics, 163
   headings, in Outline view, 48
   pictures, 163
   tables, 133
   text, xli, 39
multicolored text. See WordArt
Multilevel List gallery, 91
multilevel lists, xlvi. See also bulleted lists; lists; numbered lists
Multiplication Sign button, 182

N

name bar
   buttons on, 3
   defined, 354
navigating
   comments, lix, 288–89
   Document Map, 20
   documents, 11–12
   in Excel worksheets, 202
   Open dialog box, 13
   revisions, 284, 287
   Save As dialog box, 27
   with scroll bars, 11
   tables, 134
nested lists, xlvi, 87. See also bulleted lists; lists; numbered lists
nested tables, 150, 153, 352
New Address List dialog box, 271
New Blog Account dialog box, 316
New Comment button, 287, 289
New dialog box, 108
newspaper layout. See columns
Next button, 287
Next Page break, 118
Next Page button, 11, 14, 18, 30
Next Record button, 268
Next Screen button, 21
Next Section button, 114
non-printing characters, xxxix, 16, 22. See also paragraph marks
non-standard characters
   adding to gallery, 182
   inserting, lii, 180
   keyboard combinations for, 179
Normal document template, 104
note separators, 352
Notepad, 321
notes. See comments
numbered lists. See also bulleted lists; lists
   converting to bulleted lists, xlv
   creating, 86
   ending, 87
   number format, changing, 90
   number style, changing, 87
   when to use, 86
Numbering button, 89
Numbering gallery, 89
numbers, page, 117. See also building blocks

O

objects, drawing, 157, 350, 352. See also graphics; pictures
  attributes of, 171–72
  automatic selection of, 171
  colors, changing, 173
  commonly used, 170
  copying, lii, 173
  drawing canvases (see drawing canvases)
  grouping, lii, 172, 174
  height and width, creating equal, 172
  inserting, 170, 172
  moving, li, 174
  resizing, li
  rotating, 174
  selecting multiple, 174
Odd Page break, 118
Office menu, 6, 352
Office Online Web site templates, 105
Open dialog box, 10, 13
opening
  AutoCorrect dialog box, 93
  documents, xl, 10, 13
  drawing canvases, 171
  files, xxxix, 11
  Microsoft Clip Organizer, 164
  Notepad, 321
  PDF files, 307
  templates, 107
  Web browsers, to home page, 319
  Web documents, in Web browsers, 314
organizing clip art, 164
orientation
  changing, 28, 30
  defined, 352
Orientation button, 28
orphans
  avoiding, xlviii, 117, 119
  defined, 352
Outline button, 21, 47
Outline view, 15
  closing, 49
  collapsing levels in, 21, 47
  defined, 352
  expanding headings in, 48
  heading levels, xlii
  moving headings in, 48
  moving text in, xlii
  showing all levels in, 49
  switching to, xlii, 21, 46, 47

Outlining tab, 46
outlining text, 71
outlining WordArt, 167
Outlook contacts list as data source for mail merge, 262
overlapping graphics, 176
Overtype mode, 35

P

Page Break button, 119, 228
page breaks. See also section breaks
  deleting, 118
  inserting, xlix, 116, 118–19
  manual, 116, 352
  options for, 117
  preventing, 118, 120
  repagination of, 117
  soft, 116, 353
  in tables of contents, 228, 229
Page Color button, 9, 97
page layout
  changing, 29
  in columns (see columns)
  tables and, 150
Page Layout tab, 7
Page Number Format dialog box, 117
page numbers. See also building blocks
  different numbering, selecting, 117
  display options, 117
  formatting, xlviii, 117
  inserting, xlviii, 117
  style, changing, 117
page orientation, 28, 30, 352
Page Setup dialog box, 8, 30
page titles. See headers and footers
pagination, 116–17
paper size, 28
Paper Size gallery, 28
paragraph alignment, xlv, 77. See also justifying text
paragraph borders, 78, 84
Paragraph dialog box, 78, 312
paragraph formatting, 75, 352
paragraph indentation, xlv, 81
  first-line, xlv, 79
  left, 80
  right, 80
paragraph marks. See also non-printing characters
  deleting, 39
  displaying/hiding, 20, 142

paragraph styles, 66
    applying, 67
    defined, 352
    galleries of (see Quick Styles)
paragraphs
    applying formatting to subsequent, 78
    borders, xlv
    centering, 77, 79
    defined, 75, 352
    first letter, formatting differently, 170, 350
    framing, 84
    justifying, 77
    keeping with next, 118, 120
    lists, formatting as, xlv
    merging, 39
    page breaks and, 118, 120
    selecting, xli, 35, 36, 39
    settings for, 75
    shading, 78
    spacing between, 78, 83
parent folders, 352
passwords, 294
    entering, 295
    guidelines for, 295
    removing, lxi, 296
    setting, lx, 295
Paste All button, 40
Paste button, 38, 146, 222, 318
Paste Options button, 38
Paste Special dialog box, 147, 222
pasting
    automatic space insertion, turning on/off, 38
    from Clipboard, 40
    drawing objects, lii, 173
    Excel worksheets, as links, 147
    Excel worksheets, into Word documents, 144, 146
    formatting, xliv, 70, 128
    graphics, 163
    index entries, 234
    vs. linking or embedding, 151
    text, xli, 36–38
    text, unformatted, 222
patterns, background, 96–97
PDF files, 307
permissions, 352
personal information, finding and removing, xliii, 60, 62
personalizing
    e-mail messages, lviii
    Office, 331

Picture button, 158, 159
Picture Options dialog box, 317
Picture Styles gallery, 160
picture watermarks, xlvi, 100. See also watermarks
    adding, xlvi, 97, 100
    color, adding, 99
    defined, 96, 354
pictures. See also drawing objects; graphics
    arranging text around, 176
    brightness, adjusting, 160
    contrast, adjusting, 160
    copying, 163
    defined, 352
    inserting, 158, 159
    moving, 163
    resizing, 163
pie charts, 205, 352. See also charts
placeholders, 105
    in headers and footers, 115
    linked, 108
    replacing, 105, 108
plot area in charts
    defined, 352
    formatting, 208
pointer, 4
points, 352
Portable Document Format (PDF) files. See PDF files
portrait orientation, 28, 30, 352
Position button, 174
Position gallery, 174
positioning text with rulers, 75
posts, blog, 314. See also blogs
    creating, 316
    defined, 352
    editing, 319
    naming, 318
    publishing, 318, 319
    titles, creating, 318
pre-designed documents. See templates
predefined tables. See quick tables
Preview Results button, 273
previewing
    command effects (see live preview)
    documents, before printing, xl, 27
    greeting lines in form letters, 272
    mail merge, 268, 273
    Quick Styles, 66
    styles, 66
    themes, 8
    Web documents, 311

Previous Page button, 11
Previous Section button, 115
previous versions, ensuring compatibility with, 60
Print dialog box, 27, 30, 277
Print Layout view, 15, 17, 352
print merge. See mail merge
Print Preview, xl, 27–28
Printed Watermark dialog box, 98
printer settings
   changing, 27
   paper size, 28
printers, changing, 27, 31
printing, 27
   with custom settings, xl
   with default settings, xl
   envelopes, 270
   labels, 276
   mail merge, lviii
   multiple copies, 31
   previewing before, xl, 27–28
process diagrams. See also diagrams
   creating, 190
   defined, 188, 352
program options, lxiii, 311, 330, 338
program window status bar
   defined, 4, 353
   hiding items on, 4
   insertion point location displayed on, 12
Promote button, 48
promoting
   defined, 352
   heading levels in Outline view, xlii
   headings, 48
proofreading. See checking spelling
properties, inserting, 232
Properties dialog box, 61
Protect Document button, 297
protecting documents, 296. See also passwords; read-only documents
Publish arrow, 318
Publish As PDF Or XPS dialog box, 308
Publish Entry button, 319
publishing
   blog posts, lxii, 318, 319
   blogs, via e-mail, 315
   PDF files, online, 308
pull quotes, 222. See also building blocks
pyramid diagrams, 188, 352. See also diagrams
Pythagorean theorem, inserting, 180

Q

quadratic formula, inserting, 180
Quick Access Toolbar
   buttons, adding, lxiii, 338
   buttons, default, 337
   defined, 3, 353
   displaying below Ribbon, 337
   resetting to default, 341
   separators, adding, 339
   for specific document, customizing, 342
Quick Parts. See also building blocks
   creating, 40
   defined, 349
   deleting from Building Blocks Organizer, 225
   inserting, xli, 40
   saving, 41
   saving text as, xli, 40
Quick Parts button, 41, 221
Quick Parts gallery, 40, 221
Quick Styles
   charts, 160
   graphics, 160
   previewing effects of, 66
   saving, 110
   sets, changing, xliii
   SmartArt, 160
   tables, 160
   text, 160
Quick Tables, l
   defined, l, 138, 353
   inserting, 139
quote blocks. See also building blocks
   formatting, 223
   inserting, 222
   moving, 223
quote boxes, inserting, 222

R

read-only documents
   defined, 294, 353
   opening, 296
read-only files
   defined, 353
   opening, 11
ready-made parts. See building blocks
recalculating formulas, 145
Recolor button, 160
Recolor gallery, 160

rulers **373**

records in mail merge data source, 256
red underlined words. See checking spelling
Redo button, 37
redoing actions, 37
reference marks, 247, 353
reference materials, xlii, 45. See also thesaurus
references, formatting, 249
references, legal, 218
   APA style, conforming with, 253
   categories, changing, 231
   citing, 248
   creating, 249
   editing, 250
   entering in Source Manager, 248
   formatting, 249
   inserting, lvi, 231, 251
   making available in current document, 251
   storage of, 248
   table of, creating (see tables of authorities)
   tracking, 246
References tab, 9
registering blogs, lxii, 314, 316. See also blogs
rejecting tracked changes, lix, 284
relationship diagrams, 188, 353
relatively positioning graphics, 176
renaming files, 26
reordering
   bulleted lists, 91
   lists, xlvi, 87
   mail merge data source, lvii
   mail merge recipient list, 260
   table data, 133
Repeat button, 69, 128
repeating formatting, 128
Replace button, 86
replacing styles, 112
replacing text, xliii, 38, 50, 52
   all instances of, 53
   as you type, 35
   options for, 50
Research button, 45
Research services, xlii, 45. See also thesaurus
Research task pane, 44, 45
Reset Graphic button, 193
resetting
   diagrams, to original version, 193
   Quick Access Toolbar, to default settings, 341
resizing
   clip art, 163
   diagram pane, 191

diagrams, 196
drawing canvases, 174
Excel worksheet columns, 201
graphics, li, 159
pictures, 163
tables, 132, 137
viewing pane, 288
WordArt, 167
Restore Down/Maximize button, 3
restoring actions, 37
Restrict Formatting And Editing task pane, 297
restricting
   editing, lxi, 298
   styles, 297
reverting changes, xli, 37, 39
Review tab, 10
reviewing pane, lix, 288–90
Reviewing Pane button, 289
revisions. See also tracking changes
   in balloons, displaying, 283, 286
   defined, 283, 353
   displaying, lix
   displaying all, 293
   displaying certain types of, 284
   hiding, lx, 284, 286
   navigating through, 284, 287
   from specific reviewer, displaying, 293
Ribbon
   defined, 3, 353
   minimizing, 337
Rich Text Format (RTF) documents, 307
right indent, 77, 80
Right Tab stop, 130
Rotate button, 174
rotating drawing objects, 174
row headings in worksheets, 353
rows, table
   breaking across pages, 138
   deleting, 132
   height, changing, 132, 138
   inserting, l, 132, 135
   selecting, 132, 134
   text direction, changing, 138
RTF documents, 307
rulers
   displaying/hiding, 19
   positioning text with, 75
   setting tab stops with, 76, 81

S

Save Address List dialog box, 272
Save As dialog box, 24, 25, 27, 108, 269, 313, 318
Save As Template buton, 211
Save button, 24, 25, 111, 269
Save Chart Template dialog box, 211
Save Current Theme dialog box, 103
Save As PDF Or XPS add-in, 308
saving, 24
   automatic, changing setting for, 27
   building blocks, custom, 224
   charts, as templates, 211
   creating folders for, 24
   default format for, changing, 333
   default location for, changing, 332
   form letters, without mail merge information, 264
   keyboard shortcuts, to specific template, 346
   mail merge data sources, 272
   Quick Parts, 41
   Quick Styles, 110
   templates, 108
   text, as Quick Parts, 40, 41
   themes, xlvii, 100, 103
   XML documents, 326
saving documents
   first time, xl, 24
   in different file formats, 306
   with new name, 24
   as templates, xlvii, 109
   in XML format, lxii
   as Web pages, lxi, 313
Schema button, 322
Schema Settings dialog box, 322
schemas, XML, 320
   adding, 322
   defined, 354
   validating, 323
schemes. See themes
ScreenTip button, 245
ScreenTips
   defined, 353
   displaying, 4
   feature descriptions in, turning off, 331
   for hyperlinks, 245
scroll bars, 11
searching
   confidential information, and removing, 60, 62
   formatting, 86
   homonyms, 51
   styles, and replacing, 112

searching reference materials, 45
searching text, xliii, 49
   all forms of word, 51
   with certain formatting, 51
   homonyms and, 51
   matching case when, 51
   options for, 50
   selecting results of, 52
   whole words only, 51
   using wildcard characters when, 51
section breaks. See also page breaks
   creating, without breaking pages, 118
   defined, 118, 353
   deleting, 118
   display of, 118
   to even or odd-numbered pages, 118
   headers and footers and, 113
   inserting, xlix, 118, 120
Select Browse Object button, 12, 14
Select button, 73, 83, 119, 126, 312
Select Contacts dialog box, 262
Select Data button, 202, 214
Select Data Source dialog box, 203, 214, 258
selecting, 353
   chart elements, 208
   diagrams, 194
   documents, 36
   drawing objects, multiple, 174
   Excel worksheets, 199
   fields, 43
   headings, 69
   index entries, 238
   lines, 36, 38
   merge fields, 273
   sidebars, 224
   table cells, 132
   table columns, 132
   table rows, 132, 134
   tables, 132
selecting text, xli, 35
   adjacent, 37
   all, 126
   found, 52
   large sections of, 125
   non-adjacent, 36
   paragraphs, 35, 36, 39
   quickly, 36
   sentences, 35
   with similar formatting, xliv, 73
   turning off Mini Toolbar when, 331
   words, 35

special text effects (WordArt) 375

selection area, 36, 353
Send To Back button, 178
sending documents
   via e-mail, 280
   via fax, 283
sentences, selecting, xli, 35
Set Hyperlink ScreenTip dialog box, 245
Set Page Title dialog box, 313
Set Target Frame dialog box, 244
SGML (Standard Generalized Markup Language), 319, 353
shading
   paragraphs, 78
   table cells, 141
shadow effect (WordArt), 169
Shadow Effects button, 169
Shadow Effects gallery, 169
Shape Fill button, 167, 173
Shape Height button, 174
Shape Outline button, 167
shapes, diagram. See also drawing objects
   adding, 194
   changing, 198
   customizing, 193
   deleting, 193
   deleting words from, 194
Shapes button, 170
Shapes gallery, 170
SharePoint
   blogs and, 315
   document workspaces (see document workspaces)
Show/Hide ¶ button, 142
Show Level button, 47
Show Markup button, 293
Shrink Font button, 70
shrinking fonts, 68, 70, 351
sidebars. See also building blocks
   inserting, 223
   selecting, 224
signatures, digital, 63, 250
signature line, inserting, 63
sizing
   fonts, 68, 70, 351
   tables, 132, 137
sizing handles, 353
small caps, 73
SmartArt
   colors, changing, 197
   styles, changing, 196
SmartArt button, 189

SmartArt graphics
   creating, 189
   defined, 188, 353
SmartArt Styles gallery, 196
smart tags, 353
soft page breaks
   defined, 116, 353
   repagination of, 117
Sort button, 90
Sort Text dialog box, 90
sorting
   bulleted lists, 91
   lists, xlvi, 87
   mail merge data source, lvii
   mail merge recipient list, 260
   table data, 133
source files, 353
Source Manager, 246
   bibliography source, adding, lvi
   opening, 249
Source Manager dialog box, 248, 249
sources, 218. See also bibliographies
   APA style, conforming with, 253
   categories, changing, 231
   citing, 248
   creating, 249
   editing, 250
   entering in Source Manager, 248
   formatting, 249
   inserting, lvi, 231, 251
   making available in current document, 251
   storage of, 248
   table of, creating (see tables of authorities)
   tracking, 246
spacing between characters, 68, 72, 349
Spacing button, 167
special characters
   adding to gallery, 182
   inserting, lii, 180
   keyboard combinations for, 179
special text effects (WordArt)
   3-D effects, adding, 169
   color, changing, 167
   contextual tabs for, 165
   converting text into, 167
   creating, 165
   defined, 354
   inserting, lii, 165
   outline, adding to text, 167
   resizing, 167

special text effects (WordArt) (continued)
  shadow effect, applying, 169
  shape, changing, 168
  spacing between letters, changing, 167
Spelling & Grammar button, 57
spelling, checking, xliii
  automatically (see AutoCorrect)
  dictionary, adding words to, 59
  of entire document, 55
  ignoring errors during, 58
  settings, changing, 332
Spelling And Grammar dialog box, 55, 57
splitting table cells, 133
stacked graphics
  changing position of, 176
  defined, 353
Standard Generalized Markup Language (SGML), 319, 353
Start button, 6, 321
Start Enforcing Protection dialog box, 299
Start Mail Merge button, 258
starting Word, xxxix, 6
status bar
  defined, 4, 353
  hiding items on, 4
  insertion point location displayed on, 12
Stop Inking button (Tablet PC), 291
strong text, 69, 73, 129
Style arrow, 249
styles. See also character styles; paragraph styles; table styles
  applying, xliii, 67
  creating, xlvii
  creating, from existing formatting, 143 (see also Quick Styles)
  custom, 143
  defined, 353
  finding and replacing, 112
  galleries of (see Quick Styles)
  previewing effects of, 66
  repeating, 69
  replacing, when applying new template, 112
  restricting, 297
  scrolling through, 67
  sets of (see themes)
  sets of, applying, 68
  for tables of contents, 227, 229
  themes for (see Quick Styles)
  viewing available, 67

subentries in indexes
  defined, 232, 353
  marking, 236
suppressing. See hiding
Switch Windows button, 153
switching document windows, xl
Symbol button, 180
Symbol dialog box, 180
Symbol gallery, 180, 181
symbols
  adding to gallery, 182
  inserting, lii, 180
  keyboard combinations for, 179
synonyms, finding. See thesaurus

T

tab leaders
  defined, 353
  in indexes, 234
  in tables of contents, 229
  setting, 77
tab stops
  alignment of, changing, 130
  bar tabs, 128
  for decimal points, 82
  default placement of, 76
  defined, 76, 353
  moving insertion point between, 77
  options for setting, 76
  removing, 76
  repositioning, xlv, 76
  separating columns with (see tabular lists)
  setting, xlv, 81, 130
  setting leaders, 77
  setting, with rulers, 76
Table button, 130, 133, 139, 152
table cells, 130
  aligning text, 138
  deleting, 132
  inserting, 132
  margins, setting, 138
  merging, l, 132, 134
  selecting, 132
  shading, 141
  splitting, 133
  width, specifying, 138

table columns
  deleting, 132
  headings, repeating on each page, 138
  selecting, 132
  totaling, l
  width, adjusting to fit longest line, 137
  width, specifying, 132, 138
Table Of Authorities dialog box, 231
Table Of Contents button, 227
Table Of Contents dialog box, 227–28
Table Of Contents gallery, 227
Table Of Figures dialog box, 230
Table Properties dialog box, 138
table rows
  breaking across pages, 138
  deleting, 132
  inserting, l, 132, 135
  height, changing, 132, 138
  selecting, 132, 134
tables
  borders, applying, 141
  calculating in (see formulas)
  captions, creating table of (see tables of figures)
  captions, inserting, 230
  centering text in, 134
  contextual tabs for, 131
  converting text into, l, 136
  creating, 133
  creating, by drawing, 152
  creating, from existing text, 136
  cutting and pasting, 133
  Draft view, items not visible in, 131
  drawing, li, 152
  elements of, 131
  entering text in, 132, 134
  gridlines in, 131
  headings, turning sideways, 138
  inserting, l, 130, 133
  mathematical calculations in, 131
  mathematical expressions in (see formulas)
  moving, 133
  navigating, 134
  nested, 150, 153, 352
  for page layout, 150
  predefined (see quick tables)
  properties, changing, 138
  quick (see quick tables)
  selecting, 132
  sizing, 132, 137
  sorting data in, 133
  templates for (see quick tables)
  text direction, changing, 138
  text formatting in, 139
  title, creating, 134
  updating fields in, 145
  width, specifying, 138
tables of authorities
  creating, 231
  defined, 230, 354
tables of contents
  creating, lv, 228
  default creation of, 226
  defined, 217, 226, 354
  deleting, 228
  formatting, 227
  headings and, 226
  jumping to entries in, 229
  options, 227
  page breaks, inserting, 228, 229
  styles, 227, 229
  tab leader style, selecting, 229
  updating, lv, 227, 229
tables of figures, 230, 354
table styles, 138
  applying, l, 140
  creating, 143
Table Styles gallery, 140
Tablet PC, entering changes with, 291
tabs
  defined, 3, 353
  displaying hidden groups on, 4
  groups in, 4
Tabs dialog box, 77
tabular lists
  aligning columns in, 128
  column width in, 128
  creating, xlix, 128
  custom tab stops for, 128, 130
  defined, 128, 354
  formatting paragraphs in, 129
  setting up with columns, 123
tags, 354
tags, HTML, 310
templates
  applying, xlviii, 112
  changing, 112
  charts, saving as, 211
  Compatibility Mode, 106

templates (continued)
  creating, 106
  default storage location, 108
  default with Word, 105
  defined, 104, 354
  documents, creating from, xlvii
  downloading, 105
  information included in, 105
  modifying, 106
  Normal, 104
  from Office Online Web site, 105
  opening, 107
  placeholders in, 105, 108
  saving, 108
  saving documents as, xlvii, 109
  for tables (see quick tables)
  viewing installed, 106

Templates And Add-Ins dialog box, 112, 309, 322

text. See also fonts
  aligning, on right and left margin, 77, 79, 124, 126, 351
  arranging around pictures, 176
  bolding, 69, 73, 129
  centering, 126
  clearing formatting, xliv
  color, xliv, 68, 72, 350
  in columns (see columns)
  copying, xli, 36–38
  cutting, 39, 223
  cutting and pasting, xli
  deleting, xli, 35, 38
  deselecting, 36
  in diagrams, adding, 194
  dragging, xli, 39
  fancy (see WordArt)
  finding (see finding text)
  hiding, 16, 234
  inserting, 34
  justifying, 79
  moving, xli, 36
  outlining, 71
  pasting, xli, 37, 38
  positioning, with rulers, 75
  Quick Parts, saving as, xli
  removing formatting from, 72
  replacing, 38 (see replacing text)
  saved, inserting (see Quick Parts)
  saving, as Quick Part, 40–41
  selected, Mini Toolbar for formatting, 69
  selecting (see selecting text)

  special effects for (see WordArt)
  tables, converting into, l, 136
  in tables, formatting, 139
  translating, xlii
  underlining, 69
  unformatted, pasting, 222
  watermarks (see watermarks)
  WordArt, converting into, 167
  wrapping, 25, 176, 354

text boxes, inserting, 222
Text Direction button, 138
text documents, 307
text editor, 321
text effects (WordArt)
  3-D effects, adding, 169
  color, changing, 167
  contextual tabs for, 165
  converting text into, 167
  creating, 165
  defined, 354
  inserting, lii, 165
  outline, adding to text, 167
  resizing, 167
  shadow effect, applying, 169
  shape, changing, 168
  spacing between letters, changing, 167

text flow, 350
text wrapping breaks, 75, 354
Text Wrapping button, 174, 177
textures, background, 97
Theme Colors button, 102
Theme Colors gallery, 102, 197
Theme Fonts button, 102
Theme Fonts gallery, 102
themes
  applying, xlvii, 100, 102
  colors, changing, 102, 331
  defined, 100, 354
  fonts in, changing, 102
  mix and matching, 100, 102
  previewing, 8
  saving new, xlvii, 100, 103
  storage location of, 101
  for styles (see Quick Styles)

Themes button, 8, 101
Themes gallery, 9, 101
thesaurus
  defined, 43, 354
  finding synonyms with, 44

Thesaurus button, 44

3-D Effects button, 169
3-D Effects gallery, 169
three-dimensional text. See WordArt
thumbnails, xxxix, 5, 354
tick-mark labels, in charts, 206, 354
time, 43
title bar
  buttons on, 3
  defined, 354
titles, table, 134
toggling field code display, 43
toolbars. See Ribbon; specific toolbars
Track Changes button, 285
tracking changes. See also revisions
  accepting/rejecting, lix, 284, 287
  accepting all, lx
  balloons, showing in, lix, 283, 286
  editors, viewing names of, 286
  highlighting in, 7, 10
  turning on/off, lix, 283, 285
transforms, XML, 354
Translate button, 46
translating text, xlii, 46
Trust Center, 335
trusted locations, 335
Two Pages button, 115
typefaces. See fonts

U

Underline button, 69
underlining text, 69
Undo button, 37, 39, 48, 72, 178
undoing, xli, 37, 39
unformatted text, pasting, 222
Uniform Resource Locators (URLs), 243
unloading add-ins, 309
unsupported features, checking for, 60
Update Index button, 238
Update Table button, 229
Update Table Of Contents dialog box, 229
updating
  bibliographies, 248
  cross-references, 242
  date and time, automatically, 43
  document workspaces, 302
  fields, 43
  fields, in tables, 145
  indexes, 234, 238
  tables of contents, lv, 227, 229

uppercase, 74. See also small caps
URLs (Uniform Resource Locators), 243
user environment
  colors, applying, 9
  defined, 3
user name
  AutoText entry for, changing, 221
  changing, 331

V

validating XML schemas, 323
verifying documents, 63, 250
version control. See document workspaces
View tab, 10, 16
View toolbar, 5, 354
viewing
  two pages at once, xxxix, 18
  windows, all in one window, 22
views. See also specific views
  switching, xl
  switching among, 16

W

Watermark button, 97
watermarks
  adding, xlvi, 97, 99–100
  color, adding, 99
  defined, 96, 354
  graphics as, xlvii, 100
Web browsers
  home page, opening to, 319
  viewing documents as displayed in (see Web Layout view)
  Web documents, opening in, 314
Web documents
  defined, 354
  file formats, 310
  formatting, 312
  indentation, changing, 312
  Internet Explorer compatibility, 311
  naming, 313
  opening in Web browsers, 314
  previewing, 311
  saving Web pages as, lxi
  settings, changing, 334
  text, adding, 313

Web Layout button, 21, 311
Web Layout view
    defined, 15, 354
    switching to, 21
Web links, 218, 242
    appearance of, 243
    deleting, 243
    e-mail, 245
    editing, lvi, 243, 245
    inserting, lvi, 242, 243, 245
    jumping to, lvi, 243, 244
    new windows, opening in, 244
    ScreenTips, adding to, 245
    target frame, setting, 242, 244
    to URLs, 243
Web logs (blogs), 305, 313, 349. See also blog posts
    accounts, setting up, 315
    picture upload ability, enabling, 317
    publishing, lxii, 315
    recent entries, displaying, 319
    registering, 314, 316
    setting up, 315
    SharePoint and, 315
    text, formatting, 318
Web Options dialog box, 310, 311
Web pages, 305
    defined, 354
    documents, saving as, lxii (see also Web documents)
white space
    at top/bottom of page, hiding/displaying, 17
    surrounding text (see margins)
widows
    avoiding, xlviii, 117, 119
    defined, 354
wildcard characters, 51, 354
windows. See also document window
    maximizing, 23
    switching, 22, 153
    viewing all together, 22
Windows Live Spaces
    blog space, creating on, 315
    blogs, registering, 314
Word
    closing, 12
    importing data to Excel worksheet, 212
    starting, xxxix, 6

Word 2003, 336
WordArt
    color, changing, 167
    contextual tabs for, 165
    converting text into, 167
    creating, 165
    defined, 354
    inserting, lii, 165
    outline, adding to text, 167
    resizing, 167
    shadow effect, applying, 169
    shape, changing, 168
    spacing between letters, changing, 167
    3-D effects, adding, 169
WordArt button, 165
WordArt gallery, 165
Word Count button, 59
Word Count dialog box, 59
Word Options window, 35, 311, 330, 338
word processing, 3, 354
word wrap, 23, 25, 176, 354
words. See also text
    displaying number of in document, 59
    finding whole, 51
    red and underlined (see checking spelling)
    selecting, xli, 35
worksheets, Excel
    cell ranges in, 201
    column headings, 349
    columns, resizing, 201
    copying and pasting into Word documents, 144, 146
    copying data to, 212
    data, deleting, 201
    data, editing, 204
    data, entering, 201
    embedding in Word documents, 144
    inserting, l, 143
    keyboard commands for, 202
    linking to, 144, 147
    methods of inserting, 151
    navigating in, 202
    range for data source, editing, 203
    row headings, 353
    selecting, 199
    structure of, 199
    updating, 199
wrapping text, 23, 25, 176, 354

X

XML (Extensible Markup Language), 319, 324–25
XML documents, 305
   class elements, applying, 324
   creating, 320
   defined, 350
   invalid structure, saving with, 326
   saving, lxii, 326
   tags, 323
   transforms, 326, 354
XML Options dialog box, 322
XML schemas
   adding, 322
   defined, 320, 354
   validating, 323
XPS format, lxi

Z

Zoom button, 17, 99, 115, 126
Zoom dialog box, 17, 126
Zoom Out button, 19
zooming, xxxix, 16
   to exact percentage, 19, 126
   out, 78
   in Print Preview, 30
   to view two pages at once, 18

What do you think of this book?

We want to hear from you!

Do you have a few minutes to participate in a brief online survey?

Microsoft is interested in hearing your feedback so we can continually improve our books and learning resources for you.

To participate in our survey, please visit:

www.microsoft.com/learning/booksurvey/

...and enter this book's ISBN-10 or ISBN-13 number (located above barcode on back cover*). As a thank-you to survey participants in the United States and Canada, each month we'll randomly select five respondents to win one of five $100 gift certificates from a leading online merchant. At the conclusion of the survey, you can enter the drawing by providing your e-mail address, which will be used for prize notification only.

Thanks in advance for your input. Your opinion counts!

*Where to find the ISBN on back cover

ISBN-13: 000-0-0000-0000-0
ISBN-10: 0-0000-0000-0

Example only. Each book has unique ISBN.

Microsoft Press

No purchase necessary. Void where prohibited. Open only to residents of the 50 United States (includes District of Columbia) and Canada (void in Quebec). For official rules and entry dates see:

www.microsoft.com/learning/booksurvey/